27TH ANNUAL
KNIVES
2007

Edited by
Joe Kertzman

The Cover Knives

There were so many first-class knives to choose from for the cover of *Knives 2007*, the cream of the crop was having a difficult time rising to the top. Four fine pieces eventually surfaced, however, and they definitely don't disappoint the discerning eye. At far left is a mountable fillet knife from the hands of Schuyler Lovestrand, including a trophy bass scrimshawed by Lauria Lovestrand-Trout on a magnificent mammoth-ivory handle. The Persian-style double-D-guard bowie, complete with coffin handle, is a fabulous piece fashioned by Larry Harley, who wrestled wrought iron into a stupendous guard. He then forged and unfolded an accordion-mosaic-damascus blade, adding a mastodon-ivory handle and a bee's-nest buttcap of square-tile mosaic damascus. Stephen Olszewski, meanwhile, was busy building an Art Deco locking-liner folder that features a sterling-silver, 18k-gold and 14k-gold handle, fully carved by the maker, and a 440C blade. Stephen Vanderkolff wasn't just whistling Dixie. He had his hands full making "Dark Star," an art dagger delivered with a Matt Walker ladder-pattern-damascus blade and handle, and some of the finest pearl inlays ever to touch a knife grip. The butt of the knife is nearly as pointy as the tip.

©2006 Krause Publications

Published by

kp krause publications

An Imprint of F+W Publications

700 East State Street • Iola, WI 54990-0001
715-445-2214 • 888-457-2873

Our toll-free number to place an order or obtain
a free catalog is (800) 258-0929.

Library of Congress Catalog Number: 0277-0725

ISBN 13-digit: 978-0-89689-427-3
ISBN 10-digit: 0-89689-427-4

Designed by Kara Grundman and Patsy Howell
Edited by Joe Kertzman

Printed in the United States of America

Introduction

Sometimes it seems as though knifemakers should climb the highest mountains, ascend the steepest cliffs, stand at the peaks of the most visible mountain ranges and shout through the planet's largest megaphones for all the world to see and hear—"Take a look at the beautiful knives we're building! Are these not the coolest things you've ever seen, or what? Is anyone out there paying attention?"

At other times the old admonition—"Be careful what you wish for"—rears its cautious head. It is almost as if the knife industry is a secret society, or like a boy's or girl's club, or even a local fraternity, complete with password and secret handshake. It's *not* a good-old-boys network, because knifemakers are the first to share their knowledge with the world, and the hard-working gents (and ladies) are open and free enough to welcome others into their secret society. Yet, the knife industry—the handmade knife arena specifically—is the world's best-kept secret.

People who are fortunate enough to have discovered handmade knives often feel like they uncovered something no one else knows about—that they and only they hold a key to a certain kind of happiness. It is a good feeling. Do we really want to spoil it by climbing that mountain with gigantic megaphone in hand and blathering to the entire world that man's oldest tool has become an art form? Yes, we do!

It is the least we can do for knifemakers who have toiled under the masters' whips for far too long with little compensation, recognition or accommodation. Like seamstresses poking holes through fabric one needle prick at a time, stitching scraps of cloth together to make beautiful patchwork quilts, knifemakers pound hot steel, wear out grinding belts and sand their fingers to the bone building the most functional and beautiful bladed objects this side of the John Deere tractor plant.

No one ever mistook knifemaking for a get-rich-quick proposition. There isn't a guy in the world who ever looked at his wife and said, "Honey, I think if I quit my job and start making knives we'll be on Easy Street within two years." If he did, and if the little lady bought the proposition, they have worse problems than trying to figure out how to make a decent living fashioning edged tools and weapons.

Knifemakers do what they do for the love of doing what they're doing. First they build knives that work. Then, once they've perfected that end of the craft, they fashion edged tools that also look good. Once they're really on a roll, they embellish the bladed objects with scrimshaw, engraving, pat-tern-welded steel, precious stone inlays, file work, etching, leatherwork, carving, sculpting and material combinations. They take knives to a level of craftsmanship few tradesmen reach in their chosen fields. It is good old American ingenuity at its finest.

Someone should put out a yearly, all-color, glossy, 300-plus-page book showcasing these artists' works. They should call it the *Knives* annual book, and number it by year—*Knives 2005, Knives 2006, Knives 2007* and so on. They should include a "Trends" section, a "State of the Art" section and a "Factory Trends" section. The book should include the world's most complete directory of handmade knifemakers, including their contact information, websites, emails, specialties, knife patterns, technical information, prices, remarks and tang stamps.

Some innovative publisher ought to print a book with such fascinating feature subjects and intriguing titles as "Knifemakers of the Aloha State;" "The Most Famous Blades That Never Existed;" "The Golden Age of the Sword;" "Schooled in the Ways of the Willow Bow Smith;" "Recording Military History on Knives;" Befuddling Blade Shapes;" and "The Kiridashi Cometh."

Of course, there is such a book, and you have it in your hands. Sometimes it seems as though the publisher of *Knives 2007* should climb the highest mountains, ascend the steepest cliffs, stand at the peaks of the most visible mountain ranges and shout through the planet's largest megaphones for all the world to see and hear —"Take a look at the beautiful knives in this book! Are these not the coolest things you've ever seen? Is anyone out there paying attention?" Then again, you have to be careful what you wish for.

Joe Kertzman

Contents

FACTORY TRENDS

2007 WOODEN SWORD AWARD

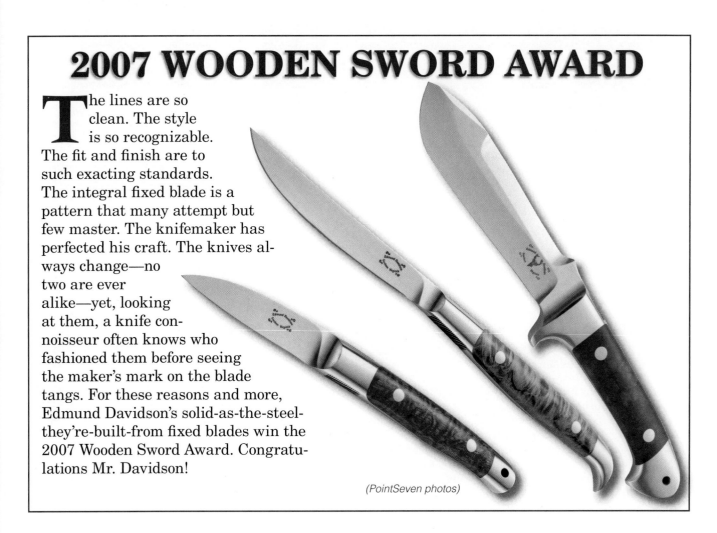

The lines are so clean. The style is so recognizable. The fit and finish are to such exacting standards. The integral fixed blade is a pattern that many attempt but few master. The knifemaker has perfected his craft. The knives always change—no two are ever alike—yet, looking at them, a knife connoisseur often knows who fashioned them before seeing the maker's mark on the blade tangs. For these reasons and more, Edmund Davidson's solid-as-the-steel-they're-built-from fixed blades win the 2007 Wooden Sword Award. Congratulations Mr. Davidson!

(PointSeven photos)

Famous Blades that Never Existed

Intangible weapons inspire our imaginations and become integral to our cultural heritages

By Dr. Louis P. Nappen

J.R.R. Tolkien's epic fantasy has grown tremendously in popularity with the release of *The Lord of the Rings* movies. One character, Gandalf, made good use of his sword, Glamdring, in *The Return Of The King*. Here he uses it in the movie's climactic battle scene. United Cutlery offers a reproduction of Glamdring, which was introduced in conjunction with the first movie in 2001. *(photo courtesy of New Line Cinema)*

Few contemporary children's poems depict the joy of knife-play. However, in 1871, Lewis Carroll penned one of the most beloved children's poems of all time—"Jabberwocky"— by doing just that. The Vorpal blade plays an integral role in the poem, with its most famous moment being when it beheads the Jabberwocky. John Tenniel's illustration makes the fantastic scene come to life.

Excalibur, Damocles, Zulfiqar, Vorpal, Amenonuhoko, Hrunting, Durendal, Balmung, Gungnir, Cryskives, the Spear of Destiny and Sting—these are some of the most famous blades of all time. Scripts and sermons have hailed their supernatural powers for centuries. Yet, as far as can be proven, the legendary blades have only existed in our myths, faiths and imaginations.

They are the most famous edged weapons that never existed.

Of course, such a list is subjective. Entire articles could be written just on the weapons depicted in video games, graphic novels or science-fiction/fantasy movies. However, this article examines the top fictional blades of the most literary significance and societal importance. These are the intangible weapons that have inspired our collective imaginations and become integral to our cultural heritages.

Vorpal Blade (or Vorpal Sword)

Few contemporary children's poems depict the joys of knife-play. However, in 1871, Lewis Carroll penned one of the most beloved children's poems of all time by doing just that. "Jabberwocky" would be just another hunting tale if it were not for Carroll's keen ear and fantastic imagination. Much of the poem is composed of nonsense words that did not exist until Carroll coined them. This can be seen in the Vorpal blade's most famous moment, when it beheads the Jabberwocky—

One, two! One, two! And through and through

The vorpal blade went snicker-snack!

He left it dead, and with its head

He went galumphing back.

"Vorpal" has become more than a playful adjective; it is this specific blade's referential designation. No one knows for sure what a Vorpal weapon can do or even what it looks like. No one knows for sure how to "snicker-snack" either, yet for over a century children have recognized the delight that comes from successfully wielding a Vorpal blade.

Hrunting

A warrior king named Beowulf is the hero of an Anglo-Saxon epic penned circa 700-1000 AD. *Beowulf* is one of the oldest surviving texts written in English; therefore a sword called Hrunting, which is given to Beowulf by a less capable warrior named Unferth, is arguably the oldest named blade in English literature. Beowulf fought many herioc battles, most noteably against the troll-like monster Grendel. Unfortunately, Hrunting, which never previously failed in battle, proves useless against Grendel's Mother, and Beowulf must find another way to win this life-threatening battle.

Sting

J.R.R. Tolkien's epic fantasy has grown tremendously in popularity with the release of The *Lord of the Rings* (*LOR*) movies. However, Sting first appeared in Tolkien's prequel to the *LOR*, The *Hobbit*. Sting is actually a long knife that made a perfect "sword" for diminutive Hobbits. Sting was forged by elves and famously glowed blue when Orcs or goblins were present. Bilbo's nephew Frodo (and Frodo's sidekick Sam) make good use of Sting throughout the *LOR*, most famously in a battle against the giant spider Shelob. Other swords of note in the *LOR* include

the wizard Gandalf's Glamdring and Elendil's Narsil, later reforged into Aragorn's Anduril.

Crysknives

As relayed in Frank Herbert's science-fiction *Dune* series, double-edged Crysknives are ground from the teeth of giant sandworms that live in the deserts of planet Arrakis. The approximately-7-inch, white knives are weilded by Arrakis' Fremen, who hold that Crysknives must draw blood each time they are unsheathed before they are permitted to be resheathed.

The more serious the reason for drawing a Crysknife, the more blood must be shed. The fable of the Crysknife's use follows the same line as the Norse swords Tyrfing and Dainsleif, which also could not be unsheathed without killing a man. Crysknives come in two types, "fixed" and "unfixed." Unfixed Crysknives must stay within the electromagentic field of a living being and cannot leave Arrakis or else they will disintegrate. Fixed Crysknives have been treated for storage.

Twelve Swords of Power

The Twelve Swords of Power are the central focus of the *Books of the Swords* by the aptly-named fantasy novelist Fred Saberhagen. The plot of the entire series revolves around the acquisition and eventual destruction of twelve magic swords. The Swords were forged by gods, then scattered for mortals to fight over. Doomgiver, Dragonslicer, Farslayer, Mindsword, Stonecutter, Sheildbreaker, Townsaver, Wayfinder and the others are ostensibly identical in design, having simple black hilts and straight crossbars.

The meter-long blades are, however, distinguishable by individual powers and white symbols etched into the sides of their hilts. For example, Coinspinner has an engraved symbol of dice and provides good luck to its weilder, and Sightblinder is engraved with the image of an eye and it alters the perceptions of those looking at the

Star Trek's well-imagined offerings include Klingon Bat'telhs (pronounced Bat'leths), yard-long crescent-shaped blades with handles inside the arcs. Renowned fantasy-knife maker Gil Hibben is recognized as the official Klingon armorer for the Star Trek, The Experience museum in the Las Vegas Hilton Hotel. Here, dressed in proper Klingon attire, he holds The Bat'telh.

swords wielder. Forged by Vulcan out of meteoric metals, the razor-sharp swords never tarnish. Of note, Woundhealer is incapable of cutting living flesh, and Soulcutter lacks a distinguishing symbol and draws light into itself, which creates a gloomy aura unto it.

Stormbringer

Over the last 40 years and several novels, author Michael Moorcock detailed the fantastic saga of the sword Stormbringer and its anti-hero possessor Elric. Similar to the strengthening effect furthered in the popular *Highlander* shows, the black Stormbringer (and its sister Mournblade) has the power to suck the souls of its victims and transfer their energies to the sword bearer. Unfortunately, Stormbringer is known to strike against its wielder's will, causing the death of the bearer's friends and lovers.

Helen Stratton's illustration "Arthur Withdraws the Sword" appears in Agnes Grozier Herbertson's *Heroic Legends*, London, 1908.

An 18th-century Icelandic manuscript depicts Odin with Gungnir. Odin was a shape-shifter who often traveled the world as a bearded man with staff and wide-brimmed hat. One of Odin's eyes was left in the purifying waters of Mimir's spring for wisdom, so he is often pictured with only one eye.
(Sam 66 Arni Magnusson Institute in Iceland image)

Subtle Knife

Arguably the most famous knife in contemporary fantasy, the Subtle Knife is featured throughout British author Philip Pullman's *His Dark Materials* trilogy (*The Golden Compass, The Subtle Knife* and *The Amber Spyglass*.) Movie adaptations are slated to premier in 2007. One edge of the 300-year-old Subtle Knife is sharp enough to slice through any known matter in the universe. The other edge can slice into other dimensions.

Careless use of the knife has led to inter-world slits being left open all over the place. The Subtle Knife's bearer often changes. Unfortunately becoming a bearer requires that the Subtle Knife "accidentally" slice off two of each bearer's fingers. The text promotes that the Subtle Knife "will be the only thing that can destroy God, to end the Authority's reign of oppression." (Now, that's a lot to ask of a knife!)

Lightsabers and Bat'telhs

Any article about culturally significant fantasy blades must mention a type of saber wielded "a long time ago in a galaxy far away." *Star Wars* Lightsabers are the primary weapon of Jedi knights. They glow in a variety of colors, can easily cut through most materials (except other Lightsabers), and can deflect shots from laser-like guns known as blasters.

An equally renowned sci-fi series deserves recognition. *Star Trek*'s well-imagined offerings include Klingon Bat'telhs (pronounced Bat'leths), or yard-long crescent-shaped blades with handles inside the arcs, and Vulcan Lirpas, short rods featuring curved blades at one end and bludgeons at the other.

Gungnir (or Odin's Spear, Sword)

The top god in Norse mythology, Odin, reigns over both wisdom and war. Odin's name, which roughly translates to "excitation" or "fury," is synonymous with warfare. Odin welcomes great warriors into "Valhalla"—heaven for fighters slain gloriously in battle. Odin is also associated with leading "The Wild Hunt," a bellowing host of warriors who charge across the sky. Odin's collection of warrior spirits are to fight in a final battle at the end of the world (known as "Ragnarök").

In order to collect the best warriors, Odin instigates wars and influences battles. Such a war god, of course, had a great weapon. Odin's spear, "Gungnir" (swaying one), was given to him by fellow god Loki. The spear always hits its target and, if thrown (like his son Thor's hammer), it returns to its master's hand.

Gram and Balmung

Norse legend relates a story about Gram, the sword with which Siegfried (Sigurd) slays the dragon Fafnir. Gram originally belonged to Siegfried's father, Sigmund, who pulled it out of a thick tree trunk called "Branstock," where Odin had forced it. Similar to Excalibur's "sword in the stone" legend, only the right person could retrieve Gram. After reforging, Gram famously clove an anvil in half. Siegfried's other sword swung in the epic Nibelungenlied was named Balmung.

Amenonuhoko

In Japanese Shinto mythology, the gods Izanagi and Izanami were responsible for creating the first land. To help them do this, they were given a bejeweled spear called "Amenonuhoko" (heavenly spear). From atop a bridge between heaven and earth, the two gods churned the ocean below with the spear. When drops of salty water fell from Amenonuhoko, they formed into the first island, "Onogoro" (self-forming), where Izanagi and Izanami resided thereafter.

Grim Reaper's Scythe

No modern image of Death personified would be complete without a black hooded robe and a scythe. The scythe was developed in 12th-century Europe to mow grass and reap crops without reapers having to bend. A scythe consists of a long wooden shaft called a "snath." A 30-or-so-inch curved blade is

Aubrey Beardsley's "How Sir Bedivere Cast the Sword Excalibur into the Water" appeared in Sir Thomas Malory's *Le Morte d'Arthur*, London: Dent, 1894.

mounted perpendicularly at the bottom of the snath. A handle in the middle of the snath controls the parallel height of the blade from the earth. A cutting motion is made by rotating one's torso.

Death's nicknames include "The Grim Reaper" and "The Harvester of Souls." Death's primary method of reaping souls is by scythe. For similar reasons, a scythe is also associated with the mythical figures of Father Time and the Four Horsemen of the Apocalypse.

Sword of Damocles

The Sword of Damocles, pronounced "Dam-ah-kleez," is not only a legend, but also a metaphor. The sword is mentioned in reference to any foreseeable peril or impending doom. For example, a scheduled IRS audit may loom like "The Sword of Damocles."

The origins of Damocles was famously described by ancient Roman Cicero in his *Tusculan Disputations*. The story tells how a courtier named Damocles praised how lucky King Dionysius was to have such wealth and rank. In response, the king let Damocles sit on his throne for a banquet.

King Dionysius, however, positioned a sharpened sword to hang by horsehair over Damocles' head throughout the evening. The king eventually explains, "I came to power by violence and I have many enemies. Every day that I rule this city, my life is in as much danger as yours is at this moment." The Myth of Damocles thereby warns us about the precarious and illusory nature of power and good fortune.

Durendal

Durendal is the sword of Charlemagne's paladin nephew Roland. According to Ludovico Ariosto's Orlando Furioso, Durendal once belonged to Hector of Troy. The Durendal legend holds that the sword opened the pass in the Pyrenees known today as Breche de Roland. In *the anonymous 11th Century epic, The Song of Roland*, Durendal is embedded with several blessed relics, including blood from Saint Basil, hair from Saint Denis, a tooth from Saint Peter, and a scrap of clothing from the Blessed Virgin Mary.

In the poem, Count Roland attempts to destroy Durendal to prevent it from being captured by invaders. However, Durendal proves indestructible, so instead he hurls it into a poisoned stream. Hauteclere is another prominent sword featured in The Song of Roland.

Shamshir-e Zomorrodnegar

According to Persian mythology, a witch named Amir Arsalan used a charm to make her demon son Fulad-zereh invulnerable to all weapons except a specific sword called "Shamshir-e Zomorrodnegar" (The Emerald-studded Sword). A wound inflicted by this sword could only be treated by a special potion made from a number of ingredients, including Fulad-zereh's brains. The blade is recognized as originally belonging to King Solomon.

Zulfiqar

The scimitar is one of the oldest, renown symbols of Islam. In all of Islam, no scimitar is more famous than Inman Ali's Zulfiqar. Zulfiqar is the sword of Muhammad and his son-in-law Caliph Ali ibn Abi Talib. Muhammad obtains the sword as booty following the Battle of Badr in 624 AD, and bequeaths it to Ali before his death.

In Arabic, "Zulfiqar" means "Cleaver of the Spine," "Double-Edged One," or the "Two-Pronged One," in deference to the "sharp distinction between right and wrong" or "the one who distinguishes between right and wrong."

Conflicting images of the sword exist. Some depict a traditional, thick, curving blade, while others project a V-shaped or parallel-edged blade. As a symbol of honor and knighthood, Zulfiqar has appeared in Islamic mythology for centuries, particularly utilized by the Abbasid Caliphate and Ottoman Empire. Islamic fundamental Shi'a, who believe that Ali was the first rightful successor to Muhammad, sometimes inscribe in Arabic on their weapons: "There is no hero except Ali, there is no sword except his sword Zulfiqar."

Spear of Destiny

Arguably, the best-known edged-weapon in Christian theology is the Spear of Destiny, which pierces the side of Jesus during his crucifixion. The spear supposedly yeilds curative powers. In some legends, the lance itself bleeds. Most famously, whoever possesses the spearhead and understands its powers supposedly holds the destiny of the world.

The spearhead has been rumored to be possessed by world leaders throughout the ages, including Constantine, Justinian, Charlemagne, Otto the Great, the Habsburg emperors and Adolf Hitler. However, no spear relic has been unquestionably authenticated as the actual piece that pierced Jesus' side.

Claíomh Solais and Caliburn

Celtic lore is rich with famous blades. "Claíomh Solais" (Sword of Light) and Spear of Lugh (Luin) are two of the "Four Treasures of

Sting first appeared in Tolkien's *The Hobbit*. Sting is actually a long knife that made a perfect "sword" for diminutive Hobbits. Sting was forged by elves and famously glowed blue when Orcs or goblins were present. United Cutlery reproduced Sting as it appeared in the *The Lord Of The Rings* movie trilogy. *(photo courtesy of New Line Cinema)*

endow Excalibur with superior sharpness and durability, making it unbreakable by anything but dishonorable acts of its user.

After Arthur is fatally wounded, Excalibur is hurled back into water and The Lady reclaims her sword. Arthur's scabbards, also supplied by The Lady, protects whoever wears it from any assault. Arthur's knife is Cernwennan and his lance Ron, short for Rhongomynad.

The lesser-known Clarent is often refered to as King Arthur's sword of peace, used for events such as knighting. According to some historians, Clarent, not Excalibur, is the sword Arthur extracts from a stone to become King of Britain.

The "Others"

Other fascinating edged weapons unfortunately did not "make the cut." Several, however, are worth mentioning, such as: Gene Wolfe's Terminus Est; Roger Zelazny's Grayswandir and Werewindle; Robert Jordan's Heron-Mark swords; Terry Brook's Sword of Shannara; C.S. Lewis' Rhindon; Edmund Spensor's Chrysaor; Luo Guanzhong's Green Dragon Crescent Moon Blade (or Frost Blade); Marvel Comics' Ebony Blade; Batarangs; the U.S.S.R.'s Crossed Hammer and Sickle; Cronus' Sickle; the Scythe of Gabriel; Poseidon's Trident; the Knife of Llawfronedd; Shiva's Trident; Satan's Trident; Achilles' Pelian Spear; Spears of the Valkyrie; the Battle Axe of Culhwch; Ysbaddadan's Javelins; Maui's Fishhook; the Viking Quernbiter; Freyr's Sword of Sharpness; Rhydderch's Dyrnwyn; Julius Caesar's Crocea Mors (The Yellow Death); the Whetstone of Tudwal; Ogier the Dane's Curtana; Gawain's Galatine; Lancelot's Secace; Sir Galahad's Sword with the Red Hilt; Charlemagne's Joiuse; Sir Percival's Grail Sword; and the other various blades brandished by Mars, Peleus, Yahweh, Baligant, St. Michael, Lady Justice....

Without doubt, fictional edged weaponry has a diverse, significant and inspiring history.

Ireland" (others being the Dagda's Cauldron and Stone of Fal). In Irish mythology, Claíomh Solais is irresistible and had the power to cut enemies in half.

Manannan mac Lir's "Fragarach" (the Answerer or Retaliator) was forged by gods and could penetrate any armor. The "Gae Bulg" (notched spear, belly spear, or lightning spear) is the weapon ZZmade from the bone of a sea monster with jagged notches (usually seven) to ensure severe damage when pulled from a victim.

"Caladbolg" or "Caladcholg" (hard belly, steel blade or hard lightning) was rumored to be as long as a rainbow, and, upon deflection in battle, it accidentally slices off three hilltops. In Geoffrey of Monmouth's "History of Kings of Britain" (circa 1100 AD), King Arthur's sword is Caliburn, not Excalibur. The sight of Caliburn spurs troops onward

and the enemy's armor proves no protection. Most historians believe Caladbolg and Caliburn provided the origins for Excalibur's name and legends.

Excalibur and Clarent

In all of Christianity, no sword is more famous than the symbol of righteous power, King Arthur's Excalibur. For all its fame, the Arthurian legends are highly muddled and unfounded. Besides whether an actual king named Arthur existed, "facts" regarding Excalibur are also contested. For example, it is unclear whether this sword possessed any magical powers or merely had a magical origin.

A mysterious water deity referred to as "The Lady of the Lake" supposedly presents Excalibur to Arthur (but, in some versions, to Arthur's father, Uther Pendragon). Most interpretations of the legend

Knifemakers of the Aloha State

Not everyone in Hawaii looks good in a grass skirt, so these craftsmen found other ways to entertain themselves—making knives

By Mike Haskew

The bolster of Stan Fujisaka's side-lock folder is beautifully engraved by Judy Beaver and complemented by an ATS-34 blade, titanium frame and mammoth-ivory grip. *(M. Fong photo)*

Living and working in paradise might be more of a challenge than a person would expect. The knifemakers of the Aloha State, however, take the sun, surf and swaying palms in stride and continually fashion some of the most dazzling custom knives to be found.

While they reside more than 2,000 miles from the U.S. mainland, the Hawaiian artisans are in touch with the mainstream of the knife industry. Often, their innovative designs, mechanics and craftsmanship set the standard. Acclaimed makers such as Stan Fujisaka and Ken Onion, for example, have become icons.

In the native language of the Hawaiian islanders, the word "Oahu" means gathering place. Today, Oahu is more than just the population center of the islands. It is also the home of the semiannual Hawaiian Historic Arms Association Great Gun Show. Each March and September, the knifemakers of the Aloha State gather to swap stories, fresh ideas and tips during the gun show. While several of them live just a few miles apart, the everyday grind can leave little time for more than an occasional telephone call or quick visit to a friend's shop.

Still, Hawaii's custom knifemakers are a close-knit group. Generous with their time and willing to share their knowledge with others, they are not only ambassadors for custom knifemaking, but also for their beautiful state.

"We all get along real well, although we are spread out across the islands," remarked Onion. "Some of us on Oahu live up to 20 miles apart. We are trying to represent Hawaii in the best fashion we can, and undermining one another doesn't portray us as we would like. Even if we weren't knifemakers, we would get along anyway."

During the last decade, Onion has become synonymous with highly successful collaborations between custom makers and manufacturers. His handiwork in concert with the factories includes dozens of models with Kershaw Knives, including a six-piece expansion of his kitchen knife

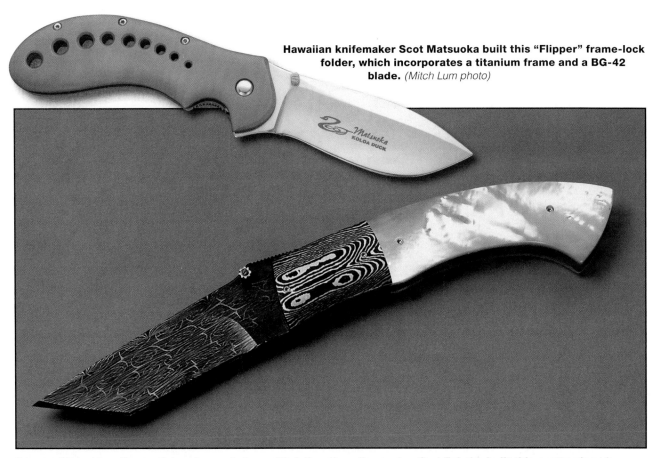

Hawaiian knifemaker Scot Matsuoka built this "Flipper" frame-lock folder, which incorporates a titanium frame and a BG-42 blade. *(Mitch Lum photo)*

George Gibo, who often collaborates on knives with fellow Hawaiian maker Carl Zakabi, built this pretty piece by himself. The folding tanto exhibits a Robert Eggerling damascus blade, a mother-of-pearl handle and mokumé fittings. *(Weyer photo)*

line, several pieces with United Cutlery, kitchen knives with Amway and a new line with Strider Knives called "Zero Tolerance."

Onion's signature folding-knife mechanism is the SpeedSafe™ Lock, but he also touts his Stud Lock as the strongest of its kind. "The SpeedSafe is something I'm known for, but I build extremely ergonomic, functional and highly unusual knives by taking the classic eight blade shapes, finding their better aspects and morphing them into something that looks unusual and functions well," he explained.

"I don't do it simply for the sake of [the knives] looking unusual," Onion continued. "If I want a classic drop-point blade, I can go out and buy one. I want to design a blade that does more. I want to be impressed with the way it cuts, minimizes mass and maximizes performance."

Preaching Precision and Tolerance

Because of high customer demand, Onion makes numerous frame-lock and locking-liner folders, using fixtures to maintain the tight tolerances inherent to the designs of the folding knives. He says the locking-liner folder is one of the simplest knives to construct, but that it can also be one of the most difficult to manufacture correctly. Precision tolerances and a locking mechanism that will last for years are absolute musts.

Helping one another to hone their skills has become a hallmark of the Hawaiian knifemakers in recent years. Ken has assisted George Gibo, Carl Zakabi, Scott Matsuoka and Ross Mitsuyuki, among others. Onion, in turn, credits Fujisaka simply with teaching him how to make knives.

"Stan's wife was my wife's teacher in high school," Onion

said. "Stan and his wife have been boyfriend and girlfriend since kindergarten. Imagine that—being with the same woman for 65 years! He is kind of like my dad away from home."

In 2006, Fujisaka celebrates his 20th year as a full-time knifemaker. For five years prior to that, he considered his work to be a hobby. As he began devoting more time to the effort, however, his popularity soared, and today he is recognized as one of the premiere locking-liner-folder makers in the world.

"I make LinerLocks® exclusively," he said, "with titanium frames, ATS-34 stainless blades, and handles of mother-of-pearl, mammoth ivory and a lot of giraffe bone, which is stable and less porous than other types of bone. I've tried every style of knife I wanted to, even making automatics, but I got away from that. I started with

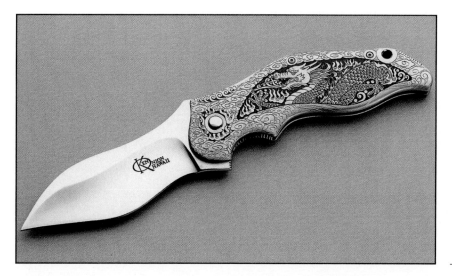

Ken Onion's "Distorted" model features a 6AL-4V-titanium handle engraved by C.J. Cai, a BG-42 blade and the SpeedSafe™ assisted-opening mechanism for which Onion's name and knives have become synonymous. *(Weyer photo)*

LinerLocks and they have been good to me. I thought LinerLocks would be a fad, but they still sell well. The attention to detail is the fun part."

In consecutive years, Fujisaka spent a week working in the Arizona shop of Butch and Judy Beaver. Early in his career, he also spent a considerable amount of time with Tom Mayo. "I'm not the initial knifemaker here," he remarked. "There was a couple here before me, like Tom and Vince Evans, the latter of whom has since moved to the mainland. But I am the eldest. I just reached my 70th birthday a few months ago."

Fujisaka estimates that more than a dozen knifemakers have spent considerable time apprenticing under him, learning the basics and sharpening their skills. Currently, he is working with Keith Ouye, a retired executive who attended his second knife show in Las Vegas last winter.

"I try to feel the young guys out first," noted Fujisaka. "I want to know that they are serious because I have had several who weren't. I spent time with them, and they just wanted to make a knife for themselves. I need to know if they are willing to invest in equipment, especially a grinder. That is the exact thing I told Ken Onion. I said if he was really serious that he would need to buy a grinder. He said he had the money and asked me what kind of grinder he should buy."

Passing the Torch

Stan does not charge his pupils. He even supplies materials and feeds them. He does explain that they will pay him back in the future when they pass their skills on to someone else. "When I started," he reasoned, "there were no books or videos. I was taught by other knifemakers, so I pass that on. You can't be a hypocrite."

Born in Tennessee, Mayo describes himself as having been "raised in the navy." He lived in California for several years before moving to Hawaii and remembers knives as a part of his life from childhood.

"My grandfather was a doctor in the small town of Martin, Tennessee, and he got me into shooting," remembered Tom. "He and my dad gave me pocketknives, and when I was 10 or 12 years old my grandfather gave me a knife made out of an old file. When I was living in California, I was into surfing, but as I got my roots a little more grounded I started going shooting and became interested in knives again. My hobby was making furniture, and that was expensive and time consuming. So, I started looking around for another hobby."

When Tom found a copy of BLADE Magazine® and subscribed, it piqued his interest in knives. He also remembers seeing Bob Loveless in Sports Illustrated. "I said to myself, 'I'm gonna do this!'" he smiled. Mayo spent two

weeks with the late Glenn Hornby, a knifemaker and detective in the Los Angeles Police Department, learning the basics of knifemaking. Mayo's current stock-in-trade includes the TNT and TMX tactical folders, along with a few neck knives. He prefers CPM S30V and CPM-154 steels along with a great deal of Stellite™ and titanium.

"After making knives for about three years, I met Stan Fujisaka," Mayo recalled. "I taught him the basics almost every weekend for about three months. Ken Onion has helped me more than just about anybody on this planet. He has a machinist's background, and I, on the other hand, made surfboards for 22 years. He knows a lot of stuff, and whenever I have a problem I call him up. One of his gifts is that he thinks in a real mechanical way. When I meet a machinist who wants to become a knifemaker, I know the guy will be a good one.

"Actually, I had been making knives but wasn't interested in going to any shows," Mayo added. "Those knives were just hunting knives for people who lived around here. Ken Onion and Duane Dwyer started bugging me about going to shows on the mainland. I finally went to one and sold 11 of the 12 knives I took. My Internet site started doing well, and I suddenly had a three-year backlog."

Mayo admits that knifemakers can be an "odd group," and says that like any other friendly

Tom Mayo says he didn't want to attend knife shows on the mainland, but preferred remaining in Hawaii and making hunting knives for friends. Fellow knifemakers Ken Onion and Duane Dwyer coaxed him into attending knife shows and displaying pieces like this titanium frame-lock folder with a damascus blade. *(Hoffman photo)*

bunch they run the risk at times of taking one another for granted. Still, the Hawaiian knifemakers, and others in their field, can count on one another.

A part-time knifemaker for 18 years, Ron Lui retired from Eastman Kodak a little more than a year ago. A mutual friend, Mel Nichiuchi, introduced Lui to Fujisaka, and for several months the two spent quite a bit of time together. It is no surprise that the locking-liner folders are Lui's favorite knives, with titanium frames and ATS-34 blade steel. He uses some mastodon ivory but prefers synthetics such as G-10 and Micarta® for handles.

Knife Patents and Partnerships

"Right now, I'm spending a couple of hours a day in the shop, and I do plan to relegate more time to making knives," related Lui. "I recently came up with my own model of an assisted-opening knife after being inspired by the success Ken Onion has had with them. My design is patentable, and I am thinking about looking for a manufacturer to partner with. I already have a patent on a fixed blade design."

Lui's projected annual knife output is around 25 pieces, and he estimates that six months of lead time would be required to produce that number. He will be attending more shows and introducing his wares to a wider audience in the future.

Five-year-old son Jamin is Zakabi's main focus these days, but he does find time to make knives, particularly fixed-blade utility and hunting knives with 440C or ATS-34 stainless steel blades and stabilized-wood or Micarta handles. Opting for stainless steel, stabilized wood and synthetic knifemaking materials is a good idea to prevent rust in the humid Hawaiian climate, Zakabi notes. He has been a part-time knifemaker since 1988 and works full time as an electrician. In the past, he produced up to 50 knives a year, and as Jamin enters school he anticipates his output to rise steadily once more.

"The first knife book I bought was Knives 1983, and then I ended up buying How To Make Knives. I made one trip to Stan Fujisaka's house and screwed up one of his blades. Then I was too ashamed to go back," Zakabi laughed. "I do come up with some weird styles, but they are so weird that people buy them.

"I would say they are fantasy knives, but not high-dollar fanta-sy, maybe working-class fantasy," Zakabi surmised. "I am hoping that my son will show an interest in knifemaking, and I like to joke that I need to find him a child's respirator to use in the shop when I am grinding."

Zakabi and Gibo are collaborating on knives now and expect to come up with one or two new models each year. While Carl lives on Oahu and George's residence is on the big island of Hawaii, the U.S. Postal Service helps bridge the distance between them.

"When we are working on a drawing together, it goes back and forth from my house to his," Zakabi commented. "George does the handle work and gets the final say on what the knife looks like. I do all the blade work and would describe the designs as combination tactical-and-executive folders. Several pieces feature high-dollar materials like Mokumé, giraffe bone or black-lip pearl, and blade lengths range from 3-to-4 ½ inches each. George and I have made a half-dozen to date over three or four years. As far as taking knife orders myself, I prefer to first review what the potential customer has in mind and see what drawings they have because I don't want to make a knife that would be short of their expectations."

Although Stan Fujisaka isn't the first Hawaiian knifemaker, having recently celebrated his 70th birthday, he guesses he's probably the oldest. Stan's side-lock folder dons a Mike Norris stainless-damascus blade, Mike Sakmar mokumé bolsters, a titanium frame and a mammoth-ivory handle scrimshawed by Linda Karst Stone.

When the affable Gibo picked up a copy of BLADE at a local newsstand, he was hooked. A part-time maker since 1996, he plans to retire from his electrician job in three years and plunge further into his knife work. Current production is between 30 and 40 knives per year, mostly folders with ATS-34, BG-42 and CPM S30V blades, and handles of pearl, mammoth ivory and giraffe bone, or carbon fiber for tactical models.

Fujisaka and Another Fledgling Maker

Gibo credits Zakabi with helping him get started, but a memorable conversation with Fujisaka put things into perspective. True to form, Fujisaka urged the fledgling maker to put his money where his mouth was.

"When I talked to Stan about getting started, he said to buy a Burr King grinder," Gibo smiled. "In those days that wasn't cheap! I didn't know Stan, but I had seen his name and phone number in BLADE Magazine, so I called him. He told me what to buy and put me in touch with the right people."

Ross Mitsuyuki's folder sports a BG-42 blade, a carbon-fiber handle and a cat's-eye thumb stud.

"I started out on my own and made my first folder, which was really crude. I showed it to Stan, and he said, 'You know what? I think maybe you should come over to my house and work a little.' I took him up on the offer and worked with him for three or four days," Gibo related. "He showed me how to fine tune my folders. Stan is so willing to teach and share information. He is just an all-around nice guy and will go out of his way to help you. Now I try to help anybody who asks. I'm just a backyard machinist, but I will share that knowledge."

One of Gibo's most memorable knives is a folder with a mammoth-ivory handle and scrimshaw work depicting the sailing ship *Endeavor*, which belonged to the famous Captain Cook. The ship was anchored in the cove on the big island where legend has it that the captain was murdered by angry Hawaiian natives. Custom orders are fulfilled in about a year, and most fancy folders range in price from $300 to $750.

According to Gibo, a number of individuals living in Hawaii are becoming interested in knifemaking. Certainly, they will find a helping hand, a ready smile and some good advice as they begin their studies. The knifemakers of the Aloha State produce outstanding work and enjoy themselves in the process. To find out more about them, just ask. They are quick with an invitation to sit and chat, to share information and to build not only knives, but friendships.

Recording Military History on Knives

Each one of Jack O'Brien's commemorative military knives is a labor of love

By Keith Spencer

Australian knifemaker Jack O'Brien crafts classy custom knives under the trademark "JOB," and sells the edged creations nationwide. Jack figured out a long time ago that Aussie knife collectors prefer "practical collectable" knives, rather than fancy art or fantasy pieces that belong in display cases. Some people who purchase practical collectables maintain them, of course, as though they are showpieces, and often display them in cabinets and cases. But in the back of their minds, most Aussie collectors like to know that, should the need arise there's a selection of practical pieces readily at hand.

O'Brien epitomizes the iconic Aussie of old—they're still around. That unworried and unhurried "she'll-be-alright" sort of bloke, who's a bit laconic and a bit of a larrikin and with a dry sense of humor that's always in the wind.

He errs on the side of gruffness and quickly gets to the point. His lingo is laced with good old-fashioned Aussie slang. That's Jack at a glance. If you can get past your first impression of him, you will discover another side to him—the inner Jack.

I discovered Jack several years ago when he was a new car salesman starting to get serious about "this knifemaking caper." He sold my daughter a car and sold my wife another car—the girls feel comfortable with Jack's easy way of doing things. I was sold on his bench-made knives. Jack was a top maker just waiting to happen in the Aussie knifemaking scene.

"'Ave you seen me Ugly?" he asked one day. Because impish Jack can be unpredictable, I wasn't sure what was about to come next. "Did I show you me Ugly?" he persisted in mock irritation.

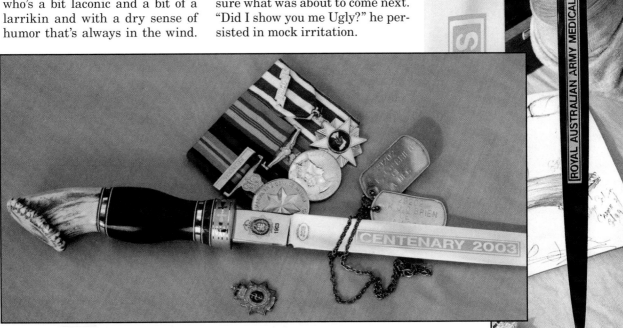

The commemorative short sword, custom crafted by Jack O'Brien, celebrates the centennial anniversary of the Royal Australian Army Medical Corps. *(Spencer photos)*

A maker of commemorative military knives, Jack O'Brien (left) presents Australian recipient of the Victoria Cross (VC), Keith Payne, with a 40th anniversary "Team Knife" featuring the four VC recipients in the Vietnam War. Decorations in the presentation case are those awarded to Payne. *(Spencer photos)*

"Err...no, I don't think so." I replied warily.

"Right!" He said sharply, and reaching into his office desk drawer, Jack removed something wrapped in a rag. He unraveled the contents onto the desk pad. There lay the "Ugly," a knife fashioned in the vein of the popular bowie pattern. Now, when you choose to make cutlery your career, you get to see a lot of bowie knives. I've seen a lot of bowies. But Jack's rendition was different. I studied the knife closely and took it into my hands to feel its usefulness.

Absorbed in examining the knife I mumbled, "You've come a long way with this one, Jack." The Ugly oozed style and practicality. But what most captured my attention was the peculiar cutaway grind, which I had not seen before, that is, not the same way Jack had applied the technique. Sure, the cutaway section enhanced the aesthetics of the knife concept, but more importantly, it lightened the blade to improve function.

Fascinated, I inquired, "How did you manage to accomplish the unusual grind?"

"With some difficulty, but I eventually worked out how to do it," Jack quipped.

He told me the secret and from that moment on I began to discover more of what Jack is about. It's been an enjoyable voyage of discovery, and in the interim, Jack has sold lots of Uglys. Why does he call them "Uglys?" I don't know. Jack nicknames people and things in accordance with personal perceptions, and as far as I am concerned, that's Jack's business.

He joined the Australian Army as a young man and served in the Vietnam War. A staunch patriot, he rises "with the sparrow's fart" for the dawn service on Anzac

Day (an Anzak is a soldier in the Australian and New Zealand Army Corps) with his military mates. He follows his early rising with a curry and rum breakfast (a heck of a way to start a day, I reckon). Once the traditional "March Past" (parade) is over, he settles into some yarn swapping with his mates over a few beers. Jack refers to booze as "direction juice." On Anzac Day, his wife Gail (Jack's best mate) expects him home when she sees him.

Get a JOB

Jack is best known for the commemorative military knives he has created. Great care goes into their production. He painstakingly experiments with prototypes until he is satisfied they faithfully fulfill their intended purpose. Without doubt, these JOB jobs are labors of love!

Jack also writes darned good articles for *Knives Australia* magazine. He writes like he talks—with catchy colloquialisms—creating challenges for an editor trying to make Jack's stories digestible for overseas readers. I know; I'm the editor! He is a natural entertainer and those who know him have come to expect the unexpected from him.

Many years ago, there used to be a "bloke-targeted" magazine called *MAN* on the newsstands in Australia. You know the type, with wild stories and scantily-clad "Sheilas," mostly fun and fiction. Jack was offshore somewhere in the army, and one day, to amuse himself, he wrote a story for *MAN* whilst sipping some "direction juice." They published it and asked

Jack O'Brien fashioned the fund-raising commemorative knife for the Viet Nam Veterans Motorcycle Club of Queensland, with proceeds going to assist the Cambodian mine clearing program. *(Spencer photos)*

Sgt. Kenneth John (Jack) O'Brien was a medic at the Vung Tau 1 Aust FD Hospital in Vietnam.

for more stories. So Jack sipped some more and wrote some more to oblige them. They loved the outlandish yarns and kept sending writer's fees in the mail. When he returned to the mainland, the editor of *MAN* and a few colleagues took Jack for a "liquid lunch." They were amazed to learn that he wasn't dreaming up fiction, but actually telling true stories!

About the same time Jack embarked upon making his first knife, a replica of the Iron Mistress Bowie that appeared in the 1952 film of the same name starring Alan Ladd. Jack was stationed on the northern side of the New Guinea coastline "...way the hell in the damn bush about three hours into the hills outside Wewak in a village called Passam. Nothing there except myself and about 120 other diggers with the object of pushing a damn road through wet, soggy jungle to Maprik for some unknown reason," he explained.

Jack drew up plans for the knife from a magazine picture, scrounged an old metal file, annealed it and, after basically shaping it with a grinder, fashioned "a fairly respectable facsimile of the original drawing." The knife was

heat treated in the camp cook's oil-fired stove and quenched in his cooking oil (without the cook's knowledge, of course). A brass strip was welded to the back of the blade and an ebony jungle-wood grip was fitted and furnished with a brass guard and pommel.

Wet and dry abrasives were used to hand sand the knife to a fine finish. In very basic conditions, Jack improvised to produce a serviceable bush knife that he carried on many trips with the army, until someone broke into his home in 1963 and stole it. The full story was published in the spring 2003 issue of *Knives Australia* magazine.

Born at Coffs Harbour Jetty in northern New South Wales, Jack was schooled at Bowral, the birthplace of Sir Donald Bradman, not far from Sydney. Jack's first job was in an underground coal mine at Berrima in the southern Highlands, just down the road from Bowral. Built in 1834, the historic Berrima jail is famous for incarcerating notorious bushrangers during the bad old days, but perhaps Berrima's greatest claim to fame goes to the Berrima Pub, which remains the oldest inn still licensed in Australia.

The area is best known, however, for being the birthplace of Australia's iron and steel industry, in 1848, at Mittagong, a town that these days merges with Bowral. Called Fitzroy Iron Works and named after the Governor General of New South Wales, Sir Charles Fitz Roy, the company was formed "for the purpose of quarrying, smelting and disposing of the ores of iron and steel to be obtained from certain mineral lands situated at Mittagong."

Given young Jack's cultural background, it isn't so surprising to find him smithing blades for a living in later life. But life had to take its course beforehand, and in the mid-1950s, young Jack signed on as a soldier in the regular army, planning to be in artillery or engineering, but became a medic instead. He served in New Guinea and Vietnam for 14 months "...and a few other places" before signing off from the army in the early '70s.

An Outback Bladesmith

Jack spent the next 25 years until his "official" retirement from the workplace, alternating between selling cars, and manufacturing kilns and furnaces for potters and mining assayers. About 15 years ago, Jack seriously looked at becoming a knifemaker. Little by little, as the years passed, he learned more and more about the art of custom knifemaking. Eventually Jack's time was his own and he became a full-time bladesmith. He even served for a period as secretary of the Western Australian Blacksmiths Association.

Independently minded, Jack sought new ways of making knives, and tested what he learned in various mediums of the craft. He was prepared to "give in order to get." Absorbing his time and money, and taxing his patience, was the time it took to develop special knifemaking techniques and accomplish individually styled, practical knives. Familiar with the needs of hunters and wilderness wanderers, Jack handcrafted a wide range of working knives,

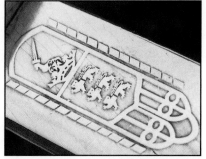 

The knife is one of Jack O'Brien's works in progress on a family heirloom. It is destined for the New South Wales lineage of the O'Brien clan's Celtic origin. Translated, the hilt inscription reads "Strongest Arm Uppermost," the O'Brien clan motto. The inscription is on the coat of arms of the O'Brien-forged cable-damascus blade, along with three lions that denote a royal connection. *(Spencer photos)*

some to the buyers' specifications, and many from cable damascus he forged.

Jack's knifemaking goal continues to be fashioning knives that he personally feels comfortable using, and thus, he figures others should also experience the same confidence with his knife in their hands.

Jack's experimental Ugly proved to be an important knife model, for it set the standard for JOB knives into the future. Jack says the Ugly evolved from the Iron Mistress replica he made in the jungle all those years before, but with improvements. He sought to construct an equally large, robust knife with which to chop, slice and pierce that weighed less and was more user-friendly.

Jack revamped the grip and removed surplus steel from the blade, restyling the grind to pro-

duce what could be described as a "sophisticated fuller." The Ugly is one of those knives that, when knife-minded folk pick it up, they instantly like it. Why? The answer they find themselves giving is "I dunno...I just do." It looks different and feels good and you sense the Ugly is functionally fantastic!

That pretty much describes the knives Jack went on to make. They look different, feel good and are functionally reliable. Jack's benevolent streak and cultural conscience emerged in his knifemaking with the advent of the new millennium, when he turned his hands to producing military commemoratives. In this medium, Jack has no peers in Australia. It is, I believe, Jack's forte to record military history on knives, dirks and swords, for clearly his heart is in creating these exquisitely inscribed and adorned objects

Jack O'Brien's so-called "Ugly" knife model set his course as a maker of note in Australia. *(Spencer photos)*

Knifemaking good-neighbor Jack O'Brien fashioned twin blades to celebrate the 21ˢᵗ birthdays of the twin girls who live next door to him. *(Spencer photos)*

d'art, utilizing his hard-learned expertise.

He has had to devote many hours to research and experimentation in order to master the art of flawless steel-etching procedures. Jack now has an etching specialist with whom he works closely to generate new ways of achieving unique images on commemorative knives. Jack has been honored in military circles, but you won't get him to elaborate on such matters. He doesn't do the things he does for official recognition, but simply because he can, and so he reasons, "Why wouldn't I?"

Pictured within this article is a JOB short sword commemorating the centennial celebration (1903-2003) of the Royal Australian Medical Corps (RAAMC). The RAAMC is steeped in history and laced with tradition. It actually traces its origins to the arrival of the First Fleet at Sydney Cove in 1788. Part of the Royal Marine light infantry on board ship was a medical team comprised of five officers under the supervision of a principal surgeon. Scalpels, it seems, were among the first knives introduced to Australia settlers.

The first hallmark in the history of the RAAMC came in 1885, when an ambulance corps, numbering 34 personnel, formed part of a contingent of 700 volunteers in New South Wales for the Sudan Campaign in South Africa. In 1899, when the Boer War broke out in South Africa, each Australian colony raised and equipped several contingents, including significant medical support of 30 officers and 338 other ranks, plus field equipment.

The Vietnam Vampire

In 1903, the army medical corps of each state and territory combined to form the Australian Army Medical Corps (AAMC). The word Royal was added in 1948, hence RAAMC. The Corps has served with distinction, courage and conviction in every conflict that Australia has been involved in since 1915 at Gallipoli in World War I. During the Vietnam War, Sgt. Kenneth John (Jack) O'Brien served as a medic at Vung Tau 1Aust Field Hospital. His call sign was "Vampire."

The centennial celebrations were carried out in Brisbane, in Queensland, in 2003, and an important part of the ceremony was the cake cutting ritual, which was performed using a custom-crafted blade that Jack generously donated. Now a significant artifact, the commemorative sword has entered the archives of the esteemed RAAMC.

Jack had to obtain special permission from the Canberra War Memorial to produce an exceptional commemorative knife to celebrate the 40th anniversary of the Australian Army Training Team Viet Nam (AATTV), often referred to as "the team." Because of the secrecy surrounding the AATTV, most people are not familiar with the role "the team" played when it was raised and sent to Vietnam in 1962, under the command of Col. F.P.Serong, until 1972, when it withdrew. The team was the first Australian unit to go into Vietnam on August 3, 1962, and was the last to leave that tragic place.

The AATTV was small, elite and unique, and its members were specially selected. For its size, the team was one of the most highly decorated units in the history of the Australian Army. A total of 1,000 soldiers served with the AATTV between 1962 and 1972, including 990 Australians and 10 New Zealanders. Casualties on record show 33 killed and 122 wounded in action. A total of 114 British and Australian military decorations were received in all ranks, including four Victoria Crosses (VC's)—the only VC's issued in the Vietnam War. Other decorations included a United States Meritorious Unit Commendation and a Unit Citation of the Vietnamese Cross of Gallantry with Palm.

I was privileged to attend a private gathering to record the presentation of a specially pre-pared 40th anniversary knife by Jack O'Brien to Keith Payne, the only surviving recipient of a VC from the AATTV. On May 24, 1969, Payne was commanding the 212th Company of the 1st Mobile Strike Force Battalion when the battalion was attacked by a numerically superior North Vietnamese force. The two forward companies were heavily riddled with rockets, mortars and machine guns from three directions simultaneously. They suffered heavy casualties.

Payne received the Victoria Cross for "his feats in dealing with this situation, affecting a withdrawal, and then rounding up the remnants of his company, including the wounded, and navigating at night back to battalion base. Four pieces of rocket shrapnel and a piece of mortar shrapnel wounded Payne in the hands, upper arm and hip."

Payne's photograph and citation are displayed in the Hall of Heroes at the John F. Kennedy Centre for Military Assistance at Fort Bragg in North Carolina. All four recipients of the VC are etched on the pile side of the commemorative blade. Jack produced a limited number of 40th anniversary knives and he allowed "the team" members to purchase them at a special price.

Biker Blades

Someone put Jack on to the Queensland chapter of the Vietnam Veterans Motorcycle Club, which led to the production of another military-orientated collectable knife. It seems that this bunch of Vietnam veteran bikers have been making regular self-funded trips to Cambodia each year, spending some months of their time and heaps of their money clearing old minefields. They heard about the problems with kids and "buffaloes" (Cambodian farm tractors) stepping and riding over live mines. A number of the Vietnam veteran club members went back to school and obtained tickets in mine clearing and associated tasks.

But obviously, too much money would never be enough to make life safer for the endangered farming

Australian knifemaker Jack O'Brien pounds hot steel on an anvil.
(Spencer photos)

families of regional Cambodia. So Jack found a way to help raise funds by building a knife the bikers could raffle, and not just any knife, but an appropriate commemorative piece. Yet again Jack went through the procedure of getting permission from the "war office" to use official insignias and an actual photo. He got exactly what he wanted—an authentic photo of a field with grunts on the ground and choppers giving cover overhead.

He and his specialist etcher (a pair of perfectionists) got their

heads together and produced a phenomenally good reproduction of a black and white war picture on the mark side of a polished knife blade. Etched on the pile side is "Viet Nam Veterans Mine Clearing Team" accompanied by the club logo "Risking Lives & Limbs To Save Lives & Limbs." Like all Jack's carefully conceived knives, this innovative piece has also fulfilled its intended purpose; it swelled the coffers to help Cambodian kids, made a collector of Australian heritage knives happy, and, oh yes, it also cuts efficiently!

The Kiridashi Cometh

The newest trend in handmade knives takes the form of the traditional Japanese kiridashi

By Michael Burch

One of my favorite things about the world of knives is the ebb and flow of trends—you never know which direction the industry is headed toward next. There will always be slip-joint folders, bowies and other classic patterns, but on occasion new blades pique the knife community's interest and spread through the industry like wildfire.

A few years ago knife enthusiasts witnessed the rise of the karambit, a Filipino martial arts blade that remains popular to this day. An increasing number of custom knifemakers and manufacturers are offering karambits and putting their own spins on the traditional design. Over the last few years, I've seen the waves of the knifemaking world splash their way to the Japanese shoreline and bring back another popular pattern that has a long history in the world of knives.

The *kiridashi* (pronounced "key-de-dah-she") is a simple-looking knife, but with clean lines that are exactly what make it such an attractive pattern to collectors and makers. The name itself breaks down to "working knife," and the pattern was designed as a utility and woodworking knife for marking and carving wood. It is also used for garden work and was once a common tool found in young students' pencil boxes to be used for crafts and sharpening pencils.

It is traditionally made of laminated steel and left with a "user" finish. Kiridashis are chisel ground (ground on only one side of the blades), and to be true kiridashi chisel grinds, the opposite sides of the blades are slightly concave to reduce friction. Of course, there are several tra-

Australian knifemaker David Winch dubbed his kiridashi the "Maxidashi." The one-of-a-kind piece is 8 inches overall and is of 5/32-inch-thick, double-ground RWL-34 blade steel. Winch used a Dremel cutoff wheel to gouge the surface, and then etched the blade and hand rubbed it to achieve an interesting textured finish. It features Winch's trademark signature—five indents, or holes, in a circle. The handle is G-10 covered in skateboard tape and wrapped with cotton cord.

ditional versions of the kiridashi built for different woodworking and utility tasks, and many of these can be found online at dedicated woodworking sites, or from Japanese blacksmiths. The kiridashi didn't just show up at the doorstep of mainstream cutlery overnight—the design has been lurking in the shadows and gaining in popularity over the last few years. Many knifemakers have tried their hands at the angular, straight-edge-style of blade. For some reason, it has been a popular year for the kiridashi. Maybe it's because knife collectors and enthusiasts enjoy a knife that is perfect for everyday tasks, or simply the fact that a knife customer can get a quality kiridashi from a great maker at a low price. Where else can you buy a blade fashioned by a master smith for under $100? Either way, the kiridashi has gone mainstream in a big way, and it has been a pleasure to see the different faces the knife can adopt under the hands of ever-creative knifemakers worldwide.

Some kiridashis stray from original patterns, but the overall concept is the same—simple, elegant knives made to be used. And though the kiridashi has a simple look to it, and it is utilitarian in nature, the kiridashi isn't one of the easiest knives to make. Because of its simple design, mistakes in the manufacture stand out like neon lights.

While there are quite a few

knifemakers building kiridashis, some reputable makers never fail to impress the masses. All five of the following knifemakers build complex blades, yet their more-affordable, simpler kiridashis still incorporate the same fit and finish that define quality knives. Following is a well-rounded sampling of what is available to customers, from traditional to contemporary kiridashis.

The Hair-Raising Kiridashi

Murray Carter's name is synonymous with "sharp." Carter is known for creating blades that can scare the hair right off your arms. In addition to being an accomplished American Bladesmith Society (ABS) master smith, Carter lived in Japan for 18 years where, for six of those years, he apprenticed under a 16th-generation bladesmith. With his teacher's blessings, Carter took over the 410-year-old family business and worked as the village bladesmith for 12 years. This is an impressive feat, and one that speaks volumes for his skills as a knifemaker.

Focusing on just one of Carter's kiridashi blades would be like only owning one knife—it's just near impossible to do.

Two of his kiridashis are traditional, hand-forged pieces in the *kataha* (two-layer steel) style, featuring Hitachi White #1 and Gokunantetsu blade steels. With ratings of 64Rc on the Rockwell Hardness Scale, the blades are tough and scream to be used. Coupled with durable, forged "user finishes" and laser-sharp edges, any knife enthusiast would appreciate their ability to handle woodwork, gardening and a variety of kitchen duties.

Carter's Muteki Series Heavy Duty Kiridashi incorporates traditional lines married with a bit of the knifemaker's style. The blade features a Hitachi steel core laminated between layers of SUS 410 stainless steel. The hammer-forged surface gives it the Carter look, and the hand-made leather sheath completes the package. The double-ground blade is ambidextrous and a great utility piece at an extremely affordable price. It would make a fine outdoor companion for any camper, backpacker or hunter.

Last of the Carter wares is his hand-forged damascus "Shumi" Kiridashi with matching *tsuka* (handle) and *saya* (scabbard). This style of kiridashi, also known as a Saya Kiridashi, is of kataha construction with Hitachi White #1 and damascus blade steels. The well-constructed piece features a beautiful ebony wood handle with a water buffalo horn spacer. The blade showcases the first piece of pattern-welded steel Carter forged at his new shop in Oregon.

Steel affects knife enthusiasts, regardless of where the good folks

Australian knifemaker Kwong Yeang, otherwise known in knife circles as "Jason Cutter," fashioned the Kiridashi-TAC. It stretches 5 inches overall and showcases a 1 ¼-inch chisel-ground blade with a convex edge, and a "reptilian" Micarta® handle. Its smooth lines and clean machine finish exemplify the attention to detail that Cutter gives all his blades.

Charles Marlowe's knives are clean, so it is no surprise that his version of a kiridashi is so elegantly simple, almost to the point of being sterile. The "Marlowe-Dashi" is a one-of-a-kind piece incorporating a 154CM blade heat-treated by Paul Bos. The blade is about 7/8-inch thick at its widest point, and stretches 4 inches in length. The razor-sharp edge is perfectly chisel ground, and like everything Marlowe does, it is crisp, clean and easy to maintain. The Marlowe-Dashi makes for a fine, compact, everyday carry knife.

Murray Carter's hand-forged damascus "Shumi" Kiridashi is of kataha (two-layer steel) construction, including Hitachi White #1 and damascus blade steels. The well-constructed piece features a matching ebony *tsuka* (handle) and *saya* (scabbard) with a water buffalo horn spacer.

Murray Carter's Muteki Series Heavy Duty Kiridashi incorporates traditional lines married with a bit of the knifemaker's style. The blade features a Hitachi steel core laminated between layers of SUS 410 stainless steel. The hammer-forged surface gives it the Carter look, and the handmade leather sheath completes the package. The double-ground blade is ambidextrous and a great utility piece at an extremely affordable price. It would make a fine outdoor companion for any camper, backpacker or hunter.

The Warren Thomas kiridashi is simply stunning. The deceptively simple-looking blade showcases an anodized 6AL-4V titanium blade and electronically welded tungsten carbide edge. With an overall length of 5 7/8 inches, the blade is 3/16-inch thick and a good size for most everyday tasks without being too cumbersome.

are from or what they do, and many knifemakers have alter egos, otherwise known as a "day jobs." Australian knifemaker Kwong Yeang, who, in blade circles, goes by the moniker "Jason Cutter," is also a full-time doctor.

In addition to spending time with his family, the Melbourne maker is a psychologist during the day and kicks up dust in his shop at night. Cutter became involved in making knives as a hobby in 2001 and creates a wide variety of blades, from ABS-style forged bowies to tactical knives, slip joints, and of course, kiridashis.

Where possible, Cutter tries to perform all the work on all aspects of his knives by himself, from forging and heat treatment to Kydex® and leather sheath work. As a voting member of the Australian Knifemakers Guild,

Cutter has a high standard to which he holds his knives, and his kiridashi blades are no exception.

His Kiridashi-TAC stretches 5 inches overall and showcases a 1 ¼-inch cutting edge. The chisel-ground blade with convex edge makes it quite a cutter (pun absolutely intended). With its "reptilian" Micarta® handle, the knife is a perfect example of a number of tactical kiridashis readily available on the market. The smooth lines and clean machine finish exemplify the attention to detail that Cutter gives all his blades.

The Steel Fuser

A full-time knifemaker for about 10 years, Warren Thomas started fashioning blades as a young kid, but as he grew older he decided to concentrate his efforts on making hard-working knives that were out of the ordinary. In 1993, Thomas experimented with fusing carbon fiber and stainless steel, spending considerable time and money researching, as well as experimenting with materials and techniques, in an effort to perfect his unique blade look.

Thomas's knives are now available across the globe, including on the Internet, and *BLADE Magazine*® has featured his work several times. His knives are hard-working blades with a definite art appeal to them that verges on "tactically-devious." His unconventional blades usually incorporate such materials as carbon fiber, titanium and tungsten carbide, and at least some of the appeal of their material makeup is that the knives are lightweight, non-magnetic and non-corrosive. Just because they have a different look doesn't mean Thomas's blades can't be used as

aggressively as other knives. His creations are built to last and are used in real-world situations by civilians and military personnel.

Though he fashions a variety of knives and employs unconventional materials, some of his patterns originate from traditional designs, making his work even more appealing. His website showcases a plethora of classically styled blades, including butterfly knives, swords, frame-lock folders and kiridashis.

The kiridashi Thomas sent me is simply stunning, and I spent a lot of time admiring the deceptively simple-looking blade with its unique anodized 6AL-4V titanium blade and electronically welded tungsten carbide edge. With an overall length of 5 7/8 inches, the blade is 3/16-inch thick and a good size for most everyday tasks without being too cumbersome. I got a good grip on the epoxy-soaked, cord-wrapped handle, and the 1 3/8-inch edge offered plenty of cutting area. It would be equally adept at opening military MRE meals and checking the daily mail.

When I take a look at Charles Marlowe's work, I think "clean."

His knives have crisp lines, solid lock-up, and great fit and finish. It was no surprise to me that his version of a kiridashi would be so elegantly simple, almost to the point of being sterile. The blade looks like it would be equally suited for cutting open boxes or in the hands of a surgeon (and it is probably sharp enough, too.)

A full-time maker for six years, Marlowe has been building knives for about 14 years and spends a lot of his time creating beautiful locking-liner folders and butterfly knives. His "Marlowe-Dashi" is a one-of-a-kind piece, but certainly not the last of its kind to come from the hands of Marlowe.

Incorporating a 154CM blade heat-treated by Paul Bos (as with all of Marlowe's stainless-steel blades), his kiridashi is a traditional design that can be relied upon in any situation. The blade is about 7/8-inch thick at its widest point, and stretches 4 inches in length. The razor-sharp edge is perfectly chisel ground, and like everything Marlowe does, it is crisp, clean and easy to maintain. The Marlowe-Dashi works perfectly with a

Two of Murray Carter's kiridashis are traditional, hand-forged pieces in the *kataha* (two-layer steel) style, featuring Hitachi White #1 and Gokunantetsu blade steels. With ratings of 64Rc on the Rockwell Hardness Scale, the blades are tough and scream to be used. Coupled with durable, forged "user finishes" and laser-sharp edges, any knife enthusiast would appreciate their ability to handle woodwork, gardening and a variety of kitchen duties.

"monkey's fist"-style lanyard (not included), and makes for a fine, compact, everyday carry knife.

The Machine Minimalist

Australian knifemaker David Winch builds beautiful blades without a workshop full of expensive machines. Though he likes to do some of his designs using CAD (Computer Aided Design) programs, his tool arsenal includes a 2x48 grinder, drill press, metal band saw, Dremel tool and a lot of elbow grease. He humorously describes his work as "hybrid tactical" that is "not fully scary, but not too gentlemanly."

Winch's full range of blades includes locking folders, neck knives, axes and much more. He employs RWL-34 blade steel, or 5160 for bigger blades. He even creates gadget-style, almost gear-like keychain knives, bottle openers and "impact"-style pieces for self-defense.

His kiridashi is a prime example of his work—clean, unique and very much a "Winch." Dubbed the "Maxidashi," this one-of-a-kind piece is 8 inches overall and is of 5/32-inch-thick, double-ground RWL-34 blade steel. Winch used a Dremel cutoff wheel to gouge the surface, and then etched the blade and hand rubbed it to achieve an interesting textured finish. It features Winch's trademark signature—five indents, or holes, in a circle. The handle is G-10 covered in skateboard tape and wrapped with cotton cord.

Being the heavyweight of the group, the Maxidashi still incorporates all the elements of a great kiridashi, just in a much larger package. The finish is impeccable on the blade flats and Winch's version of the traditional kiridashi shows off his unique take on knifemaking.

Obviously, I couldn't cover all the great knifemakers who create kiridashis. Fred Perrin, a French knifemaker who specializes in a variety of knife styles, including butterfly knives and folders, is well-known for his self-defense blades. They incorporate high-carbon-steel or damascus blades and a variety of handle materials, including paracord (parachute-type cord), wood, synthetics and more. His "Street Surgeon is one of his great kiridashi-style blades. You can see his work at www.perrinknives.com or e-mail him at bene.perrin@tiscali.fr.

Ivan Campos, a Brazilian knifemaker who has been featured in BLADE, likes to use differentially-heat-treated 5160, CPM S30V, CPM 3V and damascus blade steels. His work reflects traditional Japanese styling with cord-wrapped handles, but he also fashions more utilitarian knives with paracord handle wraps at affordable prices. You can view Ivan's knives at http://www.bladebazar.com/ivancampos.htm or e-mail him at ivan@bladebazar.com. Shinichi Watanabe is a sixth-generation bladesmith who builds beautiful, traditional kiridashi blades in a variety of styles. Based out of Japan, Shinichi offers hand-forged kiridashi knives out of his "Kintaro-Ame" steel that is achieved through forging three different steels together. You can find Watanabe's work at www.watanabeblade.com/english/ or you can e-mail him at sin@watanabeblade.com.

Get a Grip on Small Knives

Since some of the kiridashi blades are very small, a nice, knotted lanyard can give you a better grip on the blade and add a personal touch. For instance, if you've got a knife that fits in three fingers, a "monkey's fist" on a lanyard can be held tight on the outside of your fist and add a lot more security to your grip. A good sinnet knot can also become an "extension" of the knife if it is small (see the Marlowe knife). Most of the popular knots can be found online on macramé websites or through online searches. Some popular lanyard knots include:

- Flat Sinnet
- Round Sinnet
- Square Sinnet
- Monkey's Fist
- Noose/Coil Knot
- Cobra Stitch
- Twist Stitch

There are many more out there and with just a few different colors of paracord and some imagination, you can personalize your kiridashi or other small knives and make them easier to unsheathe and use.

CONTACT INFORMATION:

Murray Carter
P.O. Box 307
Vernonia, OR 97064
713.204.5192
carter.cutlery@verizon.net

Jason Cutter Bladeart
P.O. Box 351
Rosanna, VIC 3084
Australia
www.jcbknives.com
jason@jcbknives.com

You can see others of
Warren Thomas's knives at:
www.wtknives.com

Charles Marlowe
10822 Poppleton Ave.
Omaha, NE 68144
402.933.5065
www.marloweknives.com
cmarlowe1@cox.net

You can reach David Winch at
dav.winch@ozemail.com.au

Machines Make the Knifemaker

Ask any contractor or handyman, having the right tools for the job is half the battle

By Allen Elishewitz

Few articles have been written about the tools knifemakers use to fashion their edged creations. Shops vary, depending on whether a knifemaker forges blades or practices the stock-removal method of knifemaking, and whether he or she makes fixed blades or folders. It doesn't have to be that way—a shop that is well equipped, with high precision machines, allows a knifemaker to build any type of knife, as well as jewelry, pens, watches, tools and more.

No two shops are alike.

Most knife collectors see a finished product and never grasp or understand what goes into the handcrafting of an edged tool. This article should shed some light on the subject and result in more appreciation for the talented craftsmen who spend countless hours conjuring up wonderful knife designs.

Today, due to the introduction of CNC (Computer Numerically Controlled) machines and their less-expensive imported counterparts, many manual machines are available on the secondary market at attractive prices. With a good deal of knife manufacturing being outsourced overseas, manufacturers are selling machines for pennies a pound. Twenty years ago, for example, buying a Deckel GK21 pantograph could cost an individual roughly $20,000, but nowadays the machines are available used, but in good working condition, for between $1,000 and $3,500 each.

Europe is known for manufacturing quality machines, with rigidity and accuracy being held

The author uses the machines in his shop to fashion such strikingly handsome knives as the Magellan folder. It features a two-tone Damasteel blade, titanium bolsters embellished in a guilloche pattern and a silver G-10 handle.

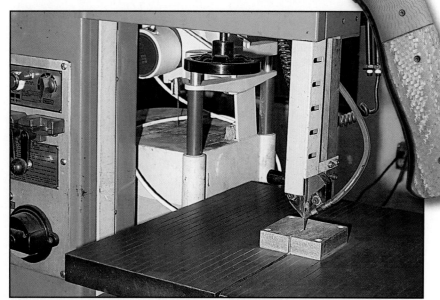

The variable speed fixed/vertical band saw is operable between 65 and 265 sfpm (surface feet per minute). The saw features a built-in welder so a knifemaker can use it to fashion his or her own band saw blades, or repair ones that break.

to a high standard. The United States also builds good machines, including designs that might not be as refined as the their European equivalents, but with accuracy that equals or surpasses them. Asian machines have had a reputation for being junk, but within the past 10 to 15 years, the Asians have developed high-precision lines that are more expensive than the cheaper units for which they had become known.

In building a knife, one of the first things a maker does is cut out his parts, including blades, handles, liners, guards and bolsters.

The parts are rough-cut to shape according to a final pattern. Most knifemakers use a metal-cutting band saw—usually a vertical saw with a blade that travels in one direction, and at a slower speed than a woodcutting band saw.

A number of saw teeth styles and variations exist, each ideal for cutting certain material. One of the more popular knifemaking band saws is a vertical/horizontal light duty cutoff machine. Such a band saw allows the user to cut material as if he or she is using a conventional band saw, or clamp the cutting medium in a built-in

The results of using a disk grinder for knifemaking applications are often better than if employing a belt grinder for the same operations. Knifemakers employ disk grinders for flat grinding blade bevels, and for flattening handles and bolsters before attaching them to blades.

The author uses a jig-bore to drill holes. A jig-bore is the most refined method of making holes, with the machine's tolerances held to a much higher standard than any other type of drill press.

vise on the base and use the machine as a horizontal chop saw. It is an inexpensive, and thus popular, machine.

When working with steel or titanium, a bi-metal saw blade is preferable. The teeth are usually tough, hard steel and the back half, or spine, of the saw blade is more flexible, softer steel. Bi-metal blades have changed cutting technology by allowing the operators to cut faster and for longer periods of time than when using standard band saw blades.

The band saw in the accompanying photograph is a fixed/vertical saw with a variable speed that allows it to be run at 65 to 265 sfpm (surface feet per minute). The saw features a built-in welder, enabling the knifemaker to fashion his or her own band saw blades, or repair the ones that break.

The Master Bevel Grinder

There is one piece of equipment that all knifemakers own regardless of what style of knives they build—a grinder. The machine is employed for profiling the handles and the blades, contouring handle material and grinding the master bevels of blades. A grinder is absolutely essential for knifemaking.

In Seki City, Japan, and in some old European cutlery towns, knifemakers use grinding stones similar to those integral to knife sharpeners in the United States. It is an age-old European tradition that is still in practice today.

Most modern U.S. knifemakers use grinding belts that come in varying grits, from 36 to 3,000 grit, and in a plethora of material make-ups, including ceramic, zirconium, silicon carbide and aluminum oxide. Each belt has specific properties well suited for grinding individual knifemaking materials.

A motor-powered belt grinder incorporates an idler wheel to control the tracking, as well as a contact wheel for grinding. A smooth wheel performs precision grinds with little vibration, but it heats the material quickly. On the other hand, a serrated wheel is more

aggressive in removing material and keeps the grinding medium cooler. A serrated wheel vibrates, though, making it difficult to control the quality of a blade finish. Idler wheels also vary in hardness, which can affect the crispness and finish of the blade surface.

The advantage of using a belt grinder is the large number of accessories available for such a machine. The average belt grinder is so versatile a knifemaker can switch from a 10-inch wheel to a 1/2-inch wheel, and then, with the same grinder, use a flat platen with a tool rest. The grinder in the accompanying photo is a typical belt grinder incorporating a DC variable-speed motor that allows the operator to control the speed of the grinder. There are numerous accessories available for this unit.

A disk grinder is another popular knifemaking machine. Specific in its design, the results of using a disk grinder for knifemaking applications are often better than if employing a belt grinder for the same operations. A disk grinder incorporates round abrasive disks that are available in the same materials and grits as belts used on a belt grinder. Each of the disks adheres to another flat, round and hard disk, and is used to grind materials flat. Knifemakers employ disk grinders for flat grinding blade bevels, and for flattening handles and bolsters before attaching them to blades.

It is Hole-drilling Time

After a maker has cut and profiled his materials, it is time to drill some holes. Drilling holes can be done using several machines, but the act of drilling the holes is always the same. Most drill bits are "spiral cutters" designed to remove material in a downward direction. In drilling through steel, the steel chips follow the spiral out of the hole.

Not one drill bit is designed for all materials, and the drill bits, themselves, come in a variety of materials, like carbide, cobalt and high-speed steel. Each of the materials has its advantages and disad-

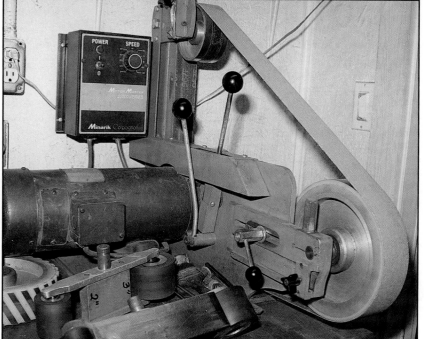

There is one piece of equipment that all knifemakers own regardless of what styles of knives they build—a grinder. The advantage of using a belt grinder is the large number of accessories available for such a machine.

vantages, and each varies in spiral type, cutting edge angle, flute number and web. The specifications also determine the application and material. Most knifemakers use drill presses—straightforward, simple machines dedicated to one operation: making holes.

The typical drill press has an adjustable table with a hand crank on the side to lower the drill bit into the cutting medium. There is another machine, however, that is better suited to drilling holes due to the rigidity and precision of its quill—a milling machine. This piece of equipment is more versatile than a drill press with the ability to perform a variety of operations.

The accompanying photo shows a jig-bore that the author uses to drill holes. A jig-bore is the most refined method of making holes, with the machine's tolerances held to a much higher standard than any other type of drill press. A co-ordinate table allows the operator to go from one position to another within an accuracy of .00005 of an inch, no problem. Basically in layman's terms, it is a glorified drill press!

A buffer is considered one of the most dangerous knifemaking machines in the shop. It might be small and unthreatening in appearance but more injury-related horror stories are connected to buffers than any other machines. A buffer is used to polish, de-burr and satin finish knife components. It can also sharpen knife blades.

A buffer—usually a motor with a shaft protruding from both ends—is mounted on a pedestal, or a bench, and there are a variety of wheels that fit over the shaft. The choices for polishing steel, for example, include sewn-muslin, loose-muslin and felt wheels. For satin finishing blades, Scotch-Brite wheels excel at their purpose.

What makes the buffer so dangerous is the combination of speed and wheels. Certain wheels have a tendency to want to grab parts. Combine that with a 3,600-rpm motor and blades can be flung across the room or even into the operator. The accompanying picture shows a 1-hp Baldor buffer with an exhaust system.

Now for the Specialty Machines ...

The above machines are what most knifemakers possess and need to fashion strikingly handsome edged tools. Other machines

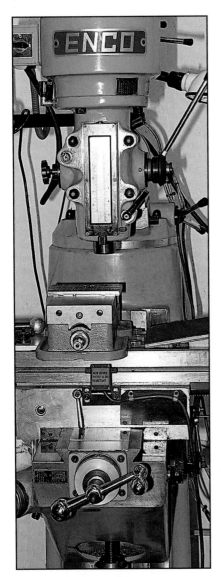

Milling machines have rotating cutters ideally suited for removing metal and other knifemaking materials. The conventional vertical knife mill features a digital readout—a coordinate measuring device.

A lathe is the opposite of a mill, in that a part is held and rotated on a lathe as a cutter is introduced to the rotating pieces. This machine produces round parts. The tool-room lathe shown here showcases a digital readout that would probably fall under the "specialty lathe" category because of the tolerance, and thus quality of the cut, to which the lathe is held.

exist that excel in specialized operations for making such things as knife mechanisms and accessories.

Milling machines have rotating cutters ideally suited for removing metal and other knifemaking materials. The cutting medium is held on a milling machine table or in a vise, and the table can be moved in three directions. A wide variety of cuts can be performed on a milling machine, such as those necessary to make slots, grooves, gears and chamfers. Since a milling machine table moves on a straight plane, only straight and square, not round, parts can be milled.

Types of milling machines include a "knee mill" with a table that moves up and down, and a "drill mill," incorporating a table in a fixed location with quill that is lowered to introduce the cutter to the part. A horizontal mill features a cutter that rotates horizontally to the surface of the table, unlike the traditional mill where the cutter is vertical to the table. A universal mill can be used both horizontally and vertically, making the milling machine the heart and soul of the specialized machine shop and the backbone of American industries.

There are more accessories for milling machines than for any other power units, so many accessories and cutting tools, in fact, that it would be impossible to mention them all in this article. They could fill a book, thus indicating the importance of the mill.

The accompanying picture is of a conventional vertical knee mill. Notice that there is a digital readout—a coordinate measuring device. Most milling machines have dials on the controls and on the hand wheels so, in theory, the operator does not need a digital readout, but having one makes life a lot easier.

A lathe is the opposite of a mill, in that a part is held and rotated on a lathe as a cutter is introduced to the rotating piece. This machine produces round parts. It does not have the variety of accessories a mill does, but by nature, the lathe produces more precision parts than a milling machine.

Most lathes incorporate tailstock, with which operators can drill the centers of spinning parts. A lathe can also be used to thread and make internal or external screws. The lathe size is determined by the swing and the length of the bed. The swing is dictated by the largest diameter that the lathe can turn. There are accessories for the lathe that will allow the operator to mill and even grind on this machine, and each of the accessories is ideally suited for specific applications.

Workhorse of Machine Shops

Lathes can be divided into three categories—engine lathes, turret lathes and specialty lathes. An engine lathe is a standard manual lathe, the workhorse of all machine shops. All turning operations can be performed on an engine lathe.

A turret lathe is usually reserved for production work for which a turret tailstock with multiple tools is assembled to achieve a set of specific operations on a production level. A specialty lathe is any lathe that is designed for a specific type of operation.

The accompanying picture shows a tool-room lathe with a digital readout that would probably fall under the "specialty lathe" category because of the tolerance, and thus quality of the cut, to which the lathe is held. It is usually reserved for the best operator making precision parts not on a production level.

A pantograph is used to duplicate parts and usually consists of two tables—a copy table and a cutting table. Upon placing a pattern on the copy table, a stylus is maneuvered to trace it. On the cutting table, a spindle rotates a cutter and cuts out the part.

A vertical spindle of a pantograph works much like a milling machine, but instead of being attached to the frame of a mill, it is attached to floating arms. The floating arms can be adjusted to change the ratio of the cut. For example, an operator can cut a 2:1 ratio, which means that the pattern will be two times larger than the actual piece being cut.

On some machines the operator has the ability to reverse the operation and cut a part twice as large as the pattern. The difference in size between the template and the part being cut influences the accuracy of the cut. With a

A pantograph is used to duplicate parts and usually consists of two tables—a copy table and a cutting table. The small die-sinking pantograph pictured here sports arms positioned at a 2:1 ratio

large pattern, there will be fewer cutting errors in the finished part than with a small pattern.

The only limitation to using a pantograph is the knifemaker's imagination! The pantograph is actually obsolete in the production industry because of the advent of CNC machines.

There are two types of pantographs—lettering pantographs and die-sinking pantographs. Lettering pantographs are usually small and light, and designed to cut letters and numbers on plastic signs and soft metals. Die sinking pantographs are designed to machine steel, and are always heavier and more rigid than lettering pantographs. Their spindles and motors are modified for heavy cuts in steel. The pantograph shown in the accompanying photo is a small die-sinking pantograph with arms positioned at a 2:1 ratio.

There are many more machines and tools being used by knifemakers. Every machine that is introduced into a knifemaker's shop opens new doors and possibilities. Machines allow the makers to create knives that take on a more unique and individual appearance than their predecessors. But every new machine introduced to the shop slows the maker's production level. The added time an operator has to put into manipulating a machine takes away from the time he or she dedicates to knifemaking.

Due to all the machines in my shop, today I am 10 times slower a knifemaker than I was seven years ago. But the outcome is well worth the trade. Machines make the knifemaker.

Befuddling Blade Shapes

Even experienced pocketknife collectors are taken back by these edged oddities

By Richard D. White

Spying an old pocketknife lying in the bottom of a glass showcase, somewhat hidden beneath a jumble of jewelry, pens and badges, gets the heart pumping. Like many outdoorsmen, knife collectors take thrill in the hunt. Outwitting fellow collectors at antique shows, being first in line, guessing what aisle the treasures are in and knowing what knife styles and brand names to look for is sweet redemption for times others beat them at their game. And having the know-how to evaluate classic pocketknives by checking for cracks in bone handles or for the amount of snap in folding blades satisfies their souls.

For some, craftsmanship of fine knives is where the attraction lies. For others, it is finely polished, hand-honed blades that snap open and closed. Still others admire the engineering of multi-blade pocketknives, particularly those with edged implements lying within centimeters of each other, yet opening and closing with unimpeded ease. The ultimate reward could be unearthing knives with tang stamps dating back to the 1880s.

The beauty of knives, however, is the main attraction for most blade admirers. Whether they have fiery, almost translucent pearl handles, gorgeous jigged-bone grips, polished hardwood exteriors or one of a striking variety of celluloid handle materials, ranging from colorful, glittery reds and yellows to swirls of blues, greens and grays, the patterns are fabulous. Some celluloid handles even resemble peacock feathers or polished tortoise shells.

Regardless of what attracts us to these fascinating edged marvels of

Three-blade and four-blade premium stockman knives are quality examples of standard blade configurations for most pocketknives. The three-blade KA-BAR stockman features (from left) a spay blade, sheepsfoot blade and master clip blade. The Wards stockman sports a sheepsfoot blade, pen blade, punch blade and master clip blade.

craftsmanship and engineering, knives are first and foremost tools designed and built for cutting.

Some people don't give much thought to the shapes of pocketknife blades, or why some knives have more than one blade in the first place. A large segment of the population figures that one blade fits all, much like your run-of-the-mill stretch pants or overalls.

Cutlery manufacturers, on the other hand, spend a great deal of time designing and developing blade styles and sizes to satisfy all cutting needs. Admittedly, for the average

The words "King Oscar Sardines" in white letters on the folder's black celluloid handle hint toward the use of the small fork—to extract sardines from a tin, and thus saving the hands from smelling like dead fish.

All photographs by the author, Mr. Richard D. White

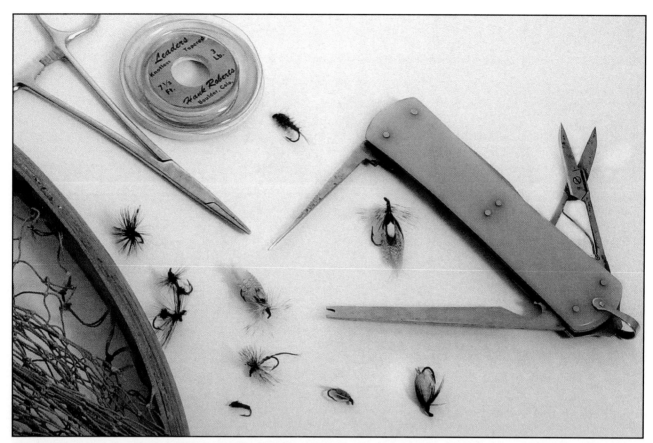

The singular design of the KA-BAR fly fishing knife includes a small scissors for trimming fly "hackle;" a combination file/hook-de-gorger; and a versatile implement (bottom) for removing hooks from fish and honing the hooks. The long awl was typically employed for such chores as untying knots in fly leader and line. Not open, or shown, in the photo is a master blade for gutting trout.

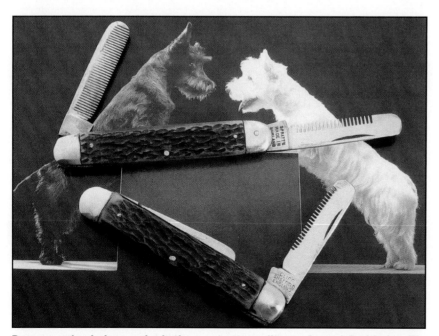

Dog-grooming knives embody the most extraordinary of specialty blades. The folders were premiums offered by the Spratts Dog Food Company of England, and used to comb burrs out of the coats of wire-haired terrier hunting dogs.

knife user, standard blade styles accomplish the majority of tasks. The typical four-blade American pocketknife, for example, includes a master blade for all-around use, a sheepsfoot blade for scribing lines and slitting material, a spay blade, which was originally designed for spaying or neutering farm animals, and either a pen blade for fine work or a leather punch.

Befuddled by Fly Fishing

Although four blades can handle most general tasks, there are hundreds of other cutting chores for which duty-specific blades have been engineered. Almost every industry and occupation claims a blade style all its own. Fly fishing knives, built specifically for those who pride themselves in the art of floating flies, handle a variety of related tasks. The master blade is designed for gutting and cleaning fish; a large "hook de-

The horseman's knife is loaded with handy implements, including a "hoof pick" for removing stones from horses' hooves. The knife features a fleam for bleeding animals, a corkscrew, saw blade, master blade, cap lifter and leather punch.

gorger" removes hooks from fish mouths, and includes a built-in cap lifter and a file for sharpening hooks; a pointed awl is engineered to remove knots from leader and line; and a small folding scissors is ideal for trimming the hackle from small flies or cutting off excess fly leader.

In addition to this assortment of specialized blades, fly fishing knives usually come with metal bails for attachment to fly fishermen's vests. Some employ standard screwdrivers protruding from the ends of the frames. So the old saying of necessity being the mother of invention is applicable to fly fishing knives and numerous other styles designed for specific applications.

In the case of English knives emblazoned with cigar advertisements, small, pointed awls similar to fly-fishing implements are used to pierce the ends of cigars. In that case, implements identical to those in fly fishing knives are engineered for totally different applications.

Somehow, the British and Germans have come up with an incredible array of blade styles and shapes. For the Germans, and many Europeans for that matter, a meal would not be complete without a glass of

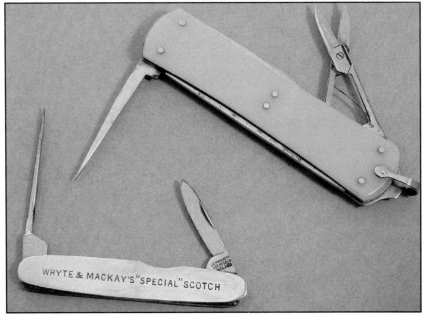

The awl of the small metal knife, although almost identical in appearance to a KA-BAR fly fishing knife awl, has a different purpose—to poke holes in the ends of cigars so that they draw air and smoke cleanly.

wine. In order to open wine bottles, corkscrews are integral to most European multi-blade pocketknives, and "champagne-bottle wire cutters" are ideal for removing the pesky wire and metal foil entwined around the mouths of champagne bottles. In fact,

corkscrews and champagne-bottle wire cutters are what often separate European camp knives, which generally have six blades, from American four-blade camp knives.

One of the strangest utensils ever built into a pocketknife appears to be

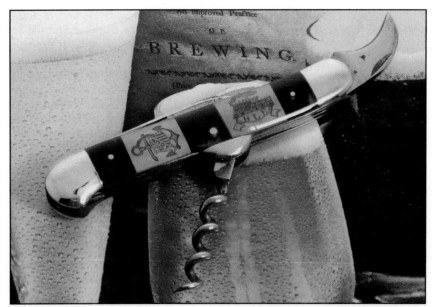

Perfect for use in the tavern or at home, the bartender's knife showcases a heavy-duty blade used to cut the foil and wire that commonly encase corks on champagne bottles.

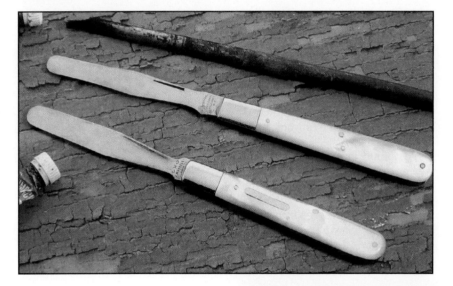

nothing more than a fork, albeit a surprisingly small fork. Though just as small as a "cigar fork," this particular example is not made to hold cigars and keep smokers from burning their fingers on glowing tobacco. The undersized fork is, indeed, used in the traditional manner—for eating food, and the clue to how it is employed lies in an advertisement touting "King Oscar Sardines" on the side of the handle. The little fork is made for spearing sardines directly out of the tin. After all, sorting slimy sardines from sharp-edged tins using one's fingers is a dangerous and daunting task.

As strange as the sardine fork might appear, there are equally odd specialty blades with purposes that only become clear upon examining the edged tools. Some clues as to the knives' uses are in advertisements, like on the King Oscar Sardines

---

The gorgeous, single-blade "palette" knives from Cattaraugus Cutlery Co. (top) and J. Russell Cutlery Co. parade pearl handles and flexible blades ideally suited for painters to mix their oils on palettes. Rare in any condition, the knives are showcase pieces.

A full-size "palette knife," the Russell Cutlery Co. folder resembles a "daddy Barlow." As the words "C.K. Williams & Co. Dry Colors Easton, PA" on the handle indicate, the piece was marketed by a maker of powdered, dry paint that was mixed with water or mineral spirits to make liquid paint. Knives made by the John Russell Cutlery Co. are exceedingly rare and this unusual folder, still with dried paint between the liners, is an exciting, recent find by the author.

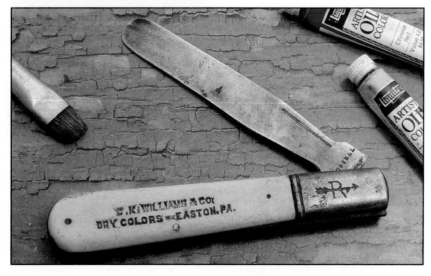

The small, pearl-handle folders incorporate unusual buttonhook implements for lacing up old-fashioned women's shoes. Such knives were probably also used by maids to tighten the laces of Victorian-era bustles.

knife, or built within the designs of the multi-blade folders.

Burrs and Cockleburs

One fascinating folder sports a pair of strange blades, each with a series of parallel grooves cut into the sides of the implements, looking much like a couple of combs. The "dog groomer's comb/knife" is stamped "SPRATTS, Made in England." An English dog and pet food company, Spratts included a dog groomer's comb in each large bag of dog food it sold.

Why would an Englishman groom a dog with a sharpened comb that resembles a pocketknife? The answer lies in the hunting sport commonly associated with the British Isles. Frequently small dogs, especially those with wiry hair, were and are used to root out rats, ground hogs and other burrowing animals during a weekend of hunting. Given the nature of Britain's hedgerows, the dogs, commonly wire-haired terriers, emerge from animal holes and undergrowth with their hair covered in cockleburs, thorns and other sticky plant material. The SPRATTS sharp-edged dog grooming combs were just the things to cut away the fur from around the burrs as the dogs were groomed. It was the only way to remove imbedded thorns and burrs without hurting the dogs.

Knives designed for oil painters are among those with befuddling blades. Known as "spatula blades," the flat, unsharpened implements were used by painters to mix various oils and pigments. Etched into the blades or handles of most spatula folders were advertisements for paint supplies and companies, the latter including the John Russell Cutlery Co., one of the oldest knife entities in the United States. John Russell is known to have made several spatula-blade folders, in particular one that is identical to a

One of the most historically interesting blades inherent to early Scout knife patterns is referred to as a "Prest-O-Lite key." As part of four-blade camp, utility or Scout knives, square holes, or keys, were most often integral to the screwdriver blades. Prest-O-Lite keys turned the valves on early automobile gaslights. They were used from about 1910-1930 and were done away with thereafter when the automobile industry went to electric lights.

large daddy Barlow pocketknife.

The spatula blade has another interesting use. As part of a slender physician's or doctor's knife, a spatula blade aided in reaching into bottles of ointment and salves that were then mixed together in preparing early prescriptions. Even today, physician's knives contain specialized spatula blades.

One of the most historically interesting blades inherent to early Scout knife patterns is referred to as a "Prest-O-Lite key." As part of four-blade camp, utility or Scout knives, square holes, or keys, were most often integral to the screwdriver blades. Prest-O-Lite keys turned the valves on early automobile gaslights. The keys were used from about 1910-1930 and were done away with thereafter when the automobile industry went to electric lights.

The list of specialty pocketknife blades is nearly endless. Outside of the common blades recognizable to

most collectors are the timber scribe; typographer's punch; glass cutter; folding ruler; cap lifter; button-hook; alligator wrench; wire stripper; survival saw; fish gaff; horse hoof pick; can opener; folding fork and spoon; pipe tamper; pipe bowl reamer; cuticle trimmer; medical fleam; scalpel; and a special Phillips screwdriver for tightening the skis outfitted to World War II 10th Mountain Division snow troops. Each of these blades was designed for a specific purpose, and each has its own unique story.

Although most collectors specialize in a particular cutlery brand name or general style, an unusual collection could be assembled with the general theme of "befuddling blades," with each knife including blades designed for specialized tasks. Such a collection would certainly uncover and encompass the true stories behind the many tasks the knives were originally designed to accomplish.

Revisit the Golden Age of the Sword

The 17th century remains the grand era of rapiers, small swords, daggers and pikes

By Edward Crews

Capt. John Smith of Jamestown, Va., fame was one of the 17th century's great soldiers. His thirst for adventure led him far from his native England, across Europe and finally to the New World. Like thousands of his contemporaries, Smith was a skilled swordsman. He knew from long military service that a sturdy blade in the hands of a determined man could easily spell the difference between victory and defeat, life and death. Not only was this true on the battlefields of Europe, but it also proved worthy in the wilds of the New World, as one anecdote exemplifies.

In the early days of the Jamestown colony, Smith quickly rose to an important leadership position thanks to his assertive personality and military skills. The colonists were fortunate to have the bold and reliable Smith. Not only was the environment they faced new and challenging, but difficulties also existed with the American Indians. In fact, relations between them and the English settlers were fragile, alternating between accommodation and warfare.

To keep the natives off balance, Smith periodically lead patrols from the palisade fort at Jamestown. On one such venture, 40 bowmen of the Paspehegh tribe, led by their chief, laid an ambush for an English patrol. The natives became rattled when they realized that Smith, who enjoyed a fierce reputation among them, was leading the unit, and they fled.

Smith sent his men back to Jamestown. Sensing correctly that the chief had remained behind, he decided to stay and hunt him down. So, the Englishman and the

While European explorers carried finely crafted metal-edged weapons, they often encountered American Indians using Stone Age technology. A sample of arrowheads shows what natives typically used for warfare and hunting.

A print of John Smith's 1612 Virginia map details the areas he explored in the New World during almost three years that he was based at Jamestown. On these explorations, he frequently carried and used a sword in encounters with Native American warriors.

Although crude by European standards, Native American knives were useful and lethal weapons in the hands of accomplished fighters.

Native Americans used simple tools and refined craftsmanship to make edged weapons. Here, a Jamestown interpreter shows the art of flint knapping, or working with stone.

native pursued one another in the forest. Smith moved from cover at one point, and when he did so, the chief reacted by positioning himself to shoot Smith with an arrow. As the chief drew his bow, Smith rushed him. The men wrestled and soon fell into a nearby river.

Smith beat and choked the chief until he surrendered. Then the Englishman pulled his enemy onto the bank, drew his sword and prepared to behead him. Before Smith acted, though, he realized that a dead chief was worth nothing. A living hostage was another matter. Smith spared the man's life and dragged him into captivity.

From beginning to end, close fierce fights like this characterized the 17th century. Arguably, it was the golden age of the sword. It was also an exciting, turbulent and violent time—a period of global exploration and continental warfare on a grand scale. The 1600s were a century of nearly constant warfare, with the largest conflict being the Thirty Years War (1618-1648). Other lesser, but no less violent, wars included the War of Devolution (1667), the Dutch War (1672) and the War of the League of Augsburg (1688).

Swarming with Swashbucklers

It was an era of swashbucklers, musketeers, adventurers and dueling masters. As Smith's story shows, no matter where they went, European soldiers carried swords and an array of other edged weapons. The arms appeared on battlefields in Poland, Austria, Germany, England and dozens of places in between.

While the sword was the 17th century's preeminent weapon, military technology made significant gains in the period. Firearms became standard weapons on battlefields and in distant colonies. At the beginning of the century, the matchlock musket had been the standard infantry longarm.

"The matchlock hung on for a long time because it was cheap, comparatively easy to mass produce, robust and anyone could fix it. The gun's dimensions varied, as did its styles and grades. It weighed about 12 pounds, maybe more, and in Europe it was fired from a rest. The matchlock was smoothbore and not particularly accurate at long ranges. At 100 yards, firing and hitting anything was largely a matter of chance," said Thomas E. Davidson, senior curator for the Jamestown-Yorktown Foundation. The foundation maintains museums at Jamestown and Yorktown, as well as a living history park at Jamestown, which interprets 17th-century life in early America.

The rapier is considered the premier weapon of the 1600s. The large, thrusting weapons saw service all over the globe and remain a steadfast prop for Hollywood films about the period.

Daggers were handy and cheap. They served well as personal defense items and on the battlefield. This picture shows a type popular in 17th-century England.

The matchlock took its name from its ignition system, a burning cord soaked in saltpeter. Firing the gun was simple. The gunner merely pushed the trigger up, causing the burning match, held in place by an arm called a "serpentine," to fall into a pan of powder. It burned through a hole in the barrel and ignited the main charge, which fired the bullet.

Matchlocks represented a huge gain in firepower but they had many shortcomings. Inventors sought a musket with higher rates of fire and better reliability. This led to the flintlock. The flintlock replaced the burning match with flint striking a piece of metal, creating sparks to fire the gun. Flintlocks were in widespread use by the 1650s and remained in service for almost 200 years.

Artillery also improved in the 17th century. Swedish King Gustavus Adolphus played a particularly important role in this advance. He not only standardized cannon by shot weight and bore diameter, but also greatly refined field artillery and used the guns to great effect on the battlefield.

Battlefield tactics in the 17th century reflected the technology at the time.

"The European battlefield of the period saw the employment of artillery and cavalry, something that didn't happen in America," Davidson said. "Battles were set-piece affairs with one side firing until the other broke. Then, the cavalry rode in and cut up the retreating force."

The model for such fighting came from Holland where the Dutch fought for independence from Spain. Soldiers throughout Europe adopted the mode of warfare, drawing on combat experience and period manuals, like "The Exercise of Arms," by Jacob DeGheyn.

Trusting Survival to the Sword

Despite the technical innovations of the 1600s, the sword remained an important military and personal defense arm during the period. The sword's popularity reflected the low fire rates and unreliability of firearms and cannons. Individual soldiers could not trust their survival in combat solely to substandard weapons. The same dilemma affected the way European colonists armed themselves in the New World, Africa and Asia. Accordingly, wherever the men went, they made sure to carry swords strapped to their sides.

Sword types varied greatly during the 1600s. Probably the best known of the era, though, is

One of the most popular edged weapons in England during the 1600s was the bill. Derived from farm implements, it featured a cutting edge and several spikes.

Pikemen constituted one of the largest elements of European armies in the early 1600s. Pikes were cheap, light and easy to make. Training was minimal. As a result and due to the poor performance of early firearms, pikes played an important role in many European campaigns.

Some swordsmen in the 1600s fought with more than one edged weapon, typically a sword and dagger. Such combat required skill, coordination and dexterity. Often sword makers built and sold matching sets of swords and daggers to discriminating clients.

the rapier. Thanks to decades of Hollywood swashbuckling adventures, modern filmgoers continue to expect stars using 17th-century period pieces to cling, clang and thrust in spirited and carefully choreographed duels. Almost always the sword of choice for film fights is a rapier with a cup hilt.

While movies frequently get historic details wrong, it is true that dueling was popular in the early 1600s. The rapier first appeared, however, in the 1500s (some historians argue that the weapon's origin was even older) and was still evolving when the 17th century began. European nobility, generals and admirals particularly liked the rapier, a fact that is self-evident to any student of upper-class European portrait painting from the era.

As the rapier developed, it became a thrusting weapon with a sharp point and no cutting edge along the blade. Blade shapes varied, but triangular and hexagonal patterns eventually appeared. While hilt types also changed, the cup hilt is well established in the public mind. Sword smiths created several others, including a distinctive hilt shaped like the letter "S." Surviving rapiers feature various decorative approaches that range from plain and utilitarian to highly ornate.

At the dawn of the 17th century, some swordsmen carried matching sets of rapiers and daggers, using them simultaneously in combat. As the century advanced, the daggers lost popularity, and rapiers became shorter and lighter. While the rapier enjoyed its heyday during the first three decades of the 1600s, the small sword gradually eclipsed it, beginning its rise to prominence during the latter part of the century and becoming especially popular during the 1700s.

Like the rapier, the small sword developed through evolution, with several varieties created in the process. The variety of small swords is staggering, making it difficult to speak categorically of the weapon's features. Generally speaking, small swords were light, thrusting weapons with sharp points and without edged blades, though some early models were cut-and-thrust weapons.

In its most basic form, the small sword was a metal pole with a sharp point, and triangular blades were common. The aristocracy wore them as ornaments and for protection. In England, the nobility's interest in the weapon supposedly had to do with the belief that King Charles II reportedly brought the weapon from France.

Some surviving examples are more works of art and less an example of the weapon makers' craft, reflecting a noble pedigree. With that said, military models did exist. Some historians argue that the small sword, not the rapier, is the great-grandfather of modern fencing swords. For all its variety and rich decoration, the small sword was a deadly weapon in the hands of a skilled fighter. Swordsmen relied on speed and dexterity rather than the laborious thrust and parries required with rapiers. A vigorous, skillful attack could, and often did, result in an opponent's death.

Decorative and Deadly

Another popular sword, first appearing in the 1500s, was the basket hilt. "Basket" refers to the sword's decorative hilt, which covered the user's hand. Such a decorative hilt was metal and formed a cage or basket to protect the hand. In the 1600s, basket hilts were popular with English, Scottish, Dalmatian and German troops, with some of the swords finding their way to Jamestown.

Turkish weapons were known to influence European sword styles, which is not unusual given the extensive campaigns fought against the Turks in Eastern Europe. Capt. Smith carried such an arm—a falchion—a single-edged cutting sword. It had a curved blade, somewhat like a Turkish scimitar, a weapon Smith had encountered in his European campaigning.

Northern European soldiers employed the falchion extensively in the 14th and 15th centuries, but the weapon's usage faded with time, and it was seen less and less on battlefields in the 16th and 17th centuries. Smith seemed to prefer the arm, with some historians theorizing that his choice was a deliberate act of self-promotion designed to draw attention to his extensive military experience.

Swords were not the only edged weapons called to action during the period. Infantry carried several types of pole arms, with the most common being the pike. A simple, solid wooden shaft parading a spearhead at one end, a pike often featured a metal butt at the other. The latter allowed the pike to be set securely in the ground to form a "hedge" to repel cavalry charges.

The weapon came in two forms: pikes, which were 14 to 16 feet long, and half pikes, about half the size. Both were simple weapons that could be produced quickly, cheaply and easily. Troops wielding pikes required little training compared to artillerymen, musketeers and cavalry.

Early in the 17th century, pike men constituted a large segment of all European armies, and some of the most accomplished pike men were mercenaries from what is today Germany. Known as "landsknecht," which means land servants, the men enjoyed a reputation across the continent for their combat skills, doggedness in battle and fierce discipline. Typically, soldiers armed with pikes also carried daggers and/or swords for close-quarters fighting. Pikes began to fade from European warfare as muskets improved in range, accuracy and reliability late in the 1600s.

Another pole arm from the period is the "bill." Like pikes, a bill featured a sturdy wooden shaft, although not as long as those used for pikes. Instead of a spearhead at one end, bills employed a wide piece of metal. On one side, parallel to the shaft, was a cutting edge. A spike was positioned opposite the blade, and another spike extended from the metal at a 90-degree angle to the cutting edge.

European infantry had two other notable edged weapons: the "partisan" and the halberd. They were more symbols of rank than weapons, yet, in a pinch, could be used for personal protection. Officers carried the partizan, an ornate spear, while non-commissioned officers toted the halberd. The halberd was a pole with an axe head mounted on it, and interestingly enough, halberds still exist as ceremonial weapons. Modern visitors to Vatican City will find the Swiss Guard, which protects the pope, armed with them.

While most 17th-century pole arms were infantry weapons, the cavalry employed one. The lance was a holdover from medieval times and, like the pike, it gradually disappeared from European battlefields as muskets improved. Lances from the 1600s were typically 10 to 14 feet long with metal spearheads.

Lance-Laden Cavalrymen

The most famous lancers included Poland's Hussaria, from which the word hussar evolved. Hussaria were accomplished cavalrymen armed with lances up to 20 feet long, six-foot swords, carbines, and bows and arrows. Hussaria wore some armor and were known for impressive "wings"—wooden projections with feathers—that they wore on their backs in battle. Hussaria repeatedly distinguished themselves in battle, especially with Turkish invaders in Europe. In one dramatic fight in the early 1600s, 2,500 Hussaria destroyed a 14,000-man Swedish army with less than 300 causalities themselves.

Arguably, the most enduring development in edged weapons during the 17th century was the bayonet. In the late 1600s, designers created a "plug bayonet," a knife with a handle that plugged snugly into a musket barrel. It allowed musketeers to pull double duty as pike men, but an obvious shortcoming was that the infantry couldn't fire their weapons with the bayonets in place.

The problem was solved with the invention of a bayonet affixed to the barrel's exterior with two rings encircling the knife handle and the barrel's exterior. It, too, eventually proved inadequate. The next refinement was the "socket bayonet"—a blade attached to a round metal attachment that fit over the barrel and locked into place. This did not impede loading and proved reliable in battle. The socket bayonet, in fact, was such a success that German and English armies adopted it in the 1690s and stopped using pikes.

In North America, local militias began carrying yet another edged weapon—the hatchet. It could be used to clear brush and obstacles or as a close fighting blade.

Given the great range of edged weapon types in the 1600s and their extensive use all over the globe, it seems safe to say that the 17th century's claim as the golden age of the sword is secure. While swords would continue to be used by armies well into the 19th century, the truth remains that improvements in artillery and firearms drastically reduced the sword's prominence in the 18th century. That leaves the 17th century as the last great era when flashing blades would dominate and shape world history.

Schooled in the Ways of the Willow Bow Smith

The author let his fingers, hands and aching muscles do the talking at Ed Fowler's knife school, and now he better appreciates hand-forged blades

By Evan F. Nappen

"To be conscious that you are ignorant is a great step to knowledge".

—Benjamin Disraeli

I have achieved "blade enlightenment." I had never made a knife before, much less heated a bar of steel to cherry red, then pounded it and ground it into the shape of a blade. I had never built an edged tool in my life, not until I became a willing participant enrolled in Ed Fowler's High Performance Knife School.

It all happened in Ed's newly built knife shop located at his longtime residence, the Willow Bow Ranch in Riverton, Wyoming. It was there that I worked trip hammers, belt grinders, ovens, forges, welding torches, buffing wheels, drill presses and a variety of other blacksmithing and knifemaking tools. Each new tool/machine was a challenge to learn how to use properly. Hours go into the process, and the hours become days invested in steel.

Muscles were worked that I did not know I had. Every night I blew unidentified black stuff out my

A student of Ed Fowler's High Performance Knife School, Evan Nappen changes a belt on a Burr King grinder (top right). Classes are held at Ed's brand-new shop (right) on the Willow Bow Ranch in Riverton, Wyoming.

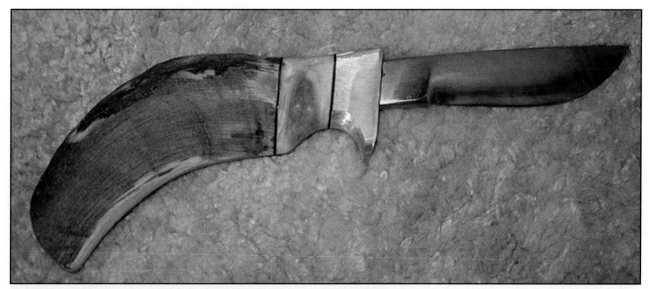
The author's first hand-forged knife is shown at 95 percent completion.

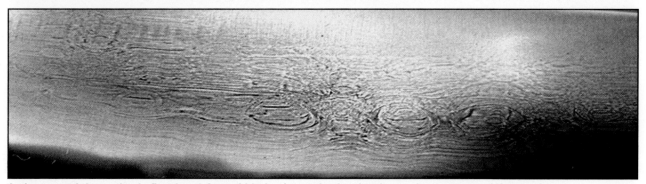
A close-up of the author's first hand-forged blade shows the fascinating grain structure of the steel.

nose. All day, the stereo in Ed's shop played the Andy Wilkinson album "Charlie Goodnight." Visitors to the shop included Rambouillet sheep, horses, cows and Ed's loyal Labrador retriever, Abraham. Every night, I breathed the wonderful scent of sagebrush and gazed at the vast starry Wyoming sky.

I had flown into Riverton from Denver via Great Lakes Airlines. Great Lakes planes haven't flown to the Great Lakes in years, but an airline representative at the gate told me, "It would be too expensive to change the name." I hoped the practice of penny-pinching wasn't also applied to airplane maintenance. The plane was a 19-seat puddle jumper that fishtailed in the sky the whole way to Riverton. (Travel tip: Wear your coat on the plane—it's cold up there! I learned the hard way.)

Upon landing at Riverton Airport, I did not confuse it with Kennedy, LaGuardia or Newark Liberty International. The Airport terminal was amazing—filled with dozens of game trophies from full-mount brown bears to mountain sheep, bespeaking a true sportsman's paradise. Riverton is the only town I have ever visited that has its own airport yet not a 7-Eleven or Dunkin' Donuts.

The gun shop in town is a combination store/outfitter/liquor store/bar and Hallmark card/gift shop. One can get a drink, some packaged goods and a gun, then write home to mother all in the same place! Riverton's claim to fame is that it is the site of the first mountain man rendezvous in 1838. That apparently was the last big event there. The Willow Bow Ranch is situated on the outskirts of town in a picturesque

location with beautiful mountains in the background and the Wind River running through it. As I drove up to the ranch house, I was greeted by a cow that came right up to the car window to check my credentials.

Once settled in, the students immediately began forging blades under Ed's guidance. Ed is a wonderful teacher and an easy guy to talk with about anything. With each new lesson, he revealed a little more of the secret recipe and its ingredients for making his style of hand-forged blades. The recipe is like a classic Western treasure map, with the hidden treasure at the end being an awesome hand-forged blade. Like searching for the Lost Dutchman mine, you will have to explore it for yourself by attending the High Performance Knife School to find exactly where "X" marks the spot.

Illustrated is how the raw handle materials and guard are put into place on the author's first hand-forged knife, but the process of finishing the materials has not yet begun.

The loud, pounding trip hammers were exhilarating to operate.

Knife school is not for everyone. It is rugged work, but even an Eastern lawyer, like your humble author, can handle it. One student quit because he couldn't deal with the physical demands of forging and the challenging hands-on approach to learning. Do not be intimidated! Just be dedicated and you will succeed. Ed has a steady stream of visitors to the Willow Bow, including former students, fellow knifemakers, ranchers and friends. All are willing to help out an admitted greenhorn, and I appreciated the advice, tips and assistance the fine folks gave me.

Laying the Hammer Down

The loud pounding trip hammers were exhilarating to operate. Some folks call them power hammers. Ed's trip hammers were made in the early 1900s, but unfortunately such great tools are no longer made in America. No stateside steel foundries are left that can pour the bases for the impressive monuments to America's once proud industrial strength. The hammers are worked by pushing foot pedals that engage the clutches, which, in turn, send the hammers slamming down.

Each foot pedal is like a car's accelerator and the further you push it down, the harder and faster the hammer hits. The hammers have different weights, but the 50-pounder seemed to be the most versatile. One of the tricks I discovered was to make sure the steel was held down firmly so it would not bounce up and take bad hits. After initially hammering out the heated steel using the classic machines, I finished the job on an anvil with a hand-held blacksmithing hammer.

Operating the Burr King belt grinder was more relaxing, yet required serious concentration to keep the blade grinds even and properly positioned. The blade can heat up quickly so I had to regularly dip it in water to cool it down, all the while being careful not to burn/overheat the tip, which will ruin its strength.

Belt choice was extremely important and working down in grit size was a methodical operation. Thumbs were my "grinding jigs" and the technique on the Burr King was fun once it "clicked." Of course, Ed is a master at the Burr King, and he worked his magic on my blade when I screwed it up (and I did screw it up.) At a couple points when I was learning to grind, I thought I had utterly messed up my forged blade beyond repair, but Ed brought it right back on the Burr King and, wow, he was amazing to watch!

Fitting the guard to the blade was challenging. It took a lot more time and work than one would think, requiring drilling, careful hand-filing and sanding to get a tight, clean fit to the blade tang. Once the guard was fitted, it was then secured to the tang using an interesting technique of silver soldering a heated blade upside down. When properly fluxed, the silver actual ran *up* into the guard, filling the gap. It was fascinating to do this and it really set the guard firmly in place.

During any downtime involved in knifemaking at the Willow Bow Ranch, I tried out a variety of Ed's great guns, including his custom handguns, tack driving rifles and smooth swinging shotguns. I borrowed his vintage Model 12 Winchester shotgun and had a great time waterfowling on the historic Wind River with fellow knifemaker Butch Deveraux, who could really call in those ducks. It was glorious to be surrounded by sagebrush and cottonwoods and hear the cattle herds mooing in the background while blasting ducks out of the clear-blue Wyoming sky. This definitely was *not* New Jersey.

Ed's Rambouillet sheep are friendly but they think all cars are Dodge Rams and occasionally they test themselves on auto body exteriors and even on visitors. The Willow Bow's hospitality was first rate and there was no pretension. Just because I was not a Wyoming native did not mean I didn't have to wipe my shoes before going into a place. Ed's collection of Rambouillet sheep horn is dazzling and it is stored, stashed, piled and hung everywhere. The "Ed Fowler Informal Museum of Knife History" is a treat, and with Ed as your guide, it beats the Smithsonian. He has knives of every type and wonderful historic pieces that trace the devolvement of his learning curve on making knives. Handling and examining each knife is an educational experience.

Willow Bow Ranch food was a delicious variety of deer, goose, duck, rabbit, elk, walleye and other fresh meat and fish. Every class day ended around midnight when "The Original Oldbury Sheep Dip Scotch," beer and chips came out

and we students discussed the world of knives, the West, freedom and philosophy with the wizard of the Willow Bow. I learned more about knifemaking and life in the West in that one week than from my entire collection of knife books and Louis L'Amour novels. Best of all, I enjoyed every moment of it. It was an experience of a lifetime and completely different from my normal "rat race" world.

The Great Escape

Knife School was a great escape—a combination of accomplishment, education and fun. As a graduate of the High Performance Knife School, I left with more than a diploma. I had Ed's secret recipe for making the finest hand-forged blades, a new understanding and appreciation of knives, and of course, memories forever to be treasured.

Knife school changed me. I now look at knives with new eyes. I see uneven plunge grinds, bent blades, scratches from belt grinders, poor polishing, bad grain structure, carbon deposits, improperly fitted

guards and dumb blade designs with silly, useless frills. I see commercial knives that claim to be great, that cannot cut hemp rope more than 1 1/2 times before they go dull. I now see through the phony hype and claims concerning blade performance. I made and tested my own hand-forged knife, so I know firsthand what really matters and what to look for in a high performance knife.

On the other hand, I now appreciate what the hand-forged blade is all about. I know the unbelievable amount of time invested in doing it right. The dedication and craftsmanship involved are awe-inspiring. I cherish the master smith's work with a deeper sense of admiration and respect. I can feel the difference at a deeper personal level when I hold a knife of true hand-forged quality. The hand-forged knives that I have purchased over the years skyrocketed in personal value to me. You cannot know what I know from reading about it. You have to do it before achieving "blade enlightenment."

The author's second forged blade, the "Pig Sticker," stretches 7 1/2 inches in length.

The large, 12-inch bowie is the author's third blade he forged at Ed Fowler's High Performance Knife School. The author had just started to grind the flats on it when the photo was taken. The small blade (the author's fourth piece) is a "Yearling" style forged but not yet ground on the Burr King grinder. There is quite a bit of scale that needs to be ground off of forged blades.

(Some of) Ed's Secret Recipe for a High Performance Hand–Forged Blade

- Start out with your steel welded to a working rod. This eliminates the need for tongs, which might slip. Next, heat the steel in a forge to above nonmagnetic temperature. (It is at this temperature that the steel will not attract a magnet.)
- Hammer the steel into shape, starting with forging the tip and the belly of the blade. (Note: Hammer blows to the spine are a waste of time and energy.) Achieve the desired blade thickness and length. Mark the tang on the anvil's hardy with the edge down.
- Lengthen the tang using the trip hammer set up with a drawing die.
- Do three accurately timed and correctly heated quenches, with the blade properly positioned, in quenching oil.
- Break off the blade from the rod to which it is welded. Taper and straighten the tang with a blacksmithing hammer on the anvil.
- Do a final inspection. (Make sure the edge is clean and the blade and tang are straight.)
- Perform two flash normalizing heat treatments. (This is where the blade is heated to a proper temperature and the cooling is observed for key indications.)
- Then complete one full normalizing process and cool to room temperature. Place the blade in the freezer for at least 24 hours.
- Remove the blade from the freezer and warm it to room temperature. Do three anneals in the oven at correct heat with appropriate cool downs. (Note: Mark blade tang after each heat treatment.)
- Remove the carbon scale on the blade with the Burr King by doing flat grinds. Profile the blade on the Burr King. Rough grind using an assortment of proper belts. (Note: Any scratch deeper than a 220-grit finish can cause a stress riser.)
- Perform three quench hardenings. These consist of accurately timed and correctly heated quenches, with the blade properly positioned, in quenching oil. Check oil depth and adjust accordingly to quench only the lower half or third of the blade. (Note: Mark the blade tang after each quench.) Heat the lower half of blade to nonmagnetic. (Note: Check regularly with a magnet!) Quench the lower half of blade in oil with rocking motion until spine cools to a black heat. Repeat at the proper intervals.
- Submerge the entire blade in a quench oil bath until the oil is room temperature. Put the blade in the freezer for 24 hours.
- Remove the blade from the freezer and warm it to room temperature. Do three tempers in the oven at correct heat and timing, then let it cool down in the oven to room temperature for the proper time. (Note: Mark blade tang after each heat treatment.) Put the blade in the freezer for 24 hours between tempering heats.
- Do the final grind on the Burr King using an assortment of proper belts.
- Test the edge. (Do a minimum of 12 edge flexes on a sharpening steel rod and perform a minimum of 200 cuts on hemp rope (one lay of 1 1/8-inch rope.)
- Continue grinding on the Burr King using an assortment of proper belts. Buff on the Burr King with the correct belt and buffing compound. Buff on the Baldor polishing wheel with a loose muslin wheel dressed with buffing compound. Wipe the blade with a clean cloth and acetone.
- Etch the blade by soaking it in a specially prepared etching solution to bring out the steel grain. Dip the blade in the special neutralizing solution to stop the etching process.
- Lightly buff the blade to an attractive finish on the Baldor. (Warning: this is one of the most dangerous operations in knifemaking because the wheel can "grab" the blade and fling it with great force, bouncing it off floors and walls, creating a live-action "ballistic knife.")
- Make a paper sheath for safe blade handling out of Kleenex Premium paper towels and masking tape. (Note: Put Breakfree oil/solution on the blade to protect it.)
- Make the guard. Cut the shoulders to the *ricasso*. Cut the guard at an angle appropriate to the blade shoulder. Mark the center. Drill holes on the angle. Fit it tight to the blade by hand filing and taking off a little material at a time. Buff out the front lines and "blisters." Peen the rear of guard to blade.
- Seal the joint to block the flux from seeping through. Remove the sheath and coat the blade with quenching oil. With the guard held in a vice, heat it using a neutral flame. With the blade pointed tip down, apply flux and let it work in. Silver solder with the blade pointed up. Shove the solder wire high up into the heated guard until full. Cool the blade and guard with a wet rag. Grab the blade with dry cloth, and cool the tang in water. Apply Breakfree to the front of the guard. Set the blade up to cool.
- Make the handle. Make the sheath. Your hand-forged knife is now completed.

Getting Knives into Soldiers' Hands

The author was instrumental in getting much-needed knives into the hands of our soldiers

By James Ayres

Soldiers need knives. But not all of them have the knives they need. Recently a family friend, home on leave from a combat zone, asked me to recommend a good knife to take back with him. I gave him a couple of suggestions, but he replied that he couldn't afford any of the knives I proposed on his pay. I had forgotten about that aspect of military life. America may love her soldiers, but she doesn't pay them much.

During the past couple of years I've received similar requests from other active-duty military personnel. I decided to do something to help these guys, even if only in a small way. With the approval of *BLADE Magazine*® editor, Steve Shackleford, I sent emails to a number of knife companies and custom knifemakers, inquiring as to their willingness to donate a knife to a soldier serving in a combat zone. Some were glad, even eager, to help out the guys on the front lines—those who risk

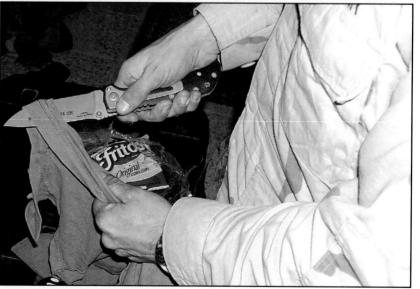

When the author sent Sgt. Kevin Gordham a Harsey Ranger knife donated to the troops by Lone Wolf Knives, the soldier wrote back with his gratitude. Though shaving isn't one of the daily tasks the knife performs, Gordham did say what he uses the knife for while stationed in Iraq. "I used the Lone Wolf to pry open a door when I didn't have a pry bar. No problem," he related. He also used it to pry open a file cabinet to retrieve classified documents while under enemy fire. Daily he uses it to cut up rags for gun cleaning, to open MRE's (Meals Ready To Eat) and for a dozen other tasks.

their lives daily to fight America's wars.

We asked the soldiers who received knives to give us their feedback on the edged tools and weapons, on what works and what doesn't in the field today, so that we could be more effective in the selection of knives we would send in the future.

We learned that some things don't change, that combat troops think of a personal knife as a last-ditch weapon, one that may never be used but that will give them some small comfort. We also learned that most service people today prefer a "tactical folder" as their primary edged tool. Many frontline troops also carry fixed blades in the 6-to-7-inch range. But the convenience of carrying a folder, combined with the strength and utility of today's tactical pieces, makes it the knife for everyday military use.

What follows are comments about the knives some of our guys received. The logistics involved in getting the knives to the troops, and the exigencies of combat precluded responses from everyone. But included is representative sampling of those we received.

Doug Hutchins of Lone Wolf Knives called me about 10 minutes after I sent him an email. He said that Lone Wolf would support our troops in any way it could. An engraved Lone Wolf Harsey Ranger was on my desk the following week, and on its way to Iraq the next day. Sgt. Kevin Gordham was the recipient of the Lone Wolf.

A Soldier Smiles

"Thank you, again, so much for this knife! It is completely above and beyond my expectations," Kevin said. "The specifications and quality are form fitted to my every need. The blade was a bit longer than I had envisioned, but after a few short minutes, I was in love. It is a comfortable weight, grip and length. I ran my thumb along my engraved name—'Sgt. Kevin M. Gordham.' It made me smile. When you share quarters with six other guys and most of your equipment looks the same, it's easy for things to come up missing. "The 'tactical' sheath seemed a bit large for wearing on my belt. But then I realized it was perfect for attachment to my body armor. The large nylon strap with the snap fits wonderfully on the Army-adopted MOLLE attachment system," he

noted. "Sometimes I make use of its strong pocket clip. But it's a little large for my pockets. I am impressed with this blade, from the drop point to the lanyard hole. Thank you again. It's incredible."

I asked Kevin if he thought of his knife as a last-ditch weapon. "Yeah," he said. "I do, definitely." But mainly Kevin, like most of the other soldiers, relies on it as his most basic tool, the one always close at hand and available for anything.

"I used the Lone Wolf to pry open a door when I didn't have a pry bar. No problem," he related. He also used it to pry open a file cabinet to retrieve classified documents while under enemy fire. Daily he uses it to cut up rags for gun cleaning, to open MRE's (Meals Ready To Eat) and for a dozen other tasks.

Kevin almost lost his Lone Wolf in an incident while training Iraqi troops. Then, in a secure compound in Mosul where he was stationed, a mess hall was bombed. As a result, he asked me if I could get him a smaller knife, one he could carry at all times. A knife wouldn't protect him from a bomb, but it might take care of a bomber inside his compound. Like most other line soldiers in regular units, he is not permitted to have a sidearm (pistol) and so a knife is about his only option as a backup weapon, and for when he doesn't have his primary weapon.

After the bombing of the mess hall in Mosul, many of the guys wrote that they were starting to take their knives with them everywhere inside their compounds, even to the showers, and for the same reason as Kevin—they are not allowed to carry side arms and a knife is the only possible secondary weapon they have.

Chris Reeve immediately volunteered to donate a Sebenza, one the finest folders made in the world today, to Kevin. Chris also engraved Kevin's name on his Sebenza.

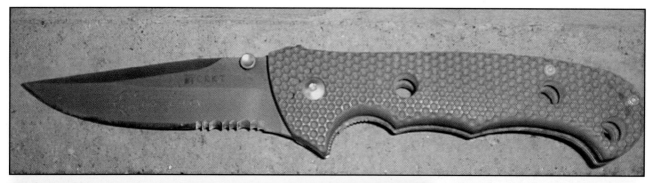

Marine Sgt. Heath Lanctot bought his Columbia River Knife & Tool folder in the PX, and was glad he did—he was forced to use it in hand-to-hand combat.

Here's what Kevin had to say about his Sebenza.

"I can't believe this knife. It's like the most perfect knife I've ever seen. I love it. Something about the polish is so smooth, and I still find myself pulling it out and just opening and closing it," Kevin said. "What kind of steel is this? It never gets dull.

"There are so many things I love about it," he added. "I'd like to give you a full review, but there's too much action right now. Another one of our Stryker's got blown up today. I'll just say this for now—it's one of three things I never let leave my side: my wedding ring, my Sebenza and my buddy Jay's KIA (Killed In Action) bracelet."

Alexandra Whitaker of Benchmade Knives sent a boxful of the company's highly regarded folders, both manuals and automatics, for the frontline troops. Following are some comments by a couple of the guys who received Benchmade folders.

Sgt. William C. Murdock III

"I got one of the automatic Benchmade folders. It is the one with the black button, not the Stryker model. The design of it is perfect. The finger grips keep it from slipping out of my hand, the blade steel is great, and I like the semi-serrated edge. When closed, the blade nestles tight inside the handle, keeping it from wobbling. I use it a lot for cutting rope and 550 cord around my vehicle. I like the option of opening the blade with my thumb or with the automatic switch. It's extremely sharp, and cuts through everything like butter.

"Most knives are pretty cheesy. This knife is an exception—a complete quality knife. I like it from tip to grip. It's the ultimate tactical knife. The Gerber Gator that the Army issued us hasn't impressed me, or the guys in my squad. The blades have play, and quite a few tips broke when used for normal applications."

Spc. James A. Tucker

"I have the Benchmade Stryker model. I use it for cutting everything that a knife should cut. It's a great utility knife, and with the tanto blade and semi-serrated edge, it's effective even when sharpeners aren't readily available. The size is perfect for all applications, whether I'm in full kit or just wearing utilities.

"It fits in my hand with just enough of the handle sticking out to make for a decent blunt object to break glass with. It also fits great in the pocket, convenient and ready. The metal pocket clip grips our slippery cotton utility pockets better than any other knife I've ever owned.

"The blade is harder to sharpen than most others, but held an edge well. Because it's an automatic folder, when the dust gets heavy around the locking mechanism, it won't fully open. The action becomes gummy, so maintenance is key when dealing with this blade."

Doug Flagg of Columbia River Knife & Tool (CRKT) also sent a large boxful of knives for the troops. Here are some comments from two combat soldiers who received CRKT folding knives.

Sgt. Nathan R. Purdy

"I like this knife. It's a good size, and I like the black blade. The clip is good for securing it to my pocket, and the small size

Marine Sgt. Heath Lanctot's team and entire squad pose for photos following an ordeal in which the sergeant was forced to use a knife in a tactical situation.

keeps it out of the way. The tanto blade is not the best for utility but I use it for everything regardless, and it works well. The steel is sturdy. I think if your life is in danger, you should have the choice of whether or not to arm yourself with a secondary weapon. And this knife would be a good weapon in a pinch. I can have it with me all the time. The security of our Forward Operating Bases is poor. There are local nationals at the gate checking IDs."

Staff Sgt. Will Pascual "I use it to pry open doors and cabinets, and to cut everything every day. When dust gets in it, it's hard to close. You have to clean it periodically. It opens quickly. The clip makes it stay in my pocket so it's easy to access, even when I have my full kit on. Everything is great with the knife."

A gentleman known only as Ragnar of Ragweed Forge (www.ragweedforge.com), specializes in fashioning Scandinavian-

style knives. Named after Ragnar of Elandris and a member of the Society of Creative Anachronism, he contributed a nice selection of his graceful knives for the guys. Here is what one of the guys had to say about the Ragnar knife, a piece that is reportedly used by the Swedish Army.

Sgt. William Franklin

"This Swedish knife is good looking and unbelievably sharp. The blade didn't seem as thick and sturdy as it should be if its main purpose is to cut during tactical situations. But it has held up under some pretty hard use, so I guess it's strong enough. It's comfortable when held and easy to sharpen. It's a good size for a fixed blade since we carry so much gear and don't have room for big knives. It would make a great outdoorsman's knife for hunting and fishing."

Bud Nealy's knives are no strangers to the world of combat, nor is Bud a guy to hesitate when asked to help American troops. Bud sent me a selection of his extremely well made fixed blades.

Spc. Marcel Baburnic grew up in the Czech Republic, came to America in February 1995, and became a citizen in May 2003. He joined the army the same month.

Spc. Marcel Baburnic

"The Bud Nealy knife fits nicely in my hand. I carry it every day, and I like the design of the blade. Unfortunately the glue that held the magnet in the sheath didn't hold so I haven't been able to evaluate how it would have worked. I keep it permanently attached to my kit as part of a thigh-worn drop pouch using 550 cord and the eyelets provided on the sheath. The plastic sheath holds the weapon tightly, but when it gets dirty, wet or dusty, the closed tip of the sheath doesn't allow for drainage. Some holes would alleviate that. I would like to carry my handgun. I would like an Army-provided one, but I'd carry my own if they let me. In the dusty environment, our M4s can jam, no matter how often you clean it. I'm glad to have this knife."

Special Forces Capt. John Smith (not his real name)

During the past 10 or 12 years, Capt. Smith has served in Bosnia, Tajikistan, Afghanistan, Iraq and other countries in the region. He is currently in non-uniformed service conducting certain activities in another Mid-Eastern country. He has had a great deal of close combat experience, and has used a knife in personal combat on two occasions.

"This small Bud Nealy knife is perfect for my needs. It replaces a boot knife I gave to a friend. I know many who prefer the tactical folders to small fixed blades. I don't. I've seen too many folding knives fail. I trust folders only for general utility," Capt. Smith said.

"If I have to use a knife to defend my life that means something has gone seriously wrong, and I am face to face with an armed enemy (or enemies), and don't have a firearm," he continued. "I don't want to worry about opening a folding knife or having a lock fail at that time. I want to be able to reach and have what I need in my hand.

"This is a great blade, but I don't use the sheath mounting system. I taped a clip from a broken Gerber to the sheath and clipped it to my underwear. Please send me Bud Nealy's address," Capt. Smith added. "I will buy another one. I trained in Escrima and like having two knives. These are small enough to conceal even under hot-weather civilian clothing."

While talking to Flagg of CRKT about the contributions his company had made to our program, he mentioned a Marine I should contact. Marine Sgt. Heath Lanctot bought his CRKT folder in the PX, and is glad that he did. After a firefight, during which his squad took out an insurgent mortar crew that had been bombarding a polling place on election day, Sgt. Lanctot went into a canal to retrieve the enemy bodies and search for any evidence.

Here are his words: "I followed the trail and, having left my weap-

on, ammo and web gear on the berm, I pulled out my CRKT folder as I made my way into the reeds. Suddenly one of the enemy popped up and grabbed my right arm."

There, cut off from any possibility of help, Sgt. Lanctot fought his enemy as men have done since the beginning of recorded history, with hand weapons and to the death. During the course of the desperate, furious fight, Lanctot dispatched his enemy with two knife thrusts to the neck.

"Did you have a Ka-Bar?" I asked him. "And if you had one, why didn't you use it instead of your folder?"

"Yeah, I have a Ka-Bar, but my folder was right there and quicker to get to," he replied.

Heath's response is understood by anyone who has gone in harm's way. Experience shows that a last-ditch weapon close at hand can save lives. From the responses we have received, it's easy to see that his wisdom is well understood by the other soldiers.

From the soldiers' responses, it is clear that military personnel use knives hard and that the edged steel is often the only tool on hand. Today's tactical folder has, in most cases, replaced the boot knife commonly used "back in the day," as my kids say.

Our modest efforts resulted in getting knives to a few dozen soldiers—hardly a drop in the bucket compared to what Spyderco has accomplished. Marketing and public relations representative Joyce Laituri informed me that Spyderco has it's own program in operation and has donated over 3,500 knives to active military members in every combat zone, an amazing and altogether admirable endeavor. But more is needed.

Soldiers need knives—good, sharp, strong, handy knives they can keep on them at all times. More than one guy wrote that he took his knife with him to the shower. If you know a serving soldier, sailor or Marine, pick out a good tactical folder, or maybe a small fixed blade, and send it to him. He'll thank you for it.

He Lives to Embellish Knives and Tomahawks

A childhood experience inspired a lifelong vocation of edged tool and weapon making, engraving, and gold and silver inlay

By Joe Szilaski

Anyone who is able to fulfill his or her childhood dream, and make a living doing so, should consider himself or herself to be very lucky. It is funny how an event can influence one's life, in particular my own.

When I was a child, history class was not, at first, my strongest subject. I do not want to make excuses, but my first history teacher would put everyone to sleep. He was not at all like my grandfather. Grandpa put some flavor into his stories, and I could listen to him all day long.

My second history teacher was a lot more fun. He arranged a class field trip to visit the museum in Budapest, Hungary, about a 2 ½-hour train ride from my hometown of Baja. It was during this trip that my whole attitude toward history changed. As we walked around the museum, I realized how much the study of history had to offer.

All of a sudden those boring dates and years were no longer so boring. I remember my jaw feeling sore as my mouth hung open, mesmerized by the museum's collection of richly decorated arms and armor.

My attention was on the swords, daggers, battle-axes and poll arms, most with ornate engraving and many with gold or silver work. My wish was to be a big sponge so I could soak up the smallest details of everything in sight.

Back at that time, I could not have imagined the amount of time, skill and effort that went into creating such works of art.

On the train ride home, I did not stop thinking about the beauty of human creativity. Deep inside I had an unexplainable feeling; I knew that one day I would have to try my hand at this type of work.

If my memory serves me correctly, most of the arms I saw that day in the museum were Hungarian or European in origin. Edged weapons from Eastern Europe often show a Turkish influence in their design and embellishment, which is not surprising, as the Turks had occupied Hungary for over a century. Turkish and Islamic weaponry is quite ornate, often decorated with silver, gold, ivory and large precious stones.

As we all know, richly decorated arms and armor date back many centuries. Stunning examples can be found from all around the world. Early weapons and armor were often decorated with mystical or religious symbols, and these ornate arms played significant roles throughout the ages, for religious ceremony, tournament and, of course, on the battlefield. Ornately decorated arms were also status symbols, often presented as fine gifts to kings and knights.

And as long as we are "tuned to the history channel," although the American experience is only a few hundred years old, in my opinion, it is one of the most fascinating histories in the world. One of the primary needs of early American colonists was to make simple, plain and functional tools and arms.

The Kentucky Rifle: An American Original

Probably the first to introduce rich embellishment to American arms were makers of the Kentucky rifle. Such early decorations had a European influence, called a "Rococo" style. With some modifications and improvements by early American craftsmen, the finely crafted and beautifully embellished guns, and the knives that went with them, evolved into part of the American culture and civilization. The Rococo style was extremely popular for quite some time.

In addition to the Kentucky rifle, American frontiersmen also saw fit to adorn other knives and tomahawks in a similar fashion. While highly decorated tomahawks were effective weapons, they were also important cer-

Joe Szilaski's pipe tomahawk showcases silver inlay and buffalo skulls carved into the pipe bowl.

It is museum-quality pieces like this officer's sword, dating back to 1876, that inspired the author to become an edged tool and weapons maker, specializing in engraving, and gold and silver inlay.

emonial items symbolizing war, peace and social rank to Native Americans.

Presentation tomahawks were more elaborately engraved and decorated with silver, gold, brass or nickel silver. Surviving examples are probably the most intricately beautiful weapons left-over from the American pioneer.

In New York City, the Metropolitan Museum of Art showcases an arms and armor exhibit with room after room of highly decorated guns, swords and knives from all over the world. Also noteworthy is the beautiful Tiffany display case with Smith & Wesson and Colt handguns featuring silver and gold grips.

Included in the Tiffany display is a lever-action repeating Winchester rifle ("the gun that won the West"), its stock masterfully adorned with embossed silver. In the 19th century, Tiffany made its mark in history with the Victorian style of gold and silver design, as well as with well-executed workmanship. The company created masterfully embellished presentation swords and knives often commissioned for presidents and generals. If you have a chance to visit the museum, you will not be disappointed.

Today's modern knifemakers are still fascinated with this type of functional art and strive to carry on the tradition. To name a memorable few, there is Bill Moran, Buster Warenski and Harvey McBurnette. Unfortunately, none of these gentlemen are still with us physically, but their works are not forgotten.

Bill was well known for his curly maple knife handles and matching scabbards with elaborate silver wire inlay work. Buster

will always be remembered for his gold inlay work and for masterfully reproducing the King Tut dagger. I have always been impressed by the work of Harvey McBurnette because of his deep-relief engraving and simple style that was pleasing to the eye. Old World craftsmanship is shown by all and many more who continue to pursue and perfect this art.

A Blacksmithing Background

Getting back to my childhood dream, I was fortunate enough to learn blacksmithing and various metalworking techniques in trade school. However, the knives I was making back then were not to be presented to kings or knights, but were simple and functional for everyday use in the local butcher shop. Do not get me wrong, a hard performing knife with well-executed form and function is in itself a work of art. Still today, I strive to develop a better working knife.

I had the desire to try my hand at ornate engraving and inlay work, and to incorporate this type of work into my knives and tomahawks. In order to do silver or gold inlay work, an artist must first learn basic engraving techniques. Functional art forms require a mixture of crafts, such as engraving, silversmithing, jewelry making, woodworking and carving, among others.

Within each of these disciplines, various techniques have

been used throughout the ages, but the basic principles of metal inlay and deep-relief engraving have not changed in hundreds of years. You can achieve such art with a hammer and various types of chisels, but technology has resulted in wonderful tools that have advanced the art further than the hammer and chisel.

One example of this is the engraving vise, an ingeniously engineered piece of equipment that can hold a work piece firmly and is able to turn 360 degrees to the left and right. With attachments, an engraving vise is capable of holding odd-shaped pieces. Prior to its invention, a generic vise was installed on a post and the engraver spent his day walking in circles around the vise to cut the design into a metal medium.

Another wonder of modern technology is the engraving machine. Engraving machines can be set to the desired impact rate per minute and are operated by a foot-controlled pedal that starts and stops a hand impact tool. The hand piece acts like a miniature jackhammer, freeing up the artist's chisel hand. With his or her free hand, an engraver is able to control the swiveling vise, and such technology has made a significant change in the steel-embellishing world.

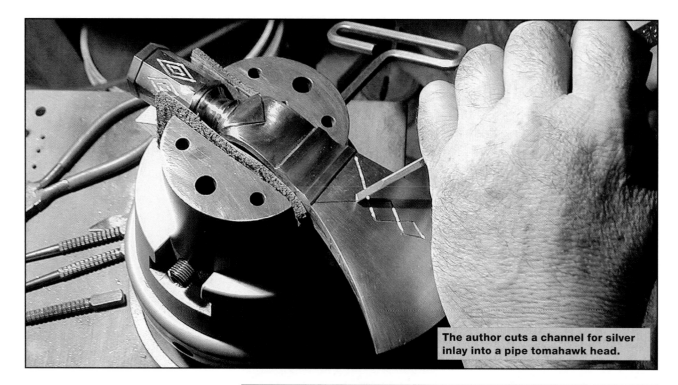

The author cuts a channel for silver inlay into a pipe tomahawk head.

While some gun and knife engravers still work with traditional hammers and chisels, the majority of the new generation has oriented to engraving machines.

Let's not make any mistake about these new engraving machines; they are not computer controlled CNC or EDM machines. The craftsman still needs to lay-out, draw and cut the design. And more importantly, the engraver has to commandeer not only the small hand piece, but also the foot pedal that controls the speed. It takes quite some time to learn how to use the machines and take full advantage of them.

Yet another invention has become indispensable for the modern engraver—high-powered magnifying glasses or instruments. With magnifiers, the craftsman or craftswoman is able to create fine, more-intricately-detailed artwork than ever. Older, more experienced engravers with strained and tired eyes can appreciate this technol-

E. Jay Hendrickson's Green River Skinner features a Masur birch handle with silver-wire inlay, and a nickel-silver dogwood flower cut out, engraved and inlaid into the wood. (PointSeven photo)

ogy. Let's face it—the older we get, the shorter our arms get.

From Blades to Banknotes

An example of how modern magnifiers have influenced engraving is Bolino or banknote engraving. It is an intricate and detailed style of engraving, difficult to do without the use of magnification. Like I say, if you can't see it, then you can't do it. Modern craftsmen can also enjoy the readily available variety of materials. And on a more lighthearted note, it is a good thing we no longer have to smelt steel or dig for gold and silver ore.

Since there are a variety of tools and materials available, knife and edged weapons makers

can enjoy more personal freedom and independence. In the last 10 or so years, it seems to me that an increasing number of knifemakers have learned to embellish their own work with carving and silver or gold inlay instead of sending their knives out to engravers or jewelers.

Engraved works, including knives incorporating silver and  gold inlay, are more appealing to the eye and represent the extra effort a craftsman puts in to create a beautiful piece of art. It is important that the craftsman or craftswoman recognize his or her

The Persian damascus blade showcases a gold-embellished handle.

limitations. Most shiny objects tend to attract people's attention, which is good for well-executed works. However, it will also draw attention to shoddy or poorly executed workmanship. In fact, the poorly executed pieces pop out like soar thumbs.

The sterling-silver-wire inlay work on the curly maple handle of a Joe Keeslar knife is superb, and complemented by decorative file work along the blade spine and an engraved "D-guard." The wire-inlaid corkscrew is the kicker.
(PointSeven photo)

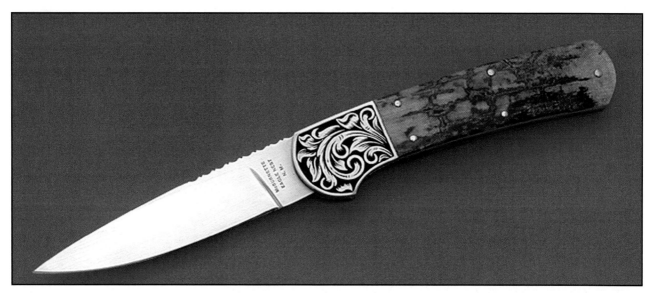

The author says he's always been impressed by the work of the late knifemaker Harvey McBurnette because of the Harvey's deep-relief engraving and simple style that was pleasing to the eye. McBurnette's folder features engraved bolsters.

As for me, that unexplainable childhood feeling is not just a feeling anymore. I owe thanks to my family for their support, especially to my wife, Lori, who understood how important it was for me to fulfill my dream. I also owe a debt of gratitude to all of my customers who support and appreciate my craft so I am able to make my living at what I love to do.

While I incorporate carving, deep-relief engraving and silver and gold inlay into my knives, tomahawks and hatchets, I try not to take away from the function of the edged tools and weapons. Function is my first and main consideration. To address the work as functional art, the design, function and embellishment have to complement each other.

While I am mostly self taught on the subject, I had an edge because of my background as a carver and sculptor, not to mention over 40 years of metalworking experience. I also had two gentlemen who would help me out by answering any of my questions.

Ron Nott, a gun engraver from Pennsylvania, was one who was generous enough to share his experience and answer any and all questions I asked of him. I have also been asking questions of a most talented knifemaker

Knifemaker Dusty Moulton engraves his own knives, like this full-tang damascus fixed blade with an engraved guard and mosaic pins. *(PointSeven photo)*

Jody Muller's pearl-handle, twist-damascus folder showcases hand engraving and gold inlay work by the maker. *(BladeGallery.com photo)*

and engraver from Montana, Rick Eaton.

Will I make history with my work? I do not think so. But this is a big country—you never know. Anything can happen. My true hope is that, one day, some youngster will see my work and it will give him enough inspiration to continue on the tradition of the art. After all, it is the craftsmen, collectors and museum curators who keep the art alive.

TRENDS

Chances are cavemen didn't foresee mammoth tooth as being a trendy knife handle material in the years 2006 and 2007. It's unlikely that Col. James Bowie predicted so many men would build bowie knives in the 21st century that photos of them could fill 10 pages of a book. When the Native Americans fell at Custer's last stand, it's doubtful their dying visions were of traditional tomahawks replicated to exacting standards. Early smelters of iron ore probably didn't envision the development of damascus patterns numbering in the thousands and counting.

So maybe all of that is a bit amazing to some, but what remains even more impressive is that knifemaking trends change from calendar year to calendar year. This year, bull-nose blades nudged their way onto the top of the trendsetting heap. Slam-dunk slip-joints remained players, as did daggers with swagger, too tough tacticals and drop-point hunters. All of those are pretty predictable, but did anyone guess that sub-hilt fighters would make a sudden comeback? And who would have foreseen the reemergence of knives with upswept tips or pearl-inlaid window-frame folders?

One new development is the blending of wood and *Micarta®*, or *Zytel®* and Micarta for knife handles and bolsters, or the pairing of several types of pearl or wood grains on one gorgeous grip. Pearl and damascus clash on more than a few folding knives, and blade diversity—those edges styled after classic patterns from across the globe—continues to rank high in the popularity polls. Garish guards, straight-back stickers and shrunken treasures (miniature knives) round out the starting lineup.

Without trends in knives, the excitement of collecting might wane. When that happens, the industry as a whole would suffer. Taking a look at the 2,000-plus names of knifemakers listed in the directory section of this book, and considering how innovative and foreword thinking many of those craftsmen are that probably won't occur for a long, long time.

Joe Kertzman

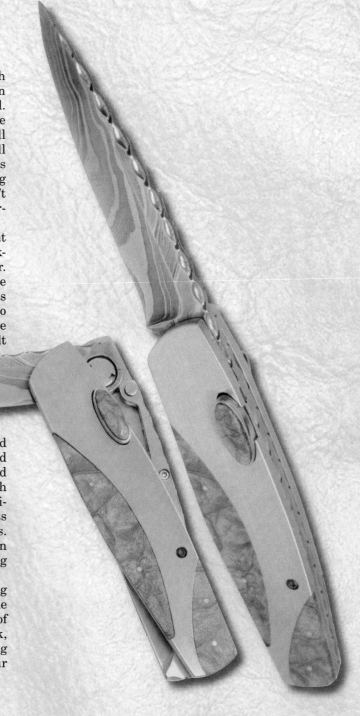

Medium-Build Bowies

He is a handsome fellow, a sharp dresser, thin and sturdy, clean cut, not rough around the edges, stands arrow-straight and of a medium build. Folks have heard tell that he's a handful when the situation calls for it, but for the most part he goes about his business without stirring up any dust. "Bowie" is what he goes by, and some say he was named after Col. James Bowie, though no one can say for certain. One thing is for sure, he is a stout fellow, not long and lean like others of his ilk. You could say he's a medium-build bowie, and no, he's not a man, but a knife.

More than just a knife, the medium-build bowie is also a trendsetter. That's right, a blade that mimics nobody—one that stands alone in defiance of the norm. While most bowie blades are 9, 10, 11, even a 12 inches or more from guard to point, the defiant one stretches its steel a mere 5 1/2-to-8 inches, and it hasn't been around for very long, either. No, he's new in town, a new breed you might say. He performs the menial chores, a utilitarian sort, not a fighter. He's low-key, seldom hard nosed, and he doesn't have nearly the chip on his shoulder as the older bowies in his family tree.

The medium-build bowie is smooth, deceptively quick, handy to have around and inconspicuous. No one seems threatened by him, but he can work as hard and long as any of his peers. This bowie is a perfect cross between his long and lean ancestors and the shorter types that like to hunt and fish. He's a medium-build bowie, a hard worker and faithful companion.

Joe Kertzman

▲ **RICK SMITH:** The 6 1/2-inch, straight-clip-point, forged O-1 blade is stocky, sturdy and sharp. The full-tang piece dons an aged-giraffe-bone, coffin-style handle.

◀ **DAN PFANENSTIEL:** Though the blade is only 5 3/4-inches long, it's of a tight 1095-and-L-6-damascus pattern and coupled with a wrought-iron and copper guard, and a stabilized-spalted-maple and ebony handle. *(SharpByCoop.com photo)*

▶ **MIKE MOONEY:** The vest bowie is decked out in a 154CM blade, nickel-silver fittings and some fossil-mammoth-ivory handle scales. *(Hoffman photo)*

▲ **MIKE RUTH:** This Ruth bowie is a babe. *(Ward photo)*

▲ **SHANE TAYLOR:** An engraved and textured guard and a perfect piece of fossil ivory beautify the 5-inch bowie-style blade. *(PointSeven photo)*

▶ **LIN RHEA:** The 6-inch damascus blade is certainly striking and in direct contrast to the creamy giraffe-bone handle. *(Ward photo)*

▲ **BILL LEVENGOOD:** He calls it a 5-inch hunter, and there's no doubt it would do the job in the field, but the blade shape is a bit "bowie" and butted up against some red amboyna burl.

▶ **TIM HANCOCK:** Not many men can make a 7 1/2-inch bowie blade look this good. The coffin-handle piece features a damascus frame, spacer and liners, a nickel-silver guard and fine filework along the blade spine. *(PointSeven photo)*

▶ **JERRY FISK:** The beige and brown stag transitions well into an engraved, copper-colored steel guard and is finally washed over by a wave of wild damascus. That's one sweet Southwest bowie. *(Ward photo)*

▲ **NICK WHEELER:** Within 4 1/2 inches of bowie blade are 1,000 layers of pattern-welded steel. *(PointSeven photo)*

▲ **STEVE HILL:** A reproduction of a small Sheffield bowie, the twist-damascus fixed blade is an ideal personal-carry size and features a classic Sambar stag grip. *(PointSeven photo)*

▶ **RAY KIRK:** Here, appearing in the chapter on medium-build bowies, is "Lil Bowie," the baddest damascus blade in town, complete with elephant-ivory handle and dazzling damascus guard. *(Ward photo)*

▲ **ART TYCER:** The "Cold Springs Bowie" boasts a 7-inch D-2 blade, nickel silver fittings and a slab of sloping stag. *(Ward photo)*

▶ **MARVIN SOLOMON:** It doesn't take two medium-build bowies to tango, but knives this handsome should be cloned. The damascus is by Devin Thomas and complemented by ebony, nickel silver and a touch of turquoise. *(Ward photo)*

▶ **GARY MULKEY:** The dog-bone bowie is fashioned from a 7 3/4-inch 1095 blade, stainless steel fittings and a blackwood handle. Vine filework climbs the bone of the dog-gone-good knife handle. *(Ward photo)*

▶ **J.R. COOK:** Though the one-of-a-kind knife took the "Best Giraffe Bone" award at the 2006 Arkansas Custom Knife Show (who knew there was a Best Giraffe Bone category?), it is a sweet little medium-build bowie even without the handsome handle. *(Ward photo)*

Material Mismatch

One of many reasons people give for the BLADE Show being world renown is that there are so many materials suppliers there. It's a perfect complement to having hundreds of knifemakers under one roof. The knifemakers need materials. They want them. They demand materials, and it wasn't always that way.

A few years ago, *BLADE Magazine®* presented the Cutlery Hall of Fame© Award to the family of Bob Schrimsher. Bob had a warehouse full of knifemaking materials long before there was such a thing as knife materials suppliers.

Schrimsher allowed knifemakers to walk into the warehouse and browse. Many of them, and by some accounts most of the craftsmen, had little or no money to buy the materials. So Schrimsher would front them the money. There were no credit applications or loan approvals. He let them walk out of his private warehouse with the materials, leaving only a promise and a handshake that they would repay him.

It's not that Schrimsher was dumb. He wasn't naïve. He may have been overly nice, but ignorance didn't play a role in his decision to bail a few knifemakers out in their time of need. He believed in what they were doing. He knew knifemaking was a burgeoning business. He knew in his heart that the craftsmen walking out of his warehouse with sacks full of supplies were embarking on worthy endeavors. He saw the beauty of knives and the intrinsic value in what the knifemakers were building. Schrimsher recognized aesthetically superior, useful tools. He understood quality and craftsmanship.

Today there are several knifemaking supplies companies, and the materials from which the knives are fashioned is increasingly exotic and interesting. In addition to steel, it has become commonplace for knifemakers to use mammoth ivory, fossil walrus ivory, black-lip pearl, pink pearl, abalone, stone, musk ox, mammoth tooth, sheep horn, water buffalo horn, stag, Micarta®, carbon fiber and Zytel®, to name a few. The newest trend, one that has upped the ante on knife design and artistry, is combining materials that complement each other. Here's to some innovative craftsmen who are practicing material mismatch.

Joe Kertzman

▼ **TIM TABOR:** Elephant ivory and cocobolo clamor to gain the attention of potential knife buyers.

▲ **ALAIN MIVILLE-DESCHENES:** Though the buffalo never met the wooly mammoth, their horns lock here on a stylish hunter.

▲ **RON HEMBROOK:** The knifemaker says a cowboy or Indian would have been equally pleased with his combination of damascus, turquoise and ironwood.

▼ **ARLAN "LANNY" HARTMAN:** Blending the browns of spalted birch and Ziricote wood worked well enough to make it into a knife book.

▲ **MARK KNAPP:** Getting up early isn't even a prerequisite to catching a musk ox and fossil-walrus-ivory sunrise. *(BladeGallery.com photo)*

HARUMI HIRAYAMA: Shell and pink-pearl flowers seemingly sprout out of a black-kaki-wood handle.

GARY SASS: She was a warthog until she met the malachite, and now she's the talk of the town.

STANLEY FUJISAKA: He eyed up amber and anodized titanium, saw they were good and built a prettified point. Bruce Shaw contributed blade engraving to the worthy cause. *(Fong photo)*

BOB PATRICK: Neither stag nor buffalo horn upstage the other, but share the limelight. *(PointSeven photo)*

▶ **JIM WHITMAN:** Both handle materials are musk ox, but one slab is from the horn and the other from the bone of the beast. *(PointSeven photo)*

▶ **BOB LAY:** The hot-handled hunter is anchored by rosewood and sheep horn. *(BladeGallery. com photo)*

▶ **HENRY HILDEN:** Green and lean is the malachite spacer between a sculpted-desert-ironwood grip and a mammoth-ivory bolster. *(BladeGallery. com photo)*

◀ **MICHAEL KANTER:** In this case, damascus was used for a patterning effect on the handle rather than on the blade, and complemented by stabilized Macassar ebony and walrus ivory. *(SharpByCoop.com photo)*

◀ **FRANK GAMBLE:** The fossil mammoth ivory is the centerpiece of the handle, but just as gripping are the stacked leather, stag and bronze. *(BladeGallery.com photo)*

▲ LOYD THOMSEN: The Scandinavian-style puukko knife is dressed out in damascus, elk antler and Amboina wood.

◀ J. NEILSON: Not a single knife collector would feel slighted by a deep-bellied damascus blade butted up against ironwood and some sea-green malachite. *(Ward photo)*

▶ LOYD THOMSEN: The handle is banksias pod, which is similar to North American pinecones, but it takes two years for the pod to develop and become hard. The leaf scars are filled with turquoise for a totally tubular look.

▼ J. NEILSON: Sambar stag and ironwood are only the beginning of a knife that dips ever so slightly down into a modified-spear-point tip.

▲ ED BRANDSEY: The horn is from a female African springbok, something you can tell from the girlish figure, the spacers are reconstituted lapis lazuli, and the stone at the butt is a yellow topaz. George Werth forged the dazzling damascus. *(SharpByCoop.com photo)*

▶ **JAMES LUCIE:** Crown stag, brass and leather come together on a Scagel-style hunter.

▶ **SCHUYLER LOVESTRAND:** The Lovestrand is a little place where mammoth teeth can get together. *(PointSeven photo)*

▶ **P.J. TOMES:** No one excelled at combining handle materials quite like the deceased William Scagel. The Scagel-style hunter sports a stag, stacked-leather, fiber and metal handle. *(BladeGallery.com)*

▲ **JURGEN STEINAU:** The mosaic pearl inlays make the innovative folder even more interesting.

▼ **CHARLIE AND HARRY MATHEWS:** The etched blade is impressive enough without adding the material mismatch, a match, you might say, made in heaven. Perhaps William Scagel saw it there. *(SharpByCoop. com)*

◀ **EDDIE STALCUP:** The bird-and-trout knife is steel, stag and canvas Micarta®.

Mammoth-Tooth

It is an old cliché that foreseeing a trend is like trying to predict the stock market. Yet, it is a cliché that makes perfect sense in this instance. Not many knife experts, purveyors, collectors or makers predicted that mammoth-tooth knife handles would become trendy. If they say they did predict it, perhaps they're tooting their own trunks. It could be they are a little woolly between the ears.

Mammoth tooth kind of snuck up on the knife industry, much like pink elephants—at first pink elephants didn't exist, and suddenly they are all around us. Well, maybe that's a bad example. Anyway, if you haven't seen mammoth-tooth knife handles before this point in time, you are in for a real treat. Heck, if you've never seen mammoth-tooth knife handles, and you are on this page of the book, you're not even reading the copy, but rather staring gape-mouthed at the drop-dead-gorgeous grips.

Astoundingly, no mammoth tooth is anything like the next.

Each one is a different color, some with stripes, others with ovals, rings and waves or curves. The hues of the beautiful biters were heretofore unimaginable on knife handles. No synthetic can mimic the natural tooth of beast.

For quite a few years, mammoth-ivory knife handles have been in existence, as well as those of mastodon ivory, walrus ivory and other ancient and legal ivories from all millennia and far reaches of the world. But mammoth tooth is just starting to sink its teeth into the industry. And what an overbite! The pearly whites are anything but white, and they are just as hard as you'd imagine mammoth choppers to be. When the woolly beasts smiled, it was a cool sight indeed. Cavemen were mesmerized, staring at the toothy grins in awe—much like you are probably entranced by the knife handles at this moment.

Joe Kertzman

◄ **SIDNEY "PETE" MOON:** Joe Mason engraved the bolsters but no one had to touch up the mammoth tooth.
(PointSeven photo)

▶ **PAT CRAWFORD:** The "Big Bite Kasper," as the maker calls it, sports a Mike Norris damascus blade and bolsters, a file-worked titanium frame and a mammoth-tooth grip.
(SharpByCoop.com photo)

▲ **DARREL RALPH:** The Mike Norris "gator-skin damascus" sports mammoth-tooth inlays for a wild look, literally. Six tritium inserts were a nice touch.

▲ **A.T. BARR:** The blade is Delbert Ealy "Bear" damascus, the bolsters are Robert Eggerling damascus and the handle scales are stabilized mammoth tooth, not that it stabilized anything on this winsome knife.
(SharpByCoop.com photo)

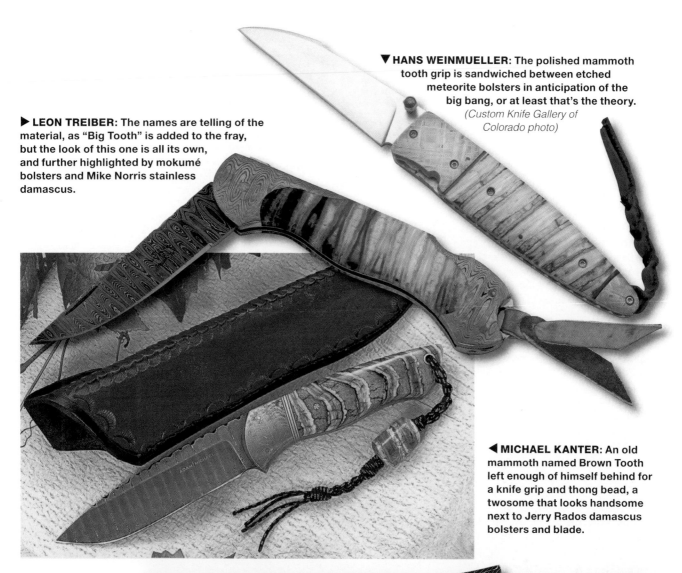

▼ **HANS WEINMUELLER:** The polished mammoth tooth grip is sandwiched between etched meteorite bolsters in anticipation of the big bang, or at least that's the theory. *(Custom Knife Gallery of Colorado photo)*

▶ **LEON TREIBER:** The names are telling of the material, as "Big Tooth" is added to the fray, but the look of this one is all its own, and further highlighted by mokumé bolsters and Mike Norris stainless damascus.

◀ **MICHAEL KANTER:** An old mammoth named Brown Tooth left enough of himself behind for a knife grip and thong bead, a twosome that looks handsome next to Jerry Rados damascus bolsters and blade.

▶ **STAN WILSON:** Inspecting the grip is like looking at a combination of ironwood, ivory and granite, all wrapped up into one pretty package—mammoth tooth. The Devin Thomas Spirograph damascus is a nice touch.

▲ **MIKE MOONEY:** It might be a gent's bowie, but the big guy who donated his tooth for the cause was a beast of a fellow. *(Hoffman photo)*

Great Guards A'mighty

Like sentinels standing watch over villages and villagers, the guards of fine fixed blades take their jobs seriously. They let no wanderers enter the danger zones. Nothing passes their steel fortresses. The objective of the guards is to halt unauthorized from breaching the confines of the edges other than approved cutting media. They have their orders and intend to carry them out dutifully.

The knife guards on this and the facing page are shaped to cradle and protect the hands that grip edged tools and weapons. They are friendly to touch without allowing wayward fingers to flail against sharp blades. Whether fighting their way through downed animal meat, thick brush, vines or enemy fortresses, the edges only skewer that for which they are intended, not those that handle them.

In war or peace, man's oldest tools remain equally useful. The objectives of knife and sword makers are as inherently important as those of sentinels guarding palaces and main streets worldwide. They build tools that work—that must work—for the safety of all who are graced by their presence. No shelter would be built, food prepared, wood shaved, fur blankets made or boardwalks built without hefty fixed blades. Freedom would never have been won without sword edges in the hands of skilled warriors.

It's no stretch to say that the guards between hilts and edges are high-ranking members of the overall company they keep. Each part is greater than the whole. They are pieces of something much larger than themselves, and they have big roles to fill. They make war-weary soldiers thank the stars above, face the heavens and express gratitude to the gods that rule the earth, not just for guards, but for the best and strongest among them—the Great Guards A'mighty.

Joe Kertzman

▲ **LYLE BRUNCKHORST:** The koa handle thought it was curly until it met the guard and realized its straightness. The blade is bewildering in its own way. *(BladeGallery.com photo)*

▲ **JAMES COOK:** Col. James, himself, would have been jealous of this highly guarded bowie with mammoth-ivory grip. *(Ward photo)*

▲ **J. NEILSON:** The "Dark Rider Bowie" set out alone in the still of the night, etched wrought iron guard at hand, to the land of Damascus where only the unknown awaited its edge. *(Ward photo)*

▲ **A.G. BARNES:** The wrought-iron guard is scrolled as tightly as the silver wire inlay of the curly maple handle. *(PointSeven photo)*

▶ **RAYMOND RYBAR JR.** Ray needed a large, scroll-like guard to keep all the fascinated fingers off the 20-inch mosaic-damascus edge of this handsome hunk of steel and walrus ivory. *(PointSeven photo)*

▲ **MICHAEL RADER:** As if the 42-inch random-pattern-damascus blade wasn't enough forged steel, the two-hand saber employs more damascus for the exceptional guard. It makes holding the zebrawood handle a worry-free pleasure. *(BladeGallery.com photo)*

▶ **RAYMOND RICHARD:** He calls it the "Caribowie" because of its inherent shape and horned handle. The wrought iron guard is just as creative and keeps the hand from slipping up onto the blade, which, by the way, was forged from a 1959 Nash Metro leaf spring. *(BladeGallery. com photo)*

▲ **JOE FLOURNOY:** The steel halfpenny guard is worth a fortune in the hands of this knifemaker, who fashioned a fine bowie with damascus blade, stag grip and aircraft aluminum butt cap and ferrules. *(Ward photo)*

◀ **RON NEWTON:** The forged and carved nickel-silver guard stands watch over a 1,500-grit, satin-finished blade. It is backed by a black-ebony Persian ball handle with 31 pearl inlays of white and gold-lip pearl, each in the shape of fleur-de-lis. *(SharpByCoop.com photo)*

Daggers with Swagger

Dust off the coffee table. Lay down a nice piece of felt or silk. Throw on an old record album, tape or CD. Leave the lights on for this one—you'll want want to see. Now, take out that dagger. It's the one with the edges—two of them—and that awesome hourglass-shaped handle. The thing looks sharp, doesn't it, and how about those lines? Man, that's a beauty. You're not taking that one to the fishing hole. This puppy is reserved for the dresser drawer or display case.

It's great to hold it. Wow—power—that's what it is, you know. It's like sighting a great, old gun, knowing that one pull of the trigger fires it. There's nothing unsavory about it, but it is a primitive feeling. There are some innate pleasures in life, and hold-ing a dagger or a Remington, Win-chester, Colt or Mauser—whatever your inclination—is one of them.

Imagine making one of these daggers. Imagine the pride swell-ing at the unveiling of the finished project. That's why the coffee table needs dusting. That's why the felt and silk need to be laid down first before resting the dag-ger on top where you can admire it. You know you'll slide the thumb ever-so-carefully across the edge. You know you'll palm the handle, slide your hand up against the guard and then back down to the pommel. You'll close the folder, sheath the fixed blade and plant it in your pocket, attach it to the belt or drape it from its bead chain around your neck, dangling there waiting for you to pull the edged object of your admiration out to see it again.

The swagger comes after in-specting the dagger. It comes upon carrying it. At that point, you can't help but swagger. Dancing would be appropriate, especially with that old album spinning in the background. But a swagger will do—a purposeful, confident strut, one that gets you noticed, one you practice only on special occasions, the walk that talks, telling people just how good you feel. A dagger can make you swagger.

Joe Kertzman

▶ **H.H. FRANK:** Golden acorns sprout from the blade of a carved push dagger. An ivory handle and gold escutcheon plate are complemented by the ivory sheath and more golden engraving. *(PointSeven photo)*

▲ **STEVE HILL:** "Black Bart" is a pirate folder inspired by the last of the golden age of piracy. Among other amenities, he boasts inscribed crossbones, a skull on a stack of 40 bones and the motto "a short and merry life" inscribed inside his handle spine. The damascus is compliments of Robert Eggerling. *(PointSeven photo)*

▲ **CHARLES STOUT:** The blackwood and damascus dagger is thorn-like and thin. *(Ward photo)*

▼ **RON HEMBROOK:** Who knew you could get red from mammoth ivory, blue from damascus and gold from guard engraving?

▲ **ALBERT TRUJILLO:** California buckeye burl has as many curves and more as the dagger-shaped ATS-34 blade. *(PointSeven photo)*

▲ **TRACY MICKLEY:** The "Scarab" is an art knife dagger, fork and horned beetle all in one.

▲ **TIM HANCOCK:** Everything about the dog-bone bowie, from its striking damascus blade to the domed pins, and damascus frame, spacers, guard and escutcheon are just as they should be in the world of swaggering daggers. *(PointSeven photo)*

▲ **RANDY DOUCETTE:** The "Centipede Dagger" might not have a lot of legs, but its S30V blade walks and talks, and the black-Micarta® handle would help it make mincemeat out of most other pests.

▼ **FRED ROWE:** The stabilized-box-elder handle, wrought-iron guard and 884-layer damascus blade define the "Pierced Black Dagger."

▲ **DAVID MIRABILE:** The tight damascus pattern is taken to new levels not only by the blade texturing, but also through the use of a wrought-iron guard, and a smooth, bulbous blue-fossil-walrus-ivory handle. *(PointSeven photo)*

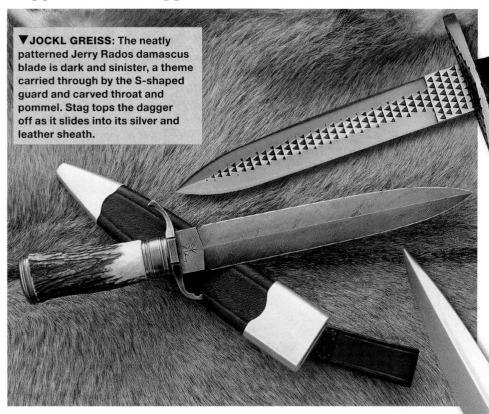

▼**JOCKL GREISS:** The neatly patterned Jerry Rados damascus blade is dark and sinister, a theme carried through by the S-shaped guard and carved throat and pommel. Stag tops the dagger off as it slides into its silver and leather sheath.

▲**STEVE STUART:** The file marks are tantalizing little triangles that set the tone for the diamond-shaped guard, dagger point and coffin handle.

▼**A.R. MAHOMEDY:** The red maple burl and sleek stainless steel elevate the dagger to a stately status.

▲ **ANDERS HOGSTROM:** Short, sweet daggers are better than long, abrasive ones. *(SharpByCoop.com photo)*

▼ PIERRE REVERDY: The Unicorn Dagger showcases a "poetic damascus" blade and handle, an enamel handle overlay, and pure silver carved into a unicorn by Nicole Reverdy Piel.

◄ DON HANSON III: Do the blue dagger swagger, as if you are the woolly mammoth that left behind the tusk for the ivory grip. *(PointSeven photo)*

► LARRY LUNN: The blue of the Siberian-mammoth-ivory handle is brought out by a blue star sapphire button, which in turn pops open the ladder-pattern-damascus blade of the double-action automatic dagger. *(Gail Lunn photo)*

◄ ALAIN MIVILLE-DESCHENES: The mighty "Aphrodite" is an ATS-34 dagger in sterling silver and copper clothing.

► P.J. TOMES: The double-edged Scagel-style dagger sports a flawless 52100 blade, a polished nickel-silver guard and a stacked-leather, fiber and crown-stag handle. *(BladeGallery.com photo)*

Bull-nose Blades

CHARLES SAUER: Mosaic damascus and mammoth ivory enliven the bull and ready it for the fight. *(PointSeven photo)*

EDMUND DAVIDSON: Bully up to an all-integral fixed blade with an Afzelia-lay grip and a BG-42 nose. *(PointSeven photo)*

JERRY FISK: The nose of this bull is ringed, the guard is carved, the stag is staggering and the pins are mosaic masterpieces. *(Ward photo)*

JOHN BARTLOW: Like those who lay mosaic tiles, some knifemakers know how to combine materials, shapes and colors. *(PointSeven photo)*

PETE FORTHOFER: Skinning knife patterns often result in bull noses, but seldom are they as handsome as this mammoth-ivory and mokumé model.

JAY FISHER: The bull was jaded but motivated by purpose.

Slam-Dunk Slip Joints

He plants his left foot, swinging his right leg around, pivoting madly, ball cupped between his palm, wrist and forearm, looking, searching for an open man, hands waving in his face, elbows jabbing his ribs, fingers dangerously close to his eyes, pivot foot planted, wrapping his free leg around those of his opponents and finally, with a final lurch, he cocks his arm and throws the ball to a teammate who slams it home through the hoop and wins the game.

It is said that knifemakers aren't typically big sports fans. Tell that to the guys who make the knives that pivot—the slip joints, those with one, two, three, four, five or more blades, all moving in and out, up and down, and sliding silently, unimpeded into handle halves that accept them smoothly, with no friction, and hide the edges within the safety of their nested liners.

The knifemakers are athletes, alright, and players, competitors, fighters and winners. They wrestle steel. They overcome hurdles, reach goals, beat clocks and practice patterns. They get up early, work out, practice, study the plays and perfect their craft.

Slip joints might be simple folding knife patterns, what without the locks, thumb studs and pocket clips to worry about, but no rookie can make them right. Like a play-off game that comes down

to the final minute, the fun is in the action, and if the action isn't smooth, the fans will walk out of the place.

Knifemakers have game, for sure, but in a more traditional sense than multi-million-dollar athletes. Those who fashion folding steel edges have passed up the contracts. They gave up their rights to health care and benefits. They don't rely on their teammates, but play singles, and they live or die by their own abilities. They pour their hearts and souls into the sport. And if they fail, it isn't "just another game."

Those who have championed the folders on this and the following pages are the most valuable players in the industry. They mastered many facets of the game and fashioned slam-dunk slip joints.

Joe Kertzman

◄ TAKESHI MATSUSAKI: The ATS-34 and stag slip joint is right smart, isn't it?

◄ KAJ EMBRETSEN: For as long as it must have taken Kaj to shape, grind, sharpen and finish the six blades, the punch and the corkscrew, he could have carved a castle. All hail the king. *(PointSeven photo)*

▲ JEFF CLAIBORNE: Take a long pull on the 52100 folding hunter blade and listen to it snap open as the stag grip nestles into the palm of your hand. *(Hoffman photo)*

▲ JOHN FRAPS: Red jigged bone beckons knife buyers to exalt in its bladed offering. *(Custom Knife Gallery of Colorado photo)*

Slam-Dunk Slip Joints

▶ **BILL BURKE:** The 52100 blades tuck neatly into the mammoth-ivory handle like a diver going into a two-and-a-half, only to un-tuck at the right moment and split the surface of the water with nary a splash. *(PointSeven photo)*

▶ **DAN BURKE:** The Anglo Saxon is the biggest of the exhibition whittlers, so, thus, the colossal mother-of-pearl handle and cloud-shaped shield. *(PointSeven photo)*

▶ **AL WARREN:** The trapper snares prey using Devin Thomas raindrop-damascus clip-point and spay blades, and its wooly-mammoth-bark-ivory body camouflages it from its own predators. *(Custom Knife Gallery of Colorado photo)*

▶ **T.R. OVEREYNDER:** The "Model 24 Jack" is anything but an ordinary jackknife. The pearl handle, gold shield and spear-point blades are exemplary for starters. *(PointSeven photo)*

▲ **TOMONARI HAMADA:** Fine cutting instruments with this many implements are significant by any standards. *(PointSeven photo)*

▲ **DON MORROW:** File work might fancy up the amber-jigged-bone wharncliffe but it is the clean fit and finish that elevate it to new levels.

▲ JACK DAVENPORT: The Joseph Rodgers-style slip joint sports a few slightly down-curved CPM 154 blades, some bust-out black-lip-pearl for the handle slabs, a sculpted-crescent-moon handle shield and bird's-eye pins. *(SharpByCoop.com photo)*

◄ DON HETHCOAT: The damascus and mammoth-ivory trapper is a credit to its kind. *(Hoffman photo)*

▲ MARK LARAMIE: The stockman is decked out in three of the prettiest damascus blades ever bestowed upon a folder.

▲ RON NEWTON: From fine engraving to gold-highlighted black-lip pearl, the reproduction of an orange-blossom pattern is nothing shy of remarkable. *(SharpByCoop.com)*

Tips Up

Avid downhill skiers know that, when riding on chairlifts, it is a good idea to keep the tips of their skis up when it comes time to unload on the exit ramps, or the ski tips will catch on the lips of the ramps and the skiers will wind up with their noses in the snow. Signs warn unwary skiers with the words "tips up."

Another winter sport (if you want to call it a sport)—ice fishing—incorporates a gadget called a "tip-up." With extra holes drilled in the ice and several lines and baited hooks dangling down into frigid waters, the resourceful ice fisherman uses spring-loaded flags to warn him of a fish—preferably a northern pike—on one of the lines. It takes a good tug to spring the flag (you wouldn't want to interrupt the card game with a weed snag, small pan fish or, worse yet, minnow.)

Whether for utility purposes, animal skinning, tactical rea-sons or just to achieve more blade belly, several knifemakers are fashioning upswept blades (with the tips up, of course.) Presumably, it makes chores like whittling or skinning a deer, rabbit or squirrel a little easier when there's more belly on the blade and a tip that reaches up and out of the way. It also makes for a dramatic, sweeping blade effect.

Fighters often have upswept blade tips, extending their reach, creating a penetrating point on the back slash and giving the belly of the blade further slashing capabilities. Japanese wakizashis are known to incorporate upswept blades, presumably for the same reasons.

Regardless of why the knives are fashioned in such a manner, there is a noticeable trend in upswept blades, with the tips up, and just in time for skiing and ice-fishing season. What a coincidence! I wonder how the knives do in chopping ice and filleting northern pike?

Joe Kertzman

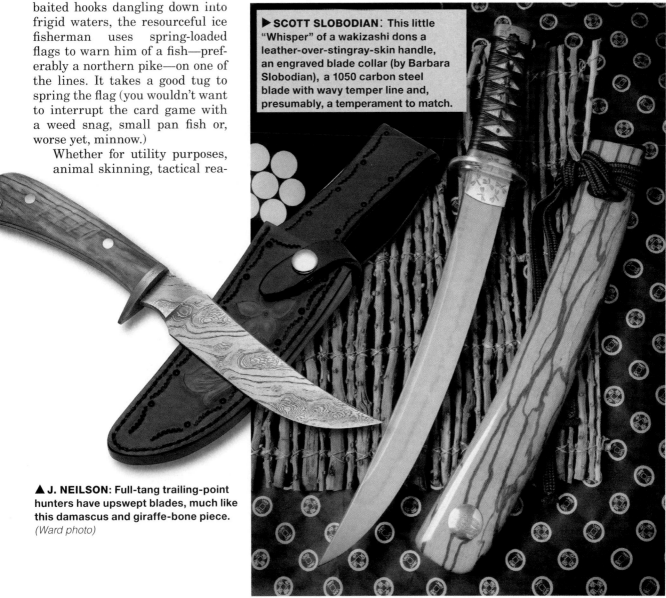

▶ SCOTT SLOBODIAN: This little "Whisper" of a wakizashi dons a leather-over-stingray-skin handle, an engraved blade collar (by Barbara Slobodian), a 1050 carbon steel blade with wavy temper line and, presumably, a temperament to match.

▲ J. NEILSON: Full-tang trailing-point hunters have upswept blades, much like this damascus and giraffe-bone piece. *(Ward photo)*

▶ **RON BEST:** The integral hunter showcases a sculpted handle with mammoth-ivory inlays and a dramatic upswept D-2 blade. *(BladeGallery.com photo)*

▶ **TODD BEGG:** A "lightning-strike" carbon fiber handle tries unsuccessfully to restrain the 6-inch blade. *(PointSeven photo)*

▶ **BOB CROWDER:** The dramatically re-curved blade of the Persian fixed blade is matched only by the highly-figured cape-buffalo-horn handle. *(PointSeven photo)*

▲ **RICK MENEFEE:** This one is a prime cutter from the tip of the damascus blade to the butt of its gemsbok handle. *(John F. Morgan photo)*

◀ **EDMUND DAVIDSON:** The stabilized box-elder handle made the blade tip stand up and take notice. *(PointSeven photo)*

▲ **NORMAN SANDOW:** The "witches whirl" damascus blade rises up at the tip like a puff of smoke emitted from a boiling pot of brew.

Heft a Hawk

▶ **RAYMOND SMITH:** The pipe hawk showcases a 200-layer 5160-and-15N20-damascus head, a tiger-stripe-maple haft, fine silver wire inlay and an Osage-orange mouthpiece.

▲ **WILLIAM MORAN AND A.G. BARNES:** True to form, the duo of masterful knifemakers crafted a W-2 and 1018 tomahawk with a colossal curly-maple haft, impeccable silver-wire inlay and a moose-antler end piece. The hawk also sports a horsehair tassel as a finishing touch. *(PointSeven photo)*

▲ **JOE SZILASKI:** With a pipe hawk and a pipe spike, you'll be smoking and swinging until the cows come home. The forged tool-steel head is inlaid and engraved, and the haft is banded and branded. *(SharpByCoop.com photo)*

▲ **DANIEL WINKLER:** Decorated by Karen Shook, the axe features a forged-1095 head and a curly maple grip, and embellishments include a hand-stitched and painted rawhide wrap, antiqued feathers, glass beads, tin cones and horsehair.

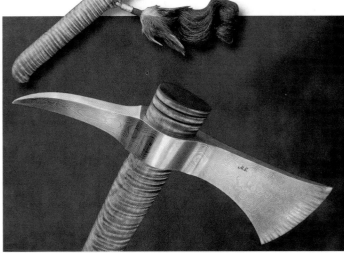

▲ **JERRY LAIRSON SR.:** The high-carbon-damascus head is given an antiqued finish to complement the deep-grained tiger-stripe-maple haft.

Too Tough Tacticals

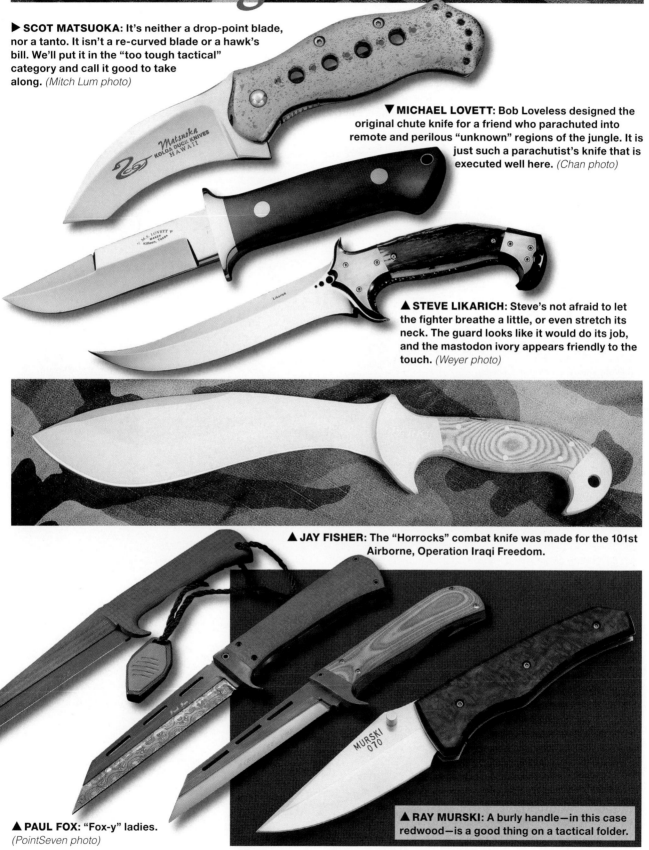

▶ **SCOT MATSUOKA:** It's neither a drop-point blade, nor a tanto. It isn't a re-curved blade or a hawk's bill. We'll put it in the "too tough tactical" category and call it good to take along. *(Mitch Lum photo)*

▼ **MICHAEL LOVETT:** Bob Loveless designed the original chute knife for a friend who parachuted into remote and perilous "unknown" regions of the jungle. It is just such a parachutist's knife that is executed well here. *(Chan photo)*

▲ **STEVE LIKARICH:** Steve's not afraid to let the fighter breathe a little, or even stretch its neck. The guard looks like it would do its job, and the mastodon ivory appears friendly to the touch. *(Weyer photo)*

▲ **JAY FISHER:** The "Horrocks" combat knife was made for the 101st Airborne, Operation Iraqi Freedom.

▲ **PAUL FOX:** "Fox-y" ladies.
(PointSeven photo)

▲ **RAY MURSKI:** A burly handle—in this case redwood—is a good thing on a tactical folder.

Too Tough Tacticals

▶ **WALLY HAYES:** The maker's mark, the shape of the blade and the fact that he left his fingerprints on the handle—all are fine reasons to like the knife. *(PointSeven photo)*

◀ **DARREL RALPH:** Two masters teamed, with Warren Thomas contributing his carbon-fiber-and-damascus blade, and Ralph designing the rest of the butterfly knife. *(PointSeven photo)*

▲ **S.R. (STEVE) JOHNSON:** This one is just begging for a reason to lash out at something. *(PointSeven photo)*

▲ **DIETMAR KRESSLER:** Gorgeous ivory gives the handle a fighting chance against the good looks of the double-ground blade. *(PointSeven photo)*

▲ **LYLE BRUNKHORST AND DAN PERREAULT:** The "Thinking Blade Folder" has a patent-pending locking mechanism that looks to have taken some thinking. *(Mitch Lum photo)*

▲ **RANDALL KING:** Some ATS-34 blade steel and a lot of grinding, shaping and polishing turned this one tactical. *(Weyer photo)*

▲ JASON KNIGHT: The secondary grind along the blade spine is called a "swedge" in knife circles, and the curly maple handle and overall knife design are declared winners by knife enthusiasts everywhere. *(Ward photo)*

▲ HOWARD VIELE: The locks are licensed to the maker by Spyderco, and ivory-Micarta® over titanium frames seems to be a common theme on the fresh knife patterns. *(PointSeven photo)*

▲ TOM MAYO: When walking into dangerous territory, you want Mayo designing your knife.

▲ TODD BEGG: This one would dive right into dinner. *(SharpByCoop.com photo)*

▲ DON NORRIS: Just obtaining the Devin Thomas damascus and the .1911 gun grips isn't enough—you still have to execute the making of the knife, and that's not nearly as easy as it looks. *(PointSeven photo)*

▲ LIN RHEA: A nice pair of brown, leather boots and the sheathed knife slipped down inside them with just the right ironwood handle sticking out results in a cocky swagger to let the world know who's feeling good today. *(Ward photo)*

Too Tough Tacticals

◄ **RANDY DOUCETTE:** They say CPM S30V is fast becoming the blade steel of choice, and this blade shape would catch on, too, if Randy wasn't the only one who could accomplish it.

◄ **MIKE DRAPER:** First there was G-10, then colored G-10 and now blue-weave G-10, and the handle material is still practically indestructible. (Mitch Lum photo)

▲ **MATT CUCCHIARA:** The "Batwing Flipper" hangs upside down at night in case any bloodletting is in order after dark. (Mitch Lum photo)

► **TIM TABOR:** The "Spec Ops" bowie boasts a 6-inch high-carbon-steel blade, a black-linen-Micarta® handle, and a nickel-silver hilt and butt.

▲ **KIRBY LAMBERT:** Marrying tan-G-10 and olive drab canvas Micarta® is akin to melding multiple blade styles into top tip shape. (PointSeven photo)

▶ **JOHN YOUNG:** The stainless and Micarta® dagger has two edges, a double guard and a couple of pins to hold the handle. *(PointSeven photo)*

▶ **ZACH WHITSON:** The martial arts knife brings out the warrior in anyone who holds it. *(Mitch Lum photo)*

◀ **RICK FRIGAULT:** A satin-finished blade, bead-blasted handle and one flabbergasted knife owner.

◀ **DICK FAUST:** Faust's fighter leaves nothing to chance. The maple-burl handle makes it a green machine.

▲ **FLAVIO YUJI R. IKOMA:** The blade was ground in thirds, the handle layered in halves and the knife dressed to the nines.

▶ **DAN PFANENSTIEL:** The 5160 fighter is a smooth operator with a more than mild temper line and ultra-fine features. *(Mitch Lum photo)*

▼**FRANK GAMBLE:** The shooting-flame-shaped blade is as textured and patterned as the fossilized-mammoth-ivory grip. *(PointSeven photo)*

▼**D.B. FRALEY:** The "Torrent" sports a torched titanium frame. *(Mitch Lum photo)*

◄**JAMES SCROGGS:** The blade facets are just one facet to this fightin' knife.

▲**YASUTAKA WADA:** The tip is needle-nose thin, the handle rolling-pin round and the guard deviled-egg oval.

►**KEITH OUYE:** This is what a wharncliffe folder looks like after a maker of tactical knives gets through with it. *(Mitch Lum photo)*

►**MACE VITALE:** Even Paracord, when applied just so, can pretty up a pair of fighters.

► **ROB BROWN:** The shapely re-curved blade of the chute knife is a slight enhancement to the original pattern, but along with the Sacramento ebony handle and stylish guard, it has more than the credence it needs. *(SharpByCoop.com photo)*

▲ **ZACK WHITSON:** The "Pakal" knife makes you want to see if you can punch through a brick building with it. *(Mitch Lum photo)*

▼ **MIKE MOONEY:** He says they're practical, not tactical, but regardless, they're emphatically radical.

▲ **MATTHEW LERCH:** The blade opens by pushing the flipper mechanism that doubles as a finger guard, and when the blade opens, the knife user's mouth naturally gapes open upon seeing the damascus pattern.

◄ **THOMAS HASLINGER:** The "Quilted Maple Fighter" sports an octagonal guard and a raindrop-damascus blade, the latter by Devin Thomas. *(SharpByCoop.com photo)*

DROP-POINT HUNTERS

► **BRAD RUTHERFORD:** It took more than will to coax this one into being, what with the smoothly shaped walrus-ivory handle and bold 1084-and-15N20 damascus blade pattern. *(PointSeven photo)*

▲ **COLTEN TIPPETTS:** The elk antler was just the right shape, and the Damasteel blade continues the taper. Bruce Shaw engraved the pommel but you'll have to imagine that part. *(PointSeven photo)*

▲ **MARVIN SOLOMON:** The black and gray damascus of the drop-point hunter color coordinates well with the lighter-gray damascus guard and even grayer giraffe-bone handle. *(Ward photo)*

▼ **MURRAY ST. AMOUR:** The style of the bolstered handle reminds one of the old "leg knives" with grips as shapely as ladies' legs in high heels. This particular drop-point hunter is a CPM S60V lady with a mammoth-ivory handle and shiny little bolsters. *(Hoffman photo)*

◄ **JEFF NIELSON:** The Alaskan hunter is a "hottie," and includes a dark, tightly patterned damascus blade and a mammoth-ivory handle.

▶ **LYNN MAXFIELD:** A groovy domestic sheep horn grip is just the beginning of this CPM S30V drop-point working and field knife. And a-hunting it could go, too.

▶ **PAT PATTERSON:** What else does a drop-point hunter need besides amboyna burl, bolsters and a file-worked blade? *(Hoffman photo)*

▲ **RUSTY POLK:** It's actually a drop-point skinner, not a hunter, but the hobby is all the same, and mammoth ivory and damascus are pretty no matter what the chore. *(Ward photo)*

◀ **CHARLES STOUT:** The rings of ironwood are interrupted by stainless spacers and dancing damascus. *(Ward photo)*

◀ **EDMUND DAVIDSON:** So solid is the all-integral drop-point hunter, only stabilized maple burl could compete. *(PointSeven photo)*

▲ **THAD BUCHANAN:** The point might drop, but the knife won't—the Micarta® handle is gripping enough. *(BladeGallery.com photo)*

▲ **WILLIAM "BILL" WEBSTER:** The snakewood-handle hunter features a satin-finished D-2 blade that's as smooth as silk.

▶ **TOM KREIN:** The "Whitetail Hunter" is well equipped with 3 inches of CPM S30V blade steel and an ironwood handle. *(Ward photo)*

▲**TRACY MICKLEY:** It's safe to assume the 4-inch "Slow Drop Point Hunters" are quick out of the gate. One sports a spalted-maple grip and the other is decked out in amboyna burl. *(SharpByCoop.com photo)*

▲ **ED BAUMGARDNER:** Having a damascus drop-point in the woods is like being with your favorite girl at a drive-in movie.

▲ **LUDWIG FRUHMANN:** The bolster, blade and tang are integral to each other and none of the parts works without the others.

▲**CHRISTOPHER MEYER:** The grind is flat, the tip is dropped and the Bocote-wood handle has hidden pins. The copper bolster was just the right touch for the tapered-tang toughie.

MICHAEL KANTER: Like a good hunting dog, the Bubinga-wood-handle BG-42 hunter has its nose to the ground. (SharpByCoop.com photo)

CRAIG CAMERER: It's all about stag, steel and stamina. (Hoffman photo)

JIM WALKER: Many knifemakers have begun with carbon steel, nickel silver and stag and haven't gotten nearly the results.

DICK FAUST: At 3/16-inch thick, the "Heavy Duty Hunter" won't crack under pressure.

ROB HUDSON: The pink ivory and spalted maple burl are colorful characters on a stainless damascus knife full of character.

▼ **SEAN O'HARE:** With a dense twist-pattern-damascus beak and stabilized-box-elder-burl body, the "Sparrow" sings like a bird.

▲ **RICK FRIGAULT:** It might be little, but it cuts like nobody's business. That's a slam-dunk slab of buckeye burl, too.

▶ **TINUS KLAASEE:** If warthog hunting is your thing, why not slide a tusk-handle hunter into a leather sheath and head out into the scrub brush?

◀ **EDDIE STALCUP:** Quilted maple shines like a beacon on a clean, shiny, new ATS-34 hunter. *(Hoffman photo)*

▲ **JIM DROUILLARD:** The tang tapers, the snakewood undulates, the bolsters dovetail and the point drops. *(SharpByCoop.com photo)*

MICK WARDELL: Most folks are afraid to embellish a bolster that's boxed in between a highly patterned damascus blade and a red-box-burl handle, but not Mick. He just ties it all in with scroll engraving.

JOHN BARTLOW: It's just another fine example of what can happen when a skilled craftsman brings stainless and stag together. *(PointSeven photo)*

PETER VAN DER WESTHUIZEN: The file-worked brass liners complement the whale-tooth grip perfectly, and the 2 ¾-inch Sandvik 12C27 blade is as swell as the rest.

J. NEILSON AND RAYMOND SMITH: Raymond Smith slipped a stag handle with file-worked butt cap onto the hot-from-the-forge damascus blade by J. Neilson before the pair allowed another Smith *(Pat)* to fashion the sheath. *(Ward photo)*

DON MCINTOSH: The stag-handle drop-point hunter is as sweet as a McIntosh apple. *(Ward photo)*

Embracing Blade Diversity

The title for this chapter evolved after hearing a conversation between two coworkers. One of them had been previously employed at a foundry where many Hmong also worked. She was telling her lunch partner how bad their food smelled, going as far as claiming that it stunk up the microwaves and people refused to use the ovens afterwards. It got worse. She blathered that "they" talked in gibberish, mimicking them as she spouted off, and that no one could understand a word they said. She just "hated them."

It is said that ignorance breeds hate, and it was immediately obvious that she had never taken the time to get to know one of "them." Had she viewed them as equals with slight cultural differences, had she made goodwill gestures toward them, had she approached them with an open mind, and a smile, her perspective would certainly have changed.

I did not waste my time wondering if she knew that Laos's Hmong tribesmen, including former CIA Special Forces soldiers, fought side-by-side with American soldiers during the Vietnam War. I barely gave the fact that Hmong people are some of the most Christianized of the hill tribes of Southeast Asia another thought. People like her prefer ignorance and blame it on "the way they were raised." No one living in the 21st century who makes generalizations about any ethnic group or race of people *has* an excuse.

In the knife industry, there are many who "embrace blade diversity." They fashion knife patterns that trace their roots to countries other than the United States. Inevitably, in doing so, a bit of each country's fashion, style, character and personality shines through in the knives. The diversity is a welcome respite from the sameness in the world. It is exotic, culturally exciting, historically significant and knife enlivening.

Embracing blade diversity is not nearly as difficult as embracing ethnic diversity among people. It takes only an appreciation for art. But should the appreciation of people who are different from us be so hard? Shouldn't we be thankful for their contributions, even if that means just their individual looks, dress and personalities? Try telling that to those who are "dug in" and set in their ways. For these purposes, it's nice to see some ethnically diverse knives. We'll take it one step, or tip, at a time.

Joe Kertzman

▶ **STEVE HILL:** The mammoth-ivory handle is marked like a calico cat, and the Robert Eggerling damascus blade features sculpted agave leaves, but the knife pattern is all Spanish *navaja*.
(PointSeven photo)

▶ **TOM FERRY:** Sculpted blackwood and a wicked damascus blade define the Persian bowie.
(Mitch Lum photo)

▲ **SCOTT SLOBODIAN:** This little "Whisper" of a knife showcases one of the prettiest damascus blades this side of Tokyo. The blade is clay tempered, and the handle is boxwood.

▲ **GERT VAN DEN ELSEN:** The "Syrian Spaniard" sports a 7 ½-inch Wootz-steel blade, made by Achim Wirtz of Germany, an African blackwood handle and a stainless-damascus guard and pommel.

▼ STEVE SCHWARZER: Using mostly Japanese sword-making techniques, Steve fashioned a Japanese-inspired gentleman's folder, including a hand-forged, clay-tempered 1070 blade, a stingray skin handle bonded to Micarta® and pre-Civil War soft iron bolsters. *(SharpByCoop.com photo)*

◄ SCOTT SLOBODIAN: The dyed-birch handle would have made any samurai die and go to heaven, or wherever samurais courted their spirits.

▼ MICHAEL RADER: The "Dha Guardian" traces its roots to Burmese and Southeast Asian mainland swords but this piece is much fancier, with 23-inch, 30-layer damascus blade and multi-colored wood grip. *(BladeGallery.com photo)*

▼ JODY MULLER: For nearly all edged-weapons makers, replicating this wakizashi, complete with 16-inch 1084 blade, wavy temper line and maple-and-blackwood handle, would be wishful thinking. *(BladeGallery.com photo)*

▲ FRED OTT: The twist-damascus tanto benefits from a copper *habaki* (blade collar) and ironwood burl handle.

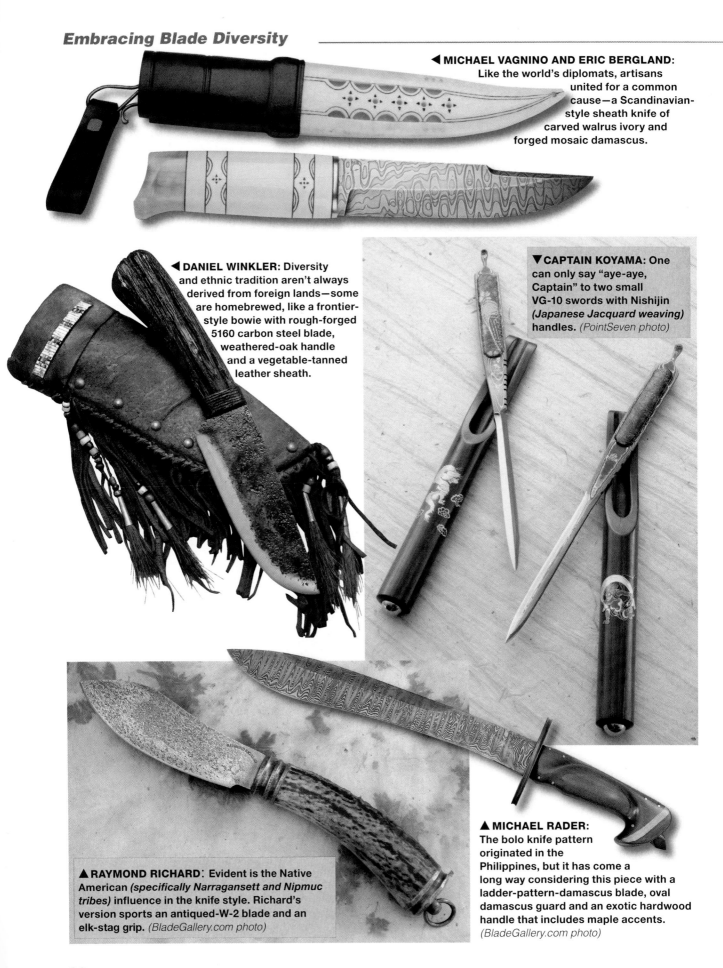

◀ **MICHAEL VAGNINO AND ERIC BERGLAND:** Like the world's diplomats, artisans united for a common cause—a Scandinavian-style sheath knife of carved walrus ivory and forged mosaic damascus.

◀ **DANIEL WINKLER:** Diversity and ethnic tradition aren't always derived from foreign lands—some are homebrewed, like a frontier-style bowie with rough-forged 5160 carbon steel blade, weathered-oak handle and a vegetable-tanned leather sheath.

▼ **CAPTAIN KOYAMA:** One can only say "aye-aye, Captain" to two small VG-10 swords with Nishijin *(Japanese Jacquard weaving)* handles. *(PointSeven photo)*

▲ **RAYMOND RICHARD:** Evident is the Native American *(specifically Narragansett and Nipmuc tribes)* influence in the knife style. Richard's version sports an antiqued-W-2 blade and an elk-stag grip. *(BladeGallery.com photo)*

▲ **MICHAEL RADER:** The bolo knife pattern originated in the Philippines, but it has come a long way considering this piece with a ladder-pattern-damascus blade, oval damascus guard and an exotic hardwood handle that includes maple accents. *(BladeGallery.com photo)*

DANIEL WATSON, ANGEL SWORD: The Scottish basket-hilt sword has an awesome amber grip, a cast-bronze guard and a Techno-Wootz damascus blade.

BAILEY BRADSHAW: Not too many replicated Japanese swords sport white handle wraps, but more will after cutlers see this damascus doozy.

KEVIN CASHEN: Though it's a small sword, it packs a lot into 34 ½ inches, including a carved-steel guard, duel-ready damascus blade and kingwood handle. *(SharpByCoop.com photo)*

JON CHRISTENSEN: Think of the blade as an Indian arrowhead and the curly maple handle and twist-damscus bolsters as the fin and feathers. *(Mitch Lum photo)*

GERT VAN DEN ELSEN: In Lapland, a *leukku* is akin to a bowie in San Antonio, Texas. This piece is decked out in etched O-1 tool steel and a stabilized-maple birch handle with an African blackwood spacer.

► **WALLY HAYES:** The damascus "Spanish Knight" is crowned with bladed helm, but his grip is all elk antler. *(PointSeven photo)*

► **RICHARD WRIGHT:** The blade of the bolster-release "Persian Dagger" is Jerry Rados Turkish-twist damascus ground to a sweeping Persian-style, folding-dagger shape. Other amenities include rubies, gold-lip mother-of-pearl and anodized titanium. *(SharpByCoop.com photo)*

▲ **PAUL JARVIS:** So many knifemakers take a liking to the Japanese style and so few execute it like Jarvis. The damascus blade is downright bewitching, and the carved grip and *saya* (sheath) are a handsome lot. *(PointSeven photo)*

▲ **JOHN LUNDEMO AND DAVID SCHLUETER:** Luck be a lady tonight. *(SharpByCoop.com photo)*

► **CHARLIE AND HARRY MATHEWS:** You'd think there would be a letdown after pulling the blade of the Scottish dirk from that impressive pierced nickel silver sheath, but then the fileworked blade and crown-stag handle would reveal themselves. *(PointSeven photo)*

▲ **JONNY WALKER NILSSON:** The Swedish Sami-style Halfhorn sports—get this—a Hwy. I-90-pattern-damascus blade, and an arctic-birch-burl and engraved-reindeer-antler handle, all using ancient Sami (Laplander) techniques.

▲ **BOB TERZUOLA:** Al Pendray's Wootz steel is world renowned, but the way it's married with an ebony handle and 24k-gold guard is equally **remarkable.** *(PointSeven photo)*

The Clash of Pearl and Damask

It isn't like when your long-lost uncle comes to town wearing a checked shirt, striped shorts, black socks pulled up to his knees and yellow Converse tennis shoes. The knives have nothing in common with the lady next door who gardens in a bright yellow muumuu, a red sun hat, blue stretch pants and brown hiking boots. The clash of pearl and damask is entirely different from the neighbor and the long-lost uncle.

It is an artistic clash, a planned mismatch of materials, a strategic marrying of dissimilar handle, blade and bolster building blocks. White mother-of-pearl contrasts completely with dark damascus blades. The pearl has a settling effect on the busy pattern-welded steel. The colorless nacre provides a respite or resting point for the eyes of knife collectors and enthusiasts. The stark-white pearl has a stabilizing effect that gives a fine folder or fixed blade appeal.

Gold-lip pearl is equally appealing when combined with a skillfully patterned blade. Damascus and black-lip pearl are instant hits in the knife industry. The translucency of pearl is a perfect match for the immediate surface patterning of the steel. The two complement each other. They are perfect bedfellows.

Part of what makes the pre-arranged marriage so ideal is that pearl and damascus are considered high-class materials reserved for the finest knives. They are first-rate, exquisite and beautiful. Their pedigrees match and combine to raise their social status to that of elitism. The coupling of pearl and damascus can mean the difference between being fine folders and ornate gent's knives suitable for suit pockets and display cases.

The clash of pearl and damask is more than utility or aesthetics. It is an elevation of folders into new markets, price ranges and classes. Consider damascus the king and pearl the queen. Suddenly the draw bridge is raised and the castle busies itself in preparation for a royal reception. The rolling out of the red carpet is certainly an appropriate act in preparation for the clash of pearl and damask.

Joe Kertzman

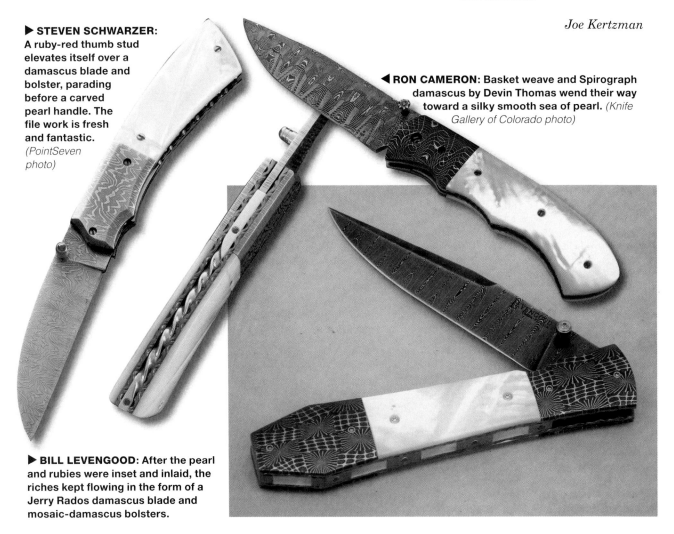

▶ **STEVEN SCHWARZER:** A ruby-red thumb stud elevates itself over a damascus blade and bolster, parading before a carved pearl handle. The file work is fresh and fantastic. *(PointSeven photo)*

◀ **RON CAMERON:** Basket weave and Spirograph damascus by Devin Thomas wend their way toward a silky smooth sea of pearl. *(Knife Gallery of Colorado photo)*

▶ **BILL LEVENGOOD:** After the pearl and rubies were inset and inlaid, the riches kept flowing in the form of a Jerry Rados damascus blade and mosaic-damascus bolsters.

LARRY NEWTON: The carved pearl swoops up while the damascus pools, waves and lines up in some semblance of order.

GEORGE BEECHEY: The Damasteel is as pretty as a pearl. *(BladeGallery.com photo)*

MURRAY STERLING: The damascus canoe is buoyed by black-lip pearl.

KAJ EMBRETSEN: Contrast is when black meets white within the confines of a fine folding knife. *(PointSeven photo)*

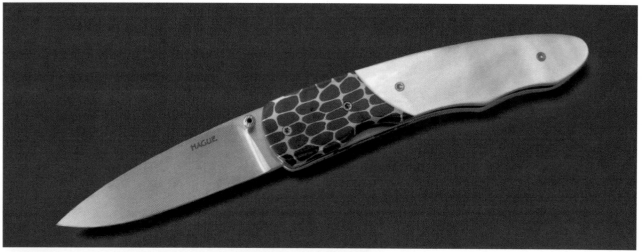

▲ **GEOFF HAGUE:** The blued-honeycomb-damascus bolsters oozed their offerings onto the honey of a gold-lip-pearl handle.

◄ **GAYLE BRADLEY:** Thirty-layer, twist-pattern Damasteel frames a black-lip-pearl inlay like the horizon frames the land. *(PointSeven photo)*

► **PAUL FOX:** The fine pearl folder gives "black and blue" a whole new meaning. *(PointSeven photo)*

Flavorful Folders

▶ SCOT MATSUOKA: The blue and purple of the bolsters play off the brown hues of the highly patterned curly koa handle. Now, let's talk about that fantastic blade shape. *(PointSeven photo)*

▼ JAMES HARRISON: The snakeskin damascus bolsters and pocket clip slither out from a scaly carbon-fiber grip and into a BG-42 tongue.

▼ TONY BOSE: Few whittlers are lockback folders, and fewer still feature Remington bone handles and such fine workmanship. *(SharpByCoop.com photo)*

▲ JEFF ISGRO: He calls the handle scales "chocolate desert ironwood," and they look good enough to eat. The blade is Odin's eye stainless damascus, in case you were watching and wondering.

▶ JOHNNY STOUT: As long as the grass is green and the blade is blued, the cutting is never dull with a mammoth-ivory-handled locking-liner folder. *(Mitch Lum photo)*

▲ **CLIFF POLK:** A toothy damascus blade was an edgy choice for a mammoth-ivory-gripped locking-liner folder.

▲ **SALVATORE PUDDU:** The shiny folder with tortoise-shell handle inlays and 18k-gold inserts completely disassembles, but who'd want to take the stunning piece apart?

◀ **DELLANA:** One of the few leading ladies of knife delivers again—this time a 324-layer-damascus lockback folder featuring textured and oxidized sterling silver bolsters overlaid with 14-karat gold, a black-lip-pearl handle and file work inside and out. *(PointSeven photo)*

▲ **ED BAUMGARDNER:** The folder is steeped in deep grains, deep damascus patterning and deeper design. *(PointSeven photo)*

▲ **TOM MAYO:** It's just Timascus and Stellite™—I mean, really, what's the big deal? *(Hoffman photo)*

▲ **JOSH SMITH:** Even the edges of the bolsters and the mammoth-ivory handle are rounded and smooth on this dual-action automatic, complete with file work along the liners. *(PointSeven photo)*

▶ **CHARLES BENNICA:** Two black-lip-pearl inlays on one side of the knife and one large inlay on the other liven up an otherwise clean, all-steel folder.

▶ **RON APPLETON:** Ron's tricked-out folders are starting to look like throwing stars, and they leave the masses starry eyed, too. *(PointSeven photo)*

◀ **STEVE HOEL:** The pocket folder features tiger-eye inlays, and that's enough for me.

▼ **J.D. BARTH:** Leave it to knifemakers to find so many winsome ways to match up mammoth-ivory and damascus patterns.

▶ **TERRY KNIPSCHIELD:** Even if there were 100 Coke Bottle Chute Folders in this book *(there probably aren't any others)* this piece would win us over with its crimson jigged-bone handle, fluted-416 stainless steel bolsters and spear-point, mirror-polished ATS-34 blade. *(Custom Knife Gallery of Colorado photo)*

► **DARREL RALPH:** The walrus that left the ivory for the handle never saw patterns this beautiful, even under the water. *(PointSeven photo)*

◄ **GEORGE GIBO AND CARL ZAKABI:** Though it sports a damascus blade, giraffe-bone handle and engraved titanium bolsters, this one is all about the smooth lines. *(PointSeven photo)*

▲ **PAT AND WES CRAWFORD:** A little jewelling, some titanium and, voila, a folding knife. Well, it took a little more than that. *(PointSeven photo)*

▲ **RON LAKE:** There were some I-shaped pieces of steel from the World Trade Center being respectfully passed around within the knifemaking community, but few knifemakers have incorporated them so beautifully into their designs as Ron did with this WTC Commemorative Series. The handles are bronze. *(SharpByCoop.com photo)*

▲ **BILL VINING:** If the Delbert Ealy dragon-pattern-damascus blade was any closer to the butterfly-damascus bolsters, we'd have dragonflies. The mammoth-ivory scales are the cream of the crop, and Joe Mason inlaid the gold.

▶ **TOM FERRY:** Imagine being the guy who has never seen a handmade knife when his buddy pulls this pair of Timascus and damascus folders out of his pants pockets. *(Mitch Lum photo)*

▲ **LYLE BRUNKHORST AND DAN PERREAULT:** The patent-pending locking mechanism holds the damascus blade right where we can see it. *(Mitch Lum photo)*

▲ **PAUL FOX:** Damascus and ivory are flavorful enough, but this rear-lock folder is bolted together and incorporates a coil pocket milled into the tang. *(PointSeven photo)*

▼ **MICHAEL WALKER:** Give the average knifemaker gold, Damasteel, Saakudo silver and titanium and he doesn't come anywhere close to this D-Lock folder. *(PointSeven photo)*

▲ **LEON TREIBER:** If you had to pick just one, which one would it be? *(Ward photo)*

▲ PETER VAN DER WESTHUIZEN: Are those cavities on the whale-tooth handle, or just neat little carvings complemented by a Mike Fellows damascus blade?

▲ CHARLES KAIN: Fancy the "Fulcrum" and its patent-pending mechanism that scissors the left handle scale 15 degrees down and back to open the blade. The presentation-grade maple and file-worked twist-damascus blade beg to be noticed, too.

► KELLY CARLSON: The fighter squadron features tritium canons, and titanium fuselages, solar collector panels and drives. And that's just the knives.

▲T.C. ROBERTS: The surface of the jasper handle reminds one of flowers floating in water, and perhaps that's why the maker chose a "damascus rose"-patterned blade. *(Ward photo)*

▲ GEORGE BEECHEY: George's amazing Technicolor dream cut includes a yellow/green tiger-eye handle, blue/green titanium bolsters and a heat-blued damascus blade. *(BladeGallery.com photo)*

▶ **REGGIE BARKER:** The gemsbok handle was groovy enough to leave the bolsters and blade plain. *(Ward photo)*

◀ **RALPH TURNBULL:** The grip might be mammoth ivory but it is the color of a killer whale and complemented by a Craig Barr damascus blade and a black-diamond thumb stud.

▶ **DON OSBORNE:** The damascus blade pattern is loose, the damascus bolster pattern is tight and the giraffe bone handle is out of sight. *(PointSeven photo)*

▲ **JOHN BARTLOW:** Sheep horn and gold-anodized titanium butt heads on a likeable locking-liner folder. *(PointSeven photo)*

▲ **JASON HOWELL:** The icy-white deer head of the mosaic damascus bolster is the perfect complement to a stark-white ivory handle and basket-weave-pattern damascus blade. *(PointSeven photo)*

The Pearl in the Window

▶ **MATT DISKIN:** Ed Schempp's flower-pot-pattern mosaic damascus sprouted some greenery within the portal of the handle. *(PointSeven photo)*

◀ **PETER MARTIN:** Gold thumb stud and bail, damascus blade, handle and bar, they all gathered to pay homage to the black pearl in the window.

◀ **ED CAFFREY:** The white mother-of-pearl is the centerpiece of a mosaic-damascus folding cutter cloaked with a carved and crackle-finished titanium handle, and 18k-gold screws.

▶ **JOSH SMITH:** The pleasing pink and green pearl is in bold contrast to the damascus blade and grip, but won't budge an inch and learns to live in unison with that of the blue hue. *(PointSeven photo)*

▲ **HOWARD HITCHMOUGH:** Mirror, mirror on the handle, who's the fairest of them all? *(PointSeven photo)*

Bowie-licious

▶ **RICK FRIGAULT:** On any other knife, the giraffe bone would be the centerpiece. On this bowie, it's the fishbone-damascus blade in spiny lines along the edge, discs in the middle and folds on top.

▶ **TOM FERRY:** There's a blade-eating man carved on the guard and he has bit off more than he can chew. *(Mitch Lum photo)*

▲ **GORDON GRAHAM:** Some elbow grease went into shaping and smoothing that blade, and ironwood was a wise choice.

▼ **ROB HUDSON:** The cut of stag is only upstaged by the filework along the blade spine.

▲ **LIN RHEA:** The bowie blade bends before you like a long-legged ballerina taking a final bow. *(Ward photo)*

▶ **ANDERS HOGSTROM AND DON HANSON III:** Don forged a 15 ½-inch damscus blade for "The Beast," and Anders outfitted it with a silver guard and walrus-ivory handle. Perhaps the ring is to hold the beast back! *(PointSeven photo)*

◀ **TERRY VANDEVENTER:** No one knows how he got the stellar sea cow rib for the handle, and everyone is afraid to ask. *(Ward photo)*

◀ **STEVE STUART:** The knifemaker smartly left the surface of the farrier's rasp intact and tactile.

◀ **J.W. RANDALL:** When replicating a Sheffield bowie, the only way to elevate it to new heights is through impeccable fit and finish. This one pierces the clouds. *(T. Randall photo)*

▲ **MARK NEVLING:** The strap of blue brings you into the blade of black and the grip of many colors.

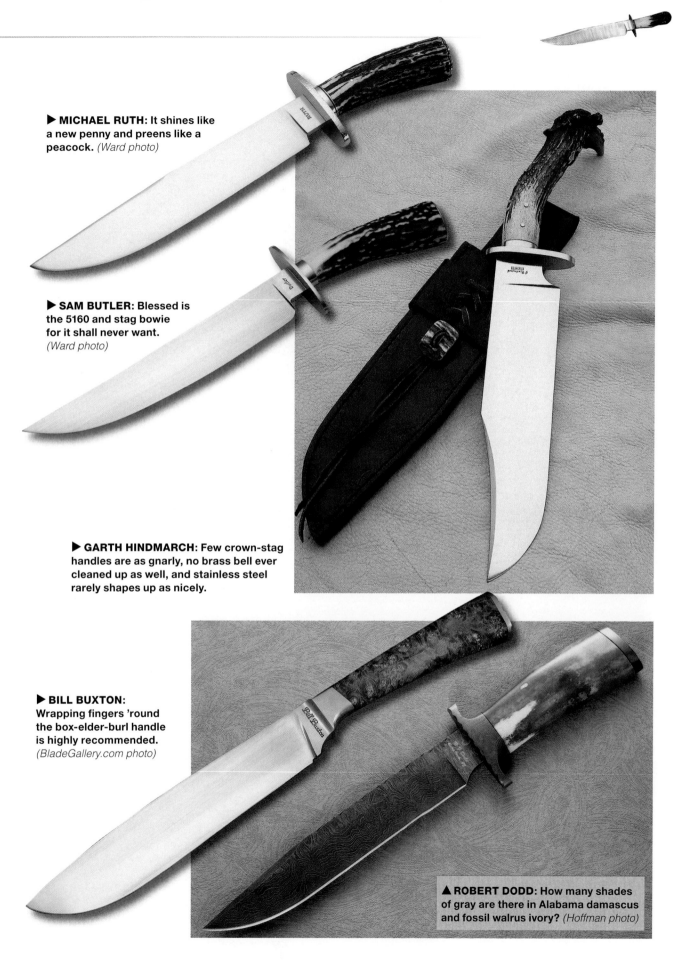

► **MICHAEL RUTH:** It shines like a new penny and preens like a peacock. *(Ward photo)*

► **SAM BUTLER:** Blessed is the 5160 and stag bowie for it shall never want. *(Ward photo)*

► **GARTH HINDMARCH:** Few crown-stag handles are as gnarly, no brass bell ever cleaned up as well, and stainless steel rarely shapes up as nicely.

► **BILL BUXTON:** Wrapping fingers 'round the box-elder-burl handle is highly recommended. *(BladeGallery.com photo)*

▲ **ROBERT DODD:** How many shades of gray are there in Alabama damascus and fossil walrus ivory? *(Hoffman photo)*

◄ TIM FOSTER: Why wouldn't a master smith forge flames into the steel of his best bowie? The stark white ivory was a nice touch for contrast and class. *(BladeGallery.com photo)*

▲ ED FOWLER: Ed is all about the grain structure of the steel, the utilitarian shape of the blade, the way the guard curls around the finger, the way the handle feels in the palm of the hand, a soft steely spine, hardened edge … well, he's about everything, really. *(Phillip LaBarbera photo)*

► P.J. TOMES: He went from satin finishing steel to sculpting walrus ivory in one knife's work. *(BladeGallery.com photo)*

◄ RED ST. CYR: Armed with a slab of steel and a well-figured slab of stag, a slab of steak shouldn't be a real problem. *(BladeGallery. com photo)*

▲ ROGER MASSEY: Catch cocobolo bowie fever and push it right to the edge.

▲ BILLY BATES: He didn't cut corners—he cut steel into corners, and brass into scrolls and stag into a slab. *(Ward photo)*

▲ KIRK REXROAT: He dug his hand files into the steel, his spurs into the bucking bronco and his tongs into the forge fire. (PointSeven photo)

▲ TIM HANCOCK: The static-stricken steel is grounded only by the smooth guard and soothing ivory handle. (PointSeven photo)

▲ JOHN FITCH AND REGGIE BARKER: It took two knifemakers to tackle this biting bowie blade. (Ward photo)

▲ DON MCINTOSH: The peaks and valleys of the damascus pattern play themselves out toward the tip of the big bowie blade. (Ward photo)

▲ STEVEN RAPP: The Joseph Rodgers replica bowie is more remarkable for its fine lines, smooth shape and fancy filework than for its material makeup. (PointSeven photo)

▲ ROB HUDSON: The cut of stag is only upstaged by the filework along the blade spine.

▲ STACY APELT: The arrowhead is symbolic of hunters harvesting stag with highly patterned steel stickers. *(PointSeven photo)*

▲ DON HANSON: When steel is differentially heat treated, the areas that take the most heat etch differently than those that don't, sometimes, when the smith knows his stuff, resulting in a temper line that wafts across the blade like clouds in the sky. *(PointSeven photo)*

▲ FUAD ACCAWI: That's some blade swedge along the spine, dipping at just the right place and giving the entire bowie another dimension. *(PointSeven photo)*

▲ BOB DOZIER: So highly figured is the walrus ivory, the blade needed only a high sheen to set the heart to beating for more. *(Weyer photo)*

▲ ROBERT BLASINGAME: A Miller-style bowie is fashioned to resemble not only the style, but the period and patina of the pretty pattern.

▶ **JON CHRISTENSEN:** English walnut has been known to class up more than a few classic knives, but never before has it left such beautiful leaf impressions on a bowie blade. *(Mitch Lum photo)*

▲ **STEVE DUNN:** A perfectly cut coffin-handle bowie with gorgeous engraving and gold inlays makes more than blips on the damascus radar screen. *(PointSeven photo)*

▲ **MACE VITALE:** When the first one turns out this well, you give it a partner and hope for baby bowies. *(PointSeven photo)*

◀ **GAYLE BRADLEY:** The grain and rings of the desert ironwood seem deeper than a surface pattern, but the blade is just as long as it looks.

▲ **CRAIG CAMERER:** The amber-colored stag handle catches the eye like sun reflecting off a bowie blade among the sandstone cliffs of Chimney Rock. *(Hoffman photo)*

Straight-Back Stickers

Their names are on the blades, their marks, logos, stamps, trademarks and signatures. The marks are what identify the makers of the knives, and make no mistake—that is important. Years from now, whether 10, 20, 50 or 200 years in the future, someone, somewhere will pick up one of the knives and look at the tang stamp. That person will investigate the mark to see who made the knife, and then the blade will have documentation, a history.

Equally important is the overall quality of the knife, and that depends on what kind of legacy the knifemaker wanted to leave behind in his or her wake. If he wanted to be known for clean, interesting, useable, fine knives, then the fit and finish, the design and workmanship will reflect those aspirations.

Take these straight-back stickers, for example. The patterns are perfect. Where the guards butt up against the blades and flow into handles can be found clean lines, fits, finishes and surfaces. The transitions are seamless. The soldered joints are practically undetectable. The curves of the blades are smooth and flowing. The handles are clean and palpable. The knives are ergonomic, sharp, exquisite and carefully fashioned. Little extras like gold pins, file work, liners and integral thong holes reveal themselves.

And the backs of the blades are perfectly straight. There is no wavering. They are straightforward, straight-back stickers that excel in their purpose and practicality. They are the types of knives people would be proud to own. They exhibit fine craftsmanship and care. The knifemakers who built them sweated over the details and left their souls in the steel. Someone 200 years from now will pick up one of these straight-back stickers and recognize it for its inherent value. That's the straight skinny on custom knifemaking.

Joe Kertzman

◀ **ROGER MASSEY:** Here's an integral stag-handle hunter of the forged-5160 kind. *(Ward photo)*

▶ **MICHAEL RUTH:** The "Trail Boss" lets his guard down but keeps his back straight. *(Ward photo)*

▲ **J.D. BARTH:** The mammoth-ivory handle is highlighted by red liners and mosaic pins, but the ATS-34 blade is as straightforward as they come.

▲ **JEROME ANDERS:** The curly maple handle and 5160 blade each bulge down in the middle, but they keep their spines straight. *(Ward photo)*

► PATRICK BURRIS: When you have armadillo armor scales, you keep your back straight.

► TIM FOSTER: With one-piece blade and guard, and a curly maple handle that fits tightly around the full blade tang, this one qualifies as an integral, and the straight-back O-1 blade is integral to the whole. *(BladeGallery.com photo)*

► NEIL MCKEE: The rifleman's belt knife is a straight shooter showcasing a 5160 blade and an elk-antler handle. *(BladeGallery.com photo)*

▲ COLTEN TIPPETTS: This one is strictly BG-42, mother-of-pearl and a little gold thrown in for good measure. *(PointSeven photo)*

◄ HENRY TORRES: As difficult as it is to keep the spine of a 7 1/2-inch blade perfectly straight, Henry accomplished just that, coupling it with a hefty desert-ironwood handle. *(Mitch Lum photo)*

► TOMMY WARE: The straight-back hunter has enough ATS-34 belly to dress out any deer, and the desert ironwood makes it right at home in the forest. *(Hoffman photo)*

Shrunken Treasures

Why would anyone limit their market, or eliminate the potential for more sales, by making miniature knives? The knife industry, including the collectors who call it home, is so inherently small. What on earth would cause a knifemaker to build tiny edges that aren't real useful to hunters, fishermen, outdoors enthusiasts, warehouse dock workers, construction workers, handymen, extreme sportsmen, daily knife users and professional ladies and gentleman who like to tote handy folders in their pockets? Are they crazy? The only folks in the market for miniature knives are collectors, and then usually only accumulators of miniature knives, and those who have an appreciation for art. I think that's where the answer lies. It's art for art's sake, isn't it?

Are you telling me that knifemakers have decided not to sell out, literally and figuratively? Could it mean that they refuse to fold under societal pressures to make money, earn a living, drive nice cars, eat in fancy restaurants, be seen in known company, strike it rich and live the American dream? Are they artists first and breadwinners second? Are they true to themselves and their arts and crafts? Do they bow to no one but the gods of knifemaking? Are they answering their own calling?

It is said that those who concentrate all their efforts into mastering certain skills become lost in their worlds. Perhaps that is going a bit too far. Yet, to make tiny knives to such exacting detail as the examples on this and the following page, the artists must temporarily shut out their surrounding environment. How else could they chisel and peen pins so small, grind such tiny blades, carve diminutive guards, cut out miniscule fittings, etch inch-long damascus blade steel, inlay millimeter-thick silver wire and engrave centimeters worth of handle frames at a time?

The makers who build miniature knives are no slouches, either. They don't allow their craft, their fits and finishes, to slide. The quality is still there. These itty-bitty knives could probably cut through bricks with enough force. They work. The knifemakers will stake their reputations on them. It makes you want to buy one, doesn't it? Perhaps knifemakers aren't limiting their market after all. They know the little loppers are worth all the effort put into them. Maybe, just maybe, the knifemakers recognize the knives as the shrunken treasures they really are.

Joe Kertzman

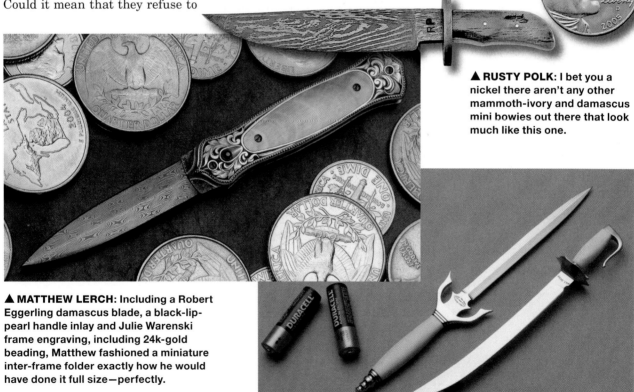

▲ **RUSTY POLK:** I bet you a nickel there aren't any other mammoth-ivory and damascus mini bowies out there that look much like this one.

▲ **MATTHEW LERCH:** Including a Robert Eggerling damascus blade, a black-lip-pearl handle inlay and Julie Warenski frame engraving, including 24k-gold beading, Matthew fashioned a miniature inter-frame folder exactly how he would have done it full size—perfectly.

▲ **BILL DUFF:** With ivory handle sword in one knuckle and dagger in the other a man can walk tall or short with equal swagger. *(Ward photo)*

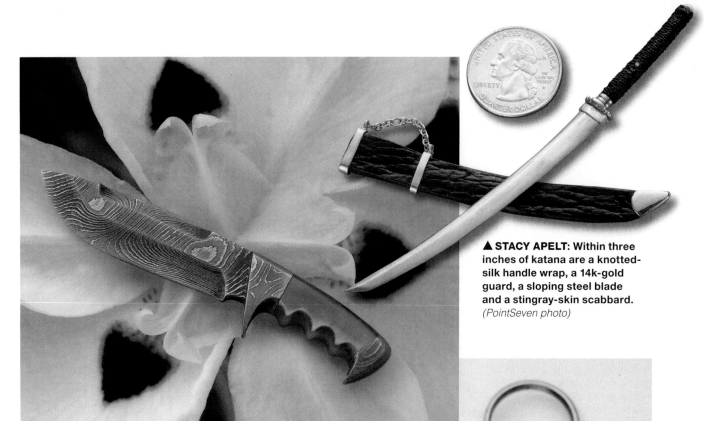

▲ **STACY APELT:** Within three inches of katana are a knotted-silk handle wrap, a 14k-gold guard, a sloping steel blade and a stingray-skin scabbard. *(PointSeven photo)*

▲ **MIKE FELLOWS:** The full integral features a twist-pattern-damascus blade and a mother-of-pearl handle, and at 34 mm long, it rests easily on the poor man's orchid.

▲ **ART TYCER:** Mastodon ivory and damascus look just as good in miniature as they do full size. *(Ward photo)*

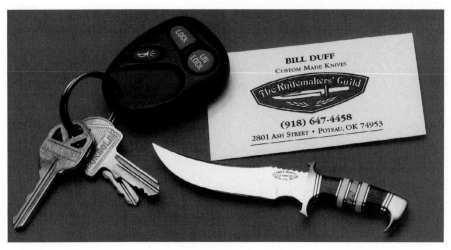

BILL DUFF
CUSTOM MADE KNIVES
The Knifemakers' Guild
(918) 647-4458
2801 ASH STREET • POTEAU, OK 74953

◄ **BILL DUFF:** The bite-size bowie dons a 440C blade and little rings of stainless steel, turquoise, ivory and cocobolo for the mini grip. *(Ward photo)*

Full-Tilt Sub-Hilts

You don't hear much about the history of the sub-hilt fighter. It is an unsung hero. It has its roots in fighting, combat, military and tactical environments. The idea behind the hilt and sub-hilt is minimum movement of the hand in tactical situations, when a life is on the line, when a human being is depending on a blade. Two guards are better than one. There isn't just one palace guard.

Specifically, a sub-hilt limits the movement or sliding of the index finger when the knife is used for slashing and cutting in a forward grip, and the pinkie when held in a reverse grip for upward thrusting. A single guard, alone, isn't always sufficient, and a person can slide his entire hand back, behind both guards, if need be, for further pointing, slashing and jabbing of the blade tip.

Now isn't all of this interesting, but what does it have to do with fine handmade knives?

Just look at that knife pattern. The blades are long, almost re-curved along the edges, but not quite. Some have swedges along the blade spines. Almost all the handles dip down at the pommels, and the full blade tangs are often tapered. Many sub-hilt blades have clip points.

They are fighting knives. Their job is not pretty, but their physical makeup and materials are enthralling. They are the point men, the leads, the commanders, the soldiers, operators, front line of defense, infantry and operatives. They go full-bore, flat out, wide open. They are the full-tilt sub-hilts. Let's roll.

Joe Kertzman

▶ **J.P. HOLMES:** This one sports a hollow-ground CPM S30V blade and a buckeye-burl handle. J.P. calls the spacer between the two hilts of the fighter "walrus tapioca," and I have no idea if he's pudding us on or not. *(SharpByCoop.com photo)*

◀ **RICARDO VELARDE:** The substantial sub-hilt fighter is full of blade, guard and ivory grip. *(PointSeven photo)*

▲ **EDMUND DAVIDSON:** Edmund's full-tilt sub-hilts are full integral and fulfilling. *(PointSeven photo)*

◀ **RICARDO VELARDE:** The stag is stained, the hilts doubled up and the blades double ground. *(PointSeven photo)*

▶ **DIETMAR KRESSLER:** It's a full-integral RWL-34 sub-hilt fighter, which basically makes it indestructible. *(PointSeven photo*

◀ **SCHUYLER LOVESTRAND:** The satin-finished, re-curved ATS-34 blade puts this sub-hilt fighter in a class of its own. *(PointSeven photo)*

▲ **MICHAEL LOVETT:** Choose your weapon. *(Stanley Chan photo)*

▲ **DICK FAUST:** The maple burl handle of the knife with two hilts is red hot. *(PointSeven photo)*

▲ **EDDIE STALCUP:** Not a traditional sub-hilt fighter, but more along the lines of an ATS-34 and ironwood hunter, this one does borrow the sub-hilt design, and rather well, too.

STATE OF THE ART

Think of the ironies. Art isn't supposed to be exacting, but on knives, it has become a science. Sculpture has no limits, but sculpted blades, bolsters and grips must embody seamless construction or the knives won't function properly. Engraving wraps itself around its subjects, yet must be contained within the boundaries of knife frames. Scrimshaw is picture-perfect artwork framed, in this case, by the parameters of knife handles. Etching allows steel to speak, but blades must quietly make their presence known. Art and knives aren't supposed to mix as freely as they do. So does that mean that artists working with knives must be more disciplined than their creative brethren? You bet your painter's palette they do.

This year has seen the rise of two embellishing techniques that have heretofore been absent in modern knives—all gray surface engraving on steel handles and blades for a less garish effect, and surface-enhanced handles resulting from the texturing of gold, steel, silver, titanium and organic grips. Just when the discerning collectors had settled on standard embellishments as the norm in handmade knives, some enterprising makers go and mix it up just for fun.

Gold and silver wire inlays haven't lost their luster, nor have precious stone insets, carved cutters, dancing damascus blades, showy sheaths, porous scrimshaw, mosaic masterpieces, checkered-pearl grips or gold and other more-garishly engraved pieces. Sit back, relax and let the art move you. It is not just art for art's sake, after all, but functional art that cuts, slashes, whittles and wows.

Joe Kertzman

Carving Up the Classics

◄ BAILEY BRADSHAW: An equine of copper and gold grew Pegasus wings and galloped up to greener pastures. *(PointSeven photo)*

▼ RON SKAGGS: The Bob Loveless and S.R. Johnson knives commemorate the golden era of the Wild West through handle carving, and gold and silver engraving and overlays. *(PointSeven photos)*

▲ CHARLIE AND HARRY MATHEWS: The handle was just an antler before the twin knifemakers carved it into fine art, similar to the artistry of the forged blade with which it is paired. *(SharpByCoop.com photo)*

▲ JOHN LEWIS JENSEN: The Siberian mastodon-ivory handle is contoured, carved and beveled, the twist-pattern-damascus bolsters are sculpted, and the laminated damascus blade is carved and beveled. The handwork is incredible, and that doesn't include all the faceting of gemstones and engraving of inlays.

Carving Up The Classics

▶ **DONALD BELL:** The Haida-inspired carving of an eagle and salmon extends from the Jerry Rados damascus blade to the gold and silver bolster and onto the mammoth-ivory handle. *(PointSeven photo)*

▲ **ROBERT WEINSTOCK:** It is Ed Schempp's damascus but Robert's rendering of it that elevates the folding dagger to heirloom quality. *(SharpByCoop.com photo)*

◀ **JULIUS MOJZIS:** Who could help but carve the beasts in steel after their ancestors left such beautiful handle material behind?

◀ **LARRY NEWTON:** Let Larry show you how damascus autos looked back when folding daggers were decorative edged implements of the upper crust. Perhaps that time is returning if not only for his efforts.

▶ **FRED OTT:** He said to himself, "I think I'll create a damascus dagger with a sea-cow-bone spacer and carved-ebony handle," and so it was willed upon the knife in exacting detail.

▶ **AUDRA DRAPER:** Carved-bronze leaves stem from a fluted-mammoth-ivory handle and highlight a dashing damascus dagger. *(PointSeven photo)*

▶ DONALD VOGT: The automatic is named "Autumn Bloom" because of the blooming flowers in the autumn colors of gold leaves and hue variations in the black-lip pearl. The scrolls in the bolsters represent the autumn winds. Devin Thomas provided the damascus. *(PointSeven photo)*

▶ ARPAD BOJTOS: The carved dragon stares down the nephrite handle at the mounted lady below.

▲ MIKE FELLOWS: The elephant-ivory handle and brass blade collar are carved to resemble a lotus flower, and the three-bar-composite-damascus blade forged to flabbergast even the most seasoned of knife veterans.

◀ JOE CORDOVA: Whimsical carved faces peer out from the stag handle unaware of the blade below them, or of the Alvin Chiwiwi engraved collar that keeps them upright. *(PointSeven photo)*

▼ **LEIF BENTZEN:** The boars-head knife bores no one.

▲ **JULIUS MOJZIS:** The stag handle is carved to depict dogs on a wild boar hunt, but the sticker has a big-horn-sheep butt.

◄ **RON APPLETON:** The carved-steel grip is as smooth as the blade and fluted as if it's the Pied Piper. *(PointSeven photo)*

► **DWIGHT TOWELL:** Dwight has one of those knifemaking styles that identifies his knives as his own, in this case complete with carved jade handle, scroll-engraved and carved blade and gold overlaid guard. *(PointSeven photo)*

▲ **STEPHEN OLSZEWSKI:** Stephen is known for his creepy crawlies, particularly scorpion-shaped knives like this auto, complete with Jerry Rados damascus main stinger, carved mammoth-ivory body and carved 14k-gold claws and secondary stingers. *(SharpByCoop.com photo)*

◄ **MIKE NORRIS AND DAVE AMMONS:** The coffin-style nickel-silver bolsters were touched up a bit with the tip and edge of a carving tool, readying them for inclusion on an elephant-ivory-handle folder with a Devin Thomas damascus blade. (PointSeven photo)

▲ **T.C. ROBERTS:** Could that be a thunderbird carved into the jade grip of a damascus push dagger? Jerry Lairson did the damascus honors, and Jody and Pat Muller engraved the nickel-silver sheath. (Ward photo)

► **DENNIS GREENBAUM:** It's a mini butterfly knife, but there's nothing diminutive about the Robert Eggerling damascus or the carved elephant-ivory scales. (SharpByCoop.com photo)

▲ **LARRY FUEGEN:** The damascus, the French grayed steel and mother-of-pearl were all carved and with equal aplomb. (PointSeven photo)

► **FRANK GAMBLE:** The 440C blade and ivory handle were carved using only files, and some fine files they must have been. (BladeGallery.com photo)

► **ARPAD BOJTOS**: The "Goddess of Victory" hoists a gold wreath over her head in celebration. She's a Damasteel lass surrounded by ivory and buffalo horn. The sheath is equally enticing and more. *(PointSeven photo)*

▲ **DONALD BELL**: It is highly unlikely that, when Tim Zowada forged a twist-pattern damascus blade, he envisioned it being twisted, pierced and carved in such a way, then married to an equally pierced and carved gold and black-lip-pearl handle. *(PointSeven photo)*

► **ARPAD BOJTOS**: If ostrich riding is your pastime, then this folder, complete with Fr. Schneider stainless-damascus blade, is for you.

▲ **PIERRE REVERDY**: The wild-boar tusk wasn't shaped that way fresh from the hunt. It took a little doing, as did the damascus blade.

▶ **LEIF BENTZEN:** How would you like to butt heads with this ram's head hunting knife? The handle is carved walrus tooth with mammoth-tooth and silver spacers.

▶ **AMAYAK STEPANYAN:** The engraving of the stainless steel handle is deep enough to make the vines jump off it, just as the damascus blade of the Owen Wood wharncliffe folder practically leaps off this page. *(SharpByCoop.com photo)*

▶ **C. GRAY TAYLOR:** The golden hue of the carved-gold-lip-pearl handle is so bright it is difficult to distinguish it from the 14k-gold liners, bolsters and pins. *(PointSeven photo)*

Textured Grips

It takes so many hours of toiling, laboring and trial and error to learn how to make a knife. The learning curve is tremendous. The number of things that can go, and will go, wrong is maddening. The skill it takes, the amount of variables to learn and memorize, the processes to master, the machines and tools to learn to use correctly, the handwork involved, the energy exerted, the pounding, grinding and polishing, and the time spent in custom craftsmanship is overwhelming. That is what makes the little "extras" knifemakers are known to throw into the mix—scrimshaw, engraving, steel etching, gemstone inlays, gold wire inlay, carving and texturing—so impressive.

Handle texturing would be the last thing on a beginning blade smith's mind. Most knifemakers probably figure if it feels good in the hand, it will do the job. But many knives that feel good in the hand also slip out of the grasps of hardworking knife users. A little texturing here or there on the handle, no matter what material is involved, goes a long way in the wilds of the knife-using world.

Texturing also adds to the aesthetic beauty of a knife. In the hands of a skilled artist, handle texturing can contribute to the smooth, flowing lines of a knife, break up the monotony of steel and other hard materials, or contrast nicely with knife parts and embellishments.

The knifemakers have forged and ground the blades, they've added the bolsters and guards, closed up any gaps between materials, polished the blades, rounded all hard corners on handles and bolsters, fit all the parts tightly together, and now they have one more task at hand—the texturing of grips. It would make one feel overwhelmed, underpaid, lonely and lost when the knifemaking tasks keep piling on, or it would give one pride and dignity in knowing a job well done. Texture those grips knifemakers and wallow in the way the palpable knives feel in your weary, work-worn hands.

Joe Kertzman

▶ **JEREMY KRAMMES:** The lines in the carved-titanium grip are like electrical charges emitted by the forge oven after it accepted the Odin's Eye damascus blade. *(SharpByCoop. com photo)*

▼ **RAY MURSKI:** As if the Robert Eggerling damascus blade and bolsters weren't enough, the poly-pearl handle is fluted, and "poly" is a crackerjack.

▲ **BRIAN TIGHE:** Now there's an excuse to go golfing if I've ever seen one! *(PointSeven photo)*

▲ **DAVID MIRABILE:** The ancient walrus ivory came that way, but the blade took some texturing to make it match. *(PointSeven photo)*

► **BILL DUFF:** Don't you love the dimples on the carved gold-lip mother-of-pearl handle? The vine filework and clean blade and bolsters add to the allure. *(Ward photo)*

▲ **ED CAFFREY;** The winding trails of the mosaic damascus lead to the carved and textured presentation-grade fossil walrus ivory, not to mention the hot-blued mild-steel guard and butt cap. *(PointSeven photo)*

▲ **BRIAN TIGHE:** No one will close their hands around the carved grips because they're too entranced by the puzzle-piece-shaped damascus inlays. The blades sport more pieces to the puzzle. *(PointSeven photo)*

► **WOLFGANG LOERCHNER:** Between the textured grip, the carved-damascus overlays and the black-lip mother-of-pearl inlays, there's plenty to hold onto. *(PointSeven photo)*

▲ **SAL MANARO:** The handle scales on the S30V "Bull's-eye" folder are "bone-linen-Micarta®," and they have some grooves for better gripping. *(SharpByCoop.com photo)*

► HARVEY DEAN: Ivory carving isn't new, but it sure is nice to see more of it on knives, and this damascus darling is as sweet as they come. *(PointSeven photo)*

▲ KELLY CARLSON: The etched and anodized copper-niobium handle does the Mike Norris stainless damascus blade justice.

► ED CAFFREY: The 6AL-4V titanium handle of the CPM S30V Progression I frame-lock folder is carved in a "Krackle" pattern and finished with lacquer and anodizing. Besides, it resembles a rainbow that broke the dried earth into hundreds of pieces.

▲ JOT SINGH KHALSA: The grips are hand stippled and carved gold, steel and pearl, all to give knife enthusiasts something with which to steady the delightful damascus blades. *(SharpByCoop.com photo)*

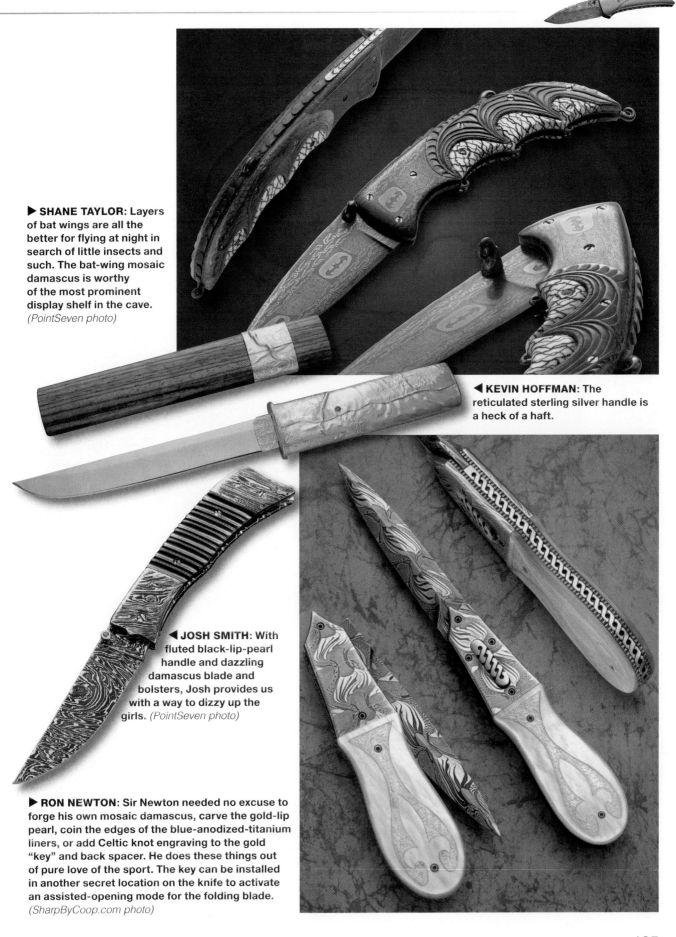

▶ **SHANE TAYLOR:** Layers of bat wings are all the better for flying at night in search of little insects and such. The bat-wing mosaic damascus is worthy of the most prominent display shelf in the cave. *(PointSeven photo)*

◀ **KEVIN HOFFMAN:** The reticulated sterling silver handle is a heck of a haft.

◀ **JOSH SMITH:** With fluted black-lip-pearl handle and dazzling damascus blade and bolsters, Josh provides us with a way to dizzy up the girls. *(PointSeven photo)*

▶ **RON NEWTON:** Sir Newton needed no excuse to forge his own mosaic damascus, carve the gold-lip pearl, coin the edges of the blue-anodized-titanium liners, or add Celtic knot engraving to the gold "key" and back spacer. He does these things out of pure love of the sport. The key can be installed in another secret location on the knife to activate an assisted-opening mode for the folding blade. *(SharpByCoop.com photo)*

Studded Stickers

► **JOHN LEWIS JENSEN:** The San Mai sticker is studded in more ways than one—with anodized titanium spikes and precious stone inlays, the latter including citrine, carnelian cabochon, apricot moonstone, amethyst, London blue topaz, sapphire, garnet and blue paua cabochon, all set in 18-k gold.

► **THOMAS HASLINGER:** Ammolite gemstones enliven an already elegant Damasteel window-frame folder. *(Murray White photo)*

▲ **DAN BURKE:** With this example measuring 5 1/4 inches closed, the Anglo Saxon whittler is the largest whittler of the English exhibition knives. Dan's version features a pink-pearl handle with lavender oyster inlays and garnets set in 14-k gold. *(PointSeven photo)*

◄ **REINHARD TSCHAGER:** Knowing the discriminating tastes of his clientele, Reinhard embellished the ATS-34 fixed blade with gold, rubies, sapphires and ivory.

Dancing Damascus

▶ **GARY HOUSE:** The combination of a matching damascus blade, guard and butt cap with a chocolaty walrus ivory handle deserves a ribbon like the one that stretches across the edged steel. *(PointSeven photo)*

◀ **CHARLES SAUER:** Damascus peaks and valleys dance across a 420-layer damascus blade, pooling up near the bridge-cable-damascus bolsters. An ironwood handle completes the piece. *(PointSeven photo)*

▲ **RODRIGO MENEZES SFREDDO:** It is as if electrical charges strike out across the 9-inch mosaic-damascus blade of the gaucho knife. Other features include a sheep-horn handle, an integral mosaic-damascus guard and sculpted mosaic-damascus pommel.

▶ **A.T. BARR:** The blued mosaic-damascus bolsters were forged by Joel Davis in a starburst pattern that left celestial fragments all across a Robert Eggerling damascus blade. *(Hoffman photo)*

▶ **STAN WILSON:** Like cells under a microscope, squares of Robert Eggerling damascus spread out across the surface of the blade and are further highlighted by a brilliantly hued mammoth-ivory handle. *(SharpByCoop.com photo)*

Dancing Damascus

▶ **KIRK REXROAT:** It is apparent that Turkish firestorm damascus turns green, purple, gold, white, blue and orange with just the right heat treat recipe. Kirk has a way with whipping up knives, and this bark-mammoth-ivory-handle locking-liner-folder is no exception. *(PointSeven photo)*

◀ **RAYMOND RYBAR:** Tama-Hagame steel showcases veins of gold, white, blue, red and gray, and is anchored by an ebony handle and D-shaped blued-damascus guard. Meteorite inlays are fitting for the fantastic knife. *(PointSeven photo)*

◀ **JOSH SMITH:** Most hot-blued damascus doesn't turn fluorescent until after the black light hits it. Josh has a way with colors, though, combining blade and double bolsters with lively ivory. *(PointSeven photo)*

▶ **STEVE HILL:** Steve says the crackle pattern in the ivory reminded him of Oriental writing, so he fashioned his first Japanese-influenced folder, complete with a damascus blade that takes the patterning to new levels. *(PointSeven photo)*

▲ **T.R. OVEREYNDER:** Owen Wood combined chevron and twist patterns for an ultimately cool damascus blade brought out of its gray shell by a pink, green, red and purple black-lip-pearl handle insert. *(PointSeven photo)*

▶ **MIKE ZSCHERNY:** The bark of the mammoth-ivory handle is so loud, the sound waves crackled across the bolsters and eventually kept a continuous pattern on the wharncliffe blade. *(Custom Knife Gallery of Colorado photo)*

▶ **THOMAS HASLINGER:** The damascus not only serves as 8 inches of chef's knife blade, but also as the handle frame over which premium mammoth ivory is laid.

◀ **TIM HANCOCK:** The blade swaggers, the guard vines around, and the handle goes stag. *(PointSeven photo)*

▶ **KAJ EMBRETSEN:** The ivory is just as milky as it gets, the folder as chiseled, rounded, shaped and filed as possible, and the blade couldn't be more dazzling if it was a dozen sunflowers in full bloom. *(PointSeven photo)*

▲ **BRAD RUTHERFORD:** Drink in the lines of the damascus and thuya burl and tell me the combination wasn't intentional. *(PointSeven photo)*

▲ **DENNIS FRIEDLY:** Like egg nests in the sand, pockets of Robert Eggerling damascus are enveloped within the lines of pattern-welded steel. *(PointSeven photo)*

Dancing Damascus

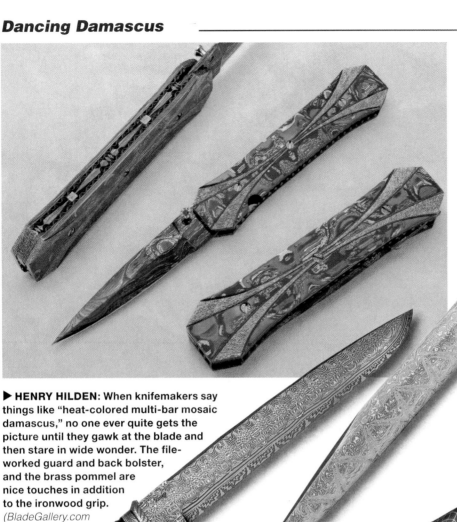

◀ **BARRY GALLAGHER:** When bearing gifts for the king, this multi-colored mosaic-damascus folding dagger would keep you away from the dungeon or gallows, and might even get you a front-row seat at the feast. *(SharpByCoop.com photo)*

◀ **JERRY FISK:** Has anyone else noticed that Jerry Fisk manipulates the patterns of damascus to conform to the blade shapes? Or maybe the blade conforms to the damascus. Either way, it's a Fisk phenomenon. Engraving and sheep horn are the encore presentation. *(Ward photo)*

▶ **HENRY HILDEN:** When knifemakers say things like "heat-colored multi-bar mosaic damascus," no one ever quite gets the picture until they gawk at the blade and then stare in wide wonder. The file-worked guard and back bolster, and the brass pommel are nice touches in addition to the ironwood grip. *(BladeGallery.com photo)*

▲ **FRED DURIO:** When Robert Eggerling whips up some damascus, he does so in a distinguished way that can only be complemented by purplish bolsters and milky mammoth-ivory handles. *(Ward photo)*

▶ **TINUS KLAASEE:** The fern-leaf-pattern damascus blade could use some misting so that it sprouts more of its kind. The padauk wood handle gives it just the right Asian look.

▲ **CHARLES GEDRAITIS:** Until now, they were called butterfly knives because of the way they flew open and closed within winged grips, not because of the colors and patterns . . . until now. The faceted gold-lip-pearl handle combines with Robert Eggerling and Al May damascus to bring the butterfly to immediate metamorphosis. *(SharpByCoop.com photo)*

◀ **CHUCK RICHARDS:** The rolled mosaic damascus looks good when stretched to 12 inches under a monster rolling pin. How about that bark-mammoth-ivory grip? Life is good. *(BladeGallery.com photo)*

▶ **DON HANSON III AND ANDERS HOGSTROM:** The design influence of Anders is especially evident on the walrus-ivory handle and sterling-silver fittings, and Hanson's damascus blade looks dashing alongside the other elements. *(PointSeven photo)*

▶ **NEIL MCKEE:** When lightning strikes Neil McKee's damascus, it cuts a swath. *(BladeGallery.com photo)*

▶ **BILL SAINDON:** Bill didn't let the overpowering Robert Eggerling twisted-crossroads pattern stop at the damascus blade, but added abalone to the hectic and eclectic mix. *(SharpByCoop.com photo)*

▼ **DANIEL WINKLER:** Daniel tossed us a bone with multi-bar primitive damascus that would make a dog's tail wag.

▼ **BUD NEALY:** Even though Daryl Meier did a bang-up job on the Turkish twist damascus, it took Bud's skilled hands at giving the blade a unique leaf shape, complete with swedge, and finger-notched bolsters. The highly figured Sambar stag is the coup de grace. *(SharpByCoop.com photo)*

Dancing Damascus

▶ **GEOFFF HAGUE:** It's not just twist damascus, it's fast twist damascus and it speeds right into a mosaic damascus bolster and ironwood grip.

▲ **ALAIN MIVILLE-DESCHENES:** The shape of the Damasteel blade mimics the buffalo horn without stealing its thunder.

▲ **JOE ZEMITIS:** The twist damascus is the definition of black-and-white contrast, and couples fantastically with a bocote-wood handle, ivory-Micarta® bolster and red spacer. I wonder where Zemitis lives.

▲ **RON NEWTON:** Enter the auto dagger done up in a damascus pattern that reminds one of the large leaves Roman slaves used to fan their masters. Then add to that a gold button, gold-wire inlay, gold file work and anodized-titanium liners, and the empire is buzzing. *(SharpByCoop. com photo)*

◀ **MICHAEL KANTER:** Trying to take in the beauty of the redwood burl and complexity of the damascus will make even the best of multi-taskers go cross-eyed.

▲ **MATT DISKIN:** A fine damascus blade of many lines is held up against a mokumé handle fashioned from fine silver and pure nickel. *(Mitch Lum photo)*

▶ **BILL DUFF:** The Thunderforged damascus pattern could be likened to a topographic map, and there's hidden treasure within the lines. *(Ward photo)*

◀ **ALAN T. BLOOMER:** The diamond shape in the center of the Des Horn mosaic-damascus bolsters is surrounded by jeweled titanium liners, a giraffe-bone handle and a George Werth damascus blade. *(SharpByCoop.com photo)*

▲ **DON MAXWELL:** You've heard of Maxwell's silver hammer? Well, this is his folding dagger, and it trumps the silver hammer any day. The Robert Eggerling damascus is only the start. The sleek leaf-shaped dagger blade leads into a mosaic damascus masterpiece of a bolster and a honey of a wooly mammoth handle that only gold wire could wrap around, all topped off with vine file work. *(Mitch Lum photo)*

◀ **MARVIN SOLOMON:** The character of the mammoth ivory is equaled by the Firestorm damascus, giving knife enthusiasts plenty to inspect. *(Ward photo)*

▶ **HARVEY DEAN:** Allowing the imagination to run wild, the damascus reveals faces, masks, demons and ghosts. The guard, engraved by Terry Theis, keeps the scrolls of time and documents the mammoth ivory. *(PointSeven photo)*

▲ **WAYNE WHITTAKER:** Cuddle up with a heat-colored, slanted-quilt-pattern damascus blade and have yourself a fine time. Robert Eggerling provided the damascus, and the maker made it "pop," complementing it with a mammoth-tooth handle and amethyst inlays. *(Custom Knife Gallery of Colorado photo)*

Showy Sheaths

▼ **VLADIMIR PULIS:** The bone sheath features a plastic intaglio of Maya lettering, an engraved silver throat and tip, sapphire inlays and a snakeskin sleeve. The knife is an integral mosaic-damascus piece decorated with plastic Mayan intaglio, and gold and palladium inlays.

▶ **PETER MARZITELLI:** Stonehenge-like images are created in custom tooled leather.

▲ **JOANN KELLEY:** There's a lot of leather to look at within the makeup of the two-tone stippled sheath.

▲ **MICHAEL WATTELET:** The belt-buckle knife and sheath are so highly embellished—with 14-k gold, amethyst cabochons and an oak-leaf and vine motif carved into the silver handle, sheath and buckle—that it's not immediately obvious it's a knife.

▼ ROBERT SCHRAP: You can almost smell the fresh leather as it is stitched, tooled and overlaid.

▲ TESS NEILSON: A carved eagle highlights a tooled leather sheath.

◀ JOE KEESLAR: Buckles, a sheriff's-style star and a Concho decorate the tooled-leather sheaths, two featuring a basket-weave pattern, and one with snakeskin inlay. Then there are those knife handles with silver wire inlay. *(PointSeven photo)*

▲ MARK NEVLING: Sheaths of burgundy alligator, camelback rattler skin and beavertail hold folding knives in the bolsters-up position.

◄ MICHAEL BELL: The scabbard shimmers from the tip to the hilt. *(BladeGallery.com photo)*

▲ DAVE COLE: The collar-style leather sheath showcases an azurite Concho to match the azurite knife-handle spacers.

► ED BRANDSEY: The fringed buckskin sheath features malachite beads, elk bur, twisted nickel silver wire, a domed 1900 Indianhead penny and a domed buffalo nickel. The bowie blade is Joe Hauk damascus and complemented by a stag and desert-ironwood handle.

◄ KAREN SHOOK: To the same degree that Daniel Winkler has mastered primitive-style knives, Karen reigns over frontier sheaths. This blade slip happens to be hand-stitched rawhide over 10-ounce vegetable-tanned leather, and it is embellished with deer hide fringe, decorative tacks, glass beads and tin cone.

Checked and Balanced Blades

It is a regal look, the checkering of knife handles, and particularly those with gold or silver pins driven into the center of each check, something called piquet work. Checking an ivory, bone or pearl handle is a skill passed down from one artisan to another. No one is born with such talent. It is not instinctual or inbred. It is a handcraft like so many other knife-related handcrafts, one that takes time, patience, desire, persistence, adaptability and concentration.

The material that is worked with files is natural and unpredictable. Countless types of pearl, all bone and every ivory carve differently. They are easily chipped or broken. Mistakes show up and ruin handle materials. The craftsmen chip away at their bladed sculptures as if molding clay into Victorian vases. One mistake and it's off to the dungeon with you young blade smiths.

When everything goes right, when the last gold pin is tapped ever so lightly into the exact center of the very last check on the pearl handle slab, and the bolsters butt up against the grip with nary a gap, when the blade is open and the knife looks fit for a king, then and only then does a knifemaker relish in a job well done.

He picks up the knife, runs a finger up and down the blade spine, slides a fingernail across the razor-sharp edge, palms the checked handle, finds the balancing point of the knife—where he can stick out an index finger, rest the knife on it, and let it teeter back and forth without falling, perfectly balanced at the bolster, guard or just behind the center line—and he grips the knife as if about to cut something. He has inspected everything, turned over every leaf and looked in every corner—the bladed beauty has been checked and balanced. Now it's time to enjoy his just desserts.

Joe Kertzman

▶ **BARRY DAVIS:** You can look all you want—there really is a tiny gold pin in the center of each small check of the black-lip-pearl handle. The spine of the knife features rope file work, the damascus blade is ground to perfection and the bolsters are filed and styled. *(PointSeven photo)*

▲ **ROGER MASSEY:** The aged bone handle of the dagger is checked, balanced and book-ended between engraved bolsters. *(Ward photo)*

▼ **BARRY DAVIS:** Damascus blade? Check! Carved 18k-gold bolsters? Check! Diamond-inlaid thumb stud? Check! Black-lip-pearl handle? Checked. *(PointSeven photo)*

▶ **C. GRAY TAYLOR:** It is the author's hope that, even though the handle checks are getting smaller, the payoff is real big. For we knife enthusiasts, it sure is! The carved 14k-gold bolsters carry out the theme. *(PointSeven photo)*

Checked and Balanced Blades

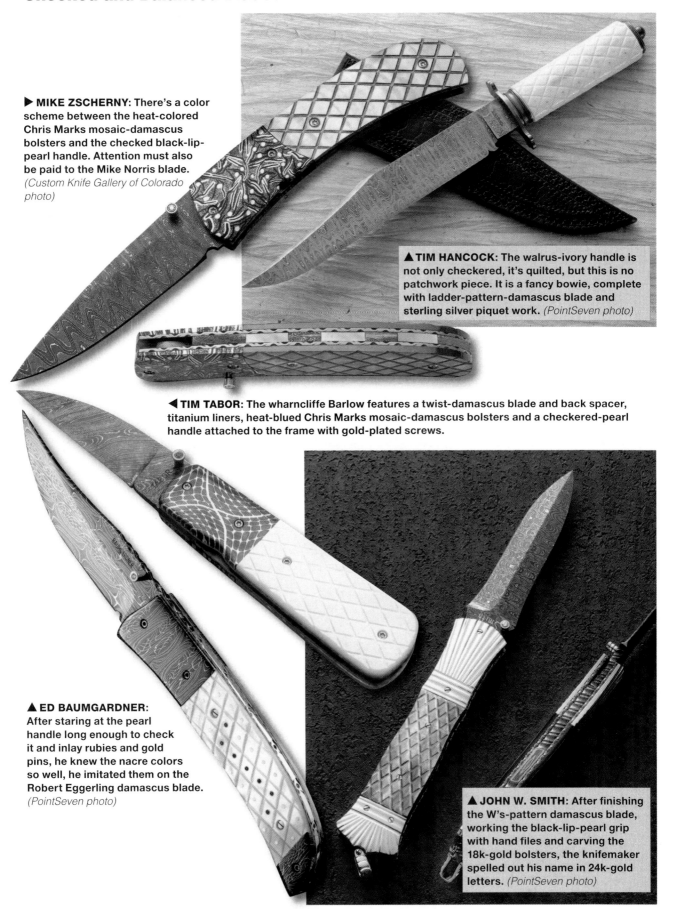

▶ **MIKE ZSCHERNY:** There's a color scheme between the heat-colored Chris Marks mosaic-damascus bolsters and the checked black-lip-pearl handle. Attention must also be paid to the Mike Norris blade. *(Custom Knife Gallery of Colorado photo)*

▲**TIM HANCOCK:** The walrus-ivory handle is not only checkered, it's quilted, but this is no patchwork piece. It is a fancy bowie, complete with ladder-pattern-damascus blade and sterling silver piquet work. *(PointSeven photo)*

◀**TIM TABOR:** The wharncliffe Barlow features a twist-damascus blade and back spacer, titanium liners, heat-blued Chris Marks mosaic-damascus bolsters and a checkered-pearl handle attached to the frame with gold-plated screws.

▲ **ED BAUMGARDNER:** After staring at the pearl handle long enough to check it and inlay rubies and gold pins, he knew the nacre colors so well, he imitated them on the Robert Eggerling damascus blade. *(PointSeven photo)*

▲ **JOHN W. SMITH:** After finishing the W's-pattern damascus blade, working the black-lip-pearl grip with hand files and carving the 18k-gold bolsters, the knifemaker spelled out his name in 24k-gold letters. *(PointSeven photo)*

All-Gray Engraving

▶ **BRUCE SHAW:** Like curlicues of wood leftover from the buckeye-burl handle of a Colten Tippetts fixed blade, the scroll engraving of the guard curls on cue. *(PointSeven photo)*

▲ **JERE DAVIDSON:** The Ron Best all-integral D-2 hunter gets a gorgeous dose of engraving all around the giraffe bone inlays. *(BladeGallery.com photo)*

▶ **MEL FASSIO:** Mammoth ivory handles are a treat, and the engraving can't be beat.

◀ **RALPH BONE:** The grays and dark grays of a Michael McClure knife, including a raindrop-damascus blade and engraved guard, give it a steely feel. *(BladeGallery.com photo)*

▲ **JAMES WHITEHEAD:** The engraving tools went wild when Whitehead was commissioned to scratch the steel of a black-jade-handle Darriel Caston wharncliffe folder. *(Custom Knife Gallery of Colorado photo)*

▶ **BRUCE BUMP:** That light-gray-engraved look, particularly when combined with a tight, lightly etched damascus blade, is the definition of exquisite. *(Mitch Lum photo)*

▶ **DARREN REEVES:** Vine-like scrolls crawl across a Charles Sauer bridge-cable-damascus fixed blade that also features a **mammoth-ivory grip.** *(PointSeven photo)*

▶ **REID SMITH:** The transition from mammoth ivory grip to damascus blade of a Steve Skiff folder is furthered by scroll **bolster engraving.** *(PointSeven photo)*

▶ **BRUCE SHAW:** You engrave a Sean O'Hare knife gingerly when trying to compete with a stabilized-juniper **handle.** *(SharpByCoop.com photo)*

▲ **CHARLES LEE:** The tiger-eye handle of the John Toner knife was so highly patterned, the bolster engraving needed to be delicate, gray and tasteful. *(PointSeven photo)*

▶ **JERRY FISK:** Some makers take classes to learn to engrave scroll and flowers of this quality, and it was time well spent. The damascus pattern changes midstream, and the walrus-ivory handle is hot. *(PointSeven photo)*

▲ **SCOT MATSUOKA:** If that's what the spider webs at Scot's house catch, then it's worth a visit. *(Mitch Lum photo)*

◀ **JIM SMALL:** It was no small favor when Jim offered to engrave a Don Cowles pearl and damascus fixed blade. *(SharpByCoop.com photo)*

▶ **JIM SMALL:** Here's an all-gray-engraved Don Cowles knife that has more scroll than a 16th-century library. *(SharpByCoop.com photo)*

▶ **VLADIMIR VANCURA:** Complementing the character of the wood with engraving on the Garth Hindmarch knife is a job well done.

▲ **BARRY LEE HANDS:** It's not how much engraving Barry added to the Mike Tyree damascus fixed blade, but the quality of the steel scratching that counts. *(PointSeven photo)*

▶ REID SMITH: Geno Denning's extended-blade version of a chute knife benefits from a superb slab of stag and a good bit of guard engraving. *(Hoffman photo)*

◄ BRUCE CHRISTENSEN: Bruce livened up the 416 stainless steel guard of Robert Dodd's pearl-handle ATS-34 hunter. *(Hoffman photo)*

▶ JULIE WARENSKI: The 130-year-old stag handle of the David Lang integral fighter deserved some window dressing in the form of guard and pommel engraving. *(BladeGallery.com photo)*

▲ JAMES WHITEHEAD: The engraved silver guard, pommel and spacer bring out the hues of an aboyna-burl and mastodon-ivory handle, and complement the carved O-1 blade. Just as smart is the engraved sterling silver sheath. *(PointSeven photo)*

▶ **REID SMITH:** As spare as the engraving is on the Jimmy Lile knife, it makes for a clean look around the wood-inlaid handle. Push the button to open the blade and push it again to close the piece. *(Hoffman photo)*

◀ **TEX SKOW:** Tex scored a hat trick with the oak leaf engraving, ebony handle and Robert Eggerling paisley-damascus blade.

▶ **BRUCE SHAW:** The dovetailed bolsters of the Mike Mooney bowie-style hunter have blossomed upon being planted next to the stabilized and dyed giraffe-bone handle.

▶ **MICK WARDELL:** The Celtic cross is engraved at the intersection of a stainless damascus blade and wood handle.

▲ **CHARLES LEE:** Gray engraving subtly smartens the bolster and spacer of a John Toner ATS-34 fixed blade with a tiger-eye handle. *(PointSeven photo)*

STATE OF THE ART **153**

All-Gray Engraving

▶ **C.J. CAI:** The grim reaper had stars in his eyes after seeing the shape of the Keith Ouye S30V blade, and a deal is being struck for him to trade in his scythe for the folding knife. *(PointSeven photo)*

◀ **RICK DUNKERLEY:** The Western-style engraving of the sterling silver handle is more subtle but definitely doesn't play second fiddle to the blued-damascus blade. *(PointSeven photo)*

▲ **JERE DAVIDSON:** The engraved D-2 bolsters and handle frame will grab you before you have a chance to grip the desert ironwood handle of the Ron Best integral hunter. *(BladeGallery. com photo)*

▼ **BRUCE CHRISTENSEN:** D' Alton Holder did up the musk-ox-handle fixed blade with tapered tang and S-shaped bolsters, calling on Mr. Christensen to christen the piece with wispy engraving. *(SharpByCoop.com photo)*

▶ **REID SMITH:** "Let the good times scroll," says Reid when asked to engrave a Charles Marlowe S30Vfolder, complete with a linen-Micarta® handle. *(Hoffman photo)*

▲ **BRUCE CHRISTENSEN:** Bruce livened up the 416 stainless steel guard of Robert Dodd's pearl-handle ATS-34 hunter. *(Hoffman photo)*

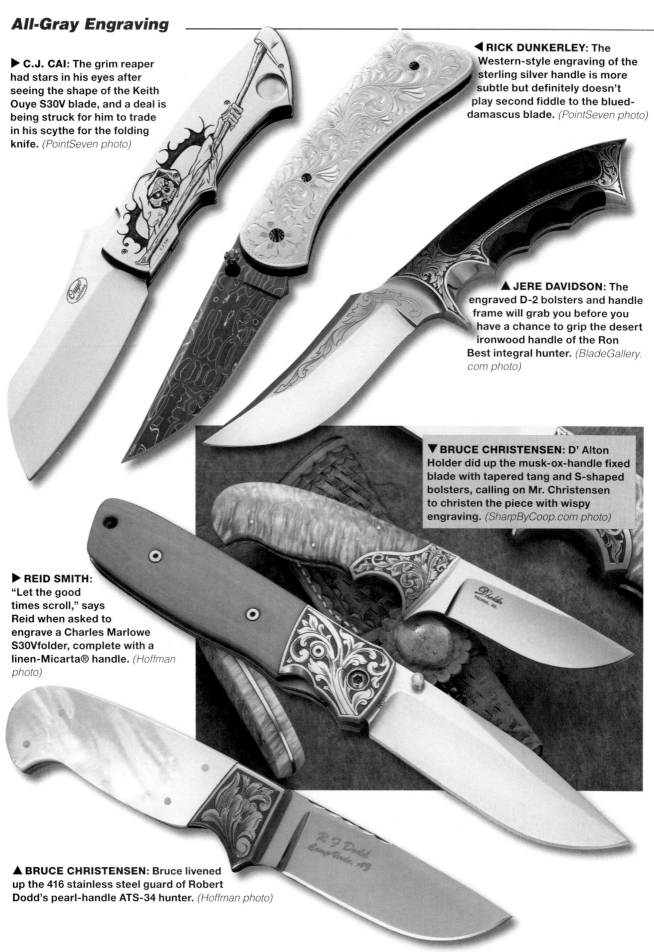

Wired and Ready

These aren't the guys who use bailing wire to fix the exhaust systems of their cars. They might or might not tackle the electrical wiring in their houses. Some have probably stooped to bending coat hangers to open car doors in the past, but it's doubtful that they use wires to dip Easter eggs into cups of dye. These artists take more inspired approaches to reaching goals. They are creative sorts who tend to be particular about how they approach certain problems and apply proven techniques.

Take wire inlay, for instance. Few folks have the creative genius it takes to inlay a wood handle with silver wire in a manner that doesn't completely destroy the grains. Innate ability is the key to fluting a wood or ivory knife handle and then wrapping it with twisted silver wire. Just twisting the silver wire would weed out the weak.

Embellishment of any kind is best left to those who excel at such things. If you've ever seen substandard scrimshaw, uninspired engraving, shoddy lapidary work or shaky gold and silver inlay, then you'd recognize a poor wiring job. It would resemble that car with the wire-suspended exhaust. The knife might still cut, but it would get a few sideways glances from friends who borrow it to slice open a box.

Not only are the following pieces inspired, but wired and ready, the types of knives that collectors seek out. Each piece showcases the kind of craftsmanship that is the envy of all who are unskilled at such things, the non-gifted, unable and noncreative types—those who have trouble drawing stick figures. It's obvious that some have it … and others are resigned to admiring the wiring.

Joe Kertzman

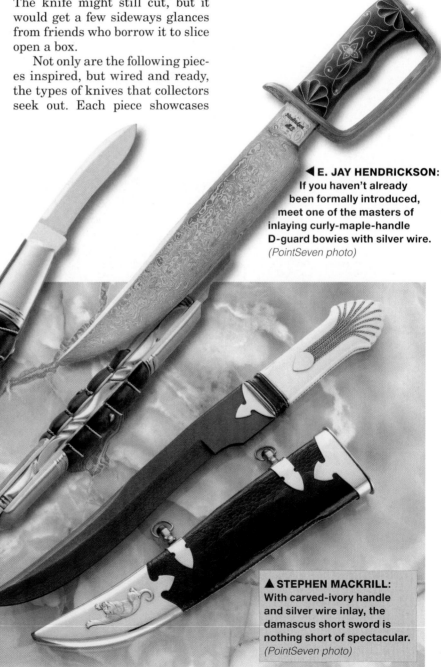

▶ **TOMONARI HAMADA:** Twisted silver wire highlights the segmented wood handle of the two-blade ATS-34 folder. *(PointSeven photo)*

◀ **E. JAY HENDRICKSON:** If you haven't already been formally introduced, meet one of the masters of inlaying curly-maple-handle D-guard bowies with silver wire. *(PointSeven photo)*

▲ **STEPHEN MACKRILL:** With carved-ivory handle and silver wire inlay, the damascus short sword is nothing short of spectacular. *(PointSeven photo)*

◄ BRUCE BUMP: Among the many embellishments inherent to the .38-caliber Matchlock Battle Axe are a Jay Hendrickson silver-wire-inlaid handle; gold wire inlay and engraving by Jere Davidson; bluing and case hardening by Doug Turnbull; barrel boring by Mark DeHass; and a serpent, designed by Bump, rising above it all. *(BladeGallery. com photo*

▼ WALLY HAYES: Less than a year before he sadly passed away, Bill Moran gave Wally written permission to replicate the ST-24 Fighter, complete with a 50-year-old, wire-inlaid curly maple handle and a 400-layer-damascus blade. *(PointSeven photo)*

▲ JOSEPH KEESLAR: The engraving, file work, silver wire inlay, damascus blade, curly maple handle, and other embellishments and techniques are all accomplished by the hands of the knifemaker. *(PointSeven photo)*

◄ A.G. BARNES: The blade almost seems secondary to the silver-wire-inlaid curly maple handle ... almost. *(Studio One photo)*

More Garish Engraving

There is a trend toward all-gray knife engraving—leaving the bolsters, blades and handles their natural steel colors, but engraving them, for a clean, steel-colored, embellished look. See pages 149 through 154 for knives with such an embellished look. The engraved pieces on this and the following seven pages do not fit into that trend. These are the more-garishly engraved knives. It's not that they are gaudy, but rather feature multi-tone embellishment of gray, silver, gold, black, red and other colors to further highlight the engravers' art. There is contrast and color.

It is only natural for an artist to start with a clean slate and add color and contrast. Knives benefit from multi-hued engraving. Thin, bending, gently curving gold inlays, engraved to match blade, handle and bolster embellishment, follow knife curves and wend their way through scrolls, flowers, faces and fauna. Fantastic figures, devilish eyes, colorful characters, brilliant wildlife, demonic beings, sexy beasts and lovely ladies emerge from steel to capture the hearts of knife aficionados everywhere.

Taking edged tools and engraving them into works of art is a fine way to spend a day. It is the ultimate irony to beautify what is supposed to be utilitarian. Such practice is the knife industry's version of an "extreme makeover." Knifemakers and engravers delight in fashioning elegant, museum-quality edged implements that bring art lovers to their knees.

No, the more garish of engraving is not gaudy. It is wrought, taut, highly sought and sometimes a little haughty or naughty, but not gaudy. Nothing so beautifully engraved is overly garish, just gorgeous.

Joe Kertzman

◄ **CHRIS DECAMILLIS:** Gold-vine engraving complements the gold pins of a single-blade W.D. Pease folder. The gold brings out the amber and black of the stag and contrasts against the black and gray flora bolster engraving. *(PointSeven photo)*

▲ **JOE MASON:** The gray, black and gold bolster engraving of Johnny Stout's locking-liner folder ties together the fossil-mammoth-ivory handle and Robert Eggerling paisley-damascus blade. *(SharpByCoop.com photo)*

▲ **JOHN W. SMITH:** The tortoise-shell handle inlay resembles the sun peaking through a black sky, and if that's the case, the clouds have golden linings. *(PointSeven photo)*

◀ **VALERIO PELI:** A gnomish face watches over a pearl-handle Reinhard Tschager dagger with gold pins, chain and pendant.

◀ **AMAYAK STEPANYAN:** The geometric Art Deco theme of an Owen Wood folder is carried through by angular white and black-lip mother-of-pearl handle inlays, two contrasting damascus patterns and Amayak's gold bolster engraving. *(SharpByCoop.com photo)*

▶ **JULIE WARENSKI:** Steven Rapp makes Julie's job of engraving a fine fixed blade difficult when he chooses such a singular gold-quartz handle for her to contend with, but she's up to the task. *(BladeGallery.com photo)*

▲ **RAY COVER JR.:** Parrots perch on a Joe Kious folding dagger, their feathers pluming the handle, fanning out at the rear bolster and ruffling collectors and their pocketbooks. *(SharpByCoop.com photo)*

▲ **H.H. FRANK:** Acorn, scroll and leaf engraving highlight three otherwise golden folding art daggers. *(PointSeven photo)*

▲ FRED HARRINGTON: Scrolled bolsters and a mother-of-pearl handle precede the Damasteel blades of a Murray Sterling pocketknife.

► VALERIO PELI: Engraving turns the Reinhard Tschager dagger into jewelry, a transition that is furthered by the black-lip mother-of-pearl handle, and gold pins, chain and pendant.

▲ JIM SMALL: It's one thing to recognize the colors of the mammoth ivory handle, but to imitate them in color engraving is quite another feat. Johnny Stout built the locking-liner folder, incorporating a Jerry Rados damascus blade and bolsters. *(SharpByCoop.com photo)*

► TIM HERMAN: Delight in the art deco dagger and all its décor. *(PointSeven photo)*

▲ RON SKAGGS: Gold carving and engraving transforms the elegant Joe Kious folding dagger into a dragon slayer. *(SharpByCoop.com photo)*

▲ **JERE DAVIDSON:** The combination of gold inlays, engraving and blue-mammoth-ivory handle qualify the Pete Forthofer fixed blade as a game bird.

▲ **C. GRAY TAYLOR:** Sleeve-board-pattern pocketknives with scissors, bolsters, pins and bell are difficult enough to fashion without embellishing an antique-tortoise-shell handle with gold engraving. Good show. *(PointSeven photo)*

▲ **JODY MULLER:** The separate entities of mosaic damascus, file work, engraving, gold inlay and black-lip-pearl combine forces on a fancy folder. *(Ward photo)*

▶ **TOM FERRY:** Does the engraving mimic the damascus pattern or vice-versa? Either way it's awesome. *(Mitch Lum photo)*

▶ **LARRY HENDRICKS:** The engraving harkens back to a time when lizard men, triceratops, dragons and Amazons roamed the earth. *(SharpByCoop.com photo)*

▶ **JUDY BEAVER:** The biker is no less an icon than Stanley Fujisaka, who built the ATS-34 side-lock folder. *(Michael Fong photo)*

▶ **RAY COVER JR. AND MANRICO TORCOLI:** Some sea creatures swim in the brilliant-blue sea, showing their true colors and eating green plant life. Others enjoy the darkness of their sea caverns, keeping company with those as beautiful as they. A set of Charles Bennica knives benefits from both types of creatures. *(SharpByCoop.com photo)*

▶ **BILLY BATES:** You've heard of a stand-up guy, well in this case, that's Billy who added stand-alone engraving to a Gerald Corbit folder. *(Ward photo)*

▲ **JON ROBYN:** Steve Hoel fashioned the fine folder but a winged seductress draped in golden sunlight stole the show. *(SharpByCoop.com photo)*

▲ **JIM ENCE:** Between the gold engraving, the gold quartz and the miner forever immortalized on the blade, the dagger hits the mother lode. *(Weyer photo)*

More Garish Engraving

▶ **DWIGHT TOWELL:** While the blade and bolsters are gorgeously engraved, the jasper handle shows off a few scrolls of its own.

◀ **JOE MASON:** The lines of a John Young knife are so clean that Joe had to take special care to make sure the engraving was just as richly refined. The double-ground ATS-34 blade and cape-buffalo-horn handle are equally hot. *(SharpByCoop.com photo)*

▲ **RAY COVER JR.:** If the hammerhead is her friend, I'd keep my distance, which would be difficult considering her inherent beauty. Matthew Lerch built the folder, including pearl inlay, and Mike Norris supplied the damascus blade.

▲ **LISA TOMLIN:** It looks like knifemaker Warren Osborne had a good hair day when he chose Lisa to apply the art to his pearl-handle folding dagger. Give her the moon, Warren. She deserves it. Mike Norris gets credit for the stainless damascus. *(SharpByCoop.com photo)*

▶ **JIM SMALL:** A couple flies and some cattails usually mean fishing, but this Don Cowles fixed blade with black-lip-pearl handle and damascus blade is display shelf material if I've ever seen it. *(SharpByCoop.com photo)*

► **TIM GEORGE:** Golden vines entwine themselves within the Damasteel pattern of a Kelly Carlson locking-liner folder.

▲ **ANDY SHINOSKY:** Enslaving engraving highlights an otherwise all-stainless-steel folder.

▲ **ANDY SHINOSKY:** English and American styles of scrollwork are separated by gold but share the limelight.

▼ **JULIE WARENSKI:** Exoticism is a Jot Singh Khalsa Kirpan featuring a Devin Thomas damascus blade, an Argentium sterling silver guard and pommel that are engraved and gold inlaid by Julie, 10 carats of diamonds and green tourmaline inlays. *(SharpByCoop.com photo)*

▲ **JASON MARCHIAFAVA:** The four diamond-shaped bolsters of the Paul Panak folding dagger are done up in medieval engraving good enough to attract knights in shining armor, dragon slayers and other men with golden shields.

▶ **CHRIS DECAMILLIS:** The mammoth tooth handle is so stunning that only the trumpet of a wooly beast, forever engraved on the bolsters of a W.D. Pease folder, could do it justice. *(PointSeven photo)*

▼ **NORIMI:** At the risk of sounding coy, not many folks could engrave a Koi fish quite like the one wading across a Scot Matsuoka folding tanto. *(Mitch Lum photo)*

▲ **NORIMI:** The BG-42 blade of the Scot Matsuoka folder was forged in the dragon's den of fire. *(Mitch Lum photo)*

▶ **JOE MASON:** The waves of a Mike Norris stainless damascus blade deposit golden leaves and black-lip-pearl upon a Warren Osborne lockback folder. If only it was that easy. *(KnifeArt.com photo)*

▲ **TIM GEORGE:** After fashioning the wharncliffe-style Damasteel folder, Howard Hitchmough called upon his pal Timothy to try his hand at some wickedly wonderful vine and leaf engraving that wraps around itself like an eel in a whirlpool. *(PointSeven photo)*

Inking Ivory Pores

The salt water sprayed over the ship railing as the boat lurched in waves that rolled all night. The sickening groan of the hull, dip of the stern, then sudden rise of the ship over the crests of waves was enough to drive men mad as the boat was tossed about like a buoy at high tide. The vessel was doomed to crash down the back sides of the waves, water rushing across the deck and pouring over the sides.

Even the hardiest of souls were below deck, queasily playing cards or lying board stiff with eyes closed. One solitary old salt sat hunched over, whale tooth in one hand, needle in the other. A glass jar of ink sat close at hand, a fair trade for fish with natives at the last island layover. Through gray eyelashes he peers, his sea-blue eyes never moving, a permanent squint leftover from too many years in the sun. Yet his hands are steady, his skill as an artist unmatched.

Through ink and ivory, a woman and another seaworthy vessel come to life. One is on the sea, the other lying across a rock, surrounded by water, marooned and naked. The woman is neither fantasy nor a vision believed true, but an entity all her own. The ship belongs in the setting; the lady lost, solitary and soulless.

This is the romanticized history of scrimshaw, a whaler's art, a seafarer's stippling of ivory, a recording of history and the beauty of life, a justification for existence.

Much of that early, scrimshawed ivory found its way onto knife handles, pendants, rings, glass display shelves and museum pedestals. Some scrimshaw saw the sea bottom and still more was carried to the grave.

Today's scrimshaw artists work in varied environs with better tools and cleaner media on which to ink ivory pores. But the tools are still rudimentary and the art unchanged. Scrimshanders continue to record fact, fiction and fantasy. They allow the seduction of the earth to bleed out of needles and into ivory with uninhibited fluidity, like salt sprays that wet the faces of stoic sea captains standing rudder straight under blood-red skies.

Joe Kertzman

◀ **SHARON BURGER:** Just as much character is revealed on the ferocious face of the warthog as on the blued-rose-damascus blade and bolsters of a George Baartman folder.

▲ **LINDA KARST STONE:** Be still bobcat, and pad lightly, the edge is sharp and the scrolls will conceal you. Knifemaker A.T. Barr commissioned Linda to scrim the cat on pre-ban elephant ivory, and Bill Bates to engrave the stainless bolsters. *(Hoffman photo)*

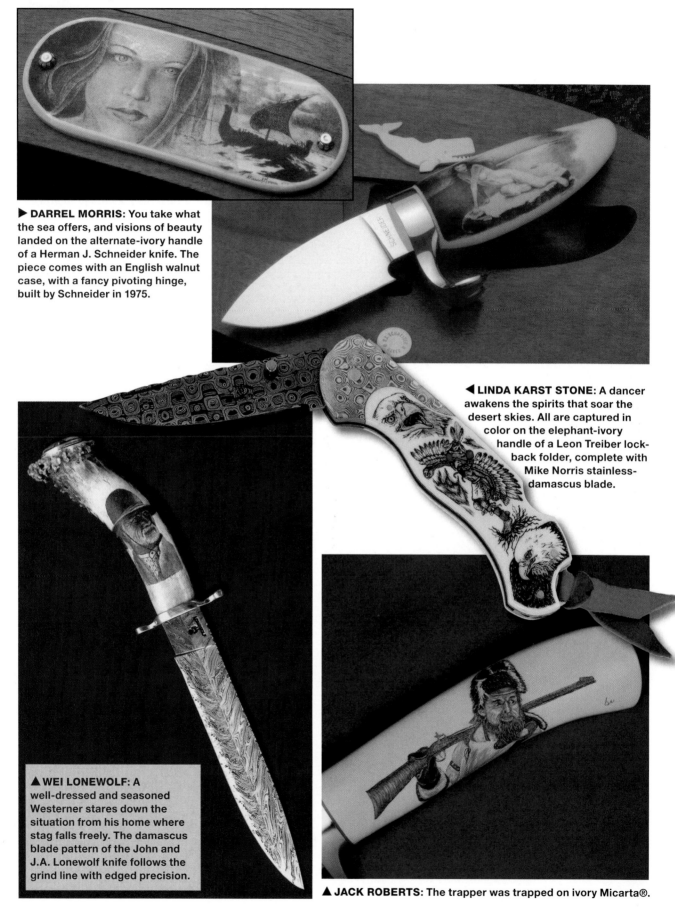

▶ **DARREL MORRIS:** You take what the sea offers, and visions of beauty landed on the alternate-ivory handle of a Herman J. Schneider knife. The piece comes with an English walnut case, with a fancy pivoting hinge, built by Schneider in 1975.

◀ **LINDA KARST STONE:** A dancer awakens the spirits that soar the desert skies. All are captured in color on the elephant-ivory handle of a Leon Treiber lockback folder, complete with Mike Norris stainless-damascus blade.

▲ **WEI LONEWOLF:** A well-dressed and seasoned Westerner stares down the situation from his home where stag falls freely. The damascus blade pattern of the John and J.A. Lonewolf knife follows the grind line with edged precision.

▲ **JACK ROBERTS:** The trapper was trapped on ivory Micarta®.

▲ **SHARON BURGER:** What a figure on the art nouveau figure. She's stippled in black on the elephant ivory handle of an A. Oliver knife.

▲ **SHARON BURGER:** A Viking apparently struts out of the mists of time and onto a large Theuns Prinsloo dagger. The image is black stipple on a rounded elephant-ivory handle.

▶ **SANDRA BRADY:** Realistically wild and uninhibited horned beasts parade across a foursome of George Trout knives. *(PointSeven photo)*

▲ **GARY WILLIAMS:** There was a stampede to Gene Baskett's table at the last knife show he attended when he pulled out the 440C fixed blade and revealed the buffalo forever scrimshawed on fossil walrus ivory. *(PointSeven photo)*

▲ **VLADIMIR PULIS:** The Amazon woman is right at home among the bone, buffalo horn and damascus of an awesome art dagger. *(Ivan Cilik photo)*

▲ **MIKE FELLOWS:** The fruits of Mike's labors are evident on the elephant-ivory handle, the bird's-eye-pattern damascus blade, damascus bolsters and titanium liners of his gentleman's dress folder.

Inking Ivory Pores

◀ **FAUSTINA MEAD:** Lowell Bray's ivory-handle damascus hunter came so close to bear in the woods, their images were forever stippled on the grip of the knife.

▶ **LINDA KARST STONE:** An abalone arrowhead inlay is the perfect touch for a Leon Treiber folder scrimshawed with a Native American girl and primitive peace pipe. Mike Norris stainless damascus, bolster engraving and vine file work complete the package.

▼ **FAUSTINA MEAD:** Steve Miller's damascus locking-liner folder is the lucky recipient of an icy stare.

▶ **VLADIMIR PULIS:** Tigers stalk the bone handle of a mosaic-damascus fixed blade. The knife features mokumé and ebony spacers.

◀ **MATT STOTHART:** The knife is the fourth in Kelly Carlson's Japanese Classic Collection of six knives commissioned and orchestrated by the Pen and The Sword. Each is provided with the original Japanese print upon which the scrimshaw is based. The blade is Delbert Ealy damascus.

Picture-Perfect Points

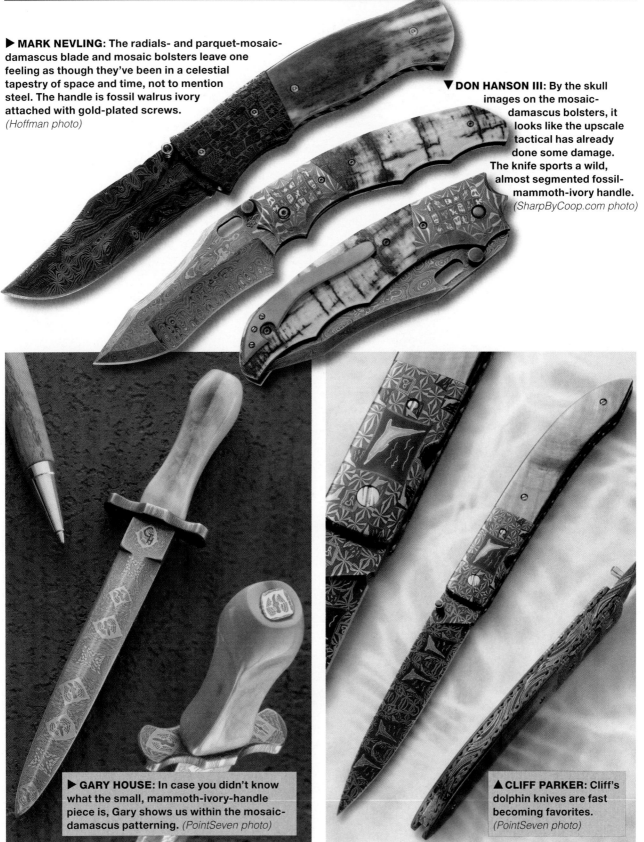

▶ **MARK NEVLING:** The radials- and parquet-mosaic-damascus blade and mosaic bolsters leave one feeling as though they've been in a celestial tapestry of space and time, not to mention steel. The handle is fossil walrus ivory attached with gold-plated screws. *(Hoffman photo)*

▼ **DON HANSON III:** By the skull images on the mosaic-damascus bolsters, it looks like the upscale tactical has already done some damage. The knife sports a wild, almost segmented fossil-mammoth-ivory handle. *(SharpByCoop.com photo)*

▶ **GARY HOUSE:** In case you didn't know what the small, mammoth-ivory-handle piece is, Gary shows us within the mosaic-damascus patterning. *(PointSeven photo)*

▲ **CLIFF PARKER:** Cliff's dolphin knives are fast becoming favorites. *(PointSeven photo)*

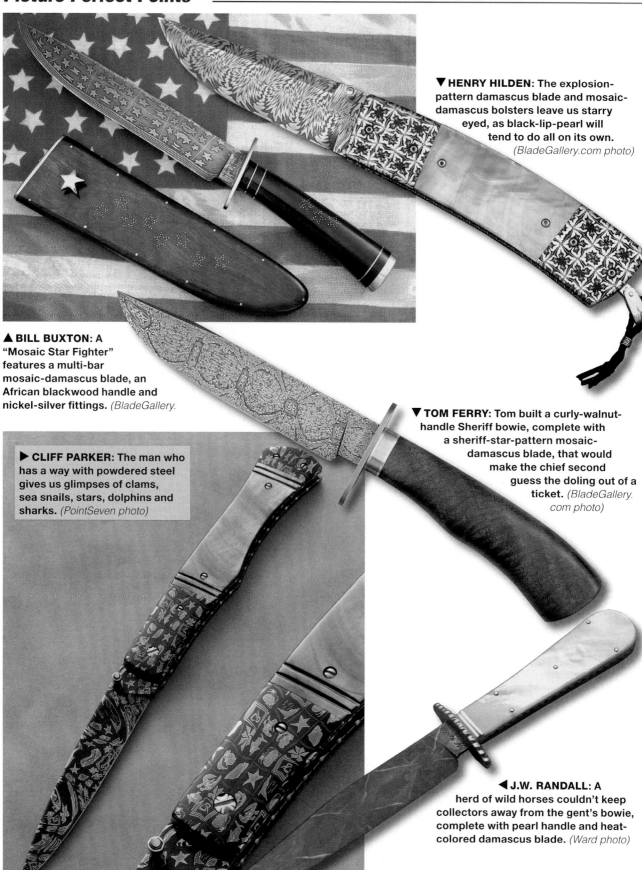

▼ HENRY HILDEN: The explosion-pattern damascus blade and mosaic-damascus bolsters leave us starry eyed, as black-lip-pearl will tend to do all on its own. *(BladeGallery.com photo)*

▲ BILL BUXTON: A "Mosaic Star Fighter" features a multi-bar mosaic-damascus blade, an African blackwood handle and nickel-silver fittings. *(BladeGallery.*

▶ CLIFF PARKER: The man who has a way with powdered steel gives us glimpses of clams, sea snails, stars, dolphins and sharks. *(PointSeven photo)*

▼ TOM FERRY: Tom built a curly-walnut-handle Sheriff bowie, complete with a sheriff-star-pattern mosaic-damascus blade, that would make the chief second guess the doling out of a ticket. *(BladeGallery. com photo)*

◀ J.W. RANDALL: A herd of wild horses couldn't keep collectors away from the gent's bowie, complete with pearl handle and heat-colored damascus blade. *(Ward photo)*

▶ **LOURENS PRINSLOO:** Forging mosaic damascus is much like spinning a web but it takes work before it starts to come naturally. There couldn't have been a prettier piece of ancient ivory with which to complement the steel. *(PointSeven photo)*

▼ **J.W. RANDALL:** The "Galaxy Bowie" is definitely stellar, and the blue blade and blue-walrus handle are more brilliant than the Southern sky. *(Tammy Randall photo)*

◀ **BILL BUXTON:** Mosaic flowers and stars cover the locking-liner folder from tip to butt. *(BladeGallery. com photo)*

▲ **STEVE SCHWARZER:** The "Face Series" folders find their way into our heads. *(PointSeven photo)*

◀ **KIRK REXROAT:** I've heard similar damascus called "ribbons" pattern, so we'll go with that, but this piece is more detailed, including heat-colored blade and handle, file-worked liners, and lots of steel imaging at which to look. *(SharpByCoop.com photo)*

FACTORY TRENDS

Computers can not be imaginative. It is impossible for a robot to be innovative. No matter how much programming goes into a CNC (Computer Numerically Controlled) machine, it can not invent. The creative aspect of knife design comes from one source and one source only—the human brain. Only it can reinvent the common everyday knife.

When does the human mind run out of ideas for new knives? That question can only be answered by custom knifemakers and the design engineers working for cutlery companies across the globe. Most of the large knife factories have research and development (R&D) teams. They are the industry's version of "think tanks," and their job is to create new, highly effective, high-tech, usable, different, comfortable, sharp, long-lasting, durable, aesthetic and appealing knives.

So far, the "ideas well" has not run dry.

This year's offerings include a whole plethora of new military knives for our soldiers fighting for this country's freedom. Call them "freedom fighters," if you will. Some of the hottest folders with forward-thinking mechanisms, locks, assisted-openers and other devices make their debuts. Hunting knives are always hot. Knives with 3-Dimensional handles are trendy this year, and butterfly knives have not lost their luster. Take a peak at all the trend-setting factory knives and relish the fact that good old American ingenuity is alive and well, displayed in brilliant color for you in the "Factory Trends" section of Knives 2007.

Joe Kertzman

Steel Magic

Heat Treatment Gives Steel Its Magic

A number of makers and factories employ a double-draw heat-treatment for D-2 and other steels. These D-2 blades are, from top, by Tom Krein, Scott Gossman, Tom Krein and Ontario/Queen. Ontario and others sometimes add a cryogenic quench, claiming it gives them optimum performance.

"Of the four elements, air, earth, water and fire, man stole only one from the gods. Fire. And with it, man forged his will upon the word." —*Anonymous, quoted on page 27 of* The Complete Bladesmith, Forging Your Way to Perfection, *by Jim Hrisoulas, Paladin Press, 1987.*

I was once asked to sharpen a friend's pocketknife. It was a small knife similar to the Buck 110. With a variety of sophisticated sharpening tools, including diamond-coated hones, I'm usually successful at it.

As most people familiar with sharpening know, a good sharpener turns the steel being removed into dust. In this case, however, my EZE-Lap pocket sharpener was taking off steel splinters. Tiny chunks of steel were abrading away!

I looked at the knife and found it was made in Pakistan, probably heat-treated over camel dung!

Seriously, even though that knife was not of the best steel, whatever heat treatment it had received was totally inadequate.

It's a simple fact: Fire gives steel its magic!

When a young boy of 10 or so, I experimented with "heat-treatment" on my own. I held the blade of a pocketknife (probably an old Camillus jackknife) in the flame of a gas kitchen stove. I thought I was sterilizing it; from the way it never quite sharpened up or held an edge again, I had apparently altered the steel's structure.

Knife writer Bill Hughes told me he once did the same thing when he was a young boy. The difference was that he plunged the blade into water and it promptly shattered!

These anecdotes show that a little heat, properly or improperly applied, can make all the difference in the way steel performs.

Any student of knives, either production or handmade, will sometimes run across claims for exotic, secret steel alloys that have amazing properties.

In the case of the Iron Mistress, the fabled first bowie knife in the novel of the same name, that blade's exotic steel could never be duplicated, because it contained a fragment of a meteorite in it.

Knives made from these leg-endary steels could be bent almost in a circle and would return to true, would hold an edge virtually forever, would rarely if ever need sharpening, and in some cases would never rust or corrode.

Of course, in reality, no such "perfect" steel exists.

There are some good steels out there, which matched to the end use of a knife, give satisfying and even superlative performance. Some will rust, if not well cared for, and will darken and discolor even when cared for.

But in this day and age, claims of "secret steels," whether stainless or not, are unlikely at best and outlandish at worst.

Using a proprietary name for a company's steel formula may also hide the fact from the public that it's a steel that most of the industry uses.

Examples over the past four decades include Razor Blade Stainless (popular in the mid-1960s to mid-1970s when stainless steel for shaving instruments had just been introduced and was getting a lot of TV advertising), Razor Grade Stainless (trying to get as close as possible to the trademarked Razor Blade name), Schrade Plus, Sword Steel, Chicago Cutlery or Special Steel, Buck Steel, Queen Steel, etc. All of these were at one time or another either 440C or 440A. The Razor Blade and Razor Grade

Some makers have found that a triple-draw during the heat-treat gives their blades maximum performance. Dan Harrison says that a blade made with a triple-draw will beat a double-draw and a cryogenic quench. Others say the third draw makes no difference. The debate goes on. From top left, these triple-drawn D-2 blades are by Jerry Halfrich of San Marcos, Texas *(the top two)*; Dan Harrison of Edom, Texas *(the bottom two)*; and, at right, Bob Dozier of Springdale, Arkansas. All are superlative performers.

Big John Fitch *(back to the camera)* cools a heat-treated blade in a bucket of ashes at a cutting school conducted by Warren Osborne in December, 2004.

names, used on competing brands, have dropped by the wayside. Others have continued, but the steel used may have changed. Buck Steel has at various times been 440C ("modified") or 440A. Currently, the standard stainless at Buck and Camillus is 420 High Carbon, a cheaper alternative to 440A. Buck, Camillus, and others use more expensive steels, such as ATS-34 or BG-42, in their premium lines.

When it comes to steel, there are no secrets. Anyone who wants may order a rather inexpensive test to determine what makes up a particular company's "secret" steel. The secrets, if any, are probably going to be in the heat treatment.

In *The Iron Mistress,* blacksmith James Black presented the first bowie to Jim Bowie, telling him, "That steel will hold an edge as none you have ever seen. I quenched it seven times. Each time in panther oil."

Custom knifemaker Dan Harrison, whose favorite using knife steel is D-2, has told this author several times that "the heat-treat is at least as important as the steel." Dan's D-2 is processed using a "triple draw."

Dan will share his process with anybody, and he says that "a triple-draw will beat a double-draw and cryo any day." Double-draw and cyrogenic heat treatment are used by many makers and factories. While it takes longer and is not as cost-effective for factories, the process helps other steels, too.

Dan designed a line of fixed-blade utility hunters for Ka-Bar a few years ago, and the company used his method of triple-draw on 440A steel. One reviewer was amazed at the performance and edge-holding of those 440A knives.

Knifemaker Jerry Halfrich of San Marcos, Texas, is convinced of the superiority of the Harrison heat-treat method. At a cutting school at Waxahachie, Texas, sponsored by Warren Osborne in December, 2004, I heard Halfrich complain that the D-2 blade of his folding semi-skinner, at a Rockwell hardness of 59Rc, didn't hold an edge the way he felt it should.

I told him about Dan and gave him his phone number. Halfrich used Dan's triple-draw heat treatment on a number of test blades of D-2, and used them on a hog hunt with fellow knifemaker Joe Kious and others. Halfrich and Kious are both guides.

"59 Rockwell is plenty," Harrison said, "if the triple-draw process is used."

Halfrich said that the triple-draw increased edge-holding by at least a third. He said Kious, who normally uses 154CM on his own knives, was also impressed.

When Harrison began using D-2 some decades ago, he bought it from a Swedish company, and learned the heat-treating method from one of that company's sales representatives.

"I've used it ever since," Harrison said.

Bob Dozier also gets superior performance from his D-2 blades by using a triple-draw. The edge-holding ability of Dozier's, Harrison's and now Halfrich's D-2 is exemplary.

Buck Knives are also noted for their edge-holding ability. According to Tom Ables' book, *The Story of Buck Knives . . . A Family Business,* by Hoyt Heath (H.H.) Buck, an apprentice blacksmith in Leavenworth, Kan., developed a superior method of tempering grub hoes so they wouldn't need resharpening as often. The process was soon transferred to knives.

When Buck Knives went commercial, "Buck Steel" became stainless rather than whatever carbon steel the company's reputation was built on. The company later said it was "440C modified." The name was to hide the fact that it was stainless, since stainless steels of previous decades had not performed well. Again, the secret is in the heat-treatment.

Likewise, when Queen Cutlery switched from industry-standard 1095 carbon steel, the company used "Queen Steel," which was 440C. Queen knows how to heat-treat stainless!

Razor Blade Stainless was Schrade's trademark for 440C. Later Schrade-Plus was 440A specially heat-treated, until the last years of the Imperial Schrade company, when it followed the industry by making 420 High Carbon their standard steel.

Jim Economos, then production manager at Schrade, told me in the early 1980s that Schrade Plus Steel was 440A that underwent a special heat treatment in which it came out of the treatment with two points more of carbon than it went in. That means the company was ending up with a steel with carbon content very close to 440C, but at a lower cost. An added plus

Knifemaker Steve Rollett forges a blade heated in a portable furnace during a demonstration at the Professional Knifemakers Association Show in Denver, in August, 2004.

was that the heat-treat gave a finer microstructure to the steel. I have otherwise identical models of the Schrade 897UH. The one I purchased around 1975 was made of 440C; the next one of Schrade Plus (specially heat-treated 440A) held an edge better and did not develop tiny chips in the edge like the earlier 440C.

Jim Barbee was one of the first great makers of folding hunting knives. He mainly used 440C for his blades, claiming that (at the time, the mid-1970s) properly heat-treated, it was the best steel for blades available.

Cold Steel's Carbon V is justly regarded as a high-performance steel. The Cold Steel catalog states that, "This steel is superior to most other steels due to its chemistry and also because of the close controls that we maintain at every stage of the manufacturing process... The final stage is a precise heat treatment sequence that was developed by Cold Steel specifically for this custom steel. This heat treatment process is one of our most closely-guarded trade secrets. It was arrived at over several years by using an exhaustive series of practical and metallurgical tests and observations."

John Fitch quenches a D-2 blade, that he just made, in transmission fluid at Warren Osborne's cutting school, December, 2004.

Bladesmith Ron Newton heats a bar of steel prior to giving a forging demonstration at the Spirit of Steel Show in Mesquite, Texas, in 2003.

Ed Fowler's articles and books (*Knife Talk: The Art & Science of Knifemaking* and *Knife Talk II*,) both compiled from Fowler's *BLADE Magazine* columns, detail his search for "the high-performance blade."

In one article, Fowler describes how a change of 30 degrees (from 385 to 415 degrees Fahrenheit), in a triple-draw on bronzed wire damascus, dramatically increased rope-cutting performance.

Fowler and Wayne Goddard, another knifemaking great, speak in another article about the advantages of triple-quenching in oil. Stock removal and forged blades were used. In their tests, they found a stock-removal triple-quenched and a forged blade triple-quenched differed a lot in performance over their single-quenched counterparts. The triple-quenched stock removal blade made 195 rope cuts, compared to 163 for the single-quenched blade. The triple-quenched forged blade made 509 cuts, compared to 269 for the single-quenched forged blade.

And there are other secrets to the magic of fire, or heat, on blades.

My first exposure to the philosophy of tempering and heat-treating was probably in a catalog I received from the late, great Bill Moran in the mid-1960s. A copy of the catalog is in the book, *Master of the Forge*, by B.R. Hughes and Houston Price, published in 1996. In the catalog, Mr. Moran states that "Moran Knives are the only blades made today in the United States that are completely hand-forged, hand-tempered, handmade in every respect. The tempering process alone can only be learned by many years' experience.

"Moran Knives are tempered in the forge itself. This technique is the same as that used by the bladesmiths of the 17th century."

Mr. Moran described his method, then rare. Now many smiths, a lot of them members of the American Bladesmith Society, use similar methods.

"The bar of steel is heated in my fieldstone forge, then forged by hand on the anvil. The hot steel is hammered slowly into shape. Each blade is heated and forged and reheated and forged dozens of times before this operation is complete. Hand forging greatly improves the blade, when properly accomplished. The blade is then ground by hand to near-final shape and it is then painstakingly hand-tempered by eye and hand in the forge.

"Tempering gives the Moran Knife special qualities, qualities no others made today possess.

"A Moran Knife is very hard from the center to the edge. The back is tempered to about the consistency of a spring. The point is slightly less hard than the edge, while the tang is annnealed for maximum tensile strength. Such unique tempering results in a blade that combines strength and edge-holding ability unattainable by any sort of production-line methods—the blade has to be tempered by hand and cannot be so tempered in a furnace."

The term had not not come into vogue at the time, but what he was describing was differential tempering, versions of what are now common among smiths. Some achieve it by quenching the edge of the blade; others by using a torch on the back of a blade to soften it and make it tougher. Others (such as in ancient Japan) temper the blade with part of it coated in clay.

The differential temper is usually evidenced by visible lines running through the blade.

I have seen some of Ed Fowler's big knives with up to seven different temper lines in the same blade.

Ken Warner, owner of Knifeware, which makes BlackJack Knives, introduced a small hunter with a 3-inch blade, called the "Small," a few years ago. The first ones were made of 52100 steel. I commented to him about them having such a custom-grade steel. He told me that the carbon steel he used might vary in the future, depending on market variables, but that whatever the steel, the knives would be given a heat-treatment that would insure good performance.

The search for the perfect heat-treat, just as the search for the perfect knife steel, continues.

As another knife writer wrote a few decades ago, "There is no magic in steel. Only fire can give steel its character. And only fire can take it away. Which, if you think about it, is magic enough."

Blades for the Blaze-Orange Crowd

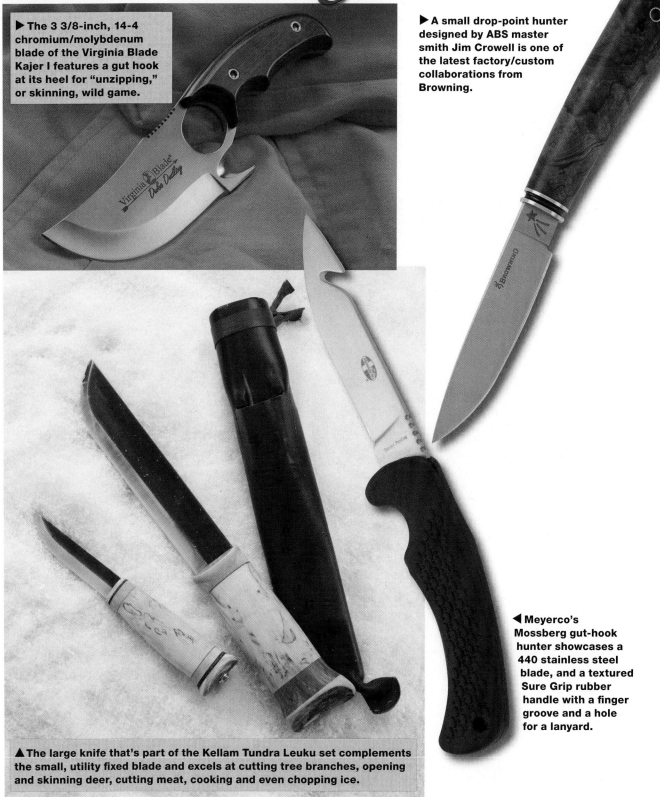

▶ The 3 3/8-inch, 14-4 chromium/molybdenum blade of the Virginia Blade Kajer I features a gut hook at its heel for "unzipping," or skinning, wild game.

▶ A small drop-point hunter designed by ABS master smith Jim Crowell is one of the latest factory/custom collaborations from Browning.

◀ Meyerco's Mossberg gut-hook hunter showcases a 440 stainless steel blade, and a textured Sure Grip rubber handle with a finger groove and a hole for a lanyard.

▲ The large knife that's part of the Kellam Tundra Leuku set complements the small, utility fixed blade and excels at cutting tree branches, opening and skinning deer, cutting meat, cooking and even chopping ice.

► Cold Steel's 60SS Sisu Finnish fixed blade sports a 4-inch, mirror-polished San Mai III™ blade, a nickel-silver bolster and pommel, a linen-Micarta® handle and a leather sheath.

▲ The Alpha Wolf from Knives of Alaska has a drop-point blade that comes in a choice of D-2 steel or CPM S30V stainless in .100-inch-thick stock for reduced drag during skinning and fleshing. A vegetable-tanned, oiled sheath is included.

▲ Outdoor Edge unveils the Shear-Knife Combo targeted toward upland-game, small-game and bird hunters.

Cut from a Finer Cloth

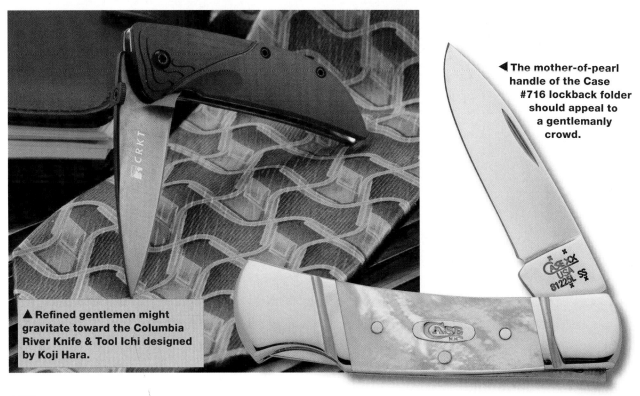

◄ The mother-of-pearl handle of the Case #716 lockback folder should appeal to a gentlemanly crowd.

▲ Refined gentlemen might gravitate toward the Columbia River Knife & Tool Ichi designed by Koji Hara.

◀ Xikar's Xi 730 Express packs form and function into a lightweight, compact frame that clips securely to any pant loop or pocket for quick access.

▶ Spyderco teams with Fox Cutlery on the Volpe folder, which features a 3 7/16-inch N690Co blade and olivewood handle inlays.

▲ An image of a trout graces the anodized-aluminum handle of the Kershaw Knives Model 1620 Trout.

▲ Buck Knives touts the Nobleman as a "contemporary, slimline, frame-lock folder."

◀ Bob Loveless designed the Lone Wolf Knives "City Knife" slip-joint folder and calls it the ideal carry knife for anyone living in a metropolitan area.

▲ Weighing between .8 and 1.1 ounces apiece, with 2 ¼-inch blades and upscale blade, handle and frame materials, the series of William Henry B4 Pikatti folders exhibits many of the characteristics knife professionals attribute to gentleman's folders.

Knife Handles in 3-D

▼ With its checkered rosewood grip, Lone Wolf Knives' U.S. 45 folding knife is styled to complement a 1911 .45 semi-automatic pistol.

▶ Ken Onion and Strider Knives teamed up to design Kershaw's Zero Tolerance ZT0301 frame-lock folder. The lock side of the handle is machined from titanium, and the non-lock side is G-10.

◀ A Joe Pardue design, the green Zytel® grip of the Ontario Utilitac feels great in the hand.

▲ The handle of Benchmade's new 151 Fixed Griptilian is co-molded from Zytel® with a soft rubber inlay for grip enhancement.

▲ What the handle of the new Buck Knives Omni 397CM folding hunter lacks in 3-D texturing, it makes up for in shape and a fully rounded contour.

Fly Like a Butterfly Knife

◄ The Spyderco Spyderfly butterfly knife dons a 440C stainless steel blade and weighs 6.562 ounces.

◄ Jeweled, blue-anodized-titanium liners peak out from beneath the skeletonized G-10 handle scales of the Benchmade Morpho.

◄ With the un-butterfly-like name of "Mayhem," the Bradley Cutlery butterfly knife features a CPM S30V blade and 6AL-4V titanium handle halves.

Singular Slip Joints

◄ The "Rancher" is a slip-joint collaboration between Queen Cutlery and custom knifemaker Dan Burke. The 3 1/8-inch clip-point blade is BG-42 stainless steel and the handle is stag.

▼ The Case 06263 SS Eisenhower sports the signature of the 34th U.S. president and World War II hero on the master blade.

▲ A four-blade congress and three-blade whittler comprise Canal Street Cutlery's "1st Year" anniversary knife set.

Knives to the Rescue

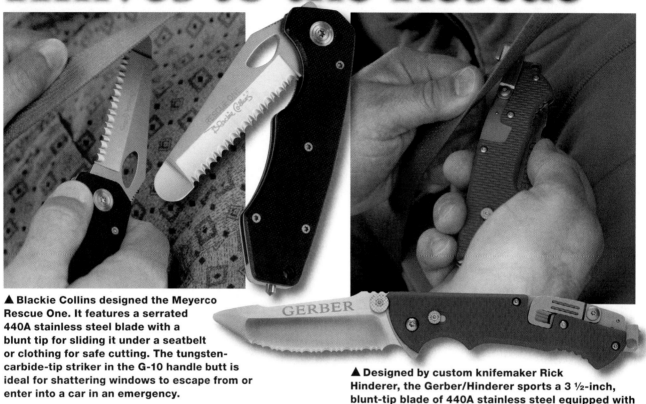

▲ Blackie Collins designed the Meyerco Rescue One. It features a serrated 440A stainless steel blade with a blunt tip for sliding it under a seatbelt or clothing for safe cutting. The tungsten-carbide-tip striker in the G-10 handle butt is ideal for shattering windows to escape from or enter into a car in an emergency.

GERBER

▲ Designed by custom knifemaker Rick Hinderer, the Gerber/Hinderer sports a 3 ½-inch, blunt-tip blade of 440A stainless steel equipped with an oversized thumb stud for one-hand opening of the blade when wearing gloves. A folding seatbelt cutter, window punch and oxygen-tank wrench are built into the handle.

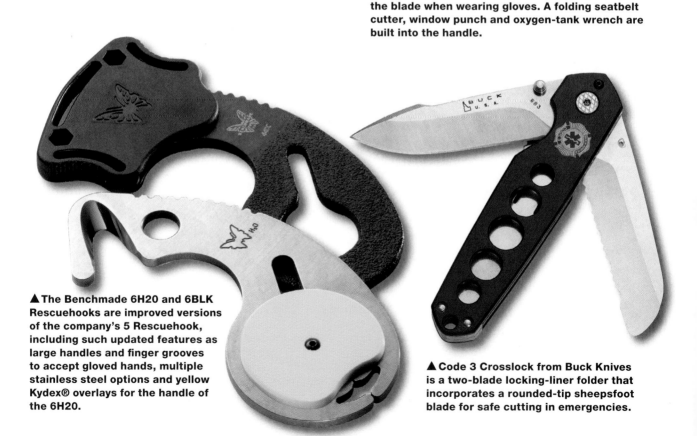

▲The Benchmade 6H20 and 6BLK Rescuehooks are improved versions of the company's 5 Rescuehook, including such updated features as large handles and finger grooves to accept gloved hands, multiple stainless steel options and yellow Kydex® overlays for the handle of the 6H20.

▲ Code 3 Crosslock from Buck Knives is a two-blade locking-liner folder that incorporates a rounded-tip sheepsfoot blade for safe cutting in emergencies.

▲ The Model 10415 Timberline Rescue Knife is a Butch Vallotton-designed locking-liner folder showcasing a partially-serrated, blunt-tipped AUS-8 blade.

▲ The Kershaw Responder has a partially serrated, blunt-tipped blade, as well as a cutting hook for slicing line, webbing, clothing and seatbelts.

▲ A hot seller to those who deal with natural disasters and other emergencies is the Smith & Wesson CKSUR7. It sports a 14-inch re-curved blade with a deep belly and a sharp point.

Folders of Forward Thinking

▶ The Kershaw ZT 0301 is designed by Ken Onion and Strider Knives and features a SpeedSafe assisted-opening mechanism.

▶ The laminated blade of the SOG Specialty Knives Arcitech folder works off the company's forward-thinking Arc-Lock.

▲ A collaborative effort between Camillus Cutlery and custom knifemaker Darrel Ralph, the 18-Xray is an automatic knife with an S.A.S. built-in safety system. The only way the blade can be deployed is by pushing down and forward on the button mechanism.

▼ United Cutlery's Ghost Lock folder is designed by custom knifemaker Gary Blanchard and features Blanchard's patented Ghost Lock "floating internal bearing lock system." A single ball bearing recessed into a cavity in the center of the 420HC stainless steel blade controls the system.

Soldier Steel

◄ Cutouts abound in Heckler & Koch's 14100 Mike Snody design, including two in the spine of the 440C drop-point blade and six—three on each molded thermoplastic handle scale—on the grip.

▶ For the new Emerson Knives CQC-15, Ernest Emerson said he tried to capture the cutting curves of his Commander model in conjunction with the strength and penetrating power of the CQC-7 tanto.

◄ Designed by Andrew Demko, Cold Steel's AK-47 was inspired by the Russian assault rifle of the same name.

▶ Boker offers the Folder I in its new Boker Plus line of economic tactical folders. The 2 5/8-inch blade is titanium-nitride-coated 440C stainless steel, and G-10 slabs are attached to the tank-body-shaped handle frame.

KNIVES MARKETPLACE

INTERESTING PRODUCT NEWS FOR BOTH THE CUTLER AND THE KNIFE ENTHUSIAST

The companies and individuals represented on the following pages will be happy to provide additional information — feel free to contact them.

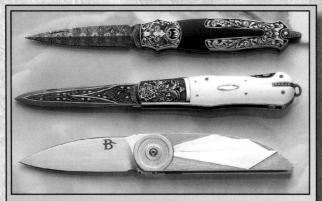
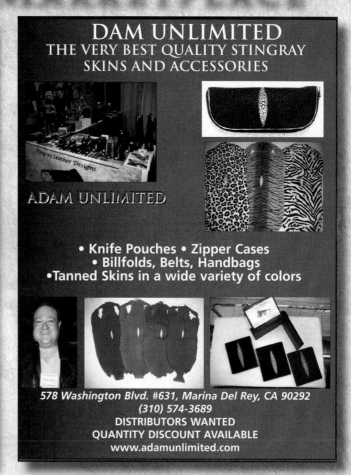

KNIVES MARKETPLACE

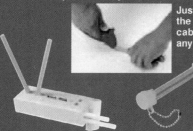

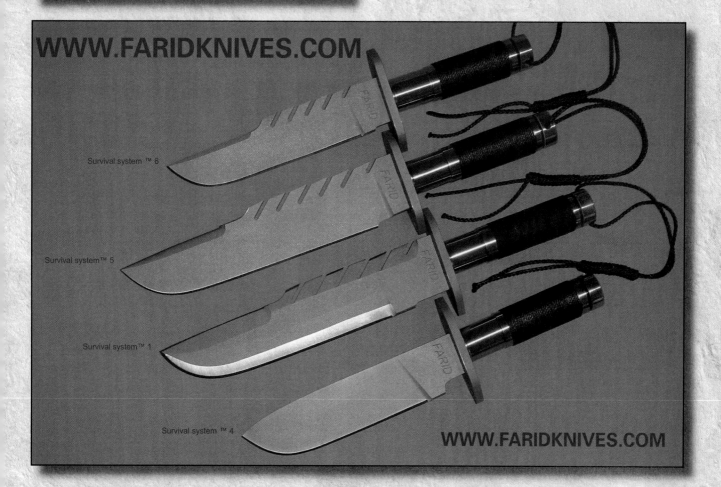

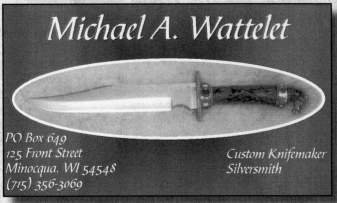

Must-Have Resources from the Writers and Editors of BLADE Magazine

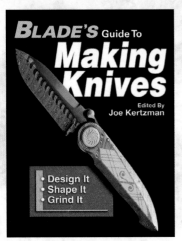
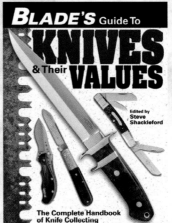

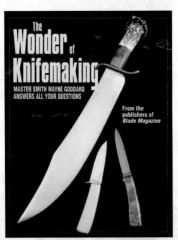
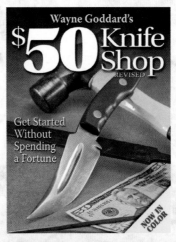

DIRECTORY

A

ABBOTT, WILLIAM M., Box 102A, RR #2, Chandlerville, IL 62627, Phone: 217-458-2325
  Specialties: High-grade edged weapons. **Patterns:** Locking folders, Bowies, working straight knives, kitchen cutlery, minis. **Technical:** Grinds D2, ATS-34, 440C and commercial Damascus. Heat-treats; Rockwell tests. Prefers natural handle materials. **Prices:** $100 to $1000. **Remarks:** Part-time maker; first knife sold in 1984. **Mark:** Name.

ABEGG, ARNIE, 5992 Kenwick Cr., Huntington Beach, CA 92648, Phone: 714-848-5697

ABERNATHY, PAUL J., 3033 Park St., Eureka, CA 95501, Phone: 707-442-3593
  Specialties: Period pieces and traditional straight knives of his design and in standard patterns. **Patterns:** Miniature daggers, fighters and swords. **Technical:** Forges and files SS, brass and sterling silver. **Prices:** $100 to $250; some to $500. **Remarks:** Part-time maker. Doing business as Abernathy's Miniatures. **Mark:** Stylized initials.

ACKERSON, ROBIN E., 119 W Smith St., Buchanan, MI 49107, Phone: 616-695-2911

ADAMS, LES, 6413 NW 200 St., Hialeah, FL 33015, Phone: 305-625-1699
  Specialties: Working straight knives of his design. **Patterns:** Fighters, tactical folders, waw enforcing autos. **Technical:** Grinds ATS-34, 440C and D2. **Prices:** $100 to $500. **Remarks:** Part-time maker; first knife sold in 1989. **Mark:** First initial, last name, Custom Knives.

ADAMS, WILLIAM D., PO Box 439, Burton, TX 77835, Phone: 713-855-5643, Fax: 713-855-5638
  Specialties: Hunter scalpels and utility knives of his design. **Patterns:** Hunters and utility/camp knives. **Technical:** Grinds 1095, 440C and 440V. Uses stabilized wood and other stabilized materials. **Prices:** $100 to $200. **Remarks:** Part-time maker; first knife sold in 1994. **Mark:** Last name in script.

ADDISON, KYLE A., 809 N. 20th St., Murray, KY 42071, Phone: 270-759-1564, kylest2@yahoo.com
  Specialties: Hand forged blades including Bowies, fighters and hunters. **Patterns:** Custom leather sheaths. **Technical:** Forges 5160, 1084, and his own Damascus. **Prices:** $175 to $1500. **Remarks:** Part-time maker, first knife sold in 1996. **Mark:** First and middle initial, last name under "Trident" with knife and hammer. **Other:** ABS member.

ADKINS, RICHARD L., 138 California Ct., Mission Viejo, CA 92692-4079

AIDA, YOSHIHITO, 26-7 Narimasu 2-chome, Itabashi-ku, Tokyo 175-0094, JAPAN, Phone: 81-3-3939-0052, Fax: 81-3-3939-0058
  Specialties: High-tech working straight knives and folders of his design. **Patterns:** Bowies, lockbacks, hunters, fighters, fishing knives, boots. **Technical:** Grinds CV-134, ATS-34; buys Damascus; works in traditional Japanese fashion for some handles and sheaths. **Prices:** $400 to $900; some higher. **Remarks:** Full-time maker; first knife sold in 1978. **Mark:** Initial logo and Riverside West.

ALBERICCI, EMILIO, 19 Via Masone, 24100, Bergamo, ITALY, Phone: 01139-35-215120
  Specialties: Folders and Bowies. **Patterns:** Collector knives. **Technical:** Uses stock removal with extreme lavoration accuracy; offers exotic and high-tech materials. **Prices:** Not currently selling. **Remarks:** Part-time maker. **Mark:** None.

ALDERMAN, ROBERT, 2655 Jewel Lake Rd., Sagle, ID 83860, Phone: 208-263-5996
  Specialties: Classic and traditional working straight knives in standard patterns or to customer specs and his design; period pieces. **Patterns:** Bowies, fighters, hunters and utility/camp knives. **Technical:** Casts, forges and grinds 1084; forges and grinds L6 and O1. Prefers an old appearance. **Prices:** $100 to $350; some to $700. **Remarks:** Full-time maker; first knife sold in 1975. Doing business as Trackers Forge. **Mark:** Deer track. **Other:** Knife-making school. Two-week course for beginners; will cover forging, stock removal, hardening, tempering, case making. All materials supplies; $1250.

ALDRETE, BOB, PO Box 1471, Lomita, CA 90717, Phone: 310-326-3041

ALEXANDER, DARREL, Box 381, Ten Sleep, WY 82442, Phone: 307-366-2699, daleywyo@tctwest.net
  Specialties: Traditional working straight knives. **Patterns:** Hunters, boots and fishing knives. **Technical:** Grinds D2, 440C, ATS-34 and 154CM. **Prices:** $75 to $120; some to $250. **Remarks:** Full-time maker; first knife sold in 1983. **Mark:** Name, city, state.

ALEXANDER, EUGENE, Box 540, Ganado, TX 77962-0540, Phone: 512-771-3727

ALEXANDER, JERED, 213 Hogg Hill Rd., Dierks, AR 71833, Phone: 870-286-2981

ALLEN, MIKE "WHISKERS", 12745 Fontenot Acres Rd., Malakoff, TX 75148, Phone: 903-489-1026, whiskersknives@aol.com Web: www.whiskersknives.com
  Specialties: Working and collector-quality lockbacks, liner locks and automatic folders to customer specs. **Patterns:** Hunters, tantos, Bowies, swords and miniatures. **Technical:** Grinds Damascus, 440C and ATS-34, engraves. **Prices:** $200 and up. **Remarks:** Full-time maker; first knife sold in 1984. **Mark:** Whiskers and date.

ALLRED, BRUCE F., 1764 N. Alder, Layton, UT 84041, Phone: 801-825-4612, allredbf@msn.com
  Specialties: Custom hunting and utility knives. **Patterns:** Custom designs that include a unique grind line, thumb and mosaic pins. **Technical:** ATS-34, 154CM and 440C. **Remarks:** The handle material include but not limited to Micarta (in various colors), natural woods and reconstituted stone.

ALVERSON, TIM (R.V.), 4874 Bobbits Bench Rd., Peck, ID 83545, Phone: 208-476-3999, trvasma@orofino-id.com
  Specialties: Fancy working knives to customer specs; other types on request. **Patterns:** Bowies, daggers, folders and miniatures. **Technical:** Grinds 440C, ATS-34; buys some Damascus. **Prices:** Start at $175. **Remarks:** Full-time maker; first knife sold in 1981. **Mark:** R.V.A. around rosebud.

AMERI, MAURO, Via Riaello No. 20, Trensasco St. Olcese, 16010 Genova, ITALY, Phone: 010-8357077
  Specialties: Working and using knives of his design. **Patterns:** Hunters, Bowies and utility/camp knives. **Technical:** Grinds 440C, ATS-34 and 154CM. Handles in wood or Micarta; offers sheaths. **Prices:** $200 to $1200. **Remarks:** Spare-time maker; first knife sold in 1982. **Mark:** Last name, city.

AMMONS, DAVID C., 6225 N. Tucson Mtn. Dr., Tucson, AZ 85743, Phone: 520-307-3585
  Specialties: Will build to suit. **Patterns:** Yours or mine. **Prices:** $250 to $2000. **Mark:** AMMONS.

AMOR JR., MIGUEL, 10730 NW 7th St. Apt B, Miami, FL 33172, Phone: 305-812-3477
  Specialties: Working and fancy straight knives in standard patterns; some to customer specs. **Patterns:** Bowies, hunters, fighters and tantos. **Technical:** Grinds 440C, ATS-34, carbon steel and commercial Damascus; forges some in high-carbon steels. **Prices:** $125 to $500; some to $1500 and higher. **Remarks:** Part-time maker; first knife sold in 1983. **Mark:** Last name. On collectors' pieces: last name, city, state.

AMOS, CHRIS, 550 S Longfellow, Tucson, AZ 85711, Phone: 520-271-9752
  Specialties: Traditional and custom, user-friendly working knives. **Patterns:** Hunters, utility, camp, and primitive. Your design or mine. **Technical:** Forged high-carbon steel, multiple quench differential hardening. **Prices:** $150 and up. **Remarks:** Part-time maker, member ABS, first knife sold in 1999. **Mark:** CAK (Chris Amos Knives).

AMOUREUX, A.W., PO Box 776, Northport, WA 99157, Phone: 509-732-6292
  Specialties: Heavy-duty working straight knives. **Patterns:** Bowies, fighters, camp knives and hunters for world-wide use. **Technical:** Grinds 440C, ATS-34 and 154CM. **Prices:** $80 to $2000. **Remarks:** Full-time maker; first knife sold in 1974. **Mark:** ALSTAR.

ANDERS, DAVID, 157 Barnes Dr., Center Ridge, AR 72027, Phone: 501-893-2294
  Specialties: Working straight knives of his design. **Patterns:** Bowies, fighters and hunters. **Technical:** Forges 5160, 1080 and Damascus. **Prices:** $225 to $3200. **Remarks:** Part-time maker; first knife sold in 1988. Doing business as Anders Knives. **Mark:** Last name/MS.

ANDERS, JEROME, 155 Barnes Dr., Center Ridge, AR 72027, Phone: 501-893-9981, web: www.andersknives.com
  Specialties: Case handles and pin work. **Patterns:** Layered and mosaic steel. **Prices:** $275 and up. **Remarks:** All his knives are truly one-of-a-kind. **Mark:** J. Anders in half moon.

ANDERSEN, HENRIK LEFOLII, Jagtvej 8, Groenholt, 3480, Fredensborg, DENMARK, Phone: 0011-45-48483026
  Specialties: Hunters and matched pairs for the serious hunter. **Technical:** Grinds A2; uses materials native to Scandinavia. **Prices:** Start at $250. **Remarks:** Part-time maker; first knife sold in 1985. **Mark:** Initials with arrow.

ANDERSON, GARY D., 2816 Reservoir Rd., Spring Grove, PA 17362-9802, Phone: 717-229-2665
Specialties: From working knives to collectors quality blades, some folders. **Patterns:** Traditional and classic designs; customer patterns welcome. **Technical:** Forges Damascus carbon and stainless steels. Offers silver inlay, mokume, filework, checkering. **Prices:** $250 and up. **Remarks:** Part-time maker; first knife sold in 1985. **Mark:** GAND, MS. **Other:** Some engraving, scrimshaw and stone work.

ANDERSON, MARK ALAN, 1176 Poplar St, Denver, CO 80220, Phone: 720-941-9276, mcantdrive65@comcast.net Web: wwwmalancustomknives.com
Specialties: Stilettos. **Prices:** $750 to $1800. **Remarks:** Most of my kives are automatic. **Mark:** Dragon head.

ANDERSON, MEL, 17158 Lee Lane, Cedaredge, CO 81413-8247, Phone: 970-856-6465, Fax: 970-856-6463, artnedge1@wmconnect.com
Specialties: Full-size, miniature and one-of-a-kind straight knives and folders of his design. **Patterns:** Bowies, daggers, fighters, hunters and pressure folders. **Technical:** Grinds 440C, 5160, D2, 1095 and Damascus; offers antler, ivory and wood carved handles. **Prices:** Start at $145. **Remarks:** Knife maker and sculptor, full-time maker; first knife sold in 1987. **Mark:** Scratchy Hand.

ANDERSON, TOM, 955 Canal Rd. Extd., Manchester, PA 17345, Phone: 717-266-6475, andersontech@suscom.net Web; www.andersoncustomknives.com
Specialties: High-tech one-hand folders. **Patterns:** Fighters, utility, and dress knives. **Technical:** Grinds BG-42, S30V and Damascus. Uses titanium, carbon fiber and select natural handle materials. **Prices:** Start at $400. **Remarks:** First knife sold in 1996. **Mark:** Stylized A over T logo with maker's name.

ANDRESS, RONNIE, 415 Audubon Dr. N, Satsuma, AL 36572, Phone: 251-675-7604
Specialties: Working straight knives in standard patterns. **Patterns:** Boots, Bowies, hunters, friction folders and camp knives. **Technical:** Forges 1095, 5160, O1 and his own Damascus. Offers filework and inlays. **Prices:** $125 to $500. **Remarks:** Part-time maker; first knife sold in 1983. Doing business as Andress Knives. **Mark:** Last name, J.S. **Other:** Jeweler, goldsmith, gold work, stone setter. Not currently making knives.

ANDREWS, ERIC, 132 Halbert Street, Grand Ledge, MI 48837, Phone: 517-627-7304
Specialties: Traditional working and using straight knives of his design. **Patterns:** Full-tang hunters, skinners and utility knives. **Technical:** Forges carbon steel; heat-treats. All knives come with sheath; most handles are of wood. **Prices:** $80 to $160. **Remarks:** Part-time maker; first knife sold in 1990. Doing business as The Tinkers Bench.

ANGELL, JON, 22516 East C. R.1474, Hawthorne, FL 32640, Phone: 352-475-5380, syrjon@aol.com

ANKROM, W.E., 14 Marquette Dr., Cody, WY 82414, Phone: 307-587-3017, Fax: 307-587-3017
Specialties: Best quality folding knives of his design. **Patterns:** Lock backs, liner locks, single high art. **Technical:** ATS-34 commercial Damascus. **Prices:** $500 and up. **Remarks:** Full-time maker; first knife sold in 1975. **Mark:** Name or name, city, state.

ANSO, JENS, GL. Skanderborgvej, 116, 8472 Sporup, DENMARK, Phone: 45 86968826, info@ansoknives.com Web: www.ansoknives.com
Specialties: Working knives of his own design. **Patterns:** Folders, baliaongs and fixedblades: Droppoints, sheepsfoots, hawkbill, tanto, recurve.**Technical:** Grinds RWL-34 Damasteel 530V. Hand rubbed or beadblasted finish. **Price:** $175 to $795, some up to $2500. **Remarks:** Full-time maker since January 2002. First knife sold 1997. Doing business as ANSOKNIVES. **Mark:** ANSO and/or ANSO with logo.

ANTONIO JR., WILLIAM J., 6 Michigan State Dr., Newark, DE 19713-1161, Phone: 302-368-8211, antonioknives@aol.com
Specialties: Fancy working straight knives of his design. **Patterns:** Hunting, survival and fishing knives. **Technical:** Grinds D2, 440C and 154CM; offers stainless Damascus. **Prices:** $125 to $395; some to $900. **Remarks:** Part-time maker; first knife sold in 1978. **Mark:** Last name.

AOUN, CHARLES, 69 Nahant St., Wakefield, MA 01880, Phone: 781-224-3353
Specialties: Classic and fancy straight knives of his design. **Patterns:** Fighters, hunters and personal knives. **Technical:** Grinds W2, 1095, ATS-34 and Damascus. Uses natural handle materials; embellishes with silver and semi-precious stones. **Prices:** Start at $290. **Remarks:** Part-time maker; first knife sold in 1995. Doing business as Galeb Knives. **Mark:** G stamped on ricasso or choil.

APELT, STACY E., 8076 Moose Ave., Norfolk, VA 23518, Phone: 757-583-5872, sapelt@cox.net
Specialties: Exotic wood and burls, ivories, bowies, custom made knives to order. **Patterns:** Bowies, hunters, fillet, professional cutlery. **Technical:** Hand forging, stock removal, scrimshaw, carbon, stainless and Damascus steels. **Prices:** $65 to $3500. **Remarks:** Professional Goldsmith. **Mark:** Stacy E. Apelt - Norfolk VA.

APPLEBY, ROBERT, 43 N. Canal St., Shickshinny, PA 18655, Phone: 570-542-4335, r.appleby@juno.com Web: www.angelfire.com/pe2/applebyknives
Specialties: Working using straight knives and folders of his own and popular and historical designs. **Patterns:** Variety of straight knives and folders. **Technical:** Hand forged or grinds O-1, 1084, 5160, 440C, ATS-34, commercial Damascus, makes own sheaths. **Prices:** Starting at $75. **Remarks:** Part-time maker; first knife sold in 1995. **Mark:** APPLEBY over SHICKSHINNY, PA.

APPLETON, RAY, 244 S. Fetzer St., Byers, CO 80103-9748, rapltn@fone.net; Web: http: //www.texinet.net/ray
Specialties: One-of-a-kind folding knives. **Patterns:** Unique folding multi-locks and high-tech patterns. **Technical:** All parts machined; D2, S7, 440C, and 6a14v. **Prices:** Start at $8500. **Remarks:** Spare-time maker; first knife sold in 1986. **Mark:** Initials within arrowhead, signed and dated.

ARBUCKLE, JAMES M., 114 Jonathan Jct., Yorktown, VA 23693, Phone: 757-867-9578, a_r_bukckle@hotmail.com
Specialties: One-of-a-kind of his design; working knives. **Patterns:** Mostly chefs knives and hunters. **Technical:** Forged and stock removal blades using exotic hardwoods, natural materials, Micarta and stabilized woods. Forge 5160, 1084 and 01; stock remove D2, ATS-34, 440C. Make own pattern welded steel. Prices; $150 to $700. **Remarks:** Forge, grind, heat-treat, finish and embellish all knives myself. Do own leatherwork and wood work. Part-time maker. **Mark:** J. Arbuckle or Arbuckle with maker below it. **Other:** ABS member; ASM member.

ARCHER, RAY AND TERRI, PO Box 129, Medicine Bow, WY 82329, Phone: 307-379-2567, archert@trib.com Web: http: //www.archersknives.com
Specialties: High finish working straight knives and small one-of-a-kind. **Patterns:** Hunters/skinners, camping. **Technical:** ATS-34, 440C, S30V. Buys Damascus. **Price:** $75 to $650. **Remarks:** Make own sheaths; first knife sold 1994. **Mark:** Last name over city and state. **Other:** Member of PKA & OK CA (Oregon Knife Collector Assoc.)

ARDWIN, COREY, 4700 North Cedar, North Little Rock, AR 72116, Phone: 501-791-0301, Fax: 501-791-2974, Boog@hotmail.com

ARM-KO KNIVES, PO Box 76280, Marble Ray 4035 KZN, South Africa, Phone: 27 31 5771451, arm-koknives.co.za Web: www.arm-koknives.co.za
Specialties: They will make what your fastidious taste desires. Be it cool collector or tenacious tactical with handles of mother of pearl, fossil & local ivories. Exotic dye/stabilized burls, giraffe bone, horns, carbon fiber, g10, and titanium etc. **Technical:** Via stock removal, grinding Damasteel, carbon & mosaic. Damascus, ATS-34, N690, 440A, 440B, 12 C 27 RWL34 and high carbon EN 8, 5160 all heat treated in house. **Prices:** From $200 and up. **Remarks:** Father a part-time maker for well over 10 years and member of knifemakers guild in SA. Son full-time maker over 3 years. **Mark:** Logo of initials A R M and H A R M "Edged Tools".

ARNOLD, JOE, 47 Patience Cres., London, Ont., CANADA N6E 2K7, Phone: 519-686-2623
Specialties: Traditional working and using straight knives of his design and to customer specs. **Patterns:** Fighters, hunters and Bowies. **Technical:** Grinds 440C, ATS-34 and 5160. **Prices:** $75 to $500; some to $2500. **Remarks:** Part-time maker; first knife sold in 1988. **Mark:** Last name, country.

ARROWOOD, DALE, 556 Lassetter Rd., Sharpsburg, GA 30277, Phone: 404-253-9672
Specialties: Fancy and traditional straight knives of his design and to customer specs. **Patterns:** Bowies, fighters and hunters. **Technical:** Grinds ATS-34 and 440C; forges high-carbon steel. Engraves and scrimshaws. **Prices:** $125 to $200; some to $245. **Remarks:** Part-time maker; first knife sold in 1989. **Mark:** Anvil with an arrow through it; Old English "Arrowood Knives".

ASHBY, DOUGLAS, 10123 Deermont, Dallas, TX 75243, Phone: 214-238-7531
Specialties: Traditional and fancy straight knives of his design or to customer specs. **Patterns:** Hunters, fighters and utility/camp knives. **Technical:** Grinds 440C, ATS-34 and commercial Damascus. **Prices:** $75 to $200; some to $500. **Remarks:** Part-time maker; first knife sold in 1990. **Mark:** Name, city.

ASHWORTH, BOYD, 1510 Bullard Place, Powder Springs, GA 30127, Phone: 770-422-9826, boydashworth@comcast.net Web: www.boydashworthknives.com
   Specialties: Turtle folders. Fancy Damascus locking folders. **Patterns:** Fighters, hunters and gents. **Technical:** Forges own Damascus; offers filework; uses exotic handle materials. **Prices:** $500 to $2500. **Remarks:** Part-time maker; first knife sold in 1993. **Mark:** Last name.

ATKINSON, DICK, General Delivery, Wausau, FL 32463, Phone: 850-638-8524
   Specialties: Working straight knives and folders of his design; some fancy. **Patterns:** Hunters, fighters, boots; locking folders in interframes. **Technical:** Grinds A2, 440C and 154CM. Likes filework. **Prices:** $85 to $300; some exceptional knives. **Remarks:** Full-time maker; first knife sold in 1977. **Mark:** Name, city, state.

AYARRAGARAY, CRISTIAN L., Buenos Aires 250, (3100) Parana-Entre Rios, ARGENTINA, Phone: 043-231753
   Specialties: Traditional working straight knives of his design. **Patterns:** Fishing and hunting knives. **Technical:** Grinds and forges carbon steel. Uses native Argentine woods and deer antler. **Prices:** $150 to $250; some to $400. **Remarks:** Full-time maker; first knife sold in 1980. **Mark:** Last name, signature.

B

BAARTMAN, GEORGE, PO Box 1116, Bela-Bela 0480, Limpopo, SOUTH AFRICA, Phone: 27 14 736 4036, Fax: 27 14 736 4036, baartmanknives@hotmail.com
   Specialties: Fancy and working liner lock folders of own design and to customers specs. Specialize in pattern filework on liners. Specialize in pattern filework on liners. **Technical:** Liner lock folders. **Technical:** Grinds 12C27, ATS-34, and Damascus, prefer working with stainless damasteel. Hollow grinds to hand-rubbed and polished satin finish. Enjoys working with mammoth, warthog tusk and pearls. **Prices:** Folders from $260 to $800. **Remarks:** Member of the Knife-makers Guild of South Africa since 1993. **Mark:** BAARTMAN.

BABCOCK, RAYMOND G., 179 Lane Rd., Vincent, OH 45784, Phone: 614-678-2688
   Specialties: Plain and fancy working straight knives. Will make knives to his design and to custom specifications. **Patterns:** Hunting knives and Bowies. **Technical:** Hollow grinds L6. **Prices:** $100 to $500. **Remarks:** Part-time maker; first knife sold in 1973. **Mark:** First initial and last name; R. Babcock.

BACHE-WIIG, TOM, N-5966, Eivindvik, NORWAY, Phone: 4757784290, Fax: 4757784122
   Specialties: High-art and working knives of his design. **Patterns:** Hunters, utility knives, hatchets, axes and art knives. **Technical:** Grinds Uddeholm Elmax, powder metallurgy tool stainless steel. Handles made of rear burls of Nordic woods stabilized with vacuum/high-pressure technique. **Prices:** $430 to $900; some to $2300. **Remarks:** Part-time maker; first knife sold 1988. **Mark:** Etched name and eagle head.

BACON, DAVID R., 906 136th St. E., Bradenton, FL 34202-9694, Phone: 813-996-4289

BAGLEY, R. KEITH, Old Pine Forge, 4415 Hope Acres Dr., White Plains, MD 20695, Phone: 301-932-0990, oldpineforge@hotmail.com
   Specialties: High-carbon Damascus with semi-precious stones set in exotic wood handle; tactical and skinner knives. **Technical:** Use ATS-34, 5160, 01, 1085, 1095. **Patterns:** Various patterns; prefer all Tool-Steel and Nickel Damascus. **Price:** Damascus from $250 to $500; stainless from $100 to $225. **Remarks:** Farrier for 25 years, blacksmith for 25 years, knife maker for 10 years.

BAILEY, JOSEPH D., 3213 Jonesboro Dr., Nashville, TN 37214, Phone: 615-889-3172, jbknfemkr@aol.com
   Specialties: Working and using straight knives; collector pieces. **Patterns:** Bowies, hunters, tactical, folders. **Technical:** 440C, ATS-34, Damascus and wire Damascus. Offers scrimshaw. **Prices:** $85 to $1200. **Remarks:** Part-time maker; first knife sold in 1988. **Mark:** Joseph D Bailey Nashville Tennessee.

BAILEY, KIRBY C., 2055 F.M. 2790 W., Lytle, TX 78052, Phone: 830-772-3376
   Specialties: All kinds of knives folders, fixed blade, fighters. **Patterns:** Hunters, folders, fighters, Bowies, miniatures. **Technical:** Does all his own work; heat treating, file work etc. **Prices:** $200 to $1000. **Remarks:** Builds any kind of hand cutlery. Have made knives for 45 years; sold knives for 28 years. **Mark:** K.C.B. and serial #. **Other:** Have sold knives in Asia and all states in US.

BAILEY, RYAN, 4185 S. St. Rt. 605, Galena, OH 43021, Phone: 740-965-9970, dr@darrelralph.com Web: www.darrelralph.com
   Specialties: Fancy, high-art, high-tech, collectible straight knives and folders of his design and to customer specs; unique mechanisms, some disassemble. **Patterns:** Daggers, fighters and swords. **Technical:** Does own Damascus and forging from high-carbon. Embellishes with file work and gold work. **Prices:** $200 to $2500. **Remarks:** Full-time maker; first knife sold in 1999. Doing business as Briar Knives. **Mark:** RLB.

BAKER, HERB, 14104 NC 87 N., Eden, NC 27288, Phone: 336-627-0338

BAKER, RAY, PO Box 303, Sapulpa, OK 74067, Phone: 918-224-8013
   Specialties: High-tech working straight knives. **Patterns:** Hunters, fighters, Bowies, skinners and boots of his design and to customer specs. **Technical:** Grinds 440C, 1095 spring steel or customer request; heat-treats. Custom-made scabbards for any knife. **Prices:** $125 to $500; some to $1000. **Remarks:** Full-time maker; first knife sold in 1981. **Mark:** First initial, last name.

BAKER, VANCE, 574 Co. Rd. 675, Riceville, TN 37370, Phone: 423-745-9157
   Specialties: Traditional working straight knives of his design and to customer specs. Prefers drop-point hunters and small Bowies. **Patterns:** Hunters, utility and kitchen knives. **Technical:** Forges Damascus, cable, L6 and 5160. **Prices:** $100 to $250; some to $500. **Remarks:** Part-time maker; first knife sold in 1985. **Mark:** Initials connected.

BAKER, WILD BILL, Box 361, Boiceville, NY 12412, Phone: 914-657-8646
   Specialties: Primitive knives, buckskinners. **Patterns:** Skinners, camp knives and Bowies. **Technical:** Works with L6, files and rasps. **Prices:** $100 to $350. **Remarks:** Part-time maker; first knife sold in 1989. **Mark:** Wild Bill Baker, Oak Leaf Forge, or both.

BALBACH, MARKUS, Heinrich - Worner - Str. 3, 35789 Weilmunster-Laubuseschbach/Ts., GERMANY 06475-8911, Fax: 912986, Web: www.schmiede-balbach.de
   Specialties: High-art knives and working/using straight knives and folders of his design and to customer specs. **Patterns:** Hunters and daggers. **Technical:** Stainless steel, one of Germany's greatest Smithies. Supplier for the forges of Solingen. **Remarks:** Full-time maker; first knife sold in 1984. Doing business as Schmiedewerkstatte M. Balbach. **Mark:** Initials stamped inside the handle.

BALDWIN, PHILLIP, PO Box 563, Snohomish, WA 98290, Phone: 425-334-5569, phb@drizzle.com
   Specialties: One-of-a-kind elegant table cutlery; exotics. **Patterns:** Elegant or exotic knives. Likes the challenge of axes, spears and specialty tools. **Technical:** Forges W2, W1 and his own pattern welded steel and mokume-gane. **Prices:** Start at $1000. **Remarks:** Full-time maker; first knife sold in 1973. **Mark:** Last initial marked with chisel.

BALL, KEN, 127 Sundown Manor, Mooresville, IN 46158, Phone: 317-834-4803
   Specialties: Classic working/using straight knives of his design and to customer specs. **Patterns:** Hunters and utility/camp knives. **Technical:** Flat-grinds ATS-34. Offers filework. **Prices:** $150 to $400. **Remarks:** Part-time maker; first knife sold in 1994. Doing business as Ball Custom Knives. **Mark:** Last name.

BALLESTRA, SANTINO, via D. Tempesta 11/17, 18039 Ventimiglia (IM), ITALY 0184-215228, ladasin@libero.it
   Specialties: Using and collecting straight knives. **Patterns:** Hunting, fighting, skinners, Bowies, medieval daggers and knives. **Technical:** Forges ATS-34, D2, O2, 1060 and his own Damascus. Uses ivory and silver. **Prices:** $500 to $2000; some higher. **Remarks:** Full-time maker; first knife sold in 1979. **Mark:** First initial, last name.

BALLEW, DALE, PO Box 1277, Bowling Green, VA 22427, Phone: 804-633-5701
   Specialties: Miniatures only to customer specs. **Patterns:** Bowies, daggers and fighters. **Technical:** Files 440C stainless; uses ivory, abalone, exotic woods and some precious stones. **Prices:** $100 to $800. **Remarks:** Part-time maker; first knife sold in 1988. **Mark:** Initials and last name.

BANKS, DAVID L., 99 Blackfoot Ave., Riverton, WY 82501, Phone: 307-856-3154/Cell: 307-851-5599
   Specialties: Heavy-duty working straight knives. **Patterns:** Hunters, Bowies and camp knives. **Technical:** Forges Damascus 1084-15N20, L-6-W1 pure nickel, 5160, 52100 and his own Damascus; differential heat treat and tempers. Handles made of horn, antlers and exotic wood. Hand-stitched harness leather sheaths. **Prices:** $300 to $2000. **Remarks:** Part-time maker. **Mark:** Banks Blackfoot forged Dave Banks and initials connected.

BARDSLEY, NORMAN P., 197 Cottage St., Pawtucket, RI 02860, Phone: 401-725-9132, www.bardsleydistinctiveweaponry.com or www.bardsleycustomknives.com
  Specialties: Working and fantasy knives. **Patterns:** Fighters, boots, fantasy, renaissance and native American in upscale and presentation fashion. **Technical:** Grinds all steels and Damascus. Uses exotic hides for sheaths. **Prices:** $100 to $15,000. **Remarks:** Full-time maker. **Mark:** Last name in script with logo.

BAREFOOT, JOE W., 117 Oakbrook Dr., Liberty, SC 29657
  Specialties: Working straight knives of his design. **Patterns:** Hunters, fighters and boots; tantos and survival knives. **Technical:** Grinds D2, 440C and ATS-34. Mirror finishes. Uses ivory and stag on customer request only. **Prices:** $50 to $160; some to $500. **Remarks:** Part-time maker; first knife sold in 1980. **Mark:** Bare footprint.

BARKER, REGGIE, 603 S. Park Dr., Springhill, LA 71075, Phone: 318-539-2958, wrbarker@cmaaccess.com Web: www.reggiebarkerknives.com
  Specialties: Camp knives and hatchets. **Patterns:** Bowie, skinning, hunting, camping, fighters, kitchen or customer design. **Technical:** Forges carbon steel and own pattern welded steels. Prices $225 to $2000. **Remarks:** Full-time maker. Winner of 1999 and 2000 Spring Hammering Cutting contest. Winner of Best Value of Show 2001; Arkansas Knife Show and Journeyman Smith. **Mark:** Barker JS. **Other:** Border Guard Forge.

BARKER, ROBERT G., 2311 Branch Rd., Bishop, GA 30621, Phone: 706-769-7827
  Specialties: Traditional working/using straight knives of his design. **Patterns:** Bowies, hunters and utility knives, ABS Journeyman Smith. **Technical:** Hand forged carbon and Damascus. Forges to shape high-carbon 5160, cable and chain. Differentially heat-treats. **Prices:** $200 to $500; some to $1000. **Remarks:** Spare-time maker; first knife sold in 1987. **Mark:** BARKER/J.S.

BARLOW, JANA POIRIER, 3820 Borland Cir., Anchorage, AK 99517, Phone: 907-243-4581

BARNES, AUBREY G., 11341 Rock Hill Rd., Hagerstown, MD 21740, Phone: 301-223-4587, a.barnes@myactv.net
  Specialties: Classic Moran style reproductions and using knives of his own design. **Patterns:** Bowies, hunters, fighters, daggers and utility/camping knives. **Technical:** Forges 5160, 1085, L6 and Damascus, Silver wire inlays. **Prices:** $300 to $2500. **Remarks:** Full-time maker; first knife sold in 1992. Doing business as Falling Waters Forge. **Mark:** First and middle initials, last name, M.S.

BARNES, ERIC, H C 74 Box 41, Mountain View, AR 72560, Phone: 501-269-3358

BARNES, GARY L., Box 138, New Windsor, MD 21776-0138, Phone: 410-635-6243, Fax: 410-635-6243
  Specialties: Ornate button lock Damascus folders. **Patterns:** Barnes original. **Technical:** Forges own Damascus. **Prices:** Average $2500. **Remarks:** ABS Master Smith since 1983. **Mark:** Hand engraved logo of letter B pierced by dagger.

BARNES, GREGORY, 266 W. Calaveras St., Altadena, CA 91001, Phone: 626-398-0053, snake@annex.com

BARNES, JACK, PO Box 1315, Whitefish, MT 59937-1315, Phone: 406-862-6078

BARNES, MARLEN R., 904 Crestview Dr.S., Atlanta, TX 75551-1854, Phone: 903-796-3668, MRBlives@worldnet.att.net
  Specialties: Hammer forges random and mosaic Damascus. **Patterns:** Hatchets, straight and folding knives. **Technical:** Hammer forges carbon steel using 5160, 1084 and 52100 with 15N20 and 203E nickel. **Prices:** $150 and up. **Remarks:** Part-time maker; first knife sold 1999. **Mark:** Script M.R.B., other side J.S.

BARNES, WENDELL, PO Box 272, Clinton, MT 59825, Phone: 406-825-0908
  Specialties: Working straight knives. **Patterns:** Hunters, folders, neck knives. **Technical:** Grinds 440C, ATS-34, D2 and Damascus. **Prices:** Start at $75. **Remarks:** Spare-time maker; first knife sold in 1996. **Mark:** First initial and last name around broken heart.

BARNES, WILLIAM, 591 Barnes Rd., Wallingford, CT 06492-1805, Phone: 860-349-0443

BARNES JR., CECIL C., 141 Barnes Dr., Center Ridge, AR 72027, Phone: 501-893-2267

BARNETT, VAN, Barnett Int'l Inc., 1135 Terminal Way Ste. #209, Reno, NV 89502, Phone: 866 ARTKNIFE or 304-727-5512, Fax: 775-201-0038, Artknife@vanBarnett.com Web: www.VanBarnett.com
  Specialties: Collector grade one-of-a-kind / embellished high art daggers and art folders. **Patterns:** Art daggers and folders. **Technical:** Forges and grinds own Damascus. **Prices:** Upscale. **Remarks:** Designs and makes one-of-a-kind highly embellished art knives using high karat gold, diamonds and other gemstones, pearls, stone and fossil ivories, carved steel guards and blades, all knives are carved and or engraved, does own engraving, carving and other embellishments, sole authorship; full-time maker since 1981. **Mark:** V. H. Barnett or Van Barnett in script. **Other:** Does one high art collaboration a year with Dellana. Voting Member of Knifemakers Guild. Member of ABS.

BARNGROVER, JERRY, RR. #4, Box 1230, Afton, OK 74331, Phone: 918-257-5076

BARR, A.T., 153 Madonna Dr., Nicholasville, KY 40356, Phone: 859-887-5400, Web: www.customknives.com
  Specialties: Fine Gent's user and collector grade liner lock folders and sheath knives. **Patterns:** Liner lock folders and sheath knives. **Technical:** Flat grinds S30V, ATS-34, D-2 commercial Damascus; all knives have a hand rubbed satin finish. Does all leather work. **Prices:** Start at $250 for folders and $200 for sheath knives. **Remarks:** Full-time maker, first knife sold in 1979. **Mark:** Full name. **Other:** Knifemakers' Guild Voting member. "Don't you buy no ugly knife."

BARR, JUDSON C., 1905 Pickwick Circle, Irving, TX 75060, Phone: 972-790-7195
  Specialties: Bowies. **Patterns:** Sheffield and Early American. **Technical:** Forged carbon steel and Damascus. Also stock removal. **Remarks:** Journeyman member of ABS **Mark:** Barr.

BARRETT, CECIL TERRY, 2514 Linda Lane, Colorado Springs, CO 80909, Phone: 719-473-8325
  Specialties: Working and using straight knives and folders of his design, to customer specs and in standard patterns. **Patterns:** Bowies, hunters, kitchen knives, locking folders and slip-joint folders. **Technical:** Grinds 440C, D2 and ATS-34. Wood and leather sheaths. **Prices:** $65 to $500; some to $750. **Remarks:** Full-time maker. **Mark:** Stamped middle name.

BARRETT, RICK L. (TOSHI HISA), 18943 CR .18, Goshen, IN 46528, Phone: 574-533-4297, barrettrick@hotmail.com
  Specialties: Japanese-style blades from sushi knives to katana and fantasy pieces. **Patterns:** Swords, axes, spears/lances, hunter and utility knives. **Technical:** Forges and grinds Damascus and carbon steels, occasionally uses stainless. **Prices:** $250 to $4000+. **Remarks:** Full-time bladesmith, jeweler. **Mark:** Japanese mei on Japanese pieces and stylized initials.

BARRON, BRIAN, 123 12th Ave., San Mateo, CA 94402, Phone: 650-341-2683
  Specialties: Traditional straight knives. **Patterns:** Daggers, hunters and swords. **Technical:** Grinds 440C, ATS-34 and 1095. Sculpts bolsters using an S-curve. **Prices:** $130 to $270; some to $1500. **Remarks:** Part-time maker; first knife sold in 1993. **Mark:** Diamond Drag "Barron".

BARRY III, JAMES J., 115 Flagler Promenade No., West Palm Beach, FL 33405, Phone: 561-832-4197
  Specialties: High-art working straight knives of his design also high art tomahawks. **Patterns:** Hunters, daggers and fishing knives. **Technical:** Grinds 440C only. Prefers exotic materials for handles. Most knives embellished with filework, carving and scrimshaw. Many pieces designed to stand unassisted. **Prices:** $500 to $10,000. **Remarks:** Part-time maker; first knife sold in 1975. Guild member (knifemakers) since 1991. **Mark:** Branded initials as a J and B together.

BARTH, J.D., 101 4th St., PO Box 186, Alberton, MT 59820, Phone: 406-722-4557, mtdeerhunter@blackfoot.net Web: www.jdbarthcustomknives.com
  Specialties: Working and fancy straight knives of his design. Liner lock folders, stainless and Damascus, fully file worked, nitre blueing. **Technical:** Grinds ATS-34, 440-C, stainless and carbon Damascus. Uses variety of natural handle materials and Micarta. Likes dovetailed bolsters. Filework on most knives, full and tapered tangs. Makes custom fit sheaths for each knife. **Mark:** Name over maker, city and state.

BARTLOW, JOHN, 5078 Coffeen Ave., Sheridan, WY 82801, Phone: 307 673-4941, jbartlow@vcn
  Specialties: New liner locks, working hunters, skinners, bird and trouts. **Patterns:** Working hunters, skinners, capers, bird and trout knives. **Technical:** Working on 6 new liner lock designs. **Prices:** $200 to $2000. **Remarks:** Full-time maker; first knife sold in 1979. Field-tests knives. **Mark:** Bartlow Sheridan, Wyo.

BARTRUG, HUGH E., 2701 34th St. N., #142, St. Petersburg, FL 33713, Phone: 813-323-1136
  Specialties: Inlaid straight knives and exotic folders; high-art knives and period pieces. **Patterns:** Hunters, Bowies and daggers; traditional patterns. **Technical:** Diffuses mokume. Forges 100 percent nickel, wrought iron, mosaic Damascus, shokeedo and O1 tool steel; grinds. **Prices:** $210 to $2500; some to $5000. **Remarks:** Retired maker; first knife sold in 1980. **Mark:** Ashley Forge or name.

BASKETT, LEE GENE, 427 Sutzer Ck. Rd., Eastview, KY 42732, Phone: 270-862-5019, baskettknives@hotmail.com Web: www.geocities.com/baskettknives
Specialties: Fancy working knives and fantasy pieces, often set up in desk stands. Patterns: Fighters, Bowies and survival knives; locking folders and traditional styles. Technical: Liner locks. Grinds O1, 440C, S-30-V; buys Damascus. Filework provided on most knives. Prices: Start at $250 and up. Remarks: Part-time maker; first knife sold in 1980. Mark: Last name.

BATLEY, MARK S., PO Box 217, Wake, VA 23176, Phone: 804 776-7794

BATSON, JAMES, 176 Brentwood Lane, Madison, AL 35758, Phone: 540-937-2318
Specialties: Forged Damascus blades and fittings in collectible period pieces. Patterns: Integral art knives, Bowies, folders, American-styled blades and miniatures. Technical: Forges carbon steel and his Damascus. Prices: $150 to $1800; some to $4500. Remarks: Semi retired full-time maker; first knife sold in 1978. Mark: Name, bladesmith with horse's head.

BATSON, RICHARD G., 6591 Waterford Rd., Rixeyville, VA 22737, Phone: 540-937-2318
Specialties: Military, utility and fighting knives in working and presentation grade. Patterns: Daggers, combat and utility knives. Technical: Grinds O1, 1095 and 440C. Etches and scrimshaws; offers polished, Parkerized finishes. Prices: Active military, please inquire. Remarks: Semi-retired, limit production. First knife sold in 1958. Mark: Bat in circle, hand-signed and serial numbered.

BATTS, KEITH, 450 Manning Rd., Hooks, TX 75561, Phone: 903-832-1140, kbatts@quixnet.net
Specialties: Working straight knives of his design or to customer specs. Patterns: Bowies, hunters, skinners, camp knives and others. Technical: Forges 5160 and his Damascus; offers filework. Prices: $245 to $895. Remarks: Part-time maker; first knife sold in 1988. Mark: Last name.

BAUCHOP, PETER, c/o Beck's Cutlery Specialties, 107 Edinburgh S #109, Cary, NC 27511, Phone: 919-460-0203, Fax: 919-460-7772, beckscutlery@mindspring.com
Specialties: Working straight knives and period pieces. Patterns: Fighters, swords and survival knives. Technical: Grinds O1, D2, G3, 440C and AST-34. Scrimshaws. Prices: $100 to $350; some to $1500. Remarks: Full-time maker; first knife sold in 1980. Mark: Bow and axe (BOW-CHOP).

BAUCHOP, ROBERT, PO Box 330, Munster, Kwazulu-Natal 4278, SOUTH AFRICA, Phone: +27 39 3192449
Specialties: Fantasy knives; working and using knives of his design and to customer specs. Patterns: Hunters, swords, utility/camp knives, diver's knives and large swords. Technical: Grinds Sandvick 12C27, D2, 440C. Uses South African hardwoods red ivory, wild olive, African blackwood, etc. on handles. Prices: $200 to $800; some to $2000. Remarks: Full-time maker; first knife sold in 1986. Doing business as Bauchop Custom Knives and swords. Mark: Viking helmet with Bauchop (bow and chopper) crest.

BAUM, RICK, 435 North Center St., Lehi, UT 84043, Phone: 801-431-7290, rick_baum@modusmedia.com

BAUMGARDNER, ED, 128 E. Main St., Glendale, KY 42740, Phone: 502-435-2675
Specialties: Working fixed blades, some folders. Patterns: Drop point and clip point hunters, fighters, small Bowies, traditional slip joint folders and lockbacks. Technical: Grinds O-1, 154CM, ATS-34, and Damascus likes using natural handle materials. Prices: $100 to $700. Remarks: Part-time maker, first knife sold in 2001. Mark: Last name.

BAXTER, DALE, 291 County Rd. 547, Trinity, AL 35673, Phone: 256-355-3626, dale@baxterknives.com
Specialties: Bowies, fighters, and hunters. Patterns: No patterns: all unique true customs. Technical: Hand forge and hand finish. Steels: 1095 and L-6 for carbon blades, 1095/L-6 for Damascus. Remarks: Full-time bladesmith and sold first knife in 1998. Mark: Dale Baxter (script) and J.S. on reverse.

BEAM, JOHN R., 1310 Foothills Rd., Kalispell, MT 59901, Phone: 406-755-2593
Specialties: Classic, high-art and working straight knives of his design. Patterns: Bowies and hunters. Technical: Grinds 440C, Damascus and scrap. Prices: $175 to $600; some to $3000. Remarks: Part-time maker; first knife sold in 1950. Doing business as Beam's Knives. Mark: Beam's Knives.

BEASLEY, GENEO, PO Box 339, Wadsworth, NV 89442, Phone: 775-575-2584

BEATTY, GORDON H., 121 Petty Rd., Seneca, SC 29672, Phone: 864-882-6278
Specialties: Working straight knives, some fancy. Patterns: Traditional patterns, mini-skinners and letter openers. Technical: Grinds 440C, D2 and ATS-34; makes knives one-at-a-time. Prices: $75 to $450; some to $450. Remarks: Part-time maker; first knife sold in 1982. Mark: Name.

BEATY, ROBERT B., CUTLER, 1995 Big Flat Rd., Missoula, MT 59804, Phone: 406-549-1818
Specialties: Plain and fancy working knives and collector pieces; will accept custom orders. Patterns: Hunters, Bowies, utility, kitchen and camp knives; locking folders. Technical: Grinds D-2, ATS-34, Dendritie D-2, makes all tool steel Damascus, forges 1095, 5160, 52100. Prices: $100 to $450; some to $1100. Remarks: Full-time maker; first knife sold 1995. Mark: Stainless: First name, middle initial, last name, city and state. Carbon: Last name stamped on Ricasso.

BEAUCHAMP, GAETAN, 125, de la Rivire, Stoneham, PQ, CANADA G0A 4P0, Phone: 418-848-1914, Fax: 418-848-6859, gaetanbeauchamp@videotron.ca web: www.beauchamp.cjb.net
Specialties: Working knives and folders of his design and to customer specs. Patterns: Hunters, fighters, fantasy knives. Technical: Grinds ATS-34, 440C, Damascus. Scrimshaws on ivory; specializes in buffalo horn and black backgrounds. Offers a variety of handle materials. Prices: Start at $125. Remarks: Full-time maker; first knife sold in 1992. Mark: Signature etched on blade.

BECKER, FRANZ, AM Kreuzberg 2, 84533, Marktl/Inn, GERMANY 08678-8020
Specialties: Stainless steel knives in working sizes. Patterns: Semi- and full-integral knives; interframe folders. Technical: Grinds stainless steels; likes natural handle materials. Prices: $200 to $2000. Mark: Name, country.

BECKER, STEVE, 201 1st Ave. N.W., Conrad, MT 59425, Phone: 406-278-7753, scbecker@marsweb.com

BECKETT, NORMAN L., 102 Tobago Ave., Satsuma, FL 32189, Phone: 386-325-3539, nbknives@yahoo.com
Specialties: Fancy, traditional and working folders and straight knives of his design. Patterns: Bowies, fighters, folders and hunters. Technical: Grinds CPM-S30V and Damascus. Fileworks blades; hollow and flat grinds. Prefers mirror finish; satin finish on working knives. Uses exotic handle material, stabilized woods and Micarta. Hand-tooled or inlaid sheaths. Prices: $125 to $900; some to $2500 and up. Remarks: Full-time maker; first knife sold in 1993. Doing business as Norm Beckett Knives. Mark: First and last name, maker, city and state.

BEERS, RAY, 8 Manorbrook Rd., Monkton, MD 21111, Phone: Summer 410-472-2229, Fax: 410-472-9136

BEERS, RAY, 2501 Lakefront Dr., Lake Wales, FL 33898, Phone: Winter 863-696-3036, Fax: 863-696-9421, rbknives@copper.net

BEETS, MARTY, 390 N. 5th Ave., Williams Lake, BC, CANADA V2G 2G4, Phone: 250-392-7199
Specialties: Working and collectable straight knives of his own design. Patterns: Hunter, skinners, Bowies and utility knives. Technical: Grinds 440C-does all his own work including heat treating Uses a variety of handle material specializing in exotic hardwoods, antler and horn. Price: $125 to $400. Remarks: Wife, Sandy does handmade/hand stitched sheaths. First knife sold in 1988. Business name Beets Handmade Knives.

BEGG, TODD M., 420 169 St. S, Spanaway, WA 98387, Phone: 253-531-2113, web: www.beggknives.com
Specialties: Hand rubbed satin finished 440c stainless steel. Mirror polished 426 stainless steel. Stabilized mardrone wood.

BEHNKE, WILLIAM, 8478 Dell Rd., Kingsley, MI 49649, Phone: 231-263-7447, wbehnke@michweb.net
Specialties: Hunters, belt knives and folders. Patterns: Traditional styling in moderate-sized straight and folding knives. Technical: Forges his own Damascus, W-2 and 1095; likes natural material. Prices: $150 to $2000. Remarks: Part-time maker. Mark: Bill Behnke Knives.

BELL, DONALD, 2 Division St., Bedford, Nova Scotia, CANADA B4A 1Y8, Phone: 902-835-2623, donbell@accesswave.ca Web: www.bellknives.com
Specialties: Fancy knives: carved and pierced folders of his own design. Patterns: Locking folders, pendant knives, jewelry knives. Technical: Grinds Damascus, pierces and carves blades. Prices: $500 to $2000, some to $3000. Remarks: Spare-time maker; first knife sold in 1993. Mark: Bell symbol with first initial inside.

BELL, MICHAEL, 88321 N. Bank Lane, Coquille, OR 97423, Phone: 541-396-3605, michael@dragonflyforge.com Web: www. Dragonflyforge.com
Specialties: Full line of combat quality Japanese swords. **Patterns:** Traditional tanto to katana. **Technical:** Handmade steel and welded cable. **Prices:** Swords from bare blades to complete high art $4500 to $28,000. **Remarks:** Studied with Japanese master Nakajima Mineyoshi. **Mark:** Dragonfly in shield or tombo kunimitsu.

BENDIK, JOHN, 7076 Fitch Rd., Olmsted Falls, OH 44138

BENJAMIN JR., GEORGE, 3001 Foxy Ln., Kissimmee, FL 34746, Phone: 407-846-7259
Specialties: Fighters in various styles to include Persian, Moro and military. **Patterns:** Daggers, skinners and one-of-a-kind grinds. **Technical:** Forges O1, D2, A2, 5160 and Damascus. Favors Pakkawood, Micarta, and mirror or Parkerized finishes. Makes unique para-military leather sheaths. **Prices:** $150 to $600; some to $1200. **Remarks:** Doing business as The Leather Box. **Mark:** Southern Pride Knives.

BENNETT, BRETT C., 1922 Morrie Ave., Cheyenne, WY 82001, Phone: 307-220-3919, brett@bennettknives.com Web: www.bennettknives.com
Specialties: Hand-rubbed finish on all blades. **Patterns:** Most fixed blade patterns. **Technical:** ATS-34, D-2, 1080/15N20 Damascus, 1080 forged. **Prices:** $100 and up. **Mark:** "B.C. Bennett" in script or "Bennett" stamped in script.

BENNETT, GLEN C., 5821 S. Stewart Blvd., Tucson, AZ 85706

BENNETT, PETER, PO Box 143, Engadine N.S.W. 2233, AUSTRALIA, Phone: 02-520-4975 (home), Fax: O2-528-8219 (work)
Specialties: Fancy and embellished working and using straight knives to customer specs and in standard patterns. **Patterns:** Fighters, hunters, bird/trout and fillet knives. **Technical:** Grinds 440C, ATS-34 and Damascus. Uses rare Australian desert timbers for handles. **Prices:** $90 to $500; some to $1500. **Remarks:** Full-time maker; first knife sold in 1985. **Mark:** First and middle initials, last name; country.

BENNICA, CHARLES, Chemin du Salet, 34190 Moules et Baucels, FRANCE, Phone: +33 4 67 73 42 40, b-ni-k@club-internet.fr
Specialties: Fixed blades and folding knives; the latter with slick closing mechanisms with push buttons to unlock blades. Unique handle shapes, signature to the maker. **Technical:** 416 stainless steel frames for folders and ATS-34 blades. Also specializes in Damascus.

BENSON, DON, 2505 Jackson St., #112, Escalon, CA 95320, Phone: 209-838-7921
Specialties: Working straight knives of his design. **Patterns:** Axes, Bowies, tantos and hunters. **Technical:** Grinds 440C. **Prices:** $100 to $150; some to $400. **Remarks:** Spare-time maker; first knife sold in 1980. **Mark:** Name.

BENTLEY, C.L., 2405 Hilltop Dr., Albany, GA 31707, Phone: 912-432-6656

BER, DAVE, 656 Miller Rd., San Juan Island, WA 98250, Phone: 206-378-7230
Specialties: Working straight and folding knives for the sportsman; welcomes customer designs. **Patterns:** Hunters, skinners, Bowies, kitchen and fishing knives. **Technical:** Forges and grinds saw blade steel, wire Damascus, O1, L6, 5160 and 440C. **Prices:** $100 to $300; some to $500. **Remarks:** Full-time maker; first knife sold in 1985. **Mark:** Last name.

BERG, LOTHAR, 37 Hillcrest Ln., Kitchener ON, CANADA NZK 1S9, Phone: 519-745-3260
519-745-3260

BERGER, MAX A., 5716 John Richard Ct., Carmichael, CA 95608, Phone: 916-972-9229, bergerknives@aol.com
Specialties: Fantasy and working/using straight knives of his design. **Patterns:** Fighters, hunters and utility/camp knives. **Technical:** Grinds ATS-34 and 440C. Offers fileworks and combinations of mirror polish and satin finish blades. **Prices:** $200 to $600; some to $2500. **Remarks:** Part-time maker; first knife sold in 1992. **Mark:** Last name.

BERGH, ROGER, Dalkarlsa 291, 91598 Bygdea, SWEDEN, Phone: 44693430061, knivroger@hotmail.com Web: www.roger-bergh.nu
Specialties: Collectible all-purpose straight-blade knives. Damascus steel blades, carving and artistic design knives are heavily influenced by nature and have an organic hand crafted feel.

BERGLIN, BRUCE D., 17441 Lake Terrace Place, Mount Vernon, WA 98274, Phone: 360-422-8603, bdb@fishersons.com
Specialties: Working and using straight knives of his own design. **Patterns:** Hunters, boots, Bowies, utility/camp knives and period pieces, some made to look old. **Technical:** Forges carbon steel, grinds carbon and stainless steel. Prefers natural handle material and micarta. **Prices:** Start at $300. **Remarks:** Part-time maker since 1998. **Mark:** First initial, middle initial and last name, sometimes surrounded with an oval.

BERTHOLUS, BERNARD, Atelier Du Brute, De Forge 21, Rue Fersen 06600, Antibes, FRANCE, Phone: 04 93 34 95 90
Specialties: Traditional working and using straight knives of his design. **Patterns:** Bowies, daggers and hunters. **Technical:** Forges ATS-34, 440, D2 and carbon steels. **Prices:** $750 to $7500. **Remarks:** Full-time maker; first knife sold in 1990. **Mark:** City and last name.

BERTOLAMI, JUAN CARLOS, Av San Juan 575, Neuquen, ARGENTINA 8300, fliabertolami@infovia.com.ar
Specialties: Hunting and country labor knives. All of them unique high quality pieces and supplies collectors too. **Technical:** Austrian stainless steel and elephant, hippopotamus and orca ivory, as well as ebony and other fine woods for the handles.

BERTUZZI, ETTORE, Via Partigiani 3, 24068 Seriate (Bergamo), ITALY, Phone: 035-294262, Fax: 035-294262
Specialties: Classic straight knives and folders of his design, to customer specs and in standard patterns. **Patterns:** Bowies, hunters and locking folders. **Technical:** Grinds ATS-34, D3, D2 and various Damascus. **Prices:** $300 to $500. **Remarks:** Part-time maker; first knife sold in 1993. **Mark:** Name etched on ricasso.

BESEDICK, FRANK E., 195 Stillwagon Rd, Ruffsdale, PA 15679, Phone: 724-696-3312, bxtr.bez3@verizon.net
Specialties: Traditional working and using straight knives of his design. **Patterns:** Hunters, utility/camp knives and miniatures; buckskinner blades and tomahawks. **Technical:** Forges and grinds 5160, O1 and Damascus. Offers filework and scrimshaw. **Prices:** $75 to $300; some to $750. **Remarks:** Part-time maker; first knife sold in 1990. **Mark:** Name or initials.

BESHARA, BRENT, 207 Cedar St., PO Box 1046, Stayner, ON, CANADA L0M 1S0, Phone: 705-428-3152, Fax: 705-428-5961, beshknives@sympatico.ca Web: www.beshknives.com
Specialties: Tactical fighting fixed knives. **Patterns:** Tantos, fighters, neck and custom designs. **Technical:** Grinds 0-1, L-6 and stainless upon request. Offers Kydex sheaths, does own Paragon heat treating. **Prices:** Start at $150. **Remarks:** Part-time maker. Active serving military bomb tech driver. **Mark:** "BESH" stamped.

BETHKE, LORA SUE, 13420 Lincoln St., Grand Haven, MI 49417, Phone: 616-842-8268, Fax: 616-844-2696, lspb@compuserve.com
Specialties: Classic and traditional straight knives of her design. **Patterns:** Boots, Bowies and hunters. **Technical:** Forges 1084 and Damascus. **Prices:** Start at $400. **Remarks:** Part-time maker; first knife sold in 1997. **Mark:** Full name - JS on reverse side. **Other:** Journeyman bladesmith, American Bladesmith Society.

BEUKES, TINUS, 83 Henry St., Risiville, Vereeniging 1939, SOUTH AFRICA, Phone: 27 16 423 2053
Specialties: Working straight knives. **Patterns:** Hunters, skinners and kitchen knives. **Technical:** Grinds D2, 440C and chain, cable and stainless Damascus. **Prices:** $80 to $180. **Remarks:** Part-time maker; first knife sold in 1993. **Mark:** Full name, city, logo.

BEVERLY II, LARRY H., PO Box 741, Spotsylvania, VA 22553, Phone: 540-898-3951
Specialties: Working straight knives, slip-joints and liner locks. Welcomes customer designs. **Patterns:** Bowies, hunters, guard less fighters and miniatures. **Technical:** Grinds 440C, A2 and O1. **Prices:** $125 to $1000. **Remarks:** Part-time maker; first knife sold in 1986. **Mark:** Initials or last name in script.

BEZUIDENHOUT, BUZZ, 30 Surlingham Ave., Malvern, Queensburgh, Natal 4093, SOUTH AFRICA, Phone: 031-4632827, Fax: 031-3631259
Specialties: Traditional working and using straight knives of his design and to customer specs. **Patterns:** Boots, hunters, kitchen knives and utility/camp knives. **Technical:** Grinds 12C27, 440C and ATS-34. Uses local hardwoods; horn; kudu, impala, buffalo; giraffe bone and ivory for handles. **Prices:** $150 to $200; some to $1500. **Remarks:** Spare-time maker; first knife sold in 1988. **Mark:** First name with a bee emblem.

BIGGERS, GARY, Ventura Knives, 1278 Colina Vista, Ventura, CA 93003, Phone: 805-658-6610, Fax: 805-658-6610
Specialties: Fixed blade knives of his design. **Patterns:** Hunters, boots/fighters, Bowies and utility knives. **Technical:** Grinds ATS-34, 01 and commercial Damascus. **Prices:** $150 to $550. **Remarks:** Part-time maker; first knife sold in 1996. Doing business as Ventura Knives. **Mark:** First and last name, city and state.

BILLGREN, PER, STALLGATAN 9, S815 76 Soderfors, SWEDEN, Phone: +46 293 30600, Fax: +46 293 30124, mail@damasteel.se
Specialties: Damasteel, stainless Damascus steels. **Patterns:** Bluetounge, Heimskringla, Muhammed's ladder, Rose twist, Odin's eye, Vinland, Hakkapelliitta. **Technical:** Modern Damascus steel made by patented powder metallurgy method. **Prices:** $80 to $180. **Remarks:** Damasteel is available through distributors around the globe.

BIRDWELL, IRA LEE, PO Box 1135, Bagdad, AZ 86321, Phone: 520-633-2516
Specialties: Special orders. **Mark:** Engraved signature.

BIRNBAUM, EDWIN, 9715 Hamocks Blvd. I 206, Miami, FL 33196

BISH, HAL, 9347 Sweetbriar Trace, Jonesboro, GA 30236, Phone: 770-477-2422, hal-bish@hp.com

BIZZELL, ROBERT, 145 Missoula Ave., Butte, MT 59701, Phone: 406-782-4403, patternweld2@cs.com
Specialties: Damascus. **Patterns:** Composite, mosaic and traditional. **Technical:** Only fixed blades at this time. **Prices:** Start at $150. **Mark:** Hand signed.

BLACK, EARL, 3466 South, 700 East, Salt Lake City, UT 84106, Phone: 801-466-8395
Specialties: High-art straight knives and folders; period pieces. **Patterns:** Boots, Bowies and daggers; lockers and gents. **Technical:** Grinds 440C and 154CM. Buys some Damascus. Scrimshaws and engraves. **Prices:** $200 to $1800; some to $2500 and higher. **Remarks:** Full-time maker; first knife sold in 1980. **Mark:** Name, city, state.

BLACK, SCOTT, 570 Malcom Rd., Covington, GA 30209
Specialties: Working/using folders of his design. **Patterns:** Daggers, hunters, utility/camp knives and friction folders. **Technical:** Forges pattern welded, cable, 1095, O1 and 5160. **Prices:** $100 to $500. **Remarks:** Part-time maker; first knife sold in 1992. Doing business as Copperhead Forge. **Mark:** Hot mark on blade, copperhead snake.

BLACK, SCOTT, 27100 Leetown Rd., Picayune, MS 39466, Phone: 601-799-5939, copperheadforge@telepak.net
Specialties: Friction folders; fighters. **Patterns:** Bowies, fighters, hunters, smoke hawks, friction folders, daggers. **Technical:** All forged, all work done by me, own hand-stitched leather work; own heat-treating. **Prices:** $100 to $2200. **Remarks:** ABS Journeyman Smith. **Mark:** Hot Mark - Copperhead Snake. **Other:** Cabel / Damascus/ High Carbone.

BLACK, TOM, 921 Grecian N.W., Albuquerque, NM 87107, Phone: 505-344-2549, tblackknives@aol.com
Specialties: Working knives to fancy straight knives of his design. **Patterns:** Drop-point skinners, folders, locking knives, Bowies and daggers. **Technical:** Grinds 440C, 154CM, ATS-34, A2, D2 and Damascus. Offers engraving and scrimshaw. **Prices:** $250 and up; some over $8500. **Remarks:** Full-time maker; first knife sold in 1970. **Mark:** Name, city.

BLACKTON, ANDREW E., 12521 Fifth Isle, Bayonet Point, FL 34667, Phone: 727-869-1406
Specialties: Straight and folding knives, some fancy. **Patterns:** Hunters, Bowies and daggers. **Technical:** Grinds D2, 440C and 154CM. Offers some embellishment. **Prices:** $125 to $450; some to $2000. **Remarks:** Full-time maker. **Mark:** Last name in script.

BLACKWOOD, NEIL, 7032 Willow Run, Lakeland, FL 33813, Phone: 863-701-0126, neil@blackwoodknives.com Web: www.blackwoodknives.com
Specialties: Fixed blades and folders. **Technical:** Blade steels d-2 Talonite, Stellite, CPM S30V and RWL 34. Handle Materials G-10 carbon fiber and Micarta in the synthetics: giraffe bone and exotic woods on the natural side. **Remarks:** Makes everything from the frames to the stop pins, pivot pins-everything but the stainless screws; one factory/custom collaboration (the Hybrid Hunter) with Outdoor Edge is in place and negotiations were under way at press time for one with Benchmade.

BLANCHARD, G.R. (GARY), PO Box 709, Pigeon Forge, TN 37868, Phone: 865-908-7466, Fax: 865-908-7466, blanchardscutlery@yahoo.com Web: www.blanchardscutlery.com
Specialties: Fancy folders with patented button blade release and high-art straight knives of his design. **Patterns:** Boots, daggers and locking folders. **Technical:** Grinds 440C and ATS-34 and Damascus. Engraves his knives. **Prices:** $1500 to $18,000 or more. **Remarks:** Full-time maker; first knife sold in 1989. **Mark:** First and middle initials, last name or last name only.

BLASINGAME, ROBERT, 281 Swanson, Kilgore, TX 75662, Phone: 903-984-8144
Specialties: Classic working and using straight knives and folders of his design and to customer specs. **Patterns:** Bowies, daggers, fighters and hunters; one-of-a-kind historic reproductions. **Technical:** Hand-forges P.W. Damascus, cable Damascus and chain Damascus. **Prices:** $150 to $1000; some to $2000. **Remarks:** Full-time maker; first knife sold in 1968. **Mark:** 'B' inside anvil.

BLAUM, ROY, 319 N. Columbia St., Covington, LA 70433, Phone: 985-893-1060
Specialties: Working straight knives and folders of his design; lightweight easy-open folders. **Patterns:** Hunters, boots, fishing and woodcarving/whittling knives. **Technical:** Grinds A2, D2, O1, 154CM and ATS-34. Offers leatherwork. **Prices:** $40 to $800; some higher.

Remarks: Full-time maker; first knife sold in 1976. **Mark:** Engraved signature or etched logo.

BLOOMER, ALAN T., 116 E. 6th St., Maquon, IL 61458, Phone: 309-875-3583
Specialties: All Damascus folders, making own Damascus. **Patterns:** Bowies, Folders, chef etc. **Technical:** Does own heat treating. **Prices:** $400 to $1000. **Remarks:** Part-time maker; Guild member. **Mark:** Stamp Bloomer. **Other:** No orders.

BLOOMQUIST, R. GORDON, 6206 Tiger Trail Dr., Olympia, WA 98512, Phone: 360-352-7162, bloomquistr@energy.wsu.edu

BLUM, CHUCK, 743 S. Brea Blvd., #10, Brea, CA 92621, Phone: 714-529-0484
Specialties: Art and investment daggers and Bowies. **Technical:** Flat-grinds; hollow-grinds 440C, ATS-34 on working knives. **Prices:** $125 to $8500. **Remarks:** Part-time maker; first knife sold in 1985. **Mark:** First and middle initials and last name with sailboat logo.

BLUM, KENNETH, 1729 Burleson, Brenham, TX 77833, Phone: 979-836-9577
Specialties: Traditional working straight knives of his design. **Patterns:** Camp knives, Hunters and Bowies. **Technical:** Forges 5160; grinds 440C and D2. Uses exotic woods and Micarta for handles. **Prices:** $150 to $300. **Remarks:** Part-time maker; first knife sold in 1978. **Mark:** Last name on ricasso.

BOARDMAN, GUY, 39 Mountain Ridge R., New Germany 3619, SOUTH AFRICA, Phone: 031-726-921
Specialties: American and South African-styles. **Patterns:** Bowies, American and South African hunters, plus more. **Technical:** Grinds Bohler steels, some ATS-34. **Prices:** $100 to $600. **Remarks:** Part-time maker; first knife sold in 1986. **Mark:** Name, city, country.

BOATRIGHT, BASEL, 11 Timber Point, New Braunfels, TX 78132, Phone: 210-609-0807
Specialties: Working and using knives of his design. **Patterns:** Hunters, skinners and utility/camp knives. **Technical:** Grinds and hand-tempers 5160. **Prices:** $75 to $300. **Remarks:** Part-time maker. **Mark:** Stamped BBB.

BOCHMAN, BRUCE, 183 Howard Place, Grants Pass, OR 97526, Phone: 503-471-1985
Specialties: Working straight knives in standard patterns. **Patterns:** Bowies, hunters, fishing and bird knives. **Technical:** 440C; mirror or satin finish. **Prices:** $140 to $250; some to $750. **Remarks:** Part-time maker; first knife sold in 1977. **Mark:** Custom blades by B. Bochman.

BODEN, HARRY, Via Gellia Mill, Bonsall Matlock, Derbyshire DE4 2AJ, ENGLAND, Phone: 0629-825176
Specialties: Traditional working straight knives and folders of his design. **Patterns:** Hunters, locking folders and utility/camp knives. **Technical:** Grinds Sandvik 12C27, D2 and O1. **Prices:** £70 to £150; some to £300. **Remarks:** Full-time maker; first knife sold in 1986. **Mark:** Full name.

BODNER, GERALD "JERRY", 4102 Spyglass Ct., Louisville, KY 40229, Phone: 502-968-5946
Specialties: Fantasy straight knives in standard patterns. **Patterns:** Bowies, fighters, hunters and micro-miniature knives. **Technical:** Grinds Damascus, 440C and D2. Offers filework. **Prices:** $35 to $180. **Remarks:** Part-time maker; first knife sold in 1993. **Mark:** Last name in script and JAB in oval above knives.

BODOLAY, ANTAL, Rua Wilson Soares Fernandes #31, Planalto, Belo Horizonte MG-31730-700, BRAZIL, Phone: 031-494-1885
Specialties: Working folders and fixed blades of his design or to customer specs; some art daggers and period pieces. **Patterns:** Daggers, hunters, locking folders, utility knives and Khukris. **Technical:** Grinds D6, high-carbon steels and 420 stainless. Forges files on request. **Prices:** $30 to $350. **Remarks:** Full-time maker; first knife sold in 1965. **Mark:** Last name in script.

BOEHLKE, GUENTER, Parkstrasse 2, 56412 Grossholbach, GERMANY 2602-5440, Boehlke-Messer@t-online.de Web: www.boehlke-messer.de
Specialties: Classic working/using straight knives of his design. **Patterns:** Hunters, utility/camp knives and ancient remakes. **Technical:** Grinds Damascus, CPM-T-440V and 440C. Inlays gemstones and ivory. **Prices:** $220 to $700; some to $2000. **Remarks:** Spare-time maker; first knife sold in 1985. **Mark:** Name, address and bow and arrow.

BOGUSZEWSKI, PHIL, PO Box 99329, Lakewood, WA 98499, Phone: 253-581-7096, knives01@aol.com
Specialties: Working folders—some fancy—mostly of his design. **Patterns:** Folders, slip-joints and lockers; also makes anodized titanium frame folders. **Technical:** Grinds BG42 and Damascus; offers filework. **Prices:** $550 to $3000. **Remarks:** Full-time maker; first knife sold in 1979. **Mark:** Name, city and state.

BOJTOS, ARPA D., Dobsinskeho 10, 98403 Lucenec, Slovakia, Phone: 00421-47 4333512, botjos@stonline.sk
    Specialties: Art Knives. **Patterns:** Daggers, fighters and hunters. **Technical:** Grinds ATS-34. Carves on steel, handle materials and sheaths. **Prices:** $2000 to $5000; some to $8000. **Remarks:** Full-time maker; first knife sold in 1990. **Mark:** AB.

BOLD, STU, 63 D'Andrea Tr., Sarnia, Ont., CANADA N7S 6H3, Phone: 519-383-7610, sbold@sar.hookup.net
    Specialties: Traditional working/using straight knives in standard patterns and to customer specs. **Patterns:** Boots, Bowies and hunters. **Technical:** Grinds ATS-34, 440C and Damascus; mosaic pins. Offers scrimshaw and hand-tooled leather sheaths. **Prices:** $140 to $500; some to $2000. **Remarks:** Part-time maker; first knife sold in 1983. **Mark:** Name, city, province.

BOLEWARE, DAVID, PO Box 96, Carson, MS 39427, Phone: 601-943-5372
    Specialties: Traditional and working/using straight knives of his design, to customer specs and in standard patterns. **Patterns:** Bowies, hunters and utility/camp knives. **Technical:** Grinds ATS-34, 440C and Damascus. **Prices:** $85 to $350; some to $600. **Remarks:** Part-time maker; first knife sold in 1989. **Mark:** First and last name, city, state.

BOLTON, CHARLES B., PO Box 6, Jonesburg, MO 63351, Phone: 636-488-5785
    Specialties: Working straight knives in standard patterns. **Patterns:** Hunters, skinners, boots and fighters. **Technical:** Grinds 440C and ATS-34. **Prices:** $100 to $300; some to $600. **Remarks:** Full-time maker; first knife sold in 1973. **Mark:** Last name.

BONASSI, FRANCO, Via Nicoletta 4, Pordenone 33170, ITALY, Phone: 0434-550821, bonassi.f@schmidt.it
    Specialties: Fancy and working one-of-a-kind straight knives of his design. **Patterns:** Hunters,utility and folders liner locks. **Technical:** Grinds CPM, ATS-34, 154CM and commercial Damascus. Uses only titanium foreguards and pommels. **Prices:** Start at $250. **Remarks:** Spare-time maker; first knife sold in 1988. Has made cutlery for several celebrities; Gen. Schwarzkopf, Fuzzy Zoeller, etc. **Mark:** FRANK.

BOOCO, GORDON, 175 Ash St., PO Box 174, Hayden, CO 81639, Phone: 970-276-3195
    Specialties: Fancy working straight knives of his design and to customer specs. **Patterns:** Hunters and Bowies. **Technical:** Grinds 440C, D2 and A2. Heat-treats. **Prices:** $150 to $350; some $600 and higher. **Remarks:** Part-time maker; first knife sold in 1984. **Mark:** Last name with push dagger artwork.

BOOS, RALPH, 5107 40 Ave., Edmonton, Alberta, CANADA T6L 1B3, Phone: 780-463-7094
    Specialties: Classic, fancy and fantasy miniature knives and swords of his design or to customer specs. **Patterns:** Bowies, daggers and swords. **Technical:** Hand files O1, stainless and Damascus. Engraves and carves. Does heat bluing and acid etching. **Prices:** $125 to $350; some to $1000. **Remarks:** Part-time maker; first knife sold in 1982. **Mark:** First initials back to back.

BOOTH, PHILIP W., 301 S. Jeffery Ave., Ithaca, MI 48847, Phone: 989-875-2844
    Specialties: Folding knives, various mechanisms, maker of the "minnow" series small folding knife. **Patterns:** Auto lock backs, liner locks, classic pattern multi-blades. **Technical:** Grinds ATS-34, 440C, 1095 and commercial Damascus. Prefers natural materials, offers file work and scrimshaw. **Prices:** $200 and up. **Remarks:** Full-time maker; first knife sold in 1991. **Mark:** Last name or name with city and map logo.

BORGER, WOLF, Benzstrasse 8, 76676 Graben-Neudorf, GERMANY, Phone: 07255-72303, Fax: 07255-72304, wolfgmesserschmied.de Web: www.messerschmied.de
    Specialties: High-tech working and using straight knives and folders, many with corkscrews or other tools, of his design. **Patterns:** Hunters, Bowies and folders with various locking systems. **Technical:** Grinds 440C, ATS-34 and CPM. Uses stainless Damascus. **Prices:** $250 to $900; some to $1500. **Remarks:** Full-time maker; first knife sold in 1975. **Mark:** Howling wolf and name; first name on Damascus blades.

BOSE, REESE, PO Box 61, Shelburn, IN 47879, Phone: 812-397-5114
    Specialties: Traditional working and using knives in standard patterns and multi-blade folders. **Patterns:** Multi-blade slip-joints. **Technical:** ATS-34, D2 and CPM 440V. **Prices:** $275 to $1500. **Remarks:** Full-time maker; first knife sold in 1992. Photos by Jack Busfield. **Mark:** R. Bose.

BOSE, TONY, 7252 N. County Rd., 300 E., Shelburn, IN 47879-9778, Phone: 812-397-5114
    Specialties: Traditional working and using knives in standard patterns; multi-blade folders. **Patterns:** Multi-blade slip-joints. **Technical:** Grinds commercial Damascus, ATS-34 and D2. **Prices:** $400 to $1200.

    Remarks: Full-time maker; first knife sold in 1972. **Mark:** First initial, last name, city, state.

BOSSAERTS, CARL, Rua Albert Einstein 906, 14051-110, Ribeirao Preto, S.P. BRAZIL, Phone: 016 633 7063
    Specialties: Working and using straight knives of his design, to customer specs and in standard patterns. **Patterns:** Hunters, fighters and utility/camp knives. **Technical:** Grinds ATS-34, 440V and 440C; does filework. **Prices:** 60 to $400. **Remarks:** Part-time maker; first knife sold in 1992. **Mark:** Initials joined together.

BOST, ROGER E., 30511 Cartier Dr, Palos Verdes, CA 90275-5629, Phone: 310- 541-6833, rogerbost@cox.net
    Specialties: Hunters, fighters, boot, utility. **Patterns:** Loveless-style. **Technical:** ATS-34, 60-61RC, stock removal and forge. **Prices:** $300 and up. **Remarks:** First knife sold in 1990. **Mark:** Diamond with initials inside and Palos Verdes California around outside. **Other:** Cal. Knifemakers Assn, ABS.

BOSTWICK, CHRIS T., 341 Robins Run, Burlington, WI 53105, c.bostwick@wi.rr.com or ceebozz @hotmail.com
    Specialties: Slipjoints ATS-34. **Patterns:** English jack, gunstock jack, doctors, stockman. **Prices:** $300 and up. **Remarks:** Enjoy traditional patterns/history multiblade slipjoints. **Mark:** CTB.

BOSWORTH, DEAN, 329 Mahogany Dr., Key Largo, FL 33037, Phone: 305-451-1564
    Specialties: Free hand hollow ground working knives with hand rubbed satin finish, filework and inlays. **Patterns:** Bird and Trout, hunters, skinners, filet, Bowies, miniatures. **Technical:** Using 440C, ATS-34, D2, Meier Damascus, custom wet formed sheaths. **Prices:** $250 and up. **Remarks:** Part-time maker; first knife made in 1985. **Mark:** BOZ stamped in block letters. **Other:** Member: Florida Knifemakers Assoc.

BOURBEAU, JEAN YVES, 15 Rue Remillard, Notre Dame, Ile Perrot, Quebec, CANADA J7V 8M9, Phone: 514-453-1069
    Specialties: Fancy/embellished and fantasy folders of his design. **Patterns:** Bowies, fighters and locking folders. **Technical:** Grinds 440C, ATS-34 and Damascus. Carves precious wood for handles. **Prices:** $150 to $1000. **Remarks:** Part-time maker; first knife sold in 1994. **Mark:** Interlaced initials.

BOUSE, D. MICHAEL, 1010 Victoria Pl., Waldorf, MD 20602, Phone: 301-843-0449
    Specialties: Traditional and working/using straight knives of his design. **Patterns:** Daggers, fighters and hunters. **Technical:** Forges 5160 and Damascus; grinds D2; differential hardened blades; decorative handle pins. **Prices:** $125 to $350. **Remarks:** Spare-time maker; first knife sold in 1992. Doing business as Michael's Handmade Knives. **Mark:** Etched last name.

BOWEN, TILTON, 189 Mt Olive Rd., Baker, WV 26801, Phone: 304-897-6159
    Specialties: Straight, stout working knives. **Patterns:** Hunters, fighters and boots; also offers buckskinner and throwing knives. All his D2-blades since 1st of year, 1997 are Deep Cryogenic processed. **Technical:** Grinds D2 and 4140. **Prices:** $60 to $275. **Remarks:** Full-time maker; first knife sold in 1982-1983. Sells wholesale to dealers. **Mark:** Initials and BOWEN BLADES, WV.

BOWLES, CHRIS, PO Box 985, Reform, AL 35481, Phone: 205-375-6162
    Specialties: Working/using straight knives, and period pieces. **Patterns:** Utility, tactical, hunting, neck knives, machetes, and swords. **Grinds:** 0-1, 154 cm, BG-42, 440V. **Prices:** $50 to $400 some higher. **Remarks:** Full-time maker. **Mark:** Bowles stamped or Bowles etched in script.

BOXER, BO, LEGEND FORGE, 6477 Hwy. 93 S #134, Whitefish, MT 59937, Phone: 505-799-0173, legendforge@aol.com Web: www.legendforgesknives.com
    Specialties: Handmade hunting knives, Damascus hunters. Most are antler handled. Also, hand forged Damascus steel. **Patterns:** Hunters and Bowies. **Prices:** $125 to $2500 on some very exceptional Damascus knives. **Mark:** The name "Legend Forge" hand engraved on every blade. **Additional:** Makes his own custom leather sheath stamped with maker stamp. His knives are used by the outdoorsman of the Smoky Mountains, North Carolina, and the Rockies of Montana and New Mexico. **Other:** Spends one-half of the year in Montana and the other part of the year in Taos New Mexico.

BOYD, FRANCIS, 1811 Prince St., Berkeley, CA 94703, Phone: 510-841-7210
    Specialties: Folders and kitchen knives; Japanese swords. **Patterns:** Push-button sturdy locking folders; San Francisco-style chef's knives. **Technical:** Forges and grinds; mostly uses high-carbon steels. **Prices:** Moderate to heavy. **Remarks:** Designer. **Mark:** Name.

BOYE, DAVID, PO Box 1238, Dolan Springs, AZ 86441, Phone: 800-853-1617, Fax: 928-767-3030, boye@ctaz.com Web: ww.boyeknives.com
 Specialties: Folders, hunting and kitchen knives. Forerunner in the use of dendritic steel and dendritic cobalt for blades. **Patterns:** BN Lockback folders, kitchen knives and hunting knives. **Technical:** Casts blades in stainless 440Cand cobalt. **Prices:** From $129 to $500. **Remarks:** Full-time maker; author of *Step-by-Step Knifemaking*; **Mark:** Name.

BOYER, MARK, 10515 Woodinville Dr., #17, Bothell, WA 98011, Phone: 206-487-9370, boyerbl@mail.eskimo.com
 Specialties: High-tech and working/using straight knives of his design. **Patterns:** Fighters and utility/camp knives. **Technical:** Grinds 1095 and D2. Offers Kydex sheaths; heat-treats. **Prices:** $45 to $120. **Remarks:** Part-time maker; first knife sold in 1994. Doing business as Boyer Blades. **Mark:** Eagle holding two swords with name.

BOYSEN, RAYMOND A., 125 E. St. Patrick, Rapid Ciy, SD 57701, Phone: 605-341-7752
 Specialties: Hunters and Bowies. **Technical:** High performance blades forged from 52100 and 5160. **Prices:** $200 and up. **Remarks:** American Bladesmith Society Journeyman Smith. **Mark:** BOYSEN. **Other:** Part-time bladesmith.

BRACK, DOUGLAS D., 119 Camino Ruiz, #71, Camirillo, CA 93012, Phone: 805-987-0490
 Specialties: Working straight knives of his design. **Patterns:** Heavy-duty skinners, fighters and boots. **Technical:** Grinds 440C, ATS-34 and 5160; forges cable. **Prices:** $90 to $180; some to $300. **Remarks:** Part-time maker; first knife sold in 1984. **Mark:** tat.

BRADBURN, GARY, BRADBURN CUSTOM CUTLERY, 1714 Park Place, Wichita, KS 67203, Phone: 316-269-4273, steeldust5@aol.com Web: www.angelfire.com/bc2bradburnknives/
 Specialties: Specialize in clay-tempered Japanese-style knives and swords. **Patterns:** Also Bowies and fighers. **Technical:** Forge and/or grind carbon steel only. **Prices:** $150 to $1200. **Mark:** Initials GB stylized to look like Japanese character.

BRADFORD, GARRICK, 582 Guelph St., Kitchener ON, CANADA N2H-5Y4, Phone: 519-576-9863

BRADLEY, DENNIS, 2410 Bradley Acres Rd., Blairsville, GA 30512, Phone: 706-745-4364
 Specialties: Working straight knives and folders, some high-art. **Patterns:** Hunters, boots and daggers; slip-joints and two-blades. **Technical:** Grinds ATS-34, D2, 440C and commercial Damascus. **Prices:** $100 to $500; some to $2000. **Remarks:** Part-time maker; first knife sold in 1973. **Mark:** BRADLEY KNIVES in double heart logo.

BRADLEY, JOHN, PO Box 37, Pomona Park, FL 32181, Phone: 904-649-4739
 Specialties: Fixed-blade using knives. **Patterns:** Skinners, Bowies, camp knives and Sgian Dubhs. **Technical:** Hand forged from 52100, 1095 and own Damascus. **Prices:** $125 to $500; some higher. **Remarks:** Part-time maker; first knife sold in 1988. **Mark:** Last name.

BRADSHAW, BAILEY, PO Box 564, Diana, TX 75640, Phone: 903-968-2029, bailey@bradshawcutlery.com
 Specialties: Traditional folders and contemporary front lock folders. **Patterns:** Single or multi-blade folders. **Technical:** Grind CPM 3V, CPM 440V, CPM 420V, Forge Damascus, 52100. **Prices:** $250 to $3000. **Remarks:** Engraves, carves and does sterling silver sheaths. **Mark:** Tori arch over initials back to back.

BRANDON, MATTHEW, 4435 Meade St., Denver, CO 80211, Phone: 303-458-0786, MTBRANDON@HOTMAIL.COM
 Specialties: Hunters, skinners, full-tang Bowies. **Prices:** $100 to $250. **Remarks:** Satisfaction or full refund. **Mark:** MTB.

BRANDSEY, EDWARD P., 335 Forest Lake Dr., Milton, WI 53563, Phone: 608-868-9010, edchar2@ticon.net
 Specialties: Large Bowies. Does own scrimshaw. See Egnath's second book. **Patterns:** Hunters, fighters, Bowies and daggers, some buckskinner-styles. Native American influence on some. An occasional tanto. **Technical:** ATS-34, 440-C, 0-1, and some Damascus. Paul Bos treating past 20 years. **Prices:** $250 to $600; some to $3000. **Remarks:** Full-time maker. First knife sold in 1973. **Mark:** Initials connected - registered Wisc. Trademark since March 1983.

BRANDT, MARTIN W., 833 Kelly Blvd., Springfield, OR 97477, Phone: 541-747-5422, oubob747@aol.com

BRANTON, ROBERT, 4976 Seewee Rd., Awendaw, SC 29429, Phone: 843-928-3624
 Specialties: Working straight knives of his design or to customer specs; throwing knives. **Patterns:** Hunters, fighters and some miniatures. **Technical:** Grinds ATS-34, A2 and 1050; forges 5160, O1. Offers hollow- or convex-grinds. **Prices:** $25 to $400. **Remarks:** Part-time maker; first knife sold in 1985. Doing business as Pro-Flyte, Inc. **Mark:** Last name; or first and last name, city, state.

BRATCHER, BRETT, 11816 County Rd. 302, Plantersville, TX 77363, Phone: 936-894-3788, Fax: (936) 894-3790, brett_bratcher@msn.com
 Specialties: Hunting and skinning knives. **Patterns:** Clip and Drop Point. Hand forged. **Technical:** Material 5160, D2, 1095 and Damascus. **Price:** $200 to $500. **Mark:** Bratcher.

BRAY JR., W. LOWELL, 6931 Manor Beach Rd., New Port Richey, FL 34652, Phone: 727-846-0830, brayknives@aol.com
 Specialties: Traditional working and using straight knives and folders of his design. **Patterns:** Hunters, fighters and utility knives. **Technical:** Grinds 440C and ATS-34; forges 52100 and Damascus. **Prices:** $100 to $500. **Remarks:** Spare-time maker; first knife sold in 1992. **Mark:** Lowell Bray Knives in shield.

BREED, KIM, 733 Jace Dr., Clarksville, TN 37040, Phone: 931-645-9171, sfbreed@yahoo.com Web: www.bwbladeworks.com
 Specialties: High end through working folders and straight knives. **Patterns:** Hunters, fighters, daggers, Bowies. His design or customers. Likes one-of-a-kind designs. **Technical:** Makes own Mosiac and regular Damascus, but will use stainless steels. Offers filework and sculpted material. **Prices:** $150 to $2000. **Remarks:** Full-time maker. First knife sold in 1990. **Mark:** Last name.

BREND, WALTER, 353 Co. Rd. 1373, Vinemont, AL 35179, Phone: 256-739-1987
 Specialties: Tactical-style knives, fighters, automatics. **Technical:** Grinds D-Z and 440C blade steels, 154CM steel. **Prices:** Micarta handles, titanium handles.

BRENNAN, JUDSON, PO Box 1165, Delta Junction, AK 99737, Phone: 907-895-5153, Fax: 907-895-5404
 Specialties: Period pieces. **Patterns:** All kinds of Bowies, rifle knives, daggers. **Technical:** Forges miscellaneous steels. **Prices:** Upscale, good value. **Remarks:** Muzzle-loading gunsmith; first knife sold in 1978. **Mark:** Name.

BRESHEARS, CLINT, 1261 Keats, Manhattan Beach, CA 90266, Phone: 310-372-0739, Fax: 310-372-0739, breshears@mindspring.com Web: www.clintknives.com
 Specialties: Working straight knives and folders. **Patterns:** Hunters, Bowies and survival knives. Folders are mostly hunters. **Technical:** Grinds 440C, 154CM and ATS-34; prefers mirror finishes. **Prices:** $125 to $750; some to $1800. **Remarks:** Part-time maker; first knife sold in 1978. **Mark:** First name.

BREUER, LONNIE, PO Box 877384, Wasilla, AK 99687-7384
 Specialties: Fancy working straight knives. **Patterns:** Hunters, camp knives and axes, folders and Bowies. **Technical:** Grinds 440C, AEB-L and D2; likes wire inlay, scrimshaw, decorative filing. **Prices:** $60 to $150; some to $300. **Remarks:** Part-time maker; first knife sold in 1977. **Mark:** Signature.

BRIGHTWELL, MARK, 21104 Crockside Dr., Leander, TX 78641, Phone: 512-267-4110
 Specialties: Fancy and plain folders of his design. **Patterns:** Fighters, hunters and gents, some traditional. **Technical:** Hollow- or flat- grinds ATS-34, D2, custom Damascus; elaborate filework; heat-treats. Extensive choice of natural handle materials; no synthetics. **Prices:** $300 to $1500. **Remarks:** Full-time maker. **Mark:** Last name.

BRITTON, TIM, 5645 Murray Rd., Winston-Salem, NC 27106, Phone: 336-922-9582 Fax: 336-923-2062, tim@trimbritton.com Web: www.trimbritton.com
 Specialties: Small and simple working knives, sgian dubhs and special tactical designs. **Technical:** Forges and grinds stainless steel. **Prices:** $110 to $600. **Remarks:** Veteran knife maker. **Mark:** Etched signature.

BROADWELL, DAVID, PO Box 4314, Wichita Falls, TX 76308, Phone: 940-692-1727, Fax: 940-692-4003, david@broadwell.com Web: www.david.broadwell.com
 Specialties: Sculpted high-art straight and folding knives. **Patterns:** Daggers, sub-hilted fighters, folders, sculpted art knives and some Bowies. **Technical:** Grinds mostly Damascus; carves; prefers natural handle materials, including stone. Some embellishment. **Prices:** $350 to $3000; some higher. **Remarks:** Part-time maker; first knife sold in 1982. **Mark:** Stylized emblem bisecting "B"/with last name below.

BROCK, KENNETH L., PO Box 375, 207 N Skinner Rd., Allenspark, CO 80510, Phone: 303-747-2547, brockknives@nedernet.net
 Specialties: Custom designs, Full-tang working knives and button lock folders of his design. **Patterns:** Hunters, miniatures and minis. **Technical:** Flat-grinds D2 and 440C; makes own sheaths; heat-treats. **Prices:** $50 to $500. **Remarks:** Full-time maker; first knife sold in 1978. **Mark:** Last name, city, state and serial number.

BRODZIAK, DAVID, 27 Stewart St, Albany, WESTERN AUSTRALIA 6330, Phone: 61 8 9841 3314, Fax: 61898115065, brodziakomninet.net.au. Web: www.brodziakcustomknives.com

BROMLEY, PETER, Bromley Knives, 1408 S Bettman, Spokane, WA 99212, Phone: 509-534-4235, Fax: 509-536-2666
 Specialties: Period Bowies, folder, hunting knives; all sizes and shapes. **Patterns:** Bowies, boot knives, hunters, utility, folder, working knives. **Technical:** High-carbon steel (1084, 1095 and 5160). Stock removal and forge. **Prices:** $85 to $750. **Remarks:** Almost full-time, first knife sold in 1987. A.B.S. Journeyman Smith. **Mark:** Bromley, Spokane, WA.

BROOKER, DENNIS, Rt. 1, Box 12A, Derby, IA 50068, Phone: 515-533-2103
 Specialties: Fancy straight knives and folders of his design. **Patterns:** Hunters, folders and boots. **Technical:** Forges and grinds. Full-time engraver and designer; instruction available. **Prices:** Moderate to upscale. **Remarks:** Part-time maker. Takes no orders; sells only completed work. **Mark:** Name.

BROOKS, BUZZ, 2345 Yosemite Dr., Los Angles, CA 90041, Phone: 323-256-2892

BROOKS, MICHAEL, 2811 64th St, Lubbock, TX 79413, Phone: 806-799-3088, chiang@nts-online.net
 Specialties: Working straight knives of his design or to customer specs. **Patterns:** Martial art, Bowies, hunters, and fighters. **Technical:** Grinds 440C, D2 and ATS-34; offers wide variety of handle materials. **Prices:** $75 & up. **Remarks:** Part-time maker; first knife sold in 1985. **Mark:** Initials.

BROOKS, STEVE R., 1610 Dunn Ave., Walkerville, MT 59701, Phone: 406-782-5114
 Specialties: Working straight knives and folders; period pieces. **Patterns:** Hunters, Bowies and camp knives; folding lockers; axes, tomahawks and buckskinner knives; swords and stilettos. **Technical:** Forges O1, Damascus and mosaic Damascus. Some knives come embellished. **Prices:** $150 to $2000. **Remarks:** Full-time maker; first knife sold in 1982. **Mark:** Lazy initials.

BROOME, THOMAS A., 1212 E. Aliak Ave., Kenai, AK 99611-8205, Phone: 907-283-9128, tomlei@ptialaska.ent Web: www.alaskanknives.com
 Specialties: Working hunters and folders **Patterns:** Traditional and custom orders. **Technical:** Grinds ATS-34, BG-42, CPM-S30V. **Prices:** $175 to $350. **Remarks:** Full-time maker; first knife sold in 1979. Doing business as Thom's Custom Knives. **Mark:** Full name, city, state. **Other:** Doing business as: Alaskan Man O; Steel Knives.

BROTHERS, ROBERT L., 989 Philpott Rd., Colville, WA 99114, Phone: 509-684-8922
 Specialties: Traditional working and using straight knives and folders of his design and to customer specs. **Patterns:** Bowies, fighters and hunters. **Technical:** Grinds D2; forges Damascus. Makes own Damascus from saw steel wire rope and chain; part-time goldsmith and stone-setter. **Prices:** $100 to $400; some higher. **Remarks:** Part-time maker; first knife sold in 1986. **Mark:** Initials and year made.

BROWER, MAX, 2016 Story St., Boone, IA 50036, Phone: 515-432-2938
 Specialties: Working/using straight knives. **Patterns:** Bowies, hunters and boots. **Technical:** Grinds 440C and ATS-34. **Prices:** Start at $150. **Remarks:** Spare-time maker; first knife sold in 1981. **Mark:** Last name.

BROWN, DENNIS G., 1633 N. 197TH Pl., Shoreline, WA 98133, Phone: 206-542-3997, denjilbro@msn.com

BROWN, JIM, 1097 Fernleigh Cove, Little Rock, AR 72210

BROWN, HAROLD E., 3654 N.W. Hwy. 72, Arcadia, FL 34266, Phone: 863-494-7514, brknives@strato.net
 Specialties: Fancy and exotic working knives. **Patterns:** Folders, sliplock, locking several kinds. **Technical:** Grinds D2, 440C and ATS-34. Embellishment available. **Prices:** $175 to $1000. **Remarks:** Part-time maker; first knife sold in 1976. **Mark:** Name and city with logo.

BROWNE, RICK, 980 West 13th St., Upland, CA 91786, Phone: 909-985-1728
 Specialties: Sheffield pattern pocket knives. **Patterns:** Hunters, fighters and daggers. No heavy-duty knives. **Technical:** Grinds ATS-34. **Prices:** Start at $450. **Remarks:** Part-time maker; first knife sold in 1975. **Mark:** R.E. Browne, Upland, CA.

BROWN, ROB E., PO Box 15107, Emerald Hill 6011, Port Elizabeth, SOUTH AFRICA, Phone: 27-41-3661086, Fax: 27-41-4511731, rbknives@global.co.za
 Specialties: Contemporary-designed straight knives and period pieces. **Patterns:** Utility knives, hunters, boots, fighters and daggers. **Technical:** Grinds 440C, D2, ATS-34 and commercial Damascus. Knives mostly mirror finished; African handle materials. **Prices:** $100 to $1500.

 Remarks: Full-time maker; first knife sold in 1985. **Mark:** Name and country.

BROWN, TROY L., 22945 W. 867 Rd., Park Hill, OK 74451, Phone: 918-457-4128
 Specialties: Working and using knives and folders. **Patterns:** Bowies, hunters, folders and scagel-style. **Technical:** Forges 5160, 52100, 1084; makes his own Damascus. Prefers stag, wood and Micarta for handles. Offers engraved bolsters and guards. **Prices:** $150 to $750. **Remarks:** Full-time maker; first knife sold in 1994. Knives. **Mark:** Troy Brown. **Other:** Doing business as Elk Creek Forge.

BROWNING, STEVEN W., 3400 Harrison Rd., Benton, AR 72015, Phone: 501-316-2450

BRUNCKHORST, LYLE, Country Village, 23706 7th Ave. SE, Ste. B, Bothell, WA 98021, Phone: 425-402-3484, bronks@net-tech.com Web: bronks.com or bronksknifeworks.com
 Specialties: Traditional working and using straight knives and folders of his design. **Patterns:** Bowies, hunters and locking folders. **Technical:** Grinds ATS-34; forges 5160 and his own Damascus. Iridescent RR spike knives. Offers scrimshaw, inlays and animal carvings in horn handles. **Prices:** $225 to $750; some to $3750. **Remarks:** Full-time maker; first knife sold in 1976. Doing business as Bronk's Knife works. **Mark:** Bucking horse.

BRUNER JR., FRED, BRUNER BLADES, E10910W Hilldale Dr., Fall Creek, WI 54742, Phone: 715-877-2496, brunerblades@msn.com
 Specialties: Pipe tomahawks, swords, may my own.**Patterns:** Drop point hunters. **Prices:** $65.00 to $1,500.00. **Remarks:** Voting member of the knifemakers guild. **Mark:** Fred Bruner.

BRUNETTA, DAVID, PO Box 4972, Laguna Beach, CA 92652, Phone: 714-497-9611
 Specialties: Straights, folders and art knives. **Patterns:** Bowies, camp/hunting, folders, fighters. **Technical:** Grinds ATS-34, D2, BG42. forges O1, 52100, 5160, 1095, makes own Damascus. **Prices:** $300 to $9000. **Mark:** Circle DB logo with last name straight or curved.

BRYAN, TOM, 14822 S Gilbert Rd., Gilbert, AZ 85296, Phone: 480-812-8529
 Specialties: Straight and folding knives. **Patterns:** Drop-point hunter fighters. **Technical:** ATS-34, 154CM, 440C and A2. **Prices:** $150 to $800. **Remarks:** Part-time maker; sold first knife in 1994. **Mark:** T. Bryan. **Other:** DBA as T. Bryan Knives.

BUCHMAN, BILL, 63312 South Rd., Bend, OR 97701, Phone: 503-382-8851
 Specialties: Working straight knives. **Patterns:** Hunters, Bowies, fighters and boots. Makes full line of leather craft and saddle maker knives. **Technical:** Forges 440C and Sandvik 15N20. Prefers 440C for saltwater. **Prices:** $95 to $400. **Remarks:** Full-time maker; first knife sold in 1982. **Mark:** Initials or last name.

BUCHNER, BILL, PO Box 73, Idleyld Park, OR 97447, Phone: 541-498-2247, blazinhammer@earthlink.net Web: www.home.earthlin.net/~blazinghammer
 Specialties: Working straight knives, kitchen knives and high-art knives of his design. **Technical:** Uses W1, L6 and his own Damascus. Invented "spectrum metal" for letter openers, folder handles and jewelry. Likes sculpturing and carving in Damascus. **Prices:** $40 to $3000; some higher. **Remarks:** Full-time maker; first knife sold in 1978. **Mark:** Signature.

BUCHOLZ, MARK A., PO Box 82, Holualoa, HI 96725, Phone: 808-322-4045
 Specialties: Liner lock folders. **Patterns:** Hunters and fighters. **Technical:** Grinds ATS-34. **Prices:** Upscale. **Remarks:** Full-time maker; first knife sold in 1976. **Mark:** Name, city and state in buffalo skull logo or signature.

BUCKBEE, DONALD M., 243 South Jackson Trail, Grayling, MI 49738, Phone: 517-348-1386
 Specialties: Working straight knives, some fancy, in standard patterns; concentrating on kitchen knives. **Patterns:** Kitchen knives, hunters, Bowies. **Technical:** Grinds D2, 440C, ATS-34. Makes ultra-lights in hunter patterns. **Prices:** $100 to $250; some to $350. **Remarks:** Part-time maker; first knife sold in 1984. **Mark:** Antlered bee—a buck bee.

BUCKNER, JIMMIE H., PO Box 162, Putney, GA 31782, Phone: 229-436-4182
 Specialties: Camp knives, Bowies (one-of-a-kind), liner-lock folders, tomahawks, camp axes, neck knives for law enforcement and hide-out knives for body guards and professional people. **Patterns:** Hunters, camp knives, Bowies. **Technical:** Forges 1084, 5160 and Damascus (own), own heat treats. **Prices:** $195 to $795 and up. **Remarks:** Full-time maker; first knife sold in 1980, ABS Master Smith. **Mark:** Name over spade.

BUEBENDORF, ROBERT E., 108 Lazybrooke Rd., Monroe, CT 06468, Phone: 203-452-1769
Specialties: Traditional and fancy straight knives of his design. **Patterns:** Hand-makes and embellishes belt buckle knives. **Technical:** Forges and grinds 440C, O1, W2, 1095, his own Damascus and 154CM. **Prices:** $200 to $500. **Remarks:** Full-time maker; first knife sold in 1978. **Mark:** First and middle initials, last name and MAKER.

BULLARD, BILL, Rt. 5, Box 35, Andalusia, AL 36420, Phone: 334-222-9003
Specialties: Traditional working and using straight knives and folders of his design. **Patterns:** Hunters, slip-joint folders and utility/camp knives and folders to customer specs. **Technical:** Forges Damascus, cable. Offers filework. **Prices:** $100 to $500; some to $1500. **Remarks:** Part-time maker; first knife sold in 1974. Doing business as Five Runs Forge. **Mark:** Last name stamped on ricasso.

BULLARD, RANDALL, 7 Mesa Dr., Canyon, TX 79015, Phone: 806-655-0590
Specialties: Working/using straight knives and folders of his design or to customer specs. **Patterns:** Hunters, locking folders and slip-joint folders. **Technical:** Grinds O1, ATS-34 and 440C. Does file work. **Prices:** $125 to $300; some to $500. **Remarks:** Part-time maker; first knife sold in 1993. Doing business as Bullard Custom Knives. **Mark:** First and middle initials, last name, maker, city and state.

BULLARD, TOM, 117 MC 8068, Flippin, AR 72634, Phone: 870-453-3421, tbullard@bullshoals.net Web: www.natconet.com/~tbullard
Specialties: Armadillo handle material on hunter and folders. **Patterns:** Bowies, hunters, single and 2-blade trappers, lockback folders. **Technical:** Grinds 440-C, ATS-34, 0-1, commercial Damascus. **Prices:** $150 and up. **Remarks:** Offers filework and engraving by Norvell Foster and Terry Thies. Does not make screw-together knives. **Mark:** T Bullard.

BUMP, BRUCE D., 1103 Rex Ln., Walla Walla, WA 99362, Phone: 509 522-2219, bruceandkaye@charter.net Web: www.brucebumpknives.com
Specialties: Traditional and Mosaic Damascus. **Patterns:** Black powder pistol/knife combinations also gun/hawk. **Technical:** Enjoy the 15th-18th century "dual threat" weapons. **Prices:** $350 to $10,000. **Remarks:** American Bladesmith Society Master Smith 2003. **Mark:** Bruce D. Bump Bruce D Bump Custom Walla Walla WA.

BURAK, CHET, KNIFE SERVICES PHOTOGRAPHER, PO Box 14383, E Providence, RI 02914, Phone: 401-431-0625, Fax: 401-434-9821

BURDEN, JAMES, 405 Kelly St., Burkburnett, TX 76354

BURGER, FRED, Box 436, Munster 4278, Kwa-Zulu Natal, SOUTH AFRICA, Phone: 27 393216, Web: www.swordcane.com
Specialties: Sword canes and tactical walking sticks. **Patterns:** 440C and carbon steel blades. **Technical:** Double hollow ground and Poniard-style blades. **Prices:** $190 to $600. **Remarks:** Full-time maker with son, Barry, since 1987. **Mark:** Last name in oval pierced by a dagger. **Other:** Member South African Guild.

BURGER, PON, 12 Glenwood Ave., Woodlands, Bulawayo, Zimbabwe 75514
Specialties: Collector's items. **Patterns:** Fighters, locking folders of traditional styles, buckles. **Technical:** Scrimshaws 440C blade. Uses polished buffalo horn with brass fittings. Cased in buffalo hide book. **Prices:** $450 to $1100. **Remarks:** Full-time maker; first knife sold in 1973. Doing business as Burger Products. **Mark:** Spirit of Africa.

BURKE, BILL, 12 chapman ln., Boise, ID 83716, Phone: 208-756-3797, burke531@salmoninternet.com
Specialties: Hand-forged working knives. **Patterns:** Fowler pronghorn, clip point and drop point hunters. **Technical:** Forges 52100 and 5160. Makes own Damascus from 15N20 and 1084. **Prices:** $450 and up. **Remarks:** Dedicated to fixed-blade high-performance knives. ABS journeyman. **Mark:** Initials connected. **Other:** Also make "Ed Fowler" miniatures.

BURKE, DAN, 22001 Ole Barn Rd., Edmond, OK 73034, Phone: 405-341-3406, Fax: 405-340-3333
Specialties: Slip joint folders. **Patterns:** Traditional folders. **Technical:** Grinds D2 and BG-42. Prefers natural handle materials; heat-treats. **Prices:** $440 to $1900. **Remarks:** Full-time maker; first knife sold in 1976. **Mark:** First initial and last name.

BURNETT, MAX, 537 Old Dug Mtn. Rd., Paris, AR 72855, Phone: 501-963-2767, mburnett@cswnet.com
Specialties: Forging with coal/charcoal; some stock removal. **Patterns:** Hunters, Bowies, camp, tactical, neck knives and kydex sheaths. **Technical:** Steels used: 1084, 1095, 52100, 5160, L6, 01 and others available. **Prices:** $50 and up for neck knives/Bowies $250 and up. **Remarks:** Full-time since March 2000. **Mark:** M.OGG and omega symbol.

BURRIS, PATRICK R., 11078 Crystal Lynn C.t, Jacksonville, FL 32226, Phone: 904-757-3938, keenedge@comcast.net
Specialties: Traditional straight knives. **Patterns:** Hunters, bowies, locking liner folders. **Technical:** Flat grinds CPM stainless and Damascus. **Remarks:** Charter member Florida Knifemakers Association. Member Knifemakers Guild. **Mark:** Last name in script.

BURROWS, CHUCK, Wild Rose Trading Co, PO Box 5174, Durango, CO 81301, Phone: 970-259-8396, chuck@wrtcleather.com Web: www.wrtcleather.com
Specialties: Presentation knives, hawks, and sheaths based on the styles of the American frontier incorporating carving, beadwork, rawhide, braintan, and other period correct materials. We also make other period style knives such as Scottish Dirks and Moorish jambiyahs. **Patterns:** Bowies, Dags, tomahawks, war clubs, and all other 18th and 19th century frontier style edged weapons and tools. **Technical:** Carbon steel only: 5160, 1080/1084, 1095, O1, Damascus-Our Frontier Shear Steel, plus other styles, available on request. Forged knives, hawks, etc. are made in collaborations with bladesmiths. Gib Guignard (under the name of Cactus Rose) and Mark Williams (under the name UB Forged). Blades are usually forge finished and all items are given an aged period look. **Prices:** $500.00 plus. **Remarks:** Full-time maker, first knife sold in 1973. 40+ years experience working leather. **Mark:** A lazy eight or lazy eight with a capital T at the center. On leather either the lazy eight with T or a WRTC makers stamp.

BURROWS, STEPHEN R., 3532 Michigan, Kansas City, MO 64109, Phone: 816-921-1573
Specialties: Fantasy straight knives of his design, to customer specs and in standard patterns; period pieces. **Patterns:** Fantasy, bird and trout knives, daggers, fighters and hunters. **Technical:** Forges 5160 and 1095 high-carbon steel, O1 and his Damascus. Offers lost wax casting in bronze or silver of cross guards and pommels. **Prices:** $65 to $600; some to $2000. **Remarks:** Full-time maker; first knife sold in 1983. Doing business as Gypsy Silk. **Mark:** Etched name.

BUSFIELD, JOHN, 153 Devonshire Circle, Roanoke Rapids, NC 27870, Phone: 252-537-3949, Fax: 252-537-8704, busfield@charter.net Web: www.busfieldknives.com
Specialties: Investor-grade folders; high-grade working straight knives. **Patterns:** Original price-style and trailing-point interframe and sculpted-frame folders, drop-point hunters and semi-skinners. **Technical:** Grinds 154CM and ATS-34. Offers interframes, gold frames and inlays; uses jade, agate and lapis. **Prices:** $275 to $2000. **Remarks:** Full-time maker; first knife sold in 1979. **Mark:** Last name and address.

BUSSE, JERRY, 11651 Co. Rd. 12, Wauseon, OH 43567, Phone: 419-923-6471
Specialties: Working straight knives. **Patterns:** Heavy combat knives and camp knives. **Technical:** Grinds D2, A2, INFI. **Prices:** $1100 to $3500. **Remarks:** Full-time maker; first knife sold in 1983. **Mark:** Last name in logo.

BUTLER, BART, 822 Seventh St., Ramona, CA 92065, Phone: 760-789-6431

BUXTON, BILL, 155 Oak Bend Rd, Kaiser, MO 65047, Phone: 573-348-3577, camper@yhti.net Web: www.geocites.com/buxtonknives
Specialties: Forged fancy and working straight knives and folders. Mostly one-of-a-kind pieces. **Patterns:** Fighters, daggers, bowies, hunters, linerlock folders, axes and tomahawks. **Technical:** Forges 52100, 0-1, 1080. Makes his own Damascus (mosaic and random patterns) from 1080, 1095, 15n20, and powdered metals 1084 and 4800a. Offers sterling silver inlay, n/s pin patterning and pewter pouring on axe and hawk handles. **Prices:** $300 to $1500. **Remarks:** Full-time maker, sold first knife in 1998. **Mark:** First and last name.

BUTLER, JOHN, 777 Tyre Rd., Havana, FL 32333, Phone: 850-539-5742
Specialties: Hunters, Bowies, period. **Technical:** Damascus, 52100, 5160, L6 steels. **Prices:** $80 and up. **Remarks:** Making knives since 1986. **Mark:** JB. **Other:** Journeyman (ABS).

BUTLER, JOHN R., 20162 6th Ave. N.E., Shoreline, WA 98155, Phone: 206-362-3847, rjjjrb@sprynet.com

BYBEE, BARRY J., 795 Lock Rd. E., Cadiz, KY 42211-8615
Specialties: Working straight knives of his design. **Patterns:** Hunters, fighters, boot knives, tantos and Bowies. **Technical:** Grinds ATS-34, 440C. Likes stag and Micarta for handle materials. **Prices:** $125 to $200; some to $1000. **Remarks:** Part-time maker; first knife sold in 1968. **Mark:** Arrowhead logo with name, city and state.

BYRD, WESLEY L., 189 Countryside Dr., Evensville, TN 37332, Phone: 423-775-3826, w.l.byrd@worldnet.att.net
Specialties: Hunters, fighters, Bowies, dirks, sign dubh, utility, and camp knives. **Patterns:** Wire rope, random patterns.Twists, W's, Ladder, Kite Tail. **Technical:** Uses 52100, 1084, 5160, L6, and 15n20. **Prices:**

Starting at $180. **Remarks:** Prefer to work with customer for their design preferences. **Mark:** BYRD, WB<X. **Other:** ABS Journeyman Smith.

C

CABE, JERRY (BUDDY), 62 McClaren Ln., Hattieville, AR 72063, Phone: 501-354-3581

CABRERA, SERGIO B., 25711 Frampton Ave. Apt. 113, Harbor City, CA 90710

CAFFREY, EDWARD J., 2608 Central Ave. West, Great Falls, MT 59404, Phone: 406-727-9102, ed@caffreyknives.net Web: www.caffreyknives.net
Specialties: One-of-a-kind, collector quality pieces, working/using knives; will accept some customer designs. **Patterns:** Folders, Bowies, hunters, fighters, camp/utility, some hawks and hatchets. **Technical:** Forges his own mosaic Damascus, 52100, 6150, 1080/1084, W-1, W-2, some cable and/or chain Damascus. Offers S30V for those who demand stainless. **Prices:** Starting at $140; typical hunters start at $350; prices for exotic mosaic Damascus pieces can range to $5000. **Remarks:** Retired military; ABS Master Smith. Full-time maker; first knife sold in 1989. **Mark:** Stamped last name with MS on straight knives. Etched last name with MS on folders.

CAIRNES JR., CARROLL B., RT. 1 Box 324, Palacios, TX 77465, Phone: 369-588-6815

CALDWELL, BILL, 255 Rebecca, West Monroe, LA 71292, Phone: 318-323-3025
Specialties: Straight knives and folders with machined bolsters and liners. **Patterns:** Fighters, Bowies, survival knives, tomahawks, razors and push knives. **Technical:** Owns and operates a very large, well-equipped blacksmith and bladesmith shop extant with six large forges and eight power hammers. **Prices:** $400 to $3500; some to $10,000. **Remarks:** Full-time maker and self-styled blacksmith; first knife sold in 1962. **Mark:** Wild Bill and Sons.

CALLAHAN, ERRETT, 2 Fredonia, Lynchburg, VA 24503, Phone: 434-528-3444
Specialties: Obsidian knives. **Patterns:** Modern-styles and Stone Age replicas. **Technical:** Flakes and knaps to order. **Prices:** $100 to $3400. **Remarks:** Part-time maker; first flint blades sold in 1974. **Mark:** Blade—engraved name, year and arrow; handle—signed edition, year and unit number.

CALLAHAN, F. TERRY, PO Box 880, Boerne, TX 78006, Phone: 830-981-8274, Fax: 830-981-8279, ftclaw@gvtc.com
Specialties: Custom hand-forged edged knives, collectible and functional. **Patterns:** Bowies, folders, daggers, hunters & camp knives . **Technical:** Forges 5160, 1095 and his own Damascus. Offers filework and handmade sheaths. **Prices:** $125 to $2000. **Remarks:** First knife sold in 1990. **Mark:** Initials inside a keystone symbol. **Other:** ABS/Journeyman Bladesmith.

CALVERT JR., ROBERT W. (BOB), 911 Julia, PO Box 858, Rayville, LA 71269, Phone: 318-728-4113, Fax: (318) 728-0000, rcalvert@bayou.com
Specialties: Using and hunting knives; your design or mine. Since 1990. **Patterns:** Forges own Damascus; all patterns. **Technical:** 5160, D2, 52100, 1084. Prefers natural handle material. **Prices:** $150 and up. **Remarks:** TOMB Member ABS, Journeyman Smith. **Mark:** Calvert (Block) J S.

CAMERER, CRAIG, 3766 Rockbridge Rd, Chesterfield, IL 62630, Phone: 618-753-2147, craig@camererknives.com Web: www.camererknives.com
Specialties: Everyday carry knives, hunters and Bowies. **Patterns:** D-guard, historical recreations and fighters. **Technical:** Most of his knives are forged to shape. **Prices:** $100 and up. **Remarks:** Member of the ABS and PKA. Journeyman Smith ABS.

CAMERON, RON G., PO Box 183, Logandale, NV 89021, Phone: 702-398-3356, rntcameron@mvdsl.com
Specialties: Fancy and embellished working/using straight knives and folders of his design. **Patterns:** Bowies, hunters and utility/camp knives. **Technical:** Grinds ATS-34, AEB-L and Devin Thomas Damascus or my own Damascus from 1084 and 15N20. Does filework, fancy pins, mokume fittings. Uses exotic hardwoods, stag and Micarta for handles. Pearl & mammoth ivory. **Prices:** $175 to $850 some to $1000. **Remarks:** Part-time maker; first knife sold in 1994. Doing business as Cameron Handmade Knives. **Mark:** Last name, town, state or last name.

CAMERON HOUSE, 2001 Delaney Rd. Se., Salem, OR 97306, Phone: 503-585-3286
Specialties: Working straight knives. **Patterns:** Hunters, Bowies, Fighters. **Technical:** Grinds ATS-34, 530V, 154CM. **Remarks:** Part-time maker, first knife. sold in 1993. **Prices:** $150 and up. **Mark:** HOUSE.

CAMPBELL, COURTNAY M., PO Box 23009, Columbia, SC 29224, Phone: 803-787-0151

CAMPBELL, DICK, 196 Garden Homes Dr, Colville, WA 99114, Phone: 509-684-6080, dicksknives@aol.com
Specialties: Working straight knives, period pieces. **Patterns:** Hunters, fighters, boots: 19th century Bowies. **Technical:** Grinds 440C, 154CM. **Prices:** $200 to $2500. **Remarks:** Full-time maker. First knife sold in 1975. **Mark:** Name.

CAMPOS, IVAN, R.XI de Agosto, 107, Tatui, SP, BRAZIL 18270-000, Phone: 00-55-15-2518092, Fax: 00-55-15-2594368, ivan@ivancampos.com Web: www.ivancompos.com
Specialties: Brazilian handmade and antique knives.

CANDRELLA, JOE, 1219 Barness Dr., Warminster, PA 18974, Phone: 215-675-0143
Specialties: Working straight knives, some fancy. **Patterns:** Daggers, boots, Bowies. **Technical:** Grinds 440C and 154CM. **Prices:** $100 to $200; some to $1000. **Remarks:** Part-time maker; first knife sold in 1985. Does business as Franjo. **Mark:** FRANJO with knife as J.

CANNADY, DANIEL L., Box 301, Allendale, SC 29810, Phone: 803-584-2813, Fax: 803-584-2813
Specialties: Working straight knives and folders in standard patterns. **Patterns:** Drop-point hunters, Bowies, skinners, fishing knives with concave grind, steak knives and kitchen cutlery. **Technical:** Grinds D2, 440C and ATS-34. **Prices:** $65 to $325; some to $1000. **Remarks:** Full-time maker; first knife sold in 1980. **Mark:** Last name above Allendale, S.C.

CANNON, DAN, 9500 Leon, Dallas, TX 75217, Phone: 972-557-0268
Specialties: Damascus, hand forged. **Patterns:** Bowies, hunters, folders. **Prices:** $300. **Remarks:** Full-time maker. **Mark:** CANNON D.

CANNON, RAYMOND W., PO Box 1412, Homer, AK 99603, Phone: 907-235-7779
Specialties: Fancy working knives, folders and swords of his design or to customer specs; many one-of-a-kind pieces. **Patterns:** Bowies, daggers and skinners. **Technical:** Forges and grinds O1, A6, 52100, 5160, his combinations for his own Damascus. **Remarks:** First knife sold in 1984. **Mark:** Cannon Alaska or "Hand forged by Wes Cannon".

CANOY, ANDREW B., 3420 Fruchey Ranch Rd., Hubbard Lake, MI 49747, Phone: 810-266-6039, canoy1@shianet.org

CANTER, RONALD E., 96 Bon Air Circle, Jackson, TN 38305, Phone: 731-668-1780, canterr@charter.net
Specialties: Traditional working knives to customer specs. **Patterns:** Beavertail skinners, Bowies, hand axes and folding lockers. **Technical:** Grinds A1, 440C and 154CM. **Prices:** $65 to $250; some $500 and higher. **Remarks:** Spare-time maker; first knife sold in 1973. **Mark:** Three last initials intertwined.

CANTRELL, KITTY D., 19720 Hwy. 78, Ramona, CA 92076, Phone: 760-788-8304

CAPDEPON, RANDY, 553 Joli Rd., Carencro, LA 70520, Phone: 318-896-4113, Fax: 318-896-8753
Specialties: Straight knives and folders of his design. **Patterns:** Hunters and locking folders. **Technical:** Grinds ATS-34, 440C and D2. **Prices:** $200 to $600. **Remarks:** Part-time maker; first knife made in 1992. Doing business as Capdepon Knives. **Mark:** Last name.

CAPDEPON, ROBERT, 829 Vatican Rd., Carencro, LA 70520, Phone: 337-896-8753, Fax: 318-896-8753
Specialties: Traditional straight knives and folders of his design. **Patterns:** Boots, hunters and locking folders. **Technical:** Grinds ATS-34, 440C and D2. Hand-rubbed finish on blades. Likes natural horn materials for handles, including ivory. Offers engraving. **Prices:** $250 to $750. **Remarks:** Full-time maker; first knife made in 1992. **Mark:** Last name.

CAREY JR., CHARLES W., 1003 Minter Rd., Griffin, GA 30223, Phone: 770-358-8994
Specialties: Working and using knives of his design and to customer specs; period pieces. **Patterns:** Fighters, hunters, utility/camp knives and forged-to-shape miniatures. **Technical:** Forges 5160, old files and cable. Offers filework; ages some of his knives. **Prices:** $35 to $400. **Remarks:** Part-time maker; first knife sold in 1991. **Mark:** Knife logo.

CARILLO, DWAINE, C/O AIRKAT KNIVES, 1021 SW 15th St, Moore, OK 73160, Phone: 405-503-5879, Web: www.airkatknives.com

CARLISLE, FRANK, 5930 Hereford, Detroit, MI 48224, Phone: 313-882-8349
Specialties: Fancy/embellished and fantasy folders of his design. **Patterns:** Hunters, locking folders and swords. **Technical:** Grinds Damascus and stainless. **Prices:** $80 to $300. **Remarks:** Full-time maker; first knife sold in 1993. Doing business as Carlisle Cutlery. **Mark:** Last name.

CARLISLE, JEFF, PO Box 282 12753 Hwy. 200, Simms, MT 59477, Phone: 406-264-5693

CARLSON, KELLY, 54 S. Holt Hill, Antrim, NH 03440, Phone: 603-588-2765, kellycarlson@tds.net Web: www.carlsonknives.com **Specialties:** Unique folders of maker's own design. **Patterns:** One-of-a-kind, artistic folders, mostly of liner-lock design, along with interpretations of traditional designs. **Technical:** Grinds and heat treats S30V, D2, ATS-34, stainless and carbon Damascus steels. Prefers hand sanded finishes and natural ivories and pearls, in conjunction with decorative accents obtained from mosaic Damascus, Damascus and various exotic materials. **Prices:** $600 to $3500. **Remarks:** Full-time maker as of 2002, first knife sold in 1975.

CARNAHAN, CHARLES A., 27 George Arnold Lane, Green Spring, WV 26722, Phone: 304-492-5891 **Specialties:** Hand forged fixed blade knives. **Patterns:** Bowies and hunters. **Technical:** Steels used; 5160, 1095, 1085, L6 and A023-E. **Prices:** $300 to $2000. **Remarks:** Part-time maker. First knife sold in 1991. Knives all made by hand forging, no stock removal. **Mark:** Last name.

CAROLINA CUSTOM KNIVES, SEE TOMMY MCNABB

CARPENTER, RONALD W., RT. 4 Box 323, Jasper, TX 75951, Phone: 409-384-4087

CARR, TIM, 3660 Pillon Rd., Muskegon, MI 49445, Phone: 231-766-3582 **Specialties:** Hunters, camp knives. **Patterns:** Mine or yours. **Technical:** Hand forged 52100 and Damascus. **Prices:** $125 to $700. **Remarks:** Part-time maker. **Mark:** The letter combined from maker's initials TRC.

CARROLL, CHAD, 12182 McClelland, Grant, MI 49327, Phone: 231-834-9183, CHAD724@msn.com **Specialties:** Hunters, Bowies, folders, swords, tomahawks. **Patterns:** Fixed blades, folders. **Prices:** $100 to $2000. **Remarks:** ABS Journeyman-May 2002. **Mark:** (a backward C next to a forward C, maker's initials).

CARSON, HAROLD J. "KIT", 1076 Brizendine Lane, Vine Grove, KY 40175, Phone: 270 877-6300, Fax: 270 877 6338, KCKnives@bbtel.com Web: http: //ww.kvnet.org/knives Web: album- www.kitcarsonknives.com/album **Specialties:** Military fixed blades and folders; art pieces. **Patterns:** Fighters, D handles, daggers, combat folders and Crosslock-styles, tactical folders, tactical fixed blades. **Technical:** Grinds Stellite 6K, Talonite, CPM steels, Damascus. **Prices:** $400 to $750; some to $5000. **Remarks:** Full-time maker; first knife sold in 1973. **Mark:** Name stamped or engraved.

CARTER, FRED, 5219 Deer Creek Rd., Wichita Falls, TX 76302, Phone: 904-723-4020 **Specialties:** High-art investor-class straight knives; some working hunters and fighters. **Patterns:** Classic daggers, Bowies; interframe, stainless and blued steel folders with gold inlay. **Technical:** Grinds a variety of steels. Uses no glue or solder. Engraves and inlays. **Prices:** Generally upscale. **Remarks:** Full-time maker. **Mark:** Signature in oval logo.

CARTER, MURRAY M., PO Box 307, Vernonia, OR 97064, Phone: 503-429-0447, m_carter-cutlery@pop06.odn.ne.jp **Specialties:** Traditional Japanese cutlery, utilizing San soh ko (3 layer) or Kata-ha (two layer) blade construction. Laminated neck knives, traditional Japanese etc. **Patterns:** Works from over 200 standard Japanese and North American designs. **Technical:** Hot Forges and cold forges Hitachi white steel #1, Hitachi blue super steel exclusively. **Prices:** $30 to $3000. **Remarks:** Full-time maker. First knife sold in 1989. Owner and designer of "Muteki" brand knives. **Mark:** Name with Japanese character on forged pieces. "Muteki" with Japanese characters on stock-removal blades.

CASHEN, KEVIN R., 5615 Tyler St., Hubbardston, MI 48845, Phone: 989-981-6780, krcashen@mvcc.com Web: www.cashenblades.com **Specialties:** Working straight knives, high art pattern welded swords, traditional renaissance and ethnic pieces. **Patterns:** Hunters, Bowies, utility knives, swords, daggers. **Technical:** Forges 1095, 1084 and his own O1/L6 Damascus. **Prices:** $100 to $4000+. **Remarks:** Full-time maker; first knife sold in 1985. Doing business as Matherton Forge. **Mark:** Black letter Old English initials and Master Smith stamp.

CASTON, DARRIEL, 3725 Duran Circle, Sacramento, CA 95821, Phone: 916-359-0613, dcaston@surewest.net **Specialties:** Investment grade jade handle folders of his design and gentleman folders. **Patterns:** Folders; slipjoints and lockback. Will be making linerlocks in the near future. **Technical:** Small gentleman folders for office and desk warriors. Grinds ATS-34, 154CM, S30V and Damascus. **Prices:** $250 to $900. **Remarks:** Part-time maker; won best new maker at first show in Sept 2004. **Mark:** Etched rocket ship with "Darriel Caston" or just "Caston" on inside spring on Damascus and engraved knives.

CASTEEL, DIANNA, P.O .Box 63, Monteagle, TN 37356, Phone: 931-723-0851, ddcasteel@charter.net Web: wwwcasteelcustomknives.com **Specialties:** Small, delicate daggers and miniatures; most knives one-of-a-kind. **Patterns:** Daggers, boot knives, fighters and miniatures. **Technical:** Grinds 440C. **Prices:** Start at $350; miniatures start at $250. **Remarks:** Full-time maker. **Mark:** Di in script.

CASTEEL, DOUGLAS, PO Box 63, Monteagle, TN 37356, Phone: 931-723-0851, Fax: 931-723-1856, ddcasteel@charter.net Web: www.casteelcustomknives.com **Specialties:** One-of-a-kind collector-class period pieces. **Patterns:** Daggers, Bowies, swords and folders. **Technical:** Grinds 440C. Offers gold and silver castings. **Prices:** Upscale. **Remarks:** Full-time maker; first knife sold in 1982. **Mark:** Last name.

CATOE, DAVID R., 4024 Heutte Dr., Norfolk, VA 23518, Phone: 757-480-3191 **Technical:** Does own forging, Damascus and heat treatments. **Price:** $200 to $500; some higher. **Remarks:** Part-time maker; trained by Dan Maragni 1985-1988; first knife sold 1989. **Mark:** Leaf of a camillia.

CAWTHORNE, CHRISTOPHER A., PO Box 604, Wrangell, AK 99929 **Specialties:** High-carbon steel, cable wire rope, silver wire inlay. **Patterns:** Forge welded Damascus and wire rope, random pattern. **Technical:** Hand forged, 50 lb. little giant power hammer, W-2, 0-1, L6, 1095. **Prices:** $650 to $2500. **Remarks:** School ABS 1985 w/bill moran, hand forged, heat treat. **Mark:** Cawthorne, forged in stamp.

CENTOFANTE, FRANK, PO Box 928, Madisonville, TN 37354-0928, Phone: 423-442-5767, frankcentofante@bellsouth.net **Specialties:** Fancy working folders. **Patterns:** Lockers and liner locks. **Technical:** Grinds ATS-34; hand-rubbed satin finish on blades. **Prices:** $600 to $1200. **Remarks:** Full-time maker; first knife sold in 1968. **Mark:** Name, city, state.

CHAFFEE, JEFF L., 14314 N. Washington St., PO Box 1, Morris, IN 47033, Phone: 812-934-6350 **Specialties:** Fancy working and utility folders and straight knives. **Patterns:** Fighters, dagger, hunter and locking folders. **Technical:** Grinds commercial Damascus, 440C, ATS-34, D2 and O1. Prefers natural handle materials. **Prices:** $350 to $2000. **Remarks:** Part-time maker; first knife sold in 1988. **Mark:** Last name.

CHAMBERLAIN, CHARLES R., PO Box 156, Barren Springs, VA 24313-0156, Phone: 703-381-5137

CHAMBERLAIN, JOHN B., 1621 Angela St., Wenatchee, WA 98801, Phone: 509-663-6720 **Specialties:** Fancy working and using straight knives mainly to customer specs, though starting to make some standard patterns. **Patterns:** Hunters, Bowies and daggers. **Technical:** Grinds D2, ATS-34, M2, M4 and L6. **Prices:** $60 to $190; some to $2500. **Remarks:** Full-time maker; first knife sold in 1943. **Mark:** Name, city, state.

CHAMBERLAIN, JON A., 15 S. Lombard, E. Wenatchee, WA 98802, Phone: 509-884-6591 **Specialties:** Working and kitchen knives to customer specs; exotics on special order. **Patterns:** Over 100 patterns in stock. **Technical:** Prefers ATS-34, D2, L6 and Damascus. **Prices:** Start at $50. **Remarks:** First knife sold in 1986. Doing business as Johnny Custom Knifemakers. **Mark:** Name in oval with city and state enclosing.

CHAMBERLIN, JOHN A., 11535 Our Rd., Anchorage, AK 99516, Phone: 907-346-1524, Fax: 907-562-4583 **Specialties:** Art and working knives. **Patterns:** Daggers and hunters; some folders. **Technical:** Grinds ATS-34, 440C, A2, D2 and Damascus. Uses Alaskan handle materials such as oosic, jade, whale jawbone, fossil ivory. **Prices:** Start at $150. **Remarks:** Does own heat treating and cryogenic deep freeze. Full-time maker; first knife sold in 1984. **Mark:** Name over English shield and dagger.

CHAMBLIN, JOEL, 960 New Hebron Church Rd., Concord, GA 30206, Phone: 770-884-9055, Web: chamblinknives.com **Specialties:** Fancy and working folders. **Patterns:** Fancy locking folders, traditional, multi-blades and utility. **Technical:** Grinds ATS-34, 440V, BG-42 and commercial Damascus. Offers filework. **Prices:** Start at $300. **Remarks:** Full-time maker; first knife sold in 1989. **Mark:** Last name.

CHAMPAGNE, PAUL, 48 Brightman Rd., Mechanicville, NY 12118, Phone: 518-664-4179 **Specialties:** Rugged, ornate straight knives in the Japanese tradition. **Patterns:** Katanas, wakizashis, tantos and some European daggers. **Technical:** Forges and hand-finishes carbon steels and his own Damascus. Makes Tamahagane for use in traditional blades; uses traditional heat-treating techniques. **Prices:** Start at $750. **Remarks:** Has passed

all traditional Japanese cutting tests. Doing business as Twilight Forge. **Mark:** Three diamonds over a stylized crown.

CHAMPION, ROBERT, 1806 Plateau Ln, Amarillo, TX 79106, Phone: 806-359-0446, championknives@arn.net
Specialties: Traditional working straight knives. **Patterns:** Hunters, skinners, camp knives, Bowies, daggers. **Technical:** Grinds 440C and D2. **Prices:** $100 to $600. **Remarks:** Part-time maker; first knife sold in 1979. **Mark:** Last name with dagger logo, city and state. **Other:** Streamline hunters.

CHAPO, WILLIAM G., 45 Wildridge Rd., Wilton, CT 06897, Phone: 203-544-9424
Specialties: Classic straight knives and folders of his design and to customer specs; period pieces. **Patterns:** Boots, Bowies and locking folders. **Technical:** Forges stainless Damascus. Offers filework. **Prices:** $750 and up. **Remarks:** Full-time maker; first knife sold in 1989. **Mark:** First and middle initials, last name, city, state.

CHARD, GORDON R., 104 S. Holiday Lane, Iola, KS 66749, Phone: 620-365-2311, Fax: 620-365-2311, gchard@cox.net
Specialties: High tech folding knives in one-of-a-kind styles. **Patterns:** Liner locking folders of own design Some fixed blades. **Technical:** Clean work with attention to fit and finish. **Prices:** $150 to $2000. **Remarks:** First knife sold in 1983. **Other:** Blade steel mostly ATS-34 and 154CM, some CPM440V Vaso Wear and Damascus.

CHASE, ALEX, 208 E. Pennsylvania Ave., DeLand, FL 32724, Phone: 386-734-9918
Specialties: Historical steels, classic and traditional straight knives of his design and to customer specs. **Patterns:** Art, fighters and hunters. **Technical:** Forges O1-L6 Damascus, meteoric Damascus, 52100, 5160; uses fossil walrus and mastodon ivory etc. **Prices:** $150 to $1000; some to $3500. **Remarks:** Part-time maker; first knife sold in 1990. Doing business as Confederate Forge. **Mark:** Stylized initials-A.C.

CHASE, JOHN E., 217 Walnut, Aledo, TX 76008, Phone: 817-441-8331, jchaseknives@earthlink.net
Specialties: Straight high-tech working knives in standard patterns or to customer specs. **Patterns:** Hunters, fighters, daggers and Bowies. **Technical:** Grinds D2, 01, 440C; offers mostly satin finishes. **Prices:** Start at $235. **Remarks:** Part-time maker; first knife sold in 1974. **Mark:** Last name in logo.

CHASTAIN, WADE, Rt. 2, Box 137-A, Horse Shoe, NC 28742, Phone: 704-891-4803
Specialties: Fancy fantasy and high-art straight knives of his design; period pieces. Known for unique mounts. **Patterns:** Bowies, daggers and fighters. **Technical:** Grinds 440C, ATS-34 and O1. Engraves; offers jewelling. **Prices:** $400 to $1200; some to $2000. **Remarks:** Full-time maker; first knife sold in 1984. Doing business as The Iron Master. **Mark:** Engraved last name.

CHAUVIN, JOHN, 200 Anna St., Scott, LA 70583, Phone: 337-237-6138, Fax: 337-230-7980
Specialties: Traditional working and using straight knives of his design, to customer specs and in standard patterns. **Patterns:** Bowies, fighters, and hunters. **Technical:** Grinds ATS-34, 440C and O1 high-carbon. Paul Bos heat treating. Uses ivory, stag, oosic and stabilized Louisiana swamp maple for handle materials. Makes sheaths using alligator and ostrich. **Prices:** $200 and up. Bowies start at $500. **Remarks:** Part-time maker; first knife sold in 1995. **Mark:** Full name, city, state.

CHAUZY, ALAIN, 1 Rue de Paris, 21140 Seur-en-Auxios, FRANCE, Phone: 03-80-97-03-30, Fax: 03-80-97-34-14
Specialties: Fixed blades, folders, hunters, Bowies-scagel-style. **Technical:** Forged blades only. Steels used XC65, 07C, and own Damascus. **Prices:** Contact maker for quote. **Remarks:** Part-time maker. **Mark:** Number 2 crossed by an arrow and name.

CHAVAR, EDWARD V., 1830 Richmond Ave., Bethlehem, PA 18018, Phone: 610-865-1806
Specialties: Working straight knives to his or customer design specifications, folders, high art pieces and some forged pieces. **Patterns:** Fighters, hunters, tactical, straight and folding knives and high art straight and folding knives for collectors. **Technical:** Grinds ATS-34, 440C, L6, Damascus from various makers and uses Damascus Steel and Mokume of his own creation. **Prices:** Standard models range from $95 to $1500, custom and specialty up to $3000. **Remarks:** Full-time maker; first knife sold in 1990. **Mark:** Name, city, state or signature.

CHEATHAM, BILL, PO Box 636, Laveen, AZ 85339, Phone: 602-237-2786, blademan76@aol.com
Specialties: Working straight knives and folders. **Patterns:** Hunters, fighters, boots and axes; locking folders. **Technical:** Grinds 440C. **Prices:** $150 to $350; exceptional knives to $600. **Remarks:** Full-time maker; first knife sold in 1976. **Mark:** Name, city, state.

CHELQUIST, CLIFF, PO Box 91, Arroyo Grande, CA 93421, Phone: 805-489-8095
Specialties: Stylish pratical knives for the outdoorsman. **Patterns:** Trout and bird to camp knives. **Technical:** Grinds ATS-34. **Prices:** $90 to $250 and up. **Remarks:** Part-time maker, first knife sold in 1983. **Mark:** First initial and last name.

CHERRY, FRANK J., 3412 Tiley N.E., Albuquerque, NM 87110, Phone: 505-883-8643

CHEW, LARRY, 515 Cleveland Rd Unit A-9, Granbury, TX 76049, Phone: 817-326-0165, larry@larrychew.com WEB: www.larrychew.com
Specialties: High-tech folding knives. **Patterns:** Double action automatic and manual folding patterns of my design. **Technical:** CAD designed folders utilizing my roller bearing pivot design known as my "VooDoo". Double action automatic folders with a variety of obvious and disguised release mechanisms, some with lock-outs. **Prices:** Manual folders start at $475, double action autos start at $675. **Remarks:** Made and sold first knife in 1988, first folder in 1989. Full-time maker since 1997. **Mark** Name and location etched in blade, Damascus autos marked on spring inside frame. Earliest knives stamped LC.

CHOATE, MILTON, 1665 W. County 17-1/2, Somerton, AZ 85350, Phone: 928-627-7251, mccustom@juno.com
Specialties: Classic working and using straight knives of his design, to customer specs and in standard patterns. **Patterns:** Bowies, hunters and utility/camp knives. **Technical:** Grinds 440C; grinds and forges 1095 and 5160. Does filework on top and guards on request. **Prices:** $200 to $800. **Remarks:** Full-time maker, first knife made in 1990. All knives come with handmade sheaths by Judy Choate. **Mark:** Knives marked "Choate".

CHRISTENSEN, JON P., 7814 Spear Dr., Shepherd, MT 59079, Phone: 406-373-0253, jbchris@aol.com Web: www.jonchristensenknives.com
Specialties: Patch knives, hunter/utility knives, Bowies, tomahawks. **Technical:** All blades forged, does all own work including sheaths. Forges 0-1, 1084, 52100, 5160. Damascus from 1084/15N20. **Prices:** $170 on up. **Remarks:** ABS Journeyman Smith, first knife sold in 1999. **Mark:** First and middle initial surrounded by last initial.

CHURCHMAN, T.W. (TIM), 475 Saddle Horn Drive, Bandera, TX 78003, Phone: 210-690-8641
Specialties: Fancy and traditional straight knives and single blade liner locking folders. Bird/trout knives of his design and to customer specs. **Patterns:** Bird/trout knives, fillet, Bowies, daggers, fighters, boot knives, some miniatures. **Technical:** Grinds 440C and D2. Offers stainless fittings, fancy filework, exotic and stabilized woods and hand sewed lined sheaths. Also flower pins as a style. **Prices:** $80 to $650; some to $1500. **Remarks:** Part-time maker; first knife made n 1981 after reading "KNIVES" "81". Doing business as "Custom Knives Churchman Made". **Mark:** Last name, dagger.

CLAIBORNE, JEFF, 1470 Roberts Rd., Franklin, IN 46131, Phone: 317-736-7443
Specialties: Multi blade slip joint folders.All one-of-a-kind by hand—no jigs or fixtures—swords, straight knives, period pieces, camp knives, hunters, fighters, ethnic swords all periods. Handle—uses stag, pearl, oosic, bone ivory, mastadon-mammoth, elephant or exotic woods. **Technical:** Forges high-carbon steel, makes Damascus, forges cable grinds, 01, 1095, 5160, 52100, L-6. **Prices:** $100 and up. **Remarks:** Part-time maker; first knife sold in 1989. **Mark:** Stylized initials in an oval.

CLAIBORNE, RON, 2918 Ellistown Rd., Knox, TN 37924, Phone: 615-524-2054, Bowie@icy.net
Specialties: Multi-blade slip joints, swords, straight knives. **Patterns:** Hunters, daggers, folders. **Technical:** Forges Damascus: mosaic, powder mosaic. Prefers bone and natural handle materials; some exotic woods. **Prices:** $125 to $2500. **Remarks:** Part-time maker; first knife sold in 1979. Doing business as Thunder Mountain Forge Claiborne Knives. **Mark:** Claiborne.

CLARK, D.E. (LUCKY), 126 Woodland St., Mineral Point, PA 15942, Phone: 814-322-4725
Specialties: Working straight knives and folders to customer specs. **Patterns:** Customer designs. **Technical:** Grinds D2, 440C, 154CM. **Prices:** $100 to $200; some higher. **Remarks:** Part-time maker; first knife sold in 1975. **Mark:** Name on one side; "Lucky" on other.

CLARK, HOWARD F., 115 35th Pl., Runnells, IA 50237, Phone: 515-966-2126, howard@mvforge.com Web: mvforge.com
Specialties: Currently Japanese-style swords. **Patterns:** Katana. **Technical:** Forges 1086, L6, 52100 and his own all tool steel Damascus; bar stock; forged blanks. **Prices:** $500 to $3000. **Remarks:** Full-time maker; first knife sold in 1979. Doing business as Morgan Valley Forge. **Prior Mark:** Block letters and serial number on folders; anvil/initials logo on straight knives. **Current Mark:** Two character kanji "Big Ear".

CLARK, NATE, 604 Baird Dr, Yoncalla, OR 97499, Phone: 541-680-5677, nateclarkknives@hotmail.com Web: www.nateclarkknives.com
 Specialties: Automatics (Push button and hidden release) ATS-34 mirror polish or satin finish, Damascus, Pearl, Ivory, Abalone, Woods, Bone, Micarta, G-10, filework and carving and sheath knives. **Prices:** $100 to $2500. **Remarks:** Fulltime knife maker since 1996. **Mark:** Nate Clark (located inside on spring).

CLARK, R.W., R.W. CLARK CUSTOM KNIVES, 1069 Golden Meadow, Corona, CA 92882, Phone: 909-279-3494, Fax: 909-279-4394, info@rwclarkknives.com Web: www.rwclarkknives.com
 Specialties: Military field knives and Asian hybrids. Hand carved leather sheaths. **Patterns:** Fixed blade hunters, field utility and military. Also presentation and collector grade knives. **Technical:** First maker to use liquid metals LM1 material in knives. Other materials include S30V, O1, stainless and carbon Damascus. **Prices:** $75 to $2000. Average price $300. **Remarks:** Started knife making in 1990 full-time in 2000. **Mark:** R.W. Clark., Custom., Corona, CA in standard football shape. Also uses three Japanese characters, spelling Clark, on Asian Hybrids.

CLAY, J.D., 65 Ellijay Rd, Greenup, KY 41144, Phone: 606-473-6769
 Specialties: Long known for cleanly finished, collector quality knives of functional design. **Patterns:** Practical hunters and locking folders. **Technical:** Grinds 440C–high mirror finishes. **Prices:** Start at $95. **Remarks:** Full-time maker; first knife sold in 1972. **Mark:** Name stamp in script on blade.

CLAY, WAYNE, Box 125B, Pelham, TN 37366, Phone: 931-467-3472, Fax: 931-467-3076
 Specialties: Working straight knives and folders in standard patterns. **Patterns:** Hunters and kitchen knives; gents and hunter patterns. **Technical:** Grinds ATS-34. **Prices:** $125 to $500; some to $1000. **Remarks:** Full-time maker; first knife sold in 1978. **Mark:** Name.

COCKERHAM, LLOYD, 1717 Carolyn Ave., Denham Springs, IA 70726, Phone: 225-665-1565

COFER, RON, 188 Ozora Rd., Loganville, GA 30052
 Specialties: Fancy working and using straight knives of his design. **Patterns:** Hunters, Bowies and fighters. **Technical:** Grinds 440C and ATS-34. Heat-treats. Some knives have carved stag handles or scrimshaw. Makes leather sheath for each knife and walnut and deer antler display stands for art knives. **Prices:** $125 to $250; some to $600. **Remarks:** Spare-time maker; first knife sold in 1991. **Mark:** Name, serial number.

COFFEY, BILL, 68 Joshua Ave, Clovis, CA 93611
 Specialties: Working and fancy straight knives and folders of his design. **Patterns:** Hunters, f fighters, utility, liner lock folders and fantasy knives. **Technical:** Grinds 440C, ATS-34, A-Z and commercial Damascus. **Prices:** $250 to $1000; some to $2500. **Remarks:** Full-time maker. First knife sold in 1993. **Mark:** First and last name, city, state.

COFFMAN, DANNY, 541 Angel Dr. S., Jacksonville, AL 36265-5787, Phone: 256-435-1619
 Specialties: Straight knives and folders of his design. Now making liner locks for $650 to $1200 with natural handles and contrasting Damascus blades and bolsters. **Patterns:** Hunters, locking and slip-joint folders. **Technical:** Grinds Damascus, 440C and D2. Offers filework and engraving. **Prices:** $100 to $400; some to $800. **Remarks:** Spare-time maker; first knife sold in 1992. Doing business as Customs by Coffman. **Mark:** Last name stamped or engraved.

COHEN, N.J. (NORM), 2408 Sugarcone Rd., Baltimore, MD 21209, Phone: 410-484-3841, njck528@bcpl.net Web: www.njcknives.com
 Specialties: Working class knives. **Patterns:** Hunters, skinners, bird knives, push daggers, boots, kitchen and practical customer designs. **Technical:** Stock removal 440C, ATS-34. Uses Micarta, Corian. Some woods in handles. **Prices:** $50 to $250. **Remarks:** Part-time maker; first knife sold in 1982. **Mark:** Etched initials or NJC MAKER.

COHEN, TERRY A., PO Box 406, Laytonville, CA 95454
 Specialties: Working straight knives and folders. **Patterns:** Bowies to boot knives and locking folders; mini-boot knives. **Technical:** Grinds stainless; hand rubs; tries for good balance. **Prices:** $85 to $150; some to $325. **Remarks:** Part-time maker; first knife sold in 1983. **Mark:** TERRY KNIVES, city and state.

COIL, JIMMIE J., 2936 Asbury Pl., Owensboro, KY 42303, Phone: 270-684-7827
 Specialties: Traditional working and straight knives of his design. **Patterns:** Hunters, Bowies and fighters. **Technical:** Grinds 440C, ATS-34 and D2. Blades are flat-ground with brush finish; most have tapered tang. Offers filework. **Prices:** $65 to $250; some to $750. **Remarks:** Spare-time maker; first knife sold in 1974. **Mark:** Name.

COLE, DAVE, 620 Poinsetta Dr., Satellite Beach, FL 32937, Phone: 321-773-1687
 Specialties: Fixed blades and friction folders of his design or customers. **Patterns:** Utility, hunters, and Bowies. **Technical:** Grinds 01, 1095.

440C stainless Damascus; prefers natural handle materials, handmade sheaths. **Prices:** $100 and up. **Remarks:** Part-time maker, member of FKA; first knife sold in 1991. **Mark:** D Cole.

COLE, JAMES M., 505 Stonewood Blvd., Bartonville, TX 76226, Phone: 817-430-0302, dogcole@swbell.net

COLE, WELBORN I., 3284 Inman Dr. N.E., Atlanta, GA 30319, Phone: 404-261-3977
 Specialties: Traditional straight knives of his design. **Patterns:** Hunters. **Technical:** Grinds 440C, ATS-34 and D2. Good wood scales. **Prices:** NA. **Remarks:** Full-time maker; first knife sold in 1983. **Mark:** Script initials.

COLEMAN, JOHN A., 7233 Camel Rock Way, Citrus Heightss, CA 95610, Phone: 916-335-1568
 Specialties: Traditional working straight knives of my design or yours. **Patterns:** Plain to fancy file back working knives hunters, bird, trout, camp knives, skinners. Trout knives miniatures of bowies and cappers. **Technical:** Grinds 440-C, ATS34, 145-CM and D2. Exotic woods bone, antler and some ivory. **Prices:** $80 to $200 some to $450. **Remarks:** Part-time maker. First knife sold in 1989. Doing business as Slim's Custom Knives. **Mark:** Cowboy setting on log whittling Slim's Custom Knives above cowboy and name and state under cowboy. **Other:** Enjoy making knives to your specs all knives come with handmade sheath by Slim's Leather.

COLEMAN, KEITH E., 5001 Starfire Pl. N.W., Albuquerque, NM 87120-2010, Phone: 505-899-3783, keith@kecenterprises.com Web: kecenterprises.com
 Specialties: Affordable collector-grade straight knives and folders; some fancy. **Patterns:** Fighters, tantos, combat fighters, gents folders and boots. **Technical:** Grinds ATS-34 and Damascus. Prefers specialty woods; offers filework. **Prices:** $150 to $700; some to $1500. **Remarks:** Full-time maker; first knife sold in 1980. **Mark:** Name, city and state.

COLLINS, HAROLD, 503 First St., West Union, OH 45693, Phone: 513-544-2982
 Specialties: Traditional using straight knives and folders of his design or to customer specs. **Patterns:** Hunters, Bowies and locking folders. **Technical:** Forges and grinds 440C, ATS-34, D2, O1 and 5160. Flat-grinds standard; filework available. **Prices:** $75 to $300. **Remarks:** Full-time maker; first knife sold in 1989. **Mark:** First initial, last name.

COLLINS, LYNN M., 138 Berkley Dr., Elyria, OH 44035, Phone: 440-366-7101
 Specialties: Working straight knives. **Patterns:** Field knives, boots and fighters. **Technical:** Grinds D2, 154CM and 440C. **Prices:** Start at $150. **Remarks:** Spare-time maker; first knife sold in 1980. **Mark:** Initials, asterisks.

COLTER, WADE, PO Box 2340, Colstrip, MT 59323, Phone: 406-748-4573
 Specialties: Fancy and embellished straight knives, folders and swords of his design; historical and period pieces. **Patterns:** Bowies, swords and folders. **Technical:** Hand forges 52100 ball bearing steel and L6, 1090, cable and chain Damascus from 5N20 and 1084. Carves and makes sheaths. **Prices:** $250 to $3500. **Remarks:** Part-time maker; first knife sold in 1990. Doing business as "Colter's Hell" Forge. **Mark:** Initials on left side ricasso.

COLTRAIN, LARRY D., PO Box 1331, Buxton, NC 27920

COMPTON, WILLIAM E., 106 N. Sequoia Ct., Sterling, VA 20164, Phone: 703-430-2129
 Specialties: Working straight knives of his design or to customer specs; some fancy knives. **Patterns:** Hunters, camp knives, Bowies and some kitchen knives. **Technical:** Also forges 5160, 1095 and make his own Damascus. **Prices:** $150 to $750, some to $1500. **Remarks:** Part-time maker, ABS Journeyman Smith, first knife sold in 1994. Doing business as Comptons Custom Knives. **Mark:** Stock removal—first and middle initials, last name, city and state. Forged first and middle initials, last name, city and state, anvil in middle.

COMUS, STEVE, PO Box 68040, Anaheim, CA 92817-9800

CONKEY, TOM, 9122 Keyser Rd., Nokesville, VA 22123, Phone: 703-791-3867
 Specialties: Classic straight knives and folders of his design and to customer specs. **Patterns:** Boots, hunters and locking folders. **Technical:** Grinds ATS-34, O1 and commercial Damascus. Lockbacks have jeweled scales and locking bars with dovetailed bolsters. Folders utilize unique 2-piece bushing of his design and manufacture. Sheaths are handmade. Presentation boxes made upon request. **Prices:** $100 to $500. **Remarks:** Part-time maker; first knife sold in 1991. Collaborates with Dan Thomas. **Mark:** Last name with "handcrafted" underneath.

CONKLIN, GEORGE L., Box 902, Ft. Benton, MT 59442, Phone: 406-622-3268, Fax: 406-622-3410, 7bbgrus@3rivers.net
    Specialties: Designer and manufacturer of the "Brisket Breaker." **Patterns:** Hunters, utility/camp knives and hatchets. **Technical:** Grinds 440C, ATS-34, D2, 1095, 154CM and 5160. Offers some forging and heat-treats for others. Offers some jewelling. **Prices:** $65 to $200; some to $1000. **Remarks:** Full-time maker. Doing business as Rocky Mountain Knives. **Mark:** Last name in script.

CONLEY, BOB, 1013 Creasy Rd., Jonesboro, TN 37659, Phone: 423-753-3302
    Specialties: Working straight knives and folders. **Patterns:** Lockers, two-blades, gents, hunters, traditional-styles, straight hunters. **Technical:** Grinds 440C, 154CM and ATS-34. Engraves. **Prices:** $250 to $450; some to $600. **Remarks:** Full-time maker; first knife sold in 1979. **Mark:** Full name, city, state.

CONN JR., C.T., 206 Highland Ave., Attalla, AL 35954, Phone: 205-538-7688
    Specialties: Working folders, some fancy. **Patterns:** Full range of folding knives. **Technical:** Grinds O2, 440C and 154CM. **Prices:** $125 to $300; some to $600. **Remarks:** Part-time maker; first knife sold in 1982. **Mark:** Name.

CONNER, ALLEN L., 6399 County Rd. 305, Fulton, MO 65251, Phone: 573-642-9200, emmorris@sockets.net

CONNOLLY, JAMES, 2486 Oro-Quincy Hwy., Oroville, CA 95966, Phone: 916-534-5363, jim@histumyani.com Web: http://www.quiknet.com/~connolly
    Specialties: Classic working and using knives of his design. **Patterns:** Boots, Bowies and daggers. **Technical:** Grinds ATS-34; forges 5160; forges and grinds O1. **Prices:** $100 to $500; some to $1500. **Remarks:** Part-time maker; first knife sold in 1980. Doing business as Gold Rush Designs. **Mark:** First initial, last name, Handmade.

CONNOR, JOHN W., PO Box 12981, Odessa, TX 79768-2981, Phone: 915-362-6901

CONNOR, MICHAEL, Box 502, Winters, TX 79567, Phone: 915-754-5602
    Specialties: Straight knives, period pieces, some folders. **Patterns:** Hunters to camp knives to traditional locking folders to Bowies. **Technical:** Forges 5160, O1, 1084 steels and his own Damascus. **Prices:** Moderate to upscale. **Remarks:** Spare-time maker; first knife sold in 1974. **Mark:** Last name, M.S. **Other:** ABS Master Smith 1983.

CONTI, JEFFREY D., 21104 75th St E, Bonney Lake, WA 98390, Phone: 253-447-4660, Fax: 253-512-8629
    Specialties: Working straight knives. **Patterns:** Fighters and survival knives; hunters, camp knives and fishing knives. **Technical:** Grinds D2, 154CM and O1. Engraves. **Prices:** Start at $80. **Remarks:** Part-time maker; first knife sold in 1980. Do my own heat treating. **Mark:** Initials, year, steel type, name and number of knife.

COOGAN, ROBERT, 1560 Craft Center Dr., Smithville, TN 37166, Phone: 615-597-6801, http://iweb.tntech.edu/rcoogan/
    Specialties: One-of-a-kind knives. **Patterns:** Unique items like ooloo-style Appalachian herb knives. **Technical:** Forges; his Damascus is made from nickel steel and W1. **Prices:** Start at $100. **Remarks:** Part-time maker; first knife sold in 1979. **Mark:** Initials or last name in script.

COOK, MIKE A., 10927 Shilton Rd., Portland, MI 48875, Phone: 517-647-2518
    Specialties: Fancy/embellished and period pieces of his design. **Patterns:** Daggers, fighters and hunters. **Technical:** Stone bladed knives in agate, obsidian and jasper. Scrimshaws; opal inlays. **Prices:** $60 to $300; some to $800. **Remarks:** Part-time maker; first knife sold in 1988. Doing business as Art of Ishi. **Mark:** Initials and year.

COOK, MIKE, 475 Robinson Ln., Ozark, IL 62972, Phone: 618-777-2932
    Specialties: Traditional working and using straight knives of his design and to customer specs. **Patterns:** Bowies, hunters and utility/camp knives. **Technical:** Forges 5160. Filework; pin work. **Prices:** Start at $50/inch. **Remarks:** Spare-time maker; first knife sold in 1991. **Mark:** First initial, last name and Journeyman stamp on one side; panther head on the other.

COOK, JAMES R., 3611 Hwy. 26 W., Nashville, AR 71852, Phone: 870 845 5173, jrcook@cswnet.com Web: www.jrcrookknives.com
    Specialties: Working straight knives and folders of his design or to customer specs. **Patterns:** Bowies, hunters and camp knives. **Technical:** Forges 1084 and high-carbon Damascus. **Prices:** $195 to $5500. **Remarks:** Full-time maker; first knife sold in 1986. **Mark:** First and middle initials, last name.

COOK, LOUISE, 475 Robinson Ln., Ozark, IL 62972, Phone: 618-777-2932
    Specialties: Working and using straight knives of her design and to customer specs; period pieces. **Patterns:** Bowies, hunters and utility/camp

knives. **Technical:** Forges 5160. Filework; pin work; silver wire inlay. **Prices:** Start at $50/inch. **Remarks:** Part-time maker; first knife sold in 1990. Doing business as Panther Creek Forge. **Mark:** First name and Journeyman stamp on one side; panther head on the other.

COOMBS JR., LAMONT, 546 State Rt. 46, Bucksport, ME 04416, Phone: 207-469-3057, Fax: 207-469-3057, theknifemaker@hotmail.com Web: www.knivesby.com/coomb-knives.html
    Specialties: Classic fancy and embellished straight knives; traditional working and using straight knives. Knives of his design and to customer specs. **Patterns:** Hunters, folders and utility/camp knives. **Technical:** Hollow- and flat-grinds ATS-34, 440C, A2, D2 and O1; grinds Damascus from other makers. **Prices:** $100 to $500; some to $3500. **Remarks:** Full-time maker; first knife sold in 1988. **Mark:** Last name on banner, handmade underneath.

COON, RAYMOND C., 21135 S.E. Tillstrom Rd., Gresham, OR 97080, Phone: 503-658-2252, Raymond@damascusknife.com Web: Damascusknife.com
    Specialties: Working straight knives in standard patterns. **Patterns:** Hunters, Bowies, daggers, boots and axes. **Technical:** Forges high-carbon steel and Damascus. **Prices:** Start at $135. **Remarks:** Full-time maker; does own leatherwork, makes own Damascus, daggers; first knife sold in 1995. **Mark:** First initial, last name.

COPELAND, GEORGE STEVE, 220 Pat Carr Lane, Alpine, TN 38543, Phone: 931-823-5214, nifmakr@twlakes.net
    Specialties: Traditional and fancy working straight knives and folders. **Patterns:** Friction folders, Congress two- and four-blade folders, button locks and one- and two-blade automatics. **Technical:** Stock removal of 440C, S300, ATS-34 and A2; heat-treats. **Prices:** $180 to $950; some higher. **Remarks:** Full-time maker; first knife sold in 1979. Doing business as Alpine Mountain Knives. **Mark:** G.S. Copeland (HANDMADE); some with four-leaf clover stamp.

COPELAND, THOM, 171 Country Line Rd. S., Nashville, AR 71852, tcope@cswnet.com
    Specialties: Hand forged fixed blades; hunters, Bowies and camp knives. **Mark:** Copeland. **Other:** Member of ABS and AKA (Arkansas Knifemakers Association).

COPPINS, DANIEL, 7303 Sherrard Rd., Cambridge, OH 43725, Phone: 740-439-4199
    Specialties: Grinds 440 C and etching toll steels, antler, bone handles. **Patterns:** Hunters patch, neck knives, primitive, tomahawk. **Prices:** $20 and up, some to $600. **Remarks:** Sold first knife in 2002. **Mark:** DC. **Other:** Made tomahawk + knives + walking stick for country music band Confederate Railroad.

CORBY, HAROLD, 218 Brandonwood Dr., Johnson City, TN 37604, Phone: 615-926-9781
    Specialties: Large fighters and Bowies; self-protection knives; art knives. Along with art knives and combat knives, Corby now has a all new automatic MO.PB1, also side lock MO LL-1 with titanium liners G-10 handles. **Patterns:** Sub-hilt fighters and hunters. **Technical:** Grinds 154CM, ATS-34 and 440C. **Prices:** $200 to $6000. **Remarks:** Full-time maker; first knife sold in 1969. Doing business as Knives by Corby. **Mark:** Last name.

CORDOVA, JOSEPH G., PO Box 977, Peralta, NM 87042, Phone: 505-869-3912, kcordova@rt66.com
    Specialties: One-of-a-kind designs, some to customer specs. **Patterns:** Fighter called the 'Gladiator', hunters, boots and cutlery. **Technical:** Forges 1095, 5160; grinds ATS-34, 440C and 154CM. **Prices:** Moderate to upscale. **Remarks:** Full-time maker; first knife sold in 1953. Past chairman of American Bladesmith Assoc. **Mark:** Cordova made.

CORKUM, STEVE, 34 Basehoar School Rd., Littlestown, PA 17340, Phone: 717-359-9563, sco7129849@aol.com Web: www.hawknives.com

CORRIGAN, DAVID P., HCR 65 Box 67, Bingham, ME 04920, Phone: 207-672-4879, outfarm@tdstelme.net

COSGROVE, CHARLES G., 2314 W. Arbook Blvd., Arlington, TX 76015, Phone: 817-472-6505
    Specialties: Traditional fixed or locking blade working knives. **Patterns:** Hunters, Bowies and locking folders. **Technical:** Stock removal using 440C, ATS-34 and D2; heat-treats. Makes heavy, hand-stitched sheaths. **Prices:** $250 to $2500. **Remarks:** Full-time maker; first knife sold in 1968. No longer accepting customer designs. **Mark:** First initial, last name, or full name over city and state.

COSTA, SCOTT, 409 Coventry Rd., Spicewood, TX 78669, Phone: 830-693-3431
    Specialties: Working straight knives. **Patterns:** Hunters, skinners, axes, trophy sets, custom boxed steak sets, carving sets and bar sets. **Technical:** Grinds D2, ATS-34, 440 and Damascus. Heat-treats. **Prices:** $225

to $2000. **Remarks:** Full-time maker; first knife sold in 1985. **Mark:** Initials connected.

COTTRILL, JAMES I., 1776 Ransburg Ave., Columbus, OH 43223, Phone: 614-274-0020
   Specialties: Working straight knives of his design. **Patterns:** Caters to the boating and hunting crowd; cutlery. **Technical:** Grinds O1, D2 and 440C. Likes filework. **Prices:** $95 to $250; some to $500. **Remarks:** Full-time maker; first knife sold in 1977. **Mark:** Name, city, state, in oval logo.

COUGHLIN, MICHAEL M., 414 Northridge Lane, Winder, GA 30680, Phone: 770-307-9509, sandman223@msn.com
   Specialties: One-of-a-kind large folders and daily carry knives. **Remarks:** Likes customer input and involvement.

COURTNEY, ELDON, 2718 Bullinger, Wichita, KS 67204, Phone: 316-838-4053
   Specialties: Working straight knives of his design. **Patterns:** Hunters, fighters and one-of-a-kinds. **Technical:** Grinds and tempers L6, 440C and spring steel. **Prices:** $100 to $500; some to $1500. **Remarks:** Full-time maker; first knife sold in 1977. **Mark:** Full name, city and state.

COURTOIS, BRYAN, 3 Lawn Avenue, Saco, ME 04072, Phone: 207-282-3977, WEB: WWW.GWI.NET/~COURTOIS/
   Specialties: Working straight knives; prefers customer designs, no standard patterns. **Patterns:** Functional hunters; everyday knives. **Technical:** Grinds 440C or customer request. Hollow-grinds with a variety of finishes. Specializes in granite handles and custom skeleton knives. **Prices:** Start at $75. **Remarks:** Part-time maker; first knife sold in 1988. Doing business as Castle Knives. **Mark:** A rook chess piece machined into blade using electrical discharge process.

COUSINO, GEORGE, 7818 Norfolk, Onsted, MI 49265, Phone: 517-467-4911, Fax: 517-467-4911, gcousino1@aol.com Web: www.cousinoknives.com
   Specialties: Hunters, Bowies using knives. **Patterns:** Hunters, Bowies, buckskinners, folders and daggers. **Technical:** Grinds 440C. **Prices:** $95 to $300. **Remarks:** Part-time maker; first knife sold in 1981. **Mark:** Last name.

COVER, RAYMOND A., Rt. 1, Box 194, Mineral Point, MO 63660, Phone: 573-749-3783
   Specialties: High-tech working straight knives and folders in standard patterns. **Patterns:** Slip joint folders, two-bladed folders. **Technical:** Grinds D2, and ATS-34. **Prices:** $165 to $250; some to $400. **Remarks:** Part-time maker; first knife sold in 1974. **Mark:** Name.

COWLES, DON, 1026 Lawndale Dr., Royal Oak, MI 48067, Phone: 248-541-4619, don@cowlesknives.com Web: www.cowlesknives.com
   Specialties: Straight, non-folding pocket knives of his design. **Patterns:** Gentlemen's pocket knives. **Technical:** Grinds ATS-34, RWL34, S30V, stainless Damascus, Talonite. Scrimshaws; pearl inlays in some handles. **Prices:** $300 to $1200. **Remarks:** Full-time maker; first knife sold in 1994. **Mark:** Full name with oak leaf.

COX, COLIN J., 107 N. Oxford Dr., Raymore, MO 64083, Phone: 816-322-1977
   Specialties: Working straight knives and folders of his design; period pieces. **Patterns:** Hunters, fighters and survival knives. Folders, two-blades, gents and hunters. **Technical:** Grinds D2, 440C, 154CM and ATS-34. **Prices:** $125 to $750; some to $4000. **Remarks:** Full-time maker; first knife sold in 1981. **Mark:** Full name, city and state.

COX, SAM, 1756 Love Springs Rd., Gaffney, SC 29341, Phone: 864-489-1892, Fax: 864-489-0403, artcutlery@yahoo.com Web: www.samcox.us
   Specialties: Classic high-art working straight knives of his design. Duck knives copyrighted. **Patterns:** Diverse. **Technical:** Grinds 154CM. **Prices:** $300 to $1400. **Remarks:** Full-time maker; first knife sold in 1983. **Mark:** Cox Call, Sam, Sam Cox, unique 2000 logo.

CRAIG, ROGER L., 2617 SW Seabrook Ave, Topeka, KS 66614, Phone: 785-249-4109
   Specialties: Working and camp knives, some fantasy; all his design. **Patterns:** Fighters, hunter. **Technical:** Grinds 1095 and 5160. Most knives have file work. **Prices:** $50 to $250. **Remarks:** Part-time maker; first knife sold in 1991. Doing business as Craig Knives. **Mark:** Last name-Craig.

CRAIN, FRANK, 1127 W. Dalke, Spokane, WA 99205, Phone: 509-325-1596

CRAIN, JACK W., PO Box 212, Granbury, TX 76048, Phone: 817-599-6414, Web: www.crainknives.com; Site 9291 jackwcrain@crainknives.com
   Specialties: Fantasy and period knives; combat and survival knives. **Patterns:** One-of-a-kind art or fantasy daggers, swords and Bowies; survival knives. **Technical:** Forges Damascus; grinds stainless steel. Carves. **Prices:** $350 to $2500; some to $20,000. **Remarks:** Full-time

maker; first knife sold in 1969. Designer and maker of the knives seen in the films *Dracula 2000, Executive Decision, Demolition Man, Predator I and II, Commando, Die Hard I and II, Road House, Ford Fairlane* and *Action Jackson,* and television shows *War of the Worlds, Air Wolf, Kung Fu: The Legend Cont.* and *Tales of the Crypt.* **Mark:** Stylized crane.

CRAWFORD, PAT AND WES, 205 N. Center, West Memphis, AR 72301, Phone: 870-732-2452, patcrawford1@earthlink.com
   Specialties: Stainless steel Damascus. High-tech working self-defense and combat types and folders. **Patterns:** Tactical-more fancy knives now. **Technical:** Grinds ATS-34, D2 and 154CM. **Prices:** $400 to $2000. **Remarks:** Full-time maker; first knife sold in 1973. **Mark:** Last name.

CRAWLEY, BRUCE R., 16 Binbrook Dr., Croydon 3136 Victoria, AUSTRALIA
   Specialties: Folders. **Patterns:** Hunters, lockback folders and Bowies. **Technical:** Grinds 440C, ATS-34 and commercial Damascus. Offers filework and mirror polish. **Prices:** $160 to $3500. **Remarks:** Part-time maker; first knife sold in 1990. **Mark:** Initials.

CRENSHAW, AL, Rt. 1, Box 717, Eufaula, OK 74432, Phone: 918-452-2128
   Specialties: Folders of his design and in standard patterns. **Patterns:** Hunters, locking folders, slip-joint folders, multi blade folders. **Technical:** Grinds 440C, D2 and ATS-34. Does filework on back springs and blades; offers scrimshaw on some handles. **Prices:** $150 to $300; some higher. **Remarks:** Full-time maker; first knife sold in 1981. Doing business as A. Crenshaw Knives. **Mark:** First initial, last name, Lake Eufaula, state stamped; first initial last name in rainbow; Lake Eufaula across bottom with Okla. in middle.

CROCKFORD, JACK, 1859 Harts Mill Rd., Chamblee, GA 30341, Phone: 770-457-4680
   Specialties: Lockback folders. **Patterns:** Hunters, fishing and camp knives, traditional folders. **Technical:** Grinds A2, D2, ATS-34 and 440C. Engraves and scrimshaws. **Prices:** Start at $175. **Remarks:** Part-time maker; first knife sold in 1975. **Mark:** Name.

CROSS, ROBERT, RMB 200B, Manilla Rd., Tamworth 2340, NSW AUSTRALIA, Phone: 067-618385

CROSSMAN, DANIEL C., Box 5236, Blakely Island, WA 98222, Phone: 360-375-6542

CROWDER, ROBERT, Box 1374, Thompson Falls, MT 59873, Phone: 406-827-4754
   Specialties: Traditional working knives to customer specs. **Patterns:** Hunters, Bowies, fighters and fillets. **Technical:** Grinds ATS-34, 154CM, 440C, Vascowear and commercial Damascus. **Prices:** $160 to $250; some to $2500. **Remarks:** Part-time maker; first knife sold in 1985. **Mark:** First initial, last name.

CROWELL, JAMES L., PO Box 822, Mtn. View, AR 72560, Phone: 870-746-4215, crowellknives@yahoo.com
   Specialties: Bowie knives; fighters and working knives. **Patterns:** Hunters, fighters, Bowies, daggers and folders. Period pieces: War hammers, Japanese and European. **Technical:** Forges 10 series carbon steels as well as 0-1, L-6 and his own Damascus. **Prices:** $425 to $4500; some to $7500. **Remarks:** Full-time maker; first knife sold in 1980. Earned ABS Master Bladesmith in 1986. **Mark:** A shooting star.

CROWTHERS, MARK F., PO Box 4641, Rolling Bay, WA 98061-0641, Phone: 206-842-7501

CULPEPPER, JOHN, 2102 Spencer Ave., Monroe, LA 71201, Phone: 318-323-3636
   Specialties: Working straight knives. **Patterns:** Hunters, Bowies and camp knives in heavy-duty patterns. **Technical:** Grinds O1, D2 and 440C; hollow-grinds. **Prices:** $75 to $200; some to $300. **Remarks:** Part-time maker; first knife sold in 1970. Doing business as Pepper Knives. **Mark:** Pepper.

CULVER, STEVE, 5682 94th St., Meriden, KS 66512, Phone: 866-505-0146, Web: www.culverart.com
   Specialties: Edged tools and weapons, collectible and functional. **Patterns:** Bowies, daggers, swords, hunters, folders and edged tools. **Technical:** Forges carbon steels and his own pattern welded steels. **Prices:** $200 to $1500; some to $4000. **Remarks:** Full-time maker; first knife sold in 1989. **Mark:** Last name, J.S.

CUMMING, BOB, CUMMING KNIVES, 35 Manana Dr., Cedar Crest, NM 87008, Phone: 505-286-0509, cumming@comcast.net Web: www.cummingknives.com
   Specialties: One of a kind exhibition grade custom bowie knives, exhibition grade and working hunters, bird & trout knives, salt and fresh water filet knives. Low country oyster knives, custom tanto's plains Indian style sheaths & custom leather, all types of exotic handle materials, scrimshaw and engraving. Coming in 206 Folders. **Prices:** $90 to $2500 and up. **Remarks:** Mentored by the late Jim Nolen, sold first knife in 1978 in

Denmark. Retired US Foreign Service Office. Member NCCKG **Mark:** Stylized CUMMING.

CUTCHIN, ROY D., 960 Hwy. 169 S., Seale, AL 36875, Phone: 334-855-3080
Specialties: Fancy and working folders of his design. **Patterns:** Locking folders. **Technical:** Grinds ATS-34 and commercial Damascus; uses anodized titanium. **Prices:** Start at $250. **Remarks:** Part-time maker. **Mark:** First initial, last name, city and state, number.

CUTE, THOMAS, State Rt. 90-7071, Cortland, NY 13045, Phone: 607-749-4055
Specialties: Working straight knives. **Patterns:** Hunters, Bowies and fighters. **Technical:** Grinds O1, 440C and ATS-34. **Prices:** $100 to $1000. **Remarks:** Full-time maker; first knife sold in 1974. **Mark:** Full name.

D

D'ANDREA, JOHN, 9321 M Santos, Citrus Springs, FL 34434, Phone: 570-420-6050
Specialties: Fancy working straight knives and folders with filework and distinctive leatherwork. **Patterns:** Hunters, fighters, daggers, folders and an occasional sword. **Technical:** Grinds ATS-34, 154CM, 440C and D2. **Prices:** $180 to $600; some to $1000. **Remarks:** Part-time maker; first knife sold in 1986. **Mark:** First name, last initial imposed on samurai sword.

D'ANGELO, LAURENCE, 14703 N.E. 17th Ave., Vancouver, WA 98686, Phone: 360-573-0546
Specialties: Straight knives of his design. **Patterns:** Bowies, hunters and locking folders. **Technical:** Grinds D2, ATS-34 and 440C. Hand makes all sheaths. **Prices:** $100 to $200. **Remarks:** Full-time maker; first knife sold in 1987. **Mark:** Football logo—first and middle initials, last name, city, state, Maker.

DAILEY, G.E., 577 Lincoln St., Seekonk, MA 02771, Phone: 508-336-5088, gedailey@msn.com Web: www.gedailey.com
Specialties: One-of-a-kind exotic designed edged weapons. **Patterns:** Folders, daggers and swords. **Technical:** Reforges and grinds Damascus; prefers hollow-grinding. Engraves, carves, offers filework and sets stones and uses exotic gems and gold. **Prices:** Start at $1100. **Remarks:** Full-time maker. First knife sold in 1982. **Mark:** Last name or stylized initialed logo.

DAKE, C.M., 19759 Chef Menteur Hwy., New Orleans, LA 70129-9602, Phone: 504-254-0357, Fax: 504-254-9501
Specialties: Fancy working folders. **Patterns:** Front-lock lockbacks, button-lock folders. **Technical:** Grinds ATS-34 and Damascus. **Prices:** $500 to $2500; some higher. **Remarks:** Full-time maker; first knife sold in 1988. Doing business as Bayou Custom Cutlery. **Mark:** Last name.

DAKE, MARY H., RT. 5 Box 287A, New Orleans, LA 70129, Phone: 504-254-0357

DALAND, B. MACGREGOR, RT. 5 Box 196, Harbeson, DE 19951, Phone: 302-945-2609

DALLYN, KELLY, 14695 Deerridge Dr. S.E., Calgary AB, CANADA T2J 6A8, Phone: 403-278-3056

DAMLOVAC, SAVA, 10292 Bradbury Dr., Indianapolis, IN 46231, Phone: 317-839-4952
Specialties: Period pieces, Fantasy, Viking, Moran type all Damascus daggers. **Patterns:** Bowies, fighters, daggers, Persian-style knives. **Technical:** Uses own Damascus, some stainless, mostly hand forges. **Prices:** $150 to $2500; some higher. **Remarks:** Full-time maker; first knife sold in 1993. **Mark:** "Sava" stamped in Damascus or etched in stainless. **Other:** Specialty, Bill Moran all Damascus dagger sets, in Moran-style wood case.

DANIEL, TRAVIS E., 1655 Carrow Rd., Chocowinity, NC 27817, Phone: 252-940-0807, dorispaul@email.com
Specialties: Traditional working straight knives of his design or to customer specs. **Patterns:** Hunters, fighters and utility/camp knives. **Technical:** Grinds ATS-34, D-2, 440-C, 154CM, forges his own Damascus. **Prices:** $90 to $1250; some to $2000. **Remarks:** Full-time maker; first knife sold in 1976. **Mark:** Carolina Custom Knives or "TED"

DANIELS, ALEX, 1416 County Rd. 415, Town Creek, AL 35672, Phone: 256-685-0943, akdknives@aol.com
Specialties: Working and using straight knives and folders; period pieces, reproduction Bowies. **Patterns:** Mostly reproduction Bowies but offer full line of knives. **Technical:** Now also using BG-42 along with 440C and ATS-34. **Prices:** $200 to $2500. **Remarks:** Full-time maker; first knife sold in 1963. **Mark:** First and middle initials, last name, city and state.

DARBY, DAVID T., 30652 S 533 Rd., Cookson, OK 74427, Phone: 918-457-4868, knfmkr@fullnet.net
Specialties: Forged blades only-All styles. **Prices:** $350.00 and up. **Mark:** Stylized quillion dagger incorporates last name (Darby). **Other:** ABS Journeyman Smith.

DARBY, JED, 7878 E. Co. Rd. 50 N., Greensburg, IN 47240, Phone: 812-663-2696
Specialties: Traditional working/using straight knives of his design and to customer specs. **Patterns:** Bowies, hunters and utility/camp knives. **Technical:** Grinds 440C, ATS-34 and Damascus. **Prices:** $70 to $550; some to $1000. **Remarks:** Full-time maker; first knife sold in 1992. Doing business as Darby Knives. **Mark:** Last name and year.

DARBY, RICK, 71 Nestingrock Ln., Levittown, PA 19054
Specialties: Working straight knives. **Patterns:** Boots, fighters and hunters with mirror finish. **Technical:** Grinds 440C and CPM440V. **Prices:** $125 to $300. **Remarks:** Part-time maker; first knife sold in 1974. **Mark:** First and middle initials, last name.

DARCEY, CHESTER L., 1608 Dominik Dr., College Station, TX 77840, Phone: 979-696-1656, DarceyKnives@yahoo.com
Specialties: Lockback, liner lock and scale release folders. **Patterns:** Bowies, hunters and utilities. **Technical:** Stock removal on carbon and stainless steels, forge own Damascus. **Prices:** $200 to $1000. **Remarks:** Part-time maker, first knife sold in 1999. **Mark:** Last name in script.

DARK, ROBERT, 2218 Huntington Court, Oxford, AL 36203, Phone: 256-831-4645, Web: www.darknives.com
Specialties: Fixed blade working knives of maker's designs. Works with customer designed specifications. **Patterns:** Hunters, Bowies, Camp Knives, Kitchen/utility, bird and trout. Standard patterns and customer designed. **Technical:** Forged and stock removal. Works with high carbon, stainless and Damascus steels. Hollow and flat grinds. **Prices:** $175 to $750. **Remarks:** Sole authorship knives and custom leather sheaths. Part-time maker. **Mark:** "R Dark" on left side of blade.

DARPINIAN, DAVE, 15219 W. 125th, Olathe, KS 66062, Phone: 913-397-8914, darpo1956@yahoo.com Web: www.darpianknives.com
Specialties: Working knives and fancy pieces to customer specs. **Patterns:** Full range of straight knives including art daggers and short swords. **Technical:** Art grinds ATS-34, 440C, 154 CM, 5160, 1095. **Prices:** $200 to $1000. **Remarks:** First knife sold in 1996, part-time maker. **Mark:** Last name.

DAVENPORT, JACK, 36842 W. Center Ave., Dade City, FL 33525, Phone: 352-521-4088
Specialties: Titanium liner lock, button-lock and release. **Patterns:** Boots and double-ground fighters. **Technical:** Grinds ATS-34, 12C27 SS and Damascus; liquid nitrogen quench; heat-treats. **Prices:** $250 to $5000. **Remarks:** Full-time maker; first knife sold in 1986. **Mark:** Last name.

DAVIDSON, EDMUND, 3345 Virginia Ave., Goshen, VA 24439, Phone: 540-997-5651, Web: www.edmunddavidson.com
Specialties: Working straight knives; many integral patterns and upgraded models. **Patterns:** Heavy-duty skinners and camp knives. **Technical:** Grinds A2, ATS-34, BG-42, S7, 440C. **Prices:** $100 to infinity. **Remarks:** Full-time maker; first knife sold in 1986. **Mark:** Name in deer head or custom logos.

DAVIDSON, LARRY, 921 Bennett St., Cedar Hill, TX 75104, Phone: 972-291-3904, dson@swbell.net Web: www.davidsonknives.com

DAVIS, BARRY L., 4262 U.S. 20, Castleton, NY 12033, Phone: 518-477-5036
Specialties: Complete sole authorship presentation grade highly complex pattern welded mosaic Damascus blade and bolster stock. **Patterns:** To date Joel has executed over 900 different mosaic Damascus patterns in the past four years anything conceived by makers imagination. Duplication of makers patterns is very rarely done, but can be if necessary. **Technical:** Uses various heat colorable "high" vibranc steels, nickel 200 and some powdered metal for bolster stock only and uses 1095, 1075 and 15N20 high carbon steels for cutting edge blade stock only. **Prices:** 15 to $50 per square inch and up, depending on complexity of patterns. **Remarks:** Full-time mosaic Damascus metal smith. Focusing strictly on never before seen mosaic patterns. Most of makers work is used for art knives ranging between $1500 to $4500.

DAVIS, CHARLIE, ANZA Knives, PO Box 710806, Santee, CA 92072, Phone: 619-561-9445, Fax: 619-390-6283, sales@anzaknives.com Web: www.anzaknives.com
Specialties: Fancy and embellished working straight knives of his design. **Patterns:** Hunters, camp and utility knives. **Technical:** Grinds high-carbon files. **Prices:** $20 to $185; custom depends. **Remarks:** Full-time maker; first knife sold in 1980. **Mark:** ANZA U.S.A. **Other:** we now offer custom.

DAVIS, DON, 8415 Coyote Run, Loveland, CO 80537-9665, Phone: 970-669-9016, Fax: 970-669-8072
Specialties: Working straight knives in standard patterns or to customer specs. **Patterns:** Hunters, utility knives, skinners and survival knives. **Technical:** Grinds 440C, ATS-34. **Prices:** $75 to $250. **Remarks:** Full-time maker; first knife sold in 1985. **Mark:** Signature, city and state.

DAVIS, JESSE W., 7398A Hwy. 3, Sarah, MS 38665, Phone: 662-382-7332, jandddvais1@earthlink.net
Specialties: Working straight knives and boots in standard patterns and to customer specs. **Patterns:** Boot knives, daggers, fighters, subhilts & bowies. **Technical:** Grinds A2, D2, 440C and commercial Damascus. **Prices:** $125 to $1000. **Remarks:** Full-time maker; first knife sold in 1977. Former member Knife Makers Guild (in good standing). **Mark:** Name or initials.

DAVIS, JOEL, 74538 165th, Albert Lea, MN 56007, Phone: 507-377-0808, joelknives@yahoo.com
Specialties: Complete sole authorship presentation grade highly complex pattern-welded mosaic Damascus blade and bolster stock. **Patterns:** To date Joel has executed over 900 different mosaic Damascus patterns in the past four years. Anything conceived by makers imagination. Duplication of makers patterns is very rarely done, but can be if necessary. **Technical:** Uses various heat colorable "high vibrancy" steels, nickel 200 and some powdered metal for bolster stock only. And uses 1095, 1075 and 15N20. High carbon steels for cutting edge blade stock only. **Prices:** 15 to $50 per square inch and up depending on complexity of pattern. **Remarks:** Full-time mosaic Damascus metal smith focusing strictly on never-before-seen mosaic patterns. Most of maker's work is used for art knives ranging between $1500 to $4500.

DAVIS, JOHN, 235 Lampe Rd., Selah, WA 98942, Phone: 509-697-3845, Fax: 509-697-8087
Specialties: Working and using straight knives of his own design, to customer specs and in standard patterns. **Patterns:** Boots, hunters, kitchen and utility/camp knives. **Technical:** Grinds ATS-34, 440C and commercial Damascus; makes own Damascus and mosaic Damascus. Embellishes with stabilized wood, mokume and nickel-silver. **Prices:** Start at $150. **Remarks:** Part-time maker; first knife sold in 1996. **Mark:** Name city and state on Damascus stamp initials.

DAVIS, STEVE, 3370 Chatsworth Way, Powder Springs, GA 30127, Phone: 770-427-5740
Specialties: Traditional Gents and Ladies folders of his design and to customer specs. **Patterns:** Slip-joint folders, locking-liner folders, lock back folders. **Technical:** Grinds ATS-34, 440C and Damascus. Offers filework; prefers hand-rubbed finishes and natural handle materials. Uses pearl, ivory, stag and exotic woods. **Prices:** $250 to $600; some to $1500. **Remarks:** Part-time maker; first knife sold in 1988. Doing business as Custom Knives by Steve Davis. **Mark:** Name engraved on blade.

DAVIS, TERRY, Box 111, Sumpter, OR 97877, Phone: 541-894-2307
Specialties: Traditional and contemporary folders. **Patterns:** Multiblade folders, whittlers and interframe multiblades; sunfish patterns. **Technical:** Flat-grinds ATS-34. **Prices:** $400 to $1000; some higher. **Remarks:** Full-time maker; first knife sold in 1985. **Mark:** Name in logo.

DAVIS, VERNON M., 2020 Behrens Circle, Waco, TX 76705, Phone: 254-799-7671
Specialties: Presentation-grade straight knives. **Patterns:** Bowies, daggers, boots, fighters, hunters and utility knives. **Technical:** Hollow-grinds 440C, ATS-34 and D2. Grinds an aesthetic grind line near choil. **Prices:** $125 to $550; some to $5000. **Remarks:** Part-time maker; first knife sold in 1980. **Mark:** Last name and city inside outline of state.

DAVIS, W.C., 19300 S. School Rd., Raymore, MO 64083, Phone: 816-331-4491
Specialties: Fancy working straight knives and folders. **Patterns:** Folding lockers and slip-joints; straight hunters, fighters and Bowies. **Technical:** Grinds A2, ATS-34 and 154, CPM T490V and CPM 530V. **Prices:** $100 to $300; some to $1000. **Remarks:** Full-time maker; first knife sold in 1972. **Mark:** Name.

DAVIS JR., JIM, 5129 Ridge St., Zephyrhills, FL 33541, Phone: 813-779-9213 813-469-4241 Cell, jimdavisknives@aol.com
Specialties: Presentation-grade fixed blade knives w/composite hidden tang handles. Employs a variety of ancient and contemporary ivories. **Patterns:** One-of-a-kind gents, personal, and executive knives and hunters w/unique cam-lock pouch sheaths and display stands. **Technical:** Flat grinds ATS-34 and stainless Damascus w/most work by hand w/ assorted files. **Prices:** $300 and up. **Remarks:** Full-time maker, first knives sold in 2000. **Mark:** Signature w/printed name over "HAND-CRAFTED".

DAVISSON, COLE, 25939 Casa Loma Ct., Hemet, CA 92544, Phone: 909-652-8588, cmd@koan.com

DAWKINS, DUDLEY L., 221 NW Broadmoor Ave., Topeka, KS 66606-1254, Phone: 785-235-0468, Fax: 785-235-3871, dawkind@sbcglobal.net
Specialties: Stylized old or "Dawkins Forged" with anvil in center. New Tang Stamps. **Patterns:** Straight knives. **Technical:** Mostly carbon steel; some Damascus-all knives forged. **Prices:** $175 and up. **Remarks:** All knives supplied with wood-lined sheaths. Also make custom wood-lined sheaths $55 and up. **Mark:** Stylized "DLD or Dawkins Forged with anvil in center. **Other:** ABS Member, sole authorship.

DAWSON, BARRY, 10A Town Plaza, Suite 303, Durango, CO 81301, LINDAD@NORTHLINK.COM Web: www.knives.com
Specialties: Samurai swords, combat knives, collector daggers, tactical, folding and hunting knives. **Patterns:** Offers over 60 different models. **Technical:** Grinds 440C, ATS-34, own heat-treatment. **Prices:** $75 to $1500; some to $5000. **Remarks:** Full-time maker; first knife sold in 1975. **Mark:** Last name, USA in print or last name in script.

DAWSON, LYNN, 10A Town Plaza, Suite 303, Durango, CO 81301, Fax: 928-772-1729, LINDAD@NORTHLINK.COM Web: www.knives.com
Specialties: Swords, hunters, utility, and art pieces. **Patterns:** Over 25 patterns to choose from. **Technical:** Grinds 440C, ATS-34, own heat treating. **Prices:** $80 to $1000. **Remarks:** Custom work and her own designs. **Mark:** The name "Lynn" in print or script.

DE MARIA JR., ANGELO, 12 Boronda Rd., Carmel Valley, CA 93924, Phone: 831-659-3381, Fax: 831-659-1315, ang@mbay.net
Specialties: Damascus, fixed and folders, sheaths. **Patterns:** Mosaic and random. **Technical:** Forging 5160, 1084 and 15N20. **Prices:** $200 +. **Remarks:** Part-time maker. **Mark:** Angelo de Maria Carmel Valley, CA etch or AdM stamp.

DE VILLIERS, ANDRE AND KIRSTEN, Postnet Suite 263, Private Bag X6, Cascades 3202, SOUTH AFRICA, Phone: 27 33 4133312, andre@knifemaker.co.za Web: www.knifemaker.co.za
Specialties: Tactical and up-market folders. **Technical:** Linerlock, buttonlocks and fixed blades. **Prices:** $300 to $1200. **Remarks:** Collectors knives are artful with filework and individual specifications. **Mark:** ADV.

DEAN, HARVEY J., 3266 CR 232, Rockdale, TX 76567, Phone: 512-446-3111, Fax: 512-446-5060, dean@tex1.net Web: www.harveydean.com
Specialties: Collectible, functional knives. **Patterns:** Bowies, hunters, folders, daggers, swords, battle axes, camp and combat knives. **Technical:** Forges 1095, O1 and his Damascus. **Prices:** $350 to $10,000. **Remarks:** Full-time maker; first knife sold in 1981. **Mark:** Last name and MS.

DEBRAGA, JOSE C., 76 Rue de La Pointe, Aux Lievres Quebec, CANADA G1K 5Y3, Phone: 418-948-0105, Fax: 418-948-0105, josecdebragaglovetrotter.net Web: www.gcaq.ga
Specialties: Art knives, fantasy pieces and working knives of his design or to customer specs. **Patterns:** Knives with sculptured or carved handles, from miniatures to full-size working knives. **Technical:** Grinds and hand-files 440C and ATS-34. A variety of steels and handle materials available. Offers lost wax casting. **Prices:** Start at $300. **Remarks:** Full-time maker; wax modeler, sculptor and knife maker; first knife sold in 1984. **Mark:** Initials in stylized script and serial number.

DEBRAGA, JOVAN, 141 Notre Dame des Victoir, Quebec, CANADA G2G 1J3, Phone: 418-948-0105, jovancdebraga@msn.com
Specialties: Art knives, fantasy pieces and working knives of his design or to customer specs. **Patterns:** Knives with sculptured or carved handles, from miniatures to full-sized working knives. **Technical:** Grinds and hand-files 440C, and Ats-34. A variety of steels and handle materials available. **Prices:** Start at $300. **Remarks:** Part-time maker. Sculptor and knife maker. First knife sold in 2003. **Mark:** Initials in stylized script and serial number.

DEFEO, ROBERT A., 403 Lost Trail Dr., Henderson, NV 89014, Phone: 702-434-3717
Specialties: Working straight knives and period pieces. **Patterns:** Hunters, fighters, daggers and Bowies. **Technical:** Grinds ATS-34 and Damascus. **Prices:** $250 to $500; some higher. **Remarks:** Part-time maker; first knife sold in 1982. **Mark:** Last name.

DEFREEST, WILLIAM G., PO Box 573, Barnwell, SC 29812, Phone: 803-259-7883
Specialties: Working straight knives and folders. **Patterns:** Fighters, hunters and boots; locking folders and slip-joints. **Technical:** Grinds 440C, 154CM and ATS-34; clean lines and mirror finishes. **Prices:** $100 to $700. **Remarks:** Full-time maker; first knife sold in 1974. **Mark:** GOR-DON.

DEL RASO, PETER, 28 Mayfield Dr., Mt. Waverly, Victoria, 3149, AUSTRALIA, Phone: 613 98060644, delrasofamily@optusnet.com.au **Specialties:** Fixed Blades, some folders, art knives. **Patterns:** Daggers, Bowies, tactical, boot, personal and working knives. **Technical:** Grinds ATS-34, commercial Damascus and any other type of steel on request. **Prices:** $100 to $1500. **Remarks:** Part-time maker, first show in 1993. **Mark:** Makers surname stamped.

DELAROSA, JIM, 343 S Eden Ct, Whitewater, WI 53190, Phone: 262-473-5652 **Specialties:** Working straight knives and folders of his design or customer specs. **Patterns:** Hunters, skinners, fillets, utility and locking folders. **Technical:** Grinds ATS-34, 440-C, D2, 01 and commercial Damascus. **Prices:** $75 to $450; some higher. **Remarks:** Part-time maker. **Mark:** First and last name, city and state.

DELL, WOLFGANG, Am Alten Berg 9, D-73277 Owen-Teck, GERMANY, Phone: 49-7021-81802, dellknives@compuserve.de Web: www.dell-knives.de **Specialties:** Fancy high-art straight of his design and to customer specs. **Patterns:** Fighters, hunters, Bowies and utility/camp knives. **Technical:** Grinds ATS-34, RWL-34, Elmax, Damascus (Fritz Schneider). Offers high gloss finish and engraving. **Prices:** $500 to $1000; some to $1600. **Remarks:** Full-time maker; first knife sold in 1992. **Mark:** Hopi hand of peace. **Other:** Member of German Knife maker Guild since 1993. Member of the Italian Knife maker Guild since 2000.

DELLANA, Starlani Int'l. Inc., 1135 Terminal Way Ste. #209, Reno, NV 89502, Phone: 877-88dellana or 304-727-5512, Fax: 303-362-7901, Dellana@KnivesByDellana.com Web: www.knivesbydellana.com **Specialties:** Collector grade fancy/embellished high art folders and art daggers. **Patterns:** Locking folders and art daggers. **Technical:** Forges her own Damascus and W-2. Engraves, does stone setting, filework, carving and gold/platinum fabrication. Prefers exotic, high karat gold, platinum, silver, gemstone and mother-of-pearl handle materials. **Price:** Upscale. **Remarks:** Sole authorship, full-time maker, first knife sold in 1994. **Mark:** First name. **Other:** Also does one high art collaboration a year with Van Barnett. Member: Art Knife Invitational and ABS; voting member: Knifemakers Guild.

DELONG, DICK, 17561 E. Ohio Circle, Aurora, CO 80017, Phone: 303-745-2652 **Specialties:** Fancy working knives and fantasy pieces. **Patterns:** Hunters and small skinners. **Technical:** Grinds and files O1, D2, 440C and Damascus. Offers cocobolo and Osage orange for handles. **Prices:** Start at $50. **Remarks:** Part-time maker. **Mark:** Last name; some unmarked. **Other:** Member of Art Knife Invitational. Voting member of Knifemakers Guild. Member of ABS.

DEMENT, LARRY, PO Box 1807, Prince Fredrick, MD 20678, Phone: 410-586-9011 **Specialties:** Fixed blades. **Technical:** Forged and stock removal. **Prices:** $75 to $200. **Remarks:** Affordable, good feelin, quality knives. **Other:** Part-time maker.

DEMPSEY, DAVID, 103 Chadwick Dr., Macon, GA 31210, Phone: 478-474-4948, dempsey@dempseyknives.com Web: www.dempseyknives.com **Specialties:** Tactical, Utility, Working, Classic straight knives. **Patterns:** Fighters, Tantos, Hunters, Neck, Utility or Customer design. **Technical:** Grinds carbon steel and stainless including S30V. (differential heat treatment), Stainless Steels. **Prices:** Start at $150 for Neck Knives. **Remarks:** Full-time maker. First knife sold 1998. **Mark:** First and last name over knives.

DEMPSEY, GORDON S., PO Box 7497, N. Kenai, AK 99635, Phone: 907-776-8425 **Specialties:** Working straight knives. **Patterns:** Pattern welded Damascus and carbon steel blades. **Technical:** Pattern welded Damascus and carbon steel. **Prices:** $80 to $250. **Remarks:** Part-time maker; first knife sold in 1974. **Mark:** Name.

DENNEHY, DAN, PO Box 2F, Del Norte, CO 81132, Phone: 719-657-2545 **Specialties:** Working knives, fighting and military knives, throwing knives. **Patterns:** Full range of straight knives, tomahawks, buckle knives. **Technical:** Forges and grinds A2, O1 and D2. **Prices:** $200 to $500. **Remarks:** Full-time maker; first knife sold in 1942. **Mark:** First name and last initial, city, state and shamrock.

DENNEHY, JOHN D., 8463 Woodlands Way, Wellington, CO 80549, Phone: 970-568-3697, jd@thewildirishrose.com **Specialties:** Working straight knives, throwers, and leatherworkers knives. **Technical:** 440C & 01, heat treats own blades, part-time maker, 1st knife sold in 1989. **Patterns:** Small hunting to presentation bowies, leatherworks round and head knives. **Prices:** $200 and up. **Remarks:** Custom sheath maker, sheath making seminars at the Blade Show.

DENNING, GENO, Caveman Engineering, 135 Allenvalley Rd., Gaston, SC 29053, Phone: 803-794-6067, cden101656@aol.com Web: www.cavemanengineering.com **Specialties:** Mirror finish. **Patterns:** Hunters, fighters, folders. **Technical:** ATS-34, 440V, S-30-V D-2. **Prices:** $100 and up. **Remarks:** Full-time maker since 1996. Sole income since 1999. Instructor at montgomery Community College (Grinding Blades). **Mark:** Troy NC. **Other:** A director of SCAK, South Carolina Association of Knifemakers.

DENT, DOUGLAS M., 1208 Chestnut St., S. Charleston, WV 25309, Phone: 304-768-3308 **Specialties:** Straight and folding sportsman's knives. **Patterns:** Hunters, boots and Bowies, interframe folders. **Technical:** Forges and grinds D2, 440C, 154CM and plain tool steels. **Prices:** $70 to $300; exceptional knives to $800. **Remarks:** Part-time maker; first knife sold in 1969. **Mark:** Last name.

DERINGER, CHRISTOPH, 625 Chemin Lower, Cookshire Quebec, CANADA J0B 1M0, Phone: 819-345-4260, cdsab@sympatico.ca **Specialties:** Traditional working/using straight knives and folders of his design and to customer specs. **Patterns:** Boots, hunters, folders, art knives, kitchen knives and utility/camp knives. **Technical:** Forges 5160, O1 and Damascus. Offers a variety of filework. **Prices:** Start at $250. **Remarks:** Full-time maker; first knife sold in 1989. **Mark:** Last name stamped/engraved.

DERR, HERBERT, 413 Woodland Dr., St. Albans, WV 25177, Phone: 304-727-3866 **Specialties:** Damascus one-of-a-kind knives, carbon steels also. **Patterns:** Birdseye, Ladder back, Mosaics. **Technical:** All styles functional as well as artistically pleasing. **Prices:** $90 to $175 carbon, Damascus $250 to $800. **Remarks:** All Damascus made by maker. **Mark:** H.K. Derr.

DETMER, PHILLIP, 14140 Bluff Rd., Breese, IL 62230, Phone: 618-526-4834 **Specialties:** Working knives. **Patterns:** Bowies, daggers and hunters. **Technical:** Grinds ATS-34 and D2. **Prices:** $60 to $400. **Remarks:** Part-time maker; first knife sold in 1977. **Mark:** Last name with dagger.

DI MARZO, RICHARD, 1417 10th St So, Birmingham, AL 35205, Phone: 205-252-3331 **Specialties:** Handle artist. Scrimshaw carvings.

DICKERSON, GAVIN, PO Box 7672, Petit 1512, SOUTH AFRICA, Phone: +27 011-965-0988, Fax: +27 011-965-0988 **Specialties:** Straight knives of his design or to customer specs. **Patterns:** Hunters, skinners, fighters and Bowies. **Technical:** Hollow-grinds D2, 440C, ATS-34, 12C27 and Damascus upon request. Prefers natural handle materials; offers synthetic handle materials. **Prices:** $190 to $2500. **Remarks:** Part-time maker; first knife sold in 1982. **Mark:** Name in full.

DICKERSON, GORDON S., 152 Laurel Ln., Hohenwald, TN 38462, Phone: 931-796-1187 **Specialties:** Traditional working straight knives; Civil War era period pieces. **Patterns:** Bowies, hunters, tactical, camp/utility knives; some folders. **Technical:** Forges carbon steel; pattern welded and cable Damascus. **Prices:** $150 to $500; some to $3000. **Mark:** Last name. **Other:** ABS member.

DICKISON, SCOTT S., 179 Taylor Rd., Fisher Circle, Portsmouth, RI 02871, Phone: 401-847-7398, squared22@cox .net; Web: http:// members.cox.net/squared22 **Specialties:** Working and using straight knives and locking folders of his design and automatics. **Patterns:** Trout knives, fishing and hunting knives. **Technical:** Forges and grinds commercial Damascus and D2, O1. Uses natural handle materials. **Prices:** $400 to $750; some higher. **Remarks:** Part-time maker; first knife sold in 1989. **Mark:** Stylized initials.

DICRISTOFANO, ANTHONY P., PO Box 2369, Northlake, IL 60164, Phone: 847-845-9598 **Specialties:** Japanese-style swords. **Patterns:** Katana, Wakizashi, Otanto, Kozuka. **Technical:** Tradition and some modern steels. All clay tempered and traditionally hand polished using Japanese wet stones. **Remarks:** Part-time maker. **Prices:** Varied, available on request. **Mark:** Blade tang signed in "Masatoni" Japanese.

DIEBEL, CHUCK, PO Box 13, Broussard, LA 70516-0013

DIETZ, HOWARD, 421 Range Rd., New Braunfels, TX 78132, Phone: 830-885-4662 **Specialties:** Lock-back folders, working straight knives. **Patterns:** Folding hunters, high-grade pocket knives. **Technical:** ATS-34, 440C, CPM 440V, D2 and stainless Damascus. **Prices:** $300 to $1000. **Remarks:** Full-time gun and knife maker; first knife sold in 1995. **Mark:** Name, city, and state.

DIETZEL, BILL, PO Box 1613, Middleburg, FL 32068, Phone: 904-282-1091
Specialties: Forged straight knives and folders. Patterns: His interpretations. Technical: Forges his Damascus and other steels. Prices: Middle ranges. Remarks: Likes natural materials; uses titanium in folder liners. Mark: Name. Other: Master Smith (1997).

DIGANGI, JOSEPH M., Box 950, Santa Cruz, NM 87567, Phone: 505-753-6414, Fax: 505-753-8144
Specialties: Kitchen and table cutlery. Patterns: French chef's knives, carving sets, steak knife sets, some camp knives and hunters. Holds patents and trademarks for "System II" kitchen cutlery set. Technical: Grinds ATS-34. Prices: $150 to $595; some to $1200. Remarks: Full-time maker; first knife sold in 1983. Mark: DiGangi Designs.

DILL, DAVE, 7404 NW 30th St., Bethany, OK 73008, Phone: 405-789-0750
Specialties: Folders of his design. Patterns: Various patterns. Technical: Hand-grinds 440C, ATS-34. Offers engraving and filework on all folders. Prices: Starting at $450. Remarks: Full-time maker; first knife sold in 1987. Mark: First initial, last name.

DILL, ROBERT, 1812 Van Buren, Loveland, CO 80538, Phone: 970-667-5144, Fax: 970-667-5144
Specialties: Fancy and working knives of his design. Patterns: Hunters, Bowies and fighters. Technical: Grinds 440C and D2. Prices: $100 to $800. Remarks: Full-time maker; first knife sold in 1984. Mark: Logo stamped into blade.

DILLUVIO, FRANK J., 7544 Ravenswood, Warren, MI 48093, Phone: 810-531-7003, fjdknives@hotmail.com Web: www.fdilluviocustomknives.com
Specialties: Traditional working straight knives, some high-tech. Patterns: Hunters, Bowies, fishing knives, sub-hilts, liner lock folders and miniatures. Technical: Grinds D2, 440C, CPM; works for precision fits—no solder. Prices: $95 to $450; some to $800. Remarks: Full-time maker; first knife sold in 1984. Mark: Name and state.

DION, GREG, 3032 S. Jackson St., Oxnard, CA 93033, Phone: 805-483-1781
Specialties: Working straight knives, some fancy. Welcomes special orders. Patterns: Hunters, fighters, camp knives, Bowies and tantos. Technical: Grinds ATS-34, 154CM and 440C. Prices: $85 to $300; some to $600. Remarks: Part-time maker; first knife sold in 1985. Mark: Name.

DIOTTE, JEFF, Diotte Knives, 159 Laurier Dr., LaSalle Ontario, CANADA N9J 1L4, Phone: 519-978-2764

DIPPOLD, AL, 90 Damascus Ln., Perryville, MO 63775, Phone: 573-547-1119, adippold@midwest.net
Specialties: Fancy one-of-a-kind locking folders. Patterns: Locking folders. Technical: Forges and grinds mosaic and pattern welded Damascus. Offers filework on all folders. Prices: $500 to $3500; some higher. Remarks: Full-time maker; first knife sold in 1980. Mark: Last name in logo inside of liner.

DISKIN, MATT, PO Box 653, Freeland, WA 98249, Phone: 360-730-0451
Specialties: Damascus autos. Patterns: Dirks and daggers. Technical: Forges mosaic Damascus using 15N20, 1084, 02, 06, L6; pure nickel. Prices: Start at $500. Remarks; Full-time maker. Mark: Last name.

DIXON JR., IRA E., PO Box 2581, Ventura, CA 93002-2581, Phone: 805-659-5867
Specialties: Utilitarian straight knives of his design. Patterns: Camp, hunters, boot, fighters. Technical: Grinds ATS-34, 440C, D2, 5160. Prices: $150 to $400. Remarks: Part-time maker; first knife sold in 1993. Mark: First name, Handmade.

DODD, ROBERT F., 4340 E Canyon Dr., Camp Verde, AZ 86322, Phone: 928-567-3333, bob@rfdknives.com Web: www.rfdknives.com
Specialties: Useable fixed blade hunter/skinners, some Bowies and collectables. Patterns: Drop point. Technical: ATS-34 stainless and Damascus. Prices: $250 and up. Remarks: Hand tooled leather sheaths, users and collectables. Mark: R. F. Dodd, Camp Verde AZ.

DOGGETT, BOB, 1310 Vinetree Rd., Brandon, FL 33510, Phone: 813-786-9057, dogman@tampabay.rr.com Web: www.doggettcustomknives.com
Specialties: Clean, functional working knives. Patterns: Classic-styled hunter, fighter and utility fixed blades; liner locking folders. Technical: Uses stainless steel and commercial Damascus, 416 stainless for bolsters and hardware, hand-rubbed satin finish, top quality handle materials and titanium liners on folders. Prices: Start at $175. Remarks: Part-time maker. Mark: Last name.

DOIRON, DONALD, 6 CHEMIN PETIT LAC DES CED, Messines PQ, CANADA JOX-2JO, Phone: 819-465-2489

DOLAN, ROBERT L., 220—B Naalae Rd., Kula, HI 96790, Phone: 808-878-6406
Specialties: Working straight knives in standard patterns, his designs or to customer specs. Patterns: Fixed blades and potter's tools, ceramic saws. Technical: Grinds O1, D2, 440C and ATS-34. Heat-treats and engraves. Prices: Start at $75. Remarks: Full-time tool and knife maker; first knife sold in 1985. Mark: Last name, USA.

DOLE, ROGER, DOLE CUSTOM KNIFE WORKS, PO Box 323, Buckley, WA 98321, Phone: 253-862-6770
Specialties: Folding knives. They include slip joint, lock back and locking liner type knives. Most have integral bolster and liners. The locking liner knives have a removable titanium side lock that is machined into the integral liner, they are also available with a split liner lock. Technical: Makes ATS-34, 440-C and BG-42 stainless steel. Has in stock or available all types of natural and synthetic handle materials. Uses 416, 303, and 304 stainless steel, 7075-T6 aluminum and titanium for the guards on the fixed blade knives and integral liners on the folding knives. The locking liner lock mechanisms are made from 6AL4V titanium. Uses the stock removal method to fabricate all of the blades produced. The blades are ground on a 2 X 72 inch belt grinder. Not a bladesmith. Patterns: 51 working designs for fixed blade knives. They include small bird and trout knives to skinning axes. Most are working designs. All come with hand crafted leather sheath Kydex sheaths; can be special ordered. Remarks: First knife sold in 1975.

DOMINY, CHUCK, PO Box 593, Colleyville, TX 76034, Phone: 817-498-4527
Specialties: Titanium liner lock folders. Patterns: Hunters, utility/camp knives and liner lock folders. Technical: Grinds 440C and ATS-34. Prices: $250 to $3000. Remarks: Full-time maker; first knife sold in 1976. Mark: Last name.

DOOLITTLE, MIKE, 13 Denise Ct., Novato, CA 94947, Phone: 415-897-3246
Specialties: Working straight knives in standard patterns. Patterns: Hunters and fishing knives. Technical: Grinds 440C, 154CM and ATS-34. Prices: $125 to $200; some to $750. Remarks: Part-time maker; first knife sold in 1981. Mark: Name, city and state.

DORNELES, LUCIANO OLIVEIRIRA, Rua 15 De Novembro 2222, Nova Petropolis, RS, BRAZIL 95150-000, Phone: 011-55-54-303-303-90, tchebufalo@hotmail.com
Specialties: Traditional "true" Brazilian-style working knives and to customer specs. Patterns: Brazilian hunters, utility and camp knives, Bowies, Dirk. A master at the making of the true "Faca Campeira Gaucha," the true camp knife of the famous Brazilian Gauchos. A Dorneles knife is 100% hand-forged with sledge hammers only. Can makes spectacular Damascus hunters/daggers. Technical: Forges only 52100 and his own Damascus, can put silver wire inlay on customer design handles on special orders; uses only natural handle materials. Prices: $250 to $1000. Mark: Symbol with L. Dorneles.

DOTSON, TRACY, 1280 Hwy. C-4A, Baker, FL 32531, Phone: 850-537-2407
Specialties: Folding fighters and small folders. Patterns: Liner lock and lockback folders. Technical: Hollow-grinds ATS-34 and commercial Damascus. Prices: Start at $250. Remarks: Part-time maker; first knife sold in 1995. Mark: Last name.

DOUCETTE, R, CUSTOM KNIVES, 112 Memorial Dr, Brantford Ontario, CANADA N3R 5S3, Phone: 519-756-9040, randy@randydoucetteknives.com Web: www.randydoucetteknives.com
Specialties: Filework, tactical designs, multiple grinds. Patterns: Bowies, daggers, tantos, karambits, short swords. Technical: All my knives are handmade. The only out sourcing is heat treatment. Prices: $200 to $2,500. Remarks: Custom orders welcome. Mark: R. Doucette

DOUGLAS, JOHN J., 506 Powell Rd., Lynch Station, VA 24571, Phone: 804-369-7196
Specialties: Fancy and traditional straight knives and folders of his design and to customer specs. Patterns: Locking folders, swords and sgian dubhs. Technical: Grinds 440C stainless, ATS-34 stainless and customer's choice. Offers newly designed non-pivot uni-lock folders. Prefers highly polished finish. Prices: $160 to $1400. Remarks: Full-time maker; first knife sold in 1975. Doing business as Douglas Keltic. Mark: Stylized initial. Folders are numbered; customs are dated.

DOURSIN, GERARD, Chemin des Croutoules, F 84210, Pernes ies Fontaines, FRANCE
Specialties: Period pieces. Patterns: Liner locks and daggers. Technical: Forges mosaic Damascus. Prices: $600 to $4000. Remarks: First knife sold in 1983. Mark: First initial, last name and I stop the lion.

DOUSSOT, LAURENT, 6262 De La Roche, Montreal, Quebec, CANADA H2H 1W9, Phone: 516-270-6992, Fax: 516-722-1641
 Specialties: Fancy and embellished folders and fantasy knives. **Patterns:** Fighters and locking folders. **Technical:** Grinds ATS-34 and commercial Damascus. Scale carvings on all knives; most bolsters are carved titanium. **Prices:** $350 to $3000. **Remarks:** Part-time maker; first knife was sold in 1992. **Mark:** Stylized initials inside circle.

DOWELL, T.M., 139 NW St. Helen's Pl., Bend, OR 97701, Phone: 541-382-8924
 Specialties: Integral construction in hunting knives. **Patterns:** Limited to featherweights, lightweights, integral hilt and caps. **Technical:** Grinds D-2, BG-42 and Vasco wear. **Prices:** $185 and up. **Remarks:** Full-time maker; first knife sold in 1967. **Mark:** Initials logo.

DOWNIE, JAMES T., 10076 Estate Dr., Port Franks, Ont., CANADA NOM 2LO, Phone: 519-243-1488, Fax: 519-243-1487, Web: www.kdg.org click on members page
 Specialties: Serviceable straight knives and folders; period pieces. **Patterns:** Hunters, Bowies, camp knives and miniatures. **Technical:** Grinds D2, 440C and ATS-34, Damasteel, stainless steel Damascus. **Prices:** $100 to $500; some higher. **Remarks:** Full-time maker, first knife sold in 1978. **Mark:** Signature of first and middle initials, last name.

DOWNING, TOM, 2675 12th St., Cuyahoga Falls, OH 44223, Phone: 330-923-7464
 Specialties: Working straight knives; period pieces. **Patterns:** Hunters, fighters and tantos. **Technical:** Grinds 440C, ATs-34 and CPM-T-440V. Prefers natural handle materials. **Prices:** $150 to $900, some to $1500. **Remarks:** Part-time maker; first knife sold in 1979. **Mark:** First and middle initials, last name.

DOWNING, LARRY, 12268 Hwy. 181N, Bremen, KY 42325, Phone: 270-525-3523, Fax: 270-525-3372, larrdowning@bellsout.net Web: www.downingcustomknives.com
 Specialties: Working straight knives and folders. **Patterns:** From mini-knives to daggers, folding lockers to interframes. **Technical:** Forges and grinds 154CM, ATS-34 and his own Damascus. **Prices:** $195 to $950; some higher. **Remarks:** Part-time maker; first knife sold in 1979. **Mark:** Name in arrowhead.

DOWNS, JAMES F., 35 Sunset Rd., Londonderry, OH 45647, Phone: 740-887-2099, jfdowns1@yahoo.com
 Specialties: Working straight knives of his design or to customer specs. **Patterns:** Folders, Bowies, boot, hunters, utility. **Technical:** Grinds 440C and other steels. Prefers mastodon ivory, all pearls, stabilized wood and elephant ivory. **Prices:** $75 to $1200. **Remarks:** Full-time maker; first knife sold in 1980. Brochures $2. **Mark:** Last name.

DOX, JAN, Zwanebloemlaan 27, B 2900 Schoten, BELGIUM, Phone: 32 3 658 77 43, jan.dox@pi.be
 Specialties: Working/using knives, from kitchen to battlefield. **Patterns:** Own designs, some based on traditional ethnic patterns (Scots, Celtic, Scandinavian and Japanese) or to customer specs. **Technical:** Grinds D2/A2 and stainless, forges carbon steels, convex edges. Handles: Wrapped in modern or traditional patterns, resin impregnated if desired. Natural or synthetic materials, some carved. **Prices:** Start at 25 to 50 Euro (USD) and up. **Remarks:** Spare-time maker, first knife sold 2001. **Mark:** Name or stylized initials.

DOZIER, BOB, PO Box 1941, Springdale, AR 72765, Phone: 888-823-0023/479-756-0023, Fax: 479-756-9139, info@dozierknives.com Web www.dozierknives.com
 Specialties: Using knives (fixed blades and folders). **Patterns:** Some fine collector-grade knives. **Technical:** Uses D2. Prefers Micarta handle material. **Prices:** Using knives: $145 to $595. **Remarks:** Full-time maker; first knife sold in 1965. **Mark:** State; last name in a circle (for fixed blades); Last name with arrow through 'D' and year over name (for folders). **Other:** Also sells a semi-handmade line of fixed blade with mark; state, knives, last name in circle.

DRAPER, AUDRA, #10 Creek Dr., Riverton, WY 82501, Phone: 307-856-6807 or 307-851-0426 cell, adraper@wyoming.com Web: www.draperknives.com
 Specialties: One-of-a-kind straight and folding knives. Also pendants, earring and bracelets of Damascus. **Patterns:** Design custom knives, using, Bowies, and mini's. **Technical:** Forge Damascus; heat-treats all knives. **Prices:** Vary depending on item. **Remarks:** Full-time maker; master bladesmith in the ABS. Member of the PKA; first knife sold in 1995. **Mark:** Audra.

DRAPER, MIKE, #10 Creek Dr., Riverton, WY 82501, Phone: 307-856-6807, adraper@wyoming.com
 Specialties: Mainly folding knives in tactical fashion, occasonal fixed blade. **Patterns:** Hunters, Bowies and camp knives, tactical survival. **Technical:** Grinds S30V stainless steel . **Prices:** Starting at $250+.

DREW, GERALD, 2 Glenn Cable, Asheville, NC 28805, Phone: 828-299-7821
 Specialties: Blade ATS-34 5 1/2". Handle spalted Maple. 10" OAL. Straight knives. **Patterns:** Hunters, camp knives, some Bowies and tactical. **Technical:** ATS-34 preferred. **Price:** $110 to $200. **Mark:** GL DREW.

DRISCOLL, MARK, 4115 Avoyer Pl., La Mesa, CA 91941, Phone: 619-670-0695
 Specialties: High-art, period pieces and working/using knives of his design or to customer specs; some fancy. **Patterns:** Swords, Bowies, Fighters, daggers, hunters and primitive (mountain man-styles). **Technical:** Forges 52100, 5160, O1, L6, 1095, and maker his own Damascus and mokume; also does multiple quench heat treating. Uses exotic hardwoods, ivory and horn, offers fancy file work, carving, scrimshaws. **Prices:** $150 to $550; some to $1500. **Remarks:** Part-time maker; first knife sold in 1986. Doing business as Mountain Man Knives. **Mark:** Double "M".

DRISKILL, BERYL, PO Box 187, Braggadocio, MO 63826, Phone: 573-757-6262
 Specialties: Fancy working knives. **Patterns:** Hunting knives, fighters, Bowies, boots, daggers and lockback folders. **Technical:** Grinds ATS-34. **Prices:** Start at $200. **Remarks:** Part-time maker; first knife sold in 1984. **Mark:** Name.
 Specialties: Working/using straight knives of his design. **Patterns:** Hunters and utility/camp knives. **Technical:** Grinds 154CM and D2. **Prices:** $125 to $5000. **Remarks:** Spare-time maker; first knife sold in 1995. **Mark:** First and middle initials, last name, maker, city and state.

DROST, MICHAEL B., Rt. 2, Box 49, French Creek, WV 26218, Phone: 304-472-7901
 Specialties: Working/using straight knives and folders of all designs. **Patterns:** Hunters, locking folders and utility/camp knives. **Technical:** Grinds ATS-34, D2 and CPM-T-440V. Offers dove-tailed bolsters and spacers, filework and scrimshaw. **Prices:** $125 to $400; some to $740. **Remarks:** Full-time maker; first knife sold in 1990. Doing business as Drost Custom Knives. **Mark:** Name, city and state.

DROST, JASON D., Rt. 2, Box 49, French Creek, WV 26218, Phone: 304-472-7901

DUBLIN, DENNIS, 728 Stanley St., Box 986, Enderby, BC, CANADA V0E 1V0, Phone: 604-838-6753
 Specialties: Working straight knives and folders, plain or fancy. **Patterns:** Hunters and Bowies, locking hunters, combination knives/axes. **Technical:** Forges and grinds high-carbon steels. **Prices:** $100 to $400; some higher. **Remarks:** Full-time maker; first knife sold in 1970. **Mark:** Name.

DUFF, BILL, 14380 Ghost Rider Dr., Reno, NV 89511, Phone: 775-851-9331
 Specialties: Straight knives and folders, some fancy. **Patterns:** Hunters, folders and miniatures. **Technical:** Grinds 440-C and commercial Damascus. **Prices:** $200 to $1000 some higher. **Remarks:** First knife some in 1976. **Mark:** Bill Duff.

DUFOUR, ARTHUR J., 8120 De Armour Rd., Anchorage, AK 99516, Phone: 907-345-1701
 Specialties: Working straight knives from standard patterns. **Patterns:** Hunters, Bowies, camp and fishing knives—grinded thin and pointed. **Technical:** Grinds 440C, ATS-34, AEB-L. Tempers 57-58R; hollow-grinds. **Prices:** $135; some to $250. **Remarks:** Part-time maker; first knife sold in 1970. **Mark:** Prospector logo.

DUGAN, BRAD M., 422 A Cribbage Ln., San Marcos, CA 92069, Phone: 760-752-4417

DUGGER, DAVE, 2504 West 51, Westwood, KS 66205, Phone: 913-831-2382
 Specialties: Working straight knives; fantasy pieces. **Patterns:** Hunters, boots and daggers in one-of-a-kind styles. **Technical:** Grinds D2, 440C and 154CM. **Prices:** $75 to $350; some to $1200. **Remarks:** Part-time maker; first knife sold in 1979. Not currently accepting orders. Doing business as Dog Knives. **Mark:** DOG.

DUNKERLEY, RICK, PO Box 582, Seeley Lake, MT 59868, Phone: 406-677-5496, rick@dunkerleyhandmadeknives.com
 Specialties: Mosaic Damascus folders and carbon steel utility knives. **Patterns:** One-of-a-kind folders, standard hunters and utility designs. **Technical:** Forges 52100, Damascus and mosaic Damascus. Prefers natural handle materials. **Prices:** $200 and up. **Remarks:** Full-time maker; first knife sold in 1984, ABS Master Smith. Doing business as Dunkerley Custom Knives. Dunkerley handmade knives, sole authorship. **Mark:** Dunkerley, MS.

DUNN, CHARLES K., 17740 GA Hwy. 116, Shiloh, GA 31826, Phone: 706-846-2666

Specialties: Fancy and working straight knives and folders of his design and to customer specs. **Patterns:** Bowies, hunters and locking folders. **Technical:** Grinds 440C and ATS-34. Engraves; filework offered. **Prices:** $75 to $300. **Remarks:** Part-time maker; first knife sold in 1988. **Mark:** First initial, last name, city, state.

DUNN, STEVE, 376 Biggerstaff Rd., Smiths Grove, KY 42171, Phone: 270-563-9830

Specialties: Working and using straight knives of his design; period pieces. **Patterns:** Hunters, skinners, Bowies, fighters, camp knives, folders, swords and battle axes. **Technical:** Forges his Damascus, O1, 5160, L6 and 1095. **Prices:** Moderate to upscale. **Remarks:** Full-time maker; first knife sold in 1990. **Mark:** Last name and MS.

DURAN, JERRY T., PO Box 80692, Albuquerque, NM 87198-0692, Phone: 505-873-4676, jtdknives@hotmail.com Website: www.kmg.org/jtdknives

Specialties: Tactical folders, Bowies, fighters, liner locks and hunters. **Patterns:** Folders, Bowies, hunters and tactical knives. **Technical:** Forges own Damascus and forges carbon steel. **Prices:** Moderate to upscale. **Remarks:** Full-time maker; first knife sold in 1978. **Mark:** Initials in elk rack logo.

DURHAM, KENNETH, BUZZARD ROOST FORGE, 10495 White Pike, Cherokee, AL 35616, Phone: 256-359-4287, www.home.hiwaay.net/~jamesd/

Specialties: Bowies, dirks, hunters. **Patterns:** Traditional patterns. **Technical:** Forges 1095, 5160, 52100 and makes own Damascus. **Prices:** $85 to $1600. **Remarks:** Began making knives about 1995. Received Journeyman stamp 1999. **Mark:** Bull's head with Ken Durham above and Cherokee AL below.

DURIO, FRED, 144 Gulino St., Opelousas, LA 70570, Phone: 337-948-4831

Specialties: Folders. **Patterns:** Liner locks; plain and fancy. **Technical:** Makes own Damascus. **Prices:** Moderate to upscale. **Remarks:** Full-time maker. **Mark:** Last name-Durio.

DUVALL, FRED, 10715 Hwy. 190, Benton, AR 72015, Phone: 501-778-9360

Specialties: Working straight knives and folders. **Patterns:** Locking folders, slip joints, hunters, fighters and Bowies. **Technical:** Grinds D2 and CPM440V; forges 5160. **Prices:** $100 to $400; some to $800. **Remarks:** Part-time maker; first knife sold in 1973. **Mark:** Last name.

DYER, DAVID, 4531 Hunters Glen, Granbury, TX 76048, Phone: 817-573-1198

Specialties: Working skinners and early period knives. **Patterns:** Customer designs, his own patterns. **Technical:** Coal forged blades; 5160 and 52100 steels. **Prices:** $150 for neck-knives and small (3" to 3-1/2"). To $600 for large blades and specialty blades. **Mark:** Last name DYER electro etched. **Other:** Grinds D-2, 1095, L-6.

DYESS, EDDIE, 1005 Hamilton, Roswell, NM 88201, Phone: 505-623-5599

Specialties: Working and using straight knives in standard patterns. **Patterns:** Hunters and fighters. **Technical:** Grinds 440C, 154CM and D2 on request. **Prices:** $85 to $135; some to $250. **Remarks:** Spare-time maker; first knife sold in 1980. **Mark:** Last name.

DYRNOE, PER, Sydskraenten 10, Tulstrup, DK 3400 Hilleroed, DENMARK, Phone: +45 42287041

Specialties: Hand-crafted knives with zirconia ceramic blades. **Patterns:** Hunters, skinners, Norwegian-style tolle knives, most in animal-like ergonomic shapes. **Technical:** Handles of exotic hardwood, horn, fossil ivory, etc. Norwegian-style sheaths. **Prices:** Start at $500. **Remarks:** Part-time maker in cooperation with Hans J. Henriksen; first knife sold in 1993. **Mark:** Initial logo.

E

EAKER, ALLEN L., 416 Clinton Ave., Dept KI, Paris, IL 61944, Phone: 217-466-5160

Specialties: Traditional straight knives and folders of his design. **Patterns:** Knives, locking folders and slip-joint folders. **Technical:** Grinds 440C; inlays. **Prices:** $125 to $325; some to $500. **Remarks:** Spare-time maker; first knife sold in 1994. **Mark:** Initials in tankard logo stamped on tang, serial number on back side.

EALY, DELBERT, PO Box 121, Indian River, MI 49749, Phone: 231-238-4705

EASLER JR., RUSSELL O., PO Box 301, Woodruff, SC 29388, Phone: 864-476-7830

Specialties: Working straight knives and folders. **Patterns:** Hunters, tantos and boots; locking folders and interframes. **Technical:** Grinds 440C, 154CM and ATS-34. **Prices:** $100 to $350; some to $800. **Remarks:** Part-time maker; first knife sold in 1973. **Mark:** Name or name with bear logo.

EATON, RICK, 9944 McCranie St., Shepherd, MT 59079 3126

Specialties: Interframe folders and one-hand-opening side locks. **Patterns:** Bowies, daggers, fighters and folders. **Technical:** Grinds 154CM, ATS-34, 440C and other maker's Damascus. Offers high-quality hand engraving, Bulino and gold inlay. **Prices:** Upscale. **Remarks:** Full-time maker; first knife sold in 1982. **Mark:** Full name or full name and address.

EBISU, HIDESAKU, 3-39-7 KOI OSAKO NISHI KU, Hiroshima City, JAPAN 733 0816

ECHOLS, ROGER, 46 Channing Rd., Nashville, AR 71852-8588, Phone: 870-451-9089, blademanechols@aol.com

Specialties: Liner locks, auto-scale release, lock backs. **Patterns:** My own or yours. **Technical:** Autos. **Prices:** $500 to $1700. **Remarks:** Likes to use pearl, ivory and Damascus the most. **Mark:** Name. **Other:** Made first knife in 1984. **Remarks:** Part-time maker; tool and die maker by trade.

EDDY, HUGH E., 211 E Oak St., Caldwell, ID 83605, Phone: 208-459-0536

EDEN, THOMAS, PO Box 57, Cranbury, NJ 08512, Phone: 609-371-0774

Patterns: Fixed blade, working patterns, hand forged. **Technical:** Damascus. **Mark:** Eden (script). **Remarks:** ABS Smith.

EDGE, TOMMY, 1244 County Road 157, Cash, AR 72421, Phone: 501-477-5210, tedge@tex.net

Specialties: Fancy/embellished working knives of his design. **Patterns:** Bowies, hunters and utility/camping knives. **Technical:** Grinds 440C, ATS-34 and D2. Makes own cable Damascus; offers filework. **Prices:** $70 to $250; some to $1500. **Remarks:** Part-time maker; first knife sold in 1973. **Mark:** Stamped first initial, last name and stenciled name, city and state in oval shape.

EDWARDS, FAIN E., PO Box 280, Topton, NC 28781, Phone: 828-321-3127

EDWARDS, MITCH, 303 New Salem Rd., Glasgow, KY 42141, Phone: 270-651-9257, medwards@glasgow-ky.com Web: www.traditionalknives.com

Specialties: Period pieces. **Patterns:** Neck knives, camp, rifleman and Bowie knives. **Technical:** All hand forged, forges own Damascus 01, 1084, 1095, L-6, 15N20. **Prices:** $200 to $1000. **Remarks:** Journeyman Smith. **Mark:** Broken heart.

EHRENBERGER, DANIEL ROBERT, 6192 Hwy 168, Shelbyville, MO 63469, Phone: 573-633-2010

Specialties: Affordable working/using straight knives of his design and to custom specs. Patterns: 10" western Bowie, fighters, hunting and skinning knives. **Technical:** Forges 1085, 1095, his own Damascus and cable Damascus. **Prices:** $80 to $500. **Remarks:** Full-time maker, first knife sold 1994. **Mark:** Ehrenberger JS.

EKLUND, MAIHKEL, Föne 1111, S-820 41 Farila, SWEDEN, info@art-knives.com Web: www.art-knives.com

Specialties: Collector-grade working straight knives. **Patterns:** Hunters, Bowies and fighters. **Technical:** Grinds ATS-34, Uddeholm and Dama steel. Engraves and scrimshaws. **Prices:** $150 to $700. **Remarks:** Full-time maker; first knife sold in 1983. **Mark:** Initials or name.

ELDER JR., PERRY B., 1321 Garretsburg Rd., Clarksville, TN 37042-2516, Phone: 931-647-9416, pbebje@aol.com

Specialties: Hunters, combat Bowies bird and trout. **Technical:** High-carbon steel and Damascus blades. **Prices:** $250 and up depending on blade desired. **Mark:** ELDER.

ELDRIDGE, ALLAN, 7731 Four Winds Dr., Ft Worth, TX 76133, Phone: 817-370-7778

Specialties: Fancy classic straight knives in standard patterns. **Patterns:** Hunters, Bowies, fighters, folders and miniatures. **Technical:** Grinds O1 and Damascus. Engraves silver-wire inlays, pearl inlays, scrimshaws and offers filework. **Prices:** $50 to $500; some to $1200. **Remarks:** Spare-time maker; first knife sold in 1965. **Mark:** Initials.

ELISHEWITZ, ALLEN, PO Box 3059, Canyon Lake, TX 78133, Phone: 830-899-5356, allen@elishewitzknives.com Web: elishewitzknives.com

Specialties: Collectible high-tech working straight knives and folders of his design. **Patterns:** Working, utility and tactical knives. **Technical:**

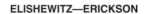

Grinds 154CM and stainless steel Damascus. All designs drafted and field-tested. **Prices:** $400 to $600. **Remarks:** Full-time maker; first knife sold in 1989. **Mark:** Last name with a Japanese crane.

ELKINS, R. VAN, PO Box 156, Bonita, LA 71223, Phone: 318-823-2124, Fax: 318-283-6802

    Specialties: High-art Bowies, fighters, folders and period daggers; all one-of-a-kind pieces. **Patterns:** Welcomes customer designs. **Technical:** Forges his own Damascus in several patterns, O1 and 5160. **Prices:** $250 to $2800. **Remarks:** First knife sold in 1984. **Mark:** Last name.

ELLEFSON, JOEL, PO Box 1016, 310 S. 1st St., Manhattan, MT 59741, Phone: 406-284-3111

    Specialties: Working straight knives, fancy daggers and one-of-a-kinds. **Patterns:** Hunters, daggers and some folders. **Technical:** Grinds A2, 440C and ATS-34. Makes own mokume in bronze, brass, silver and shibuishi; makes brass/steel blades. **Prices:** $75 to $500; some to $2000. **Remarks:** Part-time maker; first knife sold in 1978. **Mark:** Stylized last initial.

ELLERBE, W.B., 3871 Osceola Rd., Geneva, FL 32732, Phone: 407-349-5818

    Specialties: Period and primitive knives and sheaths. **Patterns:** Bowies to patch knives, some tomahawks. **Technical:** Grinds Sheffield O1 and files. **Prices:** Start at $35. **Remarks:** Full-time maker; first knife sold in 1971. Doing business as Cypress Bend Custom Knives. **Mark:** Last name or initials.

ELLIOTT, JERRY, 4507 Kanawha Ave., Charleston, WV 25304, Phone: 304-925-5045

    Specialties: Classic and traditional straight knives and folders of his design and to customer specs. **Patterns:** Hunters, locking folders and Bowies. **Technical:** Grinds ATS-34, 154CM, O1, D2 and T-440-V. All guards silver-soldered; bolsters are pinned on straight knives, spot-welded on folders. **Prices:** $80 to $265; some to $1000. **Remarks:** Full-time maker; first knife sold in 1972. **Mark:** First and middle initials, last name, knife maker, city, state.

ELLIOTT, MARCUS, Pen Dinas, Wyddfydd Rd., Great Orme, Llandudno Gwynedd, GREAT BRITAIN LL30 2QL, Phone: 01492-872747

    Specialties: Fancy working knives. **Patterns:** Boots and small hunters. **Technical:** Grinds O1, 440C and ATS-34. **Prices:** $160 to $250. **Remarks:** Spare-time maker; first knife sold in 1981. Makes only a few knives each year. **Mark:** First name, middle initial, last name, knife maker, city, state.

ELLIS, DAVE/ABS MASTERSMITH, 380 South Melrose Dr. #407, Vista, CA 92083, Phone: 760-643-4032 Eves: 760-945-7177, www.exquisiteknives.com

    Specialties: Bowies, utility and combat knives. **Patterns:** Using knives to art quality pieces. **Technical:** Forges 5160, L-6, 52100, cable and his own Damascus steels. **Prices:** $300 to $4000. **Remarks:** Part-time maker. California's first ABS Master Smith. **Mark:** Dagger-Rose with name and M.S. mark.

ELLIS, WILLIAM DEAN, 8875 N. Barton, Fresno, CA 93720, Phone: 209-299-0303, urleebird@comcast.net Web: www.billysblades.com

    Specialties: Classic and fancy knives of his design. **Patterns:** Boots, fighters and utility knives. **Technical:** Grinds ATS-34, D2 and Damascus. Offers tapered tangs and six patterns of filework; tooled multi-colored sheaths. **Prices:** $250 to $500; some to $1500. **Remarks:** Part-time maker; first knife sold in 1991. Doing business as Billy's Blades. **Mark:** "B" in a five-point star next to "Billy," city and state within a rounded-corner rectangle.

ELLIS, WILLY B., WILLY B CUSTOM STICKS and PICKS, 4941 Cardinal Trail, Palm Harbor, FL 34683, Phone: 727-942-6420, Web: www.willyb.com

    Specialties: One-of-a-kind high art and fantasy knives of his design. Occasional customs full size and miniatures. **Patterns:** Bowies, fighters, hunters and others. **Technical:** Grinds 440C, ATS-34, 1095, carbon Damascus, ivory bone, stone and metal carving. **Prices:** $175 to $15,000. **Remarks:** Full-time maker, first knife made in 1973. Probationary member Knifemakers Guild. **Mark:** Willy B. or WB"S C etched or carved. **Other:** Jewel setting inlays.

ELROD, ROGER R., 58 Dale Ave., Enterprise, AL 36330, Phone: 334-347-1863

EMBRETSEN, KAJ, FALUVAGEN 67, S-82821 Edsbyn, SWEDEN, Phone: 46-271-21057, Fax: 46-271-22961

    Specialties: High quality folders. **Patterns:** Scandinavian-style knives. **Technical:** Forges Damascus. Uses only his blades; natural materials. **Prices:** Upscale. **Remarks:** Full-time maker. **Mark:** Name.

EMERSON, ERNEST R., PO Box 4180, Torrance, CA 90510-4180, Phone: 310-212-7455, info@emersonknives.com Web: www.emersonknives.com

    Specialties: High-tech folders and combat fighters. **Patterns:** Fighters, liner lock combat folders and SPECWAR combat knives. **Technical:** Grinds 154CM and Damascus. Makes folders with titanium fittings, liners and locks. Chisel grind specialist. **Prices:** $550 to $850; some to $10,000. **Remarks:** Full-time maker; first knife sold in 1983. **Mark:** Last name and Specwar knives.

ENCE, JIM, 145 S 200 East, Richfield, UT 84701, Phone: 435-896-6206

    Specialties: High-art period pieces (spec in California knives) art knives. **Patterns:** Art, boot knives, fighters, Bowies and occasional folders. **Technical:** Grinds 440C for polish and beauty boys'; makes own Damascus. **Prices:** Upscale. **Remarks:** Full-time maker; first knife sold in 1977. Does own engraving, gold work and stone work. **Mark:** Ence, usually engraved. **Other:** Guild member since 1977. Founding member of the AKI.

ENGLAND, VIRGIL, 1340 Birchwood St., Anchorage, AK 99508, Phone: 907-274-9494, WEB: www.virgilengland.com

    Specialties: Edged weapons and equipage, one-of-a-kind only. **Patterns:** Axes, swords, lances and body armor. **Technical:** Forges and grinds as pieces dictate. Offers stainless and Damascus. **Prices:** Upscale. **Remarks:** A veteran knife maker. No commissions. **Mark:** Stylized initials.

ENGLE, WILLIAM, 16608 Oak Ridge Rd., Boonville, MO 65233, Phone: 816-882-6277

    Specialties: Traditional working and using straight knives of his design. **Patterns:** Hunters, Bowies and fighters. **Technical:** Grinds 440C, ATS-34 and 154 CM. **Prices:** $250 to $500; some higher. **Remarks:** Part-time maker; first knife sold in 1982. All knives come with certificate of authenticity. **Mark:** Last name in block lettering.

ENGLEBRETSON, GEORGE, 1209 NW 49th St., Oklahoma City, OK 73118, Phone: 405-840-4784

    Specialties: Working straight knives. **Patterns:** Hunters and Bowies. **Technical:** Grinds A2, D2, 440C and ATS-34. **Prices:** Start at $150. **Remarks:** Full-time maker; first knife sold in 1967. **Mark:** "By George," name and city.

ENGLISH, JIM, 14586 Olive Vista Dr., Jamul, CA 91935, Phone: 619-669-0833

    Specialties: Traditional working straight knives to customer specs. **Patterns:** Hunters, Bowies, fighters, tantos, daggers, boot and utility/camp knives. **Technical:** Grinds 440C, ATS-34, commercial Damascus and customer choice. **Prices:** $130 to $350. **Remarks:** Part-time maker; first knife sold in 1985. In addition to custom line, also does business as Mountain Home Knives. **Mark:** Double "A," Double "J" logo.

ENNIS, RAY, 1220S 775E, Ogden, UT 84404, Phone: 800-410-7603, Fax: 501-621-2683, nifmakr@hotmail.com web: www.ennis-entrekusa.com

ENOS III, THOMAS M., 12302 State Rd. 535, Orlando, FL 32836, Phone: 407-239-6205, tmenos3@att.net

    Specialties: Heavy-duty working straight knives; unusual designs. **Patterns:** Swords, machetes, daggers, skinners, filleting, period pieces. **Technical:** Grinds 440C, D2, 154CM. **Prices:** $75 to $1500. **Remarks:** Full-time maker; first knife sold in 1972. **Mark:** Name in knife logo and year, type of steel and serial number. **Other:** No longer accepting custom requests. Will be making his own designs. Send SASE for listing of items for sale.

ENTIN, ROBERT, 127 Pembroke St. 1, Boston, MA 02118

EPTING, RICHARD, 4021 Cody Dr., College Station, TX 77845, Phone: 979-690-6496, rgeknives@hotmail.com

    Specialties: Folders and working straight knives. **Patterns:** Hunters, Bowies, and locking folders. **Technical:** Forges high-carbon steel and his own Damascus. **Prices:** $200 to $800; some to $1800. **Remarks:** Part-time maker, first knife sold 1996. **Mark:** Name in arch logo.

ERICKSON, L.M., PO Box 132, Liberty, UT 84310, Phone: 801-745-2026

    Specialties: Straight knives; period pieces. **Patterns:** Bowies, fighters, boots and hunters. **Technical:** Grinds 440C, 154CM and commercial Damascus. **Prices:** $200 to $900; some to $5000. **Remarks:** Part-time maker; first knife sold in 1981. **Mark:** Name, city, state.

ERICKSON, WALTER E., 22280 Shelton Tr., Atlanta, MI 49709, Phone: 989-785-5262

    Specialties: Unusual survival knives and high-tech working knives. **Patterns:** Butterflies, hunters, tantos. **Technical:** Grinds ATS-34 or customer choice. **Prices:** $150 to $500; some to $1500. **Remarks:** Full-time maker; first knife sold in 1981. **Mark:** Last name in depressed area on blade.

ERIKSEN, JAMES THORLIEF, dba VIKING KNIVES, 3830 Dividend Dr., Garland, TX 75042, Phone: 972-494-3667, Fax: 972-235-4932, VikingKnives@aol.com
Specialties: Heavy-duty working and using straight knives and folders utilizing traditional, Viking original and customer specification patterns. Some high-tech and fancy/embellished knives available. **Patterns:** Bowies, hunters, skinners, boot and belt knives, utility/camp knives, fighters, daggers, locking folders, slip-joint folders and kitchen knives. **Technical:** Hollow-grinds 440C, D2, ASP-23, ATS-34, 154CM, Vascowear. **Prices:** $150 to $300; some to $600. **Remarks:** Full-time maker; first knife sold in 1985. Doing business as Viking Knives. For a color catalog showing 50 different models, mail $5 to above address. **Mark:** VIKING or VIKING USA for export.

ESSEGIAN, RICHARD, 7387 E. Tulare St., Fresno, CA 93727, Phone: 309-255-5950
Specialties: Fancy working knives of his design; art knives. **Patterns:** Bowies and some small hunters. **Technical:** Grinds A2, D2, 440C and 154CM. Engraves and inlays. **Prices:** Start at $600. **Remarks:** Part-time maker; first knife sold in 1986. **Mark:** Last name, city and state.

ETZLER, JOHN, 11200 N. Island, Grafton, OH 44044, Phone: 440-748-2460, jetzler@bright.net Web: members.tripod.com/~etzlerknives/
Specialties: High-art and fantasy straight knives and folders of his design and to customer specs. **Patterns:** Folders, daggers, fighters, utility knives. **Technical:** Forges and grinds nickel Damascus and tool steel; grinds stainless steels. Prefers exotic, natural materials. **Prices:** $250 to $1200; some to $6500. **Remarks:** Full-time maker; first knife sold in 1992. **Mark:** Name or initials.

EVANS, BRUCE A., 409 CR 1371, Booneville, MS 38829, Phone: 662-720-0193, beknives@avsia.com Web: www.bruceevans.homestead.com/open.html
Specialties: Forges blades. **Patterns:** Hunters, Bowies, or will work with customer. **Technical:** 5160, cable Damascus, pattern welded Damascus. **Prices:** $200 and up. **Mark:** Bruce A. Evans Same with JS on reverse of blade.

EVANS, CARLTON, PO Box 815, Aledo, TX 76008, Phone: 817-441-1363, carlton@crevanscustomkives.com Web: crevanscustomknives.com
Specialties: In high end folders and fixed, collectible but durable enough to carry everyday. **Patterns:** Working and hunting. **Technical:** Use the stock removal methods. The materials used are of the highest quality. **Prices:** Start from $650. **Remarks:** Part-time knifemaker. A 2003 Probationary member, eligible for voting membership August 2005 to the Knifemakers Guild.

EVANS, RONALD B., 209 Hoffer St., Middleton, PA 17057-2723, Phone: 717-944-5464

EVANS, VINCENT K. AND GRACE, 35 Beaver Creek Rd, Cathlamet, WA 98612, Phone: 360-795-0096, vevans@localnet.com
Specialties: Period pieces; swords. **Patterns:** Scottish, Viking, central Asian. **Technical:** Forges 5160 and his own Damascus. **Prices:** $300 to $2000; some to $8000. **Remarks:** Full-time maker; first knife sold in 1983. **Mark:** Last initial with fish logo.

EWING, JOHN H., 3276 Dutch Valley Rd., Clinton, TN 37716, Phone: 615-457-5757
Specialties: Working straight knives, hunters, camp knives. **Patterns:** Hunters. **Technical:** Grinds 440, Forges 5160 52100; prefers forging. **Prices:** $150 to $2000. **Remarks:** Part-time maker; first knife sold in 1985. **Mark:** First initial, last name, some embellishing done on knives.

F

FAGAN, JAMES A., 109 S 17 Ave., Lake Worth, FL 33460, Phone: 561-585-9349

FANT JR., GEORGE, 1983 CR 3214, Atlanta, TX 75551-6515, Phone: (903) 846-2938

FARR, DAN, 285 Glen Ellyn Way, Rochester, NY 14618, Phone: 585-721-1388
Specialties: Hunting, camping, fighting and utility. **Patterns:** Fixed blades. **Technical:** Forged or stock removal. **Prices:** $150 to $750.

FASSIO, MELVIN G., 420 Tyler Way, Lolo, MT 59847, Phone: 406-273-9143
Specialties: Working folders to customer specs. **Patterns:** Locking folders, hunters and traditional-style knives. **Technical:** Grinds 440C. **Prices:** $125 to $350. **Remarks:** Part-time maker; first knife sold in 1975. **Mark:** Name and city, dove logo.

FAUCHEAUX, HOWARD J., PO Box 206, Loreauville, LA 70552, Phone: 318-229-6467
Specialties: Working straight knives and folders; period pieces. Also a hatchet with capping knife in the handle. **Patterns:** Traditional locking folders, hunters, fighters and Bowies. **Technical:** Forges W2, 1095 and his own Damascus; stock removal D2. **Prices:** Start at $200. **Remarks:** Full-time maker; first knife sold in 1969. **Mark:** Last name.

FAUST, DICK, 624 Kings Hwy. N, Rochester, NY 14617, Phone: 585-544-1948
Specialties: High-performance working straight knives. **Patterns:** Hunters and utility/camp knives. **Technical:** Hollow grinds ATS-34 and 154CM full tang. Exotic woods, stag and Micarta handles. Provides a custom leather sheath with each knife. **Prices:** From $200 to $600, some higher. **Remarks:** Full-time maker. **Mark:** Signature.

FAUST, JOACHIM, Kirchgasse 10, 95497 Goldkronach, GERMANY

FECAS, STEPHEN J., 1312 Shadow Lane, Anderson, SC 29625, Phone: 864-287-4834, Fax: 864-287-4834
Specialties: Front release lock backs, liner locks. Folders only. **Patterns:** Gents folders. **Technical:** Grinds ATS-34, Damascus-Ivories and pearl handles. **Prices:** $650 to $1200. **Remarks:** Full-time maker since 1980. First knife sold in 1977. **Mark:** Last name signature. **Other:** All knives hand finished to 1500 grit.

FEIGIN, B., Liir Corp, 3037 Holly Mill Run, Marietta, GA 30062, Phone: 770-579-1631, Fax: 770-579-1199, fabei@abraxis.com

FELIX, ALEXANDER, PO Box 4036, Torrance, CA 90510, Phone: 310-320-1836
Specialties: Straight working knives, fancy ethnic designs. **Patterns:** Hunters, Bowies, daggers, period pieces. **Technical:** Forges carbon steel and Damascus; forged stainless and titanium jewelry, gold and silver casting. **Prices:** $110 and up. **Remarks:** Jeweler, ABS Journeyman Smith. **Mark:** Last name.

FELLOWS, MIKE, PO Box 166, Velddrie 7365, SOUTH AFRICA, Phone: 27 82 960 3868
Specialties: Miniatures, art knives, subhilt fighters and folders. **Patterns:** Original designs and client's specs. **Technical:** Uses own Damascus (L6 and nickel). **Other:** All knives carry strong, reliable thru-tang handles screwed and bonded together. Uses only indigenous materials for handles, i.e., various hard woods, selected horns, ivory, warthog tusk, hippo tooth, etc. Love to carve animal heads; favorite-Roses. **Mark:** "Shin" letter from Hebrew alphabet in front of Hebrew word "Karat". **Prices:** R800 to R5500 (approximately $100 to $700).

FERDINAND, DON, PO Box 1564, Shady Cove, OR 97539-1564, Phone: 503-560-3355
Specialties: One-of-a-kind working knives and period pieces; all tool steel Damascus. **Patterns:** Bowies, push knives and fishing knives. **Technical:** Forges high-carbon alloy steels L6, D2; makes his own Damascus. Exotic handle materials offered. **Prices:** $100 to $500. **Remarks:** Full-time maker since 1980. Does business as Wyvern. **Mark:** Initials connected.

FERGUSON, JIM, 32131 Via Bande, Temecula, CA 92592, Phone: 951-719-1552, jim@twistednickel.com Web: www.twisterdnickel.com
Specialties: Nickel Damascus, Bowies, Daggers, Push Blades. **Patterns:** All styles. **Technical:** Forges Damascus and sells in U.S. and Canada. **Prices:** $120 to $5000. **Remarks:** 1200 Sq. Ft. commercial shop; 75 ton press. Have mad over 10,000 lbs of Damascus. **Mark:** Jim Ferguson over push blade. Also make swords, battle axes and utilities.

FERGUSON, JIM, PO Box 764, San Angelo, TX 76902, Phone: 915-651-6656
Specialties: Straight working knives and folders. **Patterns:** Working belt knives, hunters, Bowies and some folders. **Technical:** Grinds ATS-34, D2 and Vascowear. Flat-grinds hunting knives. **Prices:** $200 to $600; some to $1000. **Remarks:** Full-time maker; first knife sold in 1987. **Mark:** First and middle initials, last name.

FERGUSON, LEE, 1993 Madison 7580, Hindsville, AR 72738, Phone: 479-443-0084, info@fergusonknives.com Web: www.fergusonknives.com
Specialties: Straight working knives and folders, some fancy. **Patterns:** Hunters, daggers, swords, locking folders and slip-joints. **Technical:** Grinds D2, 440C and ATS-34; heat-treats. **Prices:** $50 to $600; some to $4000. **Remarks:** Full-time maker; first knife sold in 1977. **Mark:** Full name.

FERRARA, THOMAS, 122 Madison Dr., Naples, FL 33942, Phone: 813-597-3363, Fax: 813-597-3363
Specialties: High-art, traditional and working straight knives and folders of all designs. **Patterns:** Boots, Bowies, daggers, fighters and hunters. **Technical:** Grinds 440C, D2 and ATS-34; heat-treats. **Prices:** $100 to $700; some to $1300. **Remarks:** Part-time maker; first knife sold in 1983. **Mark:** Last name.

FERRIER, GREGORY K., 3119 Simpson Dr., Rapid City, SD 57702, Phone: 605-342-9280

FERRIS, BILL, 186 Thornton Dr., Palm Beach Garden, FL 33418

FERRY, TOM, 16005 SE 322nd St., Auburn, WA 98092, Phone: 253-939-4468, KNFESMTH71@AOL.COM
Specialties: Damascus, fixed blades and folders. **Patterns:** Folders Damascus, and fixed blades. **Technical:** Specialize in Damascus and timascus TM (Titanium Damascus). **Prices:** $400 to $2000. **Remarks:** Name Tom Ferry DBA: Soos Creek Ironworks. **Mark:** Combined T and F in a circle and/or last name on folders. **Other:** Co-developer of Timascus TM (Titanium Damascus).

FIKES, JIMMY L., PO Box 3457, Jasper, AL 35502, Phone: 205-387-9302, Fax: 205-221-1980, oleyfermo@aol.com
Specialties: High-art working knives; artifact knives; using knives with cord-wrapped handles; swords and combat weapons. **Patterns:** Axes to buckskinners, camp knives to miniatures, tantos to tomahawks; spring less folders. **Technical:** Forges W2, O1 and his own Damascus. **Prices:** $135 to $3000; exceptional knives to $7000. **Remarks:** Full-time maker. **Mark:** Stylized initials.

FILIPPOU, IOANNIS-MINAS, 7 Krinis Str Nea Smyrni, Athens 17122, GREECE, Phone: (1) 935-2093

FINCH, RICKY D., 2446 HWY 191, West Liberty, KY 41472, Phone: 606-743-7151, finchknives@mrtc.com Web: www.finchknives.com
Specialties: Traditional working/using straight knives of his design or to customer spec. **Patterns:** Hunters, skinners and utility/camp knives. **Technical:** Grinds 440C and ATS-34, hand rubbed stain finish, use Micarta, stabilized wood; natural and exotic. **Prices:** $55 to $175; some $250. **Remarks:** Part-time maker, first knife made 1994. Doing business as Finch Knives. **Mark:** Last name inside outline of state of Kentucky.

FIORINI, BILL, E2173 Axlen Rd., DeSoto, WI 54624, Phone: 608-780-5898, fiorini.will@uwlax.edu Web: www.billfiorini.com
Specialties: Fancy working knives. **Patterns:** Hunters, boots, Japanese-style knives and kitchen/utility knives and folders. **Technical:** Forges own Damascus, mosaic and mokune-gane. **Prices:** Full range. **Remarks:** Full-time metal smith researching pattern materials. **Mark:** Orchid crest with name KOKA in Japanese.

FISHER, JAY, 1405 Edwards, Clovis, NM 88101, Phone: 505-763-2268, Fax: 505-463-2346, Web: www.JayFisher.com
Specialties: High-art, ancient and exact working and using straight knives of his design and client's designs. Military working and commemoratives. **Patterns:** Hunters, daggers, folding knives, museum pieces and high-art sculptures. **Technical:** Grinds 440C, ATS-34, 01and D2. Prolific maker of stone-handled knives and swords. **Prices:** $250 to $50,000; some higher. **Remarks:** Full-time maker; first knife sold in 1980. **Mark:** Very fine—JaFisher—Quality Custom Knives. **Other:** High resolution etching, computer and manual engraving.

FISHER, THEO (TED), 8115 Modoc Lane, Montague, CA 96064, Phone: 916-459-3804
Specialties: Moderately priced working knives in carbon steel. **Patterns:** Hunters, fighters, kitchen and buckskinner knives, Damascus miniatures. **Technical:** Grinds ATS-34, L6 and 440C. **Prices:** $65 to $165; exceptional knives to $300. **Remarks:** First knife sold in 1981. **Mark:** Name in banner logo.

FISK, JERRY, 10095 Hwy. 278 W, Nashville, AR 71852, Phone: 870-845-4456, jfisk@alltel.net Web: fisk-knives.com
Specialties: Edged weapons, collectible and functional. **Patterns:** Bowies, daggers, swords, hunters, camp knives and others. **Technical:** Forges carbon steels and his own pattern welded steels. **Prices:** $250 to $15,000. **Remarks:** National living treasure. **Mark:** Name, MS.

FISTER, JIM, PO Box 307, Simpsonville, KY 40067
Specialties: One-of-a-kind collectibles and period pieces. **Patterns:** Bowies, camp knives, hunters, buckskinners, and daggers. **Technical:** Forges, 1085, 5160, 52100, his own Damascus, pattern and turkish. **Prices:** $150 to $2500. **Remarks:** Part-time maker; first knife sold in 1982. **Mark:** Name and MS.

FITCH, JOHN S., 45 Halbrook Rd., Clinton, AR 72031-8910, Phone: 501-893-2020

FITZGERALD, DENNIS M., 4219 Alverado Dr., Fort Wayne, IN 46816-2847, Phone: 219-447-1081
Specialties: One-of-a-kind collectibles and period pieces. **Patterns:** Skinners, fighters, camp and utility knives; period pieces. **Technical:** Forges 1085, 1095, L6, 5160, 52100, his own pattern and Turkish Damascus. **Prices:** $100 to $500. **Remarks:** Part-time maker; first knife sold in 1985. Doing business as The Ringing Circle. **Mark:** Name and circle logo.

FLINT, ROBERT, 2902 Aspen, Anchorage, AK 99517, Phone: 907-243-6706
Specialties: Working straight knives and folders. **Patterns:** Utility, hunters, fighters and gents. **Technical:** Grinds ATS-34, BG-42, D2 and Damascus. **Prices:** $150 and up. **Remarks:** Part-time maker, first knife sold in 1998. **Mark:** Last name; stylized initials.

FLOURNOY, JOE, 5750 Lisbon Rd., El Dorado, AR 71730, Phone: 870-863-7208, flournoy@ipa.net
Specialties: Working straight knives and folders. **Patterns:** Hunters, Bowies, camp knives, folders and daggers. **Technical:** Forges only high-carbon steel, steel cable and his own Damascus. **Prices:** $350 Plus. **Remarks:** First knife sold in 1977. **Mark:** Last name and MS in script.

FOGARIZZU, BOITEDDU, via Crispi, 6, 07016 Pattada, ITALY
Specialties: Traditional Italian straight knives and folders. **Patterns:** Collectible folders. **Technical:** forges and grinds 12C27, ATS-34 and his Damascus. **Prices:** $200 to $3000. **Remarks:** Full-time maker; first knife sold in 1958. **Mark:** Full name and registered logo.

FOGG, DON, 40 Alma Rd., Jasper, AL 35501-8813, Phone: 205-483-0822, dfogg@dfoggknives.com; Web: www.dfoggknives.com
Specialties: Swords, daggers, Bowies and hunting knives. **Patterns:** Collectible folders. **Technical:** Hand-forged high-carbon and Damascus steel. **Prices:** $200 to $5000. **Remarks:** Full-time maker; first knife sold in 1976. **Mark:** 24K gold cherry blossom.

FONTENOT, GERALD J., 901 Maple Ave., Mamou, LA 70554, Phone: 318-468-3180

FORREST, BRIAN, FORREST KNIVES, PO Box 203, Descanso, CA 91916, Phone: 619-445-6343, Web: www.forrestknives.com
Specialties: Working straight knives, some fancy made to customer order. **Patterns:** Traditional patterns, Bowies, hunters, skinners and daggers. **Technical:** Grinds 440C, files and rasps. **Prices:** $125 and up. **Remarks:** Member of California Knifemakers Association. Full-time maker. First knife sold in 1971. **Mark:** Forrest USA.

FORSTALL, AL, 38379 Aunt Massey Rd., Pearl River, LA 70452, Phone: 504-863-2930
Specialties: Traditional working and using straight knives of his design or to customer specs. **Patterns:** Fighters, hunters and utility/camp knives. **Technical:** Grinds ATS-34, 440C, commercial Damascus and others upon request. **Prices:** $75 to $250. **Remarks:** Spare-time maker; first knife sold in 1991. **Mark:** Fleur-di-lis with name.

FORTHOFER, PETE, 5535 Hwy. 93S, Whitefish, MT 59937, Phone: 406-862-2674
Specialties: Interframes with checkered wood inlays; working straight knives. **Patterns:** Interframe folders and traditional-style knives; hunters, fighters and Bowies. **Technical:** Grinds D2, 440C, 154CM and ATS-34. **Prices:** $350 to $2500; some to $1500. **Remarks:** Part-time maker; full-time gunsmith. First knife sold in 1979. **Mark:** Name and logo.

FORTUNE PRODUCTS, INC., 205 Hickory Creek Rd., Marble Falls, TX 78654, Phone: 830-693-6111, Fax: 830-693-6394, Web: www.accusharp.com
Specialties: Knife sharpeners.

FOSTER, BURT, 23697 Archery Range Rd., Bristol, VA 24202, Phone: 276-669-0121, WEB: www.burtfoster.com
Specialties: Working straight knives, Laminated blades, and some art knives of his design. **Patterns:** Bowies, hunters, daggers. **Technical:** Forges 52100, W-2 and makes own Damascus. Does own heat treating. **Remarks:** ABS MasterSmith. Full-time maker, believes in sole authorship. **Mark:** Signed "BF" initials.

FOSTER, NORVELL C., 619 Holmgreen Rd., San Antonio, TX 78220, Phone: 210-333-1675
Specialties: Engraving; ivory handle carving. **Patterns:** American-large and small scroll-oak leaf and acorns. **Prices:** $25 to $400. **Mark:** N.C. Foster–S.A., TX and current year.

FOSTER, RONNIE E., 95 Riverview Rd., Morrilton, AR 72110, Phone: 501-354-5389
Specialties: Working, using knives, some period pieces, work with customer specs. **Patterns:** Hunters, fighters, Bowies, liner-lock folders, camp knives. **Technical:** Forge-5160, 1084, 01, 15N20-makes own Damascus. **Prices:** $200 (start). **Remarks:** Part-time maker. First knife sold 1994. **Mark:** Ronnie Foster MS.

FOSTER, TIMOTHY L., 723 Sweet Gum Acres Rd., El Dorado, AR 71730, Phone: 870-863-6188

FOSTER, AL, 118 Woodway Dr., Magnolia, TX 77355, Phone: 936-372-9297
Specialties: Straight knives and folders. **Patterns:** Hunting, fishing, folders and Bowies. **Technical:** Grinds 440-C, ATS-34 and D2. **Prices:** $100 to $1000. **Remarks:** Full-time maker; first knife sold in 1981. **Mark:** Scorpion logo and name.

FOSTER, R.L. (BOB), 745 Glendale Blvd., Mansfield, OH 44907, Phone: 419-756-6294

FOWLER, CHARLES R., 226 National Forest Rd. 48, Ft McCoy, FL 32134-9624, Phone: 904-467-3215

FOWLER, ED A., Willow Bow Ranch, PO Box 1519, Riverton, WY 82501, Phone: 307-856-9815
Specialties: High-performance working and using straight knives. **Patterns:** Hunter, camp, bird, and trout knives and Bowies. New model, the gentleman's Pronghorn. **Technical:** Low temperature forged 52100 from virgin 5 1/2 round bars, multiple quench heat treating, engraves all knives, all handles domestic sheep horn processed and aged at least 5 years. Makes heavy duty hand-stitched waxed harness leather pouch type sheathes. **Prices:** $800 to $7000. **Remarks:** Full-time maker. First knife sold in 1962. **Mark:** Initials connected.

FOWLER, JERRY, 610 FM 1660 N., Hutto, TX 78634, Phone: 512-846-2860, fowler@inetport.com
Specialties: Using straight knives of his design. **Patterns:** A variety of hunting and camp knives. Custom designs considered. **Technical:** Forges 5160, his own Damascus and cable Damascus. Makes sheaths. Prefers natural handle materials. **Prices:** Start at $150. **Remarks:** Part-time maker; first knife sold in 1986. Doing business as Fowler Forge Knife works. **Mark:** First initial, last name, date and J.S.

FOWLER, RICKY AND SUSAN, FOWLER CUSTOM KNIVES, 18535-B Co. Rd. 48, Robertsdale, AL 36567, Phone: 251-947-5648, theknlfeshop@gulftel.com Web: www.fowlerknives.net
Specialties: Traditional working/using straight knives of his design or to customer specifications. **Patterns:** Skinners, fighters, tantos, Bowies and utility/camp knives. **Technical:** Grinds O1, exclusively. **Prices:** Start at $150. **Remarks:** Full-time maker; first knife sold in 1994. Doing business as Fowler Custom Knives. **Mark:** Last name tang stamped and serial numbered.

FOX, JACK L., 7085 Canelo Hills Dr., Citrus Heights, CA 95610, Phone: 916-723-8647
Specialties: Traditional working/using straight knives of all designs. **Patterns:** Hunters, utility/camp knives and bird/fish knives. **Technical:** Grinds ATS-34, 440C and D2. **Prices:** $125 to $225; some to $350. **Remarks:** Spare-time maker; first knife sold in 1985. Doing business as Fox Knives. **Mark:** Stylized fox head.

FOX, PAUL, 4721 Rock Barn Rd., Claremont, NC 28610, Phone: 828-459-2000, Fax: 828-459-9200
Specialties: Hi-Tech. **Patterns:** Naibsek, Otnat, and Zorro (tactical) knives. **Technical:** Grinds ATS-34, 440C and D2. **Prices:** $500. **Remarks:** Spare-time maker; first knife sold in 1985. Doing business as Fox Knives. **Mark:** Laser engraved.

FOX, WENDELL, 1480 S 39th St., Springfield, OR 97478, Phone: 541-747-2126, WfoxForge@aol.com
Specialties: Large camping knives and friction folders of his design and to customer specs. One-of-a-kind prices. **Patterns:** Hunters, locking folders, slip-joint folders and utility/camp knives. **Technical:** Forges and grinds high-carbon steel only. **Prices:** $200 and up. **Remarks:** Full-time maker; first knife sold in 1952. **Mark:** Stamped name or logo. **Other:** All one-of-a-kind pieces. Specializing in early American.

FRALEY, D.B., 1355 Fairbanks Ct., Dixon, CA 95620, Phone: 707-678-0393, dbfknives@aol
Specialties: Traditional working/using straight knives and folders of his design and in standard patterns. **Patterns:** Fighters, hunters, utility/camp knives. **Technical:** Grinds ATS-34. Offers hand-stitched sheaths. **Prices:** Start at $100. **Remarks:** Part-time maker; first knife sold in 1990. **Mark:** First and middle initials, last name over buffalo.

FRAMSKI, WALTER P., 24 Rek Ln., Prospect, CT 06712, Phone: 203-758-5634

FRANCE, DAN, Box 218, Cawood, KY 40815, Phone: 606-573-6104
Specialties: Traditional working and using straight knives of his design. **Patterns:** Hunters, Bowies and utility/camp knives. **Technical:** Forges and grinds O1, 5160 and L6. **Prices:** $35 to $125; some to $350. **Remarks:** Spare-time maker; first knife sold in 1985. **Mark:** First name.

FRANCIS, JOHN D., FRANCIS KNIVES, 18 Miami St., Ft. Loramie, OH 45845, Phone: 937-295-3941, fscjohn@wcoil.com
Specialties: Utility and hunting-style fixed bladed knives of ATS-34 steel; micarta, exotic woods, and other types of handle materials. **Prices:** $100 to $150 range. **Remarks:** Exceptional quality and a value at factory prices. **Mark:** Francis-Ft. Loramie, OH stamped on tang.

FRANCIS, VANCE, 2612 Alpine Blvd., Alpine, CA 91901, Phone: 619-445-0979
Specialties: Working straight knives. **Patterns:** Bowies and utility knives. **Technical:** Uses ATS-34, A2, D2 and Damascus; differentially

tempers large blades. **Prices:** $175 to $600. **Remarks:** Part-time maker. **Mark:** First name, last name, city and state under feather in oval.

FRANK, HEINRICH H., 13868 NW Keleka Pl., Seal Rock, OR 97376, Phone: 541-563-3041, Fax: 541-563-3041
Specialties: High-art investor-class folders, handmade and engraved. **Patterns:** Folding daggers, hunter-size folders and gents. **Technical:** Grinds 07 and O1. **Prices:** $4800 to $16,000. **Remarks:** Full-time maker; first knife sold in 1965. Doing business as H.H. Frank Knives. **Mark:** Name, address and date.

FRANKL, JOHN M., 12 Holden St., Cambridge, MA 02138, Phone: 617-547-0359
Specialties: Hand forged tool steel and Damascus. **Patterns:** Camp knives, Bowies, hunters and fighters. **Technical:** Forge own Damascus, 5160 and V 1084. **Prices:** $150 to $1000. **Mark:** Last name "Frankl" on ricasso.

FRANKLIN, MIKE, 9878 Big Run Rd., Aberdeen, OH 45101, Phone: 937-549-2598
Specialties: High-tech tactical folders. **Patterns:** Tactical folders. **Technical:** Grinds CPM-T-440V, 440-C, ATS-34; titanium liners and bolsters; carbon fiber scales. Uses radical grinds and severe serrations. **Prices:** $275 to $600. **Remarks:** Full-time maker; first knife sold in 1969. **Mark:** Stylized boar with HAWG.

FRAPS, JOHN R., 3810 Wyandotte Tr., Indianpolis, IN 46240-3422, Phone: 317-849-9419, Fax: 317-842-2224, jfraps@att.net Web: www.frapsknives.com
Specialties: Working and Collector Grade liner lock and slip joint folders. **Patterns:** One-of-a kind linerlocks and traditional slip joints. **Technical:** Flat and hollow grinds ATS-34, Damascus, Talonite, CPM S30V, 154Cm, Stellite 6K; hand rubbed or mirror finish. **Prices:** $200 to $1500, some higher. **Remarks:** Full-time maker; first knife sold in 1997. **Mark:** Cougar Creek Knives and/or name.

FRAZIER, RON, 2107 Urbine Rd., Powhatan, VA 23139, Phone: 804-794-8561
Specialties: Classy working knives of his design; some high-art straight knives. **Patterns:** Wide assortment of straight knives, including miniatures and push knives. **Technical:** Grinds 440C; offers satin, mirror or sand finishes. **Prices:** $85 to $700; some to $3000. **Remarks:** Full-time maker; first knife sold in 1976. **Mark:** Name in arch logo.

FRED, REED WYLE, 3149 X S., Sacramento, CA 95817, Phone: 916-739-0237
Specialties: Working using straight knives of his design. **Patterns:** Hunting and camp knives. **Technical:** Forges any 10 series, old files and carbon steels. Offers initialing upon request; prefers natural handle materials. **Prices:** $30 to $300; some to $300. **Remarks:** Part-time maker; first knife sold in 1994. Doing business as R.W. Fred Knife maker. **Mark:** Engraved first and last initials.

FREDERICK, AARON, 459 Brooks Ln, West Liberty, KY 41472-8961, Phone: 606-7432015, aaronf@mrtc.com Web: www.frederickknives.com
Specialties: Makes most types of knives, but as for now specializes in the Damascus folder. Does all his Damascus and forging of the steel. Prefers natural handle material such as ivory and pearl. Prefers 14k gold screws in most of the knives he do. Also offers several types of file work on blades, spacers, and liners. Just recently started doing carving and can do a limited amount of engraving.

FREEMAN, JOHN, 160 Concession St., Cambridge, Ont., CANADA N1R 2H7, Phone: 519-740-2767, Fax: 519-740-2785, freeman@golden.net; Web: www.freemanknives.com
Specialties: Kitchen knives, outdoor knives, sharpeners and folders. **Patterns:** Hunters, skinners, utilities, backpackers. **Technical:** Flat ground 440C. **Prices:** Start at $135 and up. **Remarks:** Full-time maker; first knife sold in 1985. **Mark:** Last name, country.

FREER, RALPH, 114 12th St., Seal Beach, CA 90740, Phone: 562-493-4925, Fax: same, ralphfreer@adelphia.net
Specialties: Exotic folders, liner locks, folding daggers, fixed blades. **Patters:** All original. **Technical:** Lots of Damascus, ivory, pearl, jeweled, thumb studs, carving ATS-34, 420V, 530V. **Prices:** $400 to $2500 and up. **Mark:** Freer in German-style text, also Freer shield.

FREILING, ALBERT J., 3700 Niner Rd., Finksburg, MD 21048, Phone: 301-795-2880
Specialties: Working straight knives and folders; some period pieces. **Patterns:** Boots, Bowies, survival knives and tomahawks in 4130 and 440C; some locking folders and interframes; ball-bearing folders. **Technical:** Grinds O1, 440C and 154CM. **Prices:** $100 to $300; some to $500. **Remarks:** Part-time maker; first knife sold in 1966. **Mark:** Initials connected.

FREY, STEVE, 19103 131st Drive SE, Snohomish, WA 98296, Phone: 360-668-7351, sfrey2@aol.com
Remarks: Custom crafted knives-all styles.

FREY JR., W. FREDERICK, 305 Walnut St., Milton, PA 17847, Phone: 570-742-9576, wffrey@guidescape.net
Specialties: Working straight knives and folders, some fancy. **Patterns:** Wide rangeminiatures, boot knives and lock back folders. **Technical:** Grinds A2, O1 and D2; vaseo wear, cru-wear and CPM 440V. **Prices:** $100 to $250; some to $1200. **Remarks:** Spare-time maker; first knife sold in 1983. All knives include quality hand stitched sheaths. **Mark:** Last name in script.

FRIEDLY, DENNIS E., 12 Cottontail Ln. E, Cody, WY 82414, Phone: 307-527-6811, friedly_knives@hotmail.com
Specialties: Fancy working straight knives and daggers, lock back folders and liner locks. **Patterns:** Hunters, fighters, short swords, minis and miniatures; new line of full-tang hunters/boots. **Technical:** Grinds 440C, commercial Damascus, mosaic Damascus and ATS-34 blades; prefers hidden tangs. **Prices:** $135 to $900; some to $2500. **Remarks:** Full-time maker; first knife sold in 1972. **Mark:** D.E. Friedly

FRIGAULT, RICK, 3584 Rapidsview Dr., Niagara Falls ON, CANADA L2G 6C4, Phone: 905-295-6695, rfigault@cogeco.ca Web: www.rfrigaultknives.com
Specialties: Fixed blades. **Patterns:** Hunting, tactical and large Bowies. **Technical:** Grinds ATS-34, 440-C, D-2, CPMS30V, CPMS60V, CPMS90V, BG42 and Damascus. Use G-10, Micarta, ivory, antler, ironwood and other stabilized woods for carbon fiber handle material. Makes leather sheaths by hand. Tactical blades include a Concealex sheath made by "On Scene Tactical". **Remarks:** Sold first knife in 1997. Member of Canadian Knifemakers Guild. **Mark:** RFRIGAULT.

FRITZ, JESSE, 900 S. 13th St., Slaton, TX 79364, Phone: 806-828-5083
Specialties: Working and using straight knives in standard patterns. **Patterns:** Hunters, utility/camp knives and skinners with gut hook, bowie knives, kitchen carving sets by request. **Technical:** Grinds 440C, O1 and 1095. Uses 1095 steel. Fline-napped steel design, blued blades, filework and machine jewelling. Inlays handles with turquoise, coral and mother-of-pearl. Makes sheaths. **Prices:** $85 to $275; some to $500. **Mark:** Last name only (FRITZ).

FRIZZELL, TED, 14056 Low Gap Rd., West Fork, AR 72774, Phone: 501-839-2516
Specialties: Swords, axes and self-defense weapons. **Patterns:** Small skeleton knives to large swords. **Technical:** Grinds 5160 almost exclusively—1/4" to 1/2"— bars some O1 and A2 on request. All knives come with Kydex sheaths. **Prices:** $45 to $1200. **Remarks:** Full-time maker; first knife sold in 1984. Doing business as Mineral Mountain Hatchet Works. Wholesale orders welcome. **Mark:** A circle with line in the middle; MM and HW within the circle.

FRONEFIELD, DANIEL, 137 Catherine Dr., Hampton Cove, AL 35763-9732, Phone: 256-536-7827, dfronfld@hiwaay.com
Specialties: Fixed and folding knives featuring meteorites and other exotic materials. **Patterns:** San-mai Damascus, custom Damascus. **Prices:** $500 to $3000.

FROST, DEWAYNE, 1016 Van Buren Rd., Barnesville, GA 30204, Phone: 770-358-1426, lbrtyhill@aol.com
Specialties: Working straight knives and period knives. **Patterns:** Hunters, Bowies and utility knives. **Technical:** Forges own Damascus, cable, etc. as well as stock removal. **Prices:** $150 to $500. **Remarks:** Part-time maker ABS Journeyman Smith. **Mark:** Liberty Hill Forge Dewayne Frost w/liberty bell.

FRUHMANN, LUDWIG, Stegerwaldstr 8, 84489 Burghausen, GERMANY
Specialties: High-tech and working straight knives of his design. **Patterns:** Hunters, fighters and boots. **Technical:** Grinds ATS-34, CPM-T-440V and Schneider Damascus. Prefers natural handle materials. **Prices:** $200 to $1500. **Remarks:** Spare-time maker; first knife sold in 1990. **Mark:** First initial and last name.

FUEGEN, LARRY, 617 N. Coulter Circle, Prescott, AZ 86303, Phone: 928-776-8777, fuegen@cableone.net Web: www.larryfuegen.com
Specialties: High-art folders and classic and working straight knives. **Patterns:** Forged scroll folders, lockback folders and classic straight knives. **Technical:** Forges 5160, 1095 and his own Damascus. Works in exotic leather; offers elaborate filework and carving; likes natural handle materials, now offers own engraving. **Prices:** $575 to $9000. **Remarks:** Full-time maker; first knife sold in 1975. **Mark:** Initials connected. Other: Sole authorship on all knives. ABS mastersmith.

FUJIKAWA, SHUN, Sawa 1157 Kaizuka, Osaka 597 0062, JAPAN, Phone: 81-724-23-4032, Fax: 81-726-23-9229
Specialties: Folders of his design and to customer specs. **Patterns:** Locking folders. **Technical:** Grinds his own steel. **Prices:** $450 to $2500; some to $3000. **Remarks:** Part-time maker.

FUJISAKA, STANLEY, 45-004 Holowai St., Kaneohe, HI 96744, Phone: 808-247-0017
Specialties: Fancy working straight knives and folders. **Patterns:** Hunters, boots, personal knives, daggers, collectible art knives. **Technical:** Grinds 440C, 154CM and ATS-34; clean lines, inlays. **Prices:** $150 to $1200; some to $3000. **Remarks:** Full-time maker; first knife sold in 1984. **Mark:** Name, city, state.

FUKUTA, TAK, 38-Umeagae-cho, Seki-City, Gifu-Pref, JAPAN, Phone: 0575-22-0264
Specialties: Bench-made fancy straight knives and folders. **Patterns:** Sheffield-type folders, Bowies and fighters. **Technical:** Grinds commercial Damascus. **Prices:** Start at $300. **Remarks:** Full-time maker. **Mark:** Name in knife logo.

FULLER, BRUCE A., 1305 Airhart Dr., Baytown, TX 77520, Phone: 281-427-1848, fullcoforg@aol.com
Specialties: One-of-a-kind working/using straight knives and folders of his designs. **Patterns:** Bowies, hunters, folders, and utility/camp knives. **Technical:** Forges high-carbon steel and his own Damascus. Prefers El Solo Mesquite and natural materials. Offers filework. **Prices:** $200 to $500; some to $1800. **Remarks:** Spare-time maker; first knife sold in 1991. Doing business as Fullco Forge. **Mark:** Fullco, M.S.

FULLER, JACK A., 7103 Stretch Ct., New Market, MD 21774, Phone: 301-798-0119
Specialties: Straight working knives of his design and to customer specs. **Patterns:** Fighters, camp knives, hunters, tomahawks and art knives. **Technical:** Forges 5160, O1, W2 and his own Damascus. Does silver wire inlay and own leather work, wood lined sheaths for big camp knives. **Prices:** $300 to $850. **Remarks:** Part-time maker. Master Smith in ABS; first knife sold in 1979. **Mark:** Fuller's Forge, MS.

FULTON, MICKEY, 406 S Shasta St., Willows, CA 95988, Phone: 530-934-5780
Specialties: Working straight knives and folders of his design. **Patterns:** Hunters, Bowies, lockback folders and steak knife sets. **Technical:** Hand-filed, sanded, buffed ATS-34, 440C and A2. **Prices:** $65 to $600; some to $1200. **Remarks:** Full-time maker; first knife sold in 1979. **Mark:** Signature.

G

GADBERRY, EMMET, 82 Purple Plum Dr., Hattieville, AR 72063, Phone: 501-354-4842

GADDY, GARY LEE, 205 Ridgewood Lane, Washington, NC 27889, Phone: 252-946-4359
Specialties: Working/using straight knives of his design; period pieces. **Patterns:** Bowies, hunters, utility/camp knives. **Technical:** Grinds ATS-34, 01; forges 1095. **Prices:** $100 to $225; some to $400. **Remarks:** Spare-time maker; first knife sold in 1991. **Mark:** Quarter moon logo.

GAETA, ANGELO, R. Saldanha Marinho, 1295 Centro Jau, SP-17201-310, BRAZIL, Phone: 0146-224543, Fax: 0146-224543
Specialties: Straight using knives to customer specs. **Patterns:** Hunters, fighting, daggers, belt push dagger. **Technical:** Grinds D6, ATS-34 and 440C stainless. titanium nitride golden finish upon request. **Prices:** $60 to $300. **Remarks:** Full-time maker; first knife sold in 1992. **Mark:** First initial, last name.

GAETA, ROBERTO, Rua Mandi Ssununha 41, Sao Paulo, BRAZIL 05619-010, Phone: 11-37684626
Specialties: Wide range of using knives. **Patterns:** Brazilian and North American hunting and fighting knives. **Technical:** Grinds stainless steel; likes natural handle materials. **Prices:** $100 to $250; some to $600. **Remarks:** Full-time maker; first knife sold in 1979. **Mark:** BOB'G.

GAGSTAETTER, PETER, Nibelungenschmiede, Bergstrasse 2, 9306 Freidorf Tg, SWITZERLAND

GAINES, BUDDY, GAINES KNIVES, 155 Red Hill Rd., Commerce, GA 30530, Web: www.gainesknives.com
Specialties: Collectible and working folders and straight knives. **Patterns:** Folders, hunters, Bowies, tactical knives. **Technical:** Forges own Damascus, grinds ATS-34, D2, commercial Damascus. Prefers mother-of-pearl and stag. **Prices:** Start at $200. **Remarks:** Part-time maker, sold first knife in 1985. **Mark:** Last name.

GAINEY, HAL, 904 Bucklevel Rd., Greenwood, SC 29649, Phone: 864-223-0225, Web: www.scak.org
Specialties: Traditional working and using straight knives and folders. **Patterns:** Hunters, slip-joint folders and utility/camp knives. **Technical:** Hollow-grinds ATS-34 and D2; makes sheaths. **Prices:** $95 to $145; some to $500. **Remarks:** Full-time maker; first knife sold in 1975. **Mark:** Eagle head and last name.

GALLAGHER—GEVEDON

GALLAGHER, BARRY, 135 Park St., Lewistown, MT 59457, Phone: 406-538-7056, Web: www.gallagherknives.com
Specialties: One-of-a-kind Damascus folders. **Patterns:** Folders; utility to high art, some straight knives; hunter, Bowies, and art pieces. **Technical:** Forges own mosaic Damascus and carbon steel, some stainless. **Prices:** $400 to $5000+. **Remarks:** Full-time maker; first knife sold in 1993. Doing business as Gallagher Custom Knives. **Mark:** Last name.

GALLAGHER, SEAN, 24828 114th PL SE, Monroe, WA 98272-7685

GAMBLE, FRANK, 3872 Dunbar Pl., Fremont, CA 94536, Phone: 510-797-7970
Specialties: Fantasy and high-art straight knives and folders of his design. **Patterns:** Daggers, fighters, hunters and special locking folders. **Technical:** Grinds 440C and ATS-34; forges Damascus. Inlays; offers jewelling. Prices $150 to $10,000. **Remarks:** Full-time maker; first knife sold in 1976. **Mark:** First initial, last name.

GAMBLE, ROGER, 2801 65 Way N., St. Petersburg, FL 33710, Phone: 727-384-1470, rlgamble2@netzero.net
Specialties: Traditional working/using straight knives and folders of his design. **Patterns:** Liner locks and hunters. **Technical:** Grinds ATS-34 and Damascus. **Prices:** $150 to $2000. **Remarks:** Part-time maker; first knife sold in 1982. Doing business as Gamble Knives. **Mark:** First name in a fan of cards over last name.

GANSTER, JEAN-PIERRE, 18, Rue du Vieil Hopital, F-67000 Strasbourg, FRANCE, Phone: (0033) 388 32 65 61, Fax: (0033) 388 32 52 79
Specialties: Fancy and high-art miniatures of his design and to customer specs. **Patterns:** Bowies, daggers, fighters, hunters, locking folders and miniatures. **Technical:** Forges and grinds stainless Damascus, ATS-34, gold and silver. **Prices:** $100 to $380; some to $2500. **Remarks:** Part-time maker; first knife sold in 1972. **Mark:** Stylized first initials.

GARCIA, MARIO EIRAS, R. Edmundo Scanapieco, 300 Caxingui, Sao Paulo SP-05516-070, BRAZIL, Fax: 011-37214528
Specialties: Fantasy knives of his design; one-of-a-kind only. **Patterns:** Fighters, daggers, boots and two-bladed knives. **Technical:** Forges car leaf springs. Uses only natural handle material. **Prices:** $100 to $200. **Remarks:** Part-time maker; first knife sold in 1976. **Mark:** Two "B"s, one opposite the other.

GARDNER, ROB, 3381 E Rd., Loxahatchee, FL 33470, Phone: 561-784-4994
Specialties: High-art working and using knives of his design and to customer specs. **Patterns:** Daggers, hunters and ethnic-patterned knives. **Technical:** Forges Damascus, L6 and 10-series steels. Engraves and inlays. Handles and fittings may be carved. **Prices:** $175 to $500; some to $2500. **Remarks:** Full-time maker; artist blacksmith, first knife sold in 1987. Knives made by custom order only. **Mark:** Engraved or stamped initials.

GARNER, LARRY W., 13069 FM 14, Tyler, TX 75706, Phone: 903-597-6045, lwgarner@classicnet.com
Specialties: Fixed blade hunters and Bowies. **Patterns:** My designs or yours. **Technical:** Hand forges 5160. **Prices:** $200 to $500. **Remarks:** Apprentice bladesmith. **Mark:** Last name.

GARNER JR., WILLIAM O., 2803 East DeSoto St., Pensacola, FL 32503, Phone: 850-438-2009
Specialties: Working straight and art knives. **Patterns:** Hunters and folders. **Technical:** Grinds 440C and ATS-34 steels. **Prices:** $235 to $600. **Remarks:** Full-time maker; first knife sold in 1985. **Mark:** First and last name in oval logo or last name.

GARVOCK, MARK W., RR 1, Balderson, Ontario, CANADA K1G 1A0, Phone: 613-833-2545, Fax: 613-833-2208, garvock@travel-net.com
Specialties: Hunters, Bowies, Japanese, daggers and swords. **Patterns:** Cable Damascus, random pattern welded or to suit. **Technical:** Forged blades; hi-carbon. **Prices:** $250 to $900. **Remarks:** Also CKG member and ABS member. **Mark:** Big G with M in middle. **Other:** Shipping and taxes extra.

GAUDETTE, LINDEN L., 5 Hitchcock Rd., Wilbraham, MA 01095, Phone: 413-596-4896
Specialties: Traditional working knives in standard patterns. **Patterns:** Broad-bladed hunters, Bowies and camp knives; wood carver knives; locking folders. **Technical:** Grinds ATS-34, 440C and 154CM. **Prices:** $150 to $400; some higher. **Remarks:** Full-time maker; first knife sold in 1975. **Mark:** Last name in Gothic logo; used to be initials in circle.

GAULT, CLAY, #1225 PR 7022, Lexington, TX 78947, Phone: 979-773-3305
Specialties: Classic straight and folding hunting knives and multi-blade folders of his design. **Patterns:** Folders and hunting knives. **Technical:** Grinds BX-NSM 174 steel, custom rolled from billets to his specifica-

tions. Uses exotic leathers for sheaths, and fine natural materials for all knives. **Prices:** $325 to $600; some higher. **Remarks:** Full-time maker; first knife sold in 1970. **Mark:** Name or name with cattle brand.

GEDRAITIS, CHARLES J., GEDRAITIS HAND CRAFTED KNIVES, 444 Shrewsbuyn St, Holden, MA 01520, Phone: 508-886-0221, knifemaker_1999@yahoo.com Web: http: //cgknives.blademakers.com
Specialties: One of a king folders & automatics of my own design. **Patterns:** One-of-a-kind.**Technical:** Forges to shape mostly stock removal. **Prices:** $300 to $2500. **Remarks:** Full-time maker. **Mark:** 3 scallop shells with an initial inside each one. CJG

GEISLER, GARY R., PO Box 294, Clarksville, OH 45113, Phone: 937-383-4055, ggeisler@in-touch.net
Specialties: Period Bowies and such; flat ground. **Patterns:** Working knives usually modeled close after an existing antique. **Technical:** Flat grinds 440C, A2 and ATS-34. **Prices:** $300 and up. **Remarks:** Part-time maker; first knife sold in 1982. **Mark:** G.R. Geisler Maker; usually in script on reverse side because maker is left-handed.

GENSKE, JAY, 283 Doty St., Fond du Lac, WI 54935, Phone: 920-921-8019/Cell Phone 920-579-0144, jaygenske@hotmail.com
Specialties: Working/using knives and period pieces of his design and to customer specs. **Patterns:** Bowies, fighters, hunters. **Technical:** Grinds ATS-34 and 440C, 01 and 1095 forges and grinds Damascus and 1095. Offers custom-tooled sheaths, scabbards and hand carved handles. **Prices:** $95 to $500; some to $1000. **Remarks:** Full-time maker; first knife sold in 1985. Doing business as Genske Knives. **Mark:** Stamped or engraved last name.

GEORGE, HARRY, 3137 Old Camp Long Rd., Aiken, SC 29805, Phone: 803-649-1963, hdkk-george@scescape.net
Specialties: Working straight knives of his design or to customer specs. **Patterns:** Hunters, skinners and utility knives. **Technical:** Grinds ATS-34. Prefers natural handle materials, hollow-grinds and mirror finishes. **Prices:** Start at $70. **Remarks:** Part-time maker; first knife sold in 1985. Trained under George Herron. Member SCAK. Member Knifemakers Guild. **Mark:** Name, city, state.

GEORGE, LES, 1703 Payne, Wichita, KS 67203, Phone: 316-267-0736
Specialties: Classic, traditional and working/using straight knives of his design and to customer specs. **Patterns:** Fighters, hunters, swords and miniatures. **Technical:** Grinds D2; forges 5160 and Damascus. Uses mosaic handle pins and his own mokume-gane. **Prices:** $35 to $200; some to $800. **Remarks:** No orders taken at this time due to enlistment in the U.S. Marine Corps.; first knife sold in 1992. Doing business as George Custom Knives. **Mark:** Last name or initials stacked.

GEORGE, TOM, 550 Aldbury Dr., Henderson, NV 89014, tagmaker@aol.com
Specialties: Working straight knives, display knives and folders of his design. **Patterns:** Hunters, Bowies, daggers, buckskinners, swords and folders. **Technical:** Uses D2, 440C, ATS-34 and 154CM. **Prices:** $250 to $10,000. **Remarks:** Custom orders 'not' accepted. Full-time maker. **Mark:** Tom George maker.

GEPNER, DON, 2615 E. Tecumseh, Norman, OK 73071, Phone: 405-364-2750
Specialties: Traditional working and using straight knives of his design. **Patterns:** Bowies and daggers. **Technical:** Forges his Damascus, 1095 and 5160. **Prices:** $100 to $400; some to $1000. **Remarks:** Spare-time maker; first knife sold in 1991. Has been forging since 1954; first edged weapon made at 9 years old. **Mark:** Last initial.

GERNER, THOMAS, 939 German Rd., Glentui RD, Oxford, NEW ZEALAND 8253
Specialties: Forged working knives; plain steel and pattern welded. **Patterns:** Tries most patterns heard or read about. **Technical:** 5160, L6, 01, 52100 steels; Australian hardwood handles. **Prices:** $160 and up. **Remarks:** Achieved ABS Master Smith rating in 2001. **Mark:** Like a standing arrow and a leaning cross, T.G. in the Runic (Viking) alphabet.

GERUS, GERRY, PO Box 2295, G.P.O. Cairns, Qld. 4870, AUSTRALIA 070-341451, Phone: 019 617935
Specialties: Fancy working and using straight knives of his design. **Patterns:** Hunters, Bowies and fighters. **Technical:** Uses 440C, ATS-34 and commercial Damascus. **Prices:** $275 to $600; some to $1200. **Remarks:** Part-time maker; first knife sold in 1988. **Mark:** Last name; or last name, Hand Made, city, country.

GEVEDON, HANNERS (HANK), 1410 John Cash Rd., Crab Orchard, KY 40419-9770
Specialties: Traditional working and using straight knives. **Patterns:** Hunters, swords, utility and camp knives. **Technical:** Forges and grinds his own Damascus, 5160 and L6. Cast aluminum handles. **Prices:** $50 to $250; some to $400. **Remarks:** Part-time maker; first knife sold in 1983. **Mark:** Initials and LBF tang stamp.

222 KNIVES 2007

GIAGU, SALVATORE AND DEROMA MARIA ROSARIA, Via V. Emanuele 64, 07016 Pattada (SS), ITALY, Phone: 079-755918, Fax: 079-755918, coltelligiagu@jumpy.it
Specialties: Using and collecting traditional and new folders from Sardegna. **Patterns:** Folding, hunting, utility, skinners and kitchen knives. **Technical:** Forges ATS-34, 440, D2 and Damascus. **Prices:** $200 to $2000; some higher. **Mark:** First initial, last name and name of town and muflon's head.

GIBERT, PEDRO, Gutierrez 5189, 5603 Rama Caida, San Rafael Mendoza, ARGENTINA, Phone: 054-2627-441138, rosademayo@infovia.com.ar
Specialties: Hand forges: Stock removal and integral. High quality artistic knives of his design and to customer specifications. **Patterns:** Country (Argentine gaucho-style), knives, folders, Bowies, daggers, hunters. Others upon request. **Technical:** Blade: Bohler k110 Austrian steel (high resistance to waste). Handles: (Natural materials) ivory elephant, killer whale, hippo, walrus tooth, deer antler, goat, ram, buffalo horn, bone, rhea, goat, sheep, cow, exotic woods (South America native woods) hand carved and engraved guards and blades. Stainless steel guards, finely polished: semi-matte or shiny finish. Sheaths: Raw or tanned leather, hand-stitched; rawhide or cotton yarn embroidered. Box: One wood piece, hand carved. **Prices:** $400 and up. **Remarks:** Full-time maker. Supply contractors. **Mark:** Only a rose logo. Buyers initials upon request.

GIBO, GEORGE, PO Box 4304, Hilo, HI 96720, Phone: 808-987-7002, geogibo@interpac.net
Specialties: Straight knives and folders. **Patterns:** Hunters, bird and trout, utility, gentlemen and tactical folders. **Technical:** Grinds ATS-34, BG-42, Talonite, Stainless Steel Damascus. **Prices:** $250 to $1000. **Remarks:** Spare-time maker; first knife sold in 1995. **Mark:** Name, city and state around Hawaiian "Shaka" sign.

GIBSON SR., JAMES HOOT, 90 Park Place Ave., Bunnell, FL 32110, Phone: 904-437-4383
Specialties: Bowies, folders, daggers, and hunters. **Patterns:** Most all. **Technical:** ATS-440C hand cut and grind. **Prices:** $1250 to $3000. **Remarks:** 100% handmade. **Mark:** Hoot.

GILBERT, CHANTAL, 291 Rue Christophe-Colomb est. #105, Quebec City Quebec, CANADA G1K 3T1, Phone: 418-525-6961, Fax: 418-525-4666, gilbertc@medion.qc.ca WEB: www.chantalgilbert.com
Specialties: Straight art knives that may resemble creatures, often with wings, shells and antennae, always with a beak of some sort, fixed blades in a feminine style. **Technical:** ATS-34 and Damascus. Handle materials usually silver that she forms to shape via special molds and a press; ebony and fossil ivory. **Prices:** Range from $500 to $4000. **Other:** Often embellishes her art knives with rubies, meteorite, 18k gold and similar elements.

GILBREATH, RANDALL, 55 Crauswell Rd., Dora, AL 35062, Phone: 205-648-3902
Specialties: Damascus folders and fighters. **Patterns:** Folders and fixed blades. **Technical:** Forges Damascus and high-carbon; stock removal stainless steel. **Prices:** $300 to $1500. **Remarks:** Full-time maker; first knife sold in 1979. **Mark:** Name in ribbon.

GILJEVIC, BRANKO, 35 Hayley Crescent, Queanbeyan 2620, N.S.W., AUSTRALIA 0262977613
Specialties: Classic working straight knives and folders of his design. **Patterns:** Hunters, Bowies, skinners and locking folders. **Technical:** Grinds 440C. Offers acid etching, scrimshaw and leather carving. **Prices:** $150 to $1500. **Remarks:** Part-time maker; first knife sold in 1987. Doing business as Sambar Custom Knives. **Mark:** Company name in logo.

GIRTNER, JOE, 409 Catalpa Ave, Brea, CA 92821, Phone: 714-529-2388

GITTINGER, RAYMOND, 6940 S Rt. 100, Tiffin, OH 44883, Phone: 419-397-2517

GLOVER, RON, 7702 Misty Springs Ct., Mason, OH 45040, Phone: 513-398-7857
Specialties: High-tech working straight knives and folders. **Patterns:** Hunters to Bowies; some interchangeable blade models; unique locking mechanisms. **Technical:** Grinds 440C, 154CM; buys Damascus. **Prices:** $70 to $500; some to $800. **Remarks:** Part-time maker; first knife sold in 1981. **Mark:** Name in script.

GLOVER, WARREN D., dba BUBBA KNIVES, PO Box 475, Cleveland, GA 30528, Phone: 706-865-3998, Fax: 706-348-7176
Specialties: Traditional and custom working and using straight knives of his design and to customer request. **Patterns:** Hunters, skinners, bird and fish, utility and kitchen knives. **Technical:** Grinds 440, ATS-34 and stainless steel Damascus. **Prices:** $75 to $400 and up. **Remarks:** Part-time maker; sold first knife in 1995. **Mark:** Bubba, year, name, state.

GODDARD, WAYNE, 473 Durham Ave., Eugene, OR 97404, Phone: 541-689-8098, wgoddard44@comcast.net
Specialties: Working/using straight knives and folders. **Patterns:** Hunters and folders. **Technical:** Works exclusively with wire Damascus and his own-pattern welded material. **Prices:** $250 to $4000. **Remarks:** Full-time maker; first knife sold in 1963. Three-year backlog on orders. **Mark:** Blocked initials on forged blades; regular capital initials on stock removal.

GOERS, BRUCE, 3423 Royal Ct. S., Lakeland, FL 33813, Phone: 941-646-0984
Specialties: Fancy working and using straight knives of his design and to customer specs. **Patterns:** Hunters, fighters, Bowies and fantasy knives. **Technical:** Grinds ATS-34, some Damascus. **Prices:** $195 to $600; some to $1300. **Remarks:** Part-time maker; first knife sold in 1990. Doing business as Vulture Cutlery. **Mark:** Buzzard with initials.

GOERTZ, PAUL S., 201 Union Ave. SE, #207, Renton, WA 98059, Phone: 425-228-9501
Specialties: Working straight knives of his design and to customer specs. **Patterns:** Hunters, skinners, camp, bird and fish knives, camp axes, some Bowies, fighters and boots. **Technical:** Grinds ATS-34, BG42, and CPM420V. **Prices:** $75 to $500. **Remarks:** Full-time maker; first knife sold in 1985. **Mark:** Signature.

GOFOURTH, JIM, 3776 Aliso Cyn Rd., Santa Paula, CA 93060, Phone: 805-659-3814
Specialties: Period pieces and working knives. **Patterns:** Bowies, locking folders, patent lockers and others. **Technical:** Grinds A2 and 154CM. **Prices:** Moderate. **Remarks:** Spare-time maker. **Mark:** Initials interconnected.

GOGUEN, SCOTT, 166 Goguen Rd., Newport, NC 28570, Phone: 252-393-6013, goguenknives.com
Specialties: Classic and traditional working knives. **Patterns:** Kitchen, camp, hunters, Bowies. **Technical:** Forges high-carbon steel and own Damascus. Offers clay tempering and cord wrapped handles. **Prices:** $85 to $1500. **Remarks:** Spare-time maker; first knife sold in 1988. **Mark:** Last name or name in Japanese characters.

GOLDBERG, DAVID, 1120 Blyth Ct., Blue Bell, PA 19422, Phone: 215-654-7117
Specialties: Japanese-style designs, will work with special themes in Japanese Genre. **Patterns:** Kozuka, Tanto, Wakazashi, Katana, Tachi, Sword canes, Yari and Naginata. **Technical:** Forges his own Damascus and makes his own handmade steel from straw ash, iron, carbon and clay. Uses traditional materials, carves fittings handles and cases. Hardens all blades in traditional Japanese clay differential technique. **Remarks:** Full-time maker; first knife sold in 1987. **Mark:** Name (kinzan) in Japanese Kanji on Tang under handle. **Other:** Japanese swordsmanship teacher (jaido) and Japanese self-defense teach (aikido).

GOLDING, ROBIN, PO Box 267, Lathrop, CA 95330, Phone: 209-982-0839
Specialties: Working straight knives of his design. **Patterns:** Survival knives, Bowie extractions, camp knives, dive knives and skinners. **Technical:** Grinds 440C, 154CM and ATS-34. **Prices:** $95 to $250; some to $500. **Remarks:** Full-time maker; first knife sold in 1985. Up to 1-1/2 year waiting period on orders. **Mark:** Signature of last name.

GOLTZ, WARREN L., 802 4th Ave. E., Ada, MN 56510, Phone: 218-784-7721, sspexp@loretel.net
Specialties: Fancy working knives in standard patterns. **Patterns:** Hunters, Bowies and camp knives. **Technical:** Grinds 440C and ATS-34. **Prices:** $120 to $595; some to $950. **Remarks:** Part-time maker; first knife sold in 1984. **Mark:** Last name.

GONZALEZ, LEONARDO WILLIAMS, Ituzaingo 473, Maldonado, CP 20000, URUGUAY, Phone: 598 4222 1617, Fax: 598 4222 1617, willyknives@hotmail.com
Specialties: Classic high-art and fantasy straight knives; traditional working and using knives of his design, in standard patterns or to customer specs. **Patterns:** Hunters, Bowies, daggers, fighters, boots, swords and utility/camp knives. **Technical:** Forges and grinds high-carbon and stainless Bohler steels. **Prices:** $100 to $500. **Remarks:** Full-time maker; first knife sold in 1985. **Mark:** Willy, whale, R.O.U.

GOO, TAI, 5920 W Windy Lou Ln., Tucson, AZ 85742, Phone: 520-744-9777, taigoo@msn.com Web: www.taigoo.com
Specialties: High art, neo-tribal, bush and fantasy. **Technical:** hand forges, does own heat treating, makes own Damascus. **Prices:** $150 to $500 some to $10,000. **Remarks:** Full-time maker; first knife sold in 1978. **Mark:** Chiseled signature.

GOODE, BEAR, PO Box 6474, Navajo Dam, NM 87419, Phone: 505-632-8184
Specialties: Working/using straight knives of his design and in standard patterns. **Patterns:** Bowies, hunters and utility/camp knives. **Technical:** Grinds 440C, ATS-34, 154-CM; forges and grinds 1095, 5160 and other

steels on request; uses Damascus. **Prices:** $60 to $225; some to $500 and up. **Remarks:** Part-time maker; first knife sold in 1993. Doing business as Bear Knives. **Mark:** First and last name with a three-toed paw print.

GOODE, BRIAN, 104 Cider Dr., Shelby, NC 28152, Phone: 704-484-9020, web: www.bgoodeknives.com
Specialties: Flat ground working knives with etched/antique finish or hand rubbed. **Patterns:** Field, camp, hunters, skinners, survival, maker's design or yours. Currently full tang only with supplied leather sheath. Kydex can be outsourced if desired. **Technical:** 0-1, 1095, or similar high-carbon ground flatstock. Stock removal and differential heat treat preferred. Will offer handforged with the same differential heat treat method in future. Etched antique/etched satin working finish preferred. Micarta and hardwoods for strength. **Prices:** $115 to $680. **Remarks:** Part-time maker and full-time knife lover. First knife sold in 2004. **Mark:** B. Goode with NC separated by a feather.

GOODLING, RODNEY W., 6640 Old Harrisburg Rd., York Springs, PA 17372

GORDON, LARRY B., 23555 Newell Cir. W, Farmington Hills, MI 48336, Phone: 248-477-5483, lbgordon1@aol.com
Specialties: Folders, small fixed blades. **Patterns:** Rotating handle locker. **Prices:** $450 minimmum. **Mark:** Gordon. **Other:** High line materials preferred.

GORENFLO, GABE, 9145 Sullivan Rd, Baton Rouge, LA 70818, Phone: 504-261-5868

GORENFLO, JAMES T. (JT), 9145 Sullivan Rd., Baton Rouge, LA 70818, Phone: 225-261-5868
Specialties: Traditional working and using straight knives of his design. **Patterns:** Bowies, hunters and utility/camp knives. **Technical:** Forges 5160, 1095, 52100 and his own Damascus. **Prices:** Start at $200. **Remarks:** Part-time maker; first knife sold in 1992. **Mark:** Last name or initials, J.S. on reverse.

GOSSMAN, SCOTT, RAZORBACK KNIVES, PO Box 815, Forest Hill, MD 21050, Phone: 410-452-8456, scott@razorback-knives.com Web: www.razorback-knives.com
Specialties: Heavy duty knives for big game hunting and survival. **Patterns:** Drop point hunters, semi-skinners and spear point hunters. **Technical:** Grinds D-2, A2 and 5160 convex and flatgrind filework standard around full tang handles. **Price:** $100 to $350 some higher. **Remarks:** Part-time maker does business as Razorback Knives. **Mark:** First and last initials and year.

GOTTAGE, DANTE, 43227 Brooks Dr., Clinton Twp., MI 48038-5323, Phone: 810-286-7275
Specialties: Working knives of his design or to customer specs. **Patterns:** Large and small skinners, fighters, Bowies and fillet knives. **Technical:** Grinds O1, 440C and 154CM and ATS-34. **Prices:** $150 to $600. **Remarks:** Part-time maker; first knife sold in 1975. **Mark:** Full name in script letters.

GOTTAGE, JUDY, 43227 Brooks Dr., Clinton Twp., MI 48038-5323, Phone: 810-286-7275
Specialties: Custom folders of her design or to customer specs. **Patterns:** Interframes or integral. **Technical:** Stock removal. **Prices:** $300 to $3000. **Remarks:** Full-time maker; first knife sold in 1980. **Mark:** Full name, maker in script.

GOTTSCHALK, GREGORY J., 12 First St. (Ft. Pitt), Carnegie, PA 15106, Phone: 412-279-6692
Specialties: Fancy working straight knives and folders to customer specs. **Patterns:** Hunters to tantos, locking folders to minis. **Technical:** Grinds 440C, 154CM, ATS-34. Now making own Damascus. Most knives have mirror finishes. **Prices:** Start at $150. **Remarks:** Part-time maker; first knife sold in 1977. **Mark:** Full name in crescent.

GOUKER, GARY B., PO Box 955, Sitka, AK 99835, Phone: 907-747-3476
Specialties: Hunting knives for hard use. **Patterns:** Skinners, semi-skinners, and such. **Technical:** Likes natural materials, inlays, stainless steel. **Prices:** Moderate. **Remarks:** New Alaskan maker. **Mark:** Name.

GOYTIA, ENRIQUE, 2120 E Paisano Ste. 276, El Paso, TX 79905

GRAFFEO, ANTHONY I., 100 Riess Place, Chalmette, LA 70043, Phone: 504-277-1428
Specialties: Traditional working and using straight knives of his design, to customer specs and in standard patterns. **Patterns:** Hunters, utility/camp knives and fishing knives. **Technical:** Hollow- and flat-grinds ATS-34, 440C and 154CM. Handle materials include Pakkawood, Micarta and sambar stag. **Prices:** $65 to $100; some to $250. **Remarks:** Part-time maker; first knife sold in 1991. Doing business as Knives by: Graf. **Mark:** First and middle initials, last name city, state, Maker.

GRAHAM, GORDON, Rt. 3 Box 207, New Boston, TX 75570, Phone: 903-628-6337

GRANGER, PAUL J., 2820 St. Charles Ln., Kennesaw, GA 30144, Phone: 770-426-6298, grangerknives@hotmail.com Web: www.geocities.com/grangerknives Web: www.grangerknives.com
Specialties: Working straight knives of his own design and a few folders. **Patterns:** 2.75"-4.0" work knives, skinners, tactical knives and Bowies from 5"-9". **Technical:** Forges 52100 and 5160 and his own carbon steel Damascus. Offers filework. **Prices:** $95 to $400. **Remarks:** Part-time maker since 1997. Sold first knife in 1997. Doing business as Granger Knives and Pale Horse Fighters. **Mark:** "Granger" or "Palehorse Fighters." **Other:** Member of ABS and OBG.

GRAVELINE, PASCAL AND ISABELLE, 38, Rue de Kerbrezillic, 29350 Moelan-sur-Mer, FRANCE, Phone: 33 2 98 39 73 33, Fax: 33 2 98 39 73 33, atelier.graveline@wanadso.fr
Specialties: French replicas from the 17th, 18th and 19th centuries. **Patterns:** Traditional folders and multi-blade pocket knives; traveling knives, fruit knives and fork sets; puzzle knives and friend's knives; rivet less knives. **Technical:** Grind 12C27, ATS-34, Damascus and carbon steel. **Prices:** $500 to $5000; some to $2000. **Remarks:** Full-time makers; first knife sold in 1992. **Mark:** Last name over head of ram.

GRAY, BOB, 8206 N. Lucia Court, Spokane, WA 99208, Phone: 509-468-3924
Specialties: Straight working knives of his own design or to customer specs. **Patterns:** Hunter, fillet and carving knives. **Technical:** Forges 5160, L6 and some 52100; grinds 440C. **Prices:** $100 to $600. **Remarks:** Part-time maker; first knife sold in 1991. Doing business as Hi-Land Knives. **Mark:** HI-L.

GRAY, DANIEL, GRAY KNIVES, 686 Main Rd., Brownville, ME 04414, Phone: 207-965-2191, mail@grayknives.com Web: www.grayknives.com
Specialties: Straight knives, Fantasy, folders, automatics and traditional of his own design. **Patterns:** Automatics, fighters, hunters. **Technical:** Grind 01, 154CM and D2. **Prices:** From $155 to $750. **Remarks:** Full-time maker; first knife sold in 1974. **Mark:** Gray Knives.

GREBE, GORDON S., PO Box 296, Anchor Point, AK 99556-0296, Phone: 907-235-8242
Specialties: Working straight knives and folders, some fancy. **Patterns:** Tantos, Bowies, boot fighter sets, locking folders. **Technical:** Grinds stainless steels; likes 1/4" inch stock and glass-bead finishes. **Prices:** $75 to $250; some to $2000. **Remarks:** Full-time maker; first knife sold in 1968. **Mark:** Initials in lightning logo.

GRECO, JOHN, 100 Mattie Jones Rd., Greensburg, KY 42743, Phone: 270-932-3335, Fax: 270-932-2225, greco@kfbol.com Web: www.grecoknives.com
Specialties: Limited edition knives and swords. **Patterns:** Tactical, fighters, camp knives, short swords. **Technical:** Stock removal carbon steel. **Prices:** Affordable. **Remarks:** Full-time maker since1986. First knife sold in 1979. **Mark:** Greco and steroc w/mo mark.

GREEN, BILL, 706 Bradfield, Garland, TX 75042, Phone: 972-272-4748
Specialties: High-art and working straight knives and folders of his design and to customer specs. **Patterns:** Bowies, hunters, kitchen knives and locking folders. **Technical:** Grinds ATS-34, D2 and 440V. Hand-tooled custom sheaths. **Prices:** $70 to $350; some to $750. **Remarks:** Part-time maker; first knife sold in 1990. **Mark:** Last name.

GREEN, MARK, 1523 S Main St. PO Box 20, Graysville, AL 35073, Phone: 205-647-9353

GREEN, RUSS, 6013 Briercrest Ave., Lakewood, CA 90713, Phone: 562-867-2305
Specialties: Sheaths and using knives. **Technical:** Knives 440C, ATS-34, 5160, 01, cable Damascus. **Prices:** Knives: $135 to $850; sheaths: $30 to $200. **Mark:** Russ Green and year.

GREEN, WILLIAM (BILL), 46 Warren Rd., View Bank Vic., AUSTRALIA 3084, Fax: 03-9459-1529
Specialties: Traditional high-tech straight knives and folders. **Patterns:** Japanese-influenced designs, hunters, Bowies, folders and miniatures. **Technical:** Forges O1, D2 and his own Damascus. Offers lost wax castings for bolsters and pommels. Likes natural handle materials, gems, silver and gold. **Prices:** $400 to $750; some to $1200. **Remarks:** Full-time maker. **Mark:** Initials.

GREENAWAY, DON, 3325 Dinsmore Tr., Fayetteville, AR 72704, Phone: 501-521-0323

GREENE, CHRIS, 707 Cherry Lane, Shelby, NC 28150, Phone: 704-434-5620

GREENE, DAVID, 570 Malcom Rd., Covington, GA 30209, Phone: 770-784-0657
Specialties: Straight working using knives. **Patterns:** Hunters. **Technical:** Forges mosaic and twist Damascus. Prefers stag and desert ironwood for handle material.

GREENE, STEVE, DUNN KNIVES INC., PO Box 204, Rossville, KS 66533, Phone: 785-584-6856, Fax: 785-584-6856

GREENFIELD, G.O., 2605 15th St. #522, Everett, WA 98201, Phone: 425-258-1551, garyg1946@yahoo.com
Specialties: High-tech and working straight knives and folders of his design. **Patterns:** Boots, daggers, hunters and one-of-a-kinds. **Technical:** Grinds ATS-34, D2, 440C and T-440V. Makes sheaths for each knife. **Prices:** $100 to $800; some to $10,000. **Remarks:** Part-time maker; first knife sold in 1978. **Mark:** Springfield®, serial number.

GREGORY, MICHAEL, 211 Calhoun Rd., Belton, SC 29627, Phone: 864-338-8898
Specialties: Working straight knives and folders. **Patterns:** Hunters, tantos, locking folders and slip-joints, boots and fighters. **Technical:** Grinds 440C, 154CM and ATS-34; mirror finishes. **Prices:** $95 to $200; some to $1000. **Remarks:** Part-time maker; first knife sold in 1980. **Mark:** Name, city in logo.

GREINER, RICHARD, 1073 E. County Rd. 32, Green Springs, OH 44836

GREISS, JOCKL, Herrenwald 15, D 77773 Schenkenzell, GERMANY, Phone: +49 7836 95 71 69 or +49 7836 95 55 76, www.jockl-greiss-messer.de
Specialties: Classic and working using straight knives of his design. **Patterns:** Bowies, daggers and hunters. **Technical:** Uses only Jerry Rados Damascus. All knives are one-of-a-kind made by hand; no machines are used. **Prices:** $700 to $2000; some to $3000. **Remarks:** Full-time maker; first knife sold in 1984. **Mark:** An "X" with a long vertical line through it.

GREY, PIET, PO Box 363, Naboomspruit 0560, SOUTH AFRICA, Phone: 014-743-3613
Specialties: Fancy working and using straight knives of his design. **Patterns:** Fighters, hunters and utility/camp knives. **Technical:** Grinds ATS-34 and AEB-L; forges and grinds Damascus. Solder less fitting of guards. Engraves and scrimshaws. **Prices:** $125 to $750; some to $1500. **Remarks:** Part-time maker; first knife sold in 1970. **Mark:** Last name.

GRIFFIN, RENDON AND MARK, 9706 Cedardale, Houston, TX 77055, Phone: 713-468-0436
Specialties: Working folders and automatics of their designs. **Patterns:** Standard lockers and slip-joints. **Technical:** Most blade steels; stock removal. **Prices:** Start at $350. **Remarks:** Rendon's first knife sold in 1966; Mark's in 1974. **Mark:** Last name logo.

GRIFFIN, THOMAS J., 591 Quevli Ave., Windom, MN 56101, Phone: 507-831-1089
Specialties: Period pieces and fantasy straight knives of his design. **Patterns:** Daggers and swords. **Technical:** Forges 1095, 52100 and L6. Most blades are his own Damascus; turned fittings and wire-wrapped grips. **Prices:** $250 to $800; some to $2000. **Remarks:** Full-time maker; first knife sold in 1991. Doing business as Griffin Knives. **Mark:** Last name etched.

GRIFFIN JR., HOWARD A., 14299 SW 31st Ct., Davie, FL 33330, Phone: 954-474-5406, mgriffin18@aol.com
Specialties: Working straight knives and folders. **Patterns:** Hunters, Bowies, locking folders with his own push-button lock design. **Technical:** Grinds 440C. **Prices:** $100 to $200; some to $500. **Remarks:** Part-time maker; first knife sold in 1983. **Mark:** Initials.

GRIFFITH, LYNN, 5103 S Sheridan Rd. #402, Tulsa, OK 74145-7627, Phone: 918-366-8303, GriffithKN@aol.com Web: www.griffithknives.com
Specialties: Flat ground, full tang tactical knives. **Patterns:** Neck and multi-carry knives, drop and clip points, tantos and Wharncliffes. **Technical:** Grinds ATS-34 and Talonite. **Prices:** $125 to $400; some to $700. **Remarks:** Full-time knife maker; first knife sold in 1987. **Mark:** Last name over year made.

GROSPITCH, ERNIE, 18440 Amityville Dr., Orlando, FL 32820, Phone: 407-568-5438, shrpknife@aol.com web: www.erniesknives.com
Specialties: Bowies, hunting, fishing, kitchen, lockback folders, leather craft. **Patterns:** His design or customer. **Technical:** Stock removal using most available steels. **Prices:** $140 and up. **Remarks:** Full-time maker, sold first knife in 1990. Mark: Etched name/maker city and state.

GROSS, W.W., 109 Dylan Scott Dr., Archdale, NC 27263-3858
Specialties: Working knives. **Patterns:** Hunters, boots, fighters. **Technical:** Grinds. **Prices:** Moderate. **Remarks:** Full-time maker. **Mark:** Name.

GROSSMAN, STEWART, 24 Water St., #419, Clinton, MA 01510, Phone: 508-365-2291; 800-mysword
Specialties: Miniatures and full-size knives and swords. **Patterns:** One-of-a-kind miniatures—jewelry, replicas—and wire-wrapped figures. Full-size art, fantasy and combat knives, daggers and modular systems. **Technical:** Forges and grinds most metals and Damascus. Uses gems, crystals, electronics and motorized mechanisms. **Prices:** $20 to $300; some to $4500 and higher. **Remarks:** Full-time maker; first knife sold in 1985. **Mark:** G1.

GRUSSENMEYER, PAUL G., 310 Kresson Rd., Cherry Hill, NJ 08034, Phone: 856-428-1088, pgrussentne@comcast.net Web: www.pgcarvings.com
Specialties: Assembling fancy and fantasy straight knives with his own carved handles. **Patterns:** Bowies, daggers, folders, swords, hunters and miniatures. **Technical:** Uses forged steel and Damascus, stock removal and knapped obsidian blades. **Prices:** $250 to $4000. **Remarks:** Spare-time maker; first knife sold in 1991. **Mark:** First and last initial hooked together on handle.

GUARNERA, ANTHONY R., 42034 Quail Creek Dr., Quartzhill, CA 93536, Phone: 661-722-4032
Patterns: Hunters, camp, Bowies, kitchen, fighter knives. **Technical:** Forged and stock removal. **Prices:** $100 and up.

GUESS, RAYMOND L., 7214 Salineville Rd. NE, Mechanicstown, OH 44651, Phone: 330-738-2793
Specialties: Working straight knives and folders of his design or to customer specs. **Patterns:** Hunters, Bowies, fillet knives, steak and paring knife sets. **Technical:** Grinds 440C. Offers silver inlay work and mirror finishes. Custom-made leather sheath for each knife. **Prices:** $65 to $850; some to $700. **Remarks:** Spare-time maker; first knife sold in 1985. **Mark:** First initial, last name.

GUIDRY, BRUCE, 24550 Adams Ave., Murrieta, CA 92562, Phone: 909-677-2384

GUIGNARD, GIB, Box 3413, Quartzsite, AZ 85359, Phone: 928-927-4831, http: //www.cactusforge.com
Specialties: Rustic finish on primitive Bowies with stag or ironwood handles and turquoise inlay. **Patterns:** Very large in 5160 and ATS-34; Small and med. size hunting knives in ATS-34. **Technical:** Forges 5160 and grind ATS-34. **Prices:** $100 to $1000. **Remarks:** Full-time maker first knife sold in 1989. Doing business as Cactus Forge. Also do collaborations with Chuck Burrows of Wild Rose Trading Co. these collaborations are done under the name of Cactus Rose. **Mark:** Last name or G+ on period pieces and primitive.

GUNN, NELSON L., 77 Blake Rd., Epping, NH 03042, Phone: 603-679-5119
Specialties: Classic and working/using straight knives of his design. **Patterns:** Bowies, fighters and hunters. **Technical:** Grinds O1 and 440C. Carved stag handles with turquoise inlays. **Prices:** $125 to $300; some to $700. **Remarks:** Part-time maker; first knife sold in 1996. Doing business as Nelson's Custom Knives. **Mark:** First and last initial.

GUNTER, BRAD, 13 Imnaha Rd., Tijeras, NM 87059, Phone: 505-281-8080

GURGANUS, CAROL, 2553 N.C. 45 South, Colerain, NC 27924, Phone: 252-356-4831, Fax: 252-356-4650
Specialties: Working and using straight knives. **Patterns:** Fighters, hunters and kitchen knives. **Technical:** Grinds D2, ATS-34 and Damascus steel. Uses stag, and exotic wood handles. **Prices:** $100 to $300. **Remarks:** Part-time maker; first knife sold in 1992. **Mark:** Female symbol, last name, city, state.

GURGANUS, MELVIN H., 2553 N.C. 45 South, Colerain, NC 27924, Phone: 252-356-4831, Fax: 252-356-4650
Specialties: High-tech working folders. **Patterns:** Leaf-lock and back-lock designs, bolstered and interframe. **Technical:** D2 and 440C; Heat-treats, carves and offers lost wax casting. **Prices:** $300 to $3000. **Remarks:** Part-time maker; first knife sold in 1983. **Mark:** First initial, last name and maker.

GUTHRIE, GEORGE B., 1912 Puett Chapel Rd., Bassemer City, NC 28016, Phone: 704-629-3031
Specialties: Working knives of his design or to customer specs. **Patterns:** Hunters, boots, fighters, locking folders and slip-joints in traditional styles. **Technical:** Grinds D2, 440C and 154CM. **Prices:** $105 to $300; some to $450. **Remarks:** Part-time maker; first knife sold in 1978. **Mark:** Name in state.

H

HAGEN, PHILIP L., PO Box 58, 41780 Kansas Point Ln, Pelican Rapids, MN 56572, Phone: 218-863-8503, dhagen@prtel.com Web: www.dochagencustomknives.com
Specialties: Folders. **Patterns:** Defense-related straight knives; wide variety of models. **Technical:** Dual action scale release, holster release autos. **Prices:** $300 to $800; some to $3000. **Remarks:** Part-time maker; first knife sold in 1975. Make my own Damascus. **Mark:** DOC HAGEN in shield, knife, banner logo; or DOC.

HAGGERTY, GEORGE S., PO Box 88, Jacksonville, VT 05342, Phone: 802-368-7437, swewater@sover.net
Specialties: Working straight knives and folders. **Patterns:** Hunters, claws, camp and fishing knives, locking folders and backpackers. **Technical:** Forges and grinds W2, 440C and 154CM. **Prices:** $85 to $300. **Remarks:** Part-time maker; first knife sold in 1981. **Mark:** Initials or last name.

HAGUE, GEOFF, The Malt House, Hollow Ln., Wilton Marlborough, Wiltshire, ENGLAND SN8 3SR, Phone: (+44) 01672-870212, Fax: (+44) 01672 870212, geoff@hagueknives.com Web: www.hagueknives.com
Specialties: Fixed blade and folding knives. **Patterns:** Locking and friction folders, hunters and small knives. **Technical:** Grinds ATS-34, RWL34 and Damascus; others by agreement. **Prices:** Start at $200. **Remarks:** Full-time maker. **Mark:** Last name. **Other:** British voting member of the Knife Makers Guild.

HAINES, JEFF, HAINES CUSTOM KNIVES, 302 N. Mill St., Wauzeka, WI 53826, Phone: 608-875-5002
Patterns: Hunters, skinners, camp knives, customer designs welcome. **Technical:** Forges 1095, 5160, and Damascus, grinds A2. **Prices:** $40 and up. **Remarks:** Part-time maker since 1995. **Mark:** Last name.

HALFRICH, JERRY, 340 Briarwood, San Marcos, TX 78666, Phone: 512-353-2582, jerryhalfrich@earthlink.net
Specialties: Working knives and specialty utility knives for the professional and serious hunter. Uses proven designs in both straight and folding knives. Plays close attention to fit and finish. Art knives on special request. **Patterns:** Hunters, skinners, lock back liner lock. **Technical:** Grinds both flat and hollow D2, damasteel, BG42 makes high precision folders. **Prices:** $300 to $600, sometimes $1000. **Remarks:** Full-time maker since 2000. DBA Halfrich Custom Knives. **Mark:** Halfrich, San Marcos, TX in a football shape.

HALL, JEFF, PO Box 435, Los Alamitos, CA 90720, Phone: 562-594-4740, jhall10176@aol.com
Specialties: Collectible and working folders of his design. **Technical:** Grinds S30V, ATS-34, and various makers' Damascus. **Patterns:** Fighters, gentleman's, hunters and utility knives. **Prices:** $300 to $500; some to $1000. **Remarks:** Full-time maker. First knife sold 1998. **Mark:** Last name.

HALLIGAN, ED, 14 Meadow Way, Sharpsburg, GA 30277, Phone: 770-251-7720, Fax: 770-251-7720
Specialties: Working straight knives and folders, some fancy. **Patterns:** Liner locks, hunters, skinners, boots, fighters and swords. **Technical:** Grinds ATS-34; forges 5160; makes cable and pattern Damascus. **Prices:** $160 to $2500. **Remarks:** Full-time maker; first knife sold in 1985. Doing business as Halligan Knives. **Mark:** Last name, city, state and USA.

HAMLET JR., JOHNNY, 300 Billington, Clute, TX 77531, Phone: 979-265-6929, nifeman@swbell.net Web: www.hamlets-handmade-knives.com
Specialties: Working straight knives and folders. **Patterns:** Hunters, fighters, fillet and kitchen knives, locking folders. Likes upswept knives and trailing-points. **Technical:** Grinds 440C, D2, ATS-34. Makes sheaths. **Prices:** $125 and up. **Remarks:** Part-time maker; first knife sold in 1988. **Mark:** Hamlet's Handmade in script.

HAMMOND, JIM, PO Box 486, Arab, AL 35016, Phone: 256-586-4151, Fax: 256-586-0170, hammondj@otelco.net Web: www.jimhammondknives.com
Specialties: High-tech fighters and folders. **Patterns:** Proven-design fighters. **Technical:** Grinds 440C, 440V, ATS-34 and other specialty steels. **Prices:** $385 to $1200; some to $8500. **Remarks:** Full-time maker; first knife sold in 1977. Designer for Columbia River Knife and Tool. **Mark:** Full name, city, state in shield logo.

HANCOCK, TIM, 10805 N. 83rd St., Scottsdale, AZ 85260, Phone: 480-998-8849
Specialties: High-art and working straight knives and folders of his design and to customer preferences. **Patterns:** Bowies, fighters, daggers, tantos, swords, folders. **Technical:** Forges Damascus and 52100; grinds ATS-34. Makes Damascus. Silver-wire inlays; offers carved fittings and file work. **Prices:** $500 to $10,000. **Remarks:** Full-time maker; first knife sold in 1988. **Mark:** Last name or heart. **Other:** Master Smith ABS.

HAND, BILL, PO Box 773, 1103 W. 7th St., Spearman, TX 79081, Phone: 806-659-2967, Fax: 806-659-5117, klinker@arn.net
Specialties: Traditional working and using straight knives and folders of his design or to customer specs. **Patterns:** Hunters, Bowies, folders and fighters. **Technical:** Forges 5160, 52100 and Damascus. **Prices:** Start at $150. **Remarks:** Part-time maker; Journeyman Smith. Current delivery time 12 to 16 months. **Mark:** Stylized initials.

HANKINS, R., 9920 S Rural Rd. #10859, Tempe, AZ 85284, Phone: 480-940-0559, PAMHANKINS@USWEST.NET Web: http://albums.photopoint.com/j/
Specialties: Completely hand-made tactical, practical and custom Bowie knives. **Technical:** Use Damascus, ATS-34 and 440C stainless steel for blades. Stock removal method of grinding. Handle material varies from ivory, stag to Micarta, depending on application and appearance. **Remarks:** Part-time maker applying for Knifemakers Guild Int'l membership in June 2001.

HANSEN, LONNIE, PO Box 4956, Spanaway, WA 98387, Phone: 253-847-4632, LONNIEHANSEN@MSN.COM Web: lchansen.com
Specialties: Working straight knives of his design. **Patterns:** Tomahawks, tantos, hunters, filet. **Technical:** Forges 1086, 52100, grinds 440V, BG-42. **Prices:** Starting at $300. **Remarks:** Part-time maker since 1989. **Mark:** First initial and last name. Also first and last initial.

HANSEN, ROBERT W., 35701 University Ave. N.E., Cambridge, MN 55008, Phone: 612-689-3242
Specialties: Working straight knives, folders and integrals. **Patterns:** From hunters to minis, camp knives to miniatures; folding lockers and slip-joints in original styles. **Technical:** Grinds O1, 440C and 154CM; likes filework. **Prices:** $75 to $175; some to $550. **Remarks:** Part-time maker; first knife sold in 1983. **Mark:** Fish with last initial inside.

HANSON III, DON L., PO Box 13, Success, MO 65570-0013, Phone: 573-674-3045, Web: www.sunfishforge.com, www.donhansonknives.com
Specialties: One-of-a-kind Damascus folders and forged fixed blades. **Patterns:** Small, fancy pocket knives, large folding fighters and bowies. **Technical:** Forges own pattern welded Damascus, file work and carving also carbon steel bades with hamons. **Prices:** $800 and up. **Remarks:** Full-time maker, first knife sold in 1984. **Mark:** Sunfish.

HARA, KOUJI, 292-2 Ohsugi, Seki-City, Gifu-Pref. 501-32, JAPAN, Phone: 0575-24-7569, Fax: 0575-24-7569
Specialties: High-tech and working straight knives of his design; some folders. **Patterns:** Hunters, locking folders and utility/camp knives. **Technical:** Grinds Cowry X, Cowry Y and ATS-34. Prefers high mirror polish; pearl handle inlay. **Prices:** $80 to $500; some to $1000. **Remarks:** Full-time maker; first knife sold in 1980. Doing business as Knife House "Hara". **Mark:** First initial, last name in fish.

HARDY, DOUGLAS E., 114 Cypress Rd., Franklin, GA 30217, Phone: 706-675-6305

HARDY, SCOTT, 639 Myrtle Ave., Placerville, CA 95667, Phone: 530-622-5780, Web: www.innercite.com/~shardy
Specialties: Traditional working and using straight knives of his design. **Patterns:** Most anything with an edge. **Technical:** Forges carbon steels. Japanese stone polish. Offers mirror finish; differentially tempers. **Prices:** $100 to $1000. **Remarks:** Part-time maker; first knife sold in 1982. **Mark:** First initial, last name and Handmade with bird logo.

HARKINS, J.A., PO Box 218, Conner, MT 59827, Phone: 406-821-1060, kutter@customknives.net Web: customknives.net
Specialties: Investment grade folders. **Patterns:** flush buttons, lockers. **Technical:** Grinds ATS-34. Engraves; offers gem work. **Prices:** Start at $550. **Remarks:** Full-time maker and engraver; first knife sold in 1988. **Mark:** First and middle initials, last name.

HARLEY, LARRY W., 348 Deerfield Dr., Bristol, TN 37620, Phone: 423-878-5368 (shop)/Cell 423-571-0638, Fax: 276-466-6771, Web: www.lonesomepineknives.com
Specialties: One-of-a-kind Persian in one-of-a-kind Damascus. Working knives, period pieces. **Technical:** Forges and grinds ATS-34, 440c, L6, 15, 20, 1084, and 52100. **Patterns:** Full range of straight knives, tomahawks, razors, buck skinners and hog spears. **Prices:** $200 and up. **Mark:** Pine tree.

HARLEY, RICHARD, 348 Deerfield Dr., Bristol, TN 37620, Phone: 423-878-5368/423-571-0638
Specialties: Hunting knives, Bowies, friction folders, one-of-a-kind. **Technical:** Forges 1084, S160, 52100, Lg. **Prices:** $150 to $1000. **Mark:** Pine tree with name.

HARM, PAUL W., 818 Young Rd., Attica, MI 48412, Phone: 810-724-5582, harm@blclinks.net
Specialties: Early American working knives. **Patterns:** Hunters, skinners, patch knives, fighters, folders. **Technical:** Forges and grinds 1084, 01, 52100 and own Damascus. **Prices:** $75 to $1000. **Remarks:** First knife sold in 1990. **Mark:** Connected initials.

HARMON, JAY, 462 Victoria Rd., Woodstock, GA 30189, Phone: 770-928-2734
Specialties: Working straight knives and folders of his design or to customer specs; collector-grade pieces. **Patterns:** Bowies, daggers, fighters, boots, hunters and folders. **Technical:** Grinds 440C, 440V, ATS-34, D2 1095 and Damascus; heat-treats; makes own mokume. **Prices:** Start

at $185. **Remarks:** Part-time maker; first knife sold in 1984. **Mark:** Last name.

HARRINGTON, ROGER, 3 Beech Farm Cottages, Bugsell Ln., East Sussex, ENGLAND TN 32 5 EN, Phone: 44 0 1580 882194, info@bisonbushcraft.co.uk Web: www.bisonbushcraft.co.uk
Specialties: Working straight knives to his or customer's designs, flat saber Scandinavia-style grinds on full tang knives, also hollow and convex grinds. **Technical:** Grinds 01, D2, Damascus. **Prices:** $200 to $800. **Remarks:** First knife made by hand in 1997 whilst traveling around the world. **Mark:** Bison with bison written under.

HARRIS, CASS, 19855 Fraiser Hill Ln., Bluemont, VA 20135, Phone: 540-554-8774, Web: www.tdogforge.com
Prices: $160 to $500.

HARRIS, JAY, 991 Johnson St., Redwood City, CA 94061, Phone: 415-366-6077
Specialties: Traditional high-tech straight knives and folders of his design. **Patterns:** Daggers, fighters and locking folders. **Technical:** Uses 440C, ATS-34 and CPM. **Prices:** $250 to $850. **Remarks:** Spare-time maker; first knife sold in 1980.

HARRIS, JEFFERY A., 705 Olive St. Ste. 325, St. Louis, MO 63101, Phone: 314-241-2442, jeffro135@aol.com
Remarks: Purveyor and collector of handmade knives.

HARRIS, JOHN, 14131 Calle Vista, Riverside, CA 92508, Phone: 951-653-2755, johnharris@yahoo.com
Specialties: Hunters, Daggers, Bowies, Bird and Trout, period pieces, Damascus and carbon steel knives, forged and stock removal. **Prices:** $200 to $1000.

HARRIS, RALPH DEWEY, 2607 Bell Shoals Rd., Brandon, FL 33511, Phone: 813-681-5293, Fax: 813-654-8175
Specialties: Collector quality interframe folders. **Patterns:** High tech locking folders of his own design with various mechanisms. **Technical:** Grinds 440C, ATS-34 and commercial Damascus. Offers various frame materials including 416ss, and titanium; file worked frames and his own engraving. **Prices:** $400 to $3000. **Remarks:** Full-time maker; first knife sold in 1978. **Mark:** Last name, or name and city.

HARRISON, JIM (SEAMUS), 721 Fairington View Dr., St. Louis, MO 63129, Phone: 314-894-2525, seamusknives@msn.com Web: www.seamusknives.com
Specialties: Gents and fancy tactical locking-liner folders. Compact straight blades for hunting, backpacking and canoeing. **Patterns:** Liner lock folders. Compact 3 fingered fixed blades often with modified wharn-cliffes. Survival knife with mortised handles. **Technical:** Grinds 440C, talonite, S-30V, Mike Norris and Devin Thomas S.S. Damascus. Heat treats. **Prices:** Folders $325 to $700. Fixed flades $300 to $400. **Remarks:** Soon to be full time. **Mark:** Seamus

HARSEY, WILLIAM H., 82710 N. Howe Ln., Creswell, OR 97426, Phone: 519-895-4941, harseyjr@cs.com
Specialties: High-tech kitchen and outdoor knives. **Patterns:** Folding hunters, trout and bird folders; straight hunters, camp knives and axes. **Technical:** Grinds; etches. **Prices:** $125 to $300; some to $1500. Folders start at $350. **Remarks:** Full-time maker; first knife sold in 1979. **Mark:** Full name, state, U.S.A.

HART, BILL, 647 Cedar Dr., Pasadena, MD 21122, Phone: 410-255-4981
Specialties: Fur-trade era working straight knives and folders. **Patterns:** Springbuck folders, skinners, Bowies and patch knives. **Technical:** Forges and stock removes 1095 and 5160 wire Damascus. **Prices:** $100 to $600. **Remarks:** Part-time maker; first knife sold in 1986. **Mark:** Name.

HARTMAN, ARLAN (LANNY), 340 Ruddiman, N. Muskegon, MI 49445, Phone: 231-744-3635
Specialties: Working straight knives and folders. **Patterns:** Drop-point hunters, coil spring lockers, slip-joints. **Technical:** Flat-grinds D2, 440C and ATS-34. **Prices:** $300 to $2000. **Remarks:** Part-time maker; first knife sold in 1982. **Mark:** Last name.

HARTSFIELD, PHILL, PO Box 1637, Newport Beach, CA 92659-0637, Phone: 949-722-9792 and 714-636-7633, phillhartsfield@mindspring.com Web: www.phillhartsfield.com
Specialties: Heavy-duty working and using straight knives. **Patterns:** Fighters, swords and survival knives, most in Japanese profile. **Technical:** Grinds A2. **Prices:** $350 to $20,000. **Remarks:** Full-time maker; first knife sold about 1976. Doing business as A Cut Above. **Mark:** Initials, chiseled character plus register mark. **Other:** Color catalog $10.

HARVEY, HEATHER, HEAVIN FORGE, PO Box 768, Belfast 1100, SOUTH AFRICA, Phone: 27-13-253-0914, heavin.knives@mweb.co.za Web: www.africut.co.za
Specialties: Integral hand forged knives, traditional African weapons, primitive folders and by-gone forged-styles. **Patterns:** All forged knives, war axes, spears, arrows, forks, spoons, and swords. **Technical:** Own carbon Damascus and mokume. Also forges stainless, brass, copper and titanium. Traditional forging and heat-treatment methods used. **Prices:** $300 to $5000, average $1000. **Remarks:** Full-time maker and knifemaking instructor. Master bladesmith with ABS. First Damascus sold in 1995, first knife sold in 1998. Often collaborate with husband, Kevin (ABS MS) using the logo "Heavin". **Mark:** First name and sur name; oval shape with "M S" in middle.

HARVEY, KEVIN, HEAVIN FORGE, PO Box 768, Belfast 1100, SOUTH AFRICA, Phone: 27-13-253-0914, heavin.knives@mweb.co.za Web: www.africut.co.za
Specialties: Large knives of presentation quality and creative art knives. **Patterns:** Fixed blades of Bowie, dagger and fighter-styles, occasionally folders. **Technical:** Stock removal of stainless and forging of carbon steel and own Damascus. Indigenous African handle materials preferred. Stacked file worked handles. Ostrich, bull frog, fish, crocodile and snake leathers used on unique sheaths. Surface texturing and heat coloring of materials. Often collaborate with wife, Heather (ABS MS) under the logo "Heavin". **Prices:** $500 to $5000 average $1500. **Remarks:** Full-time maker and knifemaking instructor. Master bladesmith with ABS. First knife sold in 1984. **Mark:** First name and surname; oval with "M S" in the middle.

HARVEY, MAX, 14 Bass Rd., Bull Creek, Perth 6155, WESTERN AUSTRALIA, Phone: 09-332-7585
Specialties: Daggers, Bowies, fighters and fantasy knives. **Patterns:** Hunters, Bowies, tantos and skinners. **Technical:** Hollow-and flat-grinds 440C, ATS-34, 154CM and Damascus. Offers gem work. **Prices:** $250 to $4000. **Remarks:** Part-time maker; first knife sold in 1981. **Mark:** First and middle initials, last name.

HASLINGER, THOMAS, 164 Fairview Dr. SE, Calgary AB, CANADA T2H 1B3, Phone: 403-253-9628, Web: www.haslinger-knives.com
Specialties: One-of-a-kind using, working and art knives HCK signature sweeping grind liners. Differential heat treated stainless steel. **Patterns:** No fixed patterns, likes to work with customers on design. **Technical:** Grinds Various specialty alloys, including Damascus, High end satin finish. Prefers natural handle materials e.g. ancient ivory stag, pearl, abalone, stone and exotic woods. Does inlay work with stone, some sterling silver, niobium and gold wire work. Custom sheaths using matching woods or hand stitched with unique leather like sturgeon, Nile perch or carp. Offers engraving. **Prices:** Starting at $150. **Remarks:** Full-time maker; first knife sold in 1994. Doing business as Haslinger Custom Knives. **Mark:** Two marks used, high end work uses stylized initials, other uses elk antler with Thomas Haslinger, Canada, Handcrafted above.

HATCH, KEN, PO Box 203, Dinosaur, CO 81610
Specialties: Indian and early trade knives. **Patterns:** Buckskinners and period Bowies. **Technical:** Forges and grinds 1095, O1, W2, ATS-34. Prefers natural handle materials. **Prices:** $85 to $400. **Remarks:** Part-time maker, custom leather and bead work; first knife sold in 1977. **Mark:** Last name or dragonfly stamp.

HAWES, CHUCK, HAWES FORGE, PO Box 176, Weldon, IL 61882, Phone: 217-736-2479
Specialties: 95% of all work in own Damascus. **Patterns:** Slip-joints liner locks, hunters, Bowie's, swords, anything in between. **Technical:** Forges everything, uses all carbon steels, no stainless. **Prices:** $150 to $4000. **Remarks:** Like to do custom orders, his style or yours. Sells Damascus. **Mark:** Small football shape. Chuck Hawes maker Weldon, IL. **Other:** Full-time maker sine 1995.

HAWK, GRANT AND GAVIN, Box 401, Idaho City, ID 83631, Phone: 208-392-4911, Web: www.9-hawkknives.com
Specialties: Large folders with unique locking systems D.O.G. lock, toad lock. **Technical:** Grinds ATS-34, titanium folder parts. **Prices:** $450 and up. **Remarks:** Full-time maker. **Mark:** First initials and last names.

HAWK, JACK L., Rt. 1, Box 771, Ceres, VA 24318, Phone: 703-624-3878
Specialties: Fancy and embellished working and using straight knives of his design or to customer specs. **Patterns:** Hunters, Bowies and daggers. **Technical:** Hollow-grinds 440C, ATS-34 and D2; likes bone and ivory handles. **Prices:** $75 to $1200. **Remarks:** Full-time maker; first knife sold in 1982. **Mark:** Full name and initials.

HAWK, JOEY K., Rt. 1, Box 196, Ceres, VA 24318, Phone: 703-624-3282
Specialties: Working straight knives, some fancy. Welcomes customer designs. **Patterns:** Hunters, fighters, daggers, Bowies and miniatures. **Technical:** Grinds 440C or customer preference. Offers some knives with jewelling. **Prices:** $100 to $250; some to $500. **Remarks:** Part-time maker; first knife sold in 1983. **Mark:** First and middle initials, last name stamped.

custom knifemakers

HAWKINS, BUDDY, PO Box 5969, Texarkana, TX 75505-5969, Phone: 903-838-7917, buddyhawkins@cableone.net

HAWKINS, RADE, 110 Buckeye Rd., Fayetteville, GA 30214, Phone: 770-964-1023, Fax: 770-306-2877, sales@hawkinsknifemakingsupplies.com Web: www.hawkinsknifemakingsupplies.com
Specialties: Full line of knife making supplies and equipment. Catalog available $2.00. **Patterns:** All styles. **Technical:** Grinds and forges. Makes own Damascus **Prices:** Start at $190. **Remarks:** Full-time maker; first knife sold in 1972. Member knifemakers guild, ABS journeyman smith. **Mark:** Rade Hawkins Custom Knives.

HAYES, DOLORES, PO Box 41405, Los Angeles, CA 90041, Phone: 213-258-9923
Specialties: High-art working and using straight knives of her design. **Patterns:** Art knives and miniatures. **Technical:** Grinds 440C, stainless AEB, commercial Damascus and ATS-34. **Prices:** $50 to $500; some to $2000. **Remarks:** Spare-time maker; first knife sold in 1978. **Mark:** Last name.

HAYES, SCOTTY, Texarkana College, 2500 N Robinson Rd., Tesarkana, TX 75501, Phone: 903-838-4541, ext. 3236, Fax: 903-832-5030, shayes@texakanacollege.edu Web: www.americanbladesmith.com/2005ABSo/o20schedule.htm
Specialties: ABS School of Bladesmithing.

HAYES, WALLY, 1026 Old Montreal Rd., Orleans, Ont., CANADA K4A-3N2, Phone: 613-824-9520, Web: www.hayesknives.com
Specialties: Classic and fancy straight knives and folders. **Patterns:** Daggers, Bowies, fighters, tantos. **Technical:** Forges own Damascus and O1; engraves. **Prices:** $150 to $14,000. **Mark:** Last name, M.S. and serial number.

HAYNES, JERRY, 6902 Teton Ridge, San Antonio, TX 78233, Phone: 210-599-2928
Specialties: Working straight knives and folders of his design, also historical blades. **Patterns:** Hunters, skinners, carving knives, fighters, renaissance daggers, locking folders and kitchen knives. **Technical:** Grinds ATS-34, CPM, Stellite 6K, D2 and acquired Damascus. Prefers exotic handle materials. Has B.A. in design. Studied with R. Buckminster Fuller. **Prices:** $200 to $1200. **Remarks:** Part-time maker, will go full-time after retirement in 2007. First knife sold in 1953. **Mark:** Arrowhead and last name.

HAYNIE, CHARLES, 125 Cherry Lane, Toccoa, GA 30577, Phone: 706-886-8665

HAYS, MARK, Hays Handmade Knives, 1008 Kavanagh Dr., Austin, TX 78748, Phone: 512-292-4410, markhays@austin.rr.com Web: www,
Specialties: Working straight knives and folders. Patterns inspired by Randall and Stone. **Patterns:** Bowies, hunters and slip-joint folders. **Technical:** 440C stock removal. Repairs and restores Stone knives. **Prices:** Start at $200. **Remarks:** Part-time maker, brochure available, with Stone knives 1974-1983, 1990-1991. **Mark:** First initial, last name, state and serial number.

HAZEN, MARK, 9600 Surrey Rd., Charlotte, NC 28227, Phone: 704-573-0904, Fax: 704-573-0052, mhazen@carolina.rr.com
Specialties: Working/using straight knives of his design and to customer specs. **Patterns:** Hunters/skinners, fillet, utility/camp, fighters, short swords. **Technical:** Grinds 154 CM, ATS-34, 440C. **Prices:** $75 to $450; some to $1500. **Remarks:** Part-time maker. First knife sold 1982. **Mark:** Name with cross in it, stamped in blade.

HEADRICK, GARY, 122 Wilson Blvd., Juane Les Pins, FRANCE 06160, Phone: 033 0610282885
Specialties: Hi-tech folders with natural furnishings. Back lock & back spring. **Patterns:** Damascus and Mokumes. **Technical:** Self made Damascus all steel (no nickel). **Prices:** $500 to $2000. **Remarks:** Full-time maker for last 7 years. **Mark:** G/P in a circle. **Other:** 10 years active.

HEARN, TERRY L., Rt. 14 Box 7676, Lufkin, TX 75904, Phone: 936-632-5045, hearn1@lufkntx.com

HEASMAN, H.G., 28 St. Mary's Rd., Llandudno, N. Wales U.K. LL302UB, Phone: (UK)0492-876351
Specialties: Miniatures only. **Patterns:** Bowies, daggers and swords. **Technical:** Files from stock high-carbon and stainless steel. **Prices:** $400 to $600. **Remarks:** Part-time maker; first knife sold in 1975. Doing business as Reduced Reality. **Mark:** NA.

HEATH, WILLIAM, PO Box 131, Bondville, IL 61815, Phone: 217-863-2576
Specialties: Classic and working straight knives, folders. **Patterns:** Hunters and Bowies liner lock folders. **Technical:** Grinds ATS-34, 440C, 154CM, Damascus, handle materials micarta, woods to exotic materials snake skins cobra, rattle snake, African flower snake. Does own heat treating. **Prices:** $75 to $300 some $1000. **Remarks:** Full-time maker. First knife sold in 1979. **Mark:** W. D. HEATH.

HEDRICK, DON, 131 Beechwood Hills, Newport News, VA 23608, Phone: 757-877-8100, dhknife@cox.net or donaldhedrick@cox.net
Specialties: Working straight knives; period pieces and fantasy knives. **Patterns:** Hunters, boots, Bowies and miniatures. **Technical:** Grinds 440C and commercial Damascus. Also makes micro-mini Randall replicas. **Prices:** $150 to $550; some to $1200. **Remarks:** Part-time maker; first knife sold in 1982. **Mark:** First initial, last name in oval logo.

HEFLIN, CHRISTOPHER M., 6013 Jocely Hollow Rd., Nashville, TN 37205, Phone: 615-352-3909, blix@bellsouth.net

HEGWALD, J.L., 1106 Charles, Humboldt, KS 66748, Phone: 316-473-3523
Specialties: Working straight knives, some fancy. **Patterns:** Makes Bowies, miniatures. **Technical:** Forges or grinds O1, L6, 440C; mixes materials in handles. **Prices:** $35 to $200; some higher. **Remarks:** Part-time maker; first knife sold in 1983. **Mark:** First and middle initials.

HEHN, RICHARD KARL, Lehnmuehler Str. 1, 55444 Dorrebach, GERMANY, Phone: 06724 3152
Specialties: High-tech, full integral working knives. **Patterns:** Hunters, fighters and daggers. **Technical:** Grinds CPM T-440V, CPM T-420V, forges his own stainless Damascus. **Prices:** $1000 to $10,000. **Remarks:** Full-time maker; first knife sold in 1963. **Mark:** Runic last initial in logo.

HEINZ, JOHN, 611 Cafferty Rd., Upper Black Eddy, PA 18972, Phone: 610-847-8535, Web: www.herugrim.com
Specialties: Historical pieces / copies. **Technical:** Makes his own steel. **Prices:** $150 to $800. **Mark:** "H".

HEITLER, HENRY, 8106 N Albany, Tampa, FL 33604, Phone: 813-933-1645
Specialties: Traditional working and using straight knives of his design and to customer specs. **Patterns:** Fighters, hunters, utility/camp knives and fillet knives. **Technical:** Flat-grinds ATS-34; offers tapered tangs. **Prices:** $135 to $450; some to $600. **Remarks:** Part-time maker; first knife sold in 1990. **Mark:** First initial, last name, city, state circling double H's.

HELSCHER, JOHN W., 2645 Highway 1, Washington, IA 52353, Phone: 319-653-7310

HELTON, ROY, Helton Knives, 2941 Comstock St., San Diego, CA 92111, Phone: 858-277-5024

HEMBROOK, RON, HEMBROOK KNIVES, PO Box 201, Neosho, WI 53059, Phone: 920-625-3607, knifemkr@nconnect.net WEB: www.hembrookcustomknives.com
Specialties: Hunters, working knives. **Technical:** Grinds ATS-34, 440C, 01 and Damascus. **Prices:** $125 to $750, some to $1000. **Remarks:** First knife sold in 1980. **Mark:** Hembrook plus a serial number. Part-time maker, makes hunters, daggers, Bowies, folders and miniatures.

HEMPERLEY, GLEN, 13322 Country Run Rd., Willis, TX 77318, Phone: 936-228-5048, hemperley.com
Specialties: Specializes in hunting knives, does fixed and folding knives.

HENDRICKS, SAMUEL J., 2162 Van Buren Rd., Maurertown, VA 22644, Phone: 703-436-3305
Specialties: Integral hunters and skinners of thin design. **Patterns:** Boots, hunters and locking folders. **Technical:** Grinds ATS-34, 440C and D2. Integral liners and bolsters of N-S and 7075 T6 aircraft aluminum. Does leatherwork. **Prices:** $50 to $250; some to $500. **Remarks:** Full-time maker; first knife sold in 1992. **Mark:** First and middle initials, last name, city and state in football-style logo.

HENDRICKSON, E. JAY, 4204 Ballenger Creek Pike, Frederick, MD 21703, Phone: 301-663-6923, jhendrickson@xecu.net
Specialties: Classic collectors and working straight knives of his design. **Patterns:** Bowies, Kukri's, camp, hunters, and fighters. **Technical:** Forges 06, 1084, 5160, 52100, D2, L6 and W2; makes Damascus; offers silver wire inlay. Moran-styles on order. **Prices:** $400 to $5000. **Remarks:** Full-time maker; first knife sold in 1975. **Mark:** Last name, M.S.

HENDRICKSON, SHAWN, 2327 Kaetzel Rd., Knoxville, MD 21758, Phone: 301-432-4306
Specialties: Hunting knives. **Patterns:** Clip points, drop points and trailing point hunters. **Technical:** Forges 5160, 1084 and L6. **Prices:** $175 to $400.

HENDRIX, JERRY, HENDRIX CUSTOM KNIVES, 175 Skyland Dr. Ext., Clinton, SC 29325, Phone: 864-833-2659, jhendrix@backroads.net
Specialties: Traditional working straight knives of all designs. **Patterns:** Hunters, utility, boot, bird and fishing. **Technical:** grinds ATS-34 and 440C. **Prices:** $85 to $275. **Remarks:** Full-time maker. **Mark:** Full name in shape of knife. **Other:** Hand stitched, waxed leather sheaths.

HENDRIX, WAYNE, 9636 Burton's Ferry Hwy., Allendale, SC 29810, Phone: 803-584-3825, Fax: 803-584-3825, knives@barnwellsc.com Web: www.hendrixknives.com
    Specialties: Working/using knives of his design. **Patterns:** Hunters and fillet knives. **Technical:** Grinds ATS-34, D2 and 440C. **Prices:** $70 to $600. **Remarks:** Full-time maker; first knife sold in 1985. **Mark:** Last name.

HENNICKE, METALLGESTALTUNG, Wassegasse 4, 55578 Wallertheim, GERMANY, Phone: 0049 6732 930414, Fax: 0049 6732 930415, hennicke.metall@gmx.de Web: www.hennickemesser.de
    Specialties: All kinds of knives folder with titanium leiner and inlaid springs. **Patterns:** Hunting knives, Bowies, kukris, swords, daggers, camp knives. **Technical:** Forge damsteels mostly wild pattern and sanmai pattern to get strong blades. **Prices:** 400 Euro till 3000 Euro swords about 3000 to 6000 Euro. **Mark:** A mammoth walking out of the ricasso to the blade or a UH in a circle.

HENRIKSEN, HANS J., Birkegaardsvej 24, DK 3200 Helsinge, DENMARK, Fax: 45 4879 4899
    Specialties: Zirconia ceramic blades. **Patterns:** Customer designs. **Technical:** Slip-cast zirconia-water mix in plaster mould; offers hidden or full tang. **Prices:** White blades start at $10cm; colored +50 percent. **Remarks:** Part-time maker; first ceramic blade sold in 1989. **Mark:** Initial logo.

HENSLEY, WAYNE, PO Box 904, Conyers, GA 30012, Phone: 770-483-8938
    Specialties: Period pieces and fancy working knives. **Patterns:** Boots to Bowies, locking folders to miniatures. Large variety of straight knives. **Technical:** Grinds ATS-34, 440C, D2 and commercial Damascus. **Prices:** $85 and up. **Remarks:** Full-time maker; first knife sold in 1974. **Mark:** Last name.

HERBST, PETER, Komotauer Strasse 26, 91207 Lauf a.d. Pegn., GERMANY, Phone: 09123-13315, Fax: 09123-13379
    Specialties: Working/using knives and folders of his design. **Patterns:** Hunters, fighters and daggers; interframe and integral. **Technical:** Grinds CPM-T-440V, UHB-Elmax, ATS-34 and stainless Damascus. **Prices:** $300 to $3000; some to $8000. **Remarks:** Full-time maker; first knife sold in 1981. **Mark:** First initial, last name.

HERMAN, TIM, 7721 Foster, Overland Park, KS 66204, Phone: 913-649-3860, Fax: 913-649-0603
    Specialties: Investment-grade folders of his design; interframes and bolster frames. **Patterns:** Interframes and new designs in carved stainless. **Technical:** Grinds ATS-34 and damasteel Damascus. Engraves and gold inlays with pearl, jade, lapis and Australian opal. **Prices:** $1000 to $15,000. **Remarks:** Full-time maker; first knife sold in 1978. **Mark:** Etched signature.

HERNDON, WM. R. "BILL", 32520 Michigan St., Acton, CA 93510, Phone: 661-269-5860, bherndons1@earthlink.net
    Specialties: Straight knives, plain and fancy. **Technical:** Carbon steel (white and blued), Damascus, stainless steels. **Prices:** Start at $120. **Remarks:** Full-time maker; first knife sold in 1976. American Bladesmith Society journeyman smith. **Mark:** Signature and/or helm logo.

HERRING, MORRIS, Box 85, 721 W Line St., Dyer, AR 72935, Phone: 501-997-8861, morrish@ipa.com

HERRON, GEORGE, 474 Antonio Way, Springfield, SC 29146, Phone: 803-258-3914
    Specialties: High-tech working and using straight knives; some folders. **Patterns:** Hunters, fighters, boots in personal styles. **Technical:** Grinds 154CM, ATS-34. **Prices:** $400 to $2500. **Remarks:** Full-time maker; first knife sold in 1963. About 12 year back log. Not excepting orders. No catalog. **Mark:** Last name in script.

HESSER, DAVID, PO Box 1079, Dripping Springs, TX 78620, Phone: 512-894-0100
    Specialties: High-art daggers and fantasy knives of his design; court weapons of the Renaissance. **Patterns:** Daggers, swords, axes, miniatures and sheath knives. **Technical:** Forges 1065, 1095, O1, D2 and recycled tool steel. Offers custom lapidary work and stone-setting, stone handles and custom hardwood scabbards. **Prices:** $95 to $500; some to $6000. **Remarks:** Full-time maker; first knife sold in 1989. Doing business as Exotic Blades. **Mark:** Last name, year.

HETHCOAT, DON, Box 1764, Clovis, NM 88101, Phone: 505-762-5721, dhethcoat@plateautel.net
    Specialties: Liner lock-locking and multi-blade folders **Patterns:** Hunters, Bowies. **Technical:** Grinds stainless; forges Damascus. **Prices:** Moderate to upscale. **Remarks:** Full-time maker; first knife sold in 1969. **Mark:** Last name on all.

HIBBEN, DARYL, PO Box 172, LaGrange, KY 40031-0172, Phone: 502-222-0983, dhibben1@bellsouth.net
    Specialties: Working straight knives, some fancy to customer specs. **Patterns:** Hunters, fighters, Bowies, short sword, art and fantasy. **Technical:** Grinds 440C, ATS-34, 154CM, Damascus; prefers hollow-grinds. **Prices:** $175 to $3000. **Remarks:** Full-time maker; first knife sold in 1979. **Mark:** Etched full name in script.

HIBBEN, GIL, PO Box 13, LaGrange, KY 40031, Phone: 502-222-1397, Fax: 502-222-2676
    Specialties: Working knives and fantasy pieces to customer specs. **Patterns:** Full range of straight knives, including swords, axes and miniatures; some locking folders. **Technical:** Grinds ATS-34, 440C and 154CM. **Prices:** $300 to $2000; some to $10,000. **Remarks:** Full-time maker; first knife sold in 1957. Maker and designer of *Rambo III* knife; made swords for movie *Marked for Death* and throwing knife for movie *Under Seige*; made belt buckle knife and knives for movie *Perfect Weapon*; made knives featured in movie *Star Trek the Next Generation* Star Trek Nemesis 1990 inductee cutlery hall of fame; designer for United Cutlery. Official klingon armourer for Star Trek, over 34 movies and TV productions. **Mark:** Hibben Knives. City and state, or signature.

HIBBEN, JOLEEN, PO Box 172, LaGrange, KY 40031, Phone: 502-222-0983, dhibben1@bellsouth.net
    Specialties: Miniature straight knives of her design; period pieces. **Patterns:** Hunters, axes and fantasy knives. **Technical:** Grinds Damascus, 1095 tool steel and stainless 440C or ATS-34. Uses wood, ivory, bone, feathers and claws on/for handles. **Prices:** $60 to $200. **Remarks:** Spare-time maker; first knife sold in 1991. **Mark:** Initials or first name.

HIBBEN, WESTLEY G., 14101 Sunview Dr., Anchorage, AK 99515
    Specialties: Working straight knives of his design or to customer specs. **Patterns:** Hunters, fighters, daggers, combat knives and some fantasy pieces. **Technical:** Grinds 440C mostly. Filework available. **Prices:** $200 to $400; some to $3000. **Remarks:** Part-time maker; first knife sold in 1988. **Mark:** Signature.

HIGGINS, J.P. DR., ART KNIVES BY, 120 N Pheasant Run, Coupeville, WA 98239, Phone: 360-678-9269, Fax: 360-678-9269, netsuke @whidbey.net Web: www.bladegallery.com or www.2.whidbey.net/netsuke
    Specialties: Since 2003 Dr. J.P. Higgins and Tom Sterling have created a unique collaboration of one-of-a-kind, ultra-quality art knives with percussion or pressured flaked stone blades and creatively sculpted handles. Their knives are often highly influenced by the traditions of Japanese netsuke and unique fusions of cultures, reflecting stylistically integrated choices of exotic hardwoods, fossil ivories and semi-precious materials, contrasting inlays and polychromed and pyrographed details. **Prices:** $300 to $900. **Remarks:** Limited output ensures highest quality artwork and exceptional levels of craftsmanship. **Mark:** Signatures Sterling and Higgins.

HIGH, TOM, 5474 S. 112.8 Rd., Alamosa, CO 81101, Phone: 719-589-2108, www.rockymountainscrimshaw.com
    Specialties: Hunters, some fancy. **Patterns:** Drop-points in several shapes; some semi-skinners. Knives designed by and for top outfitters and guides. **Technical:** Grinds ATS-34; likes hollow-grinds, mirror finishes; prefers scrim able handles. **Prices:** $175 to $8000. **Remarks:** Full-time maker; first knife sold in 1965. Limited edition wildlife series knives. **Mark:** Initials connected; arrow through last name.

HILKER, THOMAS N., PO Box 409, Williams, OR 97544, Phone: 541-846-6461
    Specialties: Traditional working straight knives and folders. **Patterns:** Folding skinner in two sizes, Bowies, fork and knife sets, camp knives and interchangeable. **Technical:** Grinds D2, 440C and ATS-34. Heat-treats. **Prices:** $50 to $350; some to $400. Doing business as Thunderbolt Artisans. Only limited production models available; not currently taking orders. **Remarks:** Full-time maker; first knife sold in 1983. **Mark:** Last name.

HILL, HOWARD E., 111 Mission Lane, Polson, MT 59860, Phone: 406-883-3405, Fax: 406-883-3486, knifeman@bigsky.net
    Specialties: Autos, complete new design, legal in Montana (with permit). **Patterns:** Bowies, daggers, skinners and lockback folders. **Technical:** Grinds 440C; uses micro and satin finish. **Prices:** $150 to $1000. **Remarks:** Full-time maker; first knife sold in 1981. **Mark:** Persuader.

HILL, RICK, 20 Nassau, Maryville, IL 62062-5618, Phone: 618-288-4370
    Specialties: Working knives and period pieces to customer specs. **Patterns:** Hunters, locking folders, fighters and daggers. **Technical:** Grinds D2, 440C and 154CM; forges his own Damascus. **Prices:** $75 to $500; some to $3000. **Remarks:** Part-time maker; first knife sold in 1983. **Mark:** Full name in hill shape logo.

HILL, STEVE E., 40 Rand Pond Rd., Goshen, NH 03752, Phone: 603-863-4762, Fax: 603-863-4762, kingpirateboy2@juno.com
> **Specialties:** Fancy manual and automatic liner lock folders, some working grade. **Patterns:** Classic to cool folding and fixed blade designs. **Technical:** Grinds Damascus and occasional 440C, D2. Prefers natural handle materials; offers elaborate filework, carving, and inlays. **Prices:** $375 to $5000; some higher. **Remarks:** Full-time maker; first knife sold in 1978. **Mark:** First initial, last name and handmade. (4400, D2). Damascus folders: mark inside handle. **Other:** Google search: Steve Hill custom knives.

HILLMAN, CHARLES, 225 Waldoboro Rd., Friendship, ME 04547, Phone: 207-832-4634
> **Specialties:** Working knives of his own or custom design. Heavy Scagel influence. **Patterns:** Hunters, fishing, camp and general utility. Occasional folders. **Technical:** Grinds D2 and 440C. File work, blade and handle carving, engraving. Natural handle materials-antler, bone, leather, wood, horn. Sheaths made to order. **Prices:** $60 to $500. **Remarks:** Part-time maker; first knife sold 1986. **Mark:** Last name in oak leaf.

HINDERER, RICK, 5423 Kister Rd., Wooster, OH 44691, Phone: 216-263-0962, rhind64@earthlink.net Web: www.rhknives.com
> **Specialties:** Working tactical knives, and some one-of-a kind. **Patterns:** Make my own. **Technical:** Grinds CPM S30V. **Prices:** $150 to $4000. **Remarks:** Full-time maker doing business as Rick Hinderer Knives, first knife sold in 1988. **Mark:** R. Hinderer.

HINK III, LES, 1599 Aptos Lane, Stockton, CA 95206, Phone: 209-547-1292
> **Specialties:** Working straight knives and traditional folders in standard patterns or to customer specs. **Patterns:** Hunting and utility/camp knives; others on request. **Technical:** Grinds carbon and stainless steels. **Prices:** $80 to $200; some higher. **Remarks:** Part-time maker; first knife sold in 1980. **Mark:** Last name, or last name 3.

HINMAN, TED, 183 Highland Ave., Watertown, MA 02472

HINSON AND SON, R., 2419 Edgewood Rd., Columbus, GA 31906, Phone: 706-327-6801
> **Specialties:** Working straight knives and folders. **Patterns:** Locking folders, liner locks, combat knives and swords. **Technical:** Grinds 440C and commercial Damascus. **Prices:** $100 to $350; some to $1500. **Remarks:** Part-time maker; first knife sold in 1983. Son Bob is co-worker. **Mark:** HINSON, city and state.

HINTZ, GERALD M., 5402 Sahara Ct., Helena, MT 59602, Phone: 406-458-5412
> **Specialties:** Fancy, high-art, working/using knives of his design. **Patterns:** Bowies, hunters, daggers, fish fillet and utility/camp knives. **Technical:** Forges ATS-34, 440C and D2. Animal art in horn handles or in the blade. **Prices:** $75 to $400; some to $1000. **Remarks:** Part-time maker; first knife sold in 1980. Doing business as Big Joe's Custom Knives. Will take custom orders. **Mark:** F.S. or W.S. with first and middle initials and last name.

HIRAYAMA, HARUMI, 4-5-13 Kitamachi, Warabi City, Saitama Pref. 335-0001, JAPAN, Phone: 048-443-2248, Fax: 048-443-2248, Web: www.ne.jp/asahi/harumi/knives
> **Specialties:** High-tech working knives of her design. **Patterns:** Locking folders, interframes, straight gents and slip-joints. **Technical:** Grinds 440C or equivalent; uses natural handle materials and gold. **Prices:** Start at $1500. **Remarks:** Part-time maker; first knife sold in 1985. **Mark:** First initial, last name.

HIROTO, FUJIHARA, , 2-34-7 Koioosako Nishi-ku Hiroshima-city, Hiroshima, JAPAN, Phone: 082-271-8389, fjhr8363@crest.ocn.ne.jp

HITCHMOUGH, HOWARD, 95 Old Street Rd., Peterborough, NH 03458-1637, Phone: 603-924-9646, Fax: 603-924-9595, howard@hitchmoughknives.com Web: www.hitchmoughknives.com
> **Specialties:** High class folding knives. **Patterns:** Lockback folders, liner locks, pocket knives. **Technical:** Uses ATS-34, stainless Damascus, titanium, gold and gemstones. Prefers hand-rubbed finishes and natural handle materials. **Prices:** $850 to $3500; some to $4500. **Remarks:** Full-time maker; first knife sold in 1967. **Mark:** Last name.

HOBART, GENE, 100 Shedd Rd., Windsor, NY 13865, Phone: 607-655-1345

HOCKENBARY, WARREN E., 1806 Vallecito Dr., San Pedro, CA 90732

HOCKENSMITH, DAN, 33514 CR 77, Crook, CO 80726, Phone: 970-886-3404, Web: hockensmithknives.com
> **Specialties:** Traditional working and using straight knives of his design. **Patterns:** Hunters, Bowies, folders and utility/camp knives. **Technical:** Uses his Damascus, 5160, carbon steel, 52100 steel and 1084 steel. Hand forged. **Prices:** $250 to $1500; some to $1000. **Remarks:** Part-time maker; first knife sold in 1987. **Mark:** Last name or stylized "D" with H inside.

HODGE, J.B., 1100 Woodmont Ave. SE, Huntsville, AL 35801, Phone: 205-536-8388
> **Specialties:** Fancy working folders. **Patterns:** Slip-joints. **Technical:** Grinds 154CM and ATS-34. **Prices:** Start at $175. **Remarks:** Part-time maker; first knife sold in 1978. Not currently taking orders. **Mark:** Name, city and state.

HODGE III, JOHN, 422 S. 15th St., Palatka, FL 32177, Phone: 904-328-3897
> **Specialties:** Fancy straight knives and folders. **Patterns:** Various. **Technical:** Pattern-welded Damascus—"Southern-style." **Prices:** To $1000. **Remarks:** Part-time maker; first knife sold in 1981. **Mark:** JH3 logo.

HODGSON, RICHARD J., 9081 Tahoe Lane, Boulder, CO 80301, Phone: 303-666-9460
> **Specialties:** Straight knives and folders in standard patterns. **Patterns:** High-tech knives in various patterns. **Technical:** Grinds 440C, AEB-L and CPM. **Prices:** $850 to $2200. **Remarks:** Part-time maker. **Mark:** None.

HOEL, STEVE, PO Box 283, Pine, AZ 85544, Phone: 602-476-4278
> **Specialties:** Investor-class folders, straight knives and period pieces of his design. **Patterns:** Folding interframes lockers and slip-joints; straight Bowies, boots and daggers. **Technical:** Grinds 154CM, ATS-34 and commercial Damascus. **Prices:** $600 to $1200; some to $7500. **Remarks:** Full-time maker. **Mark:** Initial logo with name and address.

HOFER, LOUIS, GEN DEL, Rose Prairie BC, CANADA V0C 2H0, Phone: 250-630-2513

HOFFMAN, KEVIN L., 28 Hopeland Dr., Savannah, GA 31419, Phone: 912-920-3579, Fax: 912-920-3579, kevh052475@aol.com Web: www.KLHoffman.com
> **Specialties:** Distinctive folders and fixed blades. **Patterns:** Titanium frame lock folders. **Technical:** Sculpted guards and fittings cast in sterling silver and 14k gold. Grinds ATS-34, Damascus. Makes kydex sheaths for his fixed blade working knives. **Prices:** $400 and up. **Remarks:** Full-time maker since 1981. **Mark:** KLH.

HOFFMANN, UWE H., PO Box 60114, Vancouver, BC, CANADA V5W 4B5, Phone: 604-572-7320 (after 5 p.m.)
> **Specialties:** High-tech working knives, folders and fantasy knives of his design or to customer specs. **Patterns:** Hunters, fishing knives, combat and survival knives, folders and diver's knives. **Technical:** Grinds 440C, ATS-34, D2 and commercial Damascus. **Prices:** $95 to $900; some to $2000 and higher. **Remarks:** Full-time maker; first knife sold in 1985. **Mark:** Hoffmann Handmade Knives.

HOGAN, THOMAS R., 2802 S. Heritage Ave., Boise, ID 83709, Phone: 208-362-7848

HOGSTROM, ANDERS T., Granvagen 2, 135 52 Tyreso, SWEDEN, Phone: 46 8 798 5802, andershogstrom@hotmail.com or andershogstrom@rixmail.se Web: www.andershogstrom.com
> **Specialties:** Short and long daggers, fighters and swords For select pieces makes wooden display boxes. **Patterns:** Daggers, fighters, short knives and swords and an occasional sword. **Technical:** Grinds 1050 High Carbon, Damascus and stanless, forges own Damasus on occasion. Does clay tempering and uses exotic hardwoods. **Prices:** Start at $500. **Marks:** Last name in various typefaces.

HOKE, THOMAS M., 3103 Smith Ln., LaGrange, KY 40031, Phone: 502-222-0350
> **Specialties:** Working/using knives, straight knives. Own designs and customer specs. **Patterns:** Daggers, Bowies, hunters, fighters, short swords. **Technical:** Grind 440C, Damascus and ATS-34. Filework on all knives. Tooling on sheaths (custom fit on all knives). Any handle material, mostly exotic. **Prices:** $100 to $700; some to $1500. **Remarks:** Full-time maker; first knife sold in 1986. **Mark:** Dragon on banner which says T.M. Hoke.

HOLBROOK, H.L., PO Box 483, Sandy Hook, KY 41171, Phone: 606-738-9922 home/606-738-6842 Shop, hhknives@mrtc.com
> **Specialties:** Traditional working using straight knives and folders of his design, to customer specs and in standard patterns. Stablized wood. **Patterns:** Hunters, folders. **Technical:** Grinds 440C, ATS-34 and D2. Blades have hand-rubbed satin finish. Uses exotic woods, stag and Micarta. Hand-sewn sheath with each straight knife. **Prices:** $90 to $270; some to $400. **Remarks:** Part-time maker; first knife sold in 1983. Doing business as Holbrook knives. **Mark:** Name, city, state.

HOLDER, D'ALTON, 7148 W. Country Gables Dr., Peoria, AZ 85381, Phone: 623-878-3064, Fax: 623-878-3964, dholderknives@cox.net Web: d'holder.com
> **Specialties:** Deluxe working knives and high-art hunters. **Patterns:** Drop-point hunters, fighters, Bowies. **Technical:** Grinds ATS-34; uses amber and other materials in combination on stick tangs. **Prices:** $400 to

$1000; some to $2000. **Remarks:** Full-time maker; first knife sold in 1966. **Mark:** D'HOLDER, city and state.

HOLLAND, JOHN H., 1580 Nassau St., Titusville, FL 32780, Phone: 321-267-4378
 Specialties: Traditional and fancy working/using straight knives and folders of his design, to customer specs and in standard patterns. **Patterns:** Hunters, and slip-joint folders. **Technical:** Grinds 440V and 440C. Offers engraving. **Prices:** $200 to $500; some to $1000. **Remarks:** Part-time maker; first knife sold in 1988. doing business as Holland Knives. **Mark:** First and last name, city, state.

HOLLAR, BOB, 701 2nd Ave. SW, Great Falls, MT 59404, Phone: 406-268-8252, goshawk@imt.net
 Specialties: Working/using straight knives and folders of his design and to customer specs; period pieces. **Patterns:** Fighters, hunters, liners and back lock folders. **Technical:** Forges 52100, 5160, 15N20 and 1084 (Damascus)*. **Prices:** $225 to $650; some to $1500. **Remarks:** Full-time maker. Doing business as Goshawk Knives. **Mark:** Goshawk stamped. **Other:** *Burled woods, stag, ivory; all stabilized material for handles.

HOLLOWAY, PAUL, 714 Burksdale Rd., Norfolk, VA 23518, Phone: 804-588-7071
 Specialties: Working straight knives and folders to customer specs. **Patterns:** Lockers and slip-joints; fighters and boots; fishing and push knives, from swords to miniatures. **Technical:** Grinds A2, D2, 154CM, 440C and ATS-34. **Prices:** $125 to $400; some to $1200. **Remarks:** Part-time maker; first knife sold in 1981. **Mark:** Last name, or last name and city in logo.

HOLMES, ROBERT, 1431 S Eugene St., Baton Rouge, LA 70808-1043, Phone: 504-291-4864
 Specialties: Using straight knives and folders of his design or to customer specs. **Patterns:** Bowies, utility hunters, camp knives, skinners, slip-joint and lock-back folders. **Technical:** Forges 1065, 1095 and L6. Makes his own Damascus and cable Damascus. Offers clay tempering. **Prices:** $150 to $1500. **Remarks:** Part-time maker; first knife sold in 1988. **Mark:** DOC HOLMES, or anvil logo with last initial inside.

HORN, DES, PO Box 322, NEWLANDS, 7700 Cape Town, SOUTH AFRICA, Phone: 27283161795, Fax: 27283161795, deshorn@usa.net
 Specialties: Folding knives. **Patterns:** Ball release side lock mechanism and interframe automatics. **Technical:** Prefers working in totally stainless materials. **Prices:** $600 to $3000. **Remarks:** Full-time maker. Enjoys working in gold, titanium, meteorite, pearl and mammoth. **Mark:** Des Horn.

HORN, JESS, 2526 Lansdown Rd., Eugene, OR 97404, Phone: 541-463-1510, jandahorn@earthlink.net
 Specialties: Investor-class working folders; period pieces; collectibles. **Patterns:** High-tech design and finish in folders; liner locks, traditional slip-joints and featherweight models. **Technical:** Grinds ATS-34, 154CM. **Prices:** Start at $1000. **Remarks:** Full-time maker; first knife sold in 1968. **Mark:** Full name or last name.

HORNE, GRACE, 182 Crimicar Ln., Sheffield Britian, UNITED KINGDOM S10 4EJ, grace.horne@student.shu.ac.uk Web: www.gracehorne.co.uk
 Specialties: Knives of own design including kitchen and utility knives for people with reduced hand use. **Technical:** Working at Sheffield Hallam University researching innovative, contemporary Damascus steels using non-traditional methods of manufacture. **Remarks:** Spare-time maker/ full-time researcher. **Mark:** 'gH' and 'Sheffield'.

HORTON, SCOT, PO Box 451, Buhl, ID 83316, Phone: 208-543-4222
 Specialties: Traditional working stiff knives and folders. **Patterns:** Hunters, skinners, utility and show knives. **Technical:** Grinds ATS-34. Uses stag, abalone and exotic woods. **Prices:** $200 to $2500. **Remarks:** First knife sold in 1990. **Mark:** Full name in arch underlined with arrow, city, state.

HOSSOM, JERRY, 3585 Schilling Ridge, Duluth, GA 30096, Phone: 770-449-7809, knives@attbi.com Web: www.hossom.com
 Specialties: Working straight knives of his own design. **Patterns:** Fighters, combat knives, modern Bowies and daggers, modern swords, concealment knives for military and LE uses. **Technical:** Grinds 154CM, S30V, CPM-3V and stainless Damascus. Uses natural and synthetic handle materials. **Prices:** $250-1500, some higher. **Remarks:** Full-time maker since 1997. First knife sold in 1983. **Mark:** First initial and last name, includes city and state since 2002.

HOUSE, GARY, 2851 Pierce Rd., Ephrata, WA 98823, Phone: 509-754-3272, spindry101@aol.com
 Specialties: Mosaic Damascus bar stock. Forged blades. **Patterns:** Unlimited, SW Indian designs, geometric patterns, using 1084, 15N20 and some nickel. Bowies, hunters and daggers.**Technical:** Forge mosaic Damascus.**Prices:** $500 & up. **Remarks:** Some of the finest and most unique patterns available. ABS journeyman smith. **Marks:** Initials GTH, G hanging T, H

HOUSE, LAWRENCE, 932 Eastview Dr., Canyon Lake, TX 78133, Phone: 830-899-6932

HOWARD, DURVYN M., 4220 McLain St. S., Hokes Bluff, AL 35903, Phone: 256-492-5720
 Specialties: Collectible upscale folders; one of kinds, gentlemen's folders. Multiple patents. **Patterns:** Conceptual designs; each unique and different. **Technical:** Uses natural and exotic materials and precious metals. **Prices:** $5000 to $25,000. **Remarks:** Full-time maker; by commission or available work. **Mark:** Howard: new for 2000; Howard in Garamond Narrow "etched". **Other:** Work displayed at select shows, K.G. Show etc.

HOWE, TORI, 13000 E Stampede Rd., Athol, ID 83801

HOWELL, JASON G., 213 Buffalo Trl., Lake Jackson, TX 77566, Phone: 979-297-9454
 Specialties: Fixed blades and liner lock folders. Makes own Damascus. **Patterns:** Clip and drop point. **Prices:** $150 to $750. **Remarks:** Likes making Mosaic Damascus out of the ordinary stuff. Member of TX Knifemakers and Collectors Association; apprentice in ABS; working towards Journeyman Stamp. **Mark:** Name, city, state.

HOWELL, LEN, 550 Lee Rd. 169, Opelika, AL 36804, Phone: 334-749-1942
 Specialties: Traditional and working knives of his design and to customer specs. **Patterns:** Buckskinner, hunters and utility/camp knives. **Technical:** Forges cable Damascus, 1085 and 5160; makes own Damascus. **Mark:** Engraved last name.

HOWELL, ROBERT L., Box 1617, Kilgore, TX 75663, Phone: 903-986-4364
 Specialties: Straight knives and folders of his design. **Patterns:** Hunters and locking folders. **Technical:** Grinds D2 and ATS-34; forges and grinds Damascus. **Prices:** $75 to $200; some to $2500. **Remarks:** Part-time maker; first knife sold in 1978. Doing business as Howell Knives. **Mark:** Last name.

HOWELL, TED, 1294 Wilson Rd., Wetumpka, AL 36092, Phone: 205-569-2281, Fax: 205-569-1764
 Specialties: Working/using straight knives and folders of his design; period pieces. **Patterns:** Bowies, fighters, hunters. **Technical:** Forges 5160, 1085 and cable. Offers light engraving and scrimshaw; filework. **Prices:** $75 to $250; some to $450. **Remarks:** Part-time maker; first knife sold in 1991. Doing business as Howell Co. **Mark:** Last name, Slapout AL.

HOWSER, JOHN C., 54 Bell Ln., Frankfort, KY 40601, Phone: 502-875-3678
 Specialties: Slip joint folders (old patterns-multi blades). **Patterns:** traditional slip joint folders, lockbacks, hunters and fillet knives. **Technical:** ATS-34, S-30V, drop 440-V standard steel, will use D-2, 440V-hand rubbed satin finish natural materials. **Prices:** $100 to $400 some to $500. **Remarks:** Full-time maker; first knife sold in 1974. **Mark:** Signature or stamp.

HOY, KEN, 54744 Pinchot Dr., North Fork, CA 93643, Phone: 209-877-7805

HRISOULAS, JIM, 330 S. Decatur Ave., Suite 109, Las Vegas, NV 89107, Phone: 702-566-8551
 Specialties: Working straight knives; period pieces. **Patterns:** Swords, daggers and sgian dubhs. **Technical:** Double-edged differential heat treating. **Prices:** $85 to $175; some to $600 and higher. **Remarks:** Full-time maker; first knife sold in 1973. Author of *The Complete Bladesmith*, *The Pattern Welded Blade* and *The Master Bladesmith*. Doing business as Salamander Armory. **Mark:** 8R logo and sword and salamander.

HUCKABEE, DALE, 254 Hwy 260, Maylene, AL 35114, Phone: 205-664-2544, dalehuckabee@hotmail.com
 Specialties: Fixed blade hunter and Bowies of his design. **Technical:** Steel used: 5160, 1095, 1084 and some Damascus. **Prices:** Starting at $150 and up, depending on materials used. **Remarks:** Hand forged. Journeyman Smith. **Mark:** Stamped Huckabee J.S. **Other:** Part-time maker.

HUCKS, JERRY, KNIVES BY HUCKS, 1807 Perch Road, Moncks Corner, SC 29461, Phone: 843-761-6481, kinvesbyhucks@dycon.com
 Specialties: Oyster knives, hunters, bowies, fillets, Bowies being makers favorite with stag & ivory. **Technical:** Yours and mine. ATS-34, BG-42, makers cable Damascus also 1084 & 15N20. **Prices:** $95.00 and up. **Remarks:** Full-time maker, retired as a machinist in 1990. **Mark:** Robin Hood hat with monck corner in oval. **Other:** Making folders 4" closed, titanium liners anodized) 2-56 torx screws.

HUDSON, ANTHONY B., PO Box 368, Amanda, OH 43102, Phone: 740-969-4200, jjahudson@wmconnect.com
 Specialties: Hunting knives, fighters, survival. **Remarks:** ABS Journeyman Smith. **Mark:** A.B. HUDSON.

HUDSON, C. ROBBIN, 22280 Frazier Rd., Rock Hall, MD 21661, Phone: 410-639-7273
Specialties: High-art working knives. Patterns: Hunters, Bowies, fighters and kitchen knives. Technical: Forges W2, nickel steel, pure nickel steel, composite and mosaic Damascus; makes knives one-at-a-time. Prices: 500 to $1200; some to $5000. Remarks: Full-time maker; first knife sold in 1970. Mark: Last name and MS.

HUDSON, ROB, 340 Roush Rd., Northumberland, PA 17857, Phone: 570-473-9588, robscustknives@aol.com
Specialties: Custom hunters and bowies Technical: Grinds ATS-34, stainless, Damascus hollow grinds or flat. Filework finger groves. Engraving and scrimshaw available. (Stainless). Prices: $300 to $1200. Remarks: Full-time maker. Does business as Rob's Custom Knives. Mark: Capital R, Capital H in script.

HUDSON, ROBERT, 3802 Black Cricket Ct., Humble, TX 77396, Phone: 713-454-7207
Specialties: Working straight knives of his design. Patterns: Bowies, hunters, skinners, fighters and utility knives. Technical: Grinds D2, 440C, 154CM and commercial Damascus. Prices: $85 to $350; some to $1500. Remarks: Part-time maker; first knife sold in 1980. Mark: Full name, handmade, city and state.

HUGHES, BILL, 110 Royale Dr., Texarkana, TX 75503, Phone: 903-838-0134, chughes@tc.cc.tx.us

HUGHES, DAN, 13743 Persimmon Blvd., West Palm Beach, FL 33411
Specialties: Working straight knives to customer specs. Patterns: Hunters, fighters, fillet knives. Technical: Grinds 440C and ATS-34. Prices: $55 to $175; some to $300. Remarks: Part-time maker; first knife sold in 1984. Mark: Initials.

HUGHES, DARYLE, 10979 Leonard, Nunica, MI 49448, Phone: 616-837-6623
Specialties: Working knives. Patterns: Buckskinners, hunters, camp knives, kitchen and fishing knives. Technical: Forges and grinds W2, O1 and D2. Prices: $40 to $100; some to $400. Remarks: Part-time maker; first knife sold in 1979. Mark: Name and city in logo.

HUGHES, ED, 280 1/2 Holly Lane, Grand Junction, CO 81503, Phone: 970-243-8547, edhughes26@msn.com
Specialties: Working and art folders. Patterns: Buys Damascus. Technical: Grinds stainless steels. Engraves. Prices: $300 and up. Remarks: Full-time maker; first knife sold in 1978. Mark: Name or initials.

HUGHES, LAWRENCE, 207 W. Crestway, Plainview, TX 79072, Phone: 806-293-5406
Specialties: Working and display knives. Patterns: Bowies, daggers, hunters, buckskinners. Technical: Grinds D2, 440C and 154CM. Prices: $125 to $300; some to $2000. Remarks: Full-time maker; first knife sold in 1979. Mark: Name with buffalo skull in center.

HULETT, STEVE, 115 Yellowstone Ave., West Yellowstone, MT 59758, Phone: 406-646-4116, Web: www.seldomseenknives.com
Specialties: Classic, working/using knives, straight knives, folders. Your design, custom specs. Patterns: Utility/camp knives, hunters, and liner lock folders. Technical: Grinds 440C stainless steel, O1 Carbon, 1095. Shop is retail and knife shop; people watch their knives being made. We do everything in house: "all but smelt the ore, or tan the hide." Prices: $125 to $7000. Remarks: Full-time maker; first knife sold in 1994. Mark: Seldom seen knives/West Yellowstone Montana.

HULL, MICHAEL J., 1330 Hermits Circle, Cottonwood, AZ 86326, Phone: 928-634-2871, mjwhull@earthlink.net
Specialties: Period pieces and working knives. Patterns: Hunters, fighters, Bowies, camp and Mediterranean knives, etc. Technical: Grinds 440C, ATS-34 and BG42 and S30V. Prices: $125 to $750; some to $1000. Remarks: Full-time maker; first knife sold in 1983. Mark: Name, city, state.

HULSEY, HOYT, 379 Shiloh, Attalla, AL 35954, Phone: 256-538-6765
Specialties: Traditional working straight knives and folders of his design. Patterns: Hunters and utility/camp knives. Technical: Grinds 440C, ATS-34, O1 and A2. Prices: $75 to $250. Remarks: Part-time maker; first knife sold in 1989. Mark: Hoyt Hulsey Attalla AL.

HUME, DON, 2731 Tramway Cir. NE, Albuquerque, NM 87122, Phone: 505-796-9451

HUMENICK, ROY, PO Box 55, Rescue, CA 95672
Specialties: Multiblade folders. Patterns: Original folder and fixed blade designs, also traditional patterns. Technical: Grinds premium steels and Damascus. Prices: $350 and up; some to $1500. Remarks: First knife sold in 1984. Mark: Last name in ARC.

HUMPHREYS, JOEL, 3260 Palmer Rd., Bowling Green, FL 33834-9801, Phone: 863-773-0439
Specialties: Traditional working/using straight knives and folders of his design and in standard patterns. Patterns: Hunters, folders and utility/

camp knives. Technical: Grinds ATS-34, D2, 440C. All knives have tapered tangs, mitered bolster/handle joints, handles of horn or bone fitted sheaths. Prices: $135 to $225; some to $350. Remarks: Part-time maker; first knife sold in 1990. Doing business as Sovereign Knives. Mark: First name or "H" pierced by arrow.

HUNT, MAURICE, 10510 N CR 650 E, Winter: 2925 Argyle Rd., Venice FL 34293, Brownsburg, IN 46112, Phone: 317-892-2982/Winter: 941-493-4027, mdhuntknives@juno.com
Patterns: Bowies, hunters, fighters. Prices: $200 to $800. Remarks: Part-time maker. Other: Journeyman Smith.

HUNTER, HYRUM, 285 N. 300 W, PO Box 179, Aurora, UT 84620, Phone: 435-529-7244
Specialties: Working straight knives of his design or to customer specs. Patterns: Drop and clip, fighters dagger, some folders. Technical: Forged from two piece Damascus. Prices: Prices are adjusted according to size, complexity and material used. Remarks: Will consider any design you have. Part-time maker; first knife sold in 1990. Mark: Initials encircled with first initial and last name and city, then state. Some patterns are numbered.

HUNTER, RICHARD D., 7230 NW 200th Ter., Alachua, FL 32615, Phone: 386-462-3150
Specialties: Traditional working/using knives of his design or customer suggestions; filework. Patterns: Folders of various types, Bowies, hunters, daggers. Technical: Traditional blacksmith; hand forges high-carbon steel (5160, 1084, 52100) and makes own Damascus; grinds 440C and ATS-34. Prices: $200 and up. Remarks: Part-time maker; first knife sold in 1992. Mark: Last name in capital letters.

HURST, COLE, 1583 Tedford, E. Wenatchee, WA 98802, Phone: 509-884-9206
Specialties: Fantasy, high-art and traditional straight knives. Patterns: Bowies, daggers and hunters. Technical: Blades are made of stone; handles are made of stone, wood or ivory and embellished with fancy woods, ivory or antlers. Prices: $100 to $300; some to $2000. Remarks: Spare-time maker; first knife sold in 1985. Mark: Name and year.

HURST, JEFF, PO Box 247, Rutledge, TN 37861, Phone: 865-828-5729, jhurst@esper.com
Specialties: Working straight knives and folders of his design. Patterns: Tomahawks, hunters, boots, folders and fighters. Technical: Forges W2, O1 and his own Damascus. Makes mokume. Prices: $175 to $350; some to $500. Remarks: Full-time maker; first knife sold in 1984. Doing business as Buzzard's Knob Forge. Mark: Last name; partnered knives are marked with Newman L. Smith, handle artisan, and SH in script.

HURT, WILLIAM R., 9222 Oak Tree Cir., Frederick, MD 21701, Phone: 301-898-7143
Specialties: Traditional and working/using straight knives. Patterns: Bowies, hunters, fighters and utility knives. Technical: Forges 5160, O1 and O6; makes own Damascus. Offers silver wire inlay. Prices: $200 to $600; some higher. Remarks: Full-time maker; first knife sold in 1989. Mark: First and middle initials, last name.

HUSIAK, MYRON, PO Box 238, Altona 3018, Victoria, AUSTRALIA, Phone: 03-315-6752
Specialties: Straight knives and folders of his design or to customer specs. Patterns: Hunters, fighters, lock-back folders, skinners and boots. Technical: forges and grinds his own Damascus, 440C and ATS-34. Prices: $200 to $900. Remarks: Part-time maker; first knife sold in 1974. Mark: First initial, last name in logo and serial number.

HUTCHESON, JOHN, SURSUM KNIFE WORKS, 1237 Brown's Ferry Rd., Chattanooga, TN 37419, Phone: 423-667-6193, sursum5071@aol.com Web: www.sursumknife.com
Specialties: Straight working knives, hunters. Patterns: Customer designs, hunting, speciality working knives. Technical: Grinds D2, S7, 01 and 5160, ATS-34 on request. Prices: $100 to $300, some to $600. Remarks: First knife sold 1985, also produces a mid-tech line. Mark: Family crest boar's head over 3 arrows. Other: Doing business as Sursum Knife Works.

HYDE, JIMMY, 5094 Stagecoach Rd., Ellenwood, GA 30049, Phone: 404-968-1951, Fax: 404-209-1741
Specialties: Working straight knives of any design; period pieces. Patterns: Bowies, hunters and utility knives. Technical: Grinds 440C; forges 5160, 1095 and O1. Makes his own Damascus and cable Damascus. Prices: $150 to $600. Remarks: Part-time maker; first knife sold in 1978. Mark: First initial, last name.

HYTOVICK, JOE "HY", 14872 SW 111th St., Dunnellon, FL 34432, Phone: 800-749-5339, Fax: 352-489-3732, hyclassknives@aol.com
Specialties: Straight, Folder and Miniature. Technical: Blades from Wootz, Damascus and Alloy steel. Prices: To $5000. Mark: HY.

I

IKOMA, FLAVIO YUJI, R. MANOEL R. TEIXEIRA, 108, 108, Centro Presidente Prudente, SP-19031-220, BRAZIL, Phone: 0182-22-0115, ikomaknives@hotmail.com
Specialties: Straight knives and folders of all designs. **Patterns:** Fighters, hunters, Bowies, swords, folders, skinners, utility and defense knives. **Technical:** Grinds and forges D6, 440C, high-carbon steels and Damascus. **Prices:** $60 to $350; some to $3300. **Remarks:** Full-time maker; first knife sold in 1991. All stainless steel blades are ultra sub-zero quenched. **Mark:** Ikoma Knives beside eagle.

IMBODEN II, HOWARD L., 620 Deauville Dr., Dayton, OH 45429, Phone: 513-439-1536
Specialties: One-of-a-kind hunting, flint, steel and art knives. **Technical:** Forges and grinds stainless, high-carbon and Damascus. Uses obsidian, cast sterling silver, 14K and 18K gold guards. Carves ivory animals and more. **Prices:** $65 to $25,000. **Remarks:** Full-time maker; first knife sold in 1986. Doing business as Hill Originals. **Mark:** First and last initials, II.

IMEL, BILLY MACE, 1616 Bundy Ave., New Castle, IN 47362, Phone: 765-529-1651
Specialties: High-art working knives, period pieces and personal cutlery. **Patterns:** Daggers, fighters, hunters; locking folders and slip-joints with interframes. **Technical:** Grinds D2, 440C and 154CM. **Prices:** $300 to $2000; some to $6000. **Remarks:** Part-time maker; first knife sold in 1973. **Mark:** Name in monogram.

IRIE, MICHAEL L., MIKE IRIE HANDCRAFT, 1606 Auburn Dr., Colorado Springs, CO 80909, Phone: 719-572-5330, mikeirie@aol.com
Specialties: Working fixed blade knives and handcrafted blades for the do-it-yourselfer. **Patterns:** Twenty standard designs along with custom. **Technical:** Blades are ATS-34, BG-43, 440C with some outside Damascus. **Prices:** Fixed blades $95 and up, blade work $45 and up. **Remarks:** Formerly dba Wood, Irie and Co. with Barry Wood. Full-time maker since 1991. **Mark:** Name.

IRON WOLF FORGE, SEE NELSON, KEN,

ISAO, OHBUCHI, , 702-1 Nouso Yame-City, Fukuoka, JAPAN, Phone: 0943-23-4439, www.5d.biglobe.ne.jp/~ohisao/

ISGRO, JEFFERY, 1516 First St., West Babylon, NY 11704, Phone: 631-587-7516
Specialties: File work, glass beading, kydex, leather. **Patterns:** Tactical use knives, skinners, capers, Bowies, camp, hunters. **Technical:** ATS-34, 440C and D2. **Price:** $120 to $600. **Remarks:** Part-time maker. **Mark:** First name, last name, Long Island, NY.

ISHIHARA, HANK, 86-18 Motomachi, Sakura City, Chiba Pref., JAPAN, Phone: 043-485-3208, Fax: 043-485-3208
Specialties: Fantasy working straight knives and folders of his design. **Patterns:** Boots, Bowies, daggers, fighters, hunters, fishing, locking folders and utility camp knives. **Technical:** Grinds ATS-34, 440C, D2, 440V, CV-134, COS25 and Damascus. Engraves. **Prices:** $250 to $1000; some to $10,000. **Remarks:** Full-time maker; first knife sold in 1987. **Mark:** HANK.

J

JACKS, JIM, 344 S. Hollenbeck Ave., Covina, CA 91723-2513, Phone: 626-331-5665
Specialties: Working straight knives in standard patterns. **Patterns:** Bowies, hunters, fighters, fishing and camp knives, miniatures. **Technical:** Grinds Stellite 6K, 440C and ATS-34. **Prices:** Start at $100. **Remarks:** Spare-time maker; first knife sold in 1980. **Mark:** Initials in diamond logo.

JACKSON, CHARLTON R., 6811 Leyland Dr., San Antonio, TX 78239, Phone: 210-601-5112

JACKSON, DAVID, 214 Oleander Ave., Lemoore, CA 93245, Phone: 559-925-8547, jnbcrea@lemoorenet.com
Specialties: Forged steel. **Patterns:** Hunters, camp knives, Bowies. **Prices:** $150 and up. **Mark:** G.D. Jackson - Maker - Lemoore CA.

JACKSON, JIM, 7 Donnington Close, Chapel Row Bucklebury RG7 6PU, ENGLAND, Phone: 011-89-712743, Fax: 011-89-710495, jlandsejackson@aol.com
Specialties: Large Bowies, concentrating on form and balance; collector quality Damascus daggers. **Patterns:** With fancy filework and engraving available. **Technical:** Forges O1, 5160 and CS70 and 15N20 Damascus. **Prices:** From $1000. **Remarks:** Part-time maker. **Mark:** Jackson England with in a circle M.S. **Other:** All knives come with a custom tooled leather swivel sheath or exotic materials.

JAKSIK JR., MICHAEL, 427 Marschall Creek Rd., Fredericksburg, TX 78624, Phone: 830-997-1119
Mark: MJ or M. Jaksik.

JANIGA, MATTHEW A., 2090 Church Rd., Hummelstown, PA 17036-9796, Phone: 717-533-5916
Specialties: Period pieces, swords, daggers. **Patterns:** Daggers, fighters and swords. **Technical:** Forges and Damascus. Does own heat treating. Forges own pattern-welded steel. **Prices:** $100 to $1000; some to $5000. **Remarks:** Spare-time maker; first knife sold in 1991. **Mark:** Interwoven initials.

JARVIS, PAUL M., 30 Chalk St., Cambridge, MA 02139, Phone: 617-547-4355 or 617-666-9090
Specialties: High-art knives and period pieces of his design. **Patterns:** Japanese and Mid-Eastern knives. **Technical:** Grinds Myer Damascus, ATS-34, D2 and O1. Specializes in height-relief Japanese-style carving. Works with silver, gold and gems. **Prices:** $200 to $17,000. **Remarks:** Part-time maker; first knife sold in 1978.

JEAN, GERRY, 25B Cliffside Dr., Manchester, CT 06040, Phone: 860-649-6449
Specialties: Historic replicas. **Patterns:** Survival and camp knives. **Technical:** Grinds A2, 440C and 154CM. Handle slabs applied in unique tongue-and-groove method. **Prices:** $125 to $250; some to $1000. **Remarks:** Spare-time maker; first knife sold in 1973. **Mark:** Initials and serial number.

JEFFRIES, ROBERT W., Route 2, Box 227, Red House, WV 25168, Phone: 304-586-9780
Specialties: Straight knives and folders. **Patterns:** Hunters, skinners and folders. **Technical:** Uses 440C, ATS-34; makes his own Damascus. **Prices:** Moderate. **Remarks:** Part-time maker; first knife sold in 1988. **Mark:** NA.

JENSEN, JOHN LEWIS, dba MAGNUS DESIGN STUDIO, PO Box 60547, Pasadena, CA 91116, Phone: 626-449-1148, Fax: 626-449-1148, john@jensenknives.com Web: www.jensenknives.com
Specialties: Designer and fabricator of modern, unique, elegant, innovative, original, one-of-a-kind, hand crafted, custom ornamental edged weaponry. Combines skill, precision, distinction and the finest materials, geared toward the discriminating art collector. **Patterns:** Folding knives and fixed blades, daggers, fighters and swords. **Technical:** High embellishment, BFA 96 Rhode Island School of Design: Jewelry and metalsmithing. Grinds 440C, ATS-34, Damascus. Works with custom made Damascus to his specs. Uses gold, silver, gemstones, pearl, titanium, fossil mastodon and walrus ivories. Carving, file work, soldering, deep etches Damascus, engraving, layers, bevels, blood grooves Also forges his own Damascus. **Prices:** Start at $3500. **Remarks:** Available on a first come basis and via commission based on his designs Knifemakers guild voting member and ABS apprenticesmith and member of the Society of North American Goldsmiths. **Mark:** Maltese cross/butterfly shield.

JENSEN JR., CARL A., 1130 Colfax St., Blair, NE 68008, Phone: 402-426-3353
Specialties: Working knives of his design; some customer designs. **Patterns:** Hunters, fighters, boots and Bowies. **Technical:** Grinds A2, D2, O1, 440C, 5160 and ATS-34; recycles old files, leaf springs; heat-treats. **Prices:** $35 to $350. **Remarks:** Part-time maker; first knife sold in 1980. **Mark:** Stamp "BEAR'S CUTLERY" or etch of letters "BEAR" forming silhouette of a Bear.

JERNIGAN, STEVE, 3082 Tunnel Rd., Milton, FL 32571, Phone: 850-994-0802, Fax: 850-994-0802, jerniganknives@mchsi.com
Specialties: Investor-class folders and various theme pieces. **Patterns:** Array of models and sizes in side plate locking interframes and conventional liner construction. **Technical:** Grinds ATS-34, CPM-T-440V and Damascus. Inlays mokume (and minerals) in blades and sculpts marble cases. **Prices:** $650 to $1800; some to $6000. **Remarks:** Full-time maker; first knife sold in 1982. Takes orders for folders only. **Mark:** Last name.

JOBIN, JACQUES, 46 St. Dominique, Levis Quebec, CANADA G6V 2M7, Phone: 418-833-0283, Fax: 418-833-8378
Specialties: Fancy and working straight knives and folders; miniatures. **Patterns:** Minis, fantasy knives, fighters and some hunters. **Technical:** ATS-34, some Damascus and titanium. Likes native snake wood. Heat-treats. **Prices:** Start at $250. **Remarks:** Full-time maker; first knife sold in 1986. **Mark:** Signature on blade.

JOEHNK, BERND, Posadowskystrasse 22, 24148 Kiel, GERMANY, Phone: 0431-7297705, Fax: 0431-7297705
Specialties: One-of-a-kind fancy/embellished and traditional straight knives of his design and from customer drawing. **Patterns:** Daggers, fighters, hunters and letter openers. **Technical:** Grinds and file 440C, ATS-34, powder metal orgical, commercial Damascus and various stainless and corrosion-resistant steels. **Prices:** Upscale. **Remarks:** Likes filework. Leather sheaths. Offers engraving. Part-time maker; first knife

sold in1990. **Other:** Doing business as metal design kiel. All knives made by hand. **Mark:** From 2005 full name and city, with certificate.

JOHANNING CUSTOM KNIVES, TOM, 1735 Apex Rd., Sarasota, FL 34240 9386, Phone: 941-371-2104, Fax: 941-378-9427, Web: www.survivalknives.com
    Specialties: Survival knives. **Prices:** $375 to $775.

JOHANSSON, ANDERS, Konstvartarevagen 9, S-772 40 Grangesberg, SWEDEN, Phone: 46 240 23204, Fax: +46 21 358778, www.scrimart.u.se
    Specialties: Scandinavian traditional and modern straight knives. **Patterns:** Hunters, fighters and fantasy knives. **Technical:** Grinds stainless steel and makes own Damascus. Prefers water buffalo and mammoth for handle material. **Prices:** Start at $100. **Remarks:** Spare-time maker; first knife sold in 1994. Works together with scrimshander Viveca Sahlin. **Mark:** Stylized initials.

JOHNS, ROB, 1423 S. Second, Enid, OK 73701, Phone: 405-242-2707
    Specialties: Classic and fantasy straight knives of his design or to customer specs; fighters for use at Medieval fairs. **Patterns:** Bowies, daggers and swords. **Technical:** Forges and grinds 440C, D2 and 5160. Handles of nylon, walnut or wire-wrap. **Prices:** $150 to $350; some to $2500. **Remarks:** Full-time maker; first knife sold in 1980. **Mark:** Medieval Customs, initials.

JOHNSON, C.E. GENE, 5648 Redwood Ave., Portage, IN 46368, Phone: 219-762-5461
    Specialties: Lock-back folders and springers of his design or to customer specs. **Patterns:** Hunters, Bowies, survival lock-back folders. **Technical:** Grinds D2, 440C, A18, O1, Damascus; likes filework. **Prices:** $100 to $2000. **Remarks:** Full-time maker; first knife sold in 1975. **Mark:** "Gene" city, state and serial number.

JOHNSON, DAVID A., 1791 Defeated Creek Rd., Pleasant Shade, TN 37145, Phone: 615-774-3596, artsmith@mwsi.net

JOHNSON, DURRELL CARMON, PO Box 594, Sparr, FL 32192, Phone: 352-622-5498
    Specialties: Old-fashioned working straight knives and folders of his design or to customer specs. **Patterns:** Bowies, hunters, fighters, daggers, camp knives and Damascus miniatures. **Technical:** Forges 5160, his own Damascus, W2, wrought iron, nickel and horseshoe rasps. Offers filework. **Prices:** $100 to $2000. **Remarks:** Full-time maker and blacksmith; first knife sold in 1957. **Mark:** Middle name.

JOHNSON, GORDEN W., 5426 Sweetbriar, Houston, TX 77017, Phone: 713-645-8990
    Specialties: Working knives and period pieces. **Patterns:** Hunters, boots and Bowies. **Technical:** Flat-grinds 440C; most knives have narrow tang. **Prices:** $90 to $450. **Remarks:** Full-time maker; first knife sold in 1974. **Mark:** Name, city, state.

JOHNSON, JOHN R., 5535 Bob Smith Ave., Plant City, FL 33565, Phone: 813-986-4478, rottyjohn@msn.com
    Specialties: Hand forged and stock removal. **Technical:** High tec. Folders. **Mark:** J.R. Johnson Plant City, FL.

JOHNSON, MIKE, 38200 Main Rd, Orient, NY 11957, Phone: 631-323-3509, mjohnsoncustomknives@hotmail.com
    Specialties: Large bowie knives and cutters, fighters and working knives to customer specs. **Technical:** Forges 5160, O1. **Prices:** $325 to $1200. **Remarks:** Full-time bladesmith. **Mark:** Johnson.

JOHNSON, R.B., Box 11, Clearwater, MN 55320, Phone: 320-558-6128
    Specialties: Liner Locks with Titanium-Mosaic Damascus. **Patterns:** Liner lock folders, skeleton hunters, frontier Bowies. **Technical:** Damascus, Mosaic Damascus, A-2, O-1, 1095. **Prices:** $200 and up. **Remarks:** Full-time maker since 1973. Not accepting orders. **Mark:** R B Johnson (signature).

JOHNSON, RANDY, 2575 E. Canal Dr., Turlock, CA 95380, Phone: 209-632-5401
    Specialties: Folders. **Patterns:** Locking folders. **Technical:** Grinds Damascus. **Prices:** $200 to $400. **Remarks:** Spare-time maker; first knife sold in 1989. Doing business as Puedo Knifeworks. **Mark:** PUEDO.

JOHNSON, RICHARD, W165 N10196 Wagon Trail, Germantown, WI 53022, Phone: 262-251-5772, rlj@execpc.com web: http://www.execpc.com/~rlj/index.html
    Specialties: Custom knives and knife repair.

JOHNSON, RUFFIN, 215 LaFonda Dr., Houston, TX 77060, Phone: 281-448-4407
    Specialties: Working straight knives and folders. **Patterns:** Hunters, fighters and locking folders. **Technical:** Grinds 440C and 154CM; hidden tangs and fancy handles. **Prices:** $200 to $400; some to $1095. **Remarks:** Full-time maker; first knife sold in 1972. **Mark:** Wolf head logo and signature.

JOHNSON, RYAN M., 7320 Foster Hixson Cemetery Rd., Hixson, TN 37343, Phone: 615-842-9323
    Specialties: Working and using straight knives of his design and to customer specs. **Patterns:** Bowies, hunters and utility/camp knives. **Technical:** Forges 5160, Damascus and files. Prices; $70 to $400; some to $800. **Remarks:** Full-time maker; first knife sold in 1986. **Mark:** Sledgehammer with halo.

JOHNSON, STEVEN R., 202 E. 200 N., PO Box 5, Manti, UT 84642, Phone: 435-835-7941, srj@mail.manti.com Web: www.srjknives.com
    Specialties: Investor-class working knives. **Patterns:** Hunters, fighters, boots and folders of locking liner variety. **Technical:** Grinds ATS-34, 440-C, RWL-34. **Prices:** $500 to $5000. **Remarks:** Full-time maker; first knife sold in 1972. **Mark:** Name, city, state and optional signature mark.

JOHNSTON, DR. ROBT., PO Box 9887, 1 Lomb Mem Dr., Rochester, NY 14623

JOKERST, CHARLES, 9312 Spaulding, Omaha, NE 68134, Phone: 402-571-2536
    Specialties: Working knives in standard patterns. **Patterns:** Hunters, fighters and pocketknives. **Technical:** Grinds 440C, ATS-34. **Prices:** $90 to $170. **Remarks:** Spare-time maker; first knife sold in 1984. **Mark:** Early work marked RCJ; current work marked with last name and city.

JONES, BARRY M. AND PHILLIP G., 221 North Ave., Danville, VA 24540, Phone: 804-793-5282
    Specialties: Working and using straight knives and folders of their design and to customer specs; combat and self-defense knives. **Patterns:** Bowies, fighters, daggers, swords, hunters and liner lock knives. **Technical:** Grinds 440C, ATS-34 and D2; flat-grinds only. All blades hand polished. **Prices:** $100 to $1000, some higher. **Remarks:** Part-time makers; first knife sold in 1989. **Mark:** Jones Knives, city, state.

JONES, BOB, 6219 Aztec NE, Albuquerque, NM 87110, Phone: 505-881-4472
    Specialties: Fancy working knives of his design. **Patterns:** Mountain man/buckskinner-type knives; multi-blade folders, locking folders, and slip-joints. **Technical:** Grinds A2, O1, 1095 and commercial Damascus; uses no stainless steel. Engraves. **Prices:** $100 to $500; some to $1500. **Remarks:** Full-time maker; first knife sold in 1960. **Mark:** Initials on fixed blades; initials encircled on folders.

JONES, CHARLES ANTHONY, 36 Broadgate Close, Bellaire Barnstaple, No. Devon E31 4AL, ENGLAND, Phone: 0271-75328
    Specialties: Working straight knives. **Patterns:** Simple hunters, fighters and utility knives. **Technical:** Grinds 440C, O1 and D2; filework offered. Engraves. **Prices:** $100 to $500; engraving higher. **Remarks:** Spare-time maker; first knife sold in 1987. **Mark:** Tony engraved.

JONES, CURTIS J., 39909 176th St. E., Palmdale, CA 93591, Phone: 805-264-2753
    Specialties: Big Bowies, daggers, his own style of hunters. **Patterns:** Bowies, daggers, hunters, swords, boots and miniatures. **Technical:** Grinds 440C, ATS-34 and D2. Fitted guards only; does not solder. Heat-treats. Custom sheaths-hand-tooled and stitched. **Prices:** $125 to $1500; some to $3000. **Remarks:** Full-time maker; first knife sold in 1975. Mail orders accepted. **Mark:** Stylized initials on either side of three triangles interconnected.

JONES, ENOCH, 7278 Moss Ln., Warrenton, VA 20187, Phone: 540-341-0292
    Specialties: Fancy working straight knives. **Patterns:** Hunters, fighters, boots and Bowies. **Technical:** Forges and grinds O1, W2, 440C and Damascus. **Prices:** $100 to $350; some to $1000. **Remarks:** Part-time maker; first knife sold in 1982. **Mark:** First name.

JONES, FRANKLIN (FRANK) W., 6030 Old Dominion Rd., Columbus, GA 31909, Phone: 706-563-6051, frankscuba@peoplepc.com
    Specialties: Traditional/working/tactical/period straight knives of his or your design. **Patterns:** Hunters, skinners, utility/camp, Bowies, fighters, kitchen, neck knives. **Technical:** Forges using 5160, 01, 52100, 1084 1095 and Damascus. Also stock removal of stainless steel. **Prices:** $150 to $1000. **Remarks:** Full-time, American Bladesmith Society Journeyman Smith. **Mark:** F.W. Jones, Columbus, GA.

JONES, JOHN, 12 Schooner Circuit, Manly West, QLD 4179, AUSTRALIA, Phone: 07-339-33390
    Specialties: Straight knives and folders. **Patterns:** Working hunters, folding lockbacks, fancy daggers and miniatures. **Technical:** Grinds 440C, O1 and L6. **Prices:** $180 to $1200; some to $2000. **Remarks:** Part-time maker; first knife sold in 1986. **Mark:** Jones.

JONES, JOHN A., 779 SW 131 HWY, Holden, MO 64040, Phone: 816-850-4318
    Specialties: Working, using knives. Hunters, skinners and fighters. **Technical:** Grinds D2, 01, 440C, 1095. Prefers forging; creates own Damascus. File working on most blades. **Prices:** $50 to $500. **Remarks:**

Part-time maker; first knife sold in 1996. Doing business as Old John Knives. **Mark:** OLD JOHN and serial number.

JONES, ROGER MUDBONE, GREENMAN WORKSHOP, PO Box 367, Waverly, OH 45690, Phone: 740-947-5684, greenmanworkshop@yahoo.com

Specialties: Working in cutlery to suit working woodsman and fine collector. **Patterns:** Bowies, hunters, folders, hatchets in both period and modern style, scale miniatures a specialty. **Technical:** All cutlery hand forged to shape with traditional methods; multiple quench and draws, limited Damascus production hand carves wildlife and historic themes in stag/antler/ivory, full line of functional and high art leather. All work sole authorship. **Prices:** $50 to $5000 **Remarks:** Full-time maker/first knife sold in 1979. **Mark:** Stamped R. Jones hand made or hand engraved sig. W/Bowie knife mark.

JUSTICE, SHANE, 425 South Brooks St., Sheridan, WY 82801, Phone: 307-673-4432

Specialties: Fixed blade working knives. **Patterns:** Hunters, skinners and camp knives. Other designs produced on a limited basis. **Technical:** Hand forged 5160 and 52100. **Remarks:** Part-time maker. Sole author. **Mark:** Cross over a crescent.

K

K B S, KNIVES, RSD 181, North Castlemaine, Vic 3450, AUSTRALIA, Phone: 0011 61 3 54 705864, Fax: 0011 61 3 54 706233

Specialties: Bowies, daggers and miniatures. **Patterns:** Art daggers, traditional Bowies, fancy folders and miniatures. Hollow or flat grind, most steels. **Prices:** $200 to $600+. **Remarks:** Full-time maker; first knife sold in 1983. **Mark:** Initials and address in Southern Cross motif.

KACZOR, TOM, 375 Wharncliffe Rd. N., Upper London, Ont., CANADA N6G 1E4, Phone: 519-645-7640

KADASAH, AHMED BIN, PO Box 1969, Jeddah 21441, SAUDI ARABIA, Phone: (26) 913-0082

KAGAWA, KOICHI, 1556 Horiyamashita, Hatano-Shi, Kanagawa, JAPAN

Specialties: Fancy high-tech straight knives and folders to customer specs. **Patterns:** Hunters, locking folders and slip-joints. **Technical:** Uses 440C and ATS-34. **Prices:** $500 to $2000; some to $20,000. **Remarks:** Part-time maker; first knife sold in 1986. **Mark:** First initial, last name-YOKOHAMA.

KAIN, CHARLES, KAIN DESIGNS, 38 South Main St, Indianapolis, IN 4627, Phone: 317-781-8556, Web: www.kaincustomknives.com

Specialties: Unique damascus Art Folders. **Patterns:** Any. **Technical:** Specialized & Patented Mechanisms. **Remarks:** Unique knife & knife mechanism desgin. **Mark:** Kain and Signet stamp for unique pieces.

KAJIN, AL, PO Box 1047, Forsyth, MT 59327, Phone: 406-346-2442, kajinknives@calemt.net

Specialties: Utility/working knives, kitchen cutlery; makes own Damascus steel. **Patterns:** All types except fantasy styles. **Technical:** Maker since 1989, ABS member since 1995. Does won differential heat treating on carbon steel and Damascus with double tempering. Cryogenic soaking on stainless with double tempering. **Prices:** Stock removal starting at $250. Forged blades/Damascus start at #300. Kitchen cutlery starts at $100. **Remarks:** Likes to work with customer on designs. **Mark:** Interlocked AK on forged blades. Stylized Kajin in outline of Montana on stock removal knives.

KANDA, MICHIO, 7-32-5 Shinzutumi-cho, Shunan-shi, Yamaguchi 7460033, JAPAN, Phone: 0834-62-1910, Fax: 011-81-83462-1910

Specialties: Fantasy knives of his design. **Patterns:** Animal knives. **Technical:** Grinds ATS-34. **Prices:** $300 to $3000. **Remarks:** Full-time maker; first knife sold in 1985. Doing business as Shusui Kanda. **Mark:** Last name inside "M".

KANKI, IWAO, 14-25 3-CHOME FUKUI MIKI, Hydugo, JAPAN 673-0433, Phone: 07948-3-2555

Specialties: Plane, knife. **Prices:** Not determined yet. **Mark:** Chiyozuru Sadahide. **Other:** Masters of traditional crafts designated by the Minister of International Trade and Industry (Japan).

KANSEI, MATSUNO, 109-8 Uenomachi Nishikaiden, Gitu-city, JAPAN 501-1168, Phone: 81-58-234-8643

Specialties: Folders of original design. **Patterns:** Liner lock folder. **Technical:** Grinds VG-10, Damascus. **Prices:** $350 to $2000. **Remarks:** Full-time maker. First knife sold in 1993. **Mark:** Name.

KANTER, MICHAEL, ADAM MICHAEL KNIVES, 14550 West Honey Ln., New Berlin, WI 53151, Phone: 262-860-1136, mike@adammichaelknives.com Web: www.adammichaelknives.com

Specialties: Fixed Blades and liner Lock Folders. **Patterns:** Drop Point hunters, and Bowies. **Technical:** My own Damascus, BG42, ATS-34 and CPMS60V. **Prices:** $200 to $1000. **Mark:** Adam Michael over wavy line or engraved Adam Michael. **Other:** Ivory, Mammoth Ivory, stabilized woods, and pearl handles.

KARP, BOB, PO Box 47304, Phoenix, AZ 85068, Phone: 602 870-1234 602 870-1234, Fax: 602-331-0283

KATO, KIYOSHI, 4-6-4 Himonya Meguro-ku, Tokyo 152, JAPAN

Specialties: Swords, Damascus knives, working knives and paper knives. **Patterns:** Traditional swords, hunters, Bowies and daggers. **Technical:** Forges his own Damascus and carbon steel. Grinds ATS-34. **Prices:** $260 to $700; some to $4000. **Remarks:** Full-time maker. **Mark:** First initial, last name.

KATO, SHINICHI, 3233-27-5-410 Kikko Taikogane, Moriyama-ku Nagoya, JAPAN 463-0004, Phone: 81-52-736-6032

Specialties: Flat grind and hand finish. **Patterns:** Bowie, fighter. Hunting knife. **Technical:** Flat grind ATS-34. **Prices:** $100 to $1500. **Remarks:** Part-time maker. First knife sold in 1995. **Mark:** Name.

KATSUMARO, SHISHIDO, , 2-6-11 Kamiseno Aki-ku, Hiroshima, JAPAN, Phone: 090-3634-9054, Fax: 082-227-4438, shishido@d8.dion.ne.jp

KAUFFMAN, DAVE, 120 Clark Creek Loop, Montana City, MT 59634, Phone: 406-442-9328

Specialties: Field grade and exhibition grade hunting knives and ultra light folders. **Patterns:** Fighters, Bowies and drop-point hunters. **Technical:** ATS-34 and Damascus. **Prices:** $60 to $1200. **Remarks:** Full-time maker; first knife sold in 1989. On the cover of Knives '94. **Mark:** First and last name, city and state.

KAUFMAN, SCOTT, 302 Green Meadows Cr., Anderson, SC 29624, Phone: 864-231-9201, scott.kaufman@ces.clemson.edu

Specialties: Classic and working/using straight knives in standard patterns. **Patterns:** Fighters, hunters and utility/camp knives. Technical Grinds ATS-34, 440C, O1. **Prices:** $100 to $500. **Remarks:** Part-time maker; first knife sold in 1987. **Mark:** Kaufman Knives with Bible in middle.

KAWASAKI, AKIHISA, 11-8-9 Chome Minamiamachi, Suzurandai Kita-Ku, Kobe, JAPAN, Phone: 078-593-0418, Fax: 078-593-0418

Specialties: Working/using knives of his design. **Patterns:** Hunters, kit camp knives. **Technical:** Forges and grinds Molybdenum Panadium. Grinds ATS-34 and stainless steel. Uses Chinese Quince wood, desert ironwood and cow leather. **Prices:** $300 to $800; some to $1000. **Remarks:** Full-time maker. **Mark:** A.K.

KAY, J. WALLACE, 332 Slab Bridge Rd., Liberty, SC 29657

KAZSUK, DAVID, PO Box 39, Perris, CA 92572-0039, Phone: 909-780-2288, ddkaz@hotmail.com

Specialties: Hand forged. **Prices:** $150+. **Mark:** Last name.

KEARNEY, JAROD, 7200 Townsend Forest Ct., Brown Summit, NC 27214, Phone: 336-656-4617, jarodk@mindspring.com Web: www.jarodsworkshop.com

KEESLAR, JOSEPH F., 391 Radio Rd., Almo, KY 42020, Phone: 270-753-7919, Fax: 270-753-7919, sjkees@apex.net

Specialties: Classic and contemporary Bowies, combat, hunters, daggers and folders. **Patterns:** Decorative filework, engraving and custom leather sheaths available. **Technical:** Forges 5160, 52100 and his own Damascus steel. **Prices:** $300 to $3000. **Remarks:** Full-time maker; first knife sold in 1976. Name, initials, last name in hammer, knife and anvil logo, M.S. **Other:** ABS Master Smith.

KEESLAR, STEVEN C., 115 Lane 216, Hamilton, IN 46742, Phone: 260-488-3161, skeeslar@juno.com

Specialties: Traditional working/using straight knives of his design and to customer specs. **Patterns:** Bowies, hunters, utility/camp knives. **Technical:** Forges 5160, files 52100 Damascus. **Prices:** $100 to $600; some to $1500. **Remarks:** Part-time maker; first knife sold in 1976. A.B.S. members. **Mark:** Fox lead in flames over Steven C Keeslar.

KEETON, WILLIAM L., 6095 Rehobeth Rd. SE, Laconia, IN 47135-9550, Phone: 812-969-2836

Specialties: Plain and fancy working knives. **Patterns:** Hunters and fighters; locking folders and slip-joints. Names patterns after Kentucky Derby winners. **Technical:** Grinds D2, ATS-34, 440C, 440V and 154CM; mirror and satin finishes. **Prices:** $95 to $2000. **Remarks:** Full-time maker; first knife sold in 1971. **Mark:** Logo of key.

KEHIAYAN, ALFREDO, Cuzco 1455, Ing. Maschwitz, CP B1623GXU Buenos Aires, ARGENTINA, Phone: 03488-4-42212, alfredo@kehiayan.com.ar Web: www.kehiayan.com.ar
Specialties: Functional straight knives. Patterns: Utility knives, skinners, hunters and boots. Technical: Forges and grinds SAE 52.100, SAE 6180, SAE 9260, SAE 5160, 440C and ATS-34, titanium with nitride. All blades mirror-polished; makes leather sheath and wood cases. Prices: $70 to $800; some to $6000. Remarks: Full-time maker; first knife sold in 1983. Mark: Name. Other: Some knives are satin finish (utility knives).

KEIDEL, GENE W. AND SCOTT J., 4661 105th Ave. SW, Dickinson, ND 58601
Specialties: Fancy/embellished and working/using straight knives of his design. Patterns: Bowies, hunters and miniatures. Technical: Grind 440C and O1 tool steel. Offer scrimshaw and filework. Prices: $95 to $500. Remarks: Full-time makers; first knife sold in1990. Doing business as Keidel Knives. Mark: Last name.

KEISUKE, GOTOH, 105 Cosumo-City, Otozu 202 Ohita-city, Ohita, JAPAN, Phone: 097-523-0750, k-u-an@ki.rim.or.jp

KELLEY, GARY, 17485 SW Pheasant Lane, Aloha, OR 97006, Phone: 503-649-7867, Web: www.reproductionblades.com
Specialties: Primitive knives and blades. Patterns: Fur trade era rifleman's knives, fur trade, cowboy action, hunting knives. Technical: Hand-forges and precision investment casts. Prices: $35 to $125. Remarks: Family business, reproduction blades. Doing business as Reproduction Blades. Mark: Fir tree logo.

KELLEY, THOMAS P., 4711 E Ashler Hill Dr., Cave Creek, AZ 85331, Phone: 480-488-3101

KELLOGG, BRIAN R., 19048 Smith Creek Rd., New Market, VA 22844, Phone: 540-740-4292
Specialties: Fancy and working straight knives of his design and to customer specs. Patterns: Fighters, hunters and utility/camp knives. Technical: Grinds 440C, D2 and A2. Offers filework and fancy pin and cable pin work. Prefers natural handle materials. Prices: $75 to $225; some to $350. Remarks: Part-time maker; first knife sold in 1983. Mark: Last name.

KELLY, LANCE, 1723 Willow Oak Dr., Edgewater, FL 32132, Phone: 904-423-4933
Specialties: Investor-class straight knives and folders. Patterns: Kelly-style in contemporary outlines. Technical: Grinds O1, D2 and 440C; engraves; inlays gold and silver. Prices: $600 to $3500. Remarks: Full-time engraver and knife maker; first knife sold in 1975. Mark: Last name.

KELSEY, NATE, 3400 E Zion Rd, Springdale, AR 72764, nkelsey@cox.net
Specialties: Hand forges or stock removal traditional working knives of own or customer design. Forges own Damascus, makes custom leather sheaths, does fine engraving and scrimshaw. Technical: Forges 52100, 1084/15N20, 5160. Grinds ATS-34, 154CM. Prefers natural handle materials. Prices $175 to $750. Remarks: Part-time maker since 1990. Mark: Name and city. Doing business as Ozark Mountain Forge. Other: Member ABS, Arkansas Knifemakers Assoc.

KELSO, JIM, 577 Collar Hill Rd., Worcester, VT 05682, Phone: 802-229-4254, Fax: 802-229-0595
Specialties: Fancy high-art straight knives and folders that mix Eastern and Western influences. Only uses own designs, but accepts suggestions for themes. Patterns: Daggers, swords and locking folders. Technical: Grinds only custom Damascus. Works with top Damascus blade smiths. Prices: $3000 to $8000; some to $15,000. Remarks: Full-time maker; first knife sold in 1980. Mark: Stylized initials.

KENNEDY JR., BILL, PO Box 850431, Yukon, OK 73085, Phone: 405-354-9150
Specialties: Working straight knives. Patterns: Hunters, fighters, minis and fishing knives. Technical: Grinds D2, 440C and Damascus. Prices: $80 and higher. Remarks: Part-time maker; first knife sold in 1980. Mark: Last name and year made.

KERN, R. W., 20824 Texas Trail W, San Antonio, TX 78257-1602, Phone: 210-698-2549, rkern@ev1.net
Specialties: Damascus, straight and folders. Patterns: Hunters, Bowies and folders. Technical: Grinds ATS-34, 440C and BG42. Forge own Damascus. Prices: $200 and up. Remarks: First knives 1980; retired; work as time permits. Mark: Outline of Alamo with kern over outline. Other: Member ABS, Texas Knifemaker and Collectors Association.

KESSLER, RALPH A., PO Box 61, Fountain Inn, SC 29644-0061
Specialties: Traditional-style knives. Patterns: Folders, hunters, fighters, Bowies and kitchen knives. Technical: Grinds D2, O1, A2 and ATS-34. Forges 1090 and 1095. Prices: $100 to $500. Remarks: Part-time maker; first knife sold in 1982. Mark: Last name or initials with last name.

KEYES, DAN, 6688 King St., Chino, CA 91710, Phone: 909-628-8329

KHALSA, JOT SINGH, 368 Village St., Millis, MA 02054, Phone: 508-376-8162, Fax: 508-376-8081, www.lifeknives.com Coming soon; www.khalsakirpans.com
Specialties: Liner locks, one-of-a-kind daggers, swords, and kirpans (Sikh daggers) all original designs. Technical: Forges own Damascus, uses others high quality Damascus including stainless, and grinds stainless steels. Uses natural handle materials frequently unusual minerals. Pieces are frequently engraved and more recently carved. Prices: Start at $700.

KHARLAMOV, YURI, Oboronnay 46, 2, Tula, 300007, RUSSIA
Specialties: Classic, fancy and traditional knives of his design. Patterns: Daggers and hunters. Technical: Forges only Damascus with nickel. Uses natural handle materials; engraves on metal, carves on nut-tree; silver and pearl inlays. Prices: $600 to $2380; some to $4000. Remarks: Full-time maker; first knife sold in 1988. Mark: Initials.

KI, SHIVA, 5222 Ritterman Ave., Baton Rouge, LA 70805, Phone: 225-356-7274, shivakicustomeknives@netzero.net Web: www.shivakicustomknives.com
Specialties: Fancy working straight knives and folders to customer specs. Patterns: Emphasis on personal defense knives, martial arts weapons. Technical: Forges and grinds; makes own Damascus; prefers natural handle materials. Prices: $135 to $850; some to $1800. Remarks: Full-time maker; first knife sold in 1981. Mark: Name with logo.

KIEFER, TONY, 112 Chateaugay Dr., Pataskala, OH 43062, Phone: 740-927-6910
Specialties: Traditional working and using straight knives in standard patterns. Patterns: Bowies, fighters and hunters. Technical: Grinds 440C and D2; forges D2. Flat-grinds Bowies; hollow-grinds drop-point and trailing-point hunters. Prices: $95 to $140; some to $200. Remarks: Spare-time maker; first knife sold in 1988. Mark: Last name.

KILBY, KEITH, 1902 29th St., Cody, WY 82414, Phone: 307-587-2732
Specialties: Works with all designs. Patterns: Mostly Bowies, camp knives and hunters of his design. Technical: Forges 52100, 5160, 1095, Damascus and mosaic Damascus. Prices: $250 to $3500. Remarks: Part-time maker; first knife sold in 1974. Doing business as Foxwood Forge. Mark: Name.

KIMBERLEY, RICHARD L., 86-B Arroyo Hondo Rd., Santa Fe, NM 87508, Phone: 505-820-2727
Specialties: Fixed-blade and period knives. Technical: O1, 52100, 9260 steels. Remarks: Member ABS. Mark: "By D. KIMBERLEY SANTA FE NM". Other: Marketed under "Kimberleys of Santa Fe".

KIMSEY, KEVIN, 198 Cass White Rd. NW, Cartersville, GA 30121, Phone: 770-387-0779 and 770-655-8879
Specialties: Tactical fixed blades and folders. Patterns: Fighters, folders, hunters and utility knives. Technical: Grinds 440C, ATS-34 and D2 carbon. Prices: $100 to $400; some to $600. Remarks: Three-time "Blade" award winner, Knife maker since 1983. Mark: Rafter and stylized KK.

KING, BILL, 14830 Shaw Rd., Tampa, FL 33625, Phone: 813-961-3455
Specialties: Folders, lockbacks, liner locks and stud openers. Patterns: Wide varieties; folders. Technical: ATS-34 and some Damascus; single and double grinds. Offers filework and jewel embellishment; nickel-silver Damascus and mokume bolsters. Prices: $150 to $475; some to $850. Remarks: Full-time maker; first knife sold in 1976. All titanium fitting on liner-locks; screw or rivet construction on lock-backs. Mark: Last name in crown.

KING, FRED, 430 Grassdale Rd., Cartersville, GA 30120, Phone: 770-382-8478, Web: http://www.fking83264@aol.com
Specialties: Fancy and embellished working straight knives and folders. Patterns: Hunters, Bowies and fighters. Technical: Grinds ATS-34 and D2; forges 5160 and Damascus. Offers filework. Prices: $100 to $3500. Remarks: Spare-time maker; first knife sold in 1984. Mark: Kings Edge.

KING, HERMAN, PO Box 122, Millington, TN 38083, Phone: 901-876-3062

KING, JASON M., 5170 Rockenham Rd, St George, KS 66423, Phone: 785-494-8377, Web: www.jasonmkingknives.com
Specialties: Working and using straight knives of his design and sometimes to customer specs. Some slip joint and lockback folders. Patterns: Hunters, Bowies, tacticals, fighters; some miniatures. Technical: Grinds D2, 440C and other Damascus. Prices: $75 to $200; some up to $500. Remarks: First knife sold in 1998. Mark: JMK. Other: Likes to use height quality stabilized wood.

KING JR., HARVEY G., 32266 Hwy K4, Alta Vista, KS 66423-0184, Phone: 785-499-5207, Web: www.harveykingknives.com
Specialties: Traditional working and using straight knives of his design and to customer specs. Patterns: Hunters, Bowies and fillet knives.

Technical: Grinds O1, A2 and D2. Prefers natural handle materials; offers leatherwork. **Prices:** Start at $70. **Remarks:** Part-time maker; first knife sold in 1988. **Mark:** Name and serial number based on steel used, year made and number of knives made that year.

KINKADE, JACOB, 197 Rd. 154, Carpenter, WY 82054, Phone: 307-649-2446
Specialties: Working/using knives of his design or to customer specs; some miniature swords, daggers and battle axes. **Patterns:** Hunters, daggers, boots; some miniatures. **Technical:** Grinds carbon and stainless and commercial Damascus. Prefers natural handle material. **Prices:** Start at $30. **Remarks:** Part-time maker; first knife sold in 1990. **Mark:** Connected initials or none.

KINKER, MIKE, 8755 E County Rd. 50 N, Greensburg, IN 47240, Phone: 812-663-5277, Fax: 812-662-8131, mokinker@hsonline.net
Specialties: Working/using knives, Straight knives. Starting to make folders. Your design. **Patterns:** Boots, daggers, hunters, skinners, hatchets. **Technical:** Grind 440C and ATS-34, others if required. Damascus, dovetail bolsters, jeweled blade. **Prices:** $125 to 375; some to $1000. **Remarks:** Part-time maker; first knife sold in 1991. Doing business as Kinker Knives. **Mark:** Kinker and Kinker plus year.

KINNIKIN, TODD, Eureka Forge, 8356 John McKeever Rd., House Springs, MO 63051, Phone: 314-938-6248
Specialties: Mosaic Damascus. **Patterns:** Hunters, fighters, folders and automatics. **Technical:** Forges own mosaic Damascus with tool steel Damascus edge. Prefers natural, fossil and artifact handle materials. **Prices:** $400 to $2400. **Remarks:** Full-time maker; first knife sold in 1994. **Mark:** Initials connected.

KIOUS, JOE, 1015 Ridge Pointe Rd., Kerrville, TX 78028, Phone: 830-367-2277, Fax: 830-367-2286, kious@ktc.com
Specialties: Investment-quality interframe and bolstered folders. **Patterns:** Folder specialist, all types. **Technical:** Both stainless and non stainless Damascus. **Prices:** $650 to $3000; some to $10,000. **Remarks:** Full-time maker; first knife sold in 1969. **Mark:** Last name, city and state or last name only.

KIRK, RAY, PO Box 1445, Tahlequah, OK 74465, Phone: 918-456-1519, ray@rakerknives.com Web: www.rakerknives.com
Specialties: Folders, skinners fighters, and bowies. **Patterns:** Neck knives and small hunters and skinners. **Technical:** Forges all knives from 52100 and own Damascus. **Prices:** $65 to $3000. **Remarks:** Started forging in 1989; makes own Damascus. Does custom steel rolling. Has some 52100 and Damascus in custom flat bar 512E3 for sale **Mark:** Stamped "Raker" on blade.

KITSMILLER, JERRY, 67277 Las Vegas Dr., Montrose, CO 81401, Phone: 970-249-4290
Specialties: Working straight knives in standard patterns. **Patterns:** Hunters, boots. **Technical:** Grinds ATS-34 and 440C only. **Prices:** $75 to $200; some to $300. **Remarks:** Spare-time maker; first knife sold in 1984. **Mark:** JandS Knives.

KNICKMEYER, HANK, 6300 Crosscreek, Cedar Hill, MO 63016, Phone: 314-285-3210
Specialties: Complex mosaic Damascus constructions. **Patterns:** Fixed blades, swords, folders and automatics. **Technical:** Mosaic Damascus with all tool steel Damascus edges. **Prices:** $500 to $2000; some $3000 and higher. **Remarks:** Part-time maker; first knife sold in 1989. Doing business as Dutch Creek Forge and Foundry. **Mark:** Initials connected.

KNICKMEYER, KURT, 6344 Crosscreek, Cedar Hill, MO 63016, Phone: 314-274-0481

KNIGHT, JASON, 110 Paradie Pond Ln., Harleyville, SC 29448, Phone: 843-452-1163
Specialties: Bowies. **Patterns:** Bowies and anything from history or his own design. **Technical:** 1084, 5160, 01, 52102, Damascus/forged blades. **Prices:** $200 and up. **Remarks:** Bladesmith. **Mark:** KNIGHT.

KNIPSCHIELD, TERRY, 808 12th Ave. NE, Rochester, MN 55906, Phone: 507-288-7829, knipper01@charter.net Web: http://webpages.charter.net/knipper01
Specialties: Folders and fixed blades. Woodcarving knives. **Patterns:** Variations of traditional patterns and my own new designs. **Technical:** Stock removal. Uses ATS-34 and stainless Damascus. **Prices:** $350 to $800 on folders. $150 to $400 for fixed blades. **Mark:** Knife with shield.

KNIPSTEIN, R.C. (JOE), 731 N. Fielder, Arlington, TX 76012, Phone: 817-265-0573;817-265-2021, Fax: 817-265-3410
Specialties: Traditional pattern folders along with custom designs. **Patterns:** Bowies, folders, fighters, utility knives. **Technical:** Grinds 440C, D2, 154CM and ATS-34. Natural handle materials and full tangs are standard. **Prices:** Start at $300. **Remarks:** Part-time maker; first knife sold in 1989. **Mark:** Last name.

KNOTT, STEVE, KNOTT KNIVES, 203 Wild Rose, Guyton, GA 31312, Phone: 912-772-7655
Technical: Uses ATS-34/440C and some commercial Damascus, single and double grinds with mirror or satin finishes. **Patters:** Hunters, boot knives, Bowies, and tantos, slip joint and lock-back folders. Uses a wide variety of handle materials to include ironwood, coca-bola and colored stabilized wood, also horn, bone and ivory upon customer request. **Remarks:** First knife sold in 1991. Part-time maker.

KNUTH, JOSEPH E., 3307 Lookout Dr., Rockford, IL 61109, Phone: 815-874-9597
Specialties: High-art working straight knives of his design or to customer specs. **Patterns:** Daggers, fighters and swords. **Technical:** Grinds 440C, ATS-34 and D2. **Prices:** $150 to $1500; some to $15,000. **Remarks:** Full-time maker; first knife sold in 1989. **Mark:** Initials on bolster face.

KOHLS, JERRY, N4725 Oak Rd., Princeton, WI 54968, Phone: 920-295-3648
Specialties: Working knives and period pieces. **Patterns:** Hunters-boots and Bowies; your designs or his. **Technical:** Grinds, ATS-34 440c 154CM and 1095 and commercial Damascus. **Remarks:** Part-time maker. **Mark:** Last name.

KOJETIN, W., 20 Bapaume Rd., Delville, Germiston 1401, SOUTH AFRICA, Phone: 27118733305/mobile 27836256208
Specialties: High-art and working straight knives of all designs. **Patterns:** Daggers, hunters and his own Man hunter Bowie. **Technical:** Grinds D2 and ATS-34; forges and grinds 440B/C. Offers "wrap-around" pava and abalone handles, scrolled wood or ivory, stacked filework and setting of faceted semi-precious stones. **Prices:** $185 to $600; some to $11,000. **Remarks:** Spare-time maker; first knife sold in 1962. **Mark:** Billy K.

KOLITZ, ROBERT, W9342 Canary Rd., Beaver Dam, WI 53916, Phone: 920-887-1287
Specialties: Working straight knives to customer specs. **Patterns:** Bowies, hunters, bird and trout knives, boots. **Technical:** Grinds O1, 440C; commercial Damascus. **Prices:** $50 to $100; some to $500. **Remarks:** Spare-time maker; first knife sold in 1979. **Mark:** Last initial.

KOMMER, RUSS, 9211 Abbott Loop Rd., Anchorage, AK 99507, Phone: 907-346-3339
Specialties: Working straight knives with the outdoorsman in mind. **Patterns:** Hunters, semi-skinners, fighters, folders and utility knives, art knives. **Technical:** Hollow-grinds ATS-34, 440C and 440V. **Prices:** $125 to $850; some to $3000. **Remarks:** Full-time maker; first knife sold in 1995. **Mark:** Bear paw—full name, city and state or full name and state.

KOPP, TODD M., PO Box 3474, Apache Jct., AZ 85217, Phone: 480-983-6143, tmkopp@msn.com
Specialties: Classic and traditional straight knives. Fluted handled daggers. **Patterns:** Bowies, boots, daggers, fighters, hunters, swords and folders. **Technical:** Grinds 5160, 440C, ATS-34. All Damascus steels, or customers choice. Some engraving and filework. **Prices:** $200 to $1200; some to $4000. **Remarks:** Part-time maker; first knife sold in 1989. **Mark:** Last name in Old English, some others name, city and state.

KOSTER, STEVEN C., 16261 Gentry Ln., Huntington Beach, CA 92647, Phone: 714-840-8621
Specialties: Bowies, daggers, skinners, camp knives. **Technical:** Use 5160, 52100, 1084, 1095 steels. **Prices:** $200 to $1000. **Remarks:** Wood and leather sheaths with silver furniture. **Mark:** Koster squeezed between lines. **Other:** ABS Journeyman 2003.

KOVACIK, ROBERT, Druzstevna 301, 98556, Tomasovce, Slovakia, Web: www.e-2brane.sk/kovacik
Specialties: Engraved hunting knives. **Prices:** USD 350, USD 1500.**Mark:** R.

KOVAR, EUGENE, 2626 W. 98th St., Evergreen Park, IL 60642, Phone: 708-636-3724
Specialties: One-of-a-kind miniature knives only. **Patterns:** Fancy to fantasy miniature knives; knife pendants and tie tacks. **Technical:** Files and grinds nails, nickel-silver and sterling silver. **Prices:** $5 to $35; some to $100. **Mark:** GK.

KOYAMA, CAPTAIN BUNSHICHI, 3-23 Shirako-cho, Nakamura-ku, Nagoya City 453-0817, JAPAN, Phone: 052-461-7070, Fax: 052-461-7070
Specialties: Innovative folding knife. **Patterns:** General purpose one hand. **Technical:** Grinds ATS-34 and Damascus. **Prices:** $400 to $900; some to $1500. **Remarks:** Part-time maker; first knife sold in 1994. **Mark:** Captain B. Koyama and the shoulder straps of CAPTAIN.

KRAFT, ELMER, 1358 Meadowlark Lane, Big Arm, MT 59910, Phone: 406-849-5086, Fax: 406-883-3056
Specialties: Traditional working/using straight knives of all designs. Patterns: Fighters, hunters, utility/camp knives. Technical: Grinds 440C, D2. Custom makes sheaths. Prices: $125 to $350; some to $500. Remarks: Part-time maker; first knife sold in 1984. Mark: Last name.

KRAFT, STEVE, 315 S.E. 6th, Abilene, KS 67410, Phone: 785-263-1411
Specialties: Folders, lockbacks, scale release auto, push button auto. Patterns: Hunters, boot knives and fighters. Technical: Grinds ATS-34, Damascus; uses titanium, pearl, ivory etc. Prices: $500 to $2500. Remarks: Part-time maker; first knife sold in 1984. Mark: Kraft.

KRAPP, DENNY, 1826 Windsor Oak Dr., Apopka, FL 32703, Phone: 407-880-7115
Specialties: Fantasy and working straight knives of his design. Patterns: Hunters, fighters and utility/camp knives. Technical: Grinds ATS-34 and 440C. Prices: $85 to $300; some $800. Remarks: Spare-time maker; first knife sold in 1988. Mark: Last name.

KRAUSE, ROY W., 22412 Corteville, St. Clair Shores, MI 48081, Phone: 810-296-3995, Fax: 810-296-2663
Specialties: Military and law enforcement/Japanese-style knives and swords. Patterns: Combat and back-up, Bowies, fighters, boot knives, daggers, tantos, wakazashis and katanas. Technical: Grinds ATS-34, A2, D2, 1045, O1 and commercial Damascus; differentially hardened Japanese-style blades. Prices: Moderate to upscale. Remarks: Full-time maker. Mark: Last name on traditional knives; initials in Japanese characters on Japanese-style knives.

KREH, LEFTY, 210 Wichersham Way, "Cockeysville", MD 21030

KREIBICH, DONALD L., 1638 Commonwealth Circle, Reno, NV 89503, Phone: 775-746-0533, dmkreno@sbcglobal.net
Specialties: Working straight knives in standard patterns. Patterns: Bowies, boots and daggers; camp and fishing knives. Technical: Grinds 440C, 154CM and ATS-34; likes integrals. Prices: $100 to $200; some to $500. Remarks: Part-time maker; first knife sold in 1980. Mark: First and middle initials, last name.

KRESSLER, D.F., Schloss Odetzhausen, Schlossberg 1-85235, Odetzhausen, GERMANY, Phone: 08134-998 7290, Fax: 08134-998 7290
Specialties: High-tech Integral and Interframe knives. Patterns: Hunters, fighters, daggers. Technical: Grinds new state-of-the-art steels; prefers natural handle materials. Prices: Upscale. Mark: Name in logo.

KRETSINGER JR., PHILIP W., 17536 Bakersville Rd., Boonsboro, MD 21713, Phone: 301-432-6771
Specialties: Fancy and traditional period pieces. Patterns: Hunters, Bowies, camp knives, daggers, carvers, fighters. Technical: Forges W2, 5160 and his own Damascus. Prices: Start at $200. Remarks: Full-time knife maker. Mark: Name.

KUBAIKO, HANK, 10765 Northvale, Beach City, OH 44608, Phone: 330-359-2418
Specialties: Reproduce antique Bowies. Distal tapering and clay zone tempering. Patterns: Bowies, fighters, fishing knives, kitchen cutlery, lockers, slip-joints, camp knives, axes and miniatures. Also makes American, European and traditional samurai swords and daggers. Technical: Grinds 440C, ATS-34 and D2; will use CPM-T-440V at extra cost. Prices: Moderate. Remarks: Full-time maker. Allow three months for sword order fulfillment. Mark: Alaskan Maid and name. Other: 25th year as a knife maker. Will be making 25 serial numbered knives-folder (liner-locks).

KUBASEK, JOHN A., 74 Northhampton St., Easthampton, MA 01027, Phone: 413-532-3288
Specialties: Left- and right-handed liner lock folders of his design or to customer specs Also new knives made with Ripcord patent. Patterns: Fighters, tantos, drop points, survival knives, neck knives and belt buckle knives. Technical: Grinds ATS-34 and Damascus. Prices: $395 to $1500. Remarks: Part-time maker; first knife sold in 1985. Mark: Name and address etched.

L

LADD, JIM S., 1120 Helen, Deer Park, TX 77536, Phone: 713-479-7286
Specialties: Working knives and period pieces. Patterns: Hunters, boots and Bowies plus other straight knives. Technical: Grinds D2, 440C and 154CM. Prices: $125 to $225; some to $550. Remarks: Part-time maker; first knife sold in 1965. Doing business as The Tinker. Mark: First and middle initials, last name.

LADD, JIMMIE LEE, 1120 Helen, Deer Park, TX 77536, Phone: 713-479-7186
Specialties: Working straight knives. Patterns: Hunters, skinners and utility knives. Technical: Grinds 440C and D2. Prices: $75 to $225. Remarks: First knife sold in 1979. Mark: First and middle initials, last name.

LAGRANGE, FANIE, 12 Canary Crescent, Table View 7441, South Africa, Phone: 27 21 55 76 805
Specialties: African-influenced styles in folders and fixed blades. Patterns: All original patterns with many one-of-a-kinds. Technical: Mostly stock removal in 12c27, ATS-34, stainless Damascus. Prices: $350 to $3000. Remarks: Professional maker. S A Guild Member 13 years. Mark: Name over spear.

LAINSON, TONY, 114 Park Ave., Council Bluffs, IA 51503, Phone: 712-322-5222
Specialties: Working straight knives, liner locking folders. Technical: Grinds 154CM, ATS-34, 440C buys Damascus. Handle materials include Micarta, carbon fiber G-10 ivory pearl and bone. Prices: $95 to $600. Remarks: Part-time maker; first knife sold in 1987. Mark: Name and state.

LAIRSON SR., JERRY, H C 68 Box 970, Ringold, OK 74754, Phone: 580-876-3426, bladesmt@brightok.net Web: www.lairson-custom-knives.net
Specialties: Fighters and hunters. Patterns: Damascus, random, raindrop, ladder, twist and others. Technical: All knives hammer forged. Prices: Carbon steel $400 and up; Damascus $600 and up. Remarks: Makes any style knife but prefer fighters and hunters.

LAKE, RON, 3360 Bendix Ave., Eugene, OR 97401, Phone: 541-484-2683
Specialties: High-tech working knives; inventor of the modern inter-frame folder. Patterns: Hunters, boots, etc.; locking folders. Technical: Grinds 154CM and ATS-34. Patented interframe with special lock release tab. Prices: $2200 to $3000; some higher. Remarks: Full-time maker; first knife sold in 1966. Mark: Last name.

LALA, PAULO RICARDO P. AND LALA, ROBERTO P., R. Daniel Martins, 636, Centro, Presidente Prudente, SP-19031-260, BRAZIL, Phone: 0182-210125, Web: http: //www.orbita.starmedia/~korth
Specialties: Straight knives and folders of all designs to customer specs. Patterns: Bowies, daggers fighters, hunters and utility knives. Technical: Grinds and forges D6, 440C, high-carbon steels and Damascus. Prices: $60 to $400; some higher. Remarks: Full-time makers; first knife sold in 1991. All stainless steel blades are ultra sub-zero quenched. Mark: Sword carved on top of anvil under KORTH.

LAMB, CURTIS J., 3336 Louisiana Ter., Ottawa, KS 66067-8996, Phone: 785-242-6657

LAMBERT, JARRELL D., 2321 FM 2982, Granado, TX 77962, Phone: 512-771-3744
Specialties: Traditional working and using straight knives of his design and to customer specs. Patterns: Bowies, hunters, tantos and utility/camp knives. Technical: Grinds ATS-34; forges W2 and his own Damascus. Makes own sheaths. Prices: $80 to $600; some to $1000. Remarks: Part-time maker; first knife sold in 1982. Mark: Etched first and middle initials, last name; or stamped last name.

LAMEY, ROBERT M., 15800 Lamey Dr., Biloxi, MS 39532, Phone: 228-396-9066, Fax: 228-396-9022, rmlamey@ametro.net Web: www.lameyknives.com
Specialties: Bowies, fighters, hard use knives. Patterns: Bowies, fighters, hunters and camp knives. Technical: Forged and stock removal. Prices: $125 to $350. Remarks: Lifetime reconditioning; will build to customer designs, specializing in hard use, affordable knives. Mark: LAMEY.

LAMPSON, FRANK G., 3215 Saddle Bag Circle, Rimrock, AZ 86335, Phone: 928-567-7395, fglampson@yahoo.com
Specialties: Working folders; one-of-a-kinds. Patterns: Folders, hunters, utility knives, fillet knives and Bowies. Technical: Grinds ATS-34, 440C and 154CM. Prices: $100 to $750; some to $3500. Remarks: Full-time maker; first knife sold in 1971. Mark: Name in fish logo.

LANCASTER, C.G., No 2 Schoonwinkel St., Parys, Free State, SOUTH AFRICA, Phone: 0568112090
Specialties: High-tech working and using knives of his design and to customer specs. Patterns: Hunters, locking folders and utility/camp knives. Technical: Grinds Sandvik 12C27, 440C and D2. Offers anodized titanium bolsters. Prices: $450 to $750; some to $1500. Remarks: Part-time maker; first knife sold in 1990. Mark: Etched logo.

LANCE, BILL, PO Box 4427, Eagle River, AK 99577, Phone: 907-694-1487
Specialties: Ooloos and working straight knives; limited issue sets. Patterns: Several ooloo patterns, drop-point skinners. Technical: Uses

ATS-34, Vascomax 350; ivory, horn and high-class wood handles. **Prices:** $85 to $300; art sets to $3000. **Remarks:** First knife sold in 1981. **Mark:** Last name over a lance.

LANDERS, JOHN, 758 Welcome Rd., Newnan, GA 30263, Phone: 404-253-5719
Specialties: High-art working straight knives and folders of his design. **Patterns:** hunters, fighters and slip-joint folders. **Technical:** Grinds 440C, ATS-34, 154CM and commercial Damascus. **Prices:** $85 to $250; some to $500. **Remarks:** Part-time maker; first knife sold in 1989. **Mark:** Last name.

LANE, BEN, 4802 Massie St., North Little Rock, AR 72218, Phone: 501-753-8238
Specialties: Fancy straight knives of his design and to customer specs; period pieces. **Patterns:** Bowies, hunters, utility/camp knives. **Technical:** Grinds D2 and 154CM; forges and grinds 1095. Offers intricate handle work including inlays and spacers. **Prices:** $120 to $450; some to $5000. **Remarks:** Part-time maker; first knife sold in 1989. **Mark:** Full name, city, state.

LANER, DEAN, 1480 Fourth St., Susanville, CA 96130, Phone: 530-310-1917, laner54knives@yahoo.com
Specialties: Fancy working fixed blades, of his design, will do custom orders. **Patterns:** Hunters, fighters, combat, fishing, Bowies, utility, and kitchen knives. **Technical:** Grinds 154-CM, ATS-34, D-2, buys Damascus. Does mostly hollow grinding, some flat grinds. Uses Micata, mastodon ivory, hippo ivory, exotic woods. Loves ding spacer work on stick tang knives. A leather or kydes sheath comes with every knife. Lifetime warrantee and free sharpening also. **Remarks:** Pat-time maker, first knife sold in 1993. **Prices:** $150 to $1000. **Mark:** LANER CUSTOM KNIVES over D nest to a tree.

LANG, KURT, 4908 S. Wildwood Dr., McHenry, IL 60050, Phone: 708-516-4649
Specialties: High-art working knives. **Patterns:** Bowies, utilitarian-type knives with rough finishes. **Technical:** Forges welded steel in European and Japanese-styles. **Prices:** Moderate to upscale. **Remarks:** Part-time maker. **Mark:** "Crazy Eye" logo.

LANGLEY, GENE H., 1022 N. Price Rd., Florence, SC 29506, Phone: 843-669-3150
Specialties: Working knives in standard patterns. **Patterns:** Hunters, boots, fighters, locking folders and slip-joints. **Technical:** Grinds 440C, 154CM and ATS-34. **Prices:** $125 to $450; some to $1000. **Remarks:** Part-time maker; first knife sold in 1979. **Mark:** Name.

LANGLEY, MICK, 1015 Centre Rd, Crescent Qualicumm Beach BC, CANADA V9K 2G6, Phone: 250-752-4261
Specialties: Period Pieces and working knives. **Patterns:** Bowies, Push daggers, fighters, boots. Some folding lockers. **Technical:** Forges 5160, 1084, W2 and his own Damascus. **Prices:** $250 to $2500. Some to $4500. **Remarks:** Full-time maker, first knife sold in 1977. **Mark:** Langley with M.S. (For ABS Master Smith)

LANKTON, SCOTT, 8065 Jackson Rd. R-11, Ann Arbor, MI 48103, Phone: 313-426-3735
Specialties: Pattern welded swords, krisses and Viking period pieces. **Patterns:** One-of-a-kind. **Technical:** Forges W2, L6 nickel and other steels. **Prices:** $600 to $12,000. **Remarks:** Part-time bladesmith, full-time smith; first knife sold in 1976. **Mark:** Last name logo.

LAOISLAV, SANTA-LASKY, Tatranska 32, 97401 Banska, Bystrica, Slovakia, santa.ladislav@pobox.sk Web: www.lasky.sk
Specialties: Damascus hunters, daggers and swords. **Patterns:** Carious Damascus patterns. **Prices:** $300 USD to $6000 USD. **Mark:** L or Lasky

LAPEN, CHARLES, Box 529, W. Brookfield, MA 01585
Specialties: Chefs knives for the culinary artist. **Patterns:** camp knives, Japanese-style swords and wood working tools, hunters. **Technical:** Forges 1075, car spring and his own Damascus. Favors narrow and Japanese tangs. **Prices:** $200 to $400; some to $2000. **Remarks:** Part-time maker; first knife sold in 1972. **Mark:** Last name.

LAPLANTE, BRETT, 4545 CR412, McKinney, TX 75071, Phone: 972-838-9191
Specialties: Working straight knives and folders to customer specs. **Patterns:** Survival knives, Bowies, skinners, hunters. **Technical:** Grinds D2 and 440C. Heat-treats. **Prices:** $175 to $600. **Remarks:** Part-time maker; first knife sold in 1987. **Mark:** Last name in Canadian maple leaf logo.

LARAMIE, MARK, 181 Woodland St., Fitchburg, MA 01420, Phone: 978-502-2726, laramieknives@verison.net Web: www.malknives.com
Specialties: Traditional folders & fancy everyday carry folders. **Patterns:** Slip-Joint, back lock L/L single and multi blades. **Technical:** Free hand ground blades of D2, 440, 8, and Damascus. **Mark:** Mall knives w/ fish logo.

LARGIN, KELGIN KNIVES, PO Box 151, Metamora, IN 47030, Phone: 765-969-5012, kelgin@hotmail.com Web: www.kelgin.com
Specialties: Meteorite knife blades. **Prices:** $100 to $8000. **Mark:** KELGIN or K.C. LARGIN.

LARSON, RICHARD, 549 E. Hawkeye Ave., Turlock, CA 95380, Phone: 209-668-1615
Specialties: Traditional working/using straight knives in standard patterns. **Patterns:** Bowies, hunters and utility/camp knives. **Technical:** Grinds ATS-34, 440C, and 154CM. Engraves and scrimshaws holsters and handles. Hand-sews sheaths with tooling. **Prices:** $150 to $300; some to $1000. **Remarks:** Part-time maker; first knife sold in 1986. Doing business as Larson Knives. **Mark:** Knife logo spelling last name.

LARY, ED, 651 Rangeline Rd., Mosinee, WI 54455, Phone: 715-693-3940, laryblades@hotmail.com
Specialties: Upscale hunters and art knives with display presentations. **Patterns:** Hunters, period pieces. **Technical:** Grinds all steels, heat treats, fancy file work and engraving. **Prices:** Upscale. **Remarks:** Since 1974. **Mark:** Hand engraved "Ed Lary" in script.

LAURENT, KERMIT, 1812 Acadia Dr., LaPlace, LA 70068, Phone: 504-652-5629
Specialties: Traditional and working straight knives and folders of his design. **Patterns:** Bowies, hunters, utilities and folders. **Technical:** Forges own Damascus, plus uses most tool steels and stainless. Specializes in altering cable patterns. Uses stabilized handle materials, especially select exotic woods. **Prices:** $100 to $2500; some to $50,000. **Remarks:** Full-time maker; first knife sold in 1982. Doing business as Kermit's Knife Works. Favorite material is meteorite Damascus. **Mark:** First name.

LAWRENCE, ALTON, 201 W Stillwell, De Queen, AR 71832, Phone: 870-642-7643, Fax: 870-642-4023, uncleal@1pa.net Web: riversidemachine.net
Specialties: Classic straight knives and folders to customer specs. **Patterns:** Bowies, hunters, folders and utility/camp knives. **Technical:** Forges 5160, 1095, 1084, Damascus and railroad spikes. **Prices:** Start at $100. **Remarks:** Part-time maker; first knife sold in 1988. **Mark:** Last name inside fish symbol.

LAY, L.J., 602 Mimosa Dr., Burkburnett, TX 76354, Phone: 817-569-1329
Specialties: Working straight knives in standard patterns; some period pieces. **Patterns:** Drop-point hunters, Bowies and fighters. **Technical:** Grinds ATS-34 to mirror finish; likes Micarta handles. **Prices:** Moderate. **Remarks:** Full-time maker; first knife sold in 1985. **Mark:** Name or name with ram head and city or stamp L J Lay.

LAY, R.J. (BOB), Box 122, Falkland BC, CANADA V0E 1W0, Phone: 250-379-2265, Fax: SAME
Specialties: Traditional-styled, fancy straight knifes of his design. Specializing in hunters. **Patterns:** Bowies, fighters and hunters. **Technical:** Grinds 440C, ATS-34, 530V, forges and grinds tool steels. Uses exotic handle and spacer material. File cut, prefers narrow tang. Sheaths available. **Price:** $200 to $500, some to $5000. **Remarks:** Full-time maker, first knife sold in 1976. Doing business as Lay's Custom Knives. **Mark:** Signature acid etched.

LEACH, MIKE J., 5377 W. Grand Blanc Rd., Swartz Creek, MI 48473, Phone: 810-655-4850
Specialties: Fancy working knives. **Patterns:** Hunters, fighters, Bowies and heavy-duty knives; slip-joint folders and integral straight patterns. **Technical:** Grinds D2, 440C and 154CM; buys Damascus. **Prices:** Start at $300 starting price. **Remarks:** Full-time maker; first knife sold in 1952. **Mark:** First initial, last name.

LEAVITT JR., EARL F., Pleasant Cove Rd., Box 306, E. Boothbay, ME 04544, Phone: 207-633-3210
Specialties: 1500-1870 working straight knives and fighters; pole arms. **Patterns:** Historically significant knives, classic/modern custom designs. **Technical:** Flat-grinds O1; heat-treats. Filework available. **Prices:** $90 to $350; some to $1000. **Remarks:** Full-time maker; first knife sold in 1981. Doing business as Old Colony Manufactory. **Mark:** Initials in oval.

LEBATARD, PAUL M., 14700 Old River Rd., Vancleave, MS 39565, Phone: 228-826-4137, Fax: 228-826-2933
Specialties: Sound working knives; lightweight folder; practical tactical knives. **Patterns:** Hunters, trout and bird knives, fish fillet knives, kitchen knives, Bowies, one and two blade folders, plus a new line of tactical sheath knives. **Technical:** Grinds ATS-34, D-2, CPM 3-V, and commercial Damascus; forges and grinds 52100. Machines folder frames from aircraft aluminum. **Prices:** $50 to $650. **Remarks:** Part-time maker; celebrating 31 years of knifemaking; first knife made in 1974. Offers knife repair, restoration and sharpening. **Mark:** Stamped last name or etched logo of last name, city, and state. **Other:** All knives are serial numbered and registered in the name of the original purchaser.

LEBER, HEINZ, Box 446, Hudson's Hope, BC, CANADA V0C 1V0, Phone: 250-783-5304
Specialties: Working straight knives of his design. **Patterns:** 20 models, form capers to Bowies. **Technical:** Hollow-grinds D2 and M2 steel; mirror-finishes and full tang only. Likes moose, elk, stone sheep for handles. **Prices:** $175 to $1000. **Remarks:** Full-time maker; first knife sold in 1975. **Mark:** Initials connected.

LECK, DAL, Box 1054, Hayden, CO 81639, Phone: 970-276-3663
Specialties: Classic, traditional and working knives of his design and in standard patterns; period pieces. **Patterns:** Boots, daggers, fighters, hunters and push daggers. **Technical:** Forges O1 and 5160; makes his own Damascus. **Prices:** $175 to $700; some to $1500. **Remarks:** Part-time maker; first knife sold in 1990. Doing business as The Moonlight Smithy. **Mark:** Stamped: hammer and anvil with initials.

LEE, RANDY, PO Box 1873, St. Johns, AZ 85936, Phone: 928-337-2594, Fax: 928-337-5002, info@randyleeknives.com Web:www.randyleeknives.com
Specialties: Traditional working and using straight knives of his design. **Patterns:** Bowies, fighters, hunters, daggers and professional throwing knives. **Technical:** Grinds ATS-34, 440C and D2. Offers sheaths. **Prices:** $235 to $1500; some to $800. **Remarks:** Part-time maker; first knife sold in 1979. **Mark:** Full name, city, state.

LELAND, STEVE, 2300 Sir Francis Drake Blvd., Fairfax, CA 94930-1118, Phone: 415-457-0318, Fax: 415-457-0995, Web: wwwstephenleland@comcast.net
Specialties: Traditional and working straight knives and folders of his design. **Patterns:** Hunters, fighters, Bowies, chefs. **Technical:** Grinds O1, ATS-34 and 440C. Does own heat treat. Makes nickel silver sheaths. **Prices:** $150 to $750; some to $1500. **Remarks:** Part-time maker; first knife sold in 1987. Doing business as Leland Handmade Knives. **Mark:** Last name.

LEMCKE, JIM L., 10649 Haddington Ste 180, Houston, TX 77043, Phone: 888-461-8632, Fax: 713-461-8221, jimll@hal-pc.org Web: www.texasknife.com
Specialties: Large supply of custom ground and factory finished blades; knife kits; leather sheaths; in-house heat treating and cryogenic tempering; exotic handle material (wood, ivory, oosik, horn, stabilized woods); machines and supplies for knife making; polishing and finishing supplies; heat treat ovens; etching equipment; bar, sheet and rod material (brass, stainless steel, nickel silver); titanium sheet material. Catalog. $4.

LEONARD, RANDY JOE, 188 Newton Rd., Sarepta, LA 71071, Phone: 318-994-2712

LEONE, NICK, 9 Georgetown, Pontoon Beach, IL 62040, Phone: 618-797-1179, nickleone@sbcglobal.net
Specialties: 18th century period straight knives. **Patterns:** skinners, hunters, neck, leg and friction folders. **Technical:** Forges 5160, W2, O1, 1098, 52100 and his own Damascus. **Prices:** t$100 to $1000; some to $3500. **Remarks:** Full-time maker; first knife sold in 1987. Doing business as Anvil Head Forge. **Mark:** Last name, NL, AHF.

LEPORE, MICHAEL J., 66 Woodcutters Dr., Bethany, CT 06524, Phone: 203-393-3823
Specialties: One-of-a-kind designs to customer specs; mostly handmade. **Patterns:** Fancy working straight knives and folders. **Technical:** Forges and grinds W2, W1 and O1; prefers natural handle materials. **Prices:** Start at $350. **Remarks:** Spare-time maker; first knife sold in 1984. **Mark:** Last name.

LERCH, MATTHEW, N88 W23462 North Lisbon Rd., Sussex, WI 53089, Phone: 262-246-6362, Web: www.lerchcustomknives.com
Specialties: Gentlemen's folders. **Patterns:** Interframe and integral folders; lock backs, slip-joints, side locks, button locks and liner locks. **Technical:** Grinds ATS-34, 1095, 440 and Damascus. Offers filework and embellished bolsters. **Prices:** $400 to $6000. **Remarks:** Part-time maker; first knife sold in 1995. **Mark:** Last name.

LEVENGOOD, BILL, 15011 Otto Rd., Tampa, FL 33624, Phone: 813-961-5688
Specialties: Working straight knives and folders. **Patterns:** Hunters, Bowies, folders and collector pieces. **Technical:** Grinds ATS-34, BG-42 and Damascus. **Prices:** $175 to $1500. **Remarks:** Part-time maker; first knife sold in 1983. **Mark:** Last name, city, state.

LEVERETT, KEN, PO Box 696, Lithia, FL 33547, Phone: 813-689-8578
Specialties: High-tech and working straight knives and folders of his design and to customer specs. **Patterns:** Bowies, hunters and locking folders. **Technical:** Grinds ATS-34, Damascus. **Prices:** $100 to $350; some to $1500. **Remarks:** Part-time maker; first knife sold in 1991. **Mark:** Name, city, state.

LEVIN, JACK, 7216 Bay Pkwy., Brooklyn, NY 11204, Phone: 718-232-8574
Specialties: Highly embellished collector knives.

LEVINE, BOB, 101 Westwood Dr., Tullahoma, TN 37388, Phone: 931-454-9943, levineknives@msn.com
Specialties: Working left- and right-handed Liner Lock® folders. **Patterns:** Hunters and folders. **Technical:** Grinds ATS-34, 440C, D2, O1 and some Damascus. Uses sheep horn, fossil ivory, Micarta and exotic woods. Provides custom leather sheath with each fixed knife. **Prices:** $125 to $500; some higher. **Remarks:** Full-time maker; first knife sold in 1984. Voting member Knife Makers Guild. **Mark:** Name and logo.

LEWIS, BILL, PO Box 63, Riverside, IA 52327, Phone: 319-629-5574
Specialties: Folders of all kins including those made from one-piece of white tail antler with or without the crown. **Patterns:** Hunters, folding hunters, fillet, Bowies, push daggers, etc. **Prices:** $20 to $200. **Remarks:** Full-time maker; first knife sold in 1978. **Mark:** W.E.L.

LEWIS, K.J., 374 Cook Rd., Lugoff, SC 29078, Phone: 803-438-4343

LEWIS, MIKE, 21 Pleasant Hill Dr., DeBary, FL 32713, Phone: 386-753-0936, dragonsteel@prodigy.net
Specialties: Traditional straight knives. **Patterns:** Swords and daggers. **Technical:** Grinds, ATS-34 and 5160. Frequently uses cast bronze and cast nickel guards and pommels. **Prices:** $100 to $750. **Remarks:** Part-time maker; first knife sold in 1988. **Mark:** Dragon Steel and serial number.

LEWIS, STEVE, Knife Dealer, PO Box 9056, Woodland Park, CO 80866, Phone: 719-686-1120 or 888-685-2322
Specialties: Buy, sell, trade and consign W. F. Moran and other fine custom-made knives. Mail order and major shows.

LEWIS, TOM R., 1613 Standpipe Rd., Carlsbad, NM 88220, Phone: 505-885-3616, Web: www.cavemen.net/lewisknives/
Specialties: Traditional working straight knives and pocketknives. **Patterns:** Outdoor knives, hunting knives and Bowies. **Technical:** Grinds ATS-34 forges 5168 and 01. Makes wire, pattern welded and chainsaw Damascus. **Prices:** $100 to $900. **Remarks:** Part-time maker; first knife sold in 1980. Doing business as TR Lewis Handmade Knives. **Mark:** Lewis family crest.

LICATA, STEVEN, LICATA CUSTOM KNIVES, 142 Orchard St., Garfield, NJ 07026, Phone: 973-341-4288, Web: steven.licata.home.att.net
Prices: $200 to $25,000.

LIEBENBERG, ANDRE, 8 Hilma Rd., Bordeauxrandburg 2196, SOUTH AFRICA, Phone: 011-787-2303
Specialties: High-art straight knives of his design. **Patterns:** Daggers, fighters and swords. **Technical:** Grinds 440C and 12C27. **Prices:** $250 to $500; some $4000 and higher. Giraffe bone handles with semi-precious stones. **Remarks:** Spare-time maker; first knife sold in 1990. **Mark:** Initials.

LIEGEY, KENNETH R., 132 Carney Dr., Millwood, WV 25262, Phone: 304-273-9545
Specialties: Traditional working/using straight knives of his design and to customer specs. **Patterns:** Hunters, utility/camp knives, miniatures. **Technical:** Grinds 440C. **Prices:** $75 to $150; some to $300. **Remarks:** Spare-time maker; first knife sold in 1977. **Mark:** First and middle initials, last name.

LIGHTFOOT, GREG, RR #2, Kitscoty AB, CANADA T0B 2P0, Phone: 780-846-2812, Pitbull@lightfootknives.com Web: www.lightfootknives.com
Specialties: Stainless steel and Damascus. **Patterns:** Boots, fighters and locking folders. **Technical:** Grinds BG-42, 440C, D2, CPM steels, Stellite 6K. Offers engraving. **Prices:** $250 to $500; some to $850. **Remarks:** Full-time maker; first knife sold in 1988. Doing business as Lightfoot Knives. **Mark:** Shark with Lightfoot Knives below.

LIKARICH, STEVE, PO Box 961, Colfax, CA 95713, Phone: 530-346-8480
Specialties: Fancy working knives; art knives of his design. **Patterns:** Hunters, fighters and art knives of his design. **Technical:** Grinds ATS-34, 154CM and 440C; likes high polishes and filework. **Prices:** $200 to $2000; some higher. **Remarks:** Full-time maker; first knife sold in 1987. **Mark:** Name.

LINKLATER, STEVE, 8 Cossar Dr., Aurora, Ont., CANADA L4G 3N8, Phone: 905-727-8929, knifman@sympatico.ca
Specialties: Traditional working/using straight knives and folders of his design. **Patterns:** Fighters, hunters and locking folders. **Technical:** Grinds ATS-34, 440V and D2. **Prices:** $125 to $350; some to $600. **Remarks:** Part-time maker; first knife sold in 1987. Doing business as Links Knives. **Mark:** LINKS.

LISTER JR., WELDON E., 9140 Sailfish Dr., Boerne, TX 78006, Phone: 210-981-2210
Specialties: One-of-a-kind fancy and embellished folders. **Patterns:** Locking and slip-joint folders. **Technical:** Commercial Damascus and O1. All knives embellished. Engraves, inlays, carves and scrimshaws.

Prices: Upscale. **Remarks:** Spare-time maker; first knife sold in 1991. **Mark:** Last name.

LITTLE, GARY M., HC84 Box 10301, PO Box 156, Broadbent, OR 97414, Phone: 503-572-2656
    Specialties: Fancy working knives. **Patterns:** Hunters, tantos, Bowies, axes and buckskinners; locking folders and interframes. **Technical:** Forges and grinds O1, L6, 1095; makes his own Damascus; bronze fittings. **Prices:** $85 to $300; some to $2500. **Remarks:** Full-time maker; first knife sold in 1979. Doing business as Conklin Meadows Forge. **Mark:** Name, city and state.

LITTLE, GUY A., 486 W Lincoln Ave., Oakhurst, NJ 07755

LITTLE, JIMMY L., PO Box 871652, Wasilla, AK 99687, Phone: 907-373-7831
    Specialties: Working straight knives; fancy period pieces. **Patterns:** Bowies, bush swords and camp knives. **Technical:** Grinds 440C, 154CM and ATS-34. **Prices:** $100 to $1000. **Remarks:** Full-time maker; first knife sold in 1984. **Mark:** First and middle initials, last name.

LITTLE, LARRY, 1A Cranberry Ln., Spencer, MA 01562, Phone: 508-885-2301
    Specialties: Working straight knives of his design or to customer specs. Likes Scagel-style. **Patterns:** Hunters, fighters...can grind other patterns. **Technical:** Grinds L6 and O1, most have file work. Prefers natural handle material especially antler. Uses nickel silver. Makes own heavy duty leather sheath. **Prices:** start at $100. **Remarks:** Part-time maker. First knife sold in 1985. Offers knife repairs. **Mark:** Last name.

LIVELY, TIM AND MARIAN, PO Box 1172, Marble Falls, TX 78654, Web: www.livelyknives.com
    Specialties: Multi-cultural primitive knives of their design on speculation. **Patterns:** Old world designs. **Technical:** Hand forges using ancient techniques; hammer finish. **Prices:** High. **Remarks:** Full-time makers; first knife sold in 1974. Offers knifemaking DVD online. **Mark:** Last name.

LIVESAY, NEWT, 3306 S. Dogwood St., Siloam Springs, AR 72761, Phone: 479-549-3356, Fax: 479-549-3357, newt@newtlivesay.com WEB: www.newtlivesay.com
    Specialties: Combat utility knives, hunting knives, titanium knives, swords, axes, KYDWX sheaths for knives and pistols, custom orders.

LIVINGSTON, ROBERT C., PO Box 6, Murphy, NC 28906, Phone: 704-837-4155
    Specialties: Art letter openers to working straight knives. **Patterns:** Minis to machetes. **Technical:** Forges and grinds most steels. **Prices:** Start at $20. **Remarks:** Full-time maker; first knife sold in 1988. Doing business as Mystik Knife works. **Mark:** MYSTIK.

LOCKE, KEITH, PMB 141, 7120 Rufe Snow Dr. Ste. 106, Watauga, TX 76148-1867, Phone: 817-514-7272
    Technical: Forges carbon steel and handcrafts sheaths for his knives. **Remarks:** Sold first knife in 1996.

LOCKETT, LOWELL C., 66653 Gunderson Rd., North Bend, OR 97459-9210, Phone: 541-756-1614, spur@outdrs.net
    Specialties: Traditional and working/using knives. **Patterns:** Bowies, hunters, utility/camp knives. **Technical:** Forges 5160, 1095, 1084, 02, L6. Makes own guards and sheaths. **Prices:** Start at $90. **Remarks:** Full-time maker. **Mark:** L C lockett (on side of blade) ABS Journeyman Smith, member OKCA.

LOCKETT, STERLING, 527 E. Amherst Dr., Burbank, CA 91504, Phone: 818-846-5799
    Specialties: Working straight knives and folders to customer specs. **Patterns:** Hunters and fighters. **Technical:** Grinds. **Prices:** Moderate. **Remarks:** Spare-time maker. **Mark:** Name, city with hearts.

LOERCHNER, WOLFGANG, WOLFE FINE KNIVES, PO Box 255, Bayfield, Ont., CANADA N0M 1G0, Phone: 519-565-2196
    Specialties: Traditional straight knives, mostly ornate. **Patterns:** Small swords, daggers and stilettos; locking folders and miniatures. **Technical:** Grinds D2, 440C and 154CM; all knives hand-filed and flat-ground. **Prices:** $300 to $5000; some to $10,000. **Remarks:** Part-time maker; first knife sold in 1983. Doing business as Wolfe Fine Knives. **Mark:** WOLFE.

LONEWOLF, J. AGUIRRE, 481 Hwy 105, Demorest, GA 30535, Phone: 706-754-4660, Fax: 706-754-8470, Web: http://hemc.net/~lonewolf
    Specialties: High-art working and using straight knives of his design. **Patterns:** Bowies, hunters, utility/camp knives and fine steel blades. **Technical:** Forges Damascus and high-carbon steel. Most knives have hand-carved moose antler handles. **Prices:** $55 to $500; some to $2000. **Remarks:** Full-time maker; first knife sold in 1980. Doing business as Lonewolf Trading Post. **Mark:** Stamp.

LONG, GLENN A., 10090 SW 186th Ave., Dunnellon, FL 34432, Phone: 352-489-4272
    Specialties: Classic working and using straight knives of his design and to customer specs. **Patterns:** Hunters, Bowies, utility. **Technical:** Grinds 440C D2 and 440V. **Prices:** $85 to $300; some to $800. **Remarks:** Part-time maker; first knife sold in 1990. **Mark:** Last name inside diamond.

LONGWORTH, DAVE, 1811 SR 774, Hamersville, OH 45130, Phone: 513-876-3637
    Specialties: High-tech working knives. **Patterns:** Locking folders, hunters, fighters and elaborate daggers. **Technical:** Grinds O1, ATS-34, 440C; buys Damascus. **Prices:** $125 to $600; some higher. **Remarks:** Part-time maker; first knife sold in 1980. **Mark:** Last name.

LOOS, HENRY C., 210 Ingraham, New Hyde Park, NY 11040, Phone: 516-354-1943, hcloos@optonline.net
    Specialties: Miniature fancy knives and period pieces of his design. **Patterns:** Bowies, daggers and swords. **Technical:** Grinds O1 and 440C. Uses sterling, 18K, rubies and emeralds. All knives come with handmade hardwood cases. **Prices:** $90 to $195; some to $250. **Remarks:** Spare-time maker; first knife sold in 1990. **Mark:** Script last initial.

LORO, GENE, 2457 State Route 93 NE, Crooksville, OH 43731, Phone: 740-982-4521, Fax: 740-982-1249, geney@aol.com
    Specialties: Hand forged knives. **Patterns:** Damascus, Random, Ladder, Twist, etc. **Technical:** ABS Journeyman Smith. **Prices:** $200 and up. **Remarks:** Loro and hand forged by Gene Loro. **Mark:** Loro. Retired engineer.

LOTT-SINCLAIR, SHERRY, 1100 Legion Park Road, Greensburg, KY 42743, Phone: 270-932-2212, 4sherrylott@msn.com
    Specialties: One-of-a-kind, usually carved handles. **Patterns:** Art. **Technical:** Carbon steel, stock removal. Prices: Moderate. **Mark:** Sherry Lott. **Other:** First knife sold in 1994.

LOVE, ED, 19443 Mill Oak, San Antonio, TX 78258, Phone: 210-497-1021, edlove@co.bexar.tx.us
    Specialties: Hunting, working knives and some art pieces. **Technical:** Grinds ATS-34, and 440C. **Prices:** $150 and up. **Remarks:** Part-time maker. First knife sold in 1980. **Mark:** Name in a weeping heart.

LOVELESS, R.W., PO Box 7836, Riverside, CA 92503, Phone: 909-689-7800
    Specialties: Working knives, fighters and hunters of his design. **Patterns:** Contemporary hunters, fighters and boots. **Technical:** Grinds 154CM and ATS-34. **Prices:** $850 to $4950. **Remarks:** Full-time maker since 1969. **Mark:** Name in logo.

LOVESTRAND, SCHUYLER, 1136 19th St. SW, Vero Beach, FL 32962, Phone: 561-778-0282, Fax: 561-466-1126
    Specialties: Fancy working straight knives of his design and to customer specs; unusual fossil ivories. **Patterns:** Hunters, fighters, Bowies and fishing knives. **Technical:** Grinds stainless steel. **Prices:** $275 and up. **Remarks:** Part-time maker; first knife sold in 1982. **Mark:** Name in logo.

LOZIER, DON, 5394 SE 168th Ave., Ocklawaha, FL 32179, Phone: 352-625-3576
    Specialties: Fancy and working straight knives of his design and in standard patterns. **Patterns:** Daggers, fighters, boot knives, and hunters. **Technical:** Grinds ATS-34, 440C and Damascus. Most pieces are highly embellished by notable artisans. Taking limited number of orders per annum. **Prices:** Start at $250; most are $1250 to $3000; some to $12,000. **Remarks:** Full-time maker. **Mark:** Name.

LUCHAK, BOB, 15705 Woodforest Blvd., Channelview, TX 77530, Phone: 281-452-1779
    Specialties: Presentation knives; start of The Survivor series. **Patterns:** Skinners, Bowies, camp axes, steak knife sets and fillet knives. **Technical:** Grinds 440C. Offers electronic etching; filework. **Prices:** $50 to $1500. **Remarks:** Full-time maker; first knife sold in 1983. Doing business as Teddybear Knives. **Mark:** Full name, city and state with Teddybear logo.

LUCHINI, BOB, 1220 Dana Ave., Palo Alto, CA 94301, Phone: 650-321-8095, rwluchin@bechtel.com

LUCIE, JAMES R., 4191 E. Fruitport Rd., Fruitport, MI 49415, Phone: 231-865-6390, Fax: 231-865-3170, scagel@netonecom.net
    Specialties: Hand-forges William Scagel-style knives. **Patterns:** Authentic scagel-style knives and miniatures. **Technical:** Forges 5160, 52100 and 1084 and forges his own pattern welded Damascus steel. **Prices:** Start at $750. **Remarks:** Full-time maker; first knife sold in 1975. Believes in sole authorship of his work. ABS Journeyman Smith. **Mark:** Scagel Kris with maker's name and address.

LUCKETT, BILL, 108 Amantes Ln., Weatherford, TX 76088, Phone: 817-613-9412
    Specialties: Uniquely patterned robust straight knives. **Patterns:** Fighters, Bowies, hunters. **Technical:** Grinds 440C and commercial Dam-

ascus; makes heavy knives with deep grinding. **Prices:** $275 to $1000; some to $2000. **Remarks:** Part-time maker; first knife sold in 1975. **Mark:** Last name over Bowie logo.

LUDWIG, RICHARD O., 57-63 65 St., Maspeth, NY 11378, Phone: 718-497-5969
   Specialties: Traditional working/using knives. **Patterns:** Boots, hunters and utility/camp knives folders. Technical Grinds 440C, ATS-34 and BG42. File work on guards and handles; silver spacers. Offers scrimshaw. **Prices:** $325 to $400; some to $2000. **Remarks:** Full-time maker. **Mark:** Stamped first initial, last name, state.

LUI, RONALD M., 4042 Harding Ave., Honolulu, HI 96816, Phone: 808-734-7746
   Specialties: Working straight knives and folders in standard patterns. **Patterns:** Hunters, boots and liner locks. **Technical:** Grinds 440C and ATS-34. **Prices:** $100 to $700. **Remarks:** Spare-time maker; first knife sold in 1988. **Mark:** Initials connected.

LUM, ROBERT W., 901 Travis Ave., Eugene, OR 97404, Phone: 541-688-2737
   Specialties: High-art working knives of his design. **Patterns:** Hunters, fighters, tantos and folders. **Technical:** Grinds 440C, 154CM and ATS-34; plans to forge soon. **Prices:** $175 to $500; some to $800. **Remarks:** Full-time maker; first knife sold in 1976. **Mark:** Chop with last name underneath.

LUMAN, JAMES R., Clear Creek Trail, Anaconda, MT 59711, Phone: 406-560-1461
   Specialties: San Mai and composite end patterns. **Patterns:** Pool and eye Spirograph southwest composite patterns. **Technical:** All patterns with blued steel; all made by him. **Prices:** $200 to $800. **Mark:** Stock blade removal. Pattern welded steel. Bottom ricasso JRL.

LUNDSTROM, JAN-AKE, Mastmostigen 8, 66010 Dals-Langed, SWEDEN, Phone: 0531-40270
   Specialties: Viking swords, axes and knives in cooperation with handle makers. **Patterns:** All traditional-styles, especially swords and inlaid blades. **Technical:** Forges his own Damascus and laminated steel. **Prices:** $200 to $1000. **Remarks:** Full-time maker; first knife sold in 1985; collaborates with museums. **Mark:** Runic.

LUNN, GAIL, PO Box 48931, St. Petersburg, FL 33743, Phone: 727-345-7455, gail@lunnknives.com Web: www.lunnknives.com
   Specialties: Fancy folders and double action autos, some straight blades. **Patterns:** One-of-a-kind; all types. **Technical:** Stock removal; hand made. **Prices:** $300 and up. **Remarks:** Fancy file work, exotic materials, inlays, stone etc. **Mark:** Name in script.

LUNN, LARRY A., PO Box 48931, St. Petersburg, FL 33743, Phone: 727-345-7455, larry@lunnknives.com Web: www.lunnknives.com
   Specialties: Fancy folders and double action autos; some straight blades. **Patterns:** All types; his own designs. **Technical:** Stock removal; commercial Damascus. **Prices:** $125 and up. **Remarks:** File work inlays and exotic materials. **Mark:** Name in script.

LUPOLE, JAMIE G., KUMA KNIVES, 285 Main St., Kirkwood, NY 13795, Phone: 607-775-9368, jlupole@stny.rr.com
   Specialties: Working and collector grade fixed blades, ethnic-styled blades. **Patterns:** Fighters, Bowies, tacticals, hunters, camp, utility, personal carry knives, some swords. **Technical:** Forges and grinds 10XX series and other high-carbon steels, grinds ATS-34 and 440C, will use just about every handle material available. **Prices:** $80 to $500 and up. **Remarks:** Part-time maker since 1999. **Marks:** "KUMA" hot stamped, name, city and state-etched, or "Daiguma saku" in kanji.

LUTZ, GREG, 127 Crescent Rd., Greenwood, SC 29646, Phone: 864-229-7340
   Specialties: Working and using knives and period pieces of his design and to customer specs. **Patterns:** Fighters, hunters and swords. **Technical:** Forges 1095 and O1; grinds ATS-34. Differentially heat-treats forged blades; uses cryogenic treatment on ATS-34. **Prices:** $50 to $350; some to $1200. **Remarks:** Part-time maker; first knife sold in 1986. Doing business as Scorpion Forge. **Mark:** First initial, last name.

LYLE III, ERNEST L., LYLE KNIVES, PO Box 1755, Chiefland, FL 32644, Phone: 352-490-6693, www.ernestlyleknives.com
   Specialties: Fancy period pieces; one-of-a-kind and limited editions. **Patterns:** Arabian/Persian influenced fighters, military knives, Bowies and Roman short swords; several styles of hunters. **Technical:** Grinds 440C, D2 and 154 CM. Engraves. **Prices:** Upscale. **Remarks:** Full-time maker; first knife sold in 1972. **Mark:** Last name in capital letters - LYLE over a much smaller Chief land.

LYTTLE, BRIAN, Box 5697, High River, AB, CANADA T1V 1M7, Phone: 403-558-3638, brianlyttle@cadvision.com
   Specialties: Fancy working straight knives and folders; art knives. **Patterns:** Bowies, daggers, dirks, Sgian Dubhs, folders, dress knives. **Technical:** Forges Damascus steel; engraving; scrimshaw; heat-treat-

ing; classes. **Prices:** $200 to $1000; some to $5000. **Remarks:** Full-time maker; first knife sold in 1983. **Mark:** Last name, country.

M

MACDONALD, DAVID, 2824 Hwy 47, Los Lunas, NM 87031, Phone: 505-866-5866

MACDONALD, JOHN, 9 David Dr., Raymond, NH 03077, Phone: 603-895-0918
   Specialties: Working/using straight knives of his design and to customer specs. **Patterns:** Japanese cutlery, Bowies, hunters and working knives. **Technical:** Grinds O1, L6 and ATS-34. Swords have matching handles and scabbards with Japanese flair. **Prices:** $70 to $250; some to $500. **Remarks:** Part-time maker; first knife sold in 1988. Wood/glass-topped custom cases. Doing business as Mac the Knife. **Mark:** Initials.

MACKIE, JOHN, 13653 Lanning, Whittier, CA 90605, Phone: 562-945-6104
   Specialties: Forged. **Patterns:** Bowie and camp knives. **Technical:** Attended ABS Bladesmith School. **Prices:** $75 to $500. **Mark:** JSM in a triangle.

MACKRILL, STEPHEN, PO Box 1580, Pinegowrie 2123, Johannesburg, SOUTH AFRICA, Phone: 27-11-886-2893, Fax: 27-11-334-6230, info@mackrill.co.za Web: www.mackrill.net
   Specialties: Art fancy, historical, collectors and corporate gifts cutlery. **Patterns:** Fighters, hunters, camp, custom lock back and liner lock folders. **Technical:** N690, 12C27, ATS-34, silver and gold inlay on handles; wooden and silver sheaths. **Prices:** $330 and upwards. **Remarks:** First knife sold in 1978. **Mark:** Oval with first initial, last name, "Maker" country of origin.

MADISON II, BILLY D., 2295 Tyler Rd., Remlap, AL 35133, Phone: 205-680-6722, littleh@bellsouth.net
   Specialties: Traditional working and using straight knives and folders of his design or yours. **Patterns:** Hunters, locking folders, utility/camp knives, and fighters. **Technical:** Grinds 440C, ATS-34, D2 and BG-42; forges some high-carbons. Prefers natural handle material. Ivory, bone, exotic woods and horns. **Prices:** $250 to $500 depending on knife. My mirror finish has to be seen to aff. **Remarks:** Limited part-time maker (disabled machinist); first knife sold in 1978. Had first knife returned a folder needed buff! Horn re-epoxied. **Mark:** Last name and year. Offers sheaths. **Other:** Wife makes sheaths. All knives have unconditional lifetime warranty. Never had a knife returned in 27 years.

MADRULLI, MME JOELLE, RESIDENCE STE CATHERINE B1, Salon De Provence, FRANCE 13330

MAE, TAKAO, 1-119, 1-4 Uenohigashi, Toyonaka, Osaka, JAPAN 560-0013, Phone: 81-6-6852-2758, Fax: 81-6-6481-1649, takamae@nifty.com
   Remarks: Distinction stylish in art-forged blades, with lacquered ergonomic handles.

MAESTRI, PETER A., S11251 Fairvlew Rd., Spring Green, WI 53588, Phone: 608-546-4481
   Specialties: Working straight knives in standard patterns. **Patterns:** Camp and fishing knives, utility green-river-styled. **Technical:** Grinds 440C, 154CM and 440A. **Prices:** $15 to $45; some to $150. **Remarks:** Full-time maker; first knife sold in 1981. Provides professional cutler service to professional cutters. **Mark:** CARISOLO, MAESTRI BROS., or signature.

MAGEE, JIM, 748 S Front #3, Salina, KS 67401, Phone: 785-820-6928
   Specialties: Working and fancy folding knives. **Patterns:** Liner locking folders, favorite is his Persian. **Technical:** Grinds ATS-34, Devin Thomas & Eggerling Damascus, titanium. Liners Prefer mother-of-pearl handles. **Prices:** Start at $225 to $1200. **Remarks:** Part-time maker, first knife sold in 2001. Purveyor since 1982. Currently President of the Professional Knifemakers Assn. **Mark:** Last name.

MAGRUDER, JASON, 10w Saint Elmo Ave, Colorado Springs, CO 80906, Phone: 719-210-1579, belstain@hotmail.com
   Specialties: Fancy/embellished and working/using knives of his own design or to customer specs. Fancy filework and carving. **Patterns:** Tactical straight knives, hunters, bowies and lockback folders. **Technical:** Flats grinds S30V, CPM3V, and 1080. Forges own Damascus. **Prices:** $150 and up. **Remarks:** Part-time maker; first knife sold in 2000. **Mark:** Magruder, or initials J M.

MAHOMEDY, A. R., PO Box 76280, Marble Ray KZN, 4035, SOUTH AFRICA, Phone: +27 31 577 1451, arm-koknives@mweb.co.za Web: www.arm-koknives.co.za
   Specialties: Daggers, elegant folders, hunters & utilities. Prefers to work to commissions, collectons & presentations. With handles of mother of pearl, fossil & local ivories. Exotic dyed/stablized burls, giraffe bone and

horns.**Technical:** Via stock removal grinds Damasteel, carbon and mosaic Damascus, ATS-34, N690, 440A, 440B, 12 C 27 and RWL 34. **Prices:** $500 and up. **Remarks:** Part-time maker. First knife sold in 1995. Member knifemakers guild of SA. **Mark:** Logo of initials A R M crowned with a "Minaret".

MAIENKNECHT, STANLEY, 38648 S.R. 800, Sardis, OH 43946

MAINES, JAY, SUNRISE RIVER CUSTOM KNIVES, 5584 266th St., Wyoming, MN 55092, Phone: 651-462-5301, jaymaines@fronternet.net Web: http://www.sunrisecustomknives.com
Specialties: Heavy duty working, classic and traditional fixed blades. Some high-tech and fancy embellished knives available. **Patterns:** Hunters, skinners, Bowies, Tantos, fillet, fighters, daggers, boot and cutlery sets. **Technical:** Hollow ground, stock removal blades of 440C, ATS-34 and CPM S-90V. Prefers natural handle materials, exotic hard woods, and stag, rams and buffalo horns. Offers dovetailed bolsters in brass, stainless steel and nickel silver. Custom sheaths from matching wood or hand-stitched from heavy duty water buffalo hide. **Prices:** Moderate to up-scale. **Remarks:** Part-time maker; first knife sold in 1992. Color brochure available upon request. Doing business as Sunrise River Custom Knives. **Mark:** Full name under a Rising Sun logo. **Other:** Offers fixed blade knives repair and handle conversions.

MAISEY, ALAN, PO Box 197, Vincentia 2540, NSW AUSTRALIA, Phone: 2-4443 7829, tosanaji@excite.com
Specialties: Daggers, especially krisses; period pieces. **Technical:** Offers knives and finished blades in Damascus and nickel Damascus. **Prices:** $75 to $2000; some higher. **Remarks:** Part-time maker; provides complete restoration service for krisses. Trained by a Javanese Kris smith. **Mark:** None, triangle in a box, or three peaks.

MAJER, MIKE, 50 Palmetto Bay Rd., Hilton Head, SC 29928, Phone: 843-681-3483

MAKOTO, KUNITOMO, 3-3-18 Imazu-cho, Fukuyama-city, Hiroshima, JAPAN, Phone: 084-933-5874, kunitomo@po.iijnet.or.jp

MALABY, RAYMOND J., 835 Calhoun Ave., Juneau, AK 99801, Phone: 907-586-6981, Fax: 907-523-8631, malaby@gci.net
Specialties: Straight working knives. **Patterns:** Hunters, skiners, bowies, and camp knives. **Technical:** Hand forged 1084, 5160, O1 and grinds ATS-34 stainless.**Prices:** $195 to $400. **Remarks:** First knife sold in 1984. **Mark:** First initial, last name, city, and state.

MALLETT, JOHN, 760 E Francis St. #N, Ontario, CA 91761, Phone: 800-532-3336/ 909-923-4116, Fax: 909-923-9932, trugrit1@aol.com Web: www.trugrit.com
Specialties: Complete line of 3/M, Norton and Hermes belts for grinding and polishing 24-2000 grit; also hard core, Bader and Burr King grinders. Baldor motors and buffers. ATS-34, 440C, BG42 and 416 stainless steel.

MALLOY, JOE, 1039 Schwabe St., Freeland, PA 18224, Phone: 570-636-2781
Specialties: Working straight knives and lock back folders—plain and fancy—of his design. **Patterns:** Hunters, utility, Bowie, survival knives, folders. **Technical:** Grinds ATS-34, 440C, D2 and A2 and Damascus. Makes own leather and kyder sheaths. **Prices:** $100 to $1800. **Remarks:** Part-time maker; first knife sold in 1982. **Mark:** First and middle initials, last name, city and state.

MANABE, MICHAEL K., 3659 Tomahawk Lane, San Diego, CA 92117, Phone: 619-483-2416
Specialties: Classic and high-art straight knives of his design or to customer specs. **Patterns:** Bowies, fighters, hunters, utility/camp knives; all knives one-of-a-kind. **Technical:** Forges and grinds 52100, 5160 and 1095. Does multiple quenching for distinctive temper lines. Each blade triple-tempered. **Prices:** Start at $200. **Remarks:** Part-time maker; first knife sold in 1994. **Mark:** First and middle initials, last name and J.S. on other side.

MANEKER, KENNETH, RR 2, Galiano Island, B.C., CANADA V0N 1P0, Phone: 604-539-2084
Specialties: Working straight knives; period pieces. **Patterns:** Camp knives and hunters; French chef knives. **Technical:** Grinds 440C, 154CM and Vascowear. **Prices:** $50 to $200; some to $300. **Remarks:** Part-time maker; first knife sold in 1981. Doing business as Water Mountain Knives. **Mark:** Japanese Kanji of initials, plus glyph.

MANKEL, KENNETH, 7836 Cannonsburg Rd., Cannonsburg, MI 49317, Phone: 616-874-6955

MANLEY, DAVID W., 3270 Six Mile Hwy., Central, SC 29630, Phone: 864-654-1125, nmanley@innova.net
Specialties: Working straight knives of his design or to custom specs. **Patterns:** Hunters, boot and fighters. **Technical:** Grinds 440C and ATS-34. **Prices:** $60 to $250. **Remarks:** Part-time maker; first knife sold in 1994. **Mark:** First initial, last name, year and serial number.

MANN, MICHAEL L., IDAHO KNIFE WORKS, PO Box 144, Spirit Lake, ID 83869, Phone: 509 994-9394, Web: www.idahoknifeworks.com
Specialties: Good working blades-historical reproduction, modern or custom design. **Patterns:** Cowboy Bowies, Mountain Man period blades, old-style folders, designer and maker of "The Cliff Knife", hunter knives, hand ax and fish fillet.**Technical:** High-carbon steel blades-hand forged 5160. Stock removed 15N20 steel. Also Damascus **Prices:** $125to $600+. **Remarks:** Made first knife in 1965. Full-time making knives as Idaho Knife Works since 1986. Functional as well as collectible. Each knife truly unique! **Mark:** Four mountain peaks are his initials MM.

MANN, TIM, BLADEWORKS, PO Box 1196, Honokaa, HI 96727, Phone: 808-775-0949, Fax: 808-775-0949, birdman@shaka.com
Specialties: Hand-forged knives and swords. **Patterns:** Bowies, Tantos, pesh kabz, daggers. **Technical:** Use 5160, 1050, 1075, 1095 and ATS-34 steels, cable Damascus. **Prices:** $200 to $800. **Remarks:** Just learning to forge Damascus. **Mark:** None yet.

MARAGNI, DAN, RD 1, Box 106, Georgetown, NY 13072, Phone: 315-662-7490
Specialties: Heavy-duty working knives, some investor class. **Patterns:** Hunters, fighters and camp knives, some Scottish types. **Technical:** Forges W2 and his own Damascus; toughness and edge-holding a high priority. **Prices:** $125 to $500; some to $1000. **Remarks:** Full-time maker; first knife sold in 1975. **Mark:** Celtic initials in circle.

MARKLEY, KEN, 7651 Cabin Creek Lane, Sparta, IL 62286, Phone: 618-443-5284
Specialties: Traditional working and using knives of his design and to customer specs. **Patterns:** Fighters, hunters and utility/camp knives. **Technical:** Forges 5160, 1095 and L6; makes his own Damascus; does file work. **Prices:** $150 to $800; some to $2000. **Remarks:** Part-time maker; first knife sold in 1991. Doing business as Cabin Creek Forge. **Mark:** Last name, JS.

MARLOWE, CHARLES, 10822 Poppleton Ave., Omaha, NE 68144, Phone: 402-933-5065, cmarlowe1@cox.net Web: www.marloweknives.com
Specialties: Folding knives and balisong. **Patterns:** Tactical pattern folders. **Technical:** Grind ATS-34, S30V, others on request. Forges/ grinds 1095 on occasion. **Prices:** Start at $350. **Remarks:** First knife sold in 1993. Full-time since 1999. **Mark:** MARLOWE.

MARLOWE, DONALD, 2554 Oakland Rd., Dover, PA 17315, Phone: 717-764-6055
Specialties: Working straight knives in standard patterns. **Patterns:** Bowies, fighters, boots and utility knives. **Technical:** Grinds D2 and 440C. Integral design hunter models. **Prices:** $120 to $525. **Remarks:** Spare-time maker; first knife sold in 1977. **Mark:** Last name.

MARSHALL, GLENN, PO Box 1099, 1117 Hofmann St., Mason, TX 76854, Phone: 915-347-6207
Specialties: Working knives and period pieces. **Patterns:** Straight and folding hunters, fighters and camp knives. **Technical:** Steel used 440C, D2, CPM and 440V. **Prices:** $90 and up according to options. **Remarks:** Full-time maker; first knife sold in 1932. **Mark:** First initial, last name, city and state with anvil logo.

MARSHALL, STEPHEN R., 975 Harkreader Rd., Mt. Juliet, TN 37122

MARTIN, BRUCE E., Rt. 6, Box 164-B, Prescott, AR 71857, Phone: 501-887-2023
Specialties: Fancy working straight knives of his design. **Patterns:** Bowies, camp knives, skinners and fighters. **Technical:** Forges 5160, 1095 and his own Damascus. Uses natural handle materials; filework available. **Prices:** $75 to $350; some to $500. **Remarks:** Full-time maker; first knife sold in 1979. **Mark:** Name in arch.

MARTIN, GENE, PO Box 396, Williams, OR 97544, Phone: 541-846-6755, bladesmith@customknife.com
Specialties: Straight knives and folders. **Patterns:** Fighters, hunters, skinners, boot knives, spring back and lock back folders. **Technical:** Grinds ATS-34, 440C, Damascus and 154CM. Forges; makes own Damascus; scrimshaws. **Prices:** $150 to $2500. **Remarks:** Full-time maker; first knife sold in 1993. Doing business as Provision Forge. **Mark:** Name and/or crossed staff and sword.

MARTIN, HAL W., 781 Hwy. 95, Morrilton, AR 72110, Phone: 501-354-1682, hmartin@ipa.net

MARTIN, JIM, 1120 S. Cadiz Ct., Oxnard, CA 93035, Phone: 805-985-9849
Specialties: Fancy and working/using folders of his design. **Patterns:** Automatics, locking folders and miniatures. **Technical:** Grinds 440C, AEB-L, 304SS and Damascus. **Prices:** $350 to $700; some to $1500. **Remarks:** Full-time maker; first knife sold in 1992. Doing business as Jim Martin Custom Knives.

MARTIN, JOHN ALEXANDER, 821 N Grand Ave., Okmulgee, OK 74447, Phone: 918-758-1099, jam773054@yahoo.com Web: www.jamblades.com
Specialties: Inlaid and engraved handles. Patterns: Bowies, fighters, hunters and traditional patterns. Technical: Forges 5160, 1084, and his own Damascus. Prices: Start at $185. Remarks: Part-time maker. Mark: Initials or two initials and last name with JS.

MARTIN, MICHAEL W., Box 572, Jefferson St., Beckville, TX 75631, Phone: 903-678-2161
Specialties: Classic working/using straight knives of his design and in standard patterns. Patterns: Hunters. Technical: Grinds ATS-34, 440C, O1 and A2. Bead blasted, Parkerized, high polish and satin finishes. Sheaths are handmade. Also hand forges cable Damascus. Prices: $185 to $280 some higher. Remarks: Part-time maker; first knife sold in 1995. Doing business as Michael W. Martin Knives. Mark: Name and city, state in arch.

MARTIN, PETER, 28220 N. Lake Dr., Waterford, WI 53185, Phone: 262-895-2815, Web: www.petermartinknives.com
Specialties: Fancy, fantasy and working straight knives and folders of his design and in standard patterns. Patterns: Bowies, fighters, hunters, locking folders and liner locks. Technical: Forges own Mosaic Damascus, powdered steel and his own Damascus. Prefers natural handle material; offers file work and carved handles. Prices: Moderate. Remarks: Part-time maker; first knife sold in 1988. Doing business as Martin Custom Products. Uses only natural handle materials. Mark: Martin Knives.

MARTIN, RANDALL J., 51 Bramblewood St, Bridgewater, MA 02324, Phone: 508-279-0682
Specialties: High tech folding and fixed blade tactical knives employing the latest blade steels and exotic materials. Employs a unique combination of 3d-CNC machining and hand work on both blades and handles. All knives are designed for hard use. Clean, radical grinds and ergonomic handles are hallmarks of RJ's work, as is his reputation for producing : Scary Sharp" knives. Technical: Grinds CPM30V, CPM 3V, CPM154CM, A2 and stainless Damascus. Other CPM alloys used on request. Performs all heat treating and cryogenic processing in-house. Remarks: Full-time maker since 2001 and materials engineer. Former helicopter designer. First knife sold in 1976.

MARTIN, ROBB, 7 Victoria St., Elmira, Ontario, CANADA N3B 1R9

MARTIN, TONY, 108 S. Main St., PO Box 324, Arcadia, MO 63621, Phone: 573-546-2254, arcadian@charter.net Web: www.arcadianforge.com
Specialties: Specializes in historical designs, esp. puukko, skean dhu. Remarks: Premium quality blades, exotic wood handles, unmatched fit and finish. Mark: RJ MARTIN incapital, outline letters.

MARTIN, WALTER E., 570 Cedar Flat Rd., Williams, OR 97544, Phone: 541-846-6755

MARZITELLI, PETER, 19929 35A Ave., Langley, BC, CANADA V3A 2R1, Phone: 604-532-8899, marzitelli@shaw.ca
Specialties: Specializes in unique functional knife shapes and designs using natural and synthetic handle materials. Patterns: Mostly folders, some daggers and art knives. Technical: Grinds ATS-34, S/S Damascus and others. Prices: $220 to $1000 (average $375). Remarks: Full-time maker; first knife sold in 1984. Mark: Stylized logo reads "Marz."

MASON, BILL, 1114 St. Louis, #33, Excelsior Springs, MO 64024, Phone: 816-637-7335
Specialties: Combat knives; some folders. Patterns: Fighters to match knife types in book *Cold Steel*. Technical: Grinds O1, 440C and ATS-34. Prices: $115 to $250; some to $350. Remarks: Spare-time maker; first knife sold in 1979. Mark: Initials connected.

MASSEY, AL, Box 14, Site 15, RR#2, Mount Uniacke, Nova Scotia, CANADA B0N 1Z0, Phone: 902-866-4754, armjan@attcanada.ca
Specialties: Working knives and period pieces. Patterns: Swords and daggers of Celtic to medieval design, Bowies. Technical: Forges 5160, 1084 and 1095. Makes own Damascus. Prices: $100 to $400, some to $900. Remarks: Part-time maker; first blade sold in 1988. Mark: Initials and JS on Ricasso.

MASSEY, ROGER, 4928 Union Rd., Texarkana, AR 71854, Phone: 870-779-1018
Specialties: Traditional and working straight knives and folders of his design and to customer specs. Patterns: Bowies, hunters, daggers and utility knives. Technical: Forges 1084 and 52100, makes his own Damascus. Offers filework and silver wire inlay in handles. Prices: $200 to $1500; some to $2500. Remarks: Part-time maker; first knife sold in 1991. Mark: Last name, M.S.

MASSEY, RON, 61638 El Reposo St., Joshua Tree, CA 92252, Phone: 760-366-9239 after 5 p.m., Fax: 763-366-4620
Specialties: Classic, traditional, fancy/embellished, high art, period pieces, working/using knives, straight knives, folders, and automatics. Your design, customer specs, about 175 standard patterns. Patterns: Automatics, hunters and fighters. All folders are side-locking folders. Unless requested as lock books slip joint he specializes or custom designs. Technical: ATS-34, 440C, D-2 upon request. Engraving, filework, scrimshaw, most of the exotic handle materials. All aspects are performed by him: inlay work in pearls or stone, hand made Pem' work. Prices: $110 to $2500; some to $6000. Remarks: Part-time maker; first knife sold in 1976.

MATA, LEONARD, 3583 Arruza St., San Diego, CA 92154, Phone: 619-690-6935

MATHEWS, CHARLIE AND HARRY, TWIN BLADES, 121 Mt Pisgah Church Rd., Statesboro, GA 30458, Phone: 912-865-9098, twinblades@bulloch.net Web: www.twinxblades.com
Specialties: Working straight knives. Patterns: Hunters, fighters, Bowies and period pieces. Technical: Grinds D2, BG42, CPMS30V, CPM3V, ATS-34 and commercial Damascus; handmade sheaths some with exotic leather, file work. Prices: Starting at $125. Remarks: Twin brothers making knives full-time under the label of Twin Blades. Charter members Georgia Custom Knifemaker's Guild. Mark: Twin Blades over crossed knives, reverse side steel type.

MATSUOKA, SCOT, 94-415 Ukalialii Place, Mililani, HI 96789, Phone: 808-625-6658, scottym@hawaii.rr.com
Specialties: Folders, fixed blades with custom hand-stitched sheaths. Patterns: Gentleman's knives, hunters, tactical folders. Technical: 440C, 154CM, BG42, bolsters, file work, and engraving. Prices: Starting price $125.00. Remarks: Part-time maker, first knife sold in 2002. Mark: Logo, name and state.

MATSUSAKI, TAKESHI, MATSUSAKI KNIVES, 151 Ono-Cho Saseboshi, Nagasaki, JAPAN, Phone: 0956-47-2938, Fax: 0956-47-2938
Specialties: Working and collector grade front look and slip joint. Patterns: Sheffierd type folders. Technical: Grinds ATS-34 k-120. Price: $250 to $1000, some to $8000. Remarks: Part-time maker, first knife sold in 1990. Mark: Name and initials.

MAXEN, MICK, 2 Huggins Welham Green, "Hatfield, Herts", UNITED KINGDOM AL97LR, Phone: 01707 261213, mmaxen@aol.com
Specialties: Damascus and Mosaic. Patterns: Medieval-style daggers and Bowies. Technical: Forges CS75 and 15N20 / nickel Damascus. Mark: Last name with axe above.

MAXFIELD, LYNN, 382 Colonial Ave., Layton, UT 84041, Phone: 801-544-4176, lcmaxfield@networld.com
Specialties: Sporting knives, some fancy. Patterns: Hunters, fishing, fillet, special purpose: some locking folders. Technical: Grinds 440-C, ATS-34, 154-CM, D2, CPM-S60V, S90V, 530V, CPM-3, Talonite, and Damascus. Prices: $125 to $400; some to $900. Remarks: Part-time maker; first knife sold in 1979. Mark: Name, city and state.

MAXWELL, DON, 1484 Celeste Ave, Clovis, CA 93611, Phone: 559-299-2197, maxwellknives@aol.com
Specialties: Fancy folding knives and fixed blades of my design. Patterns: Hunters, fighters, utility/camp knives, liner lock folders and fantasy knives. Technical: Grinds 440C, ATS-34, D2 and commercial Damascus. Prices: $250 to $1000; some to $2500. Remarks: Full-time maker; first knife sold in 1987. Mark: Last name only.

MAYNARD, LARRY JOE, PO Box 493, Crab Orchard, WV 25827
Specialties: Fancy and fantasy straight knives. Patterns: Big knives; a Bowie with a full false edge; fighting knives. Technical: Grinds standard steels. Prices: $350 to $500; some to $1000. Remarks: Full-time maker; first knife sold in 1986. Mark: Middle and last initials.

MAYNARD, WILLIAM N., 2677 John Smith Rd., Fayetteville, NC 28306, Phone: 910-425-1615
Specialties: Traditional and working straight knives of all designs. Patterns: Combat, Bowies, fighters, hunters and utility knives. Technical: Grinds 440C, ATS-34 and commercial Damascus. Offers fancy filework; handmade sheaths. Prices: $100 to $300; some to $750. Remarks: Full-time maker; first knife sold in 1988. Mark: Last name.

MAYO JR., TOM, 67-420 Alahaka St., Waialua, HI 96791, Phone: 808-637-6560, mayotool@hawaii.rr.com
Specialties: Framelocks/tactical knives. Patterns: Combat knives, hunters, Bowies and folders. Technical: Titanium/stellite/S30V. Prices: Start at $500 to $1000. Remarks: Part-time maker; first knife sold in 1983. Mark: Volcano logo with name and state.

MAYVILLE, OSCAR L., 2130 E. County Rd. 910S., Marengo, IN 47140, Phone: 812-338-3103
Specialties: Working straight knives; period pieces. Patterns: Kitchen cutlery, Bowies, camp knives and hunters. Technical: Grinds A2, O1

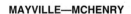

and 440C. **Prices:** $50 to $350; some to $500. **Remarks:** Full-time maker; first knife sold in 1984. **Mark:** Initials over knife logo.

MCABEE, WILLIAM, 27275 Norton Grade, Colfax, CA 95713, Phone: 530-389-8163
Specialties: Working/using knives. **Patterns:** Fighters, Bowies, Hunters. **Technical:** Grinds ATS-34. **Prices:** $75 to $200; some to $350. **Remarks:** Part-time maker; first knife sold in 1990. **Mark:** Stylized WM stamped.

MCCALLEN JR., HOWARD H., 110 Anchor Dr., So Seaside Park, NJ 08752

MCCARLEY, JOHN, 4165 Harney Rd., Taneytown, MD 21787
Specialties: Working straight knives; period pieces. **Patterns:** Hunters, Bowies, camp knives, miniatures, throwing knives. **Technical:** Forges W2, O1 and his own Damascus. **Prices:** $150 to $300; some to $1000. **Remarks:** Part-time maker; first knife sold in 1977. **Mark:** Initials in script.

MCCARTY, HARRY, 1479 Indian Ridge Rd., Blaine, TN 37709
Specialties: Period pieces. **Patterns:** Trade knives, Bowies, 18th and 19th century folders and hunting swords. **Technical:** Forges and grinds high-carbon steel. **Prices:** $75 to $1300. **Remarks:** Full-time maker; first knife sold in 1977. **Mark:** Stylized initials inside a shamrock. **Other:** Doing business as Indian Ridge Forge.

MCCLURE, MICHAEL, 803 17th Ave., Menlo Park, CA 94025, Phone: 650-323-2596, mikesknives@comcast.net
Specialties: Working/using straight knives of his design and to customer specs. **Patterns:** Bowies, hunters, skinners, utility/camp, fillets and boot knives. **Technical:** Forges high-carbon and Damascus; also grinds stainless, all grades. **Prices:** Start at $200. **Remarks:** Part-time maker; first knife sold in 1991. **Mark:** Mike McClure. **Other:** ABS Journeyman Smith.

MCCONNELL, CHARLES R., 158 Genteel Ridge, Wellsburg, WV 26070, Phone: 304-737-2015
Specialties: Working straight knives. **Patterns:** Hunters, Bowies, daggers, minis and push knives. **Technical:** Grinds 440C and 154CM; likes full tangs. **Prices:** $65 to $325; some to $800. **Remarks:** Part-time maker; first knife sold in 1977. **Mark:** Name.

MCCONNELL JR., LOYD A., 1710 Rosewood, Odessa, TX 79761, Phone: 915-363-8344, ccknives@ccknives.com Web: www.ccknives.com
Specialties: Working straight knives and folders, some fancy. **Patterns:** Hunters, boots, Bowies, locking folders and slip-joints. **Technical:** Grinds CPM Steels, ATS-34 and BG-42 and commercial Damascus. **Prices:** $175 to $900; some to $10,000. **Remarks:** Full-time maker; first knife sold in 1975. Doing business as Cactus Custom Knives. Markets product knives under name: Lone Star Knives. **Mark:** Name, city and state in cactus logo.

MCCORNOCK, CRAIG, MCC MTN OUTFITTERS, 4775 Rte. 212, Willow, NY 12495, Phone: 914-679-9758, Mccmtn@aol.com Web: www.mccmtn.com

MCCOUN, MARK, 14212 Pine Dr., DeWitt, VA 23840, Phone: 804-469-7631, markmccoun@aol.com
Specialties: Working/using straight knives of his design and in standard patterns; custom miniatures. **Patterns:** Locking liners, integrals. **Technical:** Grinds Damascus, ATS-34 and 440C. **Prices:** $150 to $500. **Remarks:** Part-time maker; first knife sold in 1989. **Mark:** Name, city and state.

MCCRACKIN, KEVIN, 3720 Hess Rd., House Spings, MO 63051, Phone: 636-677-6066

MCCRACKIN AND SON, V.J., 3720 Hess Rd., House Springs, MO 63051, Phone: 636-677-6066
Specialties: Working straight knives in standard patterns. **Patterns:** Hunters, Bowies and camp knives. **Technical:** Forges L6, 5160, his own Damascus, cable Damascus. **Prices:** $125 to $700; some to $1500. **Remarks:** Part-time maker; first knife sold in 1983. Son Kevin helps make the knives. **Mark:** Last name, M.S.

MCCULLOUGH, JERRY, 274 West Pettibone Rd., Georgiana, AL 36033, Phone: 334-382-7644, ke4er@alaweb.com
Specialties: Standard patterns or custom designs. **Technical:** Forge and grind scrap-tool and Damascus steels. Use natural handle materials and turquoise trim on some. Filework on others. **Prices:** $65 to $250 and up. **Remarks:** Part-time maker. **Mark:** Initials (JM) combined.

MCDERMOTT, MICHAEL, 151 Hwy F, Defiance, MO 63341, Phone: 314-798-2077

MCDONALD, RICH, 4590 Kirk Rd., Columbiana, OH 44408, Phone: 330-482-0007, Fax: 330-482-0007
Specialties: Traditional working/using and art knives of his design. **Patterns:** Bowies, hunters, folders, primitives and tomahawks. **Technical:**

Forges 5160, 1084, 1095, 52100 and his own Damascus. Fancy filework. **Prices:** $200 to $1500. **Remarks:** Full-time maker; first knife sold in 1994. **Mark:** First and last initials connected.

MCDONALD, ROBERT J., 14730 61 Court N., Loxahatchee, FL 33470, Phone: 561-790-1470
Specialties: Traditional working straight knives to customer specs. **Patterns:** Fighters, swords and folders. **Technical:** Grinds 440C, ATS-34 and forges own Damascus. **Prices:** $150 to $1000. **Remarks:** Part-time maker; first knife sold in 1988. **Mark:** Electro-etched name.

MCDONALD, ROBIN J., 6509 E Jeffrey Dr., Fayetteville, NC 28314
Specialties: Working knives of maker's design. **Patterns:** Bowies, hunters, camp knives and fighters. **Technical:** Forges primarily 5160. **Prices:** $100 to $500. **Remarks:** Part-time maker; first knife sold in 1999. **Mark:** Initials RJM.

MCDONALD, W.J. "JERRY", 7173 Wickshire Cove E., Germantown, TN 38138, Phone: 901-756-9924, wjmcdonaldknives@email.msn.com Web: www.mcdonaldknives.com
Specialties: Classic and working/using straight knives of his design and in standard patterns. **Patterns:** Bowies, hunters kitchen and traditional spring back pocket knives. **Technical:** Grinds ATS-34, 154CM, D2, 440V, BG42 and 440C. **Prices:** $125 to $1000. **Remarks:** Full-time maker; first knife sold in 1989. **Mark:** First and middle initials, last name, maker, city and state. Some of his knives are stamped McDonald in script.

MCFALL, KEN, PO Box 458, Lakeside, AZ 85929, Phone: 928-537-2026, Fax: 928-537-8066, knives@citlink.net
Specialties: Fancy working straight knives and some folders. **Patterns:** Daggers, boots, tantos, Bowies; some miniatures. **Technical:** Grinds D2, ATS-34 and 440C. Forges his own Damascus. **Prices:** $200 to $1200. **Remarks:** Part-time maker; first knife sold in 1984. **Mark:** Name, city and state.

MCFARLIN, ERIC E., PO Box 2188, Kodiak, AK 99615, Phone: 907-486-4799
Specialties: Working knives of his design. **Patterns:** Bowies, skinners, camp knives and hunters. **Technical:** Flat and convex grinds 440C, A2 and AEB-L. **Prices:** Start at $200. **Remarks:** Part-time maker; first knife sold in 1989. **Mark:** Name and city in rectangular logo.

MCFARLIN, J.W., 3331 Pocohantas Dr., Lake Havasu City, AZ 86404, Phone: 928-855-8095, Fax: 928-855-8095, aztheedge@redrivernet.com
Technical: Flat grinds, D2, ATS-34, 440C, Thomas and Peterson Damascus. **Remarks:** From working knives to investment. Customer designs always welcome. 100% hand made. **Prices:** $150 to $3000. **Mark:** Hand written in the blade.

MCGILL, JOHN, PO Box 302, Blairsville, GA 30512, Phone: 404-745-4686
Specialties: Working knives. **Patterns:** Traditional patterns; camp knives. **Technical:** Forges L6 and 9260; makes Damascus. **Prices:** $50 to $250; some to $500. **Remarks:** Full-time maker; first knife sold in 1982. **Mark:** XYLO.

MCGOWAN, FRANK E., 12629 Howard Lodge Dr., Sykesville, MD 21784, Phone: 410-489-4323, fmcgowan1@comcast.net
Specialties: Fancy working knives and folders to customer specs. **Patterns:** Survivor knives, fighters, fishing knives, folders and hunters. **Technical:** Grinds and forges O1, 440C, 5160, ATS-34, 52100, or customer choice. **Prices:** $100 to $1000; some more. **Remarks:** Full-time maker; first knife sold in 1986. **Mark:** Last name.

MCGRATH, PATRICK T., 8343 Kenyon Ave., Westchester, CA 90045, Phone: 310-338-8764, hidinginLA@excite.com

MCGRODER, PATRICK J., 5725 Chapin Rd., Madison, OH 44057, Phone: 216-298-3405, Fax: 216-298-3405
Specialties: Traditional working/using knives of his design. **Patterns:** Bowies, hunters and utility/camp knives. **Technical:** Grinds ATS-34, D2 and customer requests. Does reverse etching; heat-treats; prefers natural handle materials; custom made sheath with each knife. **Prices:** $125 to $250. **Remarks:** Part-time maker. **Mark:** First and middle initials, last name, maker, city and state.

MCGUANE IV, THOMAS F., 410 South 3rd Ave., Bozeman, MT 59715, Phone: 406-586-0248, Web: http://www.thomasmcguane.com
Specialties: Multi metal inlaid knives of handmade steel. **Patterns:** Lock back and liner lock folders, fancy straight knives. **Technical:** 1084/1SN20 Damascus and Mosaic steel by maker. **Prices:** $1000 and up. **Mark:** Surname or name and city, state.

MCHENRY, WILLIAM JAMES, Box 67, Wyoming, RI 02898, Phone: 401-539-8353
Specialties: Fancy high-tech folders of his design. **Patterns:** Locking folders with various mechanisms. **Technical:** One-of-a-kind only, no duplicates. Inventor of the Axis Lock. Most pieces disassemble and feature top-shelf materials including gold, silver and gems. **Prices:** Upscale.

Remarks: Full-time maker; first knife sold in 1988. Former goldsmith. **Mark:** Last name or first and last initials.

MCINTOSH, DAVID L., PO Box 948, Haines, AK 99827, Phone: 907-766-3673
Specialties: Working straight knives and folders of all designs. **Patterns:** All styles, except swords. **Technical:** Grinds ATS-34 and top name maker Damascus. Engraves; offers tooling on sheaths. Uses fossil ivory. **Prices:** $60 to $800; some to $2000. **Remarks:** Full-time maker; first knife sold in 1984. **Mark:** Last name, serial number, steel type, city and state.

MCKENZIE, DAVID BRIAN, 2311 B Ida Rd., Campbell River B, CANADA V9W-4V7

MCKIERNAN, STAN, 205 E. Park St., Vandalia, MO 63382, Phone: 573-594-6135, slmck@hotmailc.com
Specialties: Self-sheathed knives and miniatures. **Patterns:** Daggers, ethnic designs and individual styles. **Technical:** Grinds Damascus and 440C. **Prices:** $200 to $500, some to $1500. **Mark:** "River's Bend" inside two concentric circles.

MCLENDON, HUBERT W., 125 Thomas Rd., Waco, GA 30182, Phone: 770-574-9796
Specialties: Using knives; his design or customer's. **Patterns:** Bowies and hunters. **Technical:** Hand ground or forged ATS-34, 440C and D2. **Prices:** $100 to $300. **Remarks:** First knife sold in 1978. **Mark:** McLendon or Mc.

MCLUIN, TOM, 36 Fourth St., Dracut, MA 01826, Phone: 978-957-4899, tmcluin@comcast.net Web: http: //home.comcast.net/~tmcluin/
Specialties: Working straight knives and folders of his design. **Patterns:** Boots, hunters and folders. **Technical:** Grinds ATS-34, 440C, O1 and Damascus; makes his own mokume. **Prices:** $100 to $400; some to $700. **Remarks:** Part-time maker; first knife sold in 1991. **Mark:** Last name.

MCLURKIN, ANDREW, 2112 Windy Woods Dr., Raleigh, NC 27607, Phone: 919-834-4693, mclurkincustomeknives.com
Specialties: Collector grade folders, working folders, fixed blades, and miniatures. Knives made to order and to his design. **Patterns:** Locking liner and lock back folders, hunter, working and tactical designs. **Technical:** Using patterned Damascus, Mosaic Damascus, ATS-34, BG-42, and CPM steels. Prefers natural handle materials such as pearl, ancient ivory and stabilized wood. Also using synthetic materials such as carbon fiber, titanium, and G10. **Prices:** $250 and up. **Mark:** Last name. Mark is often on inside of folders.

MCMANUS, DANNY, 413 Fairhaven Drive., Taylors, SC 29687, Phone: 864-268-9849, Fax: 864-268-9699, DannyMcManus@bigfoot.com
Specialties: High-tech and traditional working/using straight knives of his design, to customer specs and in standard patterns. **Patterns:** Boots, Bowies, fighters, hunters and utility/camp knives. **Technical:** Forges stainless steel Damascus; grinds ATS-34. Offers engraving and scrimshaw. **Prices:** $300 to $2000; some to $3000. **Remarks:** Full-time maker; first knife sold in 1997. Doing business as Stamascus KnifeWorks Corp. **Mark:** Stamascus.

MCNABB, TOMMY, CAROLINA CUSTOM KNIVES, 4015 Brownsboro Rd., Winston-Salem, NC 27106, Phone: 336-924-6053, Fax: 336-924-4854, tommy@tmcnabb.com Web: carolinaknives.com

MCNEIL, JIMMY, 1175 Mt. Moriah Rd., Memphis, TN 38117, Phone: 901-544-0710 or 901-683-8133
Specialties: Fancy high-art straight knives of his design. **Patterns:** Bowies, daggers and swords. **Technical:** Grinds O1 and Damascus. Engraves, carves and inlays. **Prices:** $50 to $300; some to $2000. **Remarks:** Spare-time maker; first knife sold in 1993. Doing business as McNeil's Minerals and Knives. **Mark:** Crossed mining picks and serial number.

MCRAE, J. MICHAEL, 6100 Lake Rd, Mint Hill, NC 28227, Phone: 704-545-2929, scotia@carolina.rr.com Web: www.scotiametalwork.com
Specialties: Scottish dirks and sgian dubhs. **Patterns:** Traditional blade styles with traditional and slightly non-traditional handle treatments. **Technical:** Forges 1095, 5160 and his own Damascus. Prefers Stag and exotic hardwoods for handles, many intricately carved. **Prices:** Starting at $125, some to $3500. **Remarks:** Journeyman Smith in ABS, member of North Carolina Custom Knifemakers Guild and ABANA. Full-time maker, first knife sold in 1982. Doing business as Scotia Metalwork. **Mark:** Last name underlined with a claymore.

MEERDINK, KURT, 120 Split Rock Dr., Barryville, NY 12719, Phone: 845-557-0783
Specialties: Working straight knives. **Patterns:** Hunters, Bowies, tactical and neck knives. **Technical:** Grinds ATS-34, 440C, D2, Damascus. **Prices:** $95 to $1100. **Remarks:** Full-time maker, first knife sold in 1994. **Mark:** Meerdink Maker, Rio NY.

MEHR, FARID R, 8 Sidney Close, Tunbridge Wells, Kent, ENGLAND TN2 5QQ, Phone: 011-44-1892 520345, farid@faridknives.com
Specialties: High-tech fixed blades and titanium folders. **Patterns:** Chisel ground liner lock and integral mechanism folders. **Technical:** Grinds 440C, CPM-T-440V, CPM-420V, CPM-15V, CPMS125V, and T-1 high speed steel and Vasco-max alloy and tool steel. **Prices:** $550 to $15,000. **Remarks:** Full-time maker; first knife sold in 1991. **Mark:** First name and country.

MEIER, DARYL, 75 Forge Rd., Carbondale, IL 62901, Phone: 618-549-3234
Specialties: One-of-a-kind knives and swords. **Patterns:** Collaborates on blades. **Technical:** Forges his own Damascus, W1 and A203E, 440C, 431, nickel 200 and clad steel. **Prices:** $250 to $450; some to $6000. **Remarks:** Full-time smith and researcher since 1974; first knife sold in 1974. **Mark:** Name or circle/arrow symbol or SHAWNEE.

MELIN, GORDON C., 11259 Gladhill Rd Unit 4, Whittier, CA 90604, Phone: 562-946-5753

MELLARD, J. R., 17006 Highland Canyon Dr., Houston, TX 77095, Phone: 281-550-9464

MELOY, SEAN, 7148 Rosemary Lane, Lemon Grove, CA 91945-2105, Phone: 619-465-7173
Specialties: Traditional working straight knives of his design. **Patterns:** Bowies, fighters and utility/camp knives. **Technical:** Grinds 440C, ATS-34 and D2. **Prices:** $125 to $300. **Remarks:** Part-time maker; first knife sold in 1985. **Mark:** Broz Knives.

MENSCH, LARRY C., 578 Madison Ave., Milton, PA 17847, Phone: 570-742-9554
Specialties: Custom orders. **Patterns:** Bowies, daggers, hunters, tantos, short swords and miniatures. **Technical:** Grinds ATS-34, carbon and stainless steel Damascus; blade grinds hollow, flat and slack. Filework; bending guards and fluting handles with finger grooves. Offers engraving and scrimshaw. **Prices:** $200 and up. **Remarks:** Full-time maker; first knife sold in 1993. Doing business as Larry's Knife Shop. **Mark:** Connected capital "L" and small "m" in script.

MERCER, MIKE, 149 N. Waynesville Rd., Lebanon, OH 45036, Phone: 513-932-2837
Specialties: Jeweled gold and ivory daggers; multi-blade folders. **Patterns:** 1-1/4" folders, hunters, axes, replicas. **Technical:** Uses O1 Damascus and mokume. **Prices:** $150 to $1500. **Remarks:** Full-time maker since 1991. **Mark:** Last name in script.

MERCHANT, TED, 7 Old Garrett Ct., White Hall, MD 21161, Phone: 410-343-0380
Specialties: Traditional and classic working knives. **Patterns:** Bowies, hunters, camp knives, fighters, daggers and skinners. **Technical:** Forges W2 and 5160; makes own Damascus. Makes handles with wood, stag, horn, silver and gem stone inlay; fancy filework. **Prices:** $125 to $600; some to $1500. **Remarks:** Full-time maker; first knife sold in 1985. **Mark:** Last name.

MERZ III, ROBERT L., 1447 Winding Canyon, Katy, TX 77493, Phone: 281-391-2897
Specialties: Folders. **Technical:** Flat-grinds 440C, 154CM, ATS-34, 440V and commercial Damascus. **Prices:** $250 to $700. **Remarks:** Part-time maker; first knife sold in 1974. **Mark:** MERZ.

MESHEJIAN, MARDI, 33 Elm Dr., E. Northport, NY 11731, Phone: 631-757-4541
Specialties: One-of-a-kind fantasy and high-art straight knives of his design. **Patterns:** Swords, daggers, finger knives and other edged weapons. **Technical:** Forged Damascus and Chain Damascus. **Prices:** $150 to $2500; some to $3000. **Remarks:** Full-time maker; first knife sold in 1996. Doing business as Tooth and Nail Metalworks. **Mark:** Stamped Etched stylized "M".

MESSER, DAVID T., 134 S. Torrence St., Dayton, OH 45403-2044, Phone: 513-228-6561
Specialties: Fantasy period pieces, straight and folding, of his design. **Patterns:** Bowies, daggers and swords. **Technical:** Grinds 440C, O1, 06 and commercial Damascus. Likes fancy guards and exotic handle materials. **Prices:** $100 to $225; some to $375. **Remarks:** Spare-time maker; first knife sold in 1991. **Mark:** Name stamp.

METHENY, H.A. "WHITEY", 7750 Waterford Dr., Spotsylvania, VA 22553, Phone: 540-582-3095, Fax: 540-582-3095, hamethen4@aol.com Web: www.methenyknives.com
Specialties: Working and using straight knives of his design and to customer specs. **Patterns:** Hunters and kitchen knives. **Technical:** Grinds 440C and ATS-34. Offers filework; tooled custom sheaths. **Prices:** $200 to $350. **Remarks:** Spare-time maker; first knife sold in 1990. **Mark:** Initials/full name football logo.

METZ, GREG T., c/o James Ranch HC 83, Cascade, ID 83611, Phone: 208-382-4336
    Specialties: Hunting and utility knives. **Prices:** $300 and up. **Remarks:** Natural handle materials; hand forged blades; 1084 and 1095. **Mark:** METZ (last name).

MICHINAKA, TOSHIAKI, I-679 Koyamacho-nishi, Totton-shi, Tottori 680-0947, JAPAN, Phone: 0857-28-5911

MICHO, KANDA, 7-32-5 Shinzutsumi-cho, Shinnanyo-city, Yamaguchi, JAPAN, Phone: 0834-62-1910

MICKLEY, TRACY, 42112 Kerns Dr., North Mankato, MN 56003, Phone: 507-947-3760, tracy@mickleyknives.com Web: www.mickleyknives.com
    Specialties: Working and collectable straight knives using mammoth ivory or burl woods, liner lock folders. **Patterns:** Custom and classic hunters, utility, fighters and Bowies. **Technical:** Grinding 154-CM, BG-42 forging 01 and 52100. **Prices:** Starting at $325 **Remarks:** Part-time since 1999. **Mark:** Last name.

MILFORD, BRIAN A., RD 2 Box 294, Knox, PA 16232, Phone: 814-797-2595, Fax: 814-226-4351
    Specialties: Traditional and working/using straight knives of his design or to customer specs. **Patterns:** Fighters, hunters and utility/camp knives. **Technical:** Forges Damascus and 52100; grinds 440C. **Prices:** $50 to $300; some to $750. **Remarks:** Part-time maker; first knife sold in 1991. Doing business as BAM Forge. **Mark:** Full name or initials.

MILITANO, TOM, CUSTOM KNIVES, 77 Jason Rd., Jacksonville, AL 36265-6655, Phone: 256-435-7132, jeffkin57@aol.com
    Specialties: Fixed blade, one-of-a-kind knives. **Patterns:** Bowies, fighters, hunters and tactical knives. **Technical:** Grinds 440C, ATS-34, A2, and Damascus. Hollow grinds, flat grinds, and decorative filework. **Prices:** $150 plus. **Remarks:** Part-time maker. **Mark:** Name, city and state in oval with maker in the center. Sold first knives in the mid to late 1980s. Memberships: founding member-New England Custom Knife Association, Flint River Knife Club.

MILLARD, FRED G., 27627 Kopezyk Ln., Richland Center, WI 53581, Phone: 608-647-5376
    Specialties: Working/using straight knives of his design or to customer specs. **Patterns:** Bowies, hunters, utility/camp knives, kitchen/steak knives. **Technical:** Grinds ATS-34, O1, D2 and 440C. Makes sheaths. **Prices:** $110 to $300. **Remarks:** Full-time maker; first knife sold in 1993. Doing business as Millard Knives. **Mark:** Mallard duck in flight with serial number.

MILLER, BOB, 7659 Fine Oaks Pl., Oakville, MO 63129, Phone: 314-846-8934
    Specialties: Mosaic Damascus; collector using straight knives and folders. **Patterns:** Hunters, Bowies, utility/camp knives, daggers. **Technical:** Forges own Damascus, mosaic-Damascus and 52100. **Prices:** $125 to $500. **Remarks:** Part-time maker; first knife sold in 1983. **Mark:** First and middle initials and last name, or initials.

MILLER, DON, 1604 Harrodsburg Rd., Lexington, KY 40503, Phone: 606-276-3299

MILLER, HANFORD J., Box 97, Cowdrey, CO 80434, Phone: 970-723-4708
    Specialties: Working knives in Moran-style; period pieces. **Patterns:** Bowies, fighters, camp knives and other large straight knives. **Technical:** Forges W2, 1095, 5160 and his own Damascus; differential tempers; offers wire inlay. **Prices:** $300 to $800; some to $3000. **Remarks:** Full-time maker; first knife sold in 1968. **Mark:** Initials or name within Bowie logo.

MILLER, JAMES P., 9024 Goeller Rd., RR 2, Box 28, Fairbank, IA 50629, Phone: 319-635-2294, Web: www.damascusknives.biz
    Specialties: All tool steel Damascus; working knives and period pieces. **Patterns:** Hunters, Bowies, camp knives and daggers. **Technical:** Forges and grinds 1095, 52100, 440C and his own Damascus. **Prices:** $100 to $350; some to $1500. **Remarks:** Full-time maker; first knife sold in 1970. **Mark:** First and middle initials, last name with knife logo.

MILLER, M.A., 11625 Community Center Dr., Unit #1531, Northglenn, CO 80233, Phone: 303-280-3816
    Specialties: Using knives for hunting. 3-1/2"-4" Loveless drop-point. Made to customer specs. **Patterns:** Skinners and camp knives. **Technical:** Grinds 440C, D2, O1 and ATS-34 Damascus miniatures. **Prices:** $225 to $350; miniatures $75 to $150. **Remarks:** Part-time maker; first knife sold in 1988. **Mark:** Last name stamped in block letters or first and middle initials, last name, maker, city and state with triangles on either side etched.

MILLER, MICHAEL, 2960 E Carver Ave, Kingman, AZ 86401, Phone: 928-757-1359
    Specialties: Hunters, bowies, and skinners with exotic burl wood, stag, ivory and gemstone handles. **Patterns:** 01 and I-6 Damascus 1084 and 1095 and 01 steel knives. **Technical:** L-6 and 01 patterned Damascus.

Prices: $150 to $1000. **Remarks:** Full-time maker since 2002, first knife sold 2000; doing business as M Miller Originals. **Mark:** First initial and last name with 'handmade' underneath.

MILLER, MICHAEL E., 1400 Skyview Dr., El Reno, OK 73036, Phone: 405-422-3602
    Specialties: Traditional working/using knives of his design. **Patterns:** Bowies, hunters and kitchen knives. **Technical:** Grinds ATS-34, CPM 440V; forges Damascus and cable Damascus and 52100. Prefers scrimshaw, fancy pins, basket weave and embellished sheaths. **Prices:** $80 to $300; some to $500. **Remarks:** Part-time maker; first knife sold in 1984. Doing business as Miller Custom Knives. **Mark:** First and middle initials, last name, maker, city and state. **Other:** Member of KG A of Oklahoma and Salt Fork Blacksmith Association.

MILLER, MICHAEL K., 28510 Santiam Hwy., Sweet Home, OR 97386, Phone: 541-367-4927, miller@ptlnet.net
    Specialties: Specializes in kitchen cutlery of his design or made to customer specs. **Patterns:** Hunters, utility/camp knives and kitchen cutlery. **Technical:** Grinds ATS-34, AEBL and 440-C. Wife does scrimshaw as well. Makes custom sheaths and holsters. **Prices:** $200. **Remarks:** Full-time maker; first knife sold in 1989. **Mark:** MandM Kustom Krafts

MILLER, R.D., 10526 Estate Lane, Dallas, TX 75238, Phone: 214-348-3496
    Specialties: One-of-a-kind collector-grade knives. **Patterns:** Boots, hunters, Bowies, camp and utility knives, fishing and bird knives, miniatures. **Technical:** Grinds a variety of steels to include O1, D2, 440C, 154CM and 1095. **Prices:** $65 to $300; some to $900. **Remarks:** Full-time maker; first knife sold in 1984. **Mark:** R.D. Custom Knives with date or bow and arrow logo.

MILLER, RICK, 516 Kanaul Rd., Rockwood, PA 15557, Phone: 814-926-2059
    Specialties: Working/using straight knives of his design and in standard patterns. **Patterns:** Bowies, daggers, hunters and friction folders. **Technical:** Grinds L6. Forges 5160, L6 and Damascus. Patterns for Damascus are random, twist, rose or ladder. **Prices:** $75 to $250; some to $400. **Remarks:** Part-time maker; first knife sold in 1982. **Mark:** Script stamp "R.D.M.".

MILLER, RONALD T., 12922 127th Ave. N., Largo, FL 34644, Phone: 813-595-0378 (after 5 p.m.)
    Specialties: Working straight knives in standard patterns. **Patterns:** Combat knives, camp knives, kitchen cutlery, fillet knives, locking folders and butterflies. **Technical:** Grinds D2, 440C and ATS-34; offers brass inlays and scrimshaw. **Prices:** $45 to $325; some to $750. **Remarks:** Part-time maker; first knife sold in 1984. **Mark:** Name, city and state in palm tree logo.

MILLS, LOUIS G., 9450 Waters Rd., Ann Arbor, MI 48103, Phone: 734-668-1839
    Specialties: High-art Japanese-style period pieces. **Patterns:** Traditional tantos, daggers and swords. **Technical:** Makes steel from iron; makes his own Damascus by traditional Japanese techniques. **Prices:** $900 to $2000; some to $8000. **Remarks:** Spare-time maker. **Mark:** Yasutomo in Japanese Kanji.

MILLS, MICHAEL, 5604 Lanham Station Rd., Lanham, MD 20706-2531, Phone: 301-459-7226
    Specialties: Working knives, Hunters, Skinners, Utility and Bowies. **Technical:** Forge 5160 Differential Heat-Treats. **Prices:** $200 and up. **Remarks:** Part-time maker, ABS Journeyman. **Mark:** Last name in script.

MINK, DAN, PO Box 861, 196 Sage Circle, Crystal Beach, FL 34681, Phone: 727-786-5408, DBMink@ij.net
    Specialties: Traditional and working knives of his design. **Patterns:** Bowies, fighters, folders and hunters. **Technical:** Grinds ATS-34, 440C and D2. Blades and tanges embellished with fancy filework. Uses natural and rare handle materials. **Prices:** $125 to $450. **Remarks:** Part-time maker; first knife sold in 1985. **Mark:** Name and star encircled by custom made, city, state.

MINNICK, JIM, 144 North 7th St., Middletown, IN 47356, Phone: 765-354-4108
    Specialties: Lever-lock folding art knives, liner-locks. **Patterns:** Stilettos, Persian and one-of-a-kind folders. **Technical:** Grinds and carves Damascus, stainless, and high-carbon. **Prices:** $950 to $7000. **Remarks:** Part-time maker; first knife sold in 1976. **Mark:** Minnick and JMJ. **Other:** Husband and wife team.

MIRABILE, DAVID, 1715 Glacier Ave., Juneau, AK 99801, Phone: 907-463-3404
    Specialties: Elegant edged weapons. **Patterns:** Fighters, Bowies, claws, tklinget daggers, executive desk knives. **Technical:** Forged high-carbon steels, his own Damascus; uses ancient walrus ivory and prehistoric bone extensively, very rarely uses wood. **Prices:** $350 to $7000.

Remarks: Full-time maker. Knives sold through art gallery in Juneau, AK. **Mark:** Last name etched or engraved.

MITCHELL, JAMES A., PO Box 4646, Columbus, GA 31904, Phone: 404-322-8582
Specialties: Fancy working knives. **Patterns:** Hunters, fighters, Bowies and locking folders. **Technical:** Grinds D2, 440C and commercial Damascus. **Prices:** $100 to $400; some to $900. **Remarks:** Part-time maker; first knife sold in 1976. Sells knives in sets. **Mark:** Signature and city.

MITCHELL, MAX, DEAN AND BEN, 3803 V.F.W. Rd., Leesville, LA 71440, Phone: 318-239-6416
Specialties: Hatchet and knife sets with folder and belt and holster all match. **Patterns:** Hunters, 200 L6 steel. **Technical:** L6 steel; soft back, hand edge. **Prices:** $300 to $500. **Remarks:** Part-time makers; first knife sold in 1965. Custom orders only; no stock. **Mark:** First names.

MITCHELL, WM. DEAN, PO Box 2, Warren, TX 77664, Phone: 409-547-2213, bebo@cminet.net
Specialties: Classic and period knives. **Patterns:** Bowies, hunters, daggers and swords. **Technical:** Forged carbon steel and Damascus 52100, 1095, 5160; makes pattern, composite and mosiac Damascus; offers filework. Makes wooden display cases. **Prices:** Mid-scale. **Remarks:** Hobbist maker since 1986. First knife sold in 1986.D.B.A. The Thicket Smithy. **Mark:** Full name with anvil, MS.

MITSUYUKI, ROSS, 94-1071 Kepakepa St, C-3, Waipahu, Hawaii 96797, Phone: 808-671-3335, Fax: 808-671-3335, www.hawaiiangrinds.net
Specialties: Working straight knives and folders. **Patterns:** Hunting, fighters, utility knives and boot knives. **Technical:** 440C, BG-42, ATS-34, 530V, and Damascus. **Prices:** $100 to $500. **Remarks:** Spare-time maker, first knife sold in 1998. **Mark:** Name, state, Hawaiian sea turtle.

MIVILLE-DESCHENES, ALAIN, 1952 Charles A Parent, Quebec, CANADA G2B 4B2, Phone: 418-845-0950, Fax: 418-845-0950, amd@miville-deschenes.com Web: www.miville-deschenes.com
Specialties: Working knives of his design or to customer specs and art knives. **Patterns:** Bowies, skinner, hunter, utility, camp knives, fighters, art knives. **Technical:** Grinds ATS-34, 440C, CPM S30V, 0-1, etc. **Prices:** $175 to $500; some higher. **Remarks:** Part-time maker; first knife sold in 2001. **Mark:** Logo (small hand) and initials (AMD).

MIZE, RICHARD, FOX CREEK FORGE, 2038 Fox Creek Rd., Lawrenceburg, KY 40342, Phone: 502-859-0602, foxcreek@kih.net WEB: www.foxcreekforge.com
Specialties: Forges spring steel, 5160, 10xx steels, natural handle materials. **Patterns:** Traditional working knives, period flavor Bowies, rifle knives. **Technical:** Does own heat treating, differential temper. **Prices:** $100 to $400. **Remarks:** Strongly advocates sole authorship. **Mark:** Initial M hot stamped.

MOJZIS, JULIUS, B. S. Timravy 6, 98511 Halic, Slovakia, Web: www.m-art.sk
Specialties: Art Knives. **Prices:** USD $2000. **Mark:** MOJZIS

MOMCILOVIC, GUNNAR, Nordlysv, 16, Waipahu, NORWAY, Phone: 0111-47-3287-3586

MONCUS, MICHAEL STEVEN, 1803 US 19 N, Smithville, GA 31787, Phone: 912-846-2408

MONK, NATHAN P., 721 County Rd 1462, Cullman, AL 35055-0602, Phone: 256-737-0463
Specialties: Traditional working and using straight knives of his design and to customer specs; fancy knives. **Patterns:** Bowies, daggers, fighters, hunters, utility/camp knives, bird knives and one-of-a-kinds. **Technical:** Grinds ATS-34, 440C and A2. **Prices:** $50 to $175. **Remarks:** Spare-time maker; first knife sold in 1990. **Mark:** First and middle initials, last name, city, state.

MONTANO, GUS A., 11217 Westonhill Dr., San Diego, CA 92126-1447, Phone: 619-273-5357
Specialties: Traditional working/using straight knives of his design. **Patterns:** Boots, Bowies and fighters. **Technical:** Grinds 1095 and 5160; grinds and forges cable. Double or triple hardened and triple drawn; hand-rubbed finish. Prefers natural handle materials. **Prices:** $200 to $400; some to $600. **Remarks:** Spare-time maker; first knife sold in 1997. **Mark:** First initial and last name.

MONTEIRO, VICTOR, 31, Rue D'Opprebais, 1360 Maleves Ste Marie, BELGIUM, Phone: 010 88 0441
Specialties: Working and fancy straight knives, folders and integrals of his design. **Patterns:** Fighters, hunters and kitchen knives. **Technical:** Grinds ATS-34, 440C, D2, Damasteel and other commercial Damascus, embellishment, filework and domed pins. **Prices:** $300 to $1000, some higher. **Remarks:** Part-time maker; first knife sold in 1989. **Mark:** Logo with initials connected.

MONTJOY, CLAUDE, 706 Indian Creek Rd., Clinton, SC 29325, Phone: 864-697-6160
Specialties: Folders, slip joint, lock, lock liner and inter frame. **Patterns:** Hunters, boots, fighters, some art knives and folders. **Technical:** Grinds ATS-34 and Damascus. Offers inlaid handle scales. **Prices:** $100 to $500. **Remarks:** Full-time maker; first knife sold in 1982. **Mark:** Montjoy. **Other:** Custom orders, no catalog.

MOONEY, MIKE, 19432 E Cloud Rd, Queen Creek, AZ 85242, Phone: 480-987-3576, mike@moonblades.com
Specialties: Working straight knives of his design or customers. **Technical:** Flat-grind, S30V, ATS-34, O1, commercial Damascus. **Patterns:** Fighters, bowies, daggers, hunters, kitchen, camp. **Remarks:** Doing business as moonblades.com. **Mark:** M. Mooney followed by crescent moon.

MOORE, JAMES B., 1707 N. Gillis, Ft. Stockton, TX 79735, Phone: 915-336-2113
Specialties: Classic working straight knives and folders of his design. **Patterns:** Hunters, Bowies, daggers, fighters, boots, utility/camp knives, locking folders and slip-joint folders. **Technical:** Grinds 440C, ATS-34, D2, L6, CPM and commercial Damascus. **Prices:** $85 to $700; exceptional knives to $1500. **Remarks:** Full-time maker; first knife sold in 1972. **Mark:** Name, city and state.

MOORE, MARVE, HC 89 Box 393, Willow, AK 99688, Phone: 907-232-0478, marvemoore@aol.com
Specialties: Fixed blades forged and stock removal. **Patterns:** Gunter, skinners, fighter, short swords. **Technical:** 100% of his work is done by hand. **Prices:** $100 to $500. **Remarks:** Also makes his own sheaths. **Mark:** -MM-.

MOORE, MICHAEL ROBERT, 70 Beaulieu St., Lowell, MA 01850, Phone: 978-479-0589, Fax: 978-441-1819

MOORE, TED, 340 E Willow St., Elizabethtown, PA 17022, Phone: 717-367-3939, tedmoore@supernet.com Web: www.tedmooreknives.com
Specialties: Damascus folders, cigar cutters. **Patterns:** Locking folders and slip joint. **Technical:** Grinds Damascus, high-carbon and stainless; also ATS-34 and D2. **Prices:** $250 to $1500. **Remarks:** Part-time maker; first knife sold 1993. Knife and gun leather also. **Mark:** Moore U.S.A.

MORAN JR., WM. F., PO Box 68, Braddock Heights, MD 21714, Phone: 301-371-7543
Specialties: High-art working knives of his design. **Patterns:** Fighters, camp knives, Bowies, daggers, axes, tomahawks, push knives and miniatures. **Technical:** Forges W2, 5160 and his own Damascus; puts silver wire inlay on most handles; uses only natural handle materials. **Prices:** $400 to $7500; some to $9000. **Remarks:** Full-time maker. **Mark:** W. F. Moran Jr. Master Smith MS.

MORETT, DONALD, 116 Woodcrest Dr., Lancaster, PA 17602-1300, Phone: 717-746-4888

MORGAN, JEFF, 9200 Arnaz Way, Santee, CA 92071, Phone: 619-448-8430
Specialties: Fancy working straight knives. **Patterns:** Hunters, fighters, boots, miniatures. **Technical:** Grinds D2, 440C and ATS-34; likes exotic handles. **Prices:** $60 to $300; some to $800. **Remarks:** Full-time maker; first knife sold in 1977. **Mark:** Initials connected.

MORGAN, TOM, 14689 Ellett Rd., Beloit, OH 44609, Phone: 330-537-2023
Specialties: Working straight knives and period pieces. **Patterns:** Hunters, boots and presentation tomahawks. **Technical:** Grinds O1, 440C and 154CM. **Prices:** Knives, $65 to $200; tomahawks, $100 to $325. **Remarks:** Full-time maker; first knife sold in 1977. **Mark:** Last name and type of steel used.

MORRIS, C.H., 1590 Old Salem Rd., Frisco City, AL 36445, Phone: 334-575-7425
Specialties: Liner lock folders. **Patterns:** Interframe liner locks. **Technical:** Grinds 440C and ATS-34. **Prices:** Start at $350. **Remarks:** Full-time maker; first knife sold in 1973. Doing business as Custom Knives. **Mark:** First and middle initials, last name.

MORRIS, DARRELL PRICE, 92 Union, St. Plymouth, Devon, ENGLAND PL1 3EZ, Phone: 0752 223546
Specialties: Traditional Japanese knives, Bowies and high-art knives. **Technical:** Nickel Damascus and mokamame. **Prices:** $1000 to $4000. **Remarks:** Part-time maker; first knife sold in 1990. **Mark:** Initials and Japanese name—Kuni Shigae.

MORRIS, ERIC, 306 Ewart Ave., Beckley, WV 25801, Phone: 304-255-3951

MORTENSON, ED, 2742 Hwy. 93 N, Darby, MT 59829, Phone: 406-821-3146, Fax: 406-821-3146
Specialties: Period pieces and working/using straight knives of his design, to customer specs and in standard patterns. **Patterns:** Bowies,

hunters and kitchen knives. **Technical:** Grinds ATS-34, 5160 and 1095. Sheath combinations; flashlight/knife, hatchet/knife, etc. **Prices:** $60 to $140; some to $300. **Remarks:** Full-time maker; first knife sold in 1993. Doing business as The Blade Lair. **Mark:** M with attached O.

MOSES, STEVEN, 1610 W Hemlock Way, Santa Ana, CA 92704

MOSIER, JOSHUA J., SPRING CREEK KNIFE WORKS, PO Box 476/608 7th St, Deshler, NE 68340, scknifeworks@mail.com
Specialties: Working straight and folding knives of his designs with customer specs. **Patterns:** Hunters, utilities, locking liner folders, kitchen and camp knives. **Technical:** Forges and grinds 5160, W2, L6, simple carbon steels and his own Damascus, uses some antique materials, provides a history of the materials used in each knife. **Prices:** $55 and up. **Remarks:** Part-time maker, sold first knife in 1986. **Mark:** SCKW.

MOSSER, GARY E., 11827 NE 102nd Place, Kirkland, WA 98033-5170, Phone: 425-827-2279, themossers@msn.com
Specialties: Working knives. **Patterns:** Hunters, skinners, camp knives, some art knives. **Technical:** Stock removal method; prefers ATS-34. **Prices:** $100 to $250; special orders and art knives are higher. **Remarks:** Part-time maker; first knife sold in 1976. **Mark:** Name.

MOULTON, DUSTY, 135 Hillview Lane, Loudon, TN 37774, Phone: 865-408-9779, Web: www.moultonknives.com
Specialties: Fancy and working straight knives. **Patterns:** Hunters, fighters, fantasy and miniatures. **Technical:** Grinds ATS-34 and Damascus. **Prices:** $300 to $2000. **Remarks:** Full-time maker; first knife sold in 1991. **Mark:** Last name. **Other:** Now doing engraving on own knives as well as other makers.

MOUNT, DON, 4574 Little Finch Ln., Las Vegas, NV 89115, Phone: 702-531-2925
Specialties: High-tech working and using straight knives of his design. **Patterns:** Bowies, fighters and utility/camp knives. **Technical:** Uses 440C and ATS-34. **Prices:** $150 to $300; some to $1000. **Remarks:** Part-time maker; first knife sold in 1985. **Mark:** Name below a woodpecker.

MOUNTAIN HOME KNIVES, PO Box 167, Jamul, CA 91935, Phone: 619-669-0833
Specialties: High-quality working straight knives. **Patterns:** Hunters, fighters, skinners, tantos, utility and fillet knives, Bowies and *san-mai* Damascus Bowies. **Technical:** Hollow-grind 440C by hand. Feature linen Micarta handles, nickel-silver handle bolts and handmade sheaths. **Prices:** $65 to $270. **Remarks:** Company owned by Jim English. **Mark:** Mountain Home Knives.

MOYER, RUSS, 1266 RD 425 So, Havre, MT 59501, Phone: 406-395-4423
Specialties: Working knives to customer specs. **Patterns:** Hunters, Bowies and survival knives. **Technical:** Forges W2 & 5160. **Prices:** $150 to $350. **Remarks:** Part-time maker; first knife sold in 1976. **Mark:** Initials in logo.

MULLER, JODY, PO Box 35, Pittsburg, MO 65724, Phone: 417-852-4306/417-752-3260, Web: www.mullerforge.com
Specialties: Hand engraving, carving and inlays, fancy folders. One-of-a-kind personal carry knives with billfold cases, cleavers and oriental styles. **Patterns:** One-of-a-kind fixed blades and folders in all styles. **Technical:** Forges patterned Damascus and high carbon steel. **Prices:** $200 and up. **Remarks:** Son and father team of part-time makers. Jody made first knife at age 12. Now does fine hand-engraving, carving and inlay. **Mark:** 4 Muller J.S.**Other:** Cross reference Muller Forge. Journeyman Smith full-time knifemaker.

MULLIN, STEVE, 500 Snowberry Lane, Sandpoint, ID 83864, Phone: 208-263-7492, knives@packriver.com Web: www.packriver.com
Specialties: Damascus period pieces and folders. **Patterns:** Full range of folders, hunters and Bowies. **Technical:** Forges and grinds O1, D2, 154CM and his own Damascus. Engraves. **Prices:** $100 to $2000. **Remarks:** Full-time maker; first knife sold in 1975. Sells line of using knives under Pack River Knife Co. **Mark:** Full name, city and state.

MUNROE, DERYK C., PO Box 3454, Bozeman, MT 59772

MURRAY, BILL, 1632 Rio Mayo, Green Valley, AZ 85614

MURSKI, RAY, 12129 Captiva Ct., Reston, VA 22091-1204, Phone: 703-264-1102
Specialties: Fancy working/using folders of his design. **Patterns:** Hunters, slip-joint folders and utility/camp knives. **Technical:** Grinds CPM-3V **Prices:** $125 to $500. **Remarks:** Spare-time maker; first knife sold in 1996. **Mark:** Etched name with serial number under name.

MYERS, PAUL, 644 Maurice St., Wood River, IL 62095, Phone: 618-258-1707
Specialties: Fancy working straight knives and folders. **Patterns:** Full range of folders, straight hunters and Bowies; tie tacks; knife and fork sets. **Technical:** Grinds D2, 440C, ATS-34 and 154CM. **Prices:** $100 to

$350; some to $3000. **Remarks:** Full-time maker; first knife sold in 1974. **Mark:** Initials with setting sun on front; name and number on back.

N

NATEN, GREG, 1804 Shamrock Way, Bakersfield, CA 93304-3921
Specialties: Fancy and working/using folders of his design. **Patterns:** Fighters, hunters and locking folders. **Technical:** Grinds 440C, ATS-34 and CPM440V. Heat-treats; prefers desert ironwood, stag and mother-of-pearl. Designs and sews leather sheaths for straight knives. **Prices:** $175 to $600; some to $950. **Remarks:** Spare-time maker; first knife sold in 1992. **Mark:** Last name above battle-ax, handmade.

NAVAGATO, ANGELO, 5 Commercial Apt 2, Camp Hill, PA 17011

NEALEY, IVAN F. (FRANK), Anderson Dam Rd., Box 65, HC #87, Mt. Home, ID 83647, Phone: 208-587-4060
Specialties: Working straight knives in standard patterns. **Patterns:** Hunters, skinners and utility knives. **Technical:** Grinds D2, 440C and 154CM. **Prices:** $90 to $135; some higher. **Remarks:** Part-time maker; first knife sold in 1975. **Mark:** Name.

NEALY, BUD, 1439 Poplar Valley Rd., Stroudsburg, PA 18360, Phone: 570-402-1018, Fax: 570-402-1019, budnealy@ptd.net Web: www.budnealyknifemaker.com
Specialties: Original design concealment knives with designer multi-concealment sheath system. **Patterns:** Concealment knives, boots, combat and collector pieces. **Technical:** Grinds ATS-34; uses Damascus. **Prices:** $200 to $2500. **Remarks:** Full-time maker; first knife sold in 1980. **Mark:** Name, city, state or signature.

NEDVED, DAN, 206 Park Dr., Kalispell, MT 59901, Phone: 406-752-5060
Specialties: Slip joint folders, liner locks, straight knives. **Patterns:** Mostly traditional or modern blend with traditional lines. **Technical:** Grinds ATS-34, 440C, 1095 and uses other makers Damascus. **Prices:** $95 and up. Mostly in the $150 to $200 range. **Remarks:** Part-time maker, averages 2 a month. **Mark:** Dan Nedved or Nedved with serial # on opposite side.

NEELY, GREG, 5419 Pine St., Bellaire, TX 77401, Phone: 713-991-2677, ediiorio@houston.rr.com
Specialties: Traditional patterns and his own patterns for work and/or collecting. **Patterns:** Hunters, Bowies and utility/camp knives. **Technical:** Forges own Damascus, 1084, 5160 and some tool steels. Differentially tempers. **Prices:** $225 to $5000. **Remarks:** Part-time maker; first knife sold in 1987. **Mark:** Last name or interlocked initials, MS.

NEILSON, J., RR 2 Box 16, Wyalusing, PA 18853, Phone: 570-746-4944, mountainhollow@emcs.net Web: www.mountainhollow.net
Specialties: Working and collectable fixed blade knives. **Patterns:** Hunter/fighters, Bowies, neck knives and daggers. **Technical:** Flat and convex grinds, 1084, 5160, maker's own Damascus. **Prices:** $200 to $1500. **Remarks:** Full-time maker, first knife sold in 2000. Doing business as Neilson's Mountain Hollow. **Mark:** J. Neilson. **Other:** Each knife comes with a sheath by Tess.

NELSON, BOB, 21 Glen Rd., Sparta, NJ 07871

NELSON, DR. CARL, 2500 N Robison Rd., Texarkana, TX 75501

NELSON, KEN, 11059 Hwy 73, Pittsville, WI 54466, Phone: 715-323-0538 or 715-884-6448, Email: dwarveniron@yahoo.com
Specialties: Working straight knives, period pieces. **Patterns:** Utility, hunters, dirks, daggers, throwers, hawks, axes, swords, pole arms and blade blanks as well. **Technical:** Forges 5160, 52100, W2, 10xx, L6, carbon steels and own Damascus. Do my own heat treating. **Prices:** $50 to $350, some to $3000. **Remarks:** Part-time maker. First knife sold in 1995. Doing business as Iron Wolf Forge. **Mark:** Stylized wolf paw print.

NELSON, TOM, PO Box 2298, Wilropark 1731, Gauteng, SOUTH AFRICA, Phone: 27 11 7663991, Fax: 27 11 7687161, tom.nelson@telkomsa.net
Specialties: Own Damascus (Hosaic etc.) **Patterns:** One of akind art knives, swords and axes. **Prices:** $500 to $1000.

NETO JR., NELSON AND DE CARVALHO, HENRIQUE M., R. Joao Margarido, No. 20-V, Guerra, Braganca Paulista, SP-12900-000, BRAZIL, Phone: 011-7843-6889, Fax: 011-7843-6889
Specialties: Straight knives and folders. **Patterns:** Bowies, katanas, jambyias and others. **Technical:** Forges high-carbon steels. **Prices:** $70 to $3000. **Remarks:** Full-time makers; first knife sold in 1990. **Mark:** HandN.

NEUHAEUSLER, ERWIN, Heiligenangerstrasse 15, 86179 Augsburg, GERMANY, Phone: 0821/81 49 97, eneuhaeusl@aol.com
Specialties: Using straight knives of his design. **Patterns:** Hunters, boots, bowies and folders. **Technical:** Grinds ATS-34, RWL-34 and

Damascus. **Prices:** $200 to $750. **Remarks:** Spare-time maker; first knife sold in 1991. **Mark:** Etched logo, last name and city.

NEVLING, MARK, BURR OAK KNIVES, PO Box 9, Hume, IL 61932, Phone: 217-887-2522

Specialties: Straight knives and folders of his own design. **Patterns:** Hunters, fighters, Bowies, folders, and small executive knives. **Technical:** Convex grinds, Forges, uses only high-carbon and Damascus. **Prices:** $200 to $2000. **Remarks:** Full-time maker, first knife sold 1988.

NEWCOMB, CORBIN, 628 Woodland Ave., Moberly, MO 65270, Phone: 660-263-4639

Specialties: Working straight knives and folders; period pieces. **Patterns:** Hunters, axes, Bowies, folders, buckskinned blades and boots. **Technical:** Hollow-grinds D2, 440C and 154CM; prefers natural handle materials. Makes own Damascus; offers cable Damascus. **Prices:** $100 to $500. **Remarks:** Full-time maker; first knife sold in 1982. Doing business as Corbin Knives. **Mark:** First name and serial number.

NEWHALL, TOM, 3602 E 42nd Stravenue, Tucson, AZ 85713, Phone: 520-721-0562, gggaz@aol.com

NEWTON, LARRY, 1758 Pronghorn Ct., Jacksonville, FL 32225, Phone: 904-221-2340, Fax: 904-220-4098, CNewton1234@aol.com

Specialties: Traditional and slender high-grade gentlemen's automatic folders, locking liner type tactical, and working straight knives. **Patterns:** Front release locking folders, interframes, hunters, and skinners. **Technical:** Grinds Damascus, ATS-34, 440C and D2. **Prices:** Folders start at $350, straights start at $150. **Remarks:** Spare-time maker; first knife sold in 1989. **Mark:** Last name.

NEWTON, RON, 223 Ridge Ln., London, AR 72847, Phone: 479-293-3001, rnewton@cei.net

Specialties: Mosaic Damascus folders with accelerated actions. **Patterns:** One-of-a-kind. **Technical:** 1084-15N20 steels used in his mosaic Damascus steels. **Prices:** $1000 to $5000. **Remarks:** Also making antique Bowie repros and various fixed blades. **Mark:** All capital letters in NEWTON "Western Invitation" font.

NICHOLSON, R. KENT, PO Box 204, Phoenix, MD 21131, Phone: 410-323-6925

Specialties: Large using knives. **Patterns:** Bowies and camp knives in the Moran-style. **Technical:** Forges W2, 9260, 5160; makes Damascus. **Prices:** $150 to $995. **Remarks:** Part-time maker; first knife sold in 1984. **Mark:** Name.

NIELSON, JEFF V., PO Box 365, Monroe, UT 84754, Phone: 801-527-4242, jun1u205@hotmail.com

Specialties: Classic knives of his design and to customer specs. **Patterns:** Fighters, hunters, locking folders; miniatures. **Technical:** Grinds 440C stainless and Damascus. **Prices:** $100 to $1200. **Remarks:** Part-time maker; first knife sold in 1991. **Mark:** Name, location.

NIEMUTH, TROY, 3143 North Ave., Sheboygan, WI 53083, Phone: 414-452-2927

Specialties: Period pieces and working/using straight knives of his design and to customer specs. **Patterns:** Hunters and utility/camp knives. **Technical:** Grinds 440C, 1095 and A2. **Prices:** $85 to $350; some to $500. **Remarks:** Full-time maker; first knife sold in 1995. **Mark:** Etched last name.

NILSSON, JOHNNY WALKER, Tingsstigen 11, SE Arvidsjaur, SWEDEN, Phone: 46-960-130-48, 0960.13048@telia.com Web: www.jwnknives.com

Specialties: High-end hand-carved and engraved Sami-style horn knives with sheaths. **Patterns:** Traditional Sami and own design. **Technical:** Forges, shapes and grinds carbon and Damascus, unique horn applications like sculpted and bent horn plates. **Prices:** $800 to $6000. **Remarks:** Maker since 1988. Nordic (5 countries) champion many times. Knives inspired by 10,000 year old indigenous Sami culture, combines traditional techniques and designs with hi sown innovations. Handles in reindeer horn, birch burl. Pewter and bark spaces, bark coloring. Sheaths in reindeer horn and leather with openings, file work, and engraved inlays. Hand stitches and hand tools leather. Yearly award in his name at Nordic Championship. **Mark:** JN on sheaths, handle, and wood custom boxes. JWN on blades.

NISHIUCHI, MELVIN S., 6121 Forest Park Dr., Las Vegas, NV 89156, Phone: 702-438-2327

Specialties: Collectable quality using/working knives. **Patterns:** Locking liner folders, fighters, hunters and fancy personal knives. **Technical:** Grinds ATS-34 and Devin Thomas Damascus; prefers semi-precious stone and exotic natural handle materials. **Prices:** $375 to $2000. **Remarks:** Part-time maker; first knife sold in 1985. **Mark:** Circle with a line above it.

NIX, ROBERT T., 4194 Cadillac, Wayne, MI 48184, Phone: 734-729-6468, merlin1215@wideopenwest.com

Specialties: Hunters, skinners, art, Bowie, camp/survival/boot folders. Most are file worked. Custom leather work available also, mainly sheaths/overlays, inlays, tooling, combinations of material/leather, micarta, wood, kydex, nylon. **Technical:** Stock removal, ATS-34, stainless Damascus, 440C, 420V, 440V, BG42, D2, 01, carbon Damascus. Every blade gets Rockwelled. Likes the natural handle materials best, but will use anything available; ivory, bone, horn, pearl, stabilized woods, micarta. **Prices:** Knives from $125 to $2500. Sheaths from $40 to $400. **Remarks:** Part-time maker, first knife sold in 1993. Make each piece as if it were for me. **Mark:** R.T. Nix in script or Nix in bold face.

NOLEN, R.D. AND STEVE, 105 Flowingwells Rd, Pottsboro, TX 75076, Phone: 903-786-2454, blademaster@nolenknives.com Web: www.nolenknives.com

Specialties: Working knives; display pieces. **Patterns:** Wide variety of straight knives, butterflies and buckles. **Technical:** Grind D2, 440C and 154CM. Offer filework; make exotic handles. **Prices:** $150 to $800; some higher. **Remarks:** Part-time maker; first knife sold in 1968. Steve is third generation maker. **Mark:** NK in oval logo.

NORDELL, INGEMAR, Skarpå 2103, 82041 Färila, SWEDEN, Phone: 0651-23347

Specialties: Classic working and using straight knives. **Patterns:** Hunters, Bowies and fighters. **Technical:** Forges and grinds ATS-34, D2 and Sandvik. **Prices:** $120 to $1500. **Remarks:** Part-time maker; first knife sold in 1985. **Mark:** Initials or name.

NOREN, DOUGLAS E., 14676 Boom Rd., Springlake, MI 49456, Phone: 616-842-4247, gwenhoren@novagate.com

Specialties: Hand forged blades, custom built and made to order. Hand file work, carving and casting. Stag and stacked handles. Replicas of Scagel and Joseph Rogers. Hand tooled custom made sheaths. **Technical:** 5160, 52100 and 1084 steel. **Prices:** Start at $250. **Remarks:** Sole authorship, works in all mediums, ABS Journey man msn., all knives come with a custom hand-tooled sheath. Also makes anvils. **Other:** Enjoy the challenge and meeting people.

NORFLEET, ROSS W., 3947 Tanbark Rd., Richmond, VA 23235, Phone: 804-276-4169, rossknife@aol.com

Specialties: Classic, traditional and working/using knives of his design or in standard patterns. **Patterns:** Hunters and folders. **Technical:** Hollow-grinds 440C and ATS-34. **Prices:** $150 to $550. **Remarks:** Part-time maker; first knife sold in 1992. **Mark:** Last name.

NORRIS, DON, 8710 N Hollybrook, Tucson, AZ 85742, Phone: 520-744-2494

Specialties: Classic and traditional working/using straight knives and folders of his design, or to customer specs etc. **Patterns:** Bowies, daggers, fighters, hunters and utility/camp knives. **Technical:** Grinds and forges Damascus; grinds ATS-34 and 440C. Cast sterling guards and bolsters on Bowies. **Prices:** $350 to $2000, some to $3500. **Remarks:** Full-time maker; first knife sold in 1990. Doing business as Norris Custom Knives. **Mark:** Last name.

NORTON, DON, 95N Wilkison Ave, Port Townsend, WA 98368-2534, Phone: 306-385-1978

Specialties: Fancy and plain straight knives. **Patterns:** Hunters, small Bowies, tantos, boot knives, fillets. **Technical:** Prefers 440C, Micarta, exotic woods and other natural handle materials. Hollow-grinds all knives except fillet knives. **Prices:** $185 to $2800; average is $200. **Remarks:** Full-time maker; first knife sold in 1980. **Mark:** Full name, Hsi Shuai, city, state.

NOTT, RON P., PO Box 281, Summerdale, PA 17093, Phone: 717-732-2763, neitznott@aol.com

Specialties: High-art folders and some straight knives. **Patterns:** Scale release folders. **Technical:** Grinds ATS-34, 416 and nickel-silver. Engraves, inlays gold. **Prices:** $250 to $3000. **Remarks:** Full-time maker; first knife sold in 1993. Doing business as Knives By Nott, customer engraving. **Mark:** First initial, last name and serial number.

NOWLAND, RICK, 3677 E Bonnie Rd., Waltonville, IL 62894, Phone: 618-279-3170, ricknowland@frontiernet.net

Specialties: Slip joint folders in traditional patterns. **Patterns:** Trapper, whittler, sowbelly, toothpick and copperhead. **Technical:** Uses ATS-34, bolsters and liners have integral construction. **Prices:** $225 to $1000. **Remarks:** Part-time maker. **Mark:** Last name.

NUNN, GREGORY, HC64 Box 2107, Castle Valley, UT 84532, Phone: 435-259-8607

Specialties: High-art working and using knives of his design; new edition knife with handle made from anatomized dinosaur bone; first ever made. **Patterns:** Flaked stone knives. **Technical:** Uses gem-quality agates, jaspers and obsidians for blades. **Prices:** $250 to $2300. **Remarks:** Full-time maker; first knife sold in 1989. **Mark:** Name, knife and edition numbers, year made.

O

O'DELL, CLYDE, 176 Ouachita 404, Camden, AR 71701, Phone: 870-574-2754, abcodell@arkansas.net
Specialties: Working knives. **Patterns:** Hunters, camp knives, Bowies, daggers, tomahawks. **Technical:** Forges 5160 and 1084. **Prices:** Starting at $125. **Remarks:** Spare-time maker. **Mark:** Last name.

O'HARE, SEAN, PO Box 374, Fort Simpson, NT, CANADA X0E 0N0, Phone: 867-695-2619, sean@ohareknives.ca Web: www.ohareknives.ca
Specialties: Fixed blade hunters and tactical knives. **Patterns:** Neck knives to larger hunter and tactical knives. **Technical:** Stock removal, full and hidden tang knives. **Prices:** $115 USD to $300 USD. **Remarks:** Strives to balance aesthetics, functionality and durability. **Mark:** 1st is "OHARE KNIVES", 2nd is "NWT CANADA".

O'MALLEY, DANIEL, 4338 Evanston Ave. N, Seattle, WA 98103, Phone: 206-527-0315
Specialties: Custom chef's knives. **Remarks:** Making knives since 1997.

OBRIEN, GEORGE, 22511 Tullis Trails Ct., Katy, TX 77494-8265

OCHS, CHARLES F., 124 Emerald Lane, Largo, FL 33771, Phone: 727-536-3827, Fax: 727-536-3827, chuckandbelle@juno.com
Specialties: Working knives; period pieces. **Patterns:** Hunters, fighters, Bowies, buck skinners and folders. **Technical:** Forges 52100, 5160 and his own Damascus. **Prices:** $150 to $1800; some to $2500. **Remarks:** Full-time maker; first knife sold in 1978. **Mark:** OX Forge.

ODGEN, RANDY W., 10822 Sage Orchard, Houston, TX 77089, Phone: 713-481-3601

ODOM JR., VICTOR L., PO Box 572, North, SC 29112, Phone: 803-247-5614, vlodom@joimail.com
Specialties: Forged knives and tomahawks; stock removal knives. **Patterns:** Hunters, Bowies and folders. **Technical:** Use 1095, 5160, 52100 high carbon and alloy steels, ATS-34, and 55. **Prices:** Straight knives $60.00 and up.Folders @250.00 and up. **Remarks:** Student of Mr. George Henron. **Mark:** Steel stamp "ODOM" and etched "Odom Forge North, SC" plus a serial number. **Other:** SCAK.ORG

OGDEN, BILL, OGDEN KNIVES, PO Box 52, Avis, PA 17721, Phone: 570-753-5568
Specialties: One-of-a-kind, liner-lock folders, hunters, skinners, minis. **Technical:** Grinds ATS-34, 440-C, D2, 52100, Damascus, natural and unnatural handle materials, hand-stitched custom sheaths. **Prices:** $50 and up. **Remarks:** Part-time maker since 1992. **Marks:** Last name or "OK" stamp (Ogden Knives).

OGLETREE JR., BEN R., 2815 Israel Rd., Livingston, TX 77351, Phone: 409-327-8315
Specialties: Working/using straight knives of his design. **Patterns:** Hunters, kitchen and utility/camp knives. **Technical:** Grinds ATS-34, W1 and 1075; heat-treats. **Prices:** $200 to $400. **Remarks:** Part-time maker; first knife sold in 1955. **Mark:** Last name, city and state in oval with a tree on either side.

OLIVE, MICHAEL E., HC 78 Box 442, Leslie, AR 72645, Phone: 870-363-4452

OLIVER, TODD D., 894 Beaver Hollow, Spencer, IN 47460, Phone: 812-829-1762
Specialties: Damascus hunters and daggers. High-carbon as well. **Patterns:** Ladder, twist random. **Technical:** Sole author of all his blades. **Prices:** $350 and up. **Remarks:** Learned bladesmithing from Jim Batson at the ABS school and Damascus from Billy Merritt in Indiana. **Mark:** T.D. Oliver Spencer IN. **Other:** Two crossed swords and a battle ax.

OLOFSON, CHRIS, 29 KNIVES, 1 Kendall SQ Bldg. 600, Cambridge, MA 02139, Phone: 617-492-0451, artistacie@earthlink.net

OLSON, ROD, Box 5973, High River, AB, CANADA T1V 1P6, Phone: 403-652-2744, Fax: 403-646-5838
Specialties: Lockback folders with gold toothpicks. **Patterns:** Locking folders. **Technical:** Grinds ATS-34 blades and spring; filework; 14kt bolsters and liners. **Prices:** Mid range. **Remarks:** Part-time maker; first knife sold in 1979. **Mark:** Last name on blade.

OLSON, DARROLD E., PO Box 1539, Springfield, OR 97477, Phone: 541-726-8300/541-914-7238
Specialties: Straight knives and folders of his design and to customer specs. **Patterns:** Hunters, liner locks and locking folders. **Technical:** Grinds 440C, ATS-34 and 154CM. Uses anodized titanium; sheaths wet-molded. **Prices:** $150 to $350. **Remarks:** Part-time maker; first knife sold in 1989. **Mark:** Etched logo, year, type of steel and name.

OLSON, WAYNE C., 890 Royal Ridge Dr., Bailey, CO 80421, Phone: 303-816-9486
Specialties: High-tech working knives. **Patterns:** Hunters to folding lockers; some integral designs. **Technical:** Grinds 440C, 154CM and ATS-34; likes hand-finishes; precision-fits stainless steel fittings—no solder, no nickel silver. **Prices:** $275 to $600; some to $3000. **Remarks:** Part-time maker; first knife sold in 1979. **Mark:** Name, maker.

OLSZEWSKI, STEPHEN, 1820 Harkney Hill Rd., Coventry, RI 02816, Phone: 401-397-4774, antlers53@msn.com Web: www.olszewskiknives.com
Specialties: Lock back, liner locks, automatics (art knives). **Patterns:** One-of-a-kind art knives specializing in figurals. **Technical:** Damascus steel, titanium file worked liners, fossil ivory and pearl. **Prices:** $1800 to $6500. **Remarks:** Will custom build to your specifications. **Other:** Quality work with guarantee. **Mark:** SCO inside fish symbol. Also "Olszewski".

ONION, KENNETH J., 47-501 Hui Kelu St., Kaneohe, HI 96744, Phone: 808-239-1300, Fax: 808-289-1301, shopjunky@aol.com Web: www.kenonionknives.com
Specialties: Mostly folders featuring "speed safe", some fixed blades and miscellany. **Patterns:** Hybrid, art, fighter, utility. **Technical:** S-30X, BG-42, cowey Y, Damascus. **Prices:** $500 to $15,000. **Remarks:** Full-time maker; designer, first knife sold in 1991. **Mark:** Name and state.

ORTEGA, BEN M., 165 Dug Rd., Wyoming, PA 18644, Phone: 717-696-3234

ORTON, RICH, 3625 Fleming St., Riverside, CA 92509, Phone: 909-685-3019, ortonknifeworks@earthlink.net Web: www.ortonknifeworks.com
Specialties: Collectible folders, using and collectible straight knives. **Patterns:** Wharncliffe, gents, tactical, boot, neck knives, bird and trout, hunters, camp, Bowie. **Technical:** Grinds ATS-34, Jim Fergeson Damascus titanium liners, bolsters, anodize, lots of filework, jigged and picked bone, giraffe bone. Scrimshaw on some. **Prices:** Folders $300 to $600; straight $100 to $750. **Remarks:** Full-time maker; first knife sold in 1992. Doing business as Orton Knife Works. Now making folders. **Mark:** Rich Orton (maker) Riverside, CA.

OSBORNE, DONALD H., 5840 N McCall, Clovis, CA 93611, Phone: 559-299-9483, Fax: 559-298-1751, oforge@sbcglobal.net
Specialties: Traditional working using straight knives and folder of his design. **Patterns:** Working straight knives, Bowies, hunters, camp knives and folders. **Technical:** Forges carbon steels and makes Damascus. Grinds ATS-34, 154CM, and 440C. **Prices:** $150 and up. **Remarks:** Part-time maker. **Mark:** Last name logo and J.S.

OSBORNE, WARREN, 215 Edgefield, Waxahachie, TX 75165, Phone: 972-935-0899, Fax: 972-937-9004
Specialties: Investment grade collectible, interframes, one-of-a-kinds; unique locking mechanisms. **Patterns:** Folders; bolstered and interframes; conventional lockers, front lockers and back lockers; some slip-joints; some high-art pieces; fighters. **Technical:** Grinds ATS-34, 440 and 154; some Damascus and CPM400V. **Prices:** $400 to $2000; some to $4000. Interframes $650 to $1500. **Remarks:** Full-time maker; first knife sold in 1980. **Mark:** Last name in boomerang logo.

OTT, FRED, 1257 Rancho Durango Rd., Durango, CO 81303, Phone: 970-375-9669
Patterns: Bowies,hunters and daggers. **Technical:** Forges 1084-5160 and Damascus **Prices:** $250 to $1000. **Remarks:** Full-time maker. **Mark:** Last name.

OVEREYNDER, T.R., 1800 S. Davis Dr., Arlington, TX 76013, Phone: 817-277-4812, Fax: 817-277-4812, trovereynderknives@sbcglobal.net
Specialties: Highly finished collector-grade knives. Multi- Blades **Patterns:** Fighters, Bowies, daggers, locking folders, slip-joints and 90 percent collector-grade interframe folders. **Technical:** Grinds D2, BG-42, S-60V, S-30V, 154CM, RWL-34 vendor supplied Damascus. Has been making titanium-frame folders since 1977. **Prices:** $500 to $1500; some to $7000. **Remarks:** Full-time maker; first knife sold in 1977. Doing business as TRO Knives. **Mark:** T.R. OVEREYNDER KNIVES, city and state.

OWENS, DONALD, 2274 Lucille Ln., Melbourne, FL 32935, Phone: 321-254-9765

OWENS, JOHN, 14500 CR 270, Nathrop, CO 81236, Phone: 719-395-0870
Specialties: Hunters. **Prices:** $200 to $275; some to $650. **Remarks:** Spare-time maker. **Mark:** Last name.

OWNBY, JOHN C., 3316 Springbridge Ln., Plano, TX 75025, john@johnownby.com Web: www.johnownby.com
Specialties: Hunters, utility/camp knives. **Patterns:** Hunters, locking folders and utility/camp knives. **Technical:** 440C, D2 and ATS-34. All blades are flat ground. Prefers natural materials for handles—exotic woods, horn and antler. **Prices:** $150 to $350; some to $500. **Remarks:**

Part-time maker; first knife sold in 1993. **Mark:** Name, city, state. **Other:** Doing business as John C. Ownby Handmade Knives.

OYSTER, LOWELL R., 543 Grant Rd., Corinth, ME 04427, Phone: 207-884-8663
Specialties: Traditional and original designed multi-blade slip-joint folders. **Patterns:** Hunters, minis, camp and fishing knives. **Technical:** Grinds O1; heat-treats. **Prices:** $55 to $450; some to $750. **Remarks:** Full-time maker; first knife sold in 1981. **Mark:** A scallop shell.

P

PACHI, FRANCESCO, Via Pometta, 1, 17046 Sassello (SV), ITALY, Phone: 019 720086, Fax: 019 720086, Web: www.pachi-knives.com
Specialties: Folders and straight knives of his design. **Patterns:** Utility, hunters and skinners. **Technical:** Grinds RWL-34, CPM S30V and Damascus. **Prices:** $800 to $3500. **Remarks:** Full-time maker; first knife sold in 1991. **Mark:** Logo with last name.

PACKARD, BOB, PO Box 311, Elverta, CA 95626, Phone: 916-991-5218
Specialties: Traditional working/using straight knives of his design and to customer specs. **Patterns:** Hunters, fishing knives, utility/camp knives. **Technical:** Grinds ATS-34, 440C; Forges 52100, 5168 and cable Damascus. **Prices:** $75 to $225. **Mark:** Engraved name and year.

PADGETT JR., EDWIN L., 340 Vauxhall St., New London, CT 06320-3838, Phone: 860-443-2938
Specialties: Skinners and working knives of any design. **Patterns:** Straight and folding knives. **Technical:** Grinds ATS-34 or any tool steel upon request. **Prices:** $50 to $300. **Mark:** Name.

PADILLA, GARY, PO Box 6928, Auburn, CA 95604, Phone: 530-888-6992, gkpadilla@yahoo.com
Specialties: Unique knives of all designs and uses. **Patterns:** Hunters, kitchen knives, utility/camp knives and obsidian ceremonial knives. **Technical:** Grinds 440C, ATS-34, O1 and Damascus. **Prices:** Generally $100 to $200. **Remarks:** Part-time maker; first knife sold in 1977. Doing business as Bighorn Knifeworks. **Mark:** Stylized initials or name over company name.

PAGE, LARRY, 1200 Mackey Scott Rd., Aiken, SC 29801-7620, Phone: 803-648-0001
Specialties: Working knives of his design. **Patterns:** Hunters, boots and fighters. **Technical:** Grinds ATS-34. **Prices:** Start at $85. **Remarks:** Part-time maker; first knife sold in 1983. **Mark:** Name, city and state in oval.

PAGE, REGINALD, 6587 Groveland Hill Rd., Groveland, NY 14462, Phone: 716-243-1643
Specialties: High-art straight knives and one-of-a-kind folders of his design. **Patterns:** Hunters, locking folders and slip-joint folders. **Technical:** Forges O1, 5160 and his own Damascus. Prefers natural handle materials but will work with Micarta. **Remarks:** Spare-time maker; first knife sold in 1985. **Mark:** First initial, last name.

PAINTER, TONY, 87 Fireweed Dr, Whitehorse Yukon, CANADA Y1A 5T8, Phone: 867-633-3323, jimmies@klondiker.com Web: www.tonypainterdesigns.com
Specialties: One-of-a-kind using knives, some fancy , fixed and folders. **Patterns:** No fixed patterns. **Technical:** Grinds ATS-34, D2, O1, S30V, Damascus stain finish. Prefers to use exotic woods and other natural materials. Micarta and G10 on working knives. **Prices:** Starting at $200. **Remarks:** Full-time knife maker and carver. First knife sold in 1996. **Mark:** Two stamps used: initials TP in a circle and painter.

PALAZZO, TOM, 207-30 Jordon Dr., Bayside, NY 11360, Phone: 718-352-2170, tpknives@aol.com
Specialties: Fixed blades, custom sheaths, neck knives. **Patterns:** No fixed patterns. **Prices:** $150 and up.

PALMER, TAYLOR, TAYLOR-MADE SCENIC KNIVES INC., Box 97, Blanding, UT 84511, Phone: 435-678-2523, taylormadewoodeu@citlink.net
Specialties: Bronze carvings inside of blade area. **Prices:** $250 and up. **Mark:** Taylor Palmer Utah.

PANAK, PAUL S., 9000 Stanhope Kellogsville Rd., Kinsman, OH 44428, Phone: 330-876-8473, burn@burnknives.com Web: www.burnknives.com
Specialties: Italian-styled knives. **Patterns:** Vintage-styled Italians, fighting folders and high art gothic-styles all with various mechanisms. **Technical:** Grinds ATS-34, 154 CM, 440C and Damascus. **Prices:** $800 to $3000. **Remarks:** Full-time maker, first knife sold in 1998. **Mark:** "Burn".

PANKIEWICZ, PHILIP R., RFD #1, Waterman Rd., Lebanon, CT 06249
Specialties: Working straight knives. **Patterns:** Hunters, daggers, minis and fishing knives. **Technical:** Grinds D2, 440C and 154CM. **Prices:** $60 to $125; some to $250. **Remarks:** Spare-time maker; first knife sold in 1975. **Mark:** First initial in star.

PARDUE, JOE, PO Box 693, Spurger, TX 77660, Phone: 409-429-7074, Fax: 409-429-5657

PARDUE, MELVIN M., Rt. 1, Box 130, Repton, AL 36475, Phone: 334-248-2447, mpardue@frontiernet.net Web: www.melpardueknives.com
Specialties: Folders, collectable, combat, utility and tactical. **Patterns:** Lockback, liner lock, pushbutton; all blade and handle patterns. **Technical:** Grinds 154-CM, 440-C, 12-C-27. Forges Mokume and Damascus. Uses Titanium. **Prices:** $400 to $1600. **Remarks:** Full-time maker; Guild member, ABS member, AFC member. **Mark:** Mel Pardue or Pardue. **Other:** First knife made 1957; first knife sold professionally 1974.

PARKER, CLIFF, 6350 Tulip Dr., Zephyrhills, FL 33544, Phone: 813-973-1682
Specialties: Damascus gent knives. **Patterns:** Locking liners, some straight knives. **Technical:** Mostly use 1095, 1084, 15N20, 203E and powdered steel. **Prices:** $700 to $1800. **Remarks:** Making own Damascus and specializing in mosaics; first knife sold in 1996. **Mark:** CP. **Other:** Full-time beginning in 2000.

PARKER, J.E., 11 Domenica Cir., Clarion, PA 16214, Phone: 814-226-4837, Web: www.jimparker.knives.com
Specialties: Fancy/embellished, traditional and working straight knives of his design and to customer specs. Engraving and scrimshaw by the best in the business. **Patterns:** Bowies, hunters and liner lock folders. **Technical:** Grinds 440C, 440V, ATS-34 and nickel Damascus. Prefers mastodon, oosik, amber and malachite handle material. **Prices:** $75 to $5200. **Remarks:** Full-time maker; first knife sold in 1991. Doing business as Custom Knife. **Mark:** J E Parker and Clarion PA stamped or etched in blade.

PARKER, ROBERT NELSON, 5223 Wilhelm Rd. N.W., Rapid City, MI 49676, Fax: 248-545-8211, rnparkerknives@wowway.com
Specialties: Traditional working and using straight knives of his design. **Patterns:** Hunters, fighters, utility/camp knives; some Bowies. **Technical:** Grinds ATS-34;GB-42,S-30V forges O1, 530V, 5160, L6 hollow and flat grinds, full and hidden tangs. Hand-stitched leather sheaths. **Prices:** $350 to $500; some to $1500. **Remarks:** Full-time maker; first knife sold in 1986. **Mark:** Full name.

PARKS, BLANE C., 15908 Crest Dr., Woodbridge, VA 22191, Phone: 703-221-4680
Specialties: Knives of his design. **Patterns:** Boots, Bowies, daggers, fighters, hunters, kitchen knives, locking and slip-joint folders, utility/camp knives, letter openers and friction folders. **Technical:** Grinds ATS-34, 440C, D2 and other carbon steels. Offers filework, silver wire inlay and wooden sheaths. **Prices:** Start at $250 and up. **Remarks:** Part-time maker; first knife sold in 1993. Doing business as B.C. Parks Knives. **Mark:** First and middle initials, last name.

PARKS, JOHN, 3539 Galilee Church Rd., Jefferson, GA 30549, Phone: 706-367-4916
Specialties: Traditional working and using straight knives of his design. **Patterns:** Trout knives, hunters and integral bolsters. **Technical:** Forges 1095 and 5168. **Prices:** $175 to $450; some to $650. **Remarks:** Part-time maker; first knife sold in 1989. **Mark:** Initials.

PARLER, THOMAS O., 11 Franklin St., Charleston, SC 29401, Phone: 803-723-9433

PARRISH, ROBERT, 271 Allman Hill Rd., Weaverville, NC 28787, Phone: 828-645-2864
Specialties: Heavy-duty working knives of his design or to customer specs. **Patterns:** Survival and duty knives; hunters and fighters. **Technical:** Grinds 440C, D2, O1 and commercial Damascus. **Prices:** $200 to $300; some to $6000. **Remarks:** Part-time maker; first knife sold in 1970. **Mark:** Initials connected, sometimes with city and state.

PARRISH III, GORDON A., 940 Lakloey Dr., North Pole, AK 99705, Phone: 907-488-0357
Specialties: Classic and high-art straight knives of his design and to customer specs; working and using knives. **Patterns:** Bowies and hunters. **Technical:** Grinds tool steel and ATS-34. Uses mostly Alaskan handle materials. **Prices:** $150 to $1000. **Remarks:** Spare-time maker; first knife sold in 1980. **Mark:** Last name, state.

PARSONS, MICHAEL R., MCKEE KNIVES, 7042 McFarland Rd., Indianapolis, IN 46227, Phone: 317-784-7943, clparsons@aol.com
Specialties: Hand-forged fixed-blade knives, all fancy but all are useable knives. **Patterns:** Engraves, carves, wire inlay, and leather work. All knives one-of-a-kind. **Technical:** Blades forged from files, all work hand done. **Prices:** $350 to $2000. **Mark:** McKee.

PASSMORE, JIMMY D., 316 SE Elm, Hoxie, AR 72433, Phone: 870-886-1922

PATRICK, BOB, 12642 24A Ave., S. Surrey, B.C., CANADA V4A 8H9, Phone: 604-538-6214, Fax: 604-888-2683, bob@knivesonnet.com Web: www.knivesonnet.com
Specialties: Presentation pieces of his design only. **Patterns:** Bowies, push daggers, art pieces. **Technical:** D2, 5160, Damascus. **Prices:** Fair. **Remarks:** Full-time maker; first knife sold in 1987. Doing business as Crescent Knife Works. **Mark:** Logo with name and province or Crescent Knife Works.

PATRICK, CHUCK, PO Box 127, Brasstown, NC 28902, Phone: 828-837-7627
Specialties: Period pieces. **Patterns:** Hunters, daggers, tomahawks, pre-Civil War folders. **Technical:** Forges hardware, his own cable and Damascus, available in fancy pattern and mosaic. **Prices:** $150 to $1000; some higher. **Remarks:** Full-time maker. **Mark:** Hand-engraved name or flying owl.

PATRICK, PEGGY, PO Box 127, Brasstown, NC 28902, Phone: 828-837-7627
Specialties: Authentic period and Indian sheaths, braintan, rawhide, beads and quill work. **Technical:** Does own braintan, rawhide; uses only natural dyes for quills, old color beads.

PATRICK, WILLARD C., PO Box 5716, Helena, MT 59604, Phone: 406-458-6552, Fax: 406-458-7068, wkamar2@onewest.net
Specialties: Working straight knives and one-of-a-kind art knives of his design or to customer specs. **Patterns:** Hunters, Bowies, fish, patch and kitchen knives. **Technical:** Grinds ATS-34, 1095, O1, A2 and Damascus. **Prices:** $100 to $2,000. **Remarks:** Full-time maker; first knife sold in 1989. Doing business as Wil-A-Mar Cutlery. **Mark:** Shield with last name and a dagger.

PATTAY, RUDY, 510 E. Harrison St., Long Beach, NY 11561, Phone: 516-431-0847, dolphinp@optonline.net
Specialties: Fancy and working straight knives of his design. **Patterns:** Bowies, hunters, utility/camp knives. **Technical:** Hollow-grinds ATS-34, 440C, O1. Offers commercial Damascus, stainless steel soldered guards; fabricates guard and butt cap on lathe and milling machine. Heat-treats. Prefers synthetic handle materials. Offers hand-sewn sheaths. **Prices:** $100 to $350; some to $500. **Remarks:** Part-time maker; first knife sold in 1990. **Mark:** First initial, last name in sorcerer logo.

PATTERSON, PAT, Box 246, Barksdale, TX 78828, Phone: 830-234-3586, pat@pattersonknives.com
Specialties: Traditional fixed blades and liner lock folders. **Patterns:** Hunters and folders. **Technical:** Grinds 440C, ATS-34, D2, 01 and Damascus. **Prices:** $250 to $1000. **Remarks:** Full-time maker. First knife sold in 1991. **Mark:** Name and city.

PATTON, DICK AND ROB, 6803 View Ln., Nampa, ID 83687, Phone: 208-468-4123, grpatton@pattonknives.com Web: www.pattonknives.com
Specialties: Custom Damascus, hand forged, fighting knives-Bowie and tactical. **Patterns:** Mini Bowie, Merlin Fighter, Mandrita Fighting Bowie. **Prices:** $100 to $2000.

PAULO, FERNANDES R., Raposo Tavares, No. 213, Lencois Paulista, 18680, Sao Paulo, BRAZIL, Phone: 014-263-4281
Specialties: An apprentice of Jose Alberto Paschoarelli, his designs are heavily based on the later designs. **Technical:** Grinds tool steels and stainless steels. Part-time knife maker. **Prices:** Start from $100. **Mark:** P.R.F.

PAWLOWSKI, JOHN R., 4349 William Styron Sq N, Newport News, VA 23606, Phone: 757-223-0613, www.virginiacustomcutlery.com
Specialties: Traditional working and using straight knives and folders. **Patterns:** Hunters, Bowies, fighters and camp knives. **Technical:** Stock removal, grinds 440C, ATS-34, 154CM and buys Damascus. **Prices:** $150 to $500; some higher. **Remarks:** Part-time maker, first knife sold in 1983. **Mark:** Early mark, name over attacking Eagle and Alaska. Current mark, name over attacking Eagle and Virginia.

PEAGLER, RUSS, PO Box 1314, Moncks Corner, SC 29461, Phone: 803-761-1008
Specialties: Traditional working straight knives of his design and to customer specs. **Patterns:** Hunters, fighters, boots. **Technical:** Hollow-grinds 440C, ATS-34 and O1; uses Damascus steel. Prefers bone handles. **Prices:** $85 to $300; some to $500. **Remarks:** Spare-time maker; first knife sold in 1983. **Mark:** Initials.

PEASE, W.D., 657 Cassidy Pike, Ewing, KY 41039, Phone: 606-845-0387, Web: www.wdpeaseknives.com
Specialties: Display-quality working folders. **Patterns:** Fighters, tantos and boots; locking folders and interframes. **Technical:** Grinds ATS-34 and commercial Damascus; has own side-release lock system. **Prices:** $500 to $1000; some to $3000. **Remarks:** Full-time maker; first knife sold in 1970. **Mark** First and middle initials, last name and state. W. D. Pease Kentucky.

PEELE, BRYAN, 219 Ferry St., PO Box 1363, Thompson Falls, MT 59873, Phone: 406-827-4633
Specialties: Fancy working and using knives of his design. **Patterns:** Hunters, Bowies and fighters. **Technical:** Grinds 440C, ATS-34, D2, O1 and commercial Damascus. **Prices:** $110 to $300; some to $900. **Remarks:** Part-time maker; first knife sold in 1985. **Mark:** The Elk Rack, full name, city, state.

PENDLETON, LLOYD, 24581 Shake Ridge Rd., Volcano, CA 95689, Phone: 209-296-3353, Fax: 209-296-3353
Specialties: Contemporary working knives in standard patterns. **Patterns:** Hunters, fighters and boots. **Technical:** Grinds 154CM and ATS-34; mirror finishes. **Prices:** $400 to $725; some to $2500. **Remarks:** Full-time maker; first knife sold in 1973. **Mark:** First initial, last name logo, city and state.

PENDRAY, ALFRED H., 13950 NE 20th St., Williston, FL 32696, Phone: 352-528-6124
Specialties: Working straight knives and folders; period pieces. **Patterns:** Fighters and hunters, axes, camp knives and tomahawks. **Technical:** Forges Wootz steel; makes his own Damascus; makes traditional knives from old files and rasps. **Prices:** $125 to $1000; some to $3500. **Remarks:** Part-time maker; first knife sold in 1954. **Mark:** Last initial in horseshoe logo.

PENFOLD, MICK, PENFOLD KNIVES, 5 Highview Close, Tremar, Cornwall PL14 5SJ, ENGLAND, Phone: 01579-345783, mickpenfold@btinternet.com WEB: www.penfoldknives.co.uk
Specialties: Hunters, fighters, Bowies. **Technical:** Grinds 440C, ATS-34, and Damascus. **Prices:** $150 to $1200. **Remarks:** Part-time maker. First knives sold in 1999. **Mark:** Last name.

PENNINGTON, C.A., 163 Kainga Rd., Kainga Christchurch 8009, NEW ZEALAND, Phone: 03-3237292, capennington@xtra.co.nz
Specialties: Classic working and collectors knives. Folders a specialty. **Patterns:** Classical styling for hunters and collectors. **Technical:** Forges his own all tool steel Damascus. Grinds D2 when requested. **Prices:** $240 to $2000. **Remarks:** Full-time maker; first knife sold in 1988. **Mark:** Name, country. **Other:** Color brochure $3.

PEPIOT, STEPHAN, 73 Cornwall Blvd., Winnipeg, Man., CANADA R3J-1E9, Phone: 204-888-1499
Specialties: Working straight knives in standard patterns. **Patterns:** Hunters and camp knives. **Technical:** Grinds 440C and industrial hacksaw blades. **Prices:** $75 to $125. **Remarks:** Spare-time maker; first knife sold in 1982. Not currently taking orders. **Mark:** PEP.

PERRY, CHRIS, 1654 W. Birch, Fresno, CA 93711, Phone: 209-498-2342
Specialties: Traditional working/using straight knives of his design. **Patterns:** Boots, hunters and utility/camp knives. **Technical:** Grinds ATS-34 and 416 ss fittings. **Prices:** $190 to $225. **Remarks:** Spare-time maker. **Mark:** Name above city and state.

PERRY, JIM, Hope Star, PO Box 648, Hope, AR 71801, jenn@comfabinc.com

PERRY, JOHN, 9 South Harrell Rd., Mayflower, AR 72106, Phone: 501-470-3043
Specialties: Investment grade and working folders; some straight knives. **Patterns:** Front and rear lock folders, liner locks and hunters. **Technical:** Grinds CPM440V, D2 and making own Damascus. Offers filework. **Prices:** $375 to $950; some to $2500. **Remarks:** Part-time maker; first knife sold in 1990. Doing business as Perry Custom Knives. **Mark:** Initials or last name in high relief set in a diamond shape.

PERRY, JOHNNY, PO Box 4666, Spartanburg, SC 29305-4666, Phone: 803-578-3533, comfabinc@mindspring.com

PERSSON, CONNY, PL 588, 820 50 Loos, SWEDEN, Phone: +46 657 10305, Fax: +46 657 413 435, connyknives@swipnet.se Web: www.connyknives.com
Specialties: Mosaic Damascus. **Patterns:** Mosaic Damascus. **Technical:** Straight knives and folders. **Prices:** $1000 and up. **Mark:** C. Persson.

PETEAN, FRANCISCO AND MAURICIO, R. Dr.Carlos de Carvalho Rosa, 52, Centro, Birigui, SP-16200-000, BRAZIL, Phone: 0186-424786
Specialties: Classic knives to customer specs. **Patterns:** Bowies, boots, fighters, hunters and utility knives. **Technical:** Grinds D6, 440C and high-carbon steels. Prefers natural handle material. **Prices:** $70 to $500. **Remarks:** Full-time maker; first knife sold in 1985. **Mark:** Last name, hand made.

PETERSEN, DAN L., 10610 SW 81st, Auburn, KS 66402, Phone: 785-256-2640

Specialties: Period pieces and forged integral hilts on hunters and fighters. **Patterns:** Texas-style Bowies, boots and hunters in high-carbon and Damascus steel. **Technical:** Austempers forged high-carbon blades. Precisin heat treating using salt takns. **Prices:** $400 to $5000. **Remarks:** First knife sold in 1978. **Mark:** Stylized initials, MS.

PETERSON, CHRIS, Box 143, 2175 W. Rockyford, Salina, UT 84654, Phone: 801-529-7194

Specialties: Working straight knives of his design. **Patterns:** Large fighters, boots, hunters and some display pieces. **Technical:** Forges O1 and meteor. Makes and sells his own Damascus. Engraves, scrimshaws and inlays. **Prices:** $150 to $600; some to $1500. **Remarks:** Full-time maker; first knife sold in 1986. **Mark:** A drop in a circle with a line through it.

PETERSON, ELDON G., 260 Haugen Heights Rd., Whitefish, MT 59937, Phone: 406-862-2204, draino@digisys.net Web: http://www.kmg.org/egpeterson

Specialties: Fancy and working folders, any size. **Patterns:** Lockback interframes, integral bolster folders, liner locks, and two-blades. **Technical:** Grinds 440C and ATS-34. Offers gold inlay work, gem stone inlays and engraving. **Prices:** $285 to $5000. **Remarks:** Full-time maker; first knife sold in 1974. **Mark:** Name, city and state.

PETERSON, KAREN, THE PEN AND THE SWORD LTD., PO Box 290741, Brooklyn, NY 11229-0741, Phone: 718-382-4847, Fax: 718-376-5745, info@pensword.com WEB: www.pensword.com

PETERSON, LLOYD (PETE) C., 64 Halbrook Rd., Clinton, AR 72031, Phone: 501-893-0000, wmblade@cyberback.com

Specialties: Miniatures, and mosaic folders. **Prices:** $250 and up. **Remarks:** Lead time is 6-8 months. **Mark:** Pete.

PFANENSTIEL, DAN, 1824 Lafayette Ave., Modesto, CA 95355, Phone: 209-575-5937, dpfan@sbcglobal.net

Specialties: Japanese tanto, swords. One-of-a-kind knives. **Technical:** Forges simple carbon steels, some Damascus. **Prices:** $200 to $1000. **Mark:** Circle with wave inside.

PHILIPPE, D. A., PO Box 306, Cornish, NH 03746, Phone: 603-543-0662

Specialties: Traditional working straight knives. **Patterns:** Hunters, trout and bird, camp knives etc. **Technical:** Grinds ATS-34, 440c, A-2, Damascus, flat and hollow ground. Exotic woods and antler handles. Brass, nickel silver and stainless components. **Prices:** $125 to $800. **Remarks:** Full-time maker, first knife sold in 1984. **Mark:** First initial, last name.

PHILLIPS, DENNIS, 16411 West Bennet Rd., Independence, LA 70443, Phone: 985-878-8275

Specialties: Specializes in fixed blade military combat tacticals.

PHILLIPS, JIM, PO Box 168, Williamstown, NJ 08094, Phone: 609-567-0695

PHILLIPS, RANDY, 759 E. Francis St., Ontario, CA 91761, Phone: 909-923-4381

Specialties: Hunters, collector-grade liner locks and high-art daggers. **Technical:** Grinds D2, 440C and 154CM; embellishes. **Prices:** Start at $200. **Remarks:** Part-time maker; first knife sold in 1981. Not currently taking orders. **Mark:** Name, city and state in eagle head.

PHILLIPS, SCOTT C., 671 California Rd., Gouverneur, NY 13642, Phone: 315-287-1280, Web: www.mangusknives.com

Specialties: Sheaths in leather. Fixed blade hunters, boot knives, Bowies, buck skinners (hand forged and stock removal). **Technical:** 440C, 5160, 1095 and 52100. **Prices:** Start at $125. **Remarks:** Part-time maker; first knife sold in 1993. **Mark:** Before "2000" as above after S Mangus.

PICKENS, SELBERT, Rt. 1, Box 216, Liberty, WV 25124, Phone: 304-586-2190

Specialties: Using knives. **Patterns:** Standard sporting knives. **Technical:** Stainless steels; stock removal method. **Prices:** Moderate. **Remarks:** Part-time maker. **Mark:** Name.

PIENAAR, CONRAD, 19A Milner Rd., Bloemfontein 9300, SOUTH AFRICA, Phone: 027 514364180, Fax: 027 514364180

Specialties: Fancy working and using straight knives and folders of his design, to customer specs and in standard patterns. **Patterns:** Hunters, locking folders, cleavers, kitchen and utility/camp knives. **Technical:** Grinds 12C27, D2 and ATS-34. Uses some Damascus. Scrimshaws; inlays gold. Knives come with wooden box and custom-made leather sheath. **Prices:** $300 to $1000. **Remarks:** Part-time maker; first knife sold in 1981. Doing business as C.P. Knife maker. **Mark:** Initials and serial number. **Other:** Makes slip joint folders and liner locking folders.

PIERCE, HAROLD L., 106 Lyndon Lane, Louisville, KY 40222, Phone: 502-429-5136

Specialties: Working straight knives, some fancy. **Patterns:** Big fighters and Bowies. **Technical:** Grinds D2, 440C, 154CM; likes sub-hilts. **Prices:** $150 to $450; some to $1200. **Remarks:** Full-time maker; first knife sold in 1982. **Mark:** Last name with knife through the last initial.

PIERCE, RANDALL, 903 Wyndam, Arlington, TX 76017, Phone: 817-468-0138

PIERGALLINI, DANIEL E., 4011 N. Forbes Rd., Plant City, FL 33565, Phone: 813-754-3908, Fax: 8137543908, coolnifedad@earthlink.net

Specialties: Traditional and fancy straight knives and folders of his design or to customer's specs. **Patterns:** Hunters, fighters, three-fingered skinners, fillet, working and camp knives. **Technical:** Grinds 440C, O1, D2, ATS-34, some Damascus; forges his own mokume. Uses natural handle material. **Prices:** $450 to $800; some to $1800. **Remarks:** Part-time maker; sold first knife in 1994. **Mark:** Last name, city, state or last name in script.

PIESNER, DEAN, 1786 Sawmill Rd, Conestogo ON, CANADA N0B 1N0, Phone: 519-699-4319, Fax: 519-699-5452, dpey@kw.lgs.net Web: www.forgeandanvil.com

Specialties: Classic and period pieces of his design and to customer specs. **Patterns:** Bowies, skinners, fighters and swords. **Technical:** Forges 5160, 52100, steel Damascus and nickel-steel Damascus. Makes own mokume gane with copper, brass and nickel silver. Silver wire inlays in wood. **Prices:** Start at $150. **Remarks:** Full-time maker; first knife sold in 1990. **Mark:** First initial, last name, JS.

PIOREK, JAMES S., PO Box 335, Rexford, MT 59930, Phone: 406-889-5510, jsp@bladerigger.com; Web: http://www.bladerigger.com

Specialties: True custom and semi-custom production (SCP), specialized concealment blades; advanced sheaths and tailored body harnessing systems. **Patterns:** Tactical/personal defense fighters, swords, utility and custom patterns. **Technical:** Grinds A2 and Talonite®; heat-treats. Sheaths: Kydex or Kydex-lined leather laminated or Kydex-lined with Rigger Coat™. Exotic materials available. **Prices:** $50 to $10,000. **Remarks:** Full-time maker. Doing business as Blade Rigger L.L.C. **Mark:** For true custom: Initials with abstract cutting edge and for SCP: Blade Rigger. **Other:** Martial artist and unique defense industry tools and equipment.

PITMAN, DAVID, PO Drawer 2566, Williston, ND 58802, Phone: 701-572-3325

PITT, DAVID F., 6812 Digger Pine Ln., Anderson, CA 96007, Phone: 530-357-2393

Specialties: Fixed blade, hunters and hatchets. Flat ground mirror finish. **Patterns:** Hatchets with gut hook, small gut hooks, guards, bolsters or guard less. **Technical:** Grinds A2, 440C, 154CM, ATS-34, D2. **Prices:** $150 to $750. **Remarks:** Guild member since 1982. **Mark:** Bear paw with name David F. Pitt.

PLUNKETT, RICHARD, 29 Kirk Rd., West Cornwall, CT 06796, Phone: 860-672-3419; Toll free: 888-KNIVES-8

Specialties: Traditional, fancy folders and straight knives of his design. **Patterns:** Slip-joint folders and small straight knives. **Technical:** Grinds O1 and stainless steel. Offers many different file patterns. **Prices:** $150 to $450. **Remarks:** Full-time maker; first knife sold in 1994. **Mark:** Signature and date under handle scales.

POLK, CLIFTON, 4625 Webber Creek Rd, Van Buren, AR 72956, Phone: 479-474-3828, cliffpolkknives@aol.com Web: www.polkknives.com

Specialties: Fancy working folders. **Patterns:** One blades spring backs in five sizes, Liner Lock, Automatics, Double blades spring back folder with standard drop & clip blade or bird knife with drop and vent hook or cow boy's knives with drop and hoof pick and straight knives. **Technical:** Uses D2 & ATS-34. Makes all own Damascus using 1084, 1095, 01, 15N20, 5160. Using all kinds of exotic woods. Stage, pearls, ivory, mastodon ivory and other boon and horns. **Prices:** $200 to $3000. **Remarks:** Retired fire fighter; made knives since 1974. **Mark:** Polk.

POLK, RUSTY, 5900 Wildwood Dr., Van Buren, AR 72956, Phone: 479-410-3661, polkknives@aol.com Web: www.polkknives.com

Specialties: Skinner's, hunter's, Bowie's, fighter's and forging working knives fancy Damascus, hunting, Bowies, fighters daggers, boot knives and survival knives. **Patterns:** Drop point, and forge to shape. **Technical:** ATS-34, 440C, Damascus, D2, 51/60, 1084, 15N20, Damascus and do all his forging. **Prices:** $200 to $1000. **Remarks:** R. Polk all hand made. **Mark:** R. Polk.

POLKOWSKI, AL, 8 Cathy Ct., Chester, NJ 07930, Phone: 908-879-6030

Specialties: High-tech straight knives and folders for adventurers and professionals. **Patterns:** Fighters, side-lock folders, boots and concealment knives. **Technical:** Grinds D2 and ATS-34; features satin and

bead-blast finishes; Kydex sheaths. **Prices:** Start at $100. **Remarks:** Full-time maker; first knife sold in 1985. **Mark:** Full name, Handmade.

POLLOCK, WALLACE J., 806 Russet Vly Dr., Cedar Park, TX 78613, wpollock@austin.rr.com wjpollock@pollockn.feworks.com
Specialties: Using knives, skinner, hunter, fighting, camp knives. **Patterns:** Use his own patterns or your. Traditional hunters, daggers, fighters, camp knives. **Technical:** Grinds ATS-34, D-2, BG-42, makes own Damascus, D-2, 0-1, ATS-34, prefer D-2, handles exotic wood, horn, bone, ivory. **Remarks:** Full-time maker, sold first knife 1973. **Prices:** $250 to $2500. **Mark:** Last name, city/state.

POLZIEN, DON, 1912 Inler Suite-L, Lubbock, TX 79407, Phone: 806-791-0766, blindinglightknives.com
Specialties: Traditional Japanese-style blades; restores antique Japanese swords, scabbards and fittings. **Patterns:** Hunters, fighters, one-of-a-kind art knives. **Technical:** 1045-1050 carbon steels, 440C, D2, ATS-34, standard and cable Damascus. **Prices:** $150 to $2500. **Remarks:** Full-time maker. First knife sold in 1990. **Mark:** Oriental characters inside square border.

PONZIO, DOUG, 3212 93rd St., Pleasant Prairie, WI 53158, Phone: 262-694-3188, prfgdough@aol.com Web: www.prairie-forge.com
Specialties: Damascus; Gem stone handles. **Mark:** P.F.

POOLE, MARVIN O., PO Box 552, Commerce, GA 30529, Phone: 803-225-5970
Specialties: Traditional working/using straight knives and folders of his design and in standard patterns. **Patterns:** Bowies, fighters, hunters, locking folders, bird and trout knives. **Technical:** Grinds 440C, D2, ATS-34. **Prices:** $50 to $150; some to $750. **Remarks:** Part-time maker; first knife sold in 1980. **Mark:** First initial, last name, year, serial number.

POSKOCIL, HELMUT, Oskar Czeijastrasse 2, A-3340 Waidhofen/Ybbs, AUSTRIA, Phone: 0043-7442-54519, Fax: 0043-7442-54519
Specialties: High-art and classic straight knives and folders of his design. **Patterns:** Bowies, daggers, hunters and locking folders. **Technical:** Grinds ATS-34 and stainless and carbon Damascus. Hardwoods, fossil ivory, horn and amber for handle material; silver wire and gold inlays; silver butt caps. Offers engraving and scrimshaw. **Prices:** $350 to $850; some to $3500. **Remarks:** Part-time maker; first knife sold in 1991. **Mark:** Name.

POSNER, BARRY E., 12501 Chandler Blvd., Suite 104, N. Hollywood, CA 91607, Phone: 818-752-8005, Fax: 818-752-8006
Specialties: Working/using straight knives. **Patterns:** Hunters, kitchen and utility/camp knives. **Technical:** Grinds ATS-34; forges 1095 and nickel. **Prices:** $95 to $400. **Remarks:** Part-time maker; first knife sold in 1987. Doing business as Posner Knives. Supplier of finished mosaic handle pin stock. **Mark:** First and middle initials, last name.

POTIER, TIMOTHY F., PO Box 711, Oberlin, LA 70655, Phone: 337-639-2229, tpotier@hotmail.com
Specialties: Classic working and using straight knives to customer specs; some collectible. **Patterns:** Hunters, Bowies, utility/camp knives and belt axes. **Technical:** Forges carbon steel and his own Damascus; offers filework. **Prices:** $300 to $1800; some to $4000. **Remarks:** Part-time maker; first knife sold in 1981. **Mark:** Last name, MS.

POTOCKI, ROGER, Route 1, Box 333A, Goreville, IL 62939, Phone: 618-995-9502

POTTER, BILLY, 6280 Virginia Rd., Nashport, OH 43830, Phone: 740-454-7412, bwp@potterknives.com potterknives@voyager.net
Specialties: Working straight knives; his design or to customers patterns. **Patterns:** Bowie, fighters, utilities, skinners, hunters, folding lock blade, miniatures and tomahawks. **Technical:** Grinds and forges, carbon steel, L-6, 0-1, 1095, 5160, 1084 and 52000. Grinds 440C stainless. Forges own Damascus. Handles: prefers exotic hardwood, curly and birdseye maples. Bone, ivory, antler, pearl and horn. Some scrimshaw. **Prices:** Start at $100 up to $800. **Remarks:** Part-time maker; first knife sold 1996. **Mark:** Last name.

POWELL, JAMES, 2500 North Robinson Rd., Texarkana, TX 75501

POWELL, ROBERT CLARK, PO Box 321, 93 Gose Rd., Smarr, GA 31086, Phone: 478-994-5418
Specialties: Composite bar Damascus blades. **Patterns:** Art knives, hunters, combat, tomahawks. **Patterns:** Hand forge all blades. **Prices:** $300 and up. **Remarks:** Member ABS. **Mark:** Powell.

PRATER, MIKE, PRATER AND COMPANY, 81 Sanford Ln., Flintstone, GA 30725, cmprater@aol.com Web: www.casecustomknives.com
Specialties: Customizing factory knives. **Patterns:** Buck knives, case knives, hen and rooster knives. **Technical:** Manufacture of mica pearl. **Prices:** Varied. **Remarks:** First knife sold in 1980. **Mark:** Mica pearl.

PRESSBURGER, RAMON, 59 Driftway Rd., Howell, NJ 07731, Phone: 732-363-0816
Specialties: BG-42. Only knife maker in U.S.A. that has complete line of affordable hunting knives made from BG-42. **Patterns:** All types hunting

styles. **Technical:** Uses all steels; main steels are D-2 and BG-42. **Prices:** $75 to $500. **Remarks:** Full-time maker; has been making hunting knives for 30 years. **Mark:** NA. **Other:** Makes knives to your patterning.

PRICE, TIMMY, PO Box 906, Blairsville, GA 30514, Phone: 706-745-5111

PRIMOS, TERRY, 932 Francis Dr., Shreveport, LA 71118, Phone: 318-686-6625, tprimos@sport.rr.com or terry@primosknives.com Web: www.primosknives.com
Specialties: Traditional forged straight knives. **Patterns:** Hunters, Bowies, camp knives, and fighters. **Technical:** Forges primarily 1084 and 5160; also forges Damascus. **Prices:** $250 to $600. **Remarks:** Full-time maker; first knife sold in 1993. **Mark:** Last name.

PRINSLOO, THEUNS, PO Box 2263, Bethlehem, 9700, SOUTH AFRICA, Phone: 27824663885, theunmesa@telkomsa.net Web: www.theunsprinsloo.com
Specialties: Fancy folders. **Technical:** Own Damascus and Mokume. **Prices:** $450 to $1500.

PRITCHARD, RON, 613 Crawford Ave., Dixon, IL 61021, Phone: 815-284-6005
Specialties: Plain and fancy working knives. **Patterns:** Variety of straight knives, locking folders, interframes and miniatures. **Technical:** Grinds 440C, 154CM and commercial Damascus. **Prices:** $100 to $200; some to $1500. **Remarks:** Part-time maker; first knife sold in 1979. **Mark:** Name and city.

PROVENZANO, JOSEPH D., 3024 Ivy Place, Chalmette, LA 70043, Phone: 504-279-3154
Specialties: Working straight knives and folders in standard patterns. **Patterns:** Hunters, Bowies, folders, camp and fishing knives. **Technical:** Grinds ATS-34, 440C, 154CM, CPM 4400V, CPM420V and Damascus. Hollow-grinds hunters. **Prices:** $110 to $300; some to $1000. **Remarks:** Part-time maker; first knife sold in 1980. **Mark:** Joe-Pro.

PRYOR, STEPHEN L., HC Rt. 1, Box 1445, Boss, MO 65440, Phone: 573-626-4838, Fax: same, Knives4U3@juno.com Web: www.stevescutler.com
Specialties: Working and fancy straight knives, some to customer specs. **Patterns:** Bowies, hunting/fishing, utility/camp, fantasy/art. **Technical:** Grinds 440C, ATS-34, 1085, some Damascus, and does filework. Stag and exotic hardwood handles. **Prices:** $250 and up. **Remarks:** Full-time maker; first knife sold in 1991. **Mark:** Stylized first initial and last name over city and state.

PUDDU, SALVATORE, Via Lago Bunnari, 11 Localita Flumini, Quartu s Elena (CA), ITALY 09046, Phone: 0039070892208, salvatorepuddu@tin.it
Specialties: Collector-quality folders, straight. **Patterns:** Multi blade, folders, automatics. **Technical:** Grinds ATS-34. **Prices:** Start $1300 to $3800. **Remarks:** Full-time maker. **Mark:** Name.

PUGH, JIM, PO Box 711, Azle, TX 76020, Phone: 817-444-2679, Fax: 817-444-5455
Specialties: Fancy/embellished limited editions by request. **Patterns:** 5- to 7-inch Bowies, wildlife art pieces, hunters, daggers and fighters; some commemoratives. **Technical:** Multi color transplanting in solid 18K gold, fine gems; grinds 440C and ATS-34. Offers engraving, fancy file etching and leather sheaths for wildlife art pieces. Ivory and coco bolo handle material on limited editions. Designs animal head butt caps and paws or bear claw guards; sterling silver heads and guards. **Prices:** $60,000 to $80,000 each in the Big Five 2000 edition. **Remarks:** Full-time maker; first knife sold in 1970. **Mark:** Pugh (old English).

PULIS, VLADIMIR, Horna Ves 43/B/25, 96 701 Kremnica, SLOVAKIA, Phone: 00427 45 67 57 214, Fax: 00427 903 390076, vpulis@host.sk Web: www.upulis.host.sk
Specialties: Fancy and high-art straight knives of his design. **Patterns:** Daggers and hunters. **Technical:** Forges Damascus steel. All work done by hand. **Prices:** $250 to $3000; some to $10,000. **Remarks:** Full-time maker; first knife sold in 1990. **Mark:** Initials in sixtagon.

PULLIAM, MORRIS C., 560 Jeptha Knob Rd., Shelbyville, KY 40065, Phone: 502-633-2261, mcpulliam@fastballinternet.com
Specialties: Working knives; classic Bowies. Cherokee River pattern Damascus. **Patterns:** Bowies, hunters, and tomahawks. **Technical:** Forges L6, W2, 1095, Damascus and bar 320 layer Damascus. **Prices:** $165 to $1200. **Remarks:** Full-time maker; first knife sold in 1974. Makes knives for Native American festivals. Doing business as Knob Hill Forge. Member of Piqua Sept Shawnee of Ohio. Indian name Weshe Wapebe (The Elk) **Mark:** Small and large; Pulliam. **Other:** As a member of a state tribe, is an American Indian artist and craftsman by federal law.

PURSLEY, AARON, 8885 Coal Mine Rd., Big Sandy, MT 59520, Phone: 406-378-3200
Specialties: Fancy working knives. **Patterns:** Locking folders, straight hunters and daggers, personal wedding knives and letter openers. **Technical:** Grinds O1 and 440C; engraves. **Prices:** $900 to $2500; some to $1500. **Remarks:** Full-time maker; first knife sold in 1975. **Mark:** Initials connected with year.

PURVIS, BOB AND ELLEN, 2416 N Loretta Dr., Tucson, AZ 85716, Phone: 520-795-8290, repknives2@cox.net
Specialties: Hunter, skinners, Bowies, using knives, gentlemen's folders and collectible knives. **Technical:** Grinds ATS-34, 440C, Damascus, Dama steel, heat-treats and cryogenically quenches. We do gold-plating, salt bluing, scrimshawing, filework and fashion hand made leather sheaths. Materials used for handles include exotic woods, mammoth ivory, mother-of-pearl, G-10 and micarta. **Prices:** $165 to $800. **Remarks:** Knifemaker since retirement in 1984. Selling them since 1993. **Mark:** Script or print R.E. Purvis ~ Tucson, AZ or last name only.

PUTNAM, DONALD S., 590 Wolcott Hill Rd., Wethersfield, CT 06109, Phone: 860-563-9718, Fax: 860-563-9718, dpknives@cox.net
Specialties: Working knives for the hunter and fisherman. **Patterns:** His design or to customer specs. **Technical:** Uses stock removal method, O1, W2, D2, ATS-34, 154CM, 440C and CPM REX 20; stainless steel Damascus on request. **Prices:** $250 and up. **Remarks:** Full-time maker; first knife sold in 1985. **Mark:** Last name with a knife outline.

Q

QUAKENBUSH, THOMAS C., 2426 Butler Rd., Ft Wayne, IN 46808, Phone: 219-483-0749

QUARTON, BARR, PO Box 4335, McCall, ID 83638, Phone: 208-634-3641
Specialties: Plain and fancy working knives; period pieces. **Patterns:** Hunters, tantos and swords. **Technical:** Forges and grinds 154CM, ATS-34 and his own Damascus. **Prices:** $180 to $450; some to $4500. **Remarks:** Part-time maker; first knife sold in 1978. Doing business as Barr Custom Knives. **Mark:** First name with bear logo.

QUATTLEBAUM, CRAIG, 2 Ridgewood Ln., Searcy, AR 72143
Specialties: Traditional straight knives and one-of-a-kind knives of his design; period pieces. **Patterns:** Bowies and fighters. **Technical:** Forges 5168, 52100 and own Damascus. **Prices:** $100 to $1200. **Remarks:** Part-time maker; first knife sold in 1988. **Mark:** Stylized initials.

QUICK, MIKE, 23 Locust Ave., Kearny, NJ 07032, Phone: 201-991-6580
Specialties: Traditional working/using straight knives. **Patterns:** Bowies. **Technical:** 440C and ATS-34 for blades; Micarta, wood and stag for handles.

R

R. BOYES KNIVES, N81 W16140 Robin Hood Dr., Menomonee Falls, WI 53051, Phone: 262-255-7341, tomboyes@earthlink.net or tomboyes5@hotmail.com
Specialties: Hunters, working knives. **Technical:** Grinds ATS-34, 440C, O1 tool steel and Damascus. **Prices:** $60 to $700. **Remarks:** First knife sold in 1998. Tom Boyes changed to R. Boyes Knives.

RACHLIN, LESLIE S., 1200 W. Church St., Elmira, NY 14905, Phone: 607-733-6889
Specialties: Classic and working/using straight knives and folders of his design. **Patterns:** Hunters, locking folders and utility/camp knives. **Technical:** Grinds 440C and Damascus. **Prices:** $110 to $200; some to $450. **Remarks:** Spare-time maker; first knife sold in 1989. Doing business as Tinkermade Knives. **Mark:** Stamped initials or Tinkermade, city and state.

RADOS, JERRY F., 7523 E 5000 N Rd., Grant Park, IL 60940, Phone: 815-472-3350, Fax: 815-472-3944
Specialties: Deluxe period pieces. **Patterns:** Hunters, fighters, locking folders, daggers and camp knives. **Technical:** Forges and grinds his own Damascus which he sells commercially; makes pattern-welded Turkish Damascus. **Prices:** Start at $900. **Remarks:** Full-time maker; first knife sold in 1981. **Mark:** Last name.

RAGSDALE, JAMES D., 3002 Arabian Woods Dr., Lithonia, GA 30038, Phone: 770-482-6739
Specialties: Fancy and embellished working knives of his design or to customer specs. **Patterns:** Hunters, folders and fighters. **Technical:** Grinds 440C, ATS-34 and A2. **Prices:** $150 and up. **Remarks:** Full-time

maker; first knife sold in 1984. **Mark:** Fish symbol with name above, town below.

RAINVILLE, RICHARD, 126 Cockle Hill Rd., Salem, CT 06420, Phone: 860-859-2776, w1jo@snet.net
Specialties: Traditional working straight knives. **Patterns:** Outdoor knives, including fishing knives. **Technical:** L6, 400C, ATS-34. **Prices:** $100 to $800. **Remarks:** Full-time maker; first knife sold in 1982. **Mark:** Name, city, state in oval logo.

RALEY, R. WAYNE, 825 Poplar Acres Rd., Collierville, TN 38017, Phone: 901-853-2026

RALPH, DARREL, BRIAR KNIVES, 4185 S St. Rt. 605, Galena, OH 43021, Phone: 740-965-9970, dr@darrelralph.com Web: www.darrelralph.com
Specialties: Fancy, high-art, high-tech, collectible straight knives and folders of his design and to customer specs; unique mechanisms, some disassemble. **Patterns:** Daggers, fighters and swords. **Technical:** Forges his own Damascus, nickel and high-carbon. Uses mokume and Damascus; mosaics and special patterns. Engraves and heat-treats. Prefers pearl, ivory and abalone handle material; uses stones and jewels. **Prices:** $250 to six figures. **Remarks:** Full-time maker; first knife sold in 1987. Doing business as Briar Knives. **Mark:** DDR.

RAMEY, LARRY, 1315 Porter Morris Rd., Chapmansboro, TN 37035-5120, Phone: 615-307-4233, larryrameyknives@hotmail.com WEB: www.larryrameyknives.com
Specialties: Titanium knives. **Technical:** Pictures taken by Hawkinson Photography.

RAMEY, MARSHALL F., PO Box 2589, West Helena, AR 72390, Phone: 501-572-7436, Fax: 501-572-6245
Specialties: Traditional working knives. **Patterns:** Designs military combat knives; makes butterfly folders, camp knives and miniatures. **Technical:** Grinds D2 and 440C. **Prices:** $100 to $500. **Remarks:** Full-time maker; first knife sold in 1978. **Mark:** Name with ram's head.

RAMSEY, RICHARD A., 8525 Trout Farm Rd., Neosho, MO 64850, Phone: 417-451-1493, rams@direcway.com Web: www.ramseyknives.com
Specialties: Drop point hunters. **Patterns:** Various Damascus. **Prices:** $125 to $1500. **Mark:** RR double R also last name-RAMSEY.

RANDALL JR., JAMES W., 11606 Keith Hall Rd., Keithville, LA 71047, Phone: 318-925-6480, Fax: 318-925-1709, jw@jwrandall-knives.com
Specialties: Collectible and functional knives. **Patterns:** Bowies, hunters, daggers, swords, folders and combat knives. **Technical:** Forges 5160, 1084, 01 and his Damascus. **Prices:** $400 to $8000. **Remarks:** Part-time. First knive sold in 1998. **Mark:** J.W Randall M.S.

RANDALL MADE KNIVES, PO Box 1988, Orlando, FL 32802, Phone: 407-855-8075, Fax: 407-855-9054, Web: http: //www.randallknives.com
Specialties: Working straight knives. **Patterns:** Hunters, fighters and Bowies. **Technical:** Forges and grinds O1 and 440B. **Prices:** $170 to $550; some to $450. **Remarks:** Full-time maker; first knife sold in 1937. **Mark:** Randall made, city and state in scimitar logo.

RANDOW, RALPH, 4214 Blalock Rd., Pineville, LA 71360, Phone: 318-640-3369

RANKL, CHRISTIAN, Possenhofenerstr. 33, 81476 Munchen, GERMANY, Phone: 0049 01 71 3 66 26 79, Fax: 0049 8975967265, christian@crankl.de.
Specialties: Tail-lock knives. **Patterns:** Fighters, hunters and locking folders. **Technical:** Grinds ATS-34, D2, CPM1440V, RWL 34 also stainless Damascus. **Prices:** $450 to $950; some to $2000. **Remarks:** Full-time maker; first knife sold in 1989. **Mark:** Electrochemical etching on blade.

RAPP, STEVEN J., 7273 South 245 East, Midvale, UT 84047, Phone: 801-567-9553
Specialties: Gold quartz; mosaic handles. **Patterns:** Daggers, Bowies, fighters and San Francisco knives. **Technical:** Hollow- and flat-grinds 440C and Damascus. **Prices:** Start at $500. **Remarks:** Full-time maker; first knife sold in 1981. **Mark:** Name and state.

RAPPAZZO, RICHARD, 142 Dunsbach Ferry Rd., Cohoes, NY 12047, Phone: 518-783-6843
Specialties: Damascus locking folders and straight knives. **Patterns:** Folders, dirks, fighters and tantos in original and traditional designs. **Technical:** Hand-forges all blades; specializes in Damascus; uses only natural handle materials. **Prices:** $400 to $1500. **Remarks:** Part-time maker; first knife sold in 1985. **Mark:** Name, date, serial number.

RARDON, ARCHIE F., 1589 SE Price Dr., Polo, MO 64671, Phone: 66(354-2330
Specialties: Working knives. **Patterns:** Hunters, Bowies and miniatures. **Technical:** Grinds O1, D2, 440C, ATS-34, cable and Damascus. **Prices:** $50 to $500. **Remarks:** Part-time maker. **Mark:** Boar hog.

RARDON, A.D., 1589 SE Price Dr., Polo, MO 64671, Phone: 660-354-2330
Specialties: Folders, miniatures. **Patterns:** Hunters, buck skinners, Bowies, miniatures and daggers. **Technical:** Grinds O1, D2, 440C and ATS-34. **Prices:** $150 to $2000; some higher. **Remarks:** Full-time maker; first knife sold in 1954. **Mark:** Fox logo.

RAY, ALAN W., PO Box 479, Lovelady, TX 75851, Phone: 936-636-2350, Fax: 936-636-2931, awray@raysmfg.com Web: www.raysmfg.com
Specialties: Working straight knives of his design. **Patterns:** Hunters, camp knives, steak knives and carving sets. **Technical:** Forges L6 and 5160 for straight knives; grinds D2 and 440C for folders and kitchen cutlery. **Prices:** $200 to $1000. **Remarks:** Full-time maker; first knife sold in 1979. **Mark:** Stylized initials.

REBELLO, INDIAN GEORGE, 358 Elm St., New Bedford, MA 02740-3837, Phone: 508-999-7090, indgeo@juno.com WEB: www.indiangeorgesknives.com
Specialties: One-of-a-kind fighters and Bowies. **Patterns:** To customer's specs, hunters and utilities. **Technical:** Forges his own Damascus, 5160, 52100, 1084, 1095, cable and O-1. Grinds S30V, ATS-34, 154CM, 440C, D2 and A2. Makes own Mokumme. **Prices:** Starting at $250. **Remarks:** Full-time maker, first knife sold in 1991. Doing business as Indian George's Knives. President and founding father of the New England Custom Knives Association. **Mark:** Indian George's Knives.

RED, VERNON, 2020 Benton Cove, Conway, AR 72032, Phone: 501-450-7284, knivesvr@conwaycorp.net
Specialties: Custom design straight knives or folders of your design or mine. Love one-of-a-kind. **Patterns:** Hunters, fighters, Bowies, fillet, folders and lock-blades. **Technical:** Hollow Grind or flat grind; use 440C, D-2, ATS-34, Damascus. **Prices:** $180 and up. **Remarks:** Made first skinner in 1982, first lock blade folder in 1992. Make about 50/50. Part-time maker. Do scrimshaw on ivory and micarta. **Mark:** Last name. **Other:** Member of (AKA) Arkansas Knives Assoc., attend annual show in Feb. at Little Rock, AR. Custom Made Knives by Vernon Red.

REDDIEX, BILL, 27 Galway Ave., Palmerston North, NEW ZEALAND, Phone: 06-357-0383, Fax: 06-358-2910
Specialties: Collector-grade working straight knives. **Patterns:** Traditional-style Bowies and drop-point hunters. **Technical:** Grinds 440C, D2 and O1; offers variety of grinds and finishes. **Prices:** $130 to $750. **Remarks:** Full-time maker; first knife sold in 1980. **Mark:** Last name around kiwi bird logo.

REED, DAVE, Box 132, Brimfield, MA 01010, Phone: 413-245-3661
Specialties: Traditional styles. Makes knives from chains, rasps, gears, etc. **Patterns:** Bush swords, hunters, working minis, camp and utility knives. **Technical:** Forges 1075 and his own Damascus. **Prices:** Start at $50. **Remarks:** Part-time maker; first knife sold in 1970. **Mark:** Initials.

REED, JOHN M., 257 Navajo Dr., Oak Hill, FL 32759, Phone: 386-345-4763
Specialties: Hunter, utility, some survival knives. **Patterns:** Trailing Point, and drop point sheath knives. **Technical:** ATS-34, rockwell 60 exotic wood or natural material handles. **Prices:** $135 to $300. Depending on handle material. **Remarks:** Likes the stock removal method. "Old Fashioned trainling point blades". **Mark:** "Reed" acid etched on left side of blade. **Other:** Hand made and sewn leather sheaths.

REEVE, CHRIS, 11624 W. President Dr., Ste. B, Boise, ID 83713, Phone: 208-375-0367, Fax: 208-375-0368, crkinfo@chrisreeve.com
Specialties: Originator and designer of the One Piece range of fixed blade utility knives and of the Sebenza Integral Lock folding knives made by Chris Reeve Knives. Currently makes only one or two pieces per year himself. **Patterns:** Art folders and fixed blades; one-of-a-kind. **Technical:** Grinds specialty stainless steels, Damascus and other materials to his own design. **Prices:** $1000 and upwards. **Remarks:** Full-time in knife business; first knife sold in 1982. **Mark:** Signature and date.

REGGIO JR., SIDNEY J., PO Box 851, Sun, LA 70463, Phone: 504-886-5886
Specialties: Miniature classic and fancy straight knives of his design or in standard patterns. **Patterns:** Fighters, hunters and utility/camp knives. **Technical:** Grinds 440C, ATS-34 and commercial Damascus. Engraves; scrimshaws; offers filework. Hollow grinds most blades. Prefers natural handle material. Offers handmade sheaths. **Prices:** $85 to $250; some to $500. **Remarks:** Part-time maker; first knife sold in 1988. Doing business as Sterling Workshop. **Mark:** Initials.

REPKE, MIKE, 4191 N. Euclid Ave., Bay City, MI 48706, Phone: 517-684-3111
Specialties: Traditional working and using straight knives of their design or to customer specs; classic knives; display knives. **Patterns:** Hunters, Bowies, skinners, fighters boots, axes and swords. **Technical:** Grind 440C. Offer variety of handle materials. **Prices:** $99 to $1500. **Remarks:** Full-time makers. Doing business as Black Forest Blades. **Mark:** Knife logo.

REVERDY, PIERRE, 5 Rue de L'egalite', 26100 Romans, FRANCE, Phone: 334 75 05 10 15, Fax: 334 75 02 28 40, Web: http://www.reverdy.com
Specialties: Art knives; legend pieces. **Patterns:** Daggers, Bowies, hunters and other large patterns. **Technical:** Forges his Damascus and "poetique Damascus"; works with his own EDM machine to create any kind of pattern inside the steel with his own touch. **Prices:** $2000 and up. **Remarks:** Full-time maker; first knife sold in 1986. Nicole (wife) collaborates with enamels. **Mark:** Initials connected.

REVISHVILI, ZAZA, 2102 Linden Ave., Madison, WI 53704, Phone: 608-243-7927
Specialties: Fancy/embellished and high-art straight knives and folders of his design. **Patterns:** Daggers, swords and locking folders. **Technical:** Uses Damascus; silver filigree, silver inlay in wood; enameling. **Prices:** $1000 to $9000; some to $15,000. **Remarks:** Full-time maker; first knife sold in 1987. **Mark:** Initials, city.

REXROAT, KIRK, 527 Sweetwater Circle, Box 224, Wright, WY 82732, Phone: 307-464-0166, rexknives@vcn.com Web: www.rexroatknives.com
Specialties: Using and collectible straight knives and folders of his design or to customer specs. **Patterns:** Bowies, hunters, folders. **Technical:** Forges Damascus patterns, mosaic and 52100. **Prices:** $400 and up. **Remarks:** Part-time maker, Master Smith in the ABS; first knife sold in 1984. Doing business as Rexroat Knives. **Mark:** Last name.

REYNOLDS, DAVE, Rt. 2, Box 36, Harrisville, WV 26362, Phone: 304-643-2889, wvreynolds@hotmail.com
Specialties: Working straight knives of his design. **Patterns:** Bowies, kitchen and utility knives. **Technical:** Grinds and forges L6, 1095 and 440C. Heat-treats. **Prices:** $50 to $85; some to $175. **Remarks:** Full-time maker; first knife sold in 1980. Doing business as Terra-Gladius Knives. **Mark:** Mark on special orders only; serial number on all knives.

REYNOLDS, JOHN C., #2 Andover, HC77, Gillette, WY 82716, Phone: 307-682-6076
Specialties: Working knives, some fancy. **Patterns:** Hunters, Bowies, tomahawks and buck skinners; some folders. **Technical:** Grinds D2, ATS-34, 440C and forges own Damascus and Knifes now. Scrimshaws. **Prices:** $200 to $3000. **Remarks:** Spare-time maker; first knife sold in 1969. **Mark:** On ground blades JC Reynolds Gillette,WY, on forged blades, initials make the mark-JCR.

REYNOLDS, LEE, 5552 Dwight Ave, San Jose, CA 95118, leecreynolds@comcast.net

RHO, NESTOR LORENZO, Primera Junta 589, (6000) Junin, Buenos Aires, ARGENTINA, Phone: (02362) 15670686
Specialties: Classic and fancy straight knives of his design. **Patterns:** Bowies, fighters and hunters. **Technical:** Grinds 420C, 440C and 1050. Offers semi-precious stones on handles, acid etching on blades and blade engraving. **Prices:** $60 to $300 some to $1200. **Remarks:** Full-time maker; first knife sold in 1975. **Mark:** Name.

RHODES, JAMES D., 205 Woodpoint Ave., Hagerstown, MD 21740, Phone: 301-739-2657
Specialties: Traditional working and using straight knives of his design. **Patterns:** Bowies, fighters, hunters and kitchen knives. **Technical:** Forges 5160, 1085, and 9260; makes own Damascus. Hard edges, soft backs, dead soft tangs. Heat-treats. **Prices:** $150 to $350. **Remarks:** Part-time maker. **Mark:** Last name, JS.

RIBONI, CLAUDIO, Via L Da Vinci, Truccazzano (MI), ITALY, Phone: 02 95309010, Web: www.riboni-knives.com

RICARDO ROMANO, BERNARDES, Ruai Coronel Rennò, 1261, Itajuba MG, BRAZIL 37500, Phone: 0055-2135-622-5896
Specialties: Hunters, fighters, Bowies. **Technical:** Grinds blades of stainless and tools steels. **Patterns:** Hunters. **Prices:** $100 to $700. **Mark:** Romano.

RICHARD, RON, 4875 Calaveras Ave., Fremont, CA 94538, Phone: 510-796-9767
Specialties: High-tech working straight knives of his design. **Patterns:** Bowies, swords and locking folders. **Technical:** Forges and grinds ATS-34, 154CM and 440V. All folders have dead-bolt button locks. **Prices:** $650 to $850; some to $1400. **Remarks:** Full-time maker; first knife sold in 1968. **Mark:** Full name.

RICHARDS JR., ALVIN C., 2889 Shields Ln., Fortuna, CA 95540-3241, Phone: 707-725-2526, bldsmith@cox.net
Specialties: Fixed blade Damascus. One-of-a-kind. **Patterns:** Hunters, fighters. **Prices:** $125 to $500. **Remarks:** Like to work with customers on a truly custom knife. **Mark:** A C Richards or ACR.

RICHTER, JOHN C., 932 Bowling Green Trail, Chesapeake, VA 23320
Specialties: Hand-forged knives in original patterns. **Patterns:** Hunters, fighters, utility knives and other belt knives, folders, swords. **Technical:**

Hand-forges high-carbon and his own Damascus; makes mokume gane. **Prices:** $75 to $1500. **Remarks:** Part-time maker. **Mark:** Richter Forge.

RICHTER, SCOTT, 516 E. 2nd St., S. Boston, MA 02127, Phone: 617-269-4855

Specialties: Traditional working/using folders. **Patterns:** Locking folders, swords and kitchen knives. **Technical:** Grinds ATS-34, 5160 and A2. High-tech materials. **Prices:** $150 to $650; some to $1500. **Remarks:** Full-time maker; first knife sold in 1991. Doing business as Richter Made. **Mark:** Last name, Made.

RICKE, DAVE, 1209 Adams, West Bend, WI 53090, Phone: 262-334-5739, R.L5710@sbcglobal.net

Specialties: Working knives; period pieces. **Patterns:** Hunters, boots, Bowies; locking folders and slip-joints. **Technical:** Grinds ATS-34, A2, 440C and 154CM. **Prices:** $125 to $1600. **Remarks:** Full-time maker; first knife sold in 1976. **Mark:** Last name.

RIDER, DAVID M., PO Box 5946, Eugene, OR 97405-0911, Phone: 541-343-8747

RIEPE, RICHARD A., 17604 E 296 St., Harrisonville, MO 64701

RIETVELD, BERTIE, PO Box 53, Magaliesburg 1791, SOUTH AFRICA, Phone: +2714 5771294, Fax: +2714 5771294, bertie@batavia.co.za Web: www.batavia.co.za

Specialties: Art daggers, Bolster lock folders, persian designs, Embraces elegant designs.**Patterns:** Mostly one off's. **Technical:** Work only in own damascus, gold inlay, blued stainless fittings logo in stanhope lens; sole authorship. **Remarks:** First knife made in 1979. Annual Shows attended: ECCKS; March Blade Show, Guild Show, Milan Show, South African Guild Show.

RIGNEY JR., WILLIE, 191 Colson Dr., Bronston, KY 42518, Phone: 606-679-4227

Specialties: High-tech period pieces and fancy working knives. **Patterns:** Fighters, boots, daggers and push knives. **Technical:** Grinds 440C and 154CM; buys Damascus. Most knives are embellished. **Prices:** $150 to $1500; some to $10,000. **Remarks:** Full-time maker; first knife sold in 1978. **Mark:** First initial, last name.

RINALDI, T.H., RINALDI CUSTOM BLADES, PO Box 718, Winchester, CA 92596, Phone: 909-926-5422, Trace@thrblades.com Web: www.thrblades.com

Technical: Grinds S30V, 3V, A2 and talonite fixed blades. **Prices:** $175-600. **Remarks:** Tactical and utility for the most part.

RINKES, SIEGFRIED, Am Sportpl 2, D 91459, Markterlbach, GERMANY

RIZZI, RUSSELL J., 37 March Rd., Ashfield, MA 01330, Phone: 413-625-2842

Specialties: Fancy working and using straight knives and folders of his design or to customer specs. **Patterns:** Hunters, locking folders and fighters. **Technical:** Grinds 440C, D2 and commercial Damascus. **Prices:** $150 to $750; some to $2500. **Remarks:** Part-time maker; first knife sold in 1990. **Mark:** Last name, Ashfield, MA.

ROATH, DEAN, 3050 Winnipeg Dr., Baton Rouge, LA 70819, Phone: 225-272-5562

Specialties: Classic working knives; focusing on fillet knives for salt water fishermen. **Patterns:** Hunters, filets, canoe/trail, and boating/sailing knives. **Technical:** Grinds 440C. **Prices:** $85 to $500; some to $1500. **Remarks:** Part-time maker; first knife sold in 1978. **Mark:** Name, city and state.

ROBBINS, BILL, 299 Fairview St, Globe, AZ 85501, Phone: 928-402-0052, billrknifemaker@aol.com

Specialties: Plain and fancy working straight knives. Will make to his own designs and most anything you can draw. **Patterns:** Hunting knives, utility knives, and bowies. **Technical:** Grinds ATS-34, 440C, tool steel, high carbon, buys Damascus. **Prices:** $70 to $450. **Remarks:** Part-time maker, first knife sold in 2001. **Mark:** Last name or desert scene with name.

ROBBINS, HOWARD P., 1407 S. 217th Ave., Elkhorn, NE 68022, Phone: 402-289-4121, ARobb1407@aol.com

Specialties: High-tech working knives with clean designs, some fancy. **Patterns:** Folders, hunters and camp knives. **Technical:** Grinds 440C. Heat-treats; likes mirror finishes. Offers leatherwork. **Prices:** $100 to $500; some to $1000. **Remarks:** Full-time maker; first knife sold in 1982. **Mark:** Name, city and state.

ROBERTS, CHUCK, PO Box 7174, Golden, CO 80403, Phone: 303-642-0512, robertsart@juno.com

Specialties: Sheffield Bowies; historic-styles only. **Patterns:** Bowies and California knives. **Technical:** Grinds 440C, 5160 and ATS-34. Handles made of stag, ivory or mother-of-pearl. **Prices:** Start at $750. **Remarks:** Full-time maker. **Mark:** Last initial or last name.

ROBERTS, E. RAY, 191 Nursery Rd., Monticello, FL 32344, Phone: 850-997-4403

Specialties: High-Carbon Damascus knives and tomahawks.

ROBERTS, GEORGE A., PO Box 31228, 211 Main St., Whitehorse, YT, CANADA Y1A 5P7, Phone: 867-667-7099, Fax: 867-667-7099, Web: www.yuk-biz.com/bandit blades

Specialties: Mastadon ivory, fossil walrus ivory handled knives, scrimshawed or carved. **Patterns:** Side lockers, fancy bird and trout knives, hunters, fillet blades. **Technical:** Grinds stainless, all surgical steels. **Prices:** Up to $3500 U.S. **Remarks:** Full-time maker; first knives sold in 1986. Doing business as Bandit Blades. **Mark:** Bandit Yukon with pick and shovel crossed. **Other:** Most recent works have gold nuggets in fossilized Mastodon ivory. Something new using mosaic pins in mokume bolster and in mosaic Damascus, it creates a new look.

ROBERTS, JACK, 10811 Sagebluff Dr., Houston, TX 77089, Phone: 281-481-1784, jroberts59@houston.rr.com

Specialties: Hunting knives and folders, offers scrimshaw by wife Barbara. **Patterns:** Drop point hunters and liner lock folders. **Technical:** Grinds 440-C, offers file work, texturing, natural handle materials and micarta. **Prices:** $200 to $800 some higher. **Remarks:** Part-time maker, sold first knife in 1965. **Mark:** Name, city, state.

ROBERTS, MICHAEL, 601 Oakwood Dr., Clinton, MS 39056, Phone: 601-924-3154; Pager 601-978-8180

Specialties: Working and using knives in standard patterns and to customer specs. **Patterns:** Hunters, Bowies, tomahawks and fighters. **Technical:** Forges 5160, O1, 1095 and his own Damascus. Uses only natural handle materials. **Prices:** $145 to $500; some to $1100. **Remarks:** Part-time maker; first knife sold in 1988. **Mark:** Last name or first and last name in Celtic script.

ROBERTSON, LEO D., 3728 Pleasant Lake Dr., Indianpolis, IN 46227, Phone: 317-882-9899, ldr52@juno.com

Specialties: Hunting and folders. **Patterns:** Hunting, fillet, Bowie, utility, folders and tantos. **Technical:** Uses ATS-34, 154CM, 440C, 1095, D2 and Damascus steels. **Prices:** Fixed knives $75 to $350, folders $350 to $600. **Remarks:** Handles made with stag, wildwoods, laminates, mother-of-pearl. **Mark:** Logo with full name in oval around logo. **Other:** Made first knife in 1990. Member of American Bladesmith Society.

ROBINSON, CHARLES (DICKIE), PO Box 221, Vega, TX 79092, Phone: 806-267-2629, dickie@amaonline.com

Specialties: Classic and working/using knives. **Patterns:** Bowies, daggers, fighters, hunters and camp knives. **Technical:** Forges O1, 5160, 52100 and his own Damascus. **Prices:** $350 to $850; some to $5000. **Remarks:** Part-time maker; first knife sold in 1988. Doing business as Robinson Knives. ABS Master Smith. **Mark:** Robinson MS.

ROBINSON, CHUCK, Sea Robin Forge, 1423 Third Ave., Picayune, MS 39466, Phone: 601-798-0060, crobin@datastar.net

Specialties: Deluxe period pieces and working / using knives of his design and to customer specs. **Patterns:** Bowies, fighters, hunters, folders, utility knives and original designs. **Technical:** Forges own Damascus, 52100, 01, L6 and 1070 thru 1095. **Prices:** Start At $225. **Remarks:** First knife 1958. Recently transitioned to full-time maker. **Mark:** Fish logo, anchor and initials C.R.

ROBINSON, ROBERT W., 1569 N. Finley Pt., Polson, MT 59860, Phone: 406-887-2259, Fax: 406-887-2259

Specialties: High-art straight knives, folders and automatics of his design. **Patterns:** Hunters and locking folders. **Technical:** Grinds ATS-34, 154CM and 440V. Inlays pearl and gold; engraves sheep horn and ivory. **Prices:** $150 to $500; some to $2000. **Remarks:** Full-time maker; first knife sold in 1983. Doing business as Robbie Knife. **Mark:** Name on left side of blade.

ROBINSON III, REX R., 10531 Poe St., Leesburg, FL 34788, Phone: 352-787-4587

Specialties: One-of-a-kind high-art automatics of his design. **Patterns:** Automatics, liner locks and lock back folders. **Technical:** Uses tool steel and stainless Damascus and mokume; flat grinds. Hand carves folders. **Prices:** $1800 to $7500. **Remarks:** First knife sold in 1988. **Mark:** First name inside oval.

ROCHFORD, MICHAEL R., PO Box 577, Dresser, WI 54009, Phone: 715-755-3520, mrrochford@centurytel.net

Specialties: Working straight knives and folders. Classic Bowies and Moran traditional. **Patterns:** Bowies, fighters, hunters: slip-joint, locking and liner locking folders. **Technical:** Grinds ATS-34, 440C, 154CM and D-2; forges W2, 5160, and his own Damascus. Offers metal and metal and leather sheaths. Filework and wire inlay. **Prices:** $150 to $1000; some to $2000. **Remarks:** Part-time maker; first knife sold in 1984. **Mark:** Name.

RODEBAUGH, JAMES L., 9374 Joshua Rd., Oak Hills, CA 92345

RODEWALD, GARY, 447 Grouse Ct., Hamilton, MT 59840, Phone: 406-363-2192
  Specialties: Bowies of his design as inspired from his torical pieces. **Patterns:** Hunters, Bowies and camp/combat. Forges 5160 1084 and his own Damascus of 1084, 15N20, field grade hunters AT-34 to 440C, 440V, and BG42. **Prices:** $200 to $1500 **Remarks:** Sole author on knives, sheaths done by saddle maker. **Mark:** Rodewald.

RODKEY, DAN, 18336 Ozark Dr., Hudson, FL 34667, Phone: 727-863-8264
  Specialties: Traditional straight knives of his design and in standard patterns. **Patterns:** Boots, fighters and hunters. **Technical:** Grinds 440C, D2 and ATS-34. **Prices:** Start at $200. **Remarks:** Full-time maker; first knife sold in 1985. Doing business as Rodkey Knives. **Mark:** Etched logo on blade.

ROE JR., FRED D., 4005 Granada Dr., Huntsville, AL 35802, Phone: 205-881-6847
  Specialties: Highly finished working knives of his design; period pieces. **Patterns:** Hunters, fighters and survival knives; locking folders; specialty designs like divers' knives. **Technical:** Grinds 154CM, ATS-34 and Damascus. Field-tests all blades. **Prices:** $125 to $250; some to $2000. **Remarks:** Part-time maker; first knife sold in 1980. **Mark:** Last name.

ROGERS, CHARLES W., Rt. 1 Box 1552, Douglas, TX 75943, Phone: 409-326-4496

ROGERS, RAY, PO Box 126, Wauconda, WA 98859, Phone: 509-486-8069
  Specialties: Liner lock folders. Asian and European professional chef's knives. **Patterns:** Rayzor folders, chef's knives and cleavers of his own and traditional designs, drop point hunters and fillet knives. **Technical:** Stock removal S30V, 440, 1095, O1 Damascus and other steels. Does all heat treating, clay tempering, some forging G-10, Micarta®, Carbon fiber on folders, stabilized burl woods on fixed blades. **Prices:** $200 to $450. **Remarks:** Knives made one-at-a-time to customer's order. Maker is happy to consider customizing his knife designs to suit your preferences and sometimes create entirely new knives when necessary. As a full-time knifemaker, willing to spend as much time as it takes (usually through email) discussing the options and refining details of a knife's design to insure that you get the knife you really want.

ROGERS, RICHARD, PO Box 769, Magdalena, NM 87825, Phone: 505-854-2567, rsrogers1@yahoo.com
  Specialties: Sheffield-style folders and multi-blade folders. **Patterns:** Folders: various traditional patterns. One-of-a-kind fixed blades. Fixed blades: Bowies, daggers, hunters, utility knives. **Technical:** Mainly use ATS-34 and prefer natural handle materials. **Prices:** $400 and up. **Mark:** Last name.

ROGERS, RODNEY, 602 Osceola St., Wildwood, FL 34785, Phone: 352-748-6114
  Specialties: Traditional straight knives and folders. **Patterns:** Fighters, hunters, skinners. **Technical:** Flat-grinds ATS-34 and Damascus. Prefers natural materials. **Prices:** $150 to $1400. **Remarks:** Full-time maker; first knife sold in 1986. **Mark:** Last name, Handmade.

ROGERS JR., ROBERT P., 3979 South Main St., Acworth, GA 30101, Phone: 404-974-9982
  Specialties: Traditional working knives. **Patterns:** Hunters, 4-inch trailing-points. **Technical:** Grinds D2, 154CM and ATS-34; likes ironwood and ivory Micarta. **Prices:** $125 to $175. **Remarks:** Spare-time maker; first knife sold in 1975. **Mark:** Name.

ROGHMANS, MARK, 607 Virginia Ave., LaGrange, GA 30240, Phone: 706-885-1273
  Specialties: Classic and traditional knives of his design. **Patterns:** Bowies, daggers and fighters. **Technical:** Grinds ATS-34, D2 and 440C. **Prices:** $250 to $500. **Remarks:** Part-time maker; first knife sold in 1984. Doing business as LaGrange Knife. **Mark:** Last name and/or LaGrange Knife.

ROHN, FRED, 7675 W Happy Hill Rd., Coeur d'Alene, ID 83814, Phone: 208-667-0774
  Specialties: Hunters, boot knives, custom patterns. **Patterns:** Drop points, double edge etc. **Technical:** Grinds 440 or 154CM. **Prices:** $85 and up. **Remarks:** Part-time maker. **Mark:** Logo on blade; serial numbered.

ROLLERT, STEVE, PO Box 65, Keenesburg, CO 80643-0065, Phone: 303-732-4858, steve@doveknives.com Web: www.doveknives.com
  Specialties: Highly finished working knives. **Patterns:** Variety of straight knives; locking folders and slip-joints. **Technical:** Forges and grinds W2, 1095, ATS-34 and his pattern-welded, cable Damascus and nickel Damascus. **Prices:** $300 to $1000; some to $3000. **Remarks:** Full-time maker; first knife sold in 1980. Doing business as Dove Knives. **Mark:** Last name in script.

ROLLICK, WALTER D., 2001 Cochran Rd., Maryville, TN 37803, Phone: 423-681-6105

RONZIO, N. JACK, PO Box 248, Fruita, CO 81521, Phone: 970-858-0921

ROOT, GARY, 644 East 14th St, Erie, PA 16503, Phone: 814-459-0196
  Specialties: Damascus bowies with hand carved eagles, hawks and snakes for handles. Few folders made. **Patterns:** Daggers, fighters, hunter/field knives. **Technical:** Using handforged Damascus from Ray Bybar Jr (M.S.) and Robert Eggerling. Grinds D2, 440C, 1095 and 5160. Some 5160 is hand forged. **Prices:** $80 to $300 some to $1000. **Remarks:** Part-time maker, first knife sold in 1976. **Mark:** Name over Erie, PA.

ROSA, PEDRO GULLHERME TELES, R. das Magnolias, 45 CECAP Presidente Prudente, SP-19065-410, BRAZIL, Phone: 0182-271769
  Specialties: Using straight knives and folders to customer specs; some high-art. **Patterns:** Fighters, Bowies and daggers. **Technical:** Grinds and forges D6, 440C, high-carbon steels and Damascus. **Prices:** $60 to $400. **Remarks:** Full-time maker; first knife sold in 1991. **Mark:** A hammer over "Hammer."

ROSE, DEREK W., 14 Willow Wood Rd., Gallipolis, OH 45631, Phone: 740-446-4627

ROSENFELD, BOB, 955 Freeman Johnson Rd., Hoschton, GA 30548, Phone: 770-867-2647, www.1bladesmith@msn.com
  Specialties: Fancy and embellished working/using straight knives of his design and in standard patterns. **Patterns:** Daggers, hunters and utility/camp knives. **Technical:** Forges 52100, A203E, 1095 and L6 Damascus. Offers engraving. **Prices:** $125 to $650; some to $1000. **Remarks:** Full-time maker; first knife sold in 1984. Also makes folders; ABS Journeyman. **Mark:** Last name or full name, Knifemaker.

ROSS, D.L., 27 Kinsman St., Dunedin, NEW ZEALAND, Phone: 64 3 464 0239, Fax: 64 3 464 0239
  Specialties: Working straight knives of his design. **Patterns:** Hunters, various others. **Technical:** Grinds 440C. **Prices:** $100 to $450; some to $700 NZ dollars. **Remarks:** Part-time maker; first knife sold in 1988. **Mark:** Dave Ross, Maker, city and country.

ROSS, GREGG, 4556 Wenhart Rd., Lake Worth, FL 33463, Phone: 407-439-4681
  Specialties: Working/using straight knives. **Patterns:** Bowies, hunters and utility/camp knives. **Technical:** Forges and grinds ATS-34, Damascus and cable Damascus. Uses decorative pins. **Prices:** $125 to $250; some to $400. **Remarks:** Part-time maker; first knife sold in 1992. **Mark:** Name, city and state.

ROSS, STEPHEN, 534 Remington Dr., Evanston, WY 82930, Phone: 307-789-7104
  Specialties: One-of-a-kind collector-grade classic and contemporary straight knives and folders of his design and to customer specs; some fantasy pieces. **Patterns:** Combat and survival knives, hunters, boots and folders. **Technical:** Grinds stainless; forges spring and tool steel. Engraves, scrimshaws. Makes leather sheaths. **Prices:** $160 to $3000. **Remarks:** Part-time maker; first knife sold in 1971. **Mark:** Last name in modified Roman; sometimes in script.

ROSS, TIM, 3239 Oliver Rd, Thunder Bay, ONT, CANADA P7G 1S9, Phone: 807-935-2667, Fax: 807-935-3179
  Specialties: Fixed blades. **Patterns:** Hunting, fishing, collector. **Technical:** Uses D2, Stellite, 440C, Forges 52100, Damascus cable. **Prices:** $150 to $750, some to $5000. **Mark:** Tang stamps Ross custom knives.

ROSSDEUTSCHER, ROBERT N., 133 S Vail Ave., Arlington Heights, IL 60005, Phone: 847-577-0404, Web: www.rnrknives.com
  Specialties: Frontier-style and historically inspired knives. **Patterns:** Trade knives, Bowies, camp knives and hunting knives, tomahawks and lances. **Technical:** Most knives are hand forged, a few are stock removal. **Prices:** $135 to $1500. **Remarks:** Journeyman Smith of the American Bladesmith Society and Neo-Tribal Bladesmiths. **Mark:** Back-to-back "R's", one upside down and backwards, one right side up and forward in an oval. Sometimes with name, town and state; depending on knife style.

ROTELLA, RICHARD A., 643—75th St., Niagara Falls, NY 14304
  Specialties: Working knives of his design. **Patterns:** Various fishing, hunting and utility knives; folders. **Technical:** Grinds ATS-34. Prefers hand-rubbed finishes. **Prices:** $65 to $450; some to $900. **Remarks:** Spare-time maker; first knife sold in 1977. Not taking orders at this time; only sells locally. **Mark:** Name and city in stylized waterfall logo.

ROULIN, CHARLES, 113 B Rt. de Soral, 1233 Geneva, SWITZERLAND, Phone: 022-757-4479, Fax: 022-757-4479, coutelier@coutelier-Roulin.com Web: www.coutelier-roulin.com
  Specialties: Fancy high-art straight knives and folders of his design. **Patterns:** Bowies, locking folders, slip-joint folders and miniatures. **Technical:** Grinds 440C, ATS-34 and D2. Engraves; carves nature

custom knifemakers

scenes and detailed animals in steel, ivory, on handles and blades. **Prices:** $500 to $3000; some to $10,000. **Remarks:** Full-time maker; first knife sold in 1988. **Mark:** Symbol of fish with name or name engraved.

ROWE, FRED, BETHEL RIDGE FORGE, 3199 Roberts Rd., Amesville, OH 45711, Phone: 866-325-2164, fred.rowe@bethelridgeforge.com Web: www.bethelridgeforge.com
Specialties: Damascus and carbon steel sheath knives. **Patterns:** Bowies, hunters, fillet small kokris. **Technical:** My own Damascus, 52100, O1, L-6, 1095 carbon steels. **Prices:** $150 to $800. **Remarks:** All blades are clay hardened. **Mark:** Bethel Ridge Forge.

ROZAS, CLARK D., 1436 W "G" St., Wilmington, CA 90744, Phone: 310-518-0488
Specialties: Hand forged blades. **Patterns:** Pig stickers, toad stabbers, whackers, choppers. **Technical:** Damascus, 52100, 1095, 1084, 5160. **Prices:** $200 to $600. **Remarks:** A.B.S. member; part-time maker since 1995. **Mark:** Name over dagger.

RUANA KNIFE WORKS, Box 520, Bonner, MT 59823, Phone: 406-258-5368, www.ruanaknives.com
Specialties: Working knives and period pieces. **Patterns:** Variety of straight knives. **Technical:** Forges 5160 chrome alloy for Bowies and 1095. **Prices:** $155 and up. **Remarks:** Full-time maker; first knife sold in 1938. Currently making knife honoring the lewis and clark expedition. **Mark:** Name.

RUPERT, BOB, 301 Harshaville Rd., Clinton, PA 15026, Phone: 724-573-4569, rbrupert@aol.com
Specialties: Wrought period pieces with natural elements. **Patterns:** Elegant straight blades; friction folders. **Technical:** Forges colonial 7; 1095; 5160; diffuse mokume-gane and form Damascus. **Prices:** $150 to $1500; some higher. **Remarks:** Part-time maker; first knife sold in 1980. Evening hours studio since 1980. **Mark:** R etched in Old English. **Other:** Likes simplicity that disassembles.

RUPLE, WILLIAM H., PO Box 370, Charlotte, TX 78011, Phone: 830-277-1371
Specialties: Multi-blade folders, slip joints, some lock backs. **Patterns:** Like to reproduce old patterns. **Technical:** Grinds 440C, ATS-34, D2 and commercial Damascus. Offers filework on back springs and liners. **Prices:** $300 to $500; some to $1000. **Remarks:** Full-time maker; first knife sold in 1988. **Mark:** Ruple.

RUSS, RON, 5351 NE 160th Ave., Williston, FL 32696, Phone: 352-528-2603, RussRs@aol.com
Specialties: Damascus and Mokume. **Patterns:** Ladder, rain drop and butterfly. **Technical:** Most knives, including Damascus, are forged from 52100-E. **Prices:** $65 to $2500. **Mark:** Russ.

RUSSELL, MICK, 4 Rossini Rd., Pari Park, Port Elizabeth 6070, SOUTH AFRICA
Specialties: Art knives. **Patterns:** Working and collectible bird, trout and hunting knives, defense knives and folders. **Technical:** Grinds D2, 440C, ATS-34 and Damascus. Offers mirror or satin finishes. **Prices:** Start at $100. **Remarks:** Full-time maker; first knife sold in 1986. **Mark:** Stylized rhino incorporating initials.

RUSSELL, TOM, 6500 New Liberty Rd., Jacksonville, AL 36265, Phone: 205-492-7866
Specialties: Straight working knives of his design or to customer specs. **Patterns:** Hunters, folders, fighters, skinners, Bowies and utility knives. **Technical:** Grinds D2, 440C and ATS-34; offers filework. **Prices:** $75 to $225. **Remarks:** Part-time maker; first knife sold in 1987. Full-time tool and die maker. **Mark:** Last name with tulip stamp.

RUTH, MICHAEL G, 3101 New Boston Rd., Texarkana, TX 75501, Phone: 903-832-7166

RYBAR JR., RAYMOND B., 726 W Lynwood St., Phoenix, AZ 85007, Phone: 605-523-0201
Specialties: Fancy/embellished, high-art and traditional working using straight knives and folders of his design and in standard patterns; period pieces. **Patterns:** Daggers, fighters and swords. **Technical:** Forges Damascus. All blades have etched biblical scripture or biblical significance. **Prices:** $120 to $1200; some to $4500. **Remarks:** Full-time maker; first knife sold in 1972. Doing business as Stone Church Forge. **Mark:** Last name or business name.

RYBERG, GOTE, Faltgatan 2, S-562 00 Norrahammar, SWEDEN, Phone: 4636-61678

RYDBOM, JEFF, PO Box 548, Annandale, MN 55302, Phone: 320-274-9639, jry1890@hotmail.com
Specialties: Ring knives. **Patterns:** Hunters, fighters, Bowie and camp knives. **Technical:** Straight grinds 01, A2, 1566 and 5150 steels. **Prices:** $150 to $1000. **Remarks:** No pinning of guards or pommels. All silver brazed. **Mark:** Capital "C" with J R inside.

RYDER, BEN M., PO Box 133, Copperhill, TN 37317, Phone: 615-496-2750
Specialties: Working/using straight knives of his design and to customer specs. **Patterns:** Fighters, hunters, utility/camp knives. **Technical:** Grinds 440C, ATS-34, D2, commercial Damascus. **Prices:** $75 to $400. **Remarks:** Part-time maker; first knife sold in 1992. **Mark:** Full name in double butterfly logo.

RYUICHI, KUKI, 504-7 Tokorozawa-Shinmachi, Tokorozawa-city, Saitama, JAPAN, Phone: 042-943-3451

RZEWNICKI, GERALD, 8833 S Massbach Rd., Elizabeth, IL 61028-9714, Phone: 815-598-3239

S

SAINDON, R. BILL, 233 Rand Pond Rd., Goshen, NH 03752, Phone: 603-863-1874, dayskiev71@aol.com
Specialties: Collector-quality folders of his design or to customer specs. **Patterns:** Latch release, liner lock and lockback folders. **Technical:** Offers limited amount of own Damascus; also uses Damas makers steel. Prefers natural handle material, gold and gems. **Prices:** $500 to $4000. **Remarks:** Full-time maker; first knife sold in 1981. Doing business as Daynia Forge. **Mark:** Sun logo or engraved surname.

SAKAKIBARA, MASAKI, 20-8 Sakuragaoka, 2-Chome Setagaya-ku, Tokyo 156-0054, JAPAN, Phone: 81-3-3420-0375

SAKMAR, MIKE, 1451 Clovelly Ave., Rochester, MI 48307, Phone: 248-852-6775, Fax: 248-852-8544, mikesakmar@yahoo.com
Specialties: Mokume in various patterns and alloy combinations. **Patterns:** Bowies, fighters, hunters and integrals. **Technical:** Grinds ATS-34, Damascus and high-carbon tool steels. Uses mostly natural handle materials; elephant ivory, walrus ivory, stag, wildwood, oosic, etc. Makes mokume for resale. **Prices:** $250 to $2500; some to $4000. **Remarks:** Part-time maker; first knife sold in 1990. **Mark:** Last name. **Other:** Supplier of Mokume.

SALLEY, JOHN D., 3965 Frederick-Ginghamsburg Rd., Tipp City, OH 45371, Phone: 937-698-4588, Fax: 937-698-4131
Specialties: Fancy working knives and art pieces. **Patterns:** Hunters, fighters, daggers and some swords. **Technical:** Grinds ATS-34, 12C27 and W2; buys Damascus. **Prices:** $85 to $1000; some to $6000. **Remarks:** Part-time maker; first knife sold in 1979. **Mark:** First initial, last name.

SAMPSON, LYNN, 381 Deakins Rd., Jonesborough, TN 37659, Phone: 423-348-8373
Specialties: Highly finished working knives, mostly folders. **Patterns:** Locking folders, slip-joints, interframes and two-blades. **Technical:** Grinds D2, 440C and ATS-34; offers extensive filework. **Prices:** Start at $300. **Remarks:** Full-time maker; first knife sold in 1982. **Mark:** Name and city in logo.

SANDBERG, RONALD B., 24784 Shadowwood Ln., Browntown, MI 48134, Phone: 734-671-6866, msc@ili.net
Specialties: Good looking and functional hunting knives, filework, mixing of handle materials. **Patterns:** Hunters, skinners and Bowies. **Prices:** $120 and up. **Remarks:** Doing business as mighty Sharp Cuts. **Mark:** R.B. Sandberg.

SANDERS, A.A., 3850 72 Ave. NE, Norman, OK 73071, Phone: 405-364-8660
Specialties: Working straight knives and folders. **Patterns:** Hunters, fighters, daggers and Bowies. **Technical:** Forges his own Damascus; offers stock removal with ATS-34, 440C, A2, D2, O1, 5160 and 1095. **Prices:** $85 to $1500. **Remarks:** Full-time maker; first knife sold in 1985. Formerly known as Athern Forge. **Mark:** Name.

SANDERS, BILL, 335 Bauer Ave., PO Box 957, Mancos, CO 81328, Phone: 970-533-7223, Fax: 970-533-7390, billsand@frontier.net Web: www.billsandershandmadeknives.com
Specialties: Survival knives, working straight knives, some fancy and some fantasy, of his design. **Patterns:** Hunters, boots, utility knives, using belt knives. **Technical:** Grinds 440C, ATS-34 and commercial Damascus. Provides wide variety of handle materials. **Prices:** $170 to $800. **Remarks:** Full-time maker. Formerly of Timberline knives. **Mark:** Name, city and state.

SANDERS, MICHAEL M., PO Box 1106, Ponchatoula, LA 70454, Phone: 225-294-3601
Specialties: Working straight knives and folders, some deluxe. **Patterns:** Hunters, fighters, Bowies, daggers, large folders and deluxe Damascus miniatures. **Technical:** Grinds O1, D2, 440C, ATS-34 and Damascus. **Prices:** $75 to $650; some higher. **Remarks:** Full-time maker; first knife sold in 1967. **Mark:** Name and state.

SANDERSON, RAY, 4403 Uplands Way, Yakima, WA 98908, Phone: 509-965-0128
Specialties: One-of-a-kind Buck knives; traditional working straight knives and folders of his design. **Patterns:** Bowies, hunters and fighters. **Technical:** Grinds 440C and ATS-34. **Prices:** $200 to $750. **Remarks:** Part-time maker; first knife sold in 1984. **Mark:** Sanderson Knives in shape of Bowie.

SANDLIN, LARRY, 4580 Sunday Dr., Adamsville, AL 35005, Phone: 205-674-1816
Specialties: High-art straight knives of his design. **Patterns:** Boots, daggers, hunters and fighters. **Technical:** Forges 1095, L6, O1, carbon steel and Damascus. **Prices:** $200 to $1500; some to $5000. **Remarks:** Part-time maker; first knife sold in 1990. **Mark:** Chiseled last name in Japanese.

SANDOW, NORMAN E, 20 Redcastle Dr, Howick, Auckland, NEW ZEALAND, Phone: 09 2770916, sanknife@ezysurf.co.nz
Specialties Quality liner lock folders. Working and fancy straight knives. Some one of a kind. Embellishments available. **Patterns:** Most patterns, hunters, boot, bird and trout etc. and to customers specs. **Technical:** Predominate knife steel ATS-34. Also in use 12C27, D2 and Damascus. High class handle material used on both folders and straight knives. All blades made via the stock removal method. **Prices:** $250 to $1500. **Remarks:** Full-time maker. **Mark:** Norma E Sandow in semi-circular design.

SANDS, SCOTT, 2 Lindis Ln., New Brighton, Christchurch 9, NEW ZEALAND
Specialties: Classic working and fantasy swords. **Patterns:** Fantasy, medieval, celtic, viking, katana, some daggers. **Technical:** Forges own Damascus; 1080 and L6; 5160 and L6; 01 and L6. All hand-polished, does own heat-treating, forges non-Damascus on request. **Prices:** $1500 to $15,000+. **Remarks:** Full-time maker; first blade sold in 1996. **Mark:** Stylized Moon.

SARVIS, RANDALL J., 110 West Park Ave., Fort Pierre, SD 57532, Phone: 605-223-2772, rsarvis@sdln.net

SASS, GARY N., 2048 Buckeye Dr, Sharpsville, PA 16150, Phone: 724-866-6165, gnsass@verizon.net
Specialties: Working straight knives of his design or to customer specifications. **Patterns:** Hunters, fighters, utility knives, push daggers. **Technical:** Grinds 440C, ATS-34 and Damascus. Uses exotic wood, buffalo horn, warthog tusk and semi-precious stones. **Prices:** $50 to $250, some higher. **Remarks:** Part-time maker. First knife sold in 2003. **Mark:** Initials G.S. formed into a diamond shape.

SAWBY, SCOTT, 480 Snowberry Ln., Sandpoint, ID 83864, Phone: 208-263-4171, scotmar@imbris.net Web: www.sawbycustomknives.com
Specialties: Folders, working and fancy. **Patterns:** Locking folders, patent locking systems and interframes. **Technical:** Grinds D2, 440C, 154CM, CPM-T-440V and ATS-34. **Prices:** $500 to $1500. **Remarks:** Full-time maker; first knife sold in 1974. Engraving by wife Marian. **Mark:** Last name, city and state.

SCARROW, WIL, c/o LandW Mail Service, 919 E Hermosa Dr., San Gabriel, CA 91775, Phone: 626-286-6069, willsknife@earthlink.net
Specialties: Carving knives, also working straight knives in standard patterns or to customer specs. **Patterns:** Carving, fishing, hunting, skinning, utility, swords and Bowies. **Technical:** Forges and grinds: A2, L6, W1, D2, 5160, 1095, 440C, AEB-L, ATS-34 and others on request. Offers some filework. **Prices:** $105 to $850; some higher. Prices include sheath (carver's $40 and up). **Remarks:** Spare-time maker; first knife sold in 1983. Two to eight month construction time on custom orders. Doing business as Scarrow's Custom Stuff and Gold Hill Knife works (in Oregon). **Mark:** SC with arrow and date/year made. **Other:** Carving knives available at the 'Wild Duck' Woodcarvers Supply. Contact at duckstore@aol.com.

SCHALLER, ANTHONY BRETT, 5609 Flint Ct. NW, Albuquerque, NM 87120, Phone: 505-899-0155, brett@schallerknives.com Web: www.schallerknives.com
Specialties: Straight knives and locking-liner folders of his design and in standard patterns. **Patterns:** Boots, fighters, utility knives and folders. **Technical:** Grinds ATS-34, BG42 and stainless Damascus. Offers filework, hand-rubbed finishes and full and narrow tangs. Prefers exotic woods or Micarta for handle materials, G-10 and carbon fiber to handle materials. **Prices:** $60 to $350; some to $500. **Remarks:** Part-time maker; first knife sold in 1990. **Mark:** A.B. Schaller - Albuquerque NM - handmade.

SCHEID, MAGGIE, 124 Van Stallen St., Rochester, NY 14621-3557
Specialties: Simple working straight knives. **Patterns:** Kitchen and utility knives; some miniatures. **Technical:** Forges 5160 high-carbon steel. **Prices:** $100 to $200. **Remarks:** Part-time maker; first knife sold in 1986. **Mark:** Full name.

SCHEMPP, ED, PO Box 1181, Ephrata, WA 98823, Phone: 509-754-2963, Fax: 509-754-3212
Specialties: Mosaic Damascus and unique folder designs. **Patterns:** Primarily folders. **Technical:** Grinds CPM440V; forges many patterns of mosaic using powdered steel. **Prices:** $100 to $400; some to $2000. **Remarks:** Part-time maker; first knife sold in 1991. Doing business as Ed Schempp Knives. **Mark:** Ed Schempp Knives over five heads of wheat, city and state.

SCHEMPP, MARTIN, PO Box 1181, 5430 Baird Springs Rd. N.W., Ephrata, WA 98823, Phone: 509-754-2963, Fax: 509-754-3212
Specialties: Fantasy and traditional straight knives of his design, to customer specs and in standard patterns; Paleolithic-styles. **Patterns:** Fighters and Paleolithic designs. **Technical:** Uses opal, Mexican rainbow and obsidian. Offers scrimshaw. **Prices:** $15 to $100; some to $250. **Remarks:** Spare-time maker; first knife sold in 1995. **Mark:** Initials and date.

SCHEPERS, GEORGE B., PO Box 395, Shelton, NE 68876-0395
Specialties: Fancy period pieces of his design. **Patterns:** Bowies, swords, tomahawks; locking folders and miniatures. **Technical:** Grinds W1, W2 and his own Damascus; etches. **Prices:** $125 to $600; some higher. **Remarks:** Full-time maker; first knife sold in 1981. **Mark:** Schep.

SCHEURER, ALFREDO E. FAES, Av. Rincon de los Arcos 104, Col. Bosque Res. del Sur, C.P. 16010, MEXICO, Phone: 5676 47 63
Specialties: Fancy and fantasy knives of his design. **Patterns:** Daggers. **Technical:** Grinds stainless steel; casts and grinds silver. Sets stones in silver. **Prices:** $2000 to $3000. **Remarks:** Spare-time maker; first knife sold in 1989. **Mark:** Symbol.

SCHILLING, ELLEN, 95 Line Rd., Hamilton Square, NJ 08690, Phone: 609-448-0483

SCHIPPNICK, JIM, PO Box 326, Sanborn, NY 14132, Phone: 716-731-3715, ragnar@ragweedforge.com Web: www.ragweedforge.com
Specialties: Nordic, early American, rustic. **Mark:** Runic R. **Remarks:** Also import Nordic knives from Norway, Sweden and Finland.

SCHIRMER, MIKE, 312 E 6th St., Rosalia, WA 99170-9506, Phone: 208-523-3249, schirmer@3rivers.net
Specialties: Working straight knives of his design or to customer specs; mostly hunters and personal knives. **Patterns:** Hunters, camp, kitchen, Bowies and fighters. **Technical:** Grinds O1, D2, A2 and Damascus and Talonoite. **Prices:** Start at $150. **Remarks:** Full-time maker; first knife sold in 1992. Doing business as Ruby Mountain Knives. **Mark:** Name or name and location.

SCHLOMER, JAMES E., 2543 Wyatt Pl., Kissimmee, FL 34741, Phone: 407-348-8044
Specialties: Working and show straight knives. **Patterns:** Hunters, Bowies and skinners. **Technical:** Stock removal method, 440C. Scrimshaws; carves sambar stag handles. Works on corean and Micarta. **Prices:** $150 to $750. **Remarks:** Full-time maker. **Mark:** Name and steel number.

SCHLUETER, DAVID, PO Box 463, Syracuse, NY 13209, Phone: 315-485-0829, david@oddfrogforge.com Web: http: //www.oddfrogforge.com
Specialties: Japanese-style swords, handmade fittings, leather wraps. **Patterns:** Kozuka to Tach, blades with bo-hi and o-kissaki. **Technical:** Sole author, forges and grinds, high-carbon steels. Blades are tempered after clay-coated and water-quenched heat treatment. All fittings are handmade. **Prices:** $800 to $5000 plus. **Remarks:** Full-time maker, doing business as Odd Frog Forge. **Mark:** Full name and date.

SCHMITZ, RAYMOND E., PO Box 1787, Valley Center, CA 92082, Phone: 760-749-4318

SCHMOKER, RANDY, SPIRIT OF THE HAMMER, HC 63 Box 1085, Slana, AK 99586, Phone: 907-822-3371, spiritofthehammer@hotmail.com
Specialties: Hand carved, natural materials, mastodon ivory, moose antler. **Patterns:** Hunter, skinner, Bowie, fighter, artistic collectables. **Technical:** Hand forged. **Prices:** $300 to $600. **Remarks:** 01 tool steel, 1095, 5160, 52100. **Mark:** Sheep with an S. **Other:** Custom sheaths, display stands.

SCHNEIDER, CRAIG M., 5380 N Amity Rd., Claremont, IL 62421, Phone: 217-377-5715
Specialties: Straight knives of his own design. **Patterns:** Bowies, hunters and miniatures. **Technical:** Forged high-carbon steel and Damascus. Flat grind and differential heat treatment use a wide selection of handle, guard and bolster material also offer leather sheaths. **Prices:** $85 to $2500. **Remarks:** Part-time maker; first knife sold in 1985. **Mark:** Stylized initials.

SCHNEIDER, HERMAN, 14084 Apple Valley Rd, Apple Valley, CA 92307, Phone: 760-946-9096
Mark: H.J. Schneider-Maker.

SCHNEIDER, KARL A., 209 N. Brownleaf Rd., Newark, DE 19713, Phone: 302-737-0277
 Specialties: Traditional working and using straight knives of his design. **Patterns:** Hunters, kitchen and fillet knives. **Technical:** Grinds ATS-34. Shapes handles to fit hands; uses Micarta, Pakkawood and exotic woods. Makes hand-stitched leather cases. **Prices:** $95 to $225. **Remarks:** Part-time maker; first knife sold in 1984-85. **Mark:** Name, address; also name in shape of fish.

SCHOEMAN, CORRIE, Box 28596, Danhof 9310, SOUTH AFRICA, Phone: 027 51 4363528 Cell: 027 82-3750789, corries@intekom.co.za
 Specialties: High-tech folders of his design or to customer's specs. **Patterns:** Linerlock folders and automatics. **Technical:** ATS-34, Damascus or stainless Damascus with titanium frames; prefers exotic materials for handles. **Prices:** $650 to $2000. **Remarks:** Full-time maker; first knife sold in 1984. **Mark:** Logo in knife shape engraved on inside of back bar. **Other:** All folders come with filed liners and back and jewled inserts.

SCHOENFELD, MATTHEW A., RR #1, Galiano Island, B.C., CANADA V0N 1P0, Phone: 250-539-2806
 Specialties: Working knives of his design. **Patterns:** Kitchen cutlery, camp knives, hunters. **Technical:** Grinds 440C. **Prices:** $85 to $500. **Remarks:** Part-time maker; first knife sold in 1978. **Mark:** Signature, Galiano Is. B.C., and date.

SCHOENINGH, MIKE, 49850 Miller Rd, North Powder, OR 97867, Phone: 541-856-3239

SCHOLL, TIM, 1389 Langdon Rd., Angier, NC 27501, Phone: 910-897-2051, tscholl@surrealnet.net
 Specialties: Fancy and working/using straight knives and folders of his design and to customer specs. **Patterns:** tomahawks, swords, tantos, hunters and fantasy knives. **Technical:** Grinds ATS-34 and D2; forges carbon and tool steel and Damascus. Offers filework, engraving and scrimshaw. **Prices:** $110; some to $4000. **Remarks:** Part-time maker; first knife sold in 1990. Doing business as Tim Scholl Custom Knives. **Mark:** S pierced by arrow.

SCHRADER, ROBERT, 55532 Gross De, Bend, OR 97707, Phone: 541-598-7301
 Specialties: Hunting, utility, Bowie. **Patterns:** Fixed blade. **Prices:** $150 to $600.

SCHRAP, ROBERT G., CUSTOM LEATHER KNIFE SHEATH CO., 7024 W. Wells St., Wauwatosa, WI 53213-3717, Phone: 414-771-6472, Fax: 414-479-9765, knifesheaths@aol.com
 Specialties: Leatherwork. **Prices:** $35 to $100. **Mark:** Schrap in oval.

SCHROEN, KARL, 4042 Bones Rd., Sebastopol, CA 95472, Phone: 707-823-4057, Fax: 707-823-2914
 Specialties: Using knives made to fit. **Patterns:** Sgian dubhs, carving sets, wood-carving knives, fishing knives, kitchen knives and new cleaver design. **Technical:** Forges A2, ATS-34,D2 and L-6 cruwear S30V 590V. **Prices:** $150 to $6000. **Remarks:** Full-time maker; first knife sold in 1968. Author of *The Hand Forged Knife*. **Mark:** Last name.

SCHUCHMANN, RICK, 1500 Brandie Ln, New Richmond, OH 45157, Phone: 513-553-4316
 Specialties: Replicas of antique and out of production Scagels and Randalls, primarily miniatures. **Patterns:** All sheath knives, mostly miniatures, hunting and fighting knives, some daggers and hatchets. **Technical:** Stock removal, 440 C and 01 steel. Most knives are flat ground, some convex. **Prices:** $175 to $600 and custom to $4000. **Remarks:** Part-time maker, sold first knife in 1997. We have knives on display in the Randall Museum. Sheaths are made exclusively at Sullivan's Holster Shop, Tampa, FL **Mark:** SCAR

SCHUCKMANN, RICK, SCAR CUSTOM KNIVES, 1500 Brandie Ln, New Richmond, OH 45159, Phone: 513-553-4316

SCHULTZ, ROBERT W., PO Box 70, Cocolalla, ID 83813-0070

SCHWARZER, STEPHEN, PO Box 4, Pomona Park, FL 32181, Phone: 386-649-5026, Fax: 386-649-8585, steveschwarzer@gbso.net Web: www.steveschwarzer.com
 Specialties: Mosaic Damascus and picture mosaic in folding knives. All Japanese blades are finished working with Wally Hostetter considered the top Japanese lacquer specialist in the USA. Also produces a line of carbon steel skinning knives at $300 and a line of high end mosaic Damascus bar stock for the discriminating knife maker who wants to use the best. **Patterns:** Folders, axes and buckskinner knives. **Technical:** Specializes in picture mosaic Damascus and powder metal mosaic work. Sole authorship; all work including carving done in-house. Most knives have file work and carving. **Prices:** $1500 to $5000, some higher; carbon steel and primitive knives much less. **Remarks:** Full-time maker; first knife sold in 1976, considered by many to be one of the top mosaic Damascus specialists in the world. Mosaic Master level work. **Mark:** Schwarzer + anvil.

SCIMIO, BILL, HC 01 Box 24A, Spruce Creek, PA 16683, Phone: 814-632-3751, blackcrowforge@aol.com

SCOFIELD, EVERETT, 2873 Glass Mill Rd., Chickamauga, GA 30707, Phone: 706-375-2790
 Specialties: Historic and fantasy miniatures. **Patterns:** All patterns. **Technical:** Uses only the finest tool steels and other materials. Uses only natural, precious and semi-precious materials. **Prices:** $100 to $1500. **Remarks:** Full-time maker; first knife sold in 1971. Doing business as Three Crowns Cutlery. **Mark:** Three Crowns logo.

SCORDIA, PAOLO, Via Terralba 143, 00050 Torrimpietra, Roma, ITALY, Phone: 06-61697231, pands@mail.nexus.it Web: www.scordia-knives.com
 Specialties: Working and fantasy knives of his own design. **Patterns:** Any pattern. **Technical:** Forges own Damascus, welds own Mokume and grinds ATS-34, etc. use hardwoods and Micarta for handles, brass and nickel-silver for fittings. Makes sheaths. **Prices:** $100 to $1000. **Remarks:** Part-time maker; first knife sold in 1988. **Mark:** Initials with sun and moon logo.

SCOTT, AL, 2245 Harper Valley Rd., Harper, TX 78631, Phone: 830-864-4182
 Specialties: High-art straight knives of his design. **Patterns:** Daggers, swords, early European, Middle East and Japanese knives. **Technical:** Uses ATS-34, 440C and Damascus. Hand engraves; does file work cuts filigree in the blade; offers ivory carving and precious metal inlay. **Remarks:** Full-time maker; first knife sold in 1994. Doing business as Al Scott Maker of Fine Blade Art. **Mark:** Name engraved in old English, sometime inlaid in 24K gold.

SCROGGS, JAMES A., 108 Murray Hill Dr., Warrensburg, MO 64093, Phone: 660-747-2568
 Specialties: Straight knives, prefers light weight. **Patterns:** Hunters, hideouts, and fighters. **Technical:** Grinds CMP3V plus experiments in steels. Prefers handles of walnut in English, bastonge, American black Also uses myrtle, maple, Osage orange. **Prices:** $200 to $1000. **Remarks:** 1st knife sold in 1985. Part-time maker, no orders taken. **Mark:** SCROGGS in block or script.

SCULLEY, PETER E., 340 Sunset Dr., Rising Fawn, GA 30738, Phone: 706-398-0169

SEARS, MICK, 1697 Peach Orchard Rd. #302, Sumter, SC 29154, Phone: 803-499-5074
 Specialties: Scots and confederate reproductions; Bowies and fighters. **Patterns:** Bowies, fighters. **Technical:** Grinds 440C and 1095. **Prices:** $50 to $150; some to $300. **Remarks:** Part-time maker; first knife sold in 1975. Doing business as Mick's Custom Knives. **Mark:** First name.

SELENT, CHUCK, PO Box 1207, Bonners Ferry, ID 83805-1207, Phone: 208-267-5807
 Specialties: Period, art and fantasy miniatures; exotics; one-of-a-kinds. **Patterns:** Swords, daggers and others. **Technical:** Works in Damascus, meteorite, 440C and tool steel. Offers scrimshaw. Offers his own casting and leatherwork; uses jewelry techniques. Makes display cases for miniatures. **Prices:** $75 to $400. **Remarks:** Part-time maker; first knife sold in 1990. **Mark:** Last name and bear paw print logo scrimshawed on handles or leatherwork.

SELF, ERNIE, 950 O'Neill Ranch Rd., Dripping Springs, TX 78620-9760, Phone: 512-858-7133, ernieself@aol.com
 Specialties: Traditional and working straight knives and folders of his design and in standard patterns. **Patterns:** Hunters, locking folders and slip-joints. **Technical:** Grinds 440C, D2, 440V, ATS-34 and Damascus. Offers fancy filework. **Prices:** $125 to $500; some to $1500. **Remarks:** Full-time maker; first knife sold in 1982. **Mark:** In oval shape - Ernie Self Maker Dripping Springs TX. **Other:** Also customizes Buck 110's and 112's folding hunters.

SELLEVOLD, HARALD, S.Kleivesmau: 2, PO Box 4134, N5835 Bergen, NORWAY, Phone: 55-310682, haraldsellevold@c2i.net; Web: http://euroedge.net/sellevold
 Specialties: Norwegian-styles; collaborates with other Norse craftsmen. **Patterns:** Distinctive ferrules and other mild modifications of traditional patterns; Bowies and friction folders. **Technical:** Buys Damascus blades; blacksmiths his own blades. Semi-gemstones in handles; gemstone inlay. **Prices:** $350 to $2000. **Remarks:** Full-time maker; first knife sold in 1980. **Mark:** Name and country in logo.

SELZAM, FRANK, Martin Reinhard Str 23, 97631, Bad Koenigshofen, GERMANY, Phone: 09761-5980
 Specialties: Hunters, working knives to customers specs, hand tooled and stitched leather sheaths large stock of wood and German stag horn. **Patterns:** Mostly own design. **Technical:** Forged blades, own Damascus, also stock removal stainless. **Prices:** $250 to $1500. **Remark:** First knife sold in 1978. **Mark:** Last name stamped.

SENTZ, MARK C., 4084 Baptist Rd., Taneytown, MD 21787, Phone: 410-756-2018
Specialties: Fancy straight working knives of his design. **Patterns:** Hunters, fighters, folders and utility/camp knives. **Technical:** Forges 1085, 1095, 5160, 5155 and his Damascus. Most knives come with wood-lined leather sheath or wooden presentation sheath. **Prices:** Start at $275. **Remarks:** Full-time maker; first knife sold in 1989. Doing business as M. Charles Sentz Gunsmithing, Inc. **Mark:** Last name.

SERAFEN, STEVEN E., 24 Genesee St., New Berlin, NY 13411, Phone: 607-847-6903
Specialties: Traditional working/using straight knives of his design and to customer specs. **Patterns:** Bowies, fighters, hunters. **Technical:** Grinds ATS-34, 440C, high-carbon steel. **Prices:** $175 to $600; some to $1200. **Remarks:** Part-time maker; first knife sold in 1990. **Mark:** First and middle initial, last name in script.

SERVEN, JIM, PO Box 1, Fostoria, MI 48435, Phone: 517-795-2255
Specialties: Highly finished unique folders. **Patterns:** Fancy working folders, axes, miniatures and razors; some straight knives. **Technical:** Grinds 440C; forges his own Damascus. **Prices:** $150 to $800; some to $1500. **Remarks:** Full-time maker; first knife sold in 1971. **Mark:** Name in map logo.

SEVEY CUSTOM KNIFE, 94595 Chandler Rd., Gold Beach, OR 97444, Phone: 541-247-2649, sevey@charter.net Web: www.seveyknives.com
Specialties: Fixed blade hunters. **Patterns:** Drop point, trailing paint, clip paint, full tang, hidden tang. **Technical:** D-2, and ATS-34 blades, stock removal. Heat treatment by Paul Bos. **Prices:** $225 and up depending on overall length and grip material. **Mark:** Sevey Custom Knife.

SFREDDO, RODRITO MENEZES, Rua 15 De Novembro 2222, Nova Petropolis, RS, BRASIL 95150-000, Phone: 011-55-54-303-303-90, r.sfreddo@ig.com.br.
Specialties: Traditional Brazilian-style working and high-art knives of his design. **Patterns:** Fighters, Bowies, utility and camp knives, classic Mediterranean Dirk. Welcome customer design. **Technical:** Forges only with sledge hammers (no power hammer here) 100% to shape in 52100 and his own Damascus. Makes own sheaths in the true traditional Brazilian-style. **Remark:** Full-time maker. **Prices:** $250 to $1100 for his elaborate Mediterranean Dirk. Uses only natural handle materials. Considered by many to be Brazil's best bladesmith.

SHADLEY, EUGENE W., 26315 Norway Dr., Bovey, MN 55709, Phone: 218-245-3820, Fax: 218-245-1639, bses@uslink.net
Specialties: Classic multi-blade folders. **Patterns:** Whittlers, stockman, sowbelly, congress, trapper, etc. **Technical:** Grinds ATS-34, 416 frames. **Prices:** Start at $300. **Remarks:** Full-time maker; first knife sold in 1985. Doing business as Shadley Knives. **Mark:** Last name.

SHADMOT, BOAZ, MOSHAV PARAN D N, Arava, ISRAEL 86835, srb@arava.co.il

SHARRIGAN, MUDD, 111 Bradford Rd., Wiscasset, ME 04578-4457, Phone: 207-882-9820, Fax: 207-882-9835
Specialties: Custom designs; repair straight knives, custom leather sheaths. **Patterns:** Daggers, fighters, hunters, buckskinner, Indian crooked knives and seamen working knives; traditional Scandinavian-styles. **Technical:** Forges 1095, 52100, 5160, W2, O1. Laminates 1095 and mild steel. **Prices:** $50 to $325; some to $1200. **Remarks:** Full-time maker; first knife sold in 1982. **Mark:** First name and swallow tail carving.

SHAVER II, JAMES R., 1529 Spider Ridge Rd., Parkersburg, WV 26104, Phone: 304-422-2692, jrsknives@wirefree.com Web: www.spiderridgeforge.com
Specialties: Hunting and working straight knives in carbon and Damascus steel. **Patterns:** Bowies and daggers in Damascus and carbon steels. **Technical:** Forges 5160 carbon and Damascus in O101018 mild steel and pvee nickel. **Prices:** $85 to $225; some to $750. **Remarks:** Part-time maker; sold first knife in 1998. Believes in sole authorship. **Mark:** Last name.

SHEEHY, THOMAS J., 4131 NE 24th Ave., Portland, OR 97211-6411, Phone: 503-493-2843
Specialties: Hunting knives and ULUs. **Patterns:** Own or customer designs. **Technical:** 1095/01 and ATS-34 steel. **Prices:** $35 to $200. **Remarks:** Do own heat treating; forged or ground blades. **Mark:** Name.

SHEETS, STEVEN WILLIAM, 6 Stonehouse Rd, Mendham, NJ 07945, Phone: 201-543-5882

SHIFFER, STEVE, PO Box 582, Leakesville, MS 39451, Phone: 601-394-4425, aiifish2@yahoo.com Web: wwwchoctawplantationforge.com
Specialties: Bowies, Fighters, Hard use knives. **Patterns:** Fighters, Hunters, Combat/Utility knives Walker pattern liner lock folders. Allen pattern scale and bolster release autos. **Technical:** Most work forged, stainless stock removal. Make own Damascus. O-1 and 5160 most used also 1084, 440c, 154cm, s30v. **Prices:** $125 to $1000. **Remarks:** First

knife sold in 2000, all heat treatment done by myself. Doing business as Choctaw Plantation Forge. **Mark:** Hot mark sunrise over creek.

SHIKAYAMA, TOSHIAKI, 259-2 Suka Yoshikawa City, Saitama 342-0057, JAPAN, Phone: 04-89-81-6605, Fax: 04-89-81-6605
Specialties: Folders in standard patterns. **Patterns:** Locking and multi-blade folders. **Technical:** Grinds ATS, carbon steel, high speed steel. **Prices:** $400 to $2500; $4500 with engraving. **Remarks:** Full-time maker; first knife sold in 1952. **Mark:** First initial, last name.

SHINOSKY, ANDY, 3117 Meanderwood Dr., Canfield, OH 44406, Phone: 330-702-0299, andy@shinosky.com WEB: www.shinosky.com
Specialties: Collectible fancy folders and interframes. **Patterns:** Drop points, trailing points and daggers. **Technical:** Grinds ATS-34 and Damascus. Prefers natural handle materials. **Prices:** Start at $450. **Remarks:** Part-time maker; first knife sold in 1992. **Mark:** Name or bent folder logo.

SHIPLEY, STEVEN A., 800 Campbell Rd. Ste 137, Richardson, TX 75081, Phone: 972-644-7981, Fax: 972-644-7985, steve@shipleysphotography
Specialties: Hunters, skinners and traditional straight knives. **Technical:** Hand grinds ATS-34, 440C and Damascus steels. Each knife is custom sheathed by his son, Dan. **Prices:** $175 to $2000. **Remarks:** Part-time maker; like smooth lines and unusual handle materials. **Mark:** S A Shipley.

SHOEMAKER, CARROLL, 380 Yellowtown Rd., Northup, OH 45658, Phone: 740-446-6695
Specialties: Working/using straight knives of his design. **Patterns:** Hunters, utility/camp and early American backwoodsmen knives. **Technical:** Grinds ATS-34; forges old files, O1 and 1095. Uses some Damascus; offers scrimshaw and engraving. **Prices:** $100 to $175; some to $350. **Remarks:** Spare-time maker; first knife sold in 1977. **Mark:** Name and city or connected initials.

SHOEMAKER, SCOTT, 316 S. Main St., Miamisburg, OH 45342, Phone: 513-859-1935
Specialties: Twisted, wire-wrapped handles on swords, fighters and fantasy blades; new line of seven models with quick-draw, multi-carry Kydex sheaths. **Patterns:** Bowies, boots and one-of-a-kinds in his design or to customer specs. **Technical:** Grinds A6 and ATS-34; buys Damascus. Hand satin finish is standard. **Prices:** $100 to $1500; swords to $8000. **Remarks:** Part-time maker; first knife sold in 1984. **Mark:** Angel wings with last initial, or last name.

SHOGER, MARK O., 14780 SW Osprey Dr., Suite 345, Beaverton, OR 97007, Phone: 503-579-2495
Specialties: Working and using straight knives and folders of his design; fancy and embellished knives. **Patterns:** Hunters, Bowies, daggers and locking folders. **Technical:** Forges O1, W2 and his own pattern-welded Damascus. **Remarks:** Spare-time maker. **Mark:** Last name or stamped last initial over anvil.

SHORE, JOHN I., ALASKA KNIFEMAKER, 2901 Sheldon Jackson St., Anchorage, AK 99508, Phone: 907-272-2253, akknife@acsalaska.net Web: www.akknife.com
Specialties: Working straight knives, hatchets, and folders. **Patterns:** Hunters, skinners, Bowies, fighters, working using knives. **Technical:** Prefer using exotic steels, grinds most CPM's, Damasteel, RWL34, BG42, D2 and some ATS-34. Prefers exotic hardwoods, stabilized materials, Micarta, and Pearl. **Prices:** Start at $200. **Remarks:** Full-time maker; first knife sold in 1985. **Mark:** Name in script, Anchorage, AK.

SHOSTLE, BEN, 1121 Burlington, Muncie, IN 47302, Phone: 765-282-9073, Fax: 765-282-5270
Specialties: Fancy high-art straight knives of his design. **Patterns:** Bowies, daggers and fighters. **Technical:** Uses 440C, ATS-34 and commercial Damascus. All knives and engraved. **Prices:** $900 to $3200; some to $4000. **Remarks:** Full-time maker; first knife sold in 1987. Doing business as The Gun Room (T.G.R.). **Mark:** Last name.

SIBRIAN, AARON, 4308 Dean Dr., Ventura, CA 93003, Phone: 805-642-6950
Specialties: Tough working knives of his design and in standard patterns. **Patterns:** Makes a "Viper utility"—a kukri derivative and a variety of straight using knives. **Technical:** Grinds 440C and ATS-34. Offers traditional Japanese blades; soft backs, hard edges, temper lines. **Prices:** $60 to $100; some to $250. **Remarks:** Spare-time maker; first knife sold in 1989. **Mark:** Initials in diagonal line.

SIGMAN, CORBET R., Rt. 1, Box 260, Liberty, WV 25124, Phone: 304-586-9131
Specialties: Collectible working straight knives and folders. **Patterns:** Hunters, fighters, boots, camp knives and exotics such as sgian dubhs—distinctly Sigman lines; folders. **Technical:** Grinds D2, 154CM, plain carbon tool steel and ATS-34. **Prices:** $60 to $800; some to $4000. **Remarks:** Full-time maker; first knife sold in 1970. **Mark:** Name or initials.

custom knifemakers

SIGMAN—SMITH

SIGMAN, JAMES P., 10391 Church Rd., North Adams, MI 49262, Phone: 517-523-3028
    Specialties: High-tech working knives of his design. **Patterns:** Daggers, hunters, fighters and folders. **Technical:** Forges and grinds L6, O1, W2 and his Damascus. **Prices:** $150 to $750. **Remarks:** Part-time maker; first knife sold in 1982. **Mark:** Sig or Sig Forge.

SIMMONS, H.R., 1100 Bay City Rd., Aurora, NC 27806, Phone: 252-322-5969
    Specialties: Working/using straight knives of his design. **Patterns:** Fighters, hunters and utility/camp knives. **Technical:** Forges and grinds Damascus and L6; grinds ATS-34. **Prices:** $150 to $250; some to $400. **Remarks:** Part-time maker; first knife sold in 1987. Doing business as HRS Custom Knives, Royal Forge and Trading Company. **Mark:** Initials.

SIMONELLA, GIANLUIGI, 15, via Rosa Brustolo, 33085 Maniago, ITALY, Phone: 01139-427-730350
    Specialties: Traditional and classic folding and working/using knives of his design and to customer specs. **Patterns:** Bowies, fighters, hunters, utility/camp knives. **Technical:** Forges ATS-34, D2, 440C. **Prices:** $250 to $400; some to $1000. **Remarks:** Full-time maker; first knife sold in 1988. **Mark:** Wilson.

SIMONS, BILL, 6217 Michael Ln., Lakeland, FL 33811, Phone: 863-646-3783
    Specialties: Working folders. **Patterns:** Locking folders, liner locks, hunters, slip joints most patterns; some straight camp knives. **Technical:** Grinds D2, ATS-34 and O1. **Prices:** Start at $100. **Remarks:** Full-time maker; first knife sold in 1970. **Mark:** Last name.

SIMS, BOB, PO Box 772, Meridian, TX 76665, Phone: 254-435-6240
    Specialties: Traditional working straight knives and folders in standard patterns. **Patterns:** Locking folders, slip-joint folders and hunters. **Technical:** Grinds D2, ATS-34 and O1. Offers filework on some knives. **Prices:** $150 to $275; some to $600. **Remarks:** Full-time maker; first knife sold in 1975. **Mark:** The division sign.

SINCLAIR, J.E., 520 Francis Rd., Pittsburgh, PA 15239, Phone: 412-793-5778
    Specialties: Fancy hunters and fighters, liner locking folders. **Patterns:** Fighters, hunters and folders. **Technical:** Flat-grinds and hollow grind, prefers hand rubbed satin finish. Uses natural handle materials. **Prices:** $185 to $800. **Remarks:** Part-time maker; first knife sold in 1995. **Mark:** First and middle initials, last name and maker.

SINYARD, CLESTON S., 27522 Burkhardt Dr., Elberta, AL 36530, Phone: 334-987-1361, nimoforge1@gulftel.com Web: www.knifemakersguild
    Specialties: Working straight knives and folders of his design. **Patterns:** Hunters, buckskinners, Bowies, daggers, fighters and all-Damascus folders. **Technical:** Makes Damascus from 440C, stainless steels, D2 and regular high-carbon steel; forges "forefinger pad" into hunters and skinners. **Prices:** In Damascus $450 to $1500; some $2500. **Remarks:** Full-time maker; first knife sold in 1980. Doing business as Nimo Forge. **Mark:** Last name, U.S.A. in anvil.

SISEMORE, CHARLES RUSSEL, RR 2 Box 329AL, Mena, AR 71953, Phone: 918-383-1360

SISKA, JIM, 6 Highland Ave., Westfield, MA 01085, Phone: 413-568-9787, Fax: 413-568-6341
    Specialties: Traditional working straight knives and folders. **Patterns:** Hunters, fighters, Bowies and one-of-a-kinds; folders. **Technical:** Grinds D2 and ATS-34; buys Damascus. Likes exotic woods. **Prices:** $195 to $2500. **Remarks:** Part-time maker; first knife sold in 1983. **Mark:** Last name in Old English.

SJOSTRAND, KEVIN, 1541 S. Cain St., Visalia, CA 93292, Phone: 209-625-5254
    Specialties: Traditional and working/using straight knives and folders of his design or to customer specs. **Patterns:** Bowies, hunters, utility/camp knives, lockback, springbuck and liner lock folders. **Technical:** Grinds ATS-34, 440C and 1095. Prefers high polished blades and full tang. Natural and stabilized hardwoods, Micarta and stag handle material. **Prices:** $75 to $300. **Remarks:** Part-time maker; first knife sold in 1992. Doing business as Black Oak Blades. **Mark:** Oak tree, Black Oak Blades, name, or just last name.

SKIFF, STEVEN, SKIFF MADE BLADES, PO Box 537, Broadalbin, NY 12025, Phone: 518-883-4875, skiffmadeblades@hotmail.com Web: www.skiffmadeblades.com
    Specialties: Custom using/collector grade straight blades and liner lock folders of maker's design or customer specifications. **Patterns:** Hunters, utility/camp knives; tactical/fancy art knives **Prices:** $180 to $395 some to $325 and up. **Technical:** Stock removal hollow ground ATS-34, 154 CM, S30V, and tool steel. Damascus-Devon Thomas, Robert Eggerling, Mike Norris and Delbert Ealy. Nickel silver and stainless in-house heat treating. Handle materials man made and natural woods (stablilized). Horn shells sheaths for straight blades sews own leather and uses

sheaths by "Tree-Stump Leather". **Remarks:** First knife sold 1997. Started making folders in 2000. **Mark:** SKIFF on blade of straight blades and in inside of backspacer on folders.

SKOW, H. A. "TEX", TEX KNIVES, 3534 Gravel Springs Rd., Senatobia, MS 38668, Phone: 662-301-1568, texknives@bellsouth.net
    Specialties: One-of-a-kind daggers, Bowies, boot knives and hunters. **Patterns:** Different Damascus patterns (By Bob Eggerling). **Technical:** 440C, 58, 60 Rockwell hardness. Engraving by Joe Mason. **Prices:** Negotiable. **Mark:** TEX.

SLEE, FRED, 9 John St., Morganville, NJ 07751, Phone: 908-591-9047
    Specialties: Working straight knives, some fancy, to customer specs. **Patterns:** Hunters, fighters, boots, fancy daggers and folders. **Technical:** Grinds D2, 440C and ATS-34. **Prices:** $285 to $1100. **Remarks:** Part-time maker; first knife sold in 1980. **Mark:** Last name in old English.

SLOAN, SHANE, 4226 FM 61, Newcastle, TX 76372, Phone: 940-846-3290
    Specialties: Collector-grade straight knives and folders. **Patterns:** Uses stainless Damascus, ATS-34 and 12-C-27. Bowies, lockers, slip-joints, fancy folders, fighters and period pieces. **Technical:** Grinds D2 and ATS-34. Uses hand-rubbed satin finish. Prefers rare natural handle materials. **Prices:** $250 to $6500. **Remarks:** Full-time maker; first knife sold in 1985. **Mark:** Name and city.

SLOBODIAN, SCOTT, 4101 River Ridge Dr., PO Box 1498, San Andreas, CA 95249, Phone: 209-286-1980, Fax: 209-286-1982, scott@slobodianswords.com Web: www.slobodianswords.com
    Specialties: Japanese-style knives and swords, period pieces, fantasy pieces and miniatures. **Patterns:** Small kweikens, tantos, wakazashis, katanas, traditional samurai swords. **Technical:** Flat-grinds 1050, commercial Damascus. **Prices:** $800 to $3500; some to $7500. **Remarks:** Full-time maker; first knife sold in 1987. **Mark:** Blade signed in Japanese characters and various scripts.

SMALE, CHARLES J., 509 Grove Ave., Waukegan, IL 60085, Phone: 847-244-8013

SMALL, ED, Rt. 1, Box 178-A, Keyser, WV 26726, Phone: 304-298-4254
    Specialties: Working knives of his design; period pieces. **Patterns:** Hunters, daggers, buckskinners and camp knives; likes one-of-a-kinds. **Technical:** Forges and grinds W2, L6 and his own Damascus. **Prices:** $150 to $1500. **Remarks:** Full-time maker; first knife sold in 1978. Doing business as Iron Mountain Forge Works. **Mark:** Script initials connected.

SMALLWOOD, WAYNE, 146 Poplar Dr., Kalispell, MT 59901

SMART, STEATEN, 15815 Acorn Cir., Tavares, FL 32778, Phone: 352-343-8423

SMART, STEVE, 907 Park Row Cir., McKinney, TX 75070-3847, Phone: 214-837-4216, Fax: 214-837-4111
    Specialties: Working/using straight knives and folders of his design, to customer specs and in standard patterns. **Patterns:** Bowies, hunters, kitchen knives, locking folders, utility/camp, fishing and bird knives. **Technical:** Grinds ATS-34, D2, 440C and O1. Prefers mirror polish or satin finish; hollow-grinds all blades. All knives come with sheath. Offers some filework. **Prices:** $95 to $225; some to $500. **Remarks:** Spare-time maker; first knife sold in 1983. **Mark:** Name, Custom, city and state in oval.

SMIT, GLENN, 627 Cindy Ct., Aberdeen, MD 21001, Phone: 410-272-2959, wolfsknife@msn.com
    Specialties: Working and using straight and folding knives of his design or to customer specs. Customizes and repairs all types of cutlery. Exclusive maker of Dave Murphy Style knives. **Patterns:** Hunters, Bowies, daggers, fighters, utility/camp, folders, kitchen knives and miniatures, Murphy combat, C.H.A.I.K., Little 88 and Tiny 90-styles. **Technical:** Grinds 440C, ATS-34, O1, A2 also grinds 6AL4V titanium allox for blades. Reforges commercial Damascus and makes own Damascus, cast aluminum handles. **Prices:** Miniatures start at $30; full-size knives start at $50. **Remarks:** Spare-time maker; first knife sold in 1986. Doing business as Wolf's Knives. **Mark:** G.P. SMIT, with year on reverse side, Wolf's knives-Murphy's way with date.

SMITH, D. NOEL, 12018 NE Lonetree Ct., Poulsbo, WA 98370, Phone: 360-697-6992, blademan2@attbi.com
    Specialties: Fantasy art knives of his own design or to standard patterns. **Patterns:** Daggers, hunters and art knives. **Technical:** Grinds O1, D2, 440C stainless and Damascus. Offers natural and synthetic carved handles, engraved and acid etched blades, sculptured guards, butt caps and bases. **Prices:** Start at $250. **Remarks:** Full-time maker; first knife sold in 1990. Doing business as Minds' Eye Metal master. **Mark:** Signature.

SMITH, GREGORY H., 8607 Coddington Ct., Louisville, KY 40299, Phone: 502-491-7439
    Specialties: Traditional working straight knives and fantasy knives to customer specs. **Patterns:** Fighters and modified Bowies; camp knives

and swords. **Technical:** Grinds O1, 440C and commercial Damascus bars. **Prices:** $55 to $300. **Remarks:** Part-time maker; first knife sold in 1985. **Mark:** JAGED, plus signature.

SMITH, J.D., 69 Highland, Roxbury, MA 02119, Phone: 617-989-0723, jdsmith02119@yahoo.com
Specialties: Fighters, Bowies, Persian, locking folders and swords. **Patterns:** Bowies, fighters and locking folders. **Technical:** Forges and grinds D2, his Damascus, O1, 52100 etc. and wootz-pattern hammer steel. **Prices:** $500 to $2000; some to $5000. **Remarks:** Full-time maker; first knife sold in 1987. Doing business as Hammersmith. **Mark:** Last initial alone or in cartouche.

SMITH, JOHN M., 3450 E Beguelin Rd., Centralia, IL 62801, Phone: 618-249-6444, Fax: 618-249-6444, jknife@accessus.net
Specialties: Traditional work knives, art knives. **Patterns:** daggers, Bowies, folders. **Technical:** Forges Damascus and hi-carbon. Also uses stainless. **Prices:** $250 to $2500. **Remarks:** Full-time maker; first knife sold in 1980. **Mark:** Etched signature or logo.

SMITH, JOHN W., 1322 Cow Branch Rd., West Liberty, KY 41472, Phone: 606-743-3599, jwsknive@mrtc.com; Web: www.jwsmithknives.com
Specialties: Fancy and working locking folders of his design or to customer specs. **Patterns:** Interframes, traditional and daggers. **Technical:** Grinds 530V and his own Damascus. Offers gold inlay, engraving with gold inlay, hand-fitted mosaic pearl inlay and filework. Prefers hand-rubbed finish. Pearl and ivory available. **Prices:** Utility pieces $375 to $650. Art knives $1200 to $10,000 **Remarks:** Full-time maker. **Mark:** Initials engraved inside diamond.

SMITH, JOSH, Box 753, Frenchtown, MT 59834, Phone: 406-626-5775, josh@joshsmithknives.com Web: www.joshsmithknives.com
Specialties: Mosaic, Damascus, liner lock folders, automatics, bowies, fighters, etc. **Patterns:** All kinds. **Technical:** Advanced Mosaic and Damascus. **Prices:** $450 and up. **Mark:** JOSH. **Other:** A.B.S. Master Smith.

SMITH, LENARD C., PO Box D68, Valley Cottage, NY 10989, Phone: 914-268-7359

SMITH, MICHAEL J., 1418 Saddle Gold Ct., Brandon, FL 33511, Phone: 813-431-3790, smithknife@hotmail.com Web: www.smithknife.com
Specialties: Fancy high art folders of his design. **Patterns:** Locking locks and automatics. **Technical:** Uses ATS-34, non-stainless and stainless Damascus; hand carves folders, prefers ivory and pearl. Hand-rubbed satin finish. Liners are 6AL4V titanium. **Prices:** $500 to $3000. **Remarks:** Full-time maker; first knife sold in 1989. **Mark:** Name, city, state.

SMITH, NEWMAN L., 676 Glades Rd., Shop #3, Gatlinburg, TN 37738, Phone: 423-436-3322
Specialties: Collector-grade and working knives. **Patterns:** Hunters, slip-joint and lock-back folders, some miniatures. **Technical:** Grinds O1 and ATS-34; makes fancy sheaths. **Prices:** $110 to $450; some to $1000. **Remarks:** Full-time maker; first knife sold in 1984. Partners part-time to handle Damascus blades by Jeff Hurst; marks these with SH connected. **Mark:** First and middle initials, last name.

SMITH, RAYMOND L., 217 Red Chalk Rd., Erin, NY 14838, Phone: 607-795-5257, Web: www.theanvilsedge.com
Specialties: Working/using straight knives and folders to customer specs and in standard patterns; period pieces. **Patterns:** Bowies, hunters, skip-joints. **Technical:** Forges 5160, 52100, 1018, 15N20, 1084 Damascus and wire cable Damascus. Filework. **Prices:** $100 to $1500; estimates for custom orders. **Remarks:** Full-time maker; first knife sold in 1991. ABS Master Smith. Doing business as The Anvils Edge. **Mark:** Initials in script.

SMITH, RICK, BEAR BONE KNIVES, 1843 W Evans Creek Rd., Rogue River, OR 97537, Phone: 541-582-4144, BearBoneSmith@msn.com Web: www.bearbone.com
Specialties: Classic, historical-style Bowies for re-enactors and custom sheaths. **Patterns:** Historical-style Bowies, varied contemporary knife styles. **Technical:** Made by stock removal method; also forge weld tri-cable Damascus blades. Do own heat treating and tempering using an even heat digital kiln. Preferred steels are ATS-34, 154CM, 5160, D-2, 1095 and 01 tool and various carbon Damascus. **Prices:** $350 to $1100. **Remarks:** Full-time maker since 1997 Now forging random pattern Damascus up to 600 layers. Discontinued using BG42 steel. Serial numbers now appear under log. Damascus knives are not given a serial number. Official business name is Bear Bone Knives. Stainless steel blades sent our for cryogenic "freeze treat." **Mark:** "Bear Bone" over initials "R S" (separated by downward arrow) on blade; initials R S (separated by downward arrow) within a 3/8" circle; 2 shooting stars and a Bowie. Serial numbers appear on ricasso area of blade unless otherwise requested.

SMITH JR., JAMES B. "RED", Rt. 2, Box 1525, Morven, GA 31638, Phone: 912-775-2844
Specialties: Folders. **Patterns:** Rotating rear-lock folders. **Technical:** Grinds ATS-34, D2 and Vascomax 350. **Prices:** Start at $350. **Remarks:** Full-time maker; first knife sold in 1985. **Mark:** GA RED in cowboy hat.

SMOCK, TIMOTHY E., 1105 N Sherwood Dr., Marion, IN 46952, Phone: 765-664-0123

SMOKER, RAY, 113 Church Rd., Searcy, AR 72143, Phone: 501-796-2712
Specialties: Rugged, no nonsense working knives of his design only. **Patterns:** Hunters, skinners, utility/camp and flat-ground knives. **Technical:** Forges his own Damascus and 52100; makes sheaths. Uses improved multiple edge quench he developed. **Prices:** $450 and up; price includes sheath. **Remarks:** Semi-retired; first knife sold in 1992. **Mark:** Last name.

SNARE, MICHAEL, 3352 E. Mescal St., Phoenix, AZ 85028

SNELL, JERRY L., 539 Turkey Trl, Fortson, GA 31808, Phone: 706-324-4922
Specialties: Working straight knives of his design and in standard patterns. **Patterns:** Hunters, boots, fighters, daggers and a few folders. **Technical:** Grinds 440C, ATS-34; buys Damascus. **Prices:** $175 to $1000. **Remarks:** Part-time maker. **Mark:** Last name, or name, city and state.

SNODY, MIKE, 7169 Silk Hope Rd., Liberty, NC 27298, Phone: 888-393-9534, mnmsnody@juno.com
Specialties: High performance straight knives in traditional and Japanese-styles. **Patterns:** Skinners, hunters, tactical, Kwaiken andTantos. **Technical:** Grinds BG-42, ATS-34, 440C and A-2. Offers full or tapered tangs, upgraded handle materials such as fossil ivory, coral and exotic woods. Traditional diamond wrap over stingray on Japanese-style knives. Sheaths available in leather or Kydex. **Prices:** $100 to $1000. **Remarks:** Part-time maker; first knife sold in 1999. **Mark:** Name over knife maker.

SNOW, BILL, 4824 18th Ave., Columbus, GA 31904, Phone: 706-576-4390, tipikw@knology.net
Specialties: Traditional working/using straight knives and folders of his design and to customer specs. Offers engraving and scrimshaw. **Patterns:** Bowies, fighters, hunters and folders. **Technical:** Grinds ATS-34, 440V, 440C, 420V, CPM350, BG42, A2, D2, 5160, 52100 and O1; forges if needed. Cryogenically quenches all steels; inlaid handles; some integrals; leather or Kydex sheaths. **Prices:** $125 to $700; some to $3500. **Remarks:** Now also have 530V, 10V and 3V steels in use. Full-time maker; first knife sold in 1958. Doing business as Tipi Knife works. **Mark:** Old English scroll "S" inside a tipi.

SNYDER, MICHAEL TOM, PO Box 522, Zionsville, IN 46077-0522, Phone: 317-873-6807, wildcatcreek@indy.pr.com

SOLOMON, MARVIN, 23750 Cold Springs Rd., Paron, AR 72122, Phone: 501-821-3170, Fax: 501-821-6541, mardot@swbell.net Web: www.coldspringsforge.com
Specialties: Traditional working and using straight knives of his design and to customer specs also lock back 7 liner lock folders. **Patterns:** Single blade folders. **Technical:** Forges 5160, 1095, O1 and random Damascus. **Prices:** $125 to $1000. **Remarks:** Part-time maker; first knife sold in 1990. Doing business as Cold Springs Forge. **Mark:** Last name.

SONNTAG, DOUGLAS W., 906 N 39 ST, Nixa, MO 65714, Phone: 417-693-1640, Fax: 417-582-1392, dougsonntag@aol.com
Specialties: Working knives; art knives. **Patterns:** Hunters, boots, straight working knives; Bowies, some folders, camp/axe sets. **Technical:** Grinds D-2, ATS-34, forges own Damascus; does own heat treating. **Prices:** $225 and up. **Remarks:** Part-time maker; first knife sold in 1986. **Mark:** Etched name in arch.

SONTHEIMER, G. DOUGLAS, 12604 Bridgeton Dr., Potomac, MD 20854, Phone: 301-948-5227
Specialties: Fixed blade knives. **Patterns:** Whitetail deer, backpackers, camp, claws, filet, fighters. **Technical:** Hollow Grinds. **Price:** $500 and up. **Remarks:** Spare-time maker; first knife sold in 1976. **Mark:** LORD.

SOPPERA, ARTHUR, "Pilatusblick", Oberer Schmidberg, CH-9631 Ulisbach, SWITZERLAND, Phone: 71-988 23 27, Fax: 71-988 47 57, doublelock@hotmail.com Web: www.customknives.com/arthur.soppera
Specialties: High-art, high-tech knives of his design. **Patterns:** Mostly locking folders, some straight knives. **Technical:** Grinds ATS-34 and commercial Damascus. Folders have button lock of his own design; some are fancy folders in jeweler's fashion. Also makes jewelry with integrated small knives. **Prices:** $200 to $1000; some $2000 and higher. **Remarks:** Full-time maker; first knife sold in 1986. **Mark:** Stylized initials, name, country.

SORNBERGER, JIM, 25126 Overland Dr., Volcano, CA 95689, Phone: 209-295-7819
Specialties: Classic San Francisco-style knives. Collectible straight knives. **Patterns:** Forges 1095-1084/15W2. Makes own Damascus and powder metal. Fighters, daggers, Bowies; miniatures; hunters, custom canes, liner locks folders. **Technical:** Grinds 440C, 154CM and ATS-34; engraves, carves and embellishes. **Prices:** $500 to $20,000 in gold with gold quartz inlays. **Remarks:** Full-time maker; first knife sold in 1970. **Mark:** First initial, last name, city and state.

SOWELL, BILL, 100 Loraine Forest Ct., Macon, GA 31210, Phone: 478-994-9863, billsowell@reynoldscable.net
Specialties: Antique reproduction Bowies, forging Bowies, hunters, fighters, and most others. Also folders. **Technical:** Makes own Damascus, using 1084/15N20, also making own designs in powder metals, forges 5160-1095-1084, and other carbon steels, grinds ATS-34. **Prices:** Starting at $150 and up. **Remarks:** Part-time maker. Sold first knife in 1998. **Mark:** Iron Horse Knives; Iron Horse Forge. **Other:** Does own leather work.

SPARKS, BERNARD, PO Box 73, Dingle, ID 83233, Phone: 208-847-1883, dogknifeii@juno.com Web: www.sparksknives.com
Specialties: Maker engraved, working and art knives. Straight knives and folders of his own design. **Patterns:** Locking inner-frame folders, hunters, fighters, one-of-a-kind art knives. **Technical:** Grinds 530V steel, 440-C, 154CM, ATS-34, D-2 and forges by special order; triple temper, cryogenic soak. Mirror or hand finish. New Liquid metal steel. **Prices:** $300 to $2000. **Remarks:** Full-time maker, first knife sold in 1967. **Mark:** Last name over state with a knife logo on each end of name. Prior 1980, stamp of last name.

SPENCER, KEITH, PO Box 149, Chidlow WA, Western Australia 6556, Phone: 61 8 95727255, Fax: 61 8 95727266, spencer@knivesaustralia.com.au
Specialties: Survival & bushcraft bladeware. **Patterns:** Best known for Kakadu Bushcraft knife (since 1989). Lekira mini survival knife. (since 1993). **Prices:** $100 to $400 AV. **Mark:** Spencer Australia.

SPICKLER, GREGORY NOBLE, 5614 Mose Cir., Sharpsburg, MD 21782, Phone: 301-432-2746

SPINALE, RICHARD, 4021 Canterbury Ct., Lorain, OH 44053, Phone: 440-282-1565
Specialties: High-art working knives of his design. **Patterns:** Hunters, fighters, daggers and locking folders. **Technical:** Grinds 440C, ATS-34 and 07; engraves. Offers gold bolsters and other deluxe treatments. **Prices:** $300 to $1000; some to $3000. **Remarks:** Spare-time maker; first knife sold in 1976. **Mark:** Name, address, year and model number.

SPIVEY, JEFFERSON, 9244 W. Wilshire, Yukon, OK 73099, Phone: 405-721-4442
Specialties: The Saber tooth: a combination hatchet, saw and knife. **Patterns:** Built for the wilderness, all are one-of-a-kind. **Technical:** Grinds chromemoly steel. The saw tooth spine curves with a double row of biangular teeth. **Prices:** Start at $300. **Remarks:** First knife sold in 1977. The above Saber tooth knives are no longer in production as of Jan 1 2004. **Mark:** Name and serial number.

SPRAGG, WAYNE E., 252 Oregon Ave, 1314 3675 East Rd., Lovell, WY 82431, Phone: 307-548-7212
Specialties: Working straight knives, some fancy. **Patterns:** Folders. **Technical:** Forges carbon steel and makes Damascus. **Prices:** $110 to $400; some higher. **Remarks:** All stainless heat-treated by Paul Bos. Carbon steel in shop heat treat. **Mark:** Name, city and state with bucking horse logo.

SPROKHOLT (GATHERWOOD), ROB, Werkendelslaan 108, 1851VE Heiloo, Nederland, Europe, Phone: 0031-72-5336097, buckx@gatherwood.nl Web: www.gatherwood.nl
Specialties: One-of-a-kind stiff knives. Top materials collector grade made to use. Oiled realwood handles, intarsia wood. Characteristic one row of massive silver pins or tubes. **Patterns:** Outdoor knives (hunting, sailing, hiking), Bowies, Mans Surviving Companions MSC, big tantos. **Technical:** Stockremoval grinder; flat, hollow or confex steel; 440, RWL-34, ATS-34 powder steel Damascener, D-2, stiff knives, mostly full tang, home made mokume-gane. **Prices:** Starts at Euro 260. **Remarks:** Part-time knifemaker. Writer of first Dutch knifemaking book. **Mark:** Gatherwood in an elipse etched in the blade or stamped in an intarsia of silver in the spine. **Other:** Wife is his co-worker and goldsmith. Do everything themselves. Supply shop for knife enthusiastics. First knife sold in 2000.

SPROUSE, TERRY, 1633 Newfound Rd., Asheville, NC 28806, Phone: 704-683-3400
Specialties: Traditional and working straight knives of his design. **Patterns:** Bowies and hunters. **Technical:** Grinds ATS-34, 440C and D2. Makes sheaths. **Prices:** $85 to $125; some to $225. **Remarks:** Part-time maker; first knife sold in 1989. **Mark:** NA.

ST. AMOUR, MURRAY, RR 3, 222 Dicks Rd., Pembroke ON, CANADA K8A 6W4, Phone: 613-735-1061, knives@webhart.net Web: www.webhart.net/knives
Specialties: Working fixed blades. **Patterns:** Hunters, fish, fighters, Bowies and utility knives. **Technical:** Grinds ATS-34, 154-CM, CPM-440V and Damascus. **Prices:** $75 and up. **Remarks:** Full-time maker; sold first knife in 1992. **Mark:** Last name over Canada.

ST. CLAIR, THOMAS K., 12608 Fingerboard Rd., Monrovia, MD 21770, Phone: 301-482-0264

ST. CYR, H. RED, 1218 N Cary Ave., Wilmington, CA 90744, Phone: 310-518-9525

STAFFORD, RICHARD, 104 Marcia Ct., Warner Robins, GA 31088, Phone: 912-923-6372
Specialties: High-tech straight knives and some folders. **Patterns:** Hunters in several patterns, fighters, boots, camp knives, combat knives and period pieces. **Technical:** Grinds ATS-34 and 440C; satin finish is standard. **Prices:** Starting at $75. **Remarks:** Part-time maker; first knife sold in 1983. **Mark:** Last name.

STALCUP, EDDIE, PO Box 2200, Gallup, New Mexico 87305, Phone: 505-863-3107, sstalcup@cnetco.com
Specialties: Working and fancy hunters, bird and trout. Special custom orders. **Patterns:** Drop point hunters, locking liner and multi blade folders. **Technical:** ATS-34, 154 CM and 440C. **Prices:** $150 to $500. **Mark:** E.F. Stalcup, Gallup, NM. **Other:** Scrimshaw, Exotic handle material, wet formed sheaths. Membership Arizona Knife Collectors Association.

STANCER, CHUCK, 62 Hidden Ranch Rd. NW, Calgary AB, CANADA T3A 5S5, Phone: 403-295-7370, stancere@teluspianet.net
Specialties: Traditional and working straight knives. **Patterns:** Bowies, hunters and utility knives. **Technical:** Forges and grinds most steels. **Prices:** $175 and up. **Remarks:** Part-time maker. **Mark:** Last name.

STANLEY, JOHN, 604 Elm St., Crossett, AR 71635, Phone: 970-304-3005
Specialties: Hand forged fixed blades with engraving and carving. **Patterns:** Scottish dirks, skeans and fantasy blades. **Technical:** Forge high-carbon steel, own Damascus. Prices $70 to $500. **Remarks:** All work is sole authorship. **Mark:** Varies. **Other:** Offer engraving and carving services on other knives and handles.

STAPEL, CHUCK, Box 1617, Glendale, CA 91209, Phone: 213-66-KNIFE, Fax: 213-669-1577, www.stapelknives.com
Specialties: Working knives of his design. **Patterns:** Variety of straight knives tantos, hunters, folders and utility knives. **Technical:** Grinds D2, 440C and AEB-L. **Prices:** $185 to $12,000. **Remarks:** Full-time maker; first knife sold in 1974. **Mark:** Last name or last name, U.S.A.

STAPLETON, WILLIAM E., BUFFALO 'B' FORGE, 5425 Country Ln., Merritt Island, FL 32953, Phone: 407-452-8946, staplewe@brevard.net
Specialties: Classic and traditional knives of his design and customer spec. **Patterns:** Hunters and using knives. **Technical:** Forges, 01 and L-6 Damascus, cable Damascus and 5160; stock removal on request. **Prices:** $150 to $1000. **Remarks:** Part-time maker, first knife sold 1990. Doing business as Buffalo "B" Forge. **Mark:** Anvil with S initial in center of anvil.

STECK, VAN R., 260 W Dogwood Ave., Orange City, FL 32763, Phone: 386-775-7303
Specialties: Frame lock folders with my own lock design. Fighters, hunting & fillet, spike hawks and Asian influence on swords, sickles, spears, also traditional bowies. **Technical:** Stock removal ATS-34, D-2, forges 5160, 1050 & 1084. **Prices:** $75 to $750. **Remarks:** Free hand grinds, distal taper, hollow and chisel. Specialize in filework and Japanese handle wrapping. **Mark:** GEISHA with sword & my initials and T.H.U.D. knives.

STEFFAN, ALBERT, U Lucenecka 434/4, Filakovo 98604, Slovak Rebublic, svidi@naex.sk
Specialties: Art Knives, miniatures, Scrimshaw. **Prices:** From USD $300 to USD $2000. **Mark:** A

STEFFEN, CHUCK, 504 Dogwood Ave. NW, St. Michael, MN, Phone: 763-497-3615
Specialties: Custom hunting knives, fixed blades folders. Specializing in exotic materials. Damascus excellent fit form and finishes.

STEGALL, KEITH, 2101 W. 32nd, Anchorage, AK 99517, Phone: 907-276-6002
Specialties: Traditional working straight knives. **Patterns:** Most patterns. **Technical:** Grinds 440C and 154CM. **Prices:** $100 to $300. **Remarks:** Spare-time maker; first knife sold in 1987. **Mark:** Name and state with anchor.

STEGNER, WILBUR G., 9242 173rd Ave. SW, Rochester, WA 98579, Phone: 360-273-0937, stegner@myhome.net, Web: landru.myhome.net/stegner/
Specialties: Working/using straight knives and folders of his design. **Patterns:** Hunters and locking folders. **Technical:** Grinds ATS-34 and other tool steels. Quenches, tempers and hardness tests each blade. **Prices:** $100 to $1000; some to $5000. **Remarks:** Full-time maker; first knife sold in 1979. **Other:** Google search key words: "STEGNER KNIVES". **Mark:** First and middle initials, last name in bar over shield logo.

STEIGER, MONTE L., Box 186, Genesee, ID 83832, Phone: 208-285-1769
Specialties: Traditional working/using straight knives of all designs. **Patterns:** Hunters, utility/camp knives, filet and chefs. **Technical:** Grinds 1095, O1, 440C, ATS-34. Handles of stacked leather, natural wood, Micarta or Pakkawood. Each knife comes with right- or left-handed sheath. **Prices:** $70 to $220. **Remarks:** Spare-time maker; first knife sold in 1988. **Mark:** First initial, last name, city and state.

STEIGERWALT, KEN, 507 Savagehill Rd, Orangeville, PA 17859, Phone: 570-683-5156, Web: www.steigerwaltknives.com
Specialties: Carving on bolsters and handle material. **Patterns:** Folders, button locks and rear locks. **Technical:** Grinds ATS-34, 440C and commercial Damascus. Experiments with unique filework. **Prices:** $500 to $5000; some to $1500. **Remarks:** Full-time maker; first knife sold in 1981. **Mark:** Kasteigerwalt

STEINAU, JURGEN, Julius-Hart Strasse 44, Berlin 0-1162, GERMANY, Phone: 372-6452512, Fax: 372-645-2512
Specialties: Fantasy and high-art straight knives of his design. **Patterns:** Boots, daggers and switch-blade folders. **Technical:** Grinds 440B, 2379 and X90 Cr.Mo.V. 78. **Prices:** $1500 to $2500; some to $3500. **Remarks:** Full-time maker; first knife sold in 1984. **Mark:** Symbol, plus year, month day and serial number.

STEINBERG, AL, 5244 Duenas, Laguna Woods, CA 92653, Phone: 949-951-2889, lagknife@fsa.net
Specialties: Fancy working straight knives to customer specs. **Patterns:** Hunters, Bowies, fishing, camp knives, push knives and high end kitchen knives. **Technical:** Grinds O1, 440C and 154CM. **Prices:** $60 to $2500. **Remarks:** Full-time maker; first knife sold in 1972. **Mark:** Signature, city and state.

STEINBRECHER, MARK W., 4725 Locust Ave., Glenview, IL 60025, Phone: 847-298-5721
Specialties: Working and fancy folders. **Patterns:** Daggers, pocket knives, fighters and gents of his own design or to customer specs. **Technical:** Hollow grinds ATS-34, O-1 other makers Damascus. Uses natural handle materials: stag, ivories, mother-of-pearl. File work and some inlays. **Prices:** $500 to $1200, some to $2500. **Remarks:** Part-time maker, first folder sold in 1989. **Mark:** Name etched or handwritten on ATS-34; stamped on Damascus.

STEKETEE, CRAIG A., 871 N. Hwy. 60, Billings, MO 65610, Phone: 417-744-2770, stekknives@earthlink.net
Specialties: Classic and working straight knives and swords of his design. **Patterns:** Bowies, hunters, and Japanese-style swords. **Technical:** Forges his own Damascus; bronze, silver and Damascus fittings, offers filework. Prefers exotic and natural handle materials. **Prices:** $200 to $4000. **Remarks:** Full-time maker. **Mark:** STEK.

STEPHAN, DANIEL, 2201 S. Miller Rd., Valrico, FL 33594, Phone: 813-684-2781

STERLING, MURRAY, 693 Round Peak Church Rd., Mount Airy, NC 27030, Phone: 336-352-5110, Fax: 336-352-5105, sterck@surry.net; Web: www.sterlingcustomknives.com
Specialties: Single and dual blade folders. Interframes and integral dovetail frames. **Technical:** Grinds ATS-34 or Damascus by Mike Norris and/or Devin Thomas. **Prices:** $300 and up. **Remarks:** Full-time maker; first knife sold in 1991. **Mark:** Last name stamped.

STEWART, EDWARD L., 4297 Audrain Rd. 335, Mexico, MO 65265, Phone: 573-581-3883
Specialties: Fixed blades, working knives some art. **Patterns:** Hunters, Bowies, Utility/camp knives. **Technical:** Forging 1095-W-2-I-6-52100 makes own Damascus. **Prices:** $85 to $500. **Remarks:** Part-time maker first knife sold in 1993. **Mark:** First and last initials-last name.

STIMPS, JASON M., 374 S Shaffer St., Orange, CA 92866, Phone: 714-744-5866

STIPES, DWIGHT, 2651 SW Buena Vista Dr., Palm City, FL 34990, Phone: 772-597-0550, dwightstipes@adelphia.net
Specialties: Traditional and working straight knives in standard patterns. **Patterns:** Boots, Bowies, daggers, hunters and fighters. **Technical:** Grinds 440C, D2 and D3 tool steel. Handles of natural materials,

animal, bone or horn. **Prices:** $75 to $150. **Remarks:** Full-time maker; first knife sold in 1972. **Mark:** Stipes.

STOCKWELL, WALTER, 368 San Carlos Ave., Redwood City, CA 94061, Phone: 650-363-6069, walter@stockwellknives.com Web: www.stockwellknives.com
Specialties: Scottish dirks, sgian dubhs. **Patterns:** All knives one-of-a-kind. **Technical:** Grinds ATS-34, forges 5160, 52100, L6. **Prices:** $125 to $500. **Remarks:** Part-time maker since 1992; graduate of ABS bladesmithing school. **Mark:** Shooting star over "STOCKWELL". Pre-2000, "WKS".

STODDARD'S, INC., COPLEY PLACE, 100 Huntington Ave., Boston, MA 02116, Phone: 617-536-8688, Fax: 617-536-8689
Specialties: Cutlery (kitchen, pocket knives, Randall-made Knives, custom knives, scissors, and manicure tools), binoculars, low vision aids, personal care items (hair brushes, manicure sets, mirrors).

STODDART, W.B. BILL, 917 Smiley, Forest Park, OH 45240, Phone: 513-851-1543
Specialties: Sportsmen's working knives and multi-blade folders. **Patterns:** Hunters, camp and fish knives; multi-blade reproductions of old standards. **Technical:** Grinds A2, 440C and ATS-34; makes sheaths to match handle materials. **Prices:** $80 to $300; some to $850. **Remarks:** Part-time maker; first knife sold in 1976. **Mark:** Name, Cincinnati, state.

STOKES, ED, 22614 Cardinal Dr., Hockley, TX 77447, Phone: 713-351-1319
Specialties: Working straight knives and folders of all designs. **Patterns:** Boots, Bowies, daggers, fighters, hunters and miniatures. **Technical:** Grinds ATS-34, 440C and D2. Offers decorative butt caps, tapered spacers on handles and finger grooves, nickel-silver inlays, hand-made sheaths. **Prices:** $185 to $290; some to $350. **Remarks:** Full-time maker; first knife sold in 1973. **Mark:** First and last name, Custom Knives with Apache logo.

STONE, JERRY, PO Box 1027, Lytle, TX 78052, Phone: 512-772-4502
Specialties: Traditional working and using folders of his design and to customer specs; fancy knives. **Patterns:** Fighters, hunters, locking folders and slip-joints. **Technical:** Grinds 440C and ATS-34. Offers filework. **Prices:** $125 to $375; some to $700. **Remarks:** Full-time maker; first knife sold in 1973. **Mark:** Initials.

STORCH, ED, R.R. 4 Mannville, Alberta T0B 2W0, CANADA, Phone: 780-763-2214, storchkn@agt.net Web: www.storchknives.com
Specialties: Working knives, fancy fighting knives, kitchen cutlery and art knives. Knifemaking classes. **Patterns:** Working patterns, Bowies and folders. **Technical:** Forges his own Damascus. Grinds ATS-34. Builds friction folders. Salt heat treating. **Prices:** $45 to $750 (US). **Remarks:** Part-time maker; first knife sold in 1984. Hosts annual northwest canadian knifemakers symposium 60 to 80 knife makers and families. **Mark:** Last name.

STORMER, BOB, 10 Karabair Rd., St. Peters, MO 63376, Phone: 636-441-6807, bobstormer@sbcglobal.net
Specialties: Straight knives, using collector grade. **Patterns:** Bowies, skinners, hunters, camp knives. **Technical:** Forges 5160, 1095. **Prices:** $150 to $400. **Remarks:** Part-time maker ABS Journeyman Smith 2001. **Mark:** Setting Sun/Fall trees/Initials.

STOUT, CHARLES, RT3 178 Stout Rd., Gillham, AR 71841, Phone: 870-386-5521

STOUT, JOHNNY, 1205 Forest Trail, New Braunfels, TX 78132, Phone: 830-606-4067, johnny@stoutknives.com Web: www.stoutknives.com
Specialties: Folders, some fixed blades. Working knives, some fancy. **Patterns:** Hunters, tactical, Bowies, automatics, liner locks and slip-joints. **Technical:** Grinds stainless and carbon steels; forges own Damascus. **Prices:** $450 to $895; some to $3500. **Remarks:** Full-time maker; first knife sold in 1983. **Mark:** Name and city in logo with serial number. **Other:** Hosts semi-annual Guadalupe forge hammer-in and knifemakers rendezvous.

STOVER, HOWARD, 100 Palmetto Dr. Apt. 7, Pasadena, CA 91105, Phone: 765-452-3928

STOVER, TERRY "LEE", 1809 N. 300 E., Kokomo, IN 46901, Phone: 765-452-3928
Specialties: Damascus folders with filework; Damascus Bowies of his design or to customer specs. **Patterns:** Lockback folders and Sheffield-style Bowies. **Technical:** Forges 1095, Damascus using O2, 203E or O2, pure nickel. Makes mokume. Uses only natural handle material. **Prices:** $300 to $1700; some to $2000. **Remarks:** Part-time maker; first knife sold in 1984. **Mark:** First and middle initials, last name in knife logo; Damascus blades marked in Old English.

STRAIGHT, DON, PO Box 12, Points, WV 25437, Phone: 304-492-5471
Specialties: Traditional working straight knives of his design. **Patterns:** Hunters, Bowies and fighters. **Technical:** Grinds 440C, ATS-34 and D2.

custom knifemakers

Prices: $75 to $125; some to $225. **Remarks:** Spare-time maker; first knife sold in 1978. **Mark:** Last name.

STRAIGHT, KENNETH J., 11311 103 Lane N., Largo, FL 33773, Phone: 813-397-9817

STRANDE, POUL, Soster Svenstrup Byvej 16, Dastrup 4130 Viby Sj., DENMARK, Phone: 46 19 43 05, Fax: 46 19 53 19, Web: www.poulstrande.com
Specialties: Classic fantasy working knives; Damasceret blade, Nikkel Damasceret blade, Lamineret; Lamineret blade with Nikkel. **Patterns:** Bowies, daggers, fighters, hunters and swords. **Technical:** Uses carbon steel and 15C20 steel. **Prices:** NA. **Remarks:** Full-time maker; first knife sold in 1985. **Mark:** First and last initials.

STRICKLAND, DALE, 1440 E. Thompson View, Monroe, UT 84754, Phone: 435-896-8362
Specialties: Traditional and working straight knives and folders of his design and to customer specs. **Patterns:** Hunters, folders, miniatures and utility knives. **Technical:** Grinds Damascus and 440C. **Prices:** $120 to $350; some to $500. **Remarks:** Part-time maker; first knife sold in 1991. **Mark:** Oval stamp of name, Maker.

STRIDER, MICK, STRIDER KNIVES, 120 N Pacific Unit L-7, San Marcos, CA 92069, Phone: 760-471-8275, Fax: 503-218-7069, striderguys@striderknives.com Web: www.striderknives.com

STRONG, SCOTT, 2138 Oxmoor Dr., Beavercreek, OH 45431, Phone: 937-426-9290
Specialties: Working knives, some deluxe. **Patterns:** Hunters, fighters, survival and military-style knives, art knives. **Technical:** Forges and grinds O1, A2, D2, 440C and ATS-34. Uses no solder; most knives disassemble. **Prices:** $75 to $450; some to $1500. **Remarks:** Spare-time maker; first knife sold in 1983. **Mark:** Strong Knives.

STROYAN, ERIC, Box 218, Dalton, PA 18414, Phone: 717-563-2603
Specialties: Classic and working/using straight knives and folders of his design. **Patterns:** Hunters, locking folders, slip-joints. **Technical:** Forges Damascus; grinds ATS-34, D2. **Prices:** $200 to $600; some to $2000. **Remarks:** Part-time maker; first knife sold in 1968. **Mark:** Signature or initials stamp.

STUART, STEVE, Box 168, Gores Landing, Ont., CANADA K0K 2E0, Phone: 905-342-5617
Specialties: Straight knives. **Patterns:** Tantos, fighters, skinners, file and rasp knives. **Technical:** Uses 440C, files, Micarta and natural handle materials. **Prices:** $60 to $400. **Remarks:** Part-time maker. **Mark:** Interlocking SS with last name.

STYREFORS, MATTIAS, Unbyn 23, SE-96193 Boden, SWEDEN, infor@styrefors.com
Specialties: Damascus and mosaic Damascus. Fixed blade Nordic hunters, folders and swords. **Technical:** Forges, shapes and grinds Damascus and mosaic Damascus from mostly UHB 15N20 and 20C with contrasts in nickel and 15N20. Hardness HR 58. **Prices:** $800 to $3000. **Remarks:** Fulltime maker since 1999. International reputation for high end Damascus blades. Uses stabilized Arctic birch and willow burl, horn, fossils, exotic materials, and scrimshaw by Viveca Sahlin for knife handles. Hand tools and hand stitches leather sheaths in cow raw hide. Works in well equipped former military forgery in northern Sweden. **Mark:** MS

SUEDMEIER, HARLAN, 754 N 60th Rd, Nebraska City, NE 68410, Phone: 402-873-4372
Patterns: Straigt knives.**Technical:** Forging hi carbon Damascus. **Prices starting at $175. Remarks: Do not take orders. Mark: First initials & last name.**

SUGIHARA, KEIDOH, 4-16-1 Kamori-Cho, Kishiwada City, Osaka, F596-0042, JAPAN, Fax: 0724-44-2677
Specialties: High-tech working straight knives and folders of his design. **Patterns:** Bowies, hunters, fighters, fishing, boots, some pocket knives and liner-lock folders. **Technical:** Grinds ATS-34, COS-25, buys Damascus and high-carbon steels. Prices $60 to $4000. **Remarks:** Full-time maker, first knife sold in 1980. **Mark:** Initial logo with fish design.

SUGIYAMA, EDDY K., 2361 Nagayu, Naoirimachi Naoirigun, Ohita, JAPAN, Phone: 0974-75-2050
Specialties: One of kind, exotic-style knives. **Patterns:** Working, utility and miniatures. **Technical:** CT rind, ATS-34 and D2. **Prices:** $400 to $1200. **Remarks:** Full-time maker. **Mark:** Name or cedar mark.

SUMMERS, ARTHUR L., 1310 Hess Rd., Concord, NC 28025, Phone: 704-795-2863, arthursummers88@hotmail.com
Specialties: Collector-grade knives in drop points, clip points or straight blades. **Patterns:** Fighters, hunters, Bowies and personal knives. **Technical:** Grinds 440C, ATS-34, D2 and Damascus. **Prices:** $150 to $650;

some to $2000. **Remarks:** Full-time maker; first knife sold in 1987. **Mark:** Last name and serial number.

SUMMERS, DAN, 2675 NY Rt. 11, Whitney Pt., NY 13862, Phone: 607-692-2391, dansumm11@msn.com
Specialties: Period knives and tomahawks. **Technical:** All hand forging. **Prices:** Most $100 to $400.

SUMMERS, DENNIS K., 827 E. Cecil St., Springfield, OH 45503, Phone: 513-324-0624
Specialties: Working/using knives. **Patterns:** Fighters and personal knives. **Technical:** Grinds 440C, A2 and D2. Makes drop and clip point. **Prices:** $75 to $200. **Remarks:** Part-time maker; first knife sold in 1995. **Mark:** First and middle initials, last name, serial number.

SUNDERLAND, RICHARD, Av Infraganti 23, Col Lazaro Cardenas, Puerto Escondido Oaxaca, Mexico 71980, Phone: 011 52 94 582 1451, sunamerica@prodigy.net.mx7
Specialties: Personal and hunting knives with carved handles in oosic and ivory. **Patterns:** Hunters, Bowies, daggers, camp and personal knives. **Technical:** Grinds 440C, ATS-34 and O1. Handle materials of rosewoods, fossil mammoth ivory and oosic. **Prices:** $150 to $1000. **Remarks:** Part-time maker; first knife sold in 1983. Doing business as Sun Knife Co. **Mark:** SUN.

SUTTON, S. RUSSELL, 4900 Cypress Shores Dr., New Bern, NC 28562, Phone: 252-637-3963, srsutton@cox.net Web: www.suttoncustomknives.com
Specialties: Stralght knives and folders to customer specs and in standard patterns. **Patterns:** Boots, hunters, interframes, slip joints and locking liners. **Technical:** Grinds ATS-34, 440C and stainless Damascus. **Prices:** $185 to $650; some to $950. **Remarks:** Full-time maker; first knife sold in 1992. **Mark:** Etched last name.

SWEAZA, DENNIS, 4052 Hwy 321 E, Austin, AR 72007, Phone: 501-941-1886, knives4den@aol.com

SWEDER, JORAM, TILARU METALSMITHING, PO Box 4175, Ocala, FL 34470, Phone: 352-546-4438, tilaru@tilaru.com Web: www.tilaru.com
Specialties: Hand forged one-of-a-kind and custom pieces. **Prices:** $100 and up.

SWEENEY, COLTIN D., 1216 S 3 St. W, Missoula, MT 59801, Phone: 406-721-6782

SWYHART, ART, 509 Main St., PO Box 267, Klickitat, WA 98628, Phone: 509-369-3451, swyhart@gorge.net, Web: www.knifeoutlet.com/swyhart.htm
Specialties: Traditional working and using knives of his design. **Patterns:** Bowies, hunters and utility/camp knives. **Technical:** Forges 52100, 5160 and Damascus 1084 mixed with either 15N20 or 0186. Blades differentially heat-treated with visible temper line. **Prices:** $75 to $250; some to $350. **Remarks:** Part-time maker; first knife sold in 1983. **Mark:** First name, last initial in script.

SYMONDS, ALBERTO E., Rambla M Gandhi 485, Apt 901, Montevideo 11300, URUGUAY, Phone: 011 598 5608207, Fax: 011 598 2 7103201, albertosymonds@hotmail.com
Specialties: All sorts-including puukos, nice sheaths, leather and wood. **Prices:** $140 to $900. **Mark:** AESH and year (2005).

SYSLO, CHUCK, 3418 South 116 Ave., Omaha, NE 68144, Phone: 402-333-0647, ciscoknives@cox.net
Specialties: Hunters, working knives, daggers & misc. **Patterns:** Hunters, daggers and survival knives; locking folders. **Technical:** Flat-grinds D2, 440C and 154CM; hand polishes only. **Prices:** $250 to $1000; some to $3000. **Remarks:** Part-time maker; first knife sold in 1978. Uses many matural materials. **Mark:** CISCO in logo.

SZAREK, MARK G., 94 Oakwood Ave., Revere, MA 02151, Phone: 781-289-7102
Specialties: Classic period working and using straight knives and tools. **Patterns:** Hunting knives, American and Japanese woodworking tools. **Technical:** Forges 5160, 1050, Damascus; differentially hardens blades with fireclay. **Prices:** $50 to $750. **Remarks:** Part-time maker; first knife sold in 1989. **Mark:** Last name. **Other:** Produces Japanese alloys for sword fittings and accessories. Custom builds knife presentation boxes and cabinets.

SZILASKI, JOSEPH, 29 Carroll Dr., Wappingers Falls, NY 12590, Phone: 845-297-5397, Web: www.szilaski.com
Specialties: Straight knives, folders and tomahawks of his design, to customer specs and in standard patterns. Many pieces are one-of-a-kind. **Patterns:** Bowies, daggers, fighters, hunters, art knives and early American-styles. **Technical:** Forges A2, D2, O1 and Damascus. **Prices:** $450 to $4000; some to $10,000. **Remarks:** Full-time maker; first knife sold in 1990. **Mark:** Snake logo. **Other:** ABS Master Smith and voting member KMG.

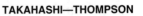

T

TAKAHASHI, KAORU, 2506 TOYO OKA YADO UEKI, Kamoto Kumamoto, JAPAN 861-01, Phone: (8196) 272-6759

TAKAHASHI, MASAO, 39-3 Sekine-machi, Maebashi-shi, Gunma 371 0047, JAPAN, Phone: 81 27 234 2223, Fax: 81 27 234 2223
Specialties: Working straight knives. **Patterns:** Daggers, fighters, hunters, fishing knives, boots. **Technical:** Grinds ATS-34 and Damascus. **Prices:** $350 to $1000 and up. **Remarks:** Full-time maker; first knife sold in 1982. **Mark:** M. Takahashi.

TALLY, GRANT, 26961 James Ave., Flat Rock, MI 48134, Phone: 734-789-8961
Specialties: Straight knives and folders of his design. **Patterns:** Bowies, daggers, fighters. **Technical:** Grinds ATS-34, 440C and D2. Offers filework. **Prices:** $250 to $1000. **Remarks:** Part-time maker; first knife sold in 1985. Doing business as Tally Knives. **Mark:** Tally (last name).

TAMBOLI, MICHAEL, 12447 N. 49 Ave., Glendale, AZ 85304, Phone: 602-978-4308
Specialties: Miniatures, some full size. **Patterns:** Miniature hunting knives to fantasy art knives. **Technical:** Grinds ATS-34. **Prices:** $75 to $500; some to $1000. **Remarks:** Part-time maker; first knife sold in 1978. **Mark:** Initials or last name, city and state, also M.T. Custom Knives.

TASMAN, KERLEY, 9 Avignon Retreat, Pt. Kennedy, 6172, Western Australia, AUSTRALIA, Phone: 61 8 9593 0554, Fax: 61 8 9593 0554, taskerley@optusnet.com.au
Specialties: Knife/harness/sheath systems for elite military personnel and body guards. **Patterns:** Utility/tactical knives, hunters small game and presentation grade knives. **Technical:** ATS-34 and 440C, Damascus, flat and hollow grids. **Prices:** US $200 to $1800. **Remarks:** Will take presentation grade commissions. **Mark:** Makers Initials. **Other:** Multi award winning maker and custom jeweler.

TAY, LARRY C-G., Siglap PO Box 315, Singapore 9145, SINGAPORE, Phone: 65-2419421, Fax: 65-2434879
Specialties: Push knives, working and using straight knives and folders of his design; Marble's Safety Knife with stained or albino Asian buffalo horn and bone or rosewood handles. **Patterns:** Fighters and utility/camp knives. **Technical:** Forges and grinds D2, truck leaf springs. **Prices:** $200 to $1000. **Remarks:** Spare-time maker; first knife sold in 1957. **Mark:** LDA/LAKELL, from 1999 initials L.T.

TAYLOR, BILLY, 10 Temple Rd., Petal, MS 39465, Phone: 601-544-0041
Specialties: Straight knives of his design. **Patterns:** Bowies, skinners, hunters and utility knives. **Technical:** Flat-grinds 440C, ATS-34 and 154CM. **Prices:** $60 to $300. **Remarks:** Part-time maker; first knife sold in 1991. **Mark:** Full name, city and state.

TAYLOR, C. GRAY, 560 Poteat Ln., Fall Branch, TN 37656, Phone: 423-348-8304, graysknives@aol.com or graysknives@hotmail.com Web: www.cgraytaylor.com
Specialties: High-art display knives; period pieces. **Patterns:** Fighters, Bowies, daggers, locking folders and interframes. **Technical:** Grinds 440C, 154CM and ATS-34. **Prices:** $350 and up. **Remarks:** Full-time maker; first knife sold in 1975. **Mark:** Name, city and state.

TAYLOR, SHANE, 18 Broken Bow Ln., Miles City, MT 59301, Phone: 406-234-7175, shane@taylorknives.com Web: www.taylorknives.com
Specialties: One-of-a-kind fancy Damascus straight knives and folders. **Patterns:** Bowies, folders and fighters. **Technical:** Forges own mosaic and pattern welded Damascus. **Prices:** $450 and up. **Remarks:** ABS Master Smith, full-time maker; first knife sold in 1982. **Mark:** First name.

TERAUCHI, TOSHIYUKI, 7649-13 219-11 Yoshida, Fujita-Cho Gobo-Shi, JAPAN

TERRILL, STEPHEN, 21363 Rd. 196, Lindsay, CA 93247, Phone: 559-562-1966, sterrill@yahoo.com
Specialties: Deluxe working straight knives and folders. **Patterns:** Fighters, tantos, boots, locking folders and axes; traditional oriental patterns. **Technical:** Forges 1095, 5160, Damascus, stock removal ATS-34. **Prices:** $250 to $1000, some $8000. **Remarks:** Full-time maker; first knife sold in 1972. **Mark:** Name, city, state in logo.

TERZUOLA, ROBERT, 3933 Agua Fria St., Santa Fe, NM 87507, Phone: 505-473-1002, Fax: 505-438-8018
Specialties: Working folders of his design; period pieces. **Patterns:** High-tech utility, defense and gentleman's folders. **Technical:** Grinds 154CM and CPM S30V. Offers titanium, carbon fiber and G10 composite for side-lock folders and tactical folders. **Prices:** $400 to $1200. **Remarks:** Full-time maker; first knife sold in 1980. **Mark:** Mayan dragon head, name.

THAYER, DANNY O., 8908S 100W, Romney, IN 47981, Phone: 765-538-3105, dot61h@juno.com
Specialties: Hunters, fighters, Bowies. **Prices:** $250 and up.

THEIS, TERRY, 21452 FM 2093, Harper, TX 78631, Phone: 830-864-4438
Specialties: All European and American engraving styles. **Prices:** $200 to $2000. **Remarks:** Engraver only.

THEVENOT, JEAN-PAUL, 16 Rue De La Prefecture, Dijon, FRANCE 21000

THIE, BRIAN, 13250 150th St, Burlington, IA 52601, Phone: 319-985-2276, bkthie@mepotelco.net Web: www.mepotelco.net/web/tknives
Specialties: Working using knives from basic to fancy. **Patterns:** Hunters, fighters, camp and folders. **Technical:** Forges blades and own Damascus. **Prices:** $100 and up. **Remarks:** Member of ABS, part-time maker. Sole author of blades including forging, heat treat, engraving and sheath making. **Mark:** Last name, anvil with last name initial inside, serial number all hand engraved into the blade.

THILL, JIM, 10242 Bear Run, Missoula, MT 59803, Phone: 406-251-5475
Specialties: Traditional and working/using knives of his design. **Patterns:** Fighters, hunters and utility/camp knives. **Technical:** Grinds D2 and ATS-34; forges 10-95-85, 52100, 5160, 10 series, reg. Damascus-mosaic. Offers hand cut sheaths with rawhide lace. **Prices:** $145 to $350; some to $1250. **Remarks:** Full-time maker; first knife sold in 1962. **Mark:** Running bear in triangle.

THOMAS, BOB G., RR 1 Box 121, Thebes, IL 62990-9718

THOMAS, DAVID E., 8502 Hwy 91, Lillian, AL 36549, Phone: 251-961-7574, redbluff@gulftel.com
Specialties: Bowies and hunters. **Technical:** Hand forged blades in 5160, 1095 and own Damascus. **Prices:** $400 and up. **Mark:** Stylized DT, maker's last name, serial number.

THOMAS, DEVIN, 90 N. 5th St., Panaca, NV 89042, Phone: 775-728-4363, hoss@devinthomas.com Web: www.devinthomas.com
Specialties: Traditional straight knives and folders in standard patterns. **Patterns:** Bowies, fighters, hunters. **Technical:** Forges stainless Damascus, nickel and 1095. Uses, makes and sells Mokume with brass, copper and nickel-silver. **Prices:** $300 to $1200. **Remarks:** Full-time maker; first knife sold in 1979. **Mark:** First and last name, city and state with anvil, or first name only.

THOMAS, KIM, PO Box 531, Seville, OH 44273, Phone: 330-769-9906
Specialties: Fancy and traditional straight knives of his design and to customer specs; period pieces. **Patterns:** Boots, daggers, fighters, swords. **Technical:** Forges own Damascus from 5160, 1010 and nickel. **Prices:** $135 to $1500; some to $3000. **Remarks:** Part-time maker; first knife sold in 1986. Doing business as Thomas Iron Works. **Mark:** KT.

THOMAS, ROCKY, 1716 Waterside Blvd., Moncks Corner, SC 29461, Phone: 843-761-7761
Specialties: Traditional working and using straight knives in standard patterns. **Patterns:** Hunters and utility/camp knives. **Technical:** Grinds 440C, ATS-34 and commercial Damascus. **Prices:** $85 to $150. **Remarks:** Spare-time maker; first knife sold in 1986. **Mark:** First name in script and/or block.

THOMPSON, KENNETH, 4887 Glenwhite Dr., Duluth, GA 30136, Phone: 770-446-6730
Specialties: Traditional working and using knives of his design. **Patterns:** Hunters, Bowies and utility/camp knives. **Technical:** Forges 5168, O1, 1095 and 52100. **Prices:** $75 to $1500; some to $2500. **Remarks:** Part-time maker; first knife sold in 1990. **Mark:** P/W; or name, P/W, city and state.

THOMPSON, LEON, 45723 S.W. Saddleback Dr., Gaston, OR 97119, Phone: 503-357-2573
Specialties: Working knives. **Patterns:** Locking folders, slip-joints and liner locks. **Technical:** Grinds ATS-34, D2 and 440C. **Prices:** $200 to $600. **Remarks:** Full-time maker; first knife sold in 1976. **Mark:** First and middle initials, last name, city and state.

THOMPSON, LLOYD, PO Box 1664, Pagosa Springs, CO 81147, Phone: 970-264-5837
Specialties: Working and collectible straight knives and folders of his design. **Patterns:** Straight blades, lock back folders and slip joint folders. **Technical:** Hollow-grinds ATS-34, D2 and O1. Uses sambar stag and exotic woods. **Prices:** $150 to upscale. **Remarks:** Full-time maker; first knife sold in 1985. Doing business as Trapper Creek Knife Co. **Remarks:** Offers three-day knife-making classes. **Mark:** Name.

THOMPSON, TOMMY, 4015 NE Hassalo, Portland, OR 97232-2607, Phone: 503-235-5762
Specialties: Fancy and working knives; mostly liner-lock folders. **Patterns:** Fighters, hunters and liner locks. **Technical:** Grinds D2, ATS-34, CPM440V and T15. Handles are either hardwood inlaid with wood band-

ing and stone or shell, or made of agate, jasper, petrified woods, etc. **Prices:** $75 to $500; some to $1000. **Remarks:** Part-time maker; first knife sold in 1987. Doing business as Stone Birds. **Mark:** First and last name, city and state. **Other:** Knife making temporarily stopped due to family obligations.

THOMSEN, LOYD W., HCR-46, Box 19, Oelrichs, SD 57763, Phone: 605-535-6162, Web: horseheadcreekknives.com
  Specialties: High-art and traditional working/using straight knives and presentation pieces of his design and to customer specs; period pieces. Hand carved animals in crown of stag on handles and carved display stands. **Patterns:** Bowies, hunters, daggers and utility/camp knives. **Technical:** Forges and grinds 1095HC, 1084, L6, 15N20, 440C stainless steel, nickel 200; special restoration process on period pieces. Makes sheaths. Uses natural materials for handles. **Prices:** $350 to $1000. **Remarks:** Full-time maker; first knife sold in 1995. Doing business as Horsehead Creek Knives. **Mark:** Initials and last name over a horse's head.

THOUROT, MICHAEL W., T-814 Co. Rd. 11, Napoleon, OH 43545, Phone: 419-533-6832, Fax: 419-533-3516, mwtknives@yahoo.com Web: wwwsafariknives.com
  Specialties: Working straight knives to customer specs. Designed two-handled skinning ax and limited edition engraved knife and art print set. **Patterns:** Fishing and fillet knives, Bowies, tantos and hunters. **Technical:** Grinds O1, D2, 440C and Damascus. **Prices:** $200 to $5000. **Remarks:** Part-time maker; first knife sold in 1968. **Mark:** Initials.

THUESEN, ED, 21211 Knolle Rd., Damon, TX 77430, Phone: 979-553-1211, Fax: 979-553-1211
  Specialties: Working straight knives. **Patterns:** Hunters, fighters and survival knives. **Technical:** Grinds D2, 440C, ATS-34 and Vascowear. **Prices:** $150 to $275; some to $600. **Remarks:** Part-time maker; first knife sold in 1979. Runs knife maker supply business. **Mark:** Last name in script.

TICHBOURNE, GEORGE, 7035 Maxwell Rd. #5, Mississauga, Ont., CANADA L5S 1R5, Phone: 905-670-0200, sales @tichbourneknives.com Web: www.tichbourneknives.com
  Specialties: Traditional working and using knives as well as unique collectibles. **Patterns:** Bowies, hunters, outdoor, kitchen, integrals, art, military, Scottish dirks, folders, kosher knives. **Technical:** Stock removal 440C, Stellite 6K, stainless Damascus, liquid metal. Handle materials include mammoth, meteorite, mother-of-pearl, Precious gems, Mosiac, Abalone, Stag, Micarta, Exotic High Resin Woods and Corian scrimshawed by George. Leather sheaths are hand stitched and tooled by George as well as the silver adornments for the Dirk Sheaths. **Prices:** $60 U.S. up to $5000 U.S. **Remarks:** Full-time maker with his OWN STORE. First knife sold in 1990. **Mark:** Full name over maple leaf.

TIENSVOLD, ALAN L., PO Box 355, Rushville, NE 69360, Phone: 308-327-2046
  Specialties: Working knives, tomahawks and period pieces, high end Damascus knives. **Patterns:** Random, ladder, twist and many more. **Technical:** Hand forged blades, we forge our own Damascus. **Prices:** Working knives start at $300. **Remarks:** Received Journeyman rating with the ABS in 2002. **Mark:** Tiensvold hand made U.S.A. on left side, JS on right. **Other:** Does own engraving and fine work.

TIENSVOLD, JASON, PO Box 795, Rushville, NE 69360, Phone: 308-327-2046, ironprik@gpcom.net
  Specialties: Working and using straight knives of his design; period pieces. Gentlemans folders, art folders. **Patterns:** Hunters, skinners, Bowies, fighters, daggers, linder locks. **Technical:** Forges own Damascus using 15N20 and 1084, 1095, nickle, custom file work. **Prices:** $200 to $4000. **Remarks:** Full-time maker, first knife sold in 1994; doing business under Tiensvold Custom Knives. **Mark:** Tiensvold USA Handmade in a circle.

TIGHE, BRIAN, 12-111 Fourth Ave, Suite 376 Ridley Square, St Catharines ON, CANADA L0S 1M0, Phone: 905-892-2734, Fax: 905-892-2734, Web: www.tigheknives.com
  Specialties: High tech tactical folders. **Patterns:** Boots, daggers, locking and slip-joint folders. **Technical:** CPM 440V and CPM 420V. Prefers natural handle material inlay; hand finishes. **Prices:** $450 to $2000. **Remarks:** Part-time maker; first knife sold in 1989. **Mark:** Etched signature.

TILL, CALVIN E. AND RUTH, 211 Chaping, Chadron, NE 69337
  Specialties: Straight knives, hunters, Bowies; no folders **Patterns:** Training point, drop point hunters, Bowies. **Technical:** ATS-34 sub zero quench RC-59, 61. **Prices:** $700 to $1200. **Remarks:** Sells only the absolute best knives they can make. **Mark:** RC Till. The R is for Ruth. **Other:** Manufactures every part in their knives.

TILTON, JOHN, 24041 HWY 383, Iowa, LA 70647, Phone: 337-582-6785, jetknives@netscape.net
  Specialties: Camp knives and skinners. **Technical:** All forged blades. **Prices:** $125 and up. **Mark:** Initials J.E.T. **Other:** ABS Journeyman Smith.

TINDERA, GEORGE, BURNING RIVER FORGE, 751 Hadcock Rd., Brunswick, OH 44212-2648, Phone: 330-220-6212
  Specialties: Straight knives; his designs. **Patterns:** Personal knives; classic Bowies and fighters. **Technical:** Hand-forged high-carbon; his own cable and pattern welded Damascus. **Prices:** $100 to $400. **Remarks:** Spare-time maker; sold first knife in 1995. **Other:** Natural handle materials.

TINGLE, DENNIS P., 19390 E Clinton Rd., Jackson, CA 95642, Phone: 209-223-4586, dtknives@webtv.net
  Specialties: Fixed-blade hunting, using knives w/guards and natural handle materials.

TIPPETTS, COLTEN, , PO Box 1436, Ketchum, ID 83340, Phone: 208-853-7779, colten@interstate-electric.com
  Specialties: Fancy and working straight knives and fancy locking folders of his own design or to customer specifications. **Patterns:** Hunters and skinners, fighters and utility. **Technical:** Grinds BG-42, high-carbon 1095 and Damascus. **Prices:** $200 to $1000. **Remarks:** Part-time maker; first knife sold in 1996. **Mark:** Fused initials.

TODD, RICHARD C., RR 1, Chambersburg, IL 62323, Phone: 217-327-4380, ktodd45@yahoo.com
  Specialties: Multi blade folders and silver sheaths. **Patterns:** Blacksmithing and tool making. **Mark:** RT with letter R crossing the T.

TOICH, NEVIO, Via Pisacane 9, Rettorgole di Caldogna, Vincenza, ITALY 36030, Phone: 0444-985065, Fax: 0444-301254
  Specialties: Working/using straight knives of his design or to customer specs. **Patterns:** Bowies, hunters, skinners and utility/camp knives. **Technical:** Grinds 440C, D2 and ATS-34. Hollow-grinds all blades and uses mirror polish. Offers hand-sewn sheaths. Uses wood and horn. **Prices:** $120 to $300; some to $450. **Remarks:** Spare-time maker; first knife sold in 1989. Doing business as Custom Toich. **Mark:** Initials and model number punched.

TOKAR, DANIEL, Box 1776, Shepherdstown, WV 25443
  Specialties: Working knives; period pieces. **Patterns:** Hunters, camp knives, buckskinners, axes, swords and battle gear. **Technical:** Forges L6, 1095 and his Damascus; makes mokume, Japanese alloys and bronze daggers; restores old edged weapons. **Prices:** $25 to $800; some to $3000. **Remarks:** Part-time maker; first knife sold in 1979. Doing business as The Willow Forge. **Mark:** Arrow over rune and date.

TOLLEFSON, BARRY A., 177 Blackfoot Trail, Gunnison, CO 81230-9720, Phone: 970-641-0752
  Specialties: Working straight knives, some fancy. **Patterns:** Hunters, skinners, fighters and camp knives. **Technical:** Grinds 440C, ATS-34 and D2. Likes mirror-finishes; offers some fancy filework. Handles made from elk, deer and exotic hardwoods. **Prices:** $75 to $300; some higher. **Remarks:** Part-time maker; first knife sold in 1990. **Mark:** Stylized initials.

TOMBERLIN, BRION R., ANVIL TOP CUSTOM KNIVES, 825 W Timberdell, Norman, OK 73072, Phone: 405-202-6832, anviltopp@aol.com
  Specialties: Hand forged blades, working pieces, standard classic patterns, some swords, custom designs. **Patterns:** Bowies, hunters, fighters, Persian and eastern-styles. Likes Japanese blades. **Technical:** Forge 1050,1075,1084,1095,5160, some forged stainless, also do some stock removal in stainless. **Prices:** Start at $150 up to $800 or higher for swords and custom pieces. **Remarks:** Part-time maker, first knife sold in 1984, member America Bladesmith Society, member Japanese Sword Society. **Mark:** "BRION" on forged blades, "ATCK" on stock removal, stainless ad early forged blades. **Other:** Prefer natural handle materials, hand rubbed finishes. Like temperlines.

TOMES, P.J., 594 High Peak Ln., Shipman, VA 22971, Phone: 434-263-8662, tomgsknives@juno.com Web: www.tomesknives.com
  Specialties: Scagel reproductions. **Patterns:** Front-lock folders. **Technical:** Forges 52100. **Prices:** $150 to $750. **Mark:** Last name, USA, MS, stamped in forged blades.

TOMEY, KATHLEEN, 146 Buford Pl., Macon, GA 31204, Phone: 478-746-8454, ktomey@tomeycustomknives.com Web: www.tomeycustomknives.com
  Specialties: Working hunters, skinners, daily users in fixed blades, plain and embellished. Tactical neck and tanto. Bowies. **Technical:** Grinds 01, ATS-34, flat or hollow grind, filework, satin and mirror polish finishes. High quality sheaths with tooling. Kydex with tactical. **Prices:** $150 to $500. **Remarks:** Almost full-time maker. **Mark:** Last name in diamond.

TOMPKINS, DAN, PO Box 398, Peotone, IL 60468, Phone: 708-258-3620

Specialties: Working knives, some deluxe, some folders. **Patterns:** Hunters, boots, daggers and push knives. **Technical:** Grinds D2, 440C, ATS-34 and 154CM. **Prices:** $85 to $150; some to $400. **Remarks:** Part-time maker; first knife sold in 1975. **Mark:** Last name, city, state.

TONER, ROGER, 531 Lightfoot Place, Pickering, Ont., CANADA L1V 5Z8, Phone: 905-420-5555

Specialties: Exotic Sword canes. **Patterns:** Bowies, daggers and fighters. **Technical:** Grinds 440C, D2 and Damascus. Scrimshaws and engraves. Silver cast pommels and guards in animal shapes; twisted silver wire inlays. Uses semi-precious stones. **Prices:** $200 to $2000; some to $3000. **Remarks:** Part-time maker; first knife sold in 1982. **Mark:** Last name.

TOPLISS, M.W. "IKE", 1668 Hermosa Ct., Montrose, CO 81401, Phone: 970-249-4703

Specialties: Working/using straight knives of his design and to customer specs. **Patterns:** Boots, hunters, utility/camp knives. **Technical:** Prefers ATS-34. Other steels available on request. Likes stabilized wood, natural hardwoods, antler and Micarta. **Prices:** $175 to $300; some to $800. **Remarks:** Part-time maker; first knife sold in 1984. **Mark:** Name, city, state.

TORGESON, SAMUEL L., 25 Alpine Ln., Sedona, AZ 86336-6809

TOSHIFUMI, KURAMOTO, 3435 Higashioda, Asakura-gun, Fukuoka, JAPAN, Phone: 0946-42-4470

TOWELL, DWIGHT L., 2375 Towell Rd., Midvale, ID 83645, Phone: 208-355-2419

Specialties: Solid, elegant working knives; art knives. **Patterns:** Hunters, Bowies, daggers; folders in several weights. **Technical:** Grinds 154CM; some engraving. **Prices:** $250 to $800; some $3500 and higher. **Remarks:** Part-time maker; first knife sold in 1970. **Mark:** Last name.

TOWNSEND, ALLEN MARK, 6 Pine Trail, Texarkana, AR 71854, Phone: 870-772-8945

TRACY, BUD, 495 Flanders Rd., Reno, NV 8951-4784

TREIBER, LEON, PO Box 342, Ingram, TX 78025, Phone: 830-367-2246, Web: www.treiberknives.com

Specialties: Folders of his design and to customer specs. **Patterns:** Locking folders. **Technical:** Grinds CPM-T-440V, D2, 440C, Damascus, 420v and ATS-34. **Prices:** $350 to $3500. **Remarks:** Part-time maker; first knife sold in 1992. Doing business as Treiber Knives. **Mark:** First initial, last name, city, state.

TREML, GLENN, RR #14, Site 11-10, Thunder Bay, Ont., CANADA P7B 5E5, Phone: 807-767-1977

Specialties: Working straight knives of his design and to customer specs. **Patterns:** Hunters, kitchen knives and double-edged survival knives. Technical Grinds 440C, ATS-34 and O1; stock removal method. Uses various woods and Micarta for handle material. **Prices:** $60 to $400; some higher. **Mark:** Stamped last name.

TRINDLE, BARRY, 1660 Ironwood Trail, Earlham, IA 50072-8611, Phone: 515-462-1237

Specialties: Engraved folders. **Patterns:** Mostly small folders, classical-styles and pocket knives. **Technical:** 440 only. Engraves. Handles of wood or mineral material. **Prices:** Start at $1000. **Mark:** Name on tang.

TRISLER, KENNETH W., 6256 Federal 80, Rayville, LA 71269, Phone: 318-728-5541

TRITZ, JEAN JOSE, Schopstrasse 23, 20255 Hamburg, GERMANY, Phone: 040-49 78 21

Specialties: Scandinavian knives, Japanese kitchen knives, friction folders, swords. **Patterns:** Puukkos, Tollekniven, Hocho, friction folders, swords. **Technical:** Forges tool steels, carbon steels, 52100 Damascus Mokume, San Maj. **Prices:** $200 to $2000; some higher. **Remarks:** Full-time maker; first knife sold in 1989. **Mark:** Initials in monogram. **Other:** Does own leatherwork, prefers natural materials. Sole authorship. Speaks French, German, English, Norwegian.

TRUDEL, PAUL, 525 Braydon Ave., Ottawa Ont., CANADA K1G 0W7

Remarks: Part-time knife maker.

TRUJILLO, ADAM, 3001 Tanglewood Dr., Anchorage, AK 99517, Phone: 907-243-6093

Specialties: Working/using straight knives of his design. **Patterns:** Hunters and utility/camp knives. **Technical:** Grinds 440C, ATS-34 and O1; ice tempers blades. Sheaths are dipped in wax and oil base. **Prices:** $200 to $500; some to $1000. **Remarks:** Spare-time maker; first knife sold in 1995. Doing business as Alaska Knife and Service Co. **Mark:** NA.

TRUJILLO, ALBERT M.B., 2035 Wasmer Cir., Bosque Farms, NM 87068, Phone: 505-869-0428

Specialties: Working/using straight knives of his design or to customer specs. **Patterns:** Hunters, skinners, fighters, working/using knives. File work offered. **Technical:** Grinds ATS-34, D2, 440C. Tapers tangs, all blades cryogenically treated. **Prices:** $75 to $500. **Remarks:** Part-time maker; first knife sold in 1997. **Mark:** First and last name under logo.

TRUJILLO, MIRANDA, 3001 Tanglewood Dr., Anchorage, AK 99517, Phone: 907-243-6093

Specialties: Working/using straight knives of her design. **Patterns:** Hunters and utility/camp knives. **Technical:** Grinds ATS-34 and 440C. Sheaths are water resistant. **Prices:** $145 to $400; some to $600. **Remarks:** Spare-time maker; first knife sold in 1989. Doing business as Alaska Knife and Service Co. **Mark:** NA.

TRUJILLO, THOMAS A., 3001 Tanglewood Dr., Anchorage, AK 99517, Phone: 907-243-6093

Specialties: High-end art knives. **Patterns:** Hunters, Bowies, daggers and locking folders. **Technical:** Grinds to customer choice, including rock and commercial Damascus. Inlays jewels and carves handles. **Prices:** $150 to $900; some to $6000. **Remarks:** Full-time maker; first knife sold in 1976. Doing business as Alaska Knife and Service Co. **Mark:** Alaska Knife and/or Thomas Anthony.

TSCHAGER, REINHARD, Piazza Parrocchia 7, I-39100 Bolzano, ITALY, Phone: 0471-970642, Fax: 0471-970642, goldtschager@dnet.it

Specialties: Classic, high-art, collector-grade straight knives of his design. **Patterns:** Hunters. **Technical:** Grinds ATS-34, D2 and Damascus. Oval pins. Gold inlay. Offers engraving. **Prices:** $500 to $1200; some to $4000. **Remarks:** Spare-time maker; first knife sold in 1979. **Mark:** Gold inlay stamped with initials.

TURCOTTE, LARRY, 1707 Evergreen, Pampa, TX 79065, Phone: 806-665-9369, 806-669-0435

Specialties: Fancy and working/using knives of his design and to customer specs. **Patterns:** Hunters, kitchen knives, utility/camp knives. **Technical:** Grinds 440C, D2, ATS-34. Engraves, scrimshaws, silver inlays. **Prices:** $150 to $350; some to $1000. **Remarks:** Part-time maker; first knife sold in 1977. Doing business as Knives by Turcotte. **Mark:** Last name.

TURECEK, JIM, 12 Elliott Rd., Ansonia, CT 06401, Phone: 203-734-8406

Specialties: Exotic folders, art knives and some miniatures. **Patterns:** Trout and bird knives with split bamboo handles and one-of-a-kind folders. **Technical:** Grinds and forges stainless and carbon Damascus. **Prices:** $750 to $1500; some to $3000. **Remarks:** Full-time maker; first knife sold in 1983. **Mark:** Last initial in script, or last name.

TURNBULL, RALPH A., 14464 Linden Dr., Spring Hill, FL 34609, Phone: 352-688-7089, tbull2000@aol.com Web: www.turnbullknives.com

Specialties: Fancy folders. **Patterns:** Primarily gents pocket knives. **Technical:** Wire EDM work on bolsters. **Prices:** $300 and up. **Remarks:** Full-time maker; first knife sold in 1973. **Mark:** Signature or initials.

TURNER, KEVIN, 17 Hunt Ave., Montrose, NY 10548, Phone: 914-739-0535

Specialties: Working straight knives of his design and to customer specs; period pieces. **Patterns:** Daggers, fighters and utility knives. **Technical:** Forges 5160 and 52100. **Prices:** $90 to $500. **Remarks:** Part-time maker; first knife sold in 1991. **Mark:** Acid-etched signed last name and year.

TYCER, ART, 23820 N Cold Springs Rd., Paron, AR 72122, Phone: 501-821-4487, blades1@tycerknives.com Web: www.tycerknives.com

Specialties: Fancy working/using straight knives of his design, to customer specs and standard patterns. **Patterns:** Boots, Bowies, daggers, fighters, hunters, kitchen and utility knives. **Technical:** Grinds ATS-34, 440C and a variety of carbon steels. Uses exotic woods with spacer material, stag and water buffalo. Offers filework. **Prices:** $150 and up depending on size and embellishments or Damascus. **Remarks:** Making and using his own Damascus and other Damascus also. **Mark:** Flying "T" over first initial inside an oval. **Other:** Full-time maker.

TYSER, ROSS, 1015 Hardee Court, Spartanburg, SC 29303, Phone: 864-585-7616

Specialties: Traditional working and using straight knives and folders of his design and in standard patterns. **Patterns:** Bowies, hunters and slip-joint folders. **Technical:** Grinds 440C and commercial Damascus. Mosaic pins; stone inlay. Does filework and scrimshaw. Offers engraving and cut-work and some inlay on sheaths. **Prices:** $45 to $125; some to $400. **Remarks:** Part-time maker; first knife sold in 1995. Doing business as RT Custom Knives. **Mark:** Stylized initials.

U

UCHIDA, CHIMATA, 977-2 Oaza Naga Shisui Ki, Kumamoto, JAPAN 861-1204

UEKAMA, NOBUYUKI, 3-2-8-302 Ochiai, Tama City, Tokyo, JAPAN

V

VAGNINO, MICHAEL, PO Box 67, Visalia, CA 93279, Phone: 559-528-2800, mvknives@lightspeed.net Web: www.mvknives.com
Specialties: Working and fancy straight knives and folders of his design and to customer specs. **Patterns:** Hunters, Bowies, camp, kitchen and folders: locking liners, slip-joint, lock-back and double-action autos. **Technical:** Forges 52100, A2, 1084 and 15N20 Damascus and grinds stainless. **Prices:** $275 to $2000 plus. **Remarks:** Full-time maker, ABS Master Smith. **Mark:** Logo, last name.

VAIL, DAVE, 554 Sloop Point Rd., Hampstead, NC 28443, Phone: 910-270-4456
Specialties: Working/using straight knives of his own design or to the customer's specs. **Patterns:** Hunters/skinners, camp/utility, fillet, Bowies. **Technical:** Grinds ATS-34, 440c, 154 CM and 1095 carbon steel. **Prices:** $90 to $450. **Remarks:** Part-time maker. Member of NC Custom Knifemakers Guild. **Mark:** Etched oval with "Dave Vail Hampstead NC" inside.

VALLOTTON, BUTCH AND AREY, 621 Fawn Ridge Dr., Oakland, OR 97462, Phone: 541-459-2216, Fax: 541-459-7473
Specialties: Quick opening knives w/complicated mechanisms. **Patterns:** Tactical, fancy, working, and some art knives. **Technical:** Grinds all steels, uses others' Damascus. Uses Spectrum Metal. **Prices:** From $350 to $4500. **Remarks:** Full-time maker since 1984; first knife sold in 1981. **Mark:** Name w/viper head in the "V". **Other:** Co/designer, Appelgate Fairbarn folding w/Bill Harsey.

VALLOTTON, RAINY D., 1295 Wolf Valley Dr., Umpqua, OR 97486, Phone: 541-459-0465
Specialties: Folders, one-handed openers and art pieces. **Patterns:** All patterns. **Technical:** Stock removal all steels; uses titanium liners and bolsters; uses all finishes. **Prices:** $350 to $3500. **Remarks:** Full-time maker. **Mark:** Name.

VALLOTTON, SHAWN, 621 Fawn Ridge Dr., Oakland, OR 97462, Phone: 503-459-2216
Specialties: Left-hand knives. **Patterns:** All styles. **Technical:** Grinds 440C, ATS-34 and Damascus. Uses titanium. Prefers bead-blasted or anodized finishes. **Prices:** $250 to $1400. **Remarks:** Full-time maker. **Mark:** Name and specialty.

VALLOTTON, THOMAS, 621 Fawn Ridge Dr., Oakland, OR 97462, Phone: 541-459-2216
Specialties: Custom autos. **Patterns:** Tactical, fancy. **Technical:** File work, uses Damascus, uses Spectrum Metal. **Prices:** From $350 to $700. **Remarks:** Full-time maker. **Mark:** T and a V mingled. **Other:** Maker of Protégé 3 canoe.

VALOIS, A. DANIEL, 3552 W. Lizard Ck. Rd., Lehighton, PA 18235, Phone: 717-386-3636
Specialties: Big working knives; various sized lock-back folders with new safety releases. **Patterns:** Fighters in survival packs, sturdy working knives, belt buckle knives, military-style knives, swords. **Technical:** Forges and grinds A2, O1 and 440C; likes full tangs. **Prices:** $65 to $240; some to $600. **Remarks:** Full-time maker; first knife sold in 1969. **Mark:** Anvil logo with last name inside.

VAN CLEVE, STEVE, Box 372, Sutton, AK 99674, Phone: 907-745-3038

VAN DE MANAKKER, THIJS, Koolweg 34, 5759 px Helenaveen, HOLLAND, Phone: 0493539369
Specialties: Classic high-art knives. **Patterns:** Swords, utility/camp knives and period pieces. **Technical:** Forges soft iron, carbon steel and Bloomery Iron. Makes own Damascus, Bloomery Iron and patterns. **Prices:** $20 to $2000; some higher. **Remarks:** Full-time maker; first knife sold in 1969. **Mark:** Stylized "V".

VAN DEN ELSEN, GERT, Purcelldreef 83, 5012 AJ Tilburg, NETHERLANDS, Phone: 013-4563200, gvdelsen@home.nl Web: www.7knifedwarfs.com
Specialties: Fancy, working/using, miniatures and integral straight knives of the maker's design or to customer specs. **Patterns:** Bowies, fighters, hunters and Japanese-style blades. **Technical:** Grinds ATS-34 and 440C; forges Damascus. Offers filework, differentially tempered blades and some mokume-gane fittings. **Prices:** $350 to $1000; some to

$4000. **Remarks:** Part-time maker; first knife sold in 1982. Doing business as G-E Knives. **Mark:** Initials GE in lozenge shape.

VAN DIJK, RICHARD, 76 Stepney Ave RD 2, Harwood Dunedin, New Zealand, Phone: 0064-3-4780401, Web: www.hoihoknives.com
Specialties: Damascus, Fantasy knives, Sigian Dubh's. **Patterns:** Mostly one-ofs, anything from bird and trout to swords, no folders. **Technical:** Forges mainly won made Damascus, some 5160, O1, 1095, L6. Prefers natural handle materials with 30 years experience as goldsmith, handle fittings are often made from sterling silver and sometimes gold, manufactured to cap the candle, use gemstones if required. Makes own sheaths. **Prices:** $300 and up. **Remarks:** Full-time maker, first knife sold in 1980. Doing business as HOIHO KNIVES. **Mark:** Stylized initials RvD in triangle.

VAN EIZENGA, JERRY W., 14227 Cleveland, Nunica, MI 49448, Phone: 616-842-2699
Specialties: Hand forged blades, Scagel patterns and other styles. **Patterns:** Camp, hunting, bird, trout, folders, axes, miniatures. **Technical:** 5160, 52100, 1084. **Prices:** Start at $250. **Remarks:** Part-time maker, sole author of knife and sheath. **Mark:** Interconnecting letters spelling VAN, city and state. **Other:** First knife made early 1970s. ABS member who believes in the beauty of simplicity.

VAN ELDIK, FRANS, Ho Flaan 3, 3632BT Loenen, NETHERLANDS, Phone: 0031 294 233 095, Fax: 0031 294 233 095
Specialties: Fancy collector-grade straight knives and folders of his design. **Patterns:** Hunters, fighters, boots and folders. **Technical:** Forges and grinds D2, 154CM, ATS-34 and stainless Damascus. **Prices:** Spare-time maker; first knife sold in 1979. Knivemaker 25 years. **Mark:** Lion with name and Amsterdam.

VAN RIJSWIJK, AAD, AVR KNIVES, Arij Koplaan 16B, 3132 AA Vlaardingen, THE NETHERLANDS, Phone: +31 10 2343227, Fax: +31 10 2343648, info@avrknives.com Web: www.avrknives.com
Specialties: High-art interframe folders of his design and in shaving sets. **Patterns:** Hunters and locking folders. **Technical:** Uses semi-precious stones, mammoth, ivory, walrus ivory, iron wood. **Prices:** $550 to $3800. **Remarks:** Full-time maker; first knife sold in 1993. **Mark:** NA.

VAN RIPER, JAMES N., PO Box 7045, Citrus Heights, CA 95621-7045, Phone: 916-721-0892

VANDERFORD, CARL G., Rt. 9, Box 238B, Columbia, TN 38401, Phone: 615-381-1488
Specialties: Traditional working straight knives and folders of his design. **Patterns:** Hunters, Bowies and locking folders. **Technical:** Forges and grinds 440C, O1 and wire Damascus. **Prices:** $60 to $125. **Remarks:** Part-time maker; first knife sold in 1987. **Mark:** Last name.

VANDEVENTER, TERRY L., 3274 Davis Rd., Terry, MS 39170-8719, Phone: 601-371-7414, tvandeventer@jam.rr.com
Specialties: Bowies, huners, camp knives, friction folders. **Technical:** 1084, 1095, 15N20 & L-6 steels, Damascus and Mokume; natural handle materials. **Prices:** $350 to $2500. **Remarks:** Sole author; makes everything here. First ABS MS from the state of Mississippi. **Mark:** T.L. Vandeventer (silhouette of snake underneath), MS on ricasso. **Other:** ABS Master Smith.

VANHOY, ED AND TANYA, 24255 N Fork River Rd., Abingdon, VA 24210, Phone: 276-944-4885, vanhoyknives@direcway.com
Specialties: Traditional and working/using straight knives of his design, make folders. **Patterns:** Fighters, straight knives, folders, hunters and art knives. **Technical:** Grinds ATS-34 and 440V; forges D2. Offers filework, engraves, acid etching, mosaic pins, decorative bolsters and custom fitted English bridle leather sheaths. **Prices:** $250 to $3000. **Remarks:** Full-time maker; first knife sold in 1977. Wife also engraves. Doing business as Van Hoy Custom Knives. **Mark:** Acid etched last name.

VASQUEZ, JOHNNY DAVID, 1552 7th St., Wyandotte, MI 48192, Phone: 734-281-2455

VAUGHAN, IAN, 351 Doe Run Rd., Manheim, PA 17545-9368, Phone: 717-665-6949

VEATCH, RICHARD, 2580 N. 35th Pl., Springfield, OR 97477, Phone: 541-747-3910
Specialties: Traditional working and using straight knives of his design and in standard patterns; period pieces. **Patterns:** Daggers, hunters, swords, utility/camp knives and minis. **Technical:** Forges and grinds his own Damascus; uses L6 and O1. Prefers natural handle materials; offers leatherwork. **Prices:** $50 to $300; some to $500. **Remarks:** Full-time maker; first knife sold in 1991. **Mark:** Stylized initials.

VEIT, MICHAEL, 3289 E. Fifth Rd., LaSalle, IL 61301, Phone: 815-223-3538, whitebear@starband.net
Specialties: Damascus folders. **Technical:** Engraver-Sole author. **Prices:** $2500 to $6500. **Remarks:** Part-time maker; first knife sold in 1985. **Mark:** Name in script.

VELARDE, RICARDO, 7240 N. Greenfield Dr., Park City, UT 84098, Phone: 435-940-1378/Cell 801-360-1413/801-361-0204, velardeknives.com
Specialties: Investment grade integrals and interframs. **Patterns:** Boots, fighters and hunters; hollow grind. **Technical:** BG on Integrals. **Prices:** $850 to $4500. **Remarks:** First knife sold in 1992. **Mark:** First initial, last name on blade; city, state, U.S.A. at bottom of tang.

VENSILD, HENRIK, GI Estrup, Randersvei 4, DK-8963 Auning, DENMARK, Phone: +45 86 48 44 48
Specialties: Classic and traditional working and using knives of his design; Scandinavian influence. **Patterns:** hunters and using knives. **Technical:** Forges Damascus. Hand makes handles, sheaths and blades. **Prices:** $350 to $1000. **Remarks:** Part-time maker; first knife sold in 1967. **Mark:** Initials.

VIALLON, HENRI, Les Belins, 63300 Thiers, FRANCE, Phone: 04-73-80-24-03, Fax: 04 73-51-02-02
Specialties: Folders and complex Damascus **Patterns:** My draws. **Technical:** Forge **Prices:** $1000 to $5000. **Mark:** H. Viallon.

VIELE, H.J., 88 Lexington Ave., Westwood, NJ 07675, Phone: 201-666-2906
Specialties: Folding knives of distinctive shapes. **Patterns:** High-tech folders. **Technical:** Grinds 440C and ATS-34. **Prices:** Start at $475. **Remarks:** Full-time maker; first knife sold in 1973. **Mark:** Last name with stylized throwing star.

VIKING KNIVES (SEE JAMES THORLIEF ERIKSEN)

VILAR, RICARDO AUGUSTO FERREIRA, Rua Alemada Dos Jasmins, NO 243, Parque Petropolis, Mairipora Sao Paulo, BRASIL 07600-000, Phone: 011-55-11-44-85-43-46, ricardovilar@ig.com.br.
Specialties: Traditional Brazilian-style working knives of the Sao Paulo state. **Patterns:** Fighters, hunters, utility, and camp knives, welcome customer design. Specialize in the "true" Brazilian camp knife "Soraca-bana." **Technical:** Forges only with sledge hammer to 100% shape in 5160 and 52100 and his own Damascus steels. Makes own sheaths in the "true" traditional "Paulista"-style of the state of Sao Paulo. **Remark:** Full-time maker. **Prices:** $250 to $600. Uses only natural handle materials. **Mark:** Special designed signature styled name R. Vilar.

VILLA, LUIZ, R. Com. Miguel Calfat, 398 Itaim Bibi, Sao Paulo, SP-04537-081, BRAZIL, Phone: 011-8290649
Specialties: One-of-a-kind straight knives and jewel knives of all designs. **Patterns:** Bowies, hunters, utility/camp knives and jewel knives. **Technical:** Grinds D6, Damascus and 440C; forges 5160. Prefers natural handle material. **Prices:** $70 to $200. **Remarks:** Part-time maker; first knife sold in 1990. **Mark:** Last name and serial number.

VILLAR, RICARDO, Al. dos Jasmins, 243, Mairipora, S.P. 07600-000, BRAZIL, Phone: 011-4851649
Specialties: Straight working knives to customer specs. **Patterns:** Bowies, fighters and utility/camp knives. **Technical:** Grinds D6, ATS-34 and 440C stainless. **Prices:** $80 to $200. **Remarks:** Part-time maker; first knife sold in 1993. **Mark:** Percor over sword and circle.

VISTE, JAMES, Edgewize Forge, 13401 Mt Elliot, Detroit, MI 48212, Phone: 313-664-7455, grumblejunky@hotmail.com
Mark: EWF touch mark.

VISTNES, TOR, N-6930 Svelgen, NORWAY, Phone: 047-57795572
Specialties: Traditional and working knives of his design. **Patterns:** Hunters and utility knives. **Technical:** Grinds Uddeholm Elmax. Handles made of rear burls of different Nordic stabilized woods. **Prices:** $300 to $1100. **Remarks:** Part-time maker; first knife sold in 1988. **Mark:** Etched name and deer head.

VITALE, MACE, 925 Rt 80, Guilford, CT 06437, Phone: 203-457-5591
Specialties: Hand forged blades. **Patterns:** Hunters, utility, chef, Bowies and fighters. **Technical:** 5160, 1095, 1084, L-6. Hand forged and finished. **Prices:** $50 to $500. **Remarks:** Full-time maker; first knife sold 2001. **Mark:** MACE.

VOGT, DONALD J., 9007 Hogans Bend, Tampa, FL 33647, Phone: 813 973-3245, vogtknives@aol.com
Specialties: Art knives, folders, automatics, large fixed blades. **Technical:** Uses Damascus steels for blade and bolsters, filework, hand carving on blade bolsters and handles. Other materials used: jewels, gold, stainless steel, mokume. Prefers to use natural handle materials. **Prices:** $800 to $7000. **Remarks:** Part-time maker; first knife sold in 1997. **Mark:** Last name.

VOGT, PATRIK, KUNGSVAGEN 83, S-30270 Halmstad, SWEDEN, Phone: 46-35-30977
Specialties: Working straight knives. **Patterns:** Bowies, hunters and fighters. **Technical:** Forges carbon steel and own Damascus. **Prices:** From $100. **Remarks:** Not currently making knives. **Mark:** Initials or last name.

VOORHIES, LES, 14511 Lk. Mazaska Tr., Faribault, MN 55021, Phone: 507-332-0736
Specialties: Steels. **Technical:** ATS-34 Damascus. **Prices:** $75 to $450.

VOSS, BEN, 362 Clark St., Galesburg, IL 61401, Phone: 309-342-6994
Specialties: Fancy working knives of his design. **Patterns:** Bowies, fighters, hunters, boots and folders. **Technical:** Grinds 440C, ATS-34 and D2. **Prices:** $35 to $1200. **Remarks:** Part-time maker; first knife sold in 1986. **Mark:** Name, city and state.

VOTAW, DAVID P., Box 327, Pioneer, OH 43554, Phone: 419-737-2774
Specialties: Working knives; period pieces. **Patterns:** Hunters, Bowies, camp knives, buckskinners and tomahawks. **Technical:** Grinds O1 and D2. **Prices:** $100 to $200; some to $500. **Remarks:** Part-time maker; took over for the late W.K. Kneubuhler. Doing business as W-K Knives. **Mark:** WK with V inside anvil.

VOWELL, DONALD J., 815 Berry Dr., Mayfield, KY 42066, Phone: 270-247-2157

W

WADA, YASUTAKA, Fujinokidai 2-6-22, Nara City, Nara prefect 631-0044, JAPAN, Phone: 0742 46-0689
Specialties: Fancy and embellished one-of-a-kind straight knives of his design. **Patterns:** Bowies, daggers and hunters. **Technical:** Grinds ATS-34, Cowry X and Cowry X L-30 laminate. **Prices:** $400 to $2500; some higher. **Remarks:** Part-time maker; first knife sold in 1990. **Mark:** Owl eyes with initial and last name underneath.

WAGAMAN, JOHN K., 107 E Railroad St., Selma, NC 27576, Phone: 919-965-9659, Fax: 919-965-9901
Specialties: Fancy working knives. **Patterns:** Bowies, miniatures, hunters, fighters and boots. **Technical:** Grinds D2, 440C, 154CM and commercial Damascus; inlays mother-of-pearl. **Prices:** $110 to $2000. **Remarks:** Part-time maker; first knife sold in 1975. **Mark:** Last name.

WALDROP, MARK, 14562 SE 1st Ave. Rd., Summerfield, FL 34491, Phone: 352-347-9034
Specialties: Period pieces. **Patterns:** Bowies and daggers. **Technical:** Uses stock removal. Engraves. **Prices:** Moderate to upscale. **Remarks:** Part-time maker; first knife sold in 1978. **Mark:** Last name.

WALKER, BILL, 431 Walker Rd., Stevensville, MD 21666, Phone: 410-643-5041

WALKER, DON, 645 Halls Chapel Rd., Burnsville, NC 28714, Phone: 828-675-9716, dlwalkernc@aol.com

WALKER, GEORGE A., PO Box 3272, 483 Aspen Hills, Alpine, WY 83128-0272, Phone: 307-883-2372, Fax: 307-883-2372, GWKNIVES@SILVERSTAR.COM
Specialties: Deluxe working knives. **Patterns:** Hunters, boots, fighters, Bowies and folders. **Technical:** Forges his own Damascus and cable; engraves, carves, scrimshaws. Makes sheaths. **Prices:** $125 to $750; some to $1000. **Remarks:** Full-time maker; first knife sold in 1979. Partners with wife. **Mark:** Name, city and state.

WALKER, JIM, 22 Walker Lane, Morrilton, AR 72110, Phone: 501-354-3175, jwalker@mail.cswnet.com
Specialties: Period pieces and working/using knives of his design and to customer specs. **Patterns:** Bowies, fighters, hunters, camp knives. **Technical:** Forges 5160, O1, L6, 52100, 1084, 1095. **Prices:** Start at $425. **Remarks:** Full-time maker; first knife sold in 1993. **Mark:** Three arrows with last name/MS.

WALKER, JOHN W., 10620 Moss Branch Rd., Bon Aqua, TN 37025, Phone: 931-670-4754
Specialties: Straight knives, daggers and folders; sterling rings, 14K gold wire wrap; some stone setting. **Patterns:** Hunters, boot knives, others. **Technical:** Grinds 440C, ATS-34, L6, etc. Buys Damascus. **Prices:** $150 to $500 some to $1500. **Remarks:** Part-time maker; first knife sold in 1982. **Mark:** Hohenzollern Eagle with name, or last name.

WALKER, MICHAEL L., PO Box 1924, Rancho de Taos, NM 87571, Phone: 505-737-3086, Fax: 505-751-0284, lockers@newmex.com
Specialties: Innovative knife designs and locking systems; Titanium and SS furniture and art. **Patterns:** Folders from utility grade to museum quality art; others upon request. **Technical:** State-of-the-art materials: titanium, stainless Damascus, gold, etc. **Prices:** $3500 and above. **Remarks:** Designer/MetalCrafts; Full-time professional knife maker since 1980; Four U.S. Patents; Invented Liner Lock® and was awarded Registered U.S. Trademark No. 1,585,333. **Mark:** Early mark MW, Walker's Lockers by M.L. Walker; current M.L. Walker or Michael Walker.

WALKER III, JOHN WADE, 2595 HWY 1647, Paintlick, KY 40461, Phone: 606-792-3498

WALLACE, ROGER L., 4902 Collins Lane, Tampa, FL 33603, Phone: 813-239-3261
Specialties: Working straight knives, Bowies and camp knives to customer specs. **Patterns:** Hunters, skinners and utility knives. **Technical:** Forges high-carbon steel. **Prices:** Start at $75. **Remarks:** Part-time maker; first knife sold in 1985. **Mark:** First initial, last name.

WALLINGFORD JR., CHARLES W., 9027 Old Union Rd, Union, KY 41091, Phone: 859-384-4141
Specialties: 18th and 19th century styles: Patch knives, Rifleman knives. **Technical:** 1084 and 5160 forged blades. **Prices:** $125 to $300. **Mark:** CW.

WALTERS, A.F., PO Box 523, 275 Crawley Rd., TyTy, GA 31795, Phone: 229-528-6207
Specialties: Working knives, some to customer specs. **Patterns:** Locking folders, straight hunters, fishing and survival knives. **Technical:** Grinds D2, 154CM and 13C26. **Prices:** Start at $200. **Remarks:** Part-time maker. Label: "The jewel knife." **Mark:** "J" in diamond and knife logo.

WARD, CHUCK, PO Box 2272, 1010 E North St, Benton, AR 72018-2272, Phone: 501-778-4329, chuckbop@aol.com
Specialties: Traditional working and using straight knives and folders of his design. **Technical:** Grinds 440C, D2, A2, ATS-34 and O1; uses natural and composite handle materials. **Prices:** $90 to $400, some higher. **Remarks:** Part-time maker; first knife sold in 1990. **Mark:** First initial, last name.

WARD, J.J., 7501 S.R. 220, Waverly, OH 45690, Phone: 614-947-5328
Specialties: Traditional and working/using straight knives and folders of his design. **Patterns:** Hunters and locking folders. **Technical:** Grinds ATS-34, 440C and Damascus. Offers handmade sheaths. **Prices:** $125 to $250; some to $500. **Remarks:** Spare-time maker; first knife sold in 1980. **Mark:** Etched name.

WARD, KEN, 5122 Lake Shastina Blvd., Weed, CA 96094, Phone: 530-938-9720
Specialties: Working knives, some to customer specs. **Patterns:** Straight and folding hunters, axes, Bowies, buckskinners and miniatures. **Technical:** Grinds ATS-34, Damascus and Stellite 6K. **Prices:** $100 to $700. **Remarks:** Part-time maker; first knife sold in 1977. **Mark:** Name.

WARD, RON, 1363 Nicholas Dr., Loveland, OH 45140, Phone: 513-722-0602
Specialties: Classic working and using straight knives, fantasy knives. **Patterns:** Bowies, hunter, fighters, and utility/camp knives. **Technical:** Grinds 440C, 154CM, ATS-34, uses composite and natural handle materials. **Prices:** $50 to $750. **Remarks:** Part-time maker, first knife sold in 1992. Doing business as Ron Ward Blades. **Mark:** Ron Ward Blades, Loveland OH.

WARD, W.C., 817 Glenn St., Clinton, TN 37716, Phone: 615-457-3568
Specialties: Working straight knives; period pieces. **Patterns:** Hunters, Bowies, swords and kitchen cutlery. **Technical:** Grinds O1. **Prices:** $85 to $150; some to $500. **Remarks:** Part-time maker; first knife sold in 1969. He styled the Tennessee Knife Maker. **Mark:** TKM.

WARDELL, MICK, 20, Clovelly Rd., Bideford, N Devon EX39 3BU, ENGLAND, Phone: 01237 475312, Fax: 01237 475312, WEB: www.wardellscustomknives.com
Specialties: Folders of his design. **Patterns:** Locking and slip-joint folders, Bowies. **Technical:** Grinds stainless Damascus and RWL34. Heat-treats. **Prices:** $200 to $2000. **Remarks:** Full-time maker; first knife sold in 1986. **Mark:** M. Wardell - England.

WARDEN, ROY A., 275 Tanglewood Rd., Union, MO 63084, Phone: 314-583-8813, rwarden@mail.usmo.com
Specialties: Complex mosaic designs of "EDM wired figures" and "Stack up" patterns and "Lazer Cut" and "Torch cut" and "Sawed" patterns combined. **Patterns:** Mostly "all mosaic" folders, automatics, fixed blades. **Technical:** Mosaic Damascus with all tool steel edges. **Prices:** $500 to $2000 and up. **Remarks:** Part-time maker; first knife sold in 1987. **Mark:** WARDEN stamped or initials connected.

WARE, TOMMY, PO Box 488, Datil, NM 87821, Phone: 505-772-5817
Specialties: Traditional working and using straight knives, folders and automatics of his design and to customer specs. **Patterns:** Hunters, automatics and locking folders. **Technical:** Grinds ATS-34, 440C and D2. Offers engraving and scrimshaw. **Prices:** $275 to $575; some to $1000. **Remarks:** Full-time maker; first knife sold in 1990. Doing business as Wano Knives. **Mark:** Last name inside oval, business name above, city and state below, year on side.

WARENSKI, BUSTER, PO Box 214, Richfield, UT 84701, Phone: 435-896-5319, Fax: 435-896-8333, buster@warenskiknives.com Web: www.warenskiknives.com
Specialties: Investor-class straight knives. **Patterns:** Daggers, swords. **Technical:** Grinds, engraves and inlays; offers surface treatments. All engraved by Julie Warenski. **Prices:** Upscale. **Remarks:** Full-time maker. **Mark:** Warenski (hand engraved on blade).

WARREN (SEE DELLANA), DELLANA

WARREN, AL, 1423 Sante Fe Circle, Roseville, CA 95678, Phone: 916-784-3217/Cell Phone 916-257-5904, al@warrenknives.com Web: www.warrenknives.com
Specialties: Working straight knives and folders, some fancy. **Patterns:** Hunters, Bowies, daggers, short swords, fillets, folders and kitchen knives. **Technical:** Grinds D2, ATS-34 and 440C, 440V. **Prices:** $110 to $1100 some to $3700. **Remarks:** Part-time maker; first knife sold in 1978. **Mark:** First and middle initials, last name.

WARREN, DANIEL, 571 Lovejoy Rd., Canton, NC 28716, Phone: 828-648-7351
Specialties: Using knives. **Patterns:** Drop point hunters. **Prices:** $200 to $500. **Mark:** Warren-Bethel NC.

WARTHER, DALE, 331 Karl Ave., Dover, OH 44622, Phone: 216-343-7513
Specialties: Working knives; period pieces. **Patterns:** Kitchen cutlery, daggers, hunters and some folders. **Technical:** Forges and grinds O1, D2 and 440C. **Prices:** $250 to $7000. **Remarks:** Full-time maker; first knife sold in 1967. Takes orders only at shows or by personal interviews at his shop. **Mark:** Warther Originals.

WASHBURN, ARTHUR D., ADW CUSTOM KNIVES, 10 Hinman St/POB 625, Pioche, NV 89043, Phone: 775-962-5463, awashburn@adwcustomknives.com; Web: www.adwcustomknives.com
Specialties: Locking liner folders. **Patterns:** Slip joint folders (single and multiplied), lock-back folders, some fixed blades. Do own heat-treating; Rockwell test each blade. **Technical:** Carbon and stainless Damascus, some 1084, 1095, ATS-34. **Prices:** $200 to $1000 and up. **Remarks:** Sold first knife in 1997. Part-time maker. **Mark:** ADW enclosed in an oval or ADW.

WASHBURN JR., ROBERT LEE, 244 Lovett Scott Rd., Adrian, GA 31002, Phone: 475-275-7926, Fax: 475-272-6849, washburn@nlamerica.com Web: www.washburnknives.com
Specialties: Hand-forged period, Bowies, tactical, boot and hunters. **Patterns:** Bowies, tantos, loot hunters, tactical and folders. **Prices:** $100 to $2500. **Remarks:** All hand forged. 52100 being his favorite steel. **Mark:** Washburn Knives W of Dublin GA.

WATANABE, WAYNE, PO Box 3563, Montebello, CA 90640, wwknives@earthlink.net Web: www.geocities.com/ww-knives
Specialties: Straight knives in Japanese-styles. One-of-a-kind designs; welcomes customer designs. **Patterns:** Tantos to katanas, Bowies. **Technical:** Flat grinds A2, O1 and ATS-34. Offers hand-rubbed finishes and wrapped handles. **Prices:** Start at $200. **Remarks:** Part-time maker. **Mark:** Name in characters with flower.

WATERS, GLENN, 11 Shinakawa Machi, Hirosaki City 036-8183, JAPAN, Phone: 172-33-8881, gwaters@luck.ocn.ne.jp Web: www.glennwaters.com
Specialties: One-of-a-kind collector-grade highly embellished art knives. Folders, fixed blades, and automatics. **Patterns:** Locking liner folders, automatics and fixed art knives. **Technical:** Grinds blades from Damasteel, and selected Damascus makers, mostly stainless. Does own engraving, gold inlaying and stone setting, filework, and carving. Gold and Japanese precious metal fabrication. Prefers exotic material, high karat gold, silver, Shyaku Dou, Shibu Ichi Gin, precious gemstones. **Prices:** Upscale. **Remarks:** Designs and makes some-of-a-kind highly embellished art knives often with fully engraved handles and blades. A jeweler by trade for 20 years before starting to make knives. Full-time since 1999, first knife sold in 1994. **Mark:** Glenn Waters maker Japan, G. Waters or Glen in Japanese writing.

WATERS, HERMAN HAROLD, 2516 Regency, Magnolia, AR 71753, Phone: 870-234-5409

WATERS, LU, 2516 Regency, Magnolia, AR 71753, Phone: 870-234-5409

WATSON, BERT, PO Box 26, Westminster, CO 80036-0026, Phone: 303-426-7577
Specialties: Working/using straight knives of his design and to customer specs. **Patterns:** Hunters, utility/camp knives. **Technical:** Grinds O1, ATS-34, 440C, D2, A2 and others. **Prices:** $50 to $250. **Remarks:** Part-time maker; first knife sold in 1974. Doing business as Game Trail Knives. **Mark:** GTK stamped or etched, sometimes with first or last name.

WATSON, BILLY, 440 Forge Rd., Deatsville, AL 36022, Phone: 334-365-1482, billy@watsonknives.com Web: www.watsonknives.com
Specialties: Working and using straight knives and folders of his design; period pieces. **Patterns:** Hunters, Bowies and utility/camp knives. **Technical:** Forges and grinds his own Damascus, 1095, 5160 and 52100. **Prices:** $40 to $1500. **Remarks:** Full-time maker; first knife sold in 1970. Doing business as Billy's Blacksmith Shop. **Mark:** Last name.

WATSON, DANIEL, 350 Jennifer Ln., Driftwood, TX 78619, Phone: 512-847-9679, info@angelsword.com Web: http: //www.angelsword.com
Specialties: One-of-a-kind knives and swords. **Patterns:** Hunters, daggers, swords. **Technical:** Hand-purify and carbonize his own high-carbon steel, pattern-welded Damascus, cable and carbon-induced crystalline Damascus. Teehno-Wootz ™Damascus steel, heat treats including cryogenic processing. European and Japanese tempering. **Prices:** $125 to $25,000. **Remarks:** Full-time maker; first knife sold in 1979. **Mark:** "Angel Sword" on forged pieces; "Bright Knight" for stock removal. Avatar on Techno-Wootz ™ Damascus. Bumon on traditional Japanese blades.

WATSON, PETER, 66 Kielblock St., La Hoff 2570, SOUTH AFRICA, Phone: 018-84942
Specialties: Traditional working and using straight knives and folders of his design. **Patterns:** Hunters, locking folders and utility/camp knives. **Technical:** Sandvik and 440C. **Prices:** $120 to $250; some to $1500. **Remarks:** Part-time maker; first knife sold in 1989. **Mark:** Buffalo head with name.

WATSON, TOM, 1103 Brenau Terrace, Panama City, FL 32405, Phone: 850-785-9209, tomwatsonknives@aol.com Web: www.tomwatsonknives.com
Specialties: Liner-lock folders. **Patterns:** Tactical, utility and art investment pieces. **Technical:** Flat-grinds ATS-34, 440-V, Damascus. **Prices:** Tactical start at $250, investment pieces $500 and up. **Remarks:** In business since 1978. **Mark:** Name and city.

WATT III, FREDDIE, PO Box 1372, Big Spring, TX 79721, Phone: 915-263-6629
Specialties: Working straight knives, some fancy. **Patterns:** Hunters, fighters and Bowies. **Technical:** Grinds A2, D2, 440C and ATS-34; prefers mirror finishes. **Prices:** $150 to $350; some to $750. **Remarks:** Full-time maker; first knife sold in 1979. **Mark:** Last name, city and state.

WATTELET, MICHAEL A., PO Box 649, 125 Front, Minocqua, WI 54548, Phone: 715-356-3069, redtroll@nnex.net
Specialties: Working and using straight knives of his design and to customer specs; fantasy knives. **Patterns:** Daggers, fighters and swords. **Technical:** Grinds 440C and L6; forges and grinds O1. Silversmith. **Prices:** $75 to $1000; some to $5000. **Remarks:** Full-time maker; first knife sold in 1966. Doing business as M and N Arts Ltd. **Mark:** First initial, last name.

WATTS, JOHNATHAN, 9560 S State Hwy 36, Gatesville, TX 76528, Phone: 254-487-2866
Specialties: Traditional folders. **Patterns:** One and two blade folders in various blade shapes. **Technical:** Grinds ATS-34 and Damascus on request. **Prices:** $120 to $400. **Remarks:** Part-time maker; first knife sold in 1997. **Mark:** J Watts.

WATTS, WALLY, 9560 S. Hwy. 36, Gatesville, TX 76528, Phone: 254-487-2866
Specialties: Unique traditional folders of his design. **Patterns:** One- to five-blade folders and single-blade gents in various blade shapes. **Technical:** Grinds ATS-34; Damascus on request. **Prices:** $165 to $500; some to $500. **Remarks:** Full-time maker; first knife sold in 1986. **Mark:** Last name.

WEDDLE JR., DEL, 2703 Green Valley Rd., St. Joseph, MO 64505, Phone: 816-364-1981
Specialties: Working knives; some period pieces. **Patterns:** Hunters, fighters, locking folders, push knives. **Technical:** Grinds D2 and 440C; can provide precious metals and set gems. Offers his own forged wire-cable Damascus in his finished knives. **Prices:** $80 to $250; some to $2000. **Remarks:** Full-time maker; first knife sold in 1972. **Mark:** Signature with last name and date.

WEHNER, RUDY, 297 William Warren Rd, Collins, MS 39428, Phone: 601-765-4997
Specialties: Reproduction antique Bowies and contemporary Bowies in full and miniature. **Patterns:** Skinners, camp knives, fighters, axes and Bowies. **Technical:** Grinds 440C, ATS-34, 154CM and Damascus. **Prices:** $100 to $500; some to $850. **Remarks:** Full-time maker; first knife sold in 1975. **Mark:** Last name on Bowies and antiques; full name, city and state on skinners.

WEILAND JR., J. REESE, PO Box 2337, Riverview, FL 33568, Phone: 813-671-0661, RWPHIL413@earthlink.net Web: www.rwcustomknive.som
Specialties: Hawk bills; tactical to fancy folders. **Patterns:** Hunters, tantos, Bowies, fantasy knives, spears and some swords. **Technical:** Grinds ATS-34, 154CM, 440C, D2, 01, A2, Damascus. Titanium hardware on locking liners and button locks. **Prices:** $150 to $4000. **Other:** Full-time maker, first knife sold in 1978. Knifemakers Guild member since 1988.

WEILER, DONALD E., PO Box 1576, Yuma, AZ 85366-9576, Phone: 928-782-1159
Specialties: Working straight knives; period pieces. **Patterns:** Strong springbuck folders, blade and spring ATS-34. **Technical:** Forges O1, W2, 5160, ATS-34, D2, 52100, L6 and cable Damascus. Makes his own high-carbon steel Damascus. **Prices:** $150 to $1000. **Remarks:** Full-time maker; first knife sold in 1952. **Mark:** Last name, city.

WEINAND, GEROME M., 14440 Harpers Bridge Rd., Missoula, MT 59808, Phone: 406-543-0845
Specialties: Working straight knives. **Patterns:** Bowies, fishing and camp knives, large special hunters. **Technical:** Grinds O1, 440C, ATS-34, 1084, L6, also stainless Damascus, Aebl and 304; makes all-tool steel Damascus; Dendritic D2 from powdered steel. Heat-treats. **Prices:** $30 to $100; some to $500. **Remarks:** Full-time maker; first knife sold in 1982. **Mark:** Last name.

WEINSTOCK, ROBERT, PO Box 170028, San Francisco, CA 94117-0028, Phone: 415-731-5968, weinstock_r@msn.com
Specialties: Fancy and high-art straight knives of his design. **Patterns:** Daggers, folders, poignards and miniatures. **Technical:** Grinds A2, O1 and 440C. Chased and hand-carved blades and handles. Also using various Damascus steels from other makers. **Prices:** $3000 to 7,000+. **Remarks:** Full-time maker; first knife sold in1994. **Mark:** Last name carved.

WEISS, CHARLES L., 18847 N. 13th Ave., Phoenix, AZ 85027, Phone: 623-582-6147, weissknife@juno.com Web: www.weissknives.com
Specialties: High-art straight knives and folders; deluxe period pieces. **Patterns:** Daggers, fighters, boots, push knives and miniatures. **Technical:** Grinds 440C, 154CM and ATS-34. **Prices:** $300 to $1200; some to $2000. **Remarks:** Full-time maker; first knife sold in 1975. **Mark:** Name and city.

WERNER JR., WILLIAM A., 336 Lands Mill, Marietta, GA 30067, Phone: 404-988-0074
Specialties: Fantasy and working/using straight knives. **Patterns:** Bowies, daggers, fighters. **Technical:** Grinds 440C stainless, 10 series carbon and Damascus. **Prices:** $150 to $400; some to $750. **Remarks:** Part-time maker. Doing business as Werner Knives. **Mark:** Last name.

WERTH, GEORGE W., 5223 Woodstock Rd., Poplar Grove, IL 61065, Phone: 815-544-4408
Specialties: Period pieces, some fancy. **Patterns:** Straight fighters, daggers and Bowies. **Technical:** Forges and grinds O1, 1095 and his Damascus, including mosaic patterns. **Prices:** $200 to $650; some higher. **Remarks:** Full-time maker. Doing business as Fox Valley Forge. **Mark:** Name in logo or initials connected.

WESCOTT, CODY, 5330 White Wing Rd., Las Cruces, NM 88012, Phone: 505-382-5008
Specialties: Fancy and presentation-grade working knives. **Patterns:** Hunters, locking folders and Bowies. **Technical:** Hollow-grinds D2 and ATS-34; all knives file worked. Offers some engraving. Makes sheaths. **Prices:** $80 to $300; some to $950. **Remarks:** Full-time maker; first knife sold in 1982. **Mark:** First initial, last name.

WEST, CHARLES A., 1315 S. Pine St., Centralia, IL 62801, Phone: 618-532-2777
Specialties: Classic, fancy, high tech, period pieces, traditional and working/using straight knives and folders. **Patterns:** Bowies, fighters and locking folders. **Technical:** Grinds ATS-34, O1 and Damascus. Prefers hot blued finishes. **Prices:** $150 to $1000; some to $2000. **Remarks:** Full-time maker; first knife sold in 1963. Doing business as West Custom Knives. **Mark:** Name or name, city and state.

WEST, PAT, PO Box 9, Charlotte, TX 78011, Phone: 830-277-1290
Specialties: Classic working and using straight knives and folders. **Patterns:** Hunters, kitchen knives, slip-joint folders. **Technical:** Grinds ATS-34, D2 and Vascowear. Offers filework and decorates liners on folders. **Prices:** $300 to $600. **Remarks:** Spare-time maker; first knife sold in 1984. **Mark:** Name.

WESTBERG, LARRY, 305 S. Western Hills Dr., Algona, IA 50511, Phone: 515-295-9276
Specialties: Traditional and working straight knives of his design and in standard patterns. **Patterns:** Bowies, hunters, fillets and folders. **Technical:** Grinds 440C, D2 and 1095. Heat-treats. Uses natural handle

custom knifemakers

materials. **Prices:** $85 to $600; some to $1000. **Remarks:** Part-time maker; first knife sold in 1987. **Mark:** Last name-town and state.

WHEELER, GARY, 351 Old Hwy 48, Clarksville, TN 37040, Phone: 931-552-3092, ir22shtr@charter.net

> **Specialties:** Working to high end fixed blades. **Patterns:** Bowies, Hunters, combat knives, daggers and a few folders. **Technical:** Forges 5160, 1080, 52100 and his own Damascus, will use stainless steels on request. **Prices:** $125 to $2000. **Remarks:** Full-time maker since 2001, first knife sold in 1985 collaborates/works at B&W blade works. **Mark:** Stamped last name.

WHEELER, ROBERT, 289 S Jefferson, Bradley, IL 60915, Phone: 815-932-5854

WHETSELL, ALEX, 1600 Palmetto Tyrone Rd., Sharpsburg, GA 30277, Phone: 770-463-4881

> **Specialties:** Knifekits.com, a source for fold locking liner type and straight knife kits. Our kits are industry standard for folding knife kits. **Technical:** Many selections of colored G10 carbon fiber and wood handle material for our kits as well as bulk sizes for the custom knife maker, heat treated folding knife pivots, screws, bushings, etc.

WHIPPLE, WESLEY A., PO Box 3771, Kodiak, AK 99615, Phone: 907-486-6737

> **Specialties:** Working straight knives, some fancy. **Patterns:** Hunters, Bowies, camp knives, fighters. **Technical:** Forges high-carbon steels, Damascus, offers relief carving and silver wire inlay checkering. **Prices:** $200 to $1400; some higher. **Remarks:** Part-time maker; first knife sold in 1989. **Mark:** Last name/JS. **Other:** A.K.A. Wilderness Knife and Forge.

WHITE, BRYCE, 1415 W Col. Glenn Rd., Little Rock, AR 72210, Phone: 501-821-2956

> **Specialties:** Hunters, fighters, makes Damascus, file work, handmade only. **Technical:** L6, 1075, 1095, 01 steels used most. **Patterns:** Will do any pattern or use his own. **Prices:** $200 to $300. Sold first knife in 1995. **Mark:** White.

WHITE, DALE, 525 CR 212, Sweetwater, TX 79556, Phone: 325-798-4178, dalew@taylortel.net

> **Specialties:** Working and using knives. **Patterns:** Hunters, skinners, utilities and Bowies. **Technical:** Grinds 440C, offers file work, fancy pins and scrimshaw by Sherry Sellers. **Prices:** From $45 to $300. **Remarks:** Sold first knife in 1975. **Mark:** Full name, city and state.

WHITE, GENE E., 6620 Briarleigh Way, Alexandria, VA 22315, Phone: 703-924-1268

> **Specialties:** Small utility/gents knives. **Patterns:** Eight standard hunters; most other patterns on commission basis. Currently no swords, axes and fantasy knives. **Technical:** Stock removal 440C and D2; others on request. Mostly hollow grinds; some flat grinds. Prefers natural handle materials. Makes own sheaths. **Prices:** Start at $85. **Remarks:** Part-time maker; first knife sold in 1971. **Mark:** First and middle initials, last name.

WHITE, LOU, 7385 Red Bud Rd. NE, Ranger, GA 30734, Phone: 706-334-2273

WHITE, RICHARD T., 359 Carver St, Grosse Pointe Farms, MI 48236, Phone: 313-881-4690

WHITE, ROBERT J., RR 1, 641 Knox Rd. 900 N., Gilson, IL 61436, Phone: 309-289-4487

> **Specialties:** Working knives, some deluxe. **Patterns:** Bird and trout knives, hunters, survival knives and locking folders. **Technical:** Grinds A2, D2 and 440C; commercial Damascus. Heat-treats. **Prices:** $125 to $250; some to $600. **Remarks:** Full-time maker; first knife sold in 1976. **Mark:** Last name in script.

WHITE JR., ROBERT J. BUTCH, RR 1, Gilson, IL 61436, Phone: 309-289-4487

> **Specialties:** Folders of all sizes. **Patterns:** Hunters, fighters, boots and folders. **Technical:** Forges Damascus; grinds tool and stainless steels. **Prices:** $500 to $1800. **Remarks:** Spare-time maker; first knife sold in 1980. **Mark:** Last name in block letters.

WHITENECT, JODY, Elderbank, Halifax County, Nova Scotia, CANADA B0N 1K0, Phone: 902-384-2511

> **Specialties:** Fancy and embellished working/using straight knives of his design and to customer specs. **Patterns:** Bowies, fighters and hunters. **Technical:** Forges 1095 and O1; forges and grinds ATS-34. Various filework on blades and bolsters. **Prices:** $200 to $400; some to $800. **Remarks:** Part-time maker; first knife sold in 1996. **Mark:** Longhorn stamp or engraved.

WHITLEY, L. WAYNE, 1675 Carrow Rd., Chocowinity, NC 27817-9495, Phone: 252-946-5648

WHITLEY, WELDON G., 1308 N Robin Ave., Odessa, TX 79764, Phone 915-584-2274

> **Specialties:** Working knives of his design or to customer specs. **Patterns:** Hunters, folders and various double-edged knives. **Technical:** Grinds 440C, 154CM and ATS-34. **Prices:** $150 to $1250. **Mark:** Name, address, road-runner logo.

WHITMAN, JIM, 21044 Salem St., Chugiak, AK 99567, Phone: 907-688-4575, Fax: 907-688-4278, Web: www.whitmanknives.com

> **Specialties:** Working straight knives and folders; some art pieces. **Patterns:** Hunters, skinners, Bowies, camp knives, working fighters, swords and hatchets. **Technical:** Grinds AEB-L Swedish, 440C, 154CM, ATS-34, and Damascus in full convex. Prefers exotic hardwoods, natural and native handle materials—whale bone, antler, ivory and horn. **Prices:** Start at $150. **Remarks:** Full-time maker; first knife sold in 1983. **Mark:** Name, city, state.

WHITMIRE, EARL T., 725 Colonial Dr., Rock Hill, SC 29730, Phone: 803-324-8384

> **Specialties:** Working straight knives, some to customer specs; some fantasy pieces. **Patterns:** Hunters, fighters and fishing knives. **Technical:** Grinds D2, 440C and 154CM. **Prices:** $40 to $200; some to $250. **Remarks:** Full-time maker; first knife sold in 1967. **Mark:** Name, city, state in oval logo.

WHITTAKER, ROBERT E., PO Box 204, Mill Creek, PA 17060

> **Specialties:** Using straight knives. Has a line of knives for buckskinners. **Patterns:** Hunters, skinners and Bowies. **Technical:** Grinds O1, A2 and D2. Offers filework. **Prices:** $35 to $100. **Remarks:** Part-time maker; first knife sold in 1980. **Mark:** Last initial or full initials.

WHITTAKER, WAYNE, 2900 Woodland Ct., Metamore, MI 48455, Phone: 810-797-5315

> **Specialties:** Folders, hunters on request. **Patterns:** Bowies, daggers and hunters. **Technical:** ATS-34 S.S. and Damascus **Prices:** $300 to $500; some to $2000. **Remarks:** Full-time maker; first knife sold in 1985. **Mark:** Etched name on one side.

WHITWORTH, KEN J., 41667 Tetley Ave., Sterling Heights, MI 48078, Phone: 313-739-5720

> **Specialties:** Working straight knives and folders. **Patterns:** Locking folders, slip-joints and boot knives. **Technical:** Grinds 440C, 154CM and D2. **Prices:** $100 to $225; some $450. **Remarks:** Part-time maker; first knife sold in 1976. **Mark:** Last name.

WICKER, DONNIE R., 2544 E. 40th Ct., Panama City, FL 32405, Phone: 904-785-9158

> **Specialties:** Traditional working and using straight knives of his design or to customer specs. **Patterns:** Hunters, fighters and slip-joint folders. **Technical:** Grinds 440C, ATS-34, D2 and 154CM. Heat-treats and does hardness testing. **Prices:** $90 to $200; some to $400. **Remarks:** Part-time maker; first knife sold in 1975. **Mark:** First and middle initials, last name.

WIGGINS, HORACE, 203 Herndon, Box 152, Mansfield, LA 71502, Phone: 318-872-4471

> **Specialties:** Fancy working knives. **Patterns:** Straight and folding hunters. **Technical:** Grinds O1, D2 and 440C. **Prices:** $90 to $275. **Remarks:** Part-time maker; first knife sold in 1970. **Mark:** Name, city and state in diamond logo.

WILCHER, WENDELL L., RR 6 Box 6573, Palestine, TX 75801, Phone: 903-549-2530

> **Specialties:** Fantasy, miniatures and working/using straight knives and folders of his design and to customer specs. **Patterns:** Fighters, hunters, locking folders. **Technical:** Hand works (hand file and hand sand knives), not grind. **Prices:** $75 to $250; some to $600. **Remarks:** Part-time maker; first knife sold in 1987. **Mark:** Initials, year, serial number.

WILE, PETER, RR 3, Bridgewater, Nova Scotia, CANADA B4V 2W2, Phone: 902-543-1373, peterwile@ns.sympatico.ca

> **Specialties:** Collector-grade one-of-a-kind file-worked folders. **Patterns:** Folders or fixed blades of his design or to customers specs. **Technical:** Grinds ATS-34, carbon and stainless Damascus. Does intricate filework on blades, spines and liners. Carves. Prefers natural handle materials. Does own heat treating. **Prices:** $350 to $2000; some to $4000. **Remarks:** Part-time maker; sold first knife in 1985; doing business as Wile Knives. **Mark:** Wile.

WILKINS, MITCHELL, 15523 Rabon Chapel Rd., Montgomery, TX 77316, Phone: 936-588-2696, mwilkins@consolidated.net

WILLEY, W.G., 14210 Sugar Hill Rd, Greenwood, DE 19950, Phone: 302-349-4070, Web: www.willeyknives.com

> **Specialties:** Fancy working straight knives. **Patterns:** Small game knives, Bowies and throwing knives. **Technical:** Grinds 440C and 154CM. **Prices:** $350 to $600; some to $1500. **Remarks:** Part-time

maker; first knife sold in 1975. Owns retail store. **Mark:** Last name inside map logo.

WILLIAMS, JASON L., PO Box 67, Wyoming, RI 02898, Phone: 401-539-8353, Fax: 401-539-0252
Specialties: Fancy and high tech folders of his design, co-inventor of the Axis Lock. **Patterns:** Fighters, locking folders, automatics and fancy pocket knives. **Technical:** Forges Damascus and other steels by request. Uses exotic handle materials and precious metals. Offers inlaid spines and gemstone thumb knobs. **Prices:** $1000 and up. **Remarks:** Full-time maker; first knife sold in 1989. **Mark:** First and last initials on pivot.

WILLIAMS, MICHAEL L., Rt. 4, PO Box 64-1, Broken Bow, OK 74728, Phone: 405-494-6326, hforge@pine-net.com
Specialties: Plain to fancy working and dress knives. **Patterns:** Hunters, Bowies, camp knives and others. **Technical:** Forges 1084, L6, 52100 and pattern-welded steel. **Prices:** $295 and up. **Remarks:** Part-time maker; first knife sold in 1989. ABS Master Smith. **Mark:** Williams.

WILLIAMS JR., RICHARD, 1440 Nancy Circle, Morristown, TN 37814, Phone: 615-581-0059
Specialties: Working and using straight knives of his design or to customer specs. **Patterns:** Hunters, dirks and utility/camp knives. **Technical:** Forges 5160 and uses file steel. Hand-finish is standard; offers filework. **Prices:** $80 to $180; some to $250. **Remarks:** Spare-time maker; first knife sold in 1985. **Mark:** Last initial or full initials.

WILLIAMSON, TONY, Rt. 3, Box 503, Siler City, NC 27344, Phone: 919-663-3551
Specialties: Flint knapping—knives made of obsidian flakes and flint with wood, antler or bone for handles. **Patterns:** Skinners, daggers and flake knives. **Technical:** Blades have width/thickness ratio of at least 4 to 1. Hafts with methods available to prehistoric man. **Prices:** $58 to $160. **Remarks:** Student of Errett Callahan. **Mark:** Initials and number code to identify year and number of knives made.

WILSON (SEE SIMONELLA, GIANLUIGI)

WILLIS, BILL, RT 7 Box 7549, Ava, MO 65608, Phone: 417-683-4326
Specialties: Forged blades, Damascus and carbon steel. **Patterns:** Cable, random or ladder lamented. **Technical:** Professionally heat treated blades. **Prices:** $75 to $600. **Remarks:** Lifetime guarantee on all blades against breakage. **Mark:** WF. **Other:** All work done by myself; including leather work.

WILSON, JAMES G., PO Box 4024, Estes Park, CO 80517, Phone: 303-586-3944
Specialties: Bronze Age knives; Medieval and Scottish-styles; tomahawks. **Patterns:** Bronze knives, daggers, swords, spears and battle axes; 12-inch steel Misericorde daggers, sgian dubhs, "his and her" skinners, bird and fish knives, capers, boots and daggers. **Technical:** Casts bronze; grinds D2, 440C and ATS-34. **Prices:** $49 to $400; some to $1300. **Remarks:** Part-time maker; first knife sold in 1975. **Mark:** WilsonHawk.

WILSON, JON J., 1826 Ruby St., Johnstown, PA 15902, Phone: 814-266-6410
Specialties: Miniatures and full size. **Patterns:** Bowies, daggers and hunters. **Technical:** Grinds Damascus, 440C and O1. Scrimshaws and carves. **Prices:** $75 to $500; some higher. **Remarks:** Full-time maker; first knife sold in 1988. **Mark:** First and middle initials, last name.

WILSON, MIKE, 1416 McDonald Rd., Hayesville, NC 28904, Phone: 828-389-8145
Specialties: Fancy working and using straight knives of his design or to customer specs, folders. **Patterns:** Hunters, Bowies, utility knives, gut hooks, skinners, fighters and miniatures. **Technical:** Hollow-grinds 440C, L-6, 01 and D2. Mirror finishes are standard. Offers filework. **Prices:** $50 to $600. **Remarks:** Full-time maker; first knife sold in 1985. **Mark:** Last name.

WILSON, PHILIP C., SEAMOUNT KNIFEWORKS, PO Box 846, Mountain Ranch, CA 95246, Phone: 209-754-1990, SEAMOUNT@BIGPLANET.COM
Specialties: Working knives; emphasis on salt water fillet knives and utility hunters of his design. **Patterns:** Fishing knives, hunters, kitchen knives. **Technical:** Grinds CPM S-30V, CPM10V, S-90V and 154CM. Heat-treats and Rockwell tests all blades. **Prices:** Start at $280. **Remarks:** First knife sold in 1985. Doing business as Sea-Mount Knife Works. **Mark:** Signature.

WILSON, R.W., PO Box 2012, Weirton, WV 26062, Phone: 304-723-2771
Specialties: Working straight knives; period pieces. **Patterns:** Bowies, tomahawks and patch knives. **Technical:** Grinds 440C; scrimshaws. **Remarks:** Part-time maker; first knife sold in 1966. Knife maker supplier. Offers free knife-making lessons. **Mark:** Name in tomahawk.

WILSON, RON, 2639 Greenwood Ave., Morro Bay, CA 93442, Phone: 805-772-3381
Specialties: Classic and fantasy straight knives of his design. **Patterns:** Daggers, fighters, swords and axes-mostly all miniatures. **Technical:** Forges and grinds Damascus and various tool steels; grinds meteorite. Uses gold, precious stones and exotic wood. **Prices:** Vary. **Remarks:** Part-time maker; first knives sold in 1995. **Mark:** Stamped first and last initials.

WIMPFF, CHRISTIAN, PO Box 700526, 70574 Stuttgart 70, GERMANY, Phone: 711 7260 749, Fax: 711 7260 749
Specialties: High-tech folders of his design. **Patterns:** Boots, locking folders and liners locks. **Technical:** Offers meteorite, bolsters and blades. **Prices:** $1000 to $2800; some to $4000. **Remarks:** Full-time maker; first knife sold in 1984. **Mark:** First initial, last name.

WINBERG, DOUGLAS R., 19720 Hwy 78, Ramona, CA 92076, Phone: 760-788-8304

WINGO, GARY, 240 Ogeechee, Ramona, OK 74061, Phone: 918-536-1067, wingg_2000@yahoo.com Web: www.geocities.com/wings_2000/gary.html
Specialties: Folder specialist. Steel 44OC, D2, others on request. Handle bone-stag, others on request. **Patterns:** Trapper three-blade stockman, four-blade congress, single- and two-blade barlows. **Prices:** 150 to $400. **Mark:** First knife sold 1994. Steer head with Wingo Knives or Straight line Wingo Knives.

WINGO, PERRY, 22 55th St., Gulfport, MS 39507, Phone: 228-863-3193
Specialties: Traditional working straight knives. **Patterns:** Hunters, skinners, Bowies and fishing knives. **Technical:** Grinds 440C. **Prices:** $75 to $1000. **Remarks:** Full-time maker; first knife sold in 1988. **Mark:** Last name.

WINKLER, DANIEL, PO Box 2166, Blowing Rock, NC 28605, Phone: 828-295-9156, daniel@winklerknives.com Web: www.winklerknives.com
Specialties: Forged cutlery styled in the tradition of an era past. **Patterns:** Fixed blades, friction folders, axes/tomahawks and war clubs. **Technical:** Forges and grinds carbon steels and his own Damascus. **Prices:** $200 to $4000. **Remarks:** Full-time maker since 1988. Exclusively offers leatherwork by Karen Shook. **Mark:** Initials connected. **Other:** ABS Master Smith; Knifemakers Guild voting member.

WINN, TRAVIS A., 558 E. 3065 S., Salt Lake City, UT 84106, Phone: 801-467-5957
Specialties: Fancy working knives and knives to customer specs. **Patterns:** Hunters, fighters, boots, Bowies and fancy daggers, some miniatures, tantos and fantasy knives. **Technical:** Grinds D2 and 440C. Embellishes. **Prices:** $125 to $500; some higher. **Remarks:** Part-time maker; first knife sold in 1976. **Mark:** TRAV stylized.

WINSTON, DAVID, 1671 Red Holly St., Starkville, MS 39759, Phone: 601-323-1028
Specialties: Fancy and traditional knives of his design and to customer specs. **Patterns:** Bowies, daggers, hunters, boot knives and folders. **Technical:** Grinds 440C, ATS-34 and D2. Offers filework; heat-treats. **Prices:** $40 to $750; some higher. **Remarks:** Part-time maker; first knife sold in 1984. Offers lifetime sharpening for original owner. **Mark:** Last name.

WINTER, GEORGE, 5940 Martin Hwy., Union City, TN 38261

WIRTZ, ACHIM, Mittelstrasse 58, WUERSELEN, D -52146, GERMANY, Phone: 0049-2405-462-486, wootz@web.de Web: www.7knifedwarfs.com
Specialties: Period pieces, Scandinavian and middle east-style knives. **Technical:** Forged blades, makes Damascus, Mossic, Woots. Stainless Woots. Mokume. **Prices:** Start at $50. **Remarks:** Spare-time maker. First knife sold in 1997. **Mark:** Stylized initials.

WISE, DONALD, 304 Bexhill Rd., St. Leonardo-On-Sea, East Sussex, TN3 8AL, ENGLAND
Specialties: Fancy and embellished working straight knives to customer specs. **Patterns:** Hunters, Bowies and daggers. **Technical:** Grinds Sandvik 12C27, D2 D3 and O1. Scrimshaws. **Prices:** $110 to $300; some to $500. **Remarks:** Full-time maker; first knife sold in 1983. **Mark:** KNIFECRAFT.

WITSAMAN, EARL, 3957 Redwing Circle, Stow, OH 44224, Phone: 330-688-4208, eawits@aol.com Web: http: //hometown.aol.com//eawits/index.html
Specialties: Straight and fantasy miniatures. **Patterns:** Wide variety—Randalls to D-guard Bowies. **Technical:** Grinds O1, 440C and 300 stainless; buys Damascus; highly detailed work. **Prices:** $85 to $300. **Remarks:** Part-time maker; first knife sold in1974. **Mark:** Initials.

WOLF, BILL, 4618 N. 79th Ave., Phoenix, AZ 85033, Phone: 623-846-3585, Fax: 623-846-3585, bwolf@cox.net
Specialties: Investor-grade folders and straight knives. **Patterns:** Lockback, slip joint and side lock interframes. **Technical:** Grinds ATS-34 and

440C. **Prices:** $400 to $10,000. **Remarks:** Full-time maker; first knife sold in 1989. **Mark:** Name.

WOLF JR., WILLIAM LYNN, 4006 Frank Rd., Lagrange, TX 78945, Phone: 409-247-4626

WOOD, ALAN, Greenfield Villa, Greenhead, Brampton CA8 7HH, ENGLAND, Phone: 016977-47303, a.wood@kivesfreeserve.co.uk Web: www.alanwoodknives.co.uk
Specialties: High-tech working straight knives of his design. **Patterns:** Hunters, utility/camp and woodcraft knives. **Technical:** Grinds 12027, RWL-34, stainless Damascus and 01. Blades are cryogenic treated. **Prices:** $200 to $800; some to $750. **Remarks:** Full-time maker; first knife sold in 1979. Not currently taking orders **Mark:** Full name and state motif.

WOOD, LARRY B., 6945 Fishburg Rd., Huber Heights, OH 45424, Phone: 513-233-6751
Specialties: Fancy working knives of his design. **Patterns:** Hunters, buckskinners, Bowies, tomahawks, locking folders and Damascus miniatures. **Technical:** Forges 1095, file steel and his own Damascus. **Prices:** $125 to $500; some to $2000. **Remarks:** Full-time maker; first knife sold in 1974. Doing business as Wood's Metal Studios. **Mark:** Variations of last name, sometimes with blacksmith logo.

WOOD, OWEN DALE, 6492 Garrison St., Arvada, CO 80004-3157, Phone: 303-466-2748, ow2knives@cs.com
Specialties: Folding knives and daggers. **Patterns:** Own Damascus, specialties in 456 composite blades. **Technical:** Materials: Damascus stainless steel, exotic metals, gold, rare handle materials. **Prices:** $1000 to $9000. **Remarks:** Folding knives in art deco and art noveau themes. **Other:** Full-time maker from 1981. **Mark:** OWEN WOOD.

WOOD, WEBSTER, 22041 Shelton Trail, Atlanta, MI 49709, Phone: 989-785-2996, littlewolf@racc2000.com
Specialties: Work mainly in stainless; art knives, Bowies, hunters and folders. **Remarks:** Full-time maker; first knife sold in 1980. Guild member since 1984. All engraving done by maker. **Mark:** Initials inside shield and name.

WOOD, WILLIAM W., PO Box 606, Seymour, TX 76380, Phone: 817-888-5832
Specialties: Exotic working knives with Middle-East flavor. **Patterns:** Fighters, boots and some utility knives. **Technical:** Grinds D2 and 440C; buys Damascus. Prefers hand-rubbed satin finishes; uses only natural handle materials. **Prices:** $300 to $600; some to $2000. **Remarks:** Full-time maker; first knife sold in 1977. **Mark:** Name, city and state.

WOODARD, WILEY, 4527 Jim Mitchell W, Colleyville, TX 76034
Specialties: Straight knives, Damascus carbon and stainless, all natural material.

WOODIWISS, DORREN, PO Box 396, Thompson Falls, MT 59873-0396, Phone: 406-827-0079

WOODWARD, WILEY, 4517 Jim Mitchell W, Colleyville, TX 76034, Phone: 817-267-3277

WOOTTON, RANDY, 83 Lafayett 254, Stamps, AR 71860, Phone: 870-533-2472

WORTHEN, BILL, 200 E 3rd, Little Rock, AR 72201-1608, Phone: 501-324-9351

WRIGHT, KEVIN, 671 Leland Valley Rd. W, Quilcene, WA 98376-9517, Phone: 360-765-3589
Specialties: Fancy working or collector knives to customer specs. **Patterns:** Hunters, boots, buckskinners, miniatures. **Technical:** Forges and grinds L6, 1095, 440C and his own Damascus. **Prices:** $75 to $500; some to $2000. **Remarks:** Part-time maker; first knife sold in 1978. **Mark:** Last initial in anvil.

WRIGHT, L.T., 1523 Pershing Ave., Steubenville, OH 43952, Phone: 740-282-4947
Specialties: Filework, hunting knives. **Patterns:** Drop point hunters, straightback hunter, small game, bird & trout. **Technical:** Grinds 440C. **Prices:** $60 to $500. **Remarks:** Part-time maker. **Mark:** First, middle initials and last name w/house logo.

WRIGHT, RICHARD S., PO Box 201, 111 Hilltop Dr., Carolina, RI 02812, Phone: 401-364-3579, rswswitchblades@hotmail.com Web: www.richards.wright.com
Specialties: Bolster release switchblades. **Patterns:** Folding fighters, gents pocket knives, one-of-a-kind high-grade automatics. **Technical:** Reforges and grinds various makers Damascus. Uses a variety of tool steels. Uses natural handle material such as ivory and pearl, extensive file-work on most knives. **Prices:** $2000 and up. **Remarks:** Part-time knife maker with background as a gunsmith. Made first folder in 1991. **Mark:** RSW on blade, all folders are serial numbered.

WRIGHT, TIMOTHY, PO Box 3746, Sedona, AZ 86340, Phone: 928-282-4180
Specialties: High-tech folders and working knives. **Patterns:** Interframe locking folders, non-inlaid folders, straight hunters and kitchen knives. **Technical:** Grinds BG-42, AEB-L, K190 and Cowry X; works with new steels. All folders can disassemble and are furnished with tools. **Prices:** $150 to $1800; some to $3000. **Remarks:** Full-time maker; first knife sold in 1975. **Mark:** Last name and type of steel used.

WUERTZ, TRAVIS, 2487 E. Hwy. 287, Casa Grande, AZ 85222, Phone: 520-723-4432

WYATT, WILLIAM R., Box 237, Rainelle, WV 25962, Phone: 304-438-5494
Specialties: Classic and working knives of all designs. **Patterns:** Hunters and utility knives. **Technical:** Forges and grinds saw blades, files and rasps. Prefers stag handles. **Prices:** $45 to $95; some to $350. **Remarks:** Part-time maker; first knife sold in 1990. **Mark:** Last name in star with knife logo.

WYMAN, MARC L., 3325 Griffin Rd. Ste. 124, Ft. Lauderdale, FL 33312, Phone: 754-234-5111, Fax: 954-964-4418
Specialties: Custom pattern welded Damascus for stock removal. **Patterns:** Tactical fighters, combat and hunting knives. **Technical:** High-carbon steels. **Prices:** Upon request. **Remarks:** Part-time maker. **Mark:** MLW over skull and cross bones. **Other:** Florida fish and wildlife hunter safety education instructs.

Y

YASHINSKI, JOHN L., 207 N Platt, PO Box 1284, Red Lodge, MT 59068, Phone: 406-446-3916
Specialties: Native American Beaded sheathes. **Prices:** Vary.

YEATES, JOE A., 730 Saddlewood Circle, Spring, TX 77381, Phone: 281-367-2765, joeyeates291@cs.com Web: www.yeatesbowies.com
Specialties: Bowies and period pieces. **Patterns:** Bowies, toothpicks and combat knives. **Technical:** Grinds 440C, D2 and ATS-34. **Prices:** $600 to $2500. **Remarks:** Full-time maker; first knife sold in 1975. **Mark:** Last initial within outline of Texas; or last initial.

YESKOO, RICHARD C., 76 Beekman Rd., Summit, NJ 07901

YORK, DAVID C., PO Box 3166, Chino Valley, AZ 86323, Phone: 928-636-1709
Specialties: Working straight knives and folders. **Patterns:** Prefers small hunters and skinners; locking folders. **Technical:** Grinds D2 and 440C; buys Damascus. **Prices:** $75 to $300; some to $600. **Remarks:** Part-time maker; first knife sold in 1975. **Mark:** Last name.

YOSHIHARA, YOSHINDO, 8-17-11 TAKASAGO, KATSUSHI, Tokyo, JAPAN

YOSHIKAZU, KAMADA, , 540-3 Kaisaki Niuta-cho, Tokushima, JAPAN, Phone: 0886-44-2319

YOSHIO, MAEDA, , 3-12-11 Chuo-cho tamashima Kurashiki-city, Okayama, JAPAN, Phone: 086-525-2375

YOUNG, BUD, Box 336, Port Hardy, BC, CANADA V0N 2P0, Phone: 250-949-6478
Specialties: Fixed blade, working knives, some fancy. **Patterns:** Drop-points to skinners. **Technical:** Hollow or flat grind, 5160, 440-C, mostly ATS-34, satin finish. **Prices:** $150 to $500 CDN. **Remarks:** Spare-time maker; making knives since 1962; first knife sold in 1985. **Mark:** Name. **Other:** Not taking orders at this time, sell as produced.

YOUNG, CLIFF, Fuente De La Cibeles No. 5, Atascadero, San Miguel De Allende, GTO., MEXICO, Phone: 37700, Fax: 011-52-415-2-57-11
Specialties: Working knives. **Patterns:** Hunters, fighters and fishing knives. **Technical:** Grinds all; offers D2, 440C and 154CM. **Prices:** Start at $250. **Remarks:** Part-time maker; first knife sold in 1980. **Mark:** Name.

YOUNG, ERROL, 4826 Storey Land, Alton, IL 62002, Phone: 618-466-4707
Specialties: Traditional working straight knives and folders. **Patterns:** Wide range, including tantos, Bowies, miniatures and multi-blade folders. **Technical:** Grinds D2, 440C and ATS-34. **Prices:** $75 to $650; some to $800. **Remarks:** Part-time maker; first knife sold in 1987. **Mark:** Last name with arrow.

YOUNG, GEORGE, 713 Pinoak Dr., Kokomo, IN 46901, Phone: 765-457-8893
Specialties: Fancy/embellished and traditional straight knives and folders of his design and to customer specs. **Patterns:** Hunters, fillet/camp knives and locking folders. **Technical:** Grinds 440C, CPM440V, and Stellite 6K. Fancy ivory, black pearl and stag for handles. Filework—all Stellite construction (6K and 25 alloys). Offers engraving. **Prices:** $350

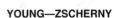
to $750; some $1500 to $3000. **Remarks:** Full-time maker; first knife sold in 1954. Doing business as Young's Knives. **Mark:** Last name integral inside Bowie.

YOUNG, PAUL A., 168 Elk Ridge Rd., Boone, NC 28607, Phone: 704-264-7048
    Specialties: Working straight knives and folders of his design or to customer specs; some art knives. **Patterns:** Small boot knives, skinners, 18th-century period pieces and folders. **Technical:** Forges O1 and file steels. Full-time embellisher—engraves and scrimshaws. Prefers floral designs; any design accepted. Does not engrave hardened metals. **Prices:** Determined by type and design. **Remarks:** Full-time maker; first knife sold in 1978. **Mark:** Initials in logo.

YOUNG, RAYMOND L., Cutler/Bladesmith, 2922 Hwy 188E, Mt. Ida, AR 71957, Phone: 870-867-3947
    Specialties: Cutler-Bladesmith, Sharpening service. **Patterns:** Hunter, skinners, fighters, no guard, no ricasso, chef tools. **Technical:** Edge tempered 1095, 516C, Mosiac handles, water buffalo and exotic woods. **Prices:** $100 and up. **Remarks:** Federal contractor since 1995. Surgical steel sharpening. **Mark:** R.

YURCO, MIKE, PO Box 712, Canfield, OH 44406, Phone: 330-533-4928, shorinki@aol.com
    Specialties: Working straight knives. **Patterns:** Hunters, utility knives, Bowies and fighters, push knives, claws and other hideouts. **Technical:** Grinds 440C, ATS-34 and 154CM; likes mirror and satin finishes. **Prices:** $20 to $500. **Remarks:** Part-time maker; first knife sold in 1983. **Mark:** Name, steel, serial number.

Z

ZACCAGNINO JR., DON, 2256 Bacom Point Rd., Pahokee, FL 33476-2622, Phone: 561-924-7032, zackknife@aol.com
    Specialties: Working knives and some period pieces of their designs. **Patterns:** Heavy-duty hunters, axes and Bowies; a line of light-weight hunters, fillets and personal knives. **Technical:** Grinds 440C and 17-4 PH—highly finished in complex handle and blade treatments. **Prices:** $165 to $500; some to $2500. **Remarks:** Part-time maker; first knife sold in 1969 by Don Zaccagnino Sr. **Mark:** ZACK, city and state inside oval.

ZAHM, KURT, 488 Rio Casa, Indialantic, FL 32903, Phone: 407-777-4860
    Specialties: Working straight knives of his design or to customer specs. **Patterns:** Daggers, fancy fighters, Bowies, hunters and utility knives. **Technical:** Grinds D2, 440C; likes filework. **Prices:** $75 to $1000. **Remarks:** Part-time maker; first knife sold in 1985. **Mark:** Last name.

ZAKABI, CARL S., PO Box 893161, Mililani Town, HI 96789-0161, Phone: 808-626-2181
    Specialties: Working and using straight knives of his design. **Patterns:** Fighters, hunters and utility/camp knives. **Technical:** Grinds 440C and ATS-34. **Prices:** $90 to $400. **Remarks:** Spare-time maker; first knife sold in 1988. Doing business as Zakabi's Knifeworks LLC. **Mark:** Last name and state inside a Hawaiian sharktooth dagger.

ZAKHAROV, GLADISTON, Bairro Rio Comprido, Rio Comprido Jacarei, Jacaret SP, BRAZIL 12302-070, Phone: 55 12 3958 4021, Fax: 55 12 3958 4103, arkhip@terra.com.br Web: www.arkhip.com.br
    Specialties: Using straight knives of his design. **Patterns:** Hunters, kitchen, utility/camp and barbecue knives. **Technical:** Grinds his own

"secret steel." **Prices:** $30 to $200. **Remarks:** Full-time maker. **Mark:** Arkhip Special Knives.

ZBORIL, TERRY, 5320 CR 130, Caldwell, TX 77836, Phone: 979-535-4157, terry.zboril@worldnet.att.net
    Specialties: ABS Journeyman Smith.

ZEMBKO III, JOHN, 140 Wilks Pond Rd., Berlin, CT 06037, Phone: 860-828-3503, zemknives@aol.com
    Specialties: Working knives of his design or to customer specs. **Patterns:** Likes to use stabilized high-figured woods. **Technical:** Grinds ATS-34, A-2, D-2; forges O-1, 1095; grinds Damasteel. **Prices:** $50 to $400; some higher. **Remarks:** First knife sold in 1987. **Mark:** Name.

ZEMITIS, JOE, 14 Currawong Rd., Cardiff Hts., 2285 Newcastle, AUSTRALIA, Phone: 0249549907
    Specialties: Traditional working straight knives. **Patterns:** Hunters, Bowies, tantos, fighters and camp knives. **Technical:** Grinds O1, D2, W2 and 440C; makes his own Damascus. Embellishes; offers engraving and scrimshaw. **Prices:** $150 to $3000. **Remarks:** Full-time maker; first knife sold in 1983. **Mark:** First initial, last name and country, or last name.

ZIMA, MICHAEL F., 732 State St., Ft. Morgan, CO 80701, Phone: 970-867-6078, Web: http: //www.zimaknives.com
    Specialties: Working straight knives and folders. **Patterns:** Hunters; utility, locking and slip-joint folders. **Technical:** Grinds D-2, 440C, ATS-34, and Specialty Damascus. **Prices:** $150 to $300; some higher. **Remarks:** Full-time maker; first knife sold in 1982. **Mark:** Last name.

ZINKER, BRAD, BZ KNIVES, 1591 NW 17 St., Homestead, FL 33030, Phone: 305-216-0404, bzknives@aol.com
    Specialties: Fillets, folders and hunters. **Technical:** Uses ATS-34 and stainless Damascus. **Prices:** $200 to $600. **Remarks:** Voting member of Knifemakers Guild and Florida Knifemakers Association. **Mark:** Offset connected initials BZ.

ZIRBES, RICHARD, Neustrasse 15, D-54526 Niederkail, GERMANY, Phone: 0049 6575 1371
    Specialties: Fancy embellished knives with engraving and self-made scrimshaw (scrimshaw made by maker). High-tech working knives and high-tech hunters, boots, fighters and folders. All knives made by hand. **Patterns:** Boots, fighters, folders, hunters. **Technical:** Uses only the best steels for blade material like CPM-T 440V, CPM-T 420V, ATS-34, D2, C440, stainless Damascus or steel according to customer's desire. **Prices:** Working knives and hunters: $200 to $600. Fancy embellished knives with engraving and/or scrimshaw: $800 to $3000. **Remarks:** Part-time maker; first knife sold in 1991. Member of the German Knife Maker Guild. **Mark:** Zirbes or R. Zirbes.

ZOWADA, TIM, 4509 E. Bear River Rd., Boyne Falls, MI 49713, Phone: 231-348-5446, knifeguy@nmo.net
    Specialties: Working knives, some fancy. **Patterns:** Hunters, camp knives, boots, swords, fighters, tantos and locking folders. **Technical:** Forges O2, L6, W2 and his own Damascus. **Prices:** $150 to $1000; some to $5000. **Remarks:** Full-time maker; first knife sold in 1980.

ZSCHERNY, MICHAEL, 1840 Rock Island Dr., Ely, IA 52227, Phone: 319-848-3629
    Specialties: Quality folding knives. **Patterns:** Liner-lock and lock-back folders in titanium, working straight knives. **Technical:** Grinds 440 and commercial Damascus, prefers natural materials such as pearls and ivory. **Prices:** Starting at $200. **Remarks:** Full-time maker, first knife sold in 1978. **Mark:** Last name, city and state; folders, last name with stars inside folding knife.

knifemakers state-by-state

AK

Barlow, Jana Poirier	Anchorage
Brennan, Judson	Delta Junction
Breuer, Lonnie	Wasilla
Broome, Thomas A.	Kenai
Cannon, Raymond W.	Homer
Cawthorne, Christopher A.	Wrangell
Chamberlin, John A.	Anchorage
Dempsey, Gordon S.	N. Kenai
Dufour, Arthur J.	Anchorage
England, Virgil	Anchorage
Flint, Robert	Anchorage
Gouker, Gary B.	Sitka
Grebe, Gordon S.	Anchor Point
Hibben, Westley G.	Anchorage
Kubaiko, Hank	Palmer
Lance, Bill	Eagle River
Little, Jimmy L.	Wasilla
Malaby, Raymond J.	Juneau
Mcfarlin, Eric E.	Kodiak
Mcintosh, David L.	Haines
Mirabile, David	Juneau
Moore, Marve	Willow
Parrish Iii, Gordon A.	North Pole
Shore, John I.	Kenai
Stegall, Keith	Wasilla
Trujillo, Adam	Anchorage
Trujillo, Miranda	Anchorage
Trujillo, Thomas A.	Anchorage
Van Cleve, Steve	Sutton
Whipple, Wesley A.	Kodiak
Whitman, Jim	Chugiak

AL

Andress, Ronnie	Satsuma
Batson, James	Madison
Baxter, Dale	Trinity
Bowles, Chris	Reform
Brend, Walter	Vinemont
Bullard, Bill	Andalusia
Coffman, Danny	Jacksonville
Conn Jr., C.T.	Attalla
Cutchin, Roy D.	Seale
Daniels, Alex	Town Creek
Dark, Robert	Oxford
Di Marzo, Richard	Birmingham
Durham, Kenneth	Cherokee
Elrod, Roger R.	Enterprise
Fikes, Jimmy L.	Jasper
Fogg, Don	Jasper
Fowler, Ricky And Susan	Robertsdale
Fronefield, Daniel	Hampton Cove
Gilbreath, Randall	Dora
Hammond, Jim	Arab
Howard, Durvyn M.	Hokes Bluff
Howell, Len	Opelika
Howell, Ted	Wetumpka
Huckabee, Dale	Maylene
Hulsey, Hoyt	Attalla
Madison Ii, Billy D.	Remlap
Mccullough, Jerry	Georgiana
Militano, Tom	Jacksonville
Monk, Nathan P.	Cullman
Morris, C.H.	Frisco City
Pardue, Melvin M.	Repton
Roe Jr., Fred D.	Huntsville
Russell, Tom	Jacksonville
Sandlin, Larry	Adamsville
Sinyard, Cleston S.	Elberta

Thomas, David E.	Lillian
Watson, Billy	Deatsville

AR

Anders, David	Center Ridge
Anders, Jerome	Center Ridge
Ardwin, Corey	North Little Rock
Barnes, Eric	Mountain View
Barnes Jr., Cecil C.	Center Ridge
Brown, Jim	Little Rock
Browning, Steven W.	Benton
Bullard, Tom	Flippin
Burnett, Max	Paris
Cabe, Jerry (Buddy)	Hattieville
Cook, James R.	Nashville
Copeland, Thom	Nashville
Crawford, Pat And Wes	West Memphis
Crowell, James L.	Mtn. View
Dozier, Bob	Springdale
Duvall, Fred	Benton
Echols, Roger	Nashville
Edge, Tommy	Cash
Ferguson, Lee	Hindsville
Ferguson, Linda	Hindsville
Fisk, Jerry	Nashville
Fitch, John S.	Clinton
Flournoy, Joe	El Dorado
Foster, Ronnie E.	Morrilton
Foster, Timothy L.	El Dorado
Frizzell, Ted	West Fork
Gadberry, Emmet	Hattieville
Greenaway, Don	Fayetteville
Herring, Morris	Dyer
Kelsey, Nate	Springdale
Lane, Ben	North Little Rock
Lawrence, Alton	De Queen
Livesay, Newt	Siloam Springs
Martin, Bruce E.	Prescott
Martin, Hal W.	Morrilton
Massey, Roger	Texarkana
Newton, Ron	London
O'Dell, Clyde	Camden
Olive, Michael E.	Leslie
Passmore, Jimmy D.	Hoxie
Perry, Jim	Hope
Perry, John	Mayflower
Peterson, Lloyd (Pete) C.	Clinton
Polk, Clifton	Van Buren
Polk, Rusty	Van Buren
Quattlebaum, Craig	Searcy
Red, Vernon	Conway
Rhea, Lin	Prattsville
Sisemore, Charles Russel	Mena
Smoker, Ray	Searcy
Solomon, Marvin	Paron
Stanley, John	Crossett
Stout, Charles	Gillham
Sweaza, Dennis	Austin
Townsend, Allen Mark	Texarkana
Tycer, Art	Paron
Walker, Jim	Morrilton
Ward, Chuck	Benton
Waters, Herman Harold	Magnolia
Waters, Lu	Magnolia
White, Bryce	Little Rock
Wootton, Randy	Stamps
Worthen, Bill	Little Rock
Young, Raymond L.	Mt Ida

AZ

Ammons, David C.	Tucson
Bennett, Glen C.	Tucson
Birdwell, Ira Lee	Bagdad
Boye, David	Dolan Springs
Bryan, Tom	Gilbert
Cheatham, Bill	Laveen
Choate, Milton	Somerton
Dawson, Lynn	Prescott Valley
Dodd, Robert F.	Camp Verde
Fuegen, Larry	Prescott
Goo, Tai	Tucson
Hancock, Tim	Scottsdale
Hankins, R.	Tempe
Hoel, Steve	Pine
Holder, D'Alton	Peoria
Hull, Michael J.	Cottonwood
Karp, Bob	Phoenix
Kelley, Thomas P.	Cave Creek
Kopp, Todd M.	Apache Jct
Lampson, Frank G.	Rimrock
Lee, Randy	St. Johns
Mcfall, Ken	Lakeside
Mcfarlin, J.W.	Lake Havasu City
Miller, Michael	Kingman
Mooney, Mike	Queen Creek
Murray, Bill	Green Valley
Newhall, Tom	Tucson
Norris, Don	Tucson
Purvis, Bob And Ellen	Tucson
Robbins, Bill	Globe
Rybar Jr., Raymond B.	Phoenix
Snare, Michael	Phoenix
Tamboli, Michael	Glendale
Tollefson, Barry A.	Tubac
Torgeson, Samuel L.	Sedona
Tyre, Michael A	Wickenburg
Weiler, Donald E.	Yuma
Weiss, Charles L.	Phoenix
Wolf, Bill	Phoenix
Wright, Timothy	Sedona
Wuertz, Travis	Casa Grande
York, David C.	Chino Valley

CA

Abegg, Arnie	Huntington Beach
Abernathy, Paul J.	Eureka
Adkins, Richard L.	Mission Viejo
Aldrete, Bob	Lomita
Athey, Steve	Riverside
Barnes, Gregory	Altadena
Barron, Brian	San Mateo
Benson, Don	Escalon
Berger, Max A.	Carmichael
Biggers, Gary	Ventura
Blum, Chuck	Brea
Bost, Roger E.	Palos Verdes
Boyd, Francis	Berkeley
Brack, Douglas D.	Camirillo
Breshears, Clint	Manhattan Beach
Brooks, Buzz	Los Angles
Browne, Rick	Upland
Brunetta, David	Laguna Beach
Butler, Bart	Ramona
Cabrera, Sergio B.	Wilmington
Cantrell, Kitty D.	Ramona
Caston, Darriel	Sacramento
Chelquist, Cliff	Arroyo Grande
Clark, R.W.	Corona

Coffey, Bill — Clovis
Cohen, Terry A. — Laytonville
Coleman, John A — Citrus Heightss
Comus, Steve — Anaheim
Connolly, James — Oroville
Davis, Charlie — Santee
De Maria Jr., Angelo — Carmel Valley
Dion, Greg — Oxnard
Dixon Jr., Ira E. — Ventura
Doolittle, Mike — Novato
Driscoll, Mark — La Mesa
Ellis, Dave/Abs Mastersmith — Vista
Ellis, William Dean — Fresno
Emerson, Ernest R. — Torrance
English, Jim — Jamul
Essegian, Richard — Fresno
Felix, Alexander — Torrance
Ferguson, Jim — Temecula
Fisher, Theo (Ted) — Montague
Forrest, Brian — Descanso
Fox, Jack L. — Citrus Heights
Fraley, D.B. — Dixon
Francis, Vance — Alpine
Fred, Reed Wyle — Sacramento
Freer, Ralph — Seal Beach
Fulton, Mickey — Willows
Girtner, Joe — Brea
Gofourth, Jim — Santa Paula
Green, Russ — Lakewood
Guarnera, Anthony R. — Quartzhill
Guidry, Bruce — Murrieta
Hall, Jeff — Los Alamitos
Hardy, Scott — Placerville
Harris, Jay — Redwood City
Harris, John — Riverside
Hartsfield, Phill — Newport Beach
Hayes, Dolores — Los Angeles
Helton, Roy — San Diego
Herndon, Wm. R. "Bill" — Acton
Hink Iii, Les — Stockton
Hockenbary, Warren E. — San Pedro
Hoy, Ken — North Fork
Humenick, Roy — Rescue
Iames, Gary — Tahoe
Jacks, Jim — Covina
Jackson, David — Lemoore
Jensen, John Lewis — Pasadena
Johnson, Randy — Turlock
Jones, Curtis J. — Palmdale
Kazsuk, David — Perris
Keyes, Dan — Chino
Koster, Steven C. — Huntington Beach
Laner, Dean — Susanville
Larson, Richard — Turlock
Leland, Steve — Fairfax
Likarich, Steve — Colfax
Lockett, Sterling — Burbank
Loveless, R.W. — Riverside
Luchini, Bob — Palo Alto
Mackie, John — Whittier
Mallett, John — Ontario
Martin, Jim — Oxnard
Massey, Ron — Joshua Tree
Mata, Leonard — San Diego
Maxwell, Don — Clovis
Mcabee, William — Colfax
Mcclure, Michael — Menlo Park
Mcgrath, Patrick T. — Westchester
Melin, Gordon C. — La Mirada
Meloy, Sean — Lemon Grove
Montano, Gus A. — San Diego
Morgan, Jeff — Santee
Moses, Steven — Santa Ana
Mountain Home Knives, — Jamul
Naten, Greg — Bakersfield

Orton, Rich — Riverside
Osborne, Donald H. — Clovis
Packard, Bob — Elverta
Padilla, Gary — Auburn
Pendleton, Lloyd — Volcano
Perry, Chris — Fresno
Pfanenstiel, Dan — Modesto
Phillips, Randy — Ontario
Pitt, David F. — Anderson
Posner, Barry E. — N. Hollywood
Richard, Ron — Fremont
Richards Jr., Alvin (Chuck) — Fortuna
Rinaldi, T.H. — Winchester
Rodebaugh, James L. — Oak Hills
Rozas, Clark D. — Wilmington
Schmitz, Raymond E. — Valley Center
Schneider, Herman — Apple Valley
Schroen, Karl — Sebastopol
Sibrian, Aaron — Ventura
Sjostrand, Kevin — Visalia
Slobodian, Scott — San Andreas
Sornberger, Jim — Volcano
St. Cyr, H. Red — Wilmington
Stapel, Chuck — Glendale
Steinberg, Al — Laguna Woods
Stimps, Jason M. — Orange
Stockwell, Walter — Redwood City
Stover, Howard — Pasadena
Strider, Mick — San Marcos
Terrill, Stephen — Lindsay
Tingle, Dennis P. — Jackson
Vagnino, Michael — Visalia
Van Riper, James N. — Citrus Heights
Ward, Ken — Weed
Warren, Al — Roseville
Watanabe, Wayne — Montebello
Weinstock, Robert — San Francisco
Wilson, Philip C. — Mountain Ranch
Wilson, Ron — Morro Bay

CO

Anderson, Mark Alan — Denver
Anderson, Mel — Hotchkiss
Barrett, Cecil Terry — Colorado Springs
Booco, Gordon — Hayden
Brandon, Matthew — Denver
Brock, Kenneth L. — Allenspark
Burrows, Chuck — Durango
Dannemann, Randy — Hotchkiss
Davis, Don — Loveland
Dawson, Barry — Durango
Delong, Dick — Aurora
Dennehy, Dan — Del Norte
Dennehy, John D — Wellington
Dill, Robert — Loveland
High, Tom — Alamosa
Hockensmith, Dan — Crook
Hughes, Ed — Grand Junction
Irie, Michael L. — Colorado Springs
Kitsmiller, Jerry — Montrose
Leck, Dal — Hayden
Magruder, Jason — Colorado Springs
Miller, Hanford J. — Cowdrey
Miller, M.A. — Northglenn
Olson, Wayne C. — Bailey
Ott, Fred — Durango
Owens, John — Nathrop
Roberts, Chuck — Golden
Rollert, Steve — Keenesburg
Ronzio, N. Jack — Fruita
Sanders, Bill — Mancos
Thompson, Lloyd — Pagosa Springs
Topliss, M.W. "Ike" — Montrose
Watson, Bert — Westminster

Wilson, James G. — Estes Park
Wood, Owen Dale — Arvada
Zima, Michael F. — Ft. Morgan

CT

Barnes, William — Wallingford
Buebendorf, Robert E. — Monroe
Chapo, William G. — Wilton
Framski, Walter P. — Prospect
Jean, Gerry — Manchester
Lepore, Michael J. — Bethany
Meyer, Christopher J. — Tolland
Padgett Jr., Edwin L. — New London
Pankiewicz, Philip R. — Lebanon
Plunkett, Richard — West Cornwall
Putnam, Donald S. — Wethersfield
Rainville, Richard — Salem
Turecek, Jim — Ansonia
Vitale, Mace — Guilford
Zembko Iii, John — Berlin

DE

Antonio Jr., William J. — Newark
Schneider, Karl A. — Newark
Willey, W.G. — Greenwood

FL

Adams, Les — Hialeah
Angell, Jon — Hawthorne
Atkinson, Dick — Wausau
Bacon, David R. — Bradenton
Barry Iii, James J. — West Palm Beach
Bartrug, Hugh E. — St. Petersburg
Beckett, Norman L. — Satsuma
Beers, Ray — Lake Wales
Benjamin Jr., George — Kissimmee
Birnbaum, Edwin — Miami
Blackton, Andrew E. — Bayonet Point
Blackwood, Neil — Lakeland
Bosworth, Dean — Key Largo
Bradley, John — Pomona Park
Bray Jr., W. Lowell — New Port Richey
Brown, Harold E. — Arcadia
Burris, Patrick R. — Jacksonville
Butler, John — Havana
Chase, Alex — DeLand
Cole, Dave — Satellite Beach
D'Andrea, John — Citrus Springs
Davenport, Jack — Dade City
Davis Jr., Jim — Zephyrhills
Dietzel, Bill — Middleburg
Doggett, Bob — Brandon
Dotson, Tracy — Baker
Ellerbe, W.B. — Geneva
Ellis, Willy B. — Palm Harbor
Enos Iii, Thomas M. — Orlando
Fagan, James A. — Lake Worth
Ferrara, Thomas — Naples
Ferris, Bill — Palm Beach Garden
Fowler, Charles R. — Ft McCoy
Gamble, Roger — St. Petersburg
Garner Jr., William O. — Pensacola
Gibson Sr., James Hoot — Bunnell
Goers, Bruce — Lakeland
Griffin Jr., Howard A. — Davie
Grospitch, Ernie — Orlando
Harris, Ralph Dewey — Brandon
Heaney, John D — Haines City
Heaney, John D — Haines City
Heitler, Henry — Tampa
Hodge Iii, John — Palatka
Holland, John H. — Titusville

Hartman, Arlan (Lanny) — N. Muskegon
Hughes, Daryle — Nunica
Krause, Roy W. — St. Clair Shores
Lankton, Scott — Ann Arbor
Leach, Mike J. — Swartz Creek
Lucie, James R. — Fruitport
Mankel, Kenneth — Cannonsburg
Mills, Louis G. — Ann Arbor
Nix, Robert T. — Wayne
Noren, Douglas E. — Springlake
Parker, Robert Nelson — Rapid City
Repke, Mike — Bay City
Sakmar, Mike — Rochester
Sandberg, Ronald B. — Browntown
Serven, Jim — Fostoria
Sigman, James P. — North Adams
Tally, Grant — Flat Rock
Van Eizenga, Jerry W. — Nunica
Vasquez, Johnny David — Wyandotte
Viste, James — Detroit
Webster, Bill — Three Rivers
Welling, Ronald L — Grand Haven
White, Richard T. — Grosse Pointe Farms
Whittaker, Wayne — Metamore
Whitworth, Ken J. — Sterling Heights
Wood, Webster — Atlanta
Zowada, Tim — Boyne Falls

MN

Davis, Joel — Albert Lea
Goltz, Warren L. — Ada
Griffin, Thomas J. — Windom
Hagen, Philip L. — Pelican Rapids
Hansen, Robert W. — Cambridge
Johnson, R.B. — Clearwater
Knipschield, Terry — Rochester
Maines, Jay — Wyoming
Mickley, Tracy — North Mankato
Rydbom, Jeff — Annandale
Shadley, Eugene W. — Bovey
Steffen, Chuck — St. Michael
Voorhies, Les — Faribault

MO

Bolton, Charles B. — Jonesburg
Buxton, Bill — Kaiser
Conner, Allen L. — Fulton
Cover, Raymond A. — Mineral Point
Cox, Colin J. — Raymore
Davis, W.C. — Raymore
Dippold, Al — Perryville
Driskill, Beryl — Braggadocio
Eaton, Frank L Jr — Farmington
Ehrenberger, Daniel Robert — Mexico
Engle, William — Boonville
Hanson Iii, Don L. — Success
Harris, Jeffery A. — St. Louis
Harrison, Jim (Seamus) — St. Louis
Jones, John A. — Holden
Kinnikin, Todd — House Springs
Knickmeyer, Hank — Cedar Hill
Knickmeyer, Kurt — Cedar Hill
Martin, Tony — Arcadia
Mason, Bill — Excelsior Springs
Mccrackin, Kevin — House Spings
Mccrackin And Son, V.J. — House Springs
Miller, Bob — Oakville
Mulkey, Gary — Branson
Muller, Jody — Pittsburg
Newcomb, Corbin — Moberly
Pryor, Stephen L. — Boss
Ramsey, Richard A. — Neosho
Rardon, A.D. — Polo

Rardon, Archie F. — Polo
Riepe, Richard A. — Harrisonville
Scroggs, James A. — Warrensburg
Sonntag, Douglas W. — Nixa
Steketee, Craig A. — Billings
Stewart, Edward L. — Mexico
Stormer, Bob — St. Peters
Warden, Roy A. — Union
Weddle Jr., Del — St. Joseph
Willis, Bill — Ava

MS

Black, Scott — Picayune
Boleware, David — Carson
Davis, Jesse W. — Sarah
Dickerson, Gordon S. — New Augusta
Evans, Bruce A. — Booneville
Lamey, Robert M. — Biloxi
Lebatard, Paul M. — Vancleave
Pickett, Terrell — Lumberton
Roberts, Michael — Clinton
Roberts, Mike — Clinton
Robinson, Chuck — Picayune
Shiffer, Steve — Leakesville
Skow, H. A. "Tex" — Senatobia
Taylor, Billy — Petal
Vandeventer, Terry L. — Terry
Vardaman, Robert — Hattiesburg
Wehner, Rudy — Collins
Wingo, Perry — Gulfport
Winston, David — Starkville

MT

Barnes, Jack — Whitefish
Barnes, Wendell — Clinton
Barth, J.D. — Alberton
Beam, John R. — Kalispell
Beaty, Robert B. — Missoula
Bell, Don — Lincoln
Bizzell, Robert — Butte
Boxer, Bo — Whitefish
Brooks, Steve R. — Walkerville
Caffrey, Edward J. — Great Falls
Carlisle, Jeff — Simms
Christensen, Jon P. — Shepherd
Colter, Wade — Colstrip
Conklin, George L. — Ft. Benton
Crowder, Robert — Thompson Falls
Dunkerley, Rick — Seeley Lake
Eaton, Rick — Shepherd
Ellefson, Joel — Manhattan
Fassio, Melvin G. — Lolo
Forthofer, Pete — Whitefish
Gallagher, Barry — Lewistown
Harkins, J.A. — Conner
Hill, Howard E. — Polson
Hintz, Gerald M. — Helena
Hulett, Steve — West Yellowstone
Kajin, Al — Forsyth
Kauffman, Dave — Montana City
Luman, James R. — Anaconda
Mcguane Iv, Thomas F. — Bozeman
Mortenson, Ed — Darby
Moyer, Russ — Havre
Munroe, Deryk C. — Bozeman
Nedved, Dan — Kalispell
Patrick, Willard C. — Helena,
Peele, Bryan — Thompson Falls
Peterson, Eldon G. — Whitefish
Piorek, James S. — Rexford
Pursley, Aaron — Big Sandy
Robinson, Robert W. — Polson
Rodewald, Gary — Hamilton

Ruana Knife Works, — Bonner
Smallwood, Wayne — Kalispell
Smith, Josh — Frenchtown
Sweeney, Coltin D. — Missoula
Taylor, Shane — Miles City
Thill, Jim — Missoula
Weinand, Gerome M. — Missoula
Woodiwiss, Dorren — Thompson Falls
Yashinski, John L. — Red Lodge

NC

Baker, Herb — Eden
Bauchop, Peter — Cary
Britton, Tim — Winston-Salem
Busfield, John — Roanoke Rapids
Chastain, Wade — Horse Shoe
Coltrain, Larry D. — Buxton
Daniel, Travis E. — Chocowinity
Drew, Gerald — Asheville
Edwards, Fain E. — Topton
Fox, Paul — Claremont
Gaddy, Gary Lee — Washington
Goguen, Scott — Newport
Goode, Brian — Shelby
Greene, Chris — Shelby
Gross, W.W. — Archdale
Gurganus, Carol — Colerain
Gurganus, Melvin H. — Colerain
Guthrie, George B. — Bassemer City
Hazen, Mark — Charlotte
Kommer, Russ — Fargo
Livingston, Robert C. — Murphy
Maynard, William N. — Fayetteville
Mcdonald, Robin J. — Fayetteville
Mclurkin, Andrew — Raleigh
Mcnabb, Tommy — Winston-Salem
Mcrae, J. Michael — Mint Hill
Parrish, Robert — Weaverville
Patrick, Chuck — Brasstown
Patrick, Peggy — Brasstown
Scholl, Tim — Angier
Simmons, H.R. — Aurora
Sprouse, Terry — Asheville
Sterling, Murray — Mount Airy
Summers, Arthur L. — Concord
Sutton, S. Russell — New Bern
Vail, Dave — Hampstead
Wagaman, John K. — Selma
Walker, Don — Burnsville
Warren, Daniel — Canton
Whitley, L. Wayne — Chocowinity
Williamson, Tony — Siler City
Wilson, Mike — Hayesville
Winkler, Daniel — Blowing Rock
Young, Paul A. — Boone

ND

Pitman, David — Williston

NE

Jokerst, Charles — Omaha
Marlowe, Charles — Omaha
Moore, Jon P — Aurora
Mosier, Joshua J. — Deshler
Robbins, Howard P. — Elkhorn
Schepers, George B. — Shelton
Suedmeier, Harlan — Nebraska City
Syslo, Chuck — Omaha
Tiensvold, Alan L. — Rushville
Tiensvold, Jason — Rushville
Till, Calvin E. And Ruth — Chadron

NH

Carlson, Kelly	Antrim
Gunn, Nelson L.	Epping
Hill, Steve E.	Goshen
Hitchmough, Howard	Peterborough
Macdonald, John	Raymond
Philippe, D. A.	Cornish
Saindon, R. Bill	Goshen

NJ

Eden, Thomas	Cranbury
Grussenmeyer, Paul G.	Cherry Hill
Kearney, Jarod	Bordentown
Licata, Steven	Noonton
Little, Guy A.	Oakhurst
Mccallen Jr., Howard H.	So Seaside Park
Nelson, Bob	Sparta
Phillips, Jim	Williamstown
Polkowski, Al	Chester
Pressburger, Ramon	Howell
Schilling, Ellen	Hamilton Square
Sheets, Steven William	Mendham
Slee, Fred	Morganville
Viele, H.J.	Westwood
Yeskoo, Richard C.	Summit

NM

Black, Tom	Albuquerque
Cherry, Frank J.	Albuquerque
Coleman, Keith E.	Albuquerque
Cordova, Joseph G.	Peralta
Cumming, Bob	Cedar Crest
Digangi, Joseph M.	Santa Cruz
Duran, Jerry T.	Albuquerque
Dyess, Eddie	Roswell
Fisher, Jay	Clovis
Goode, Bear	Navajo Dam
Gunter, Brad	Tijeras
Hethcoat, Don	Clovis
Hume, Don	Albuquerque
Jones, Bob	Albuquerque
Kimberley, Richard L.	Santa Fe
Lewis, Tom R.	Carlsbad
Macdonald, David	Los Lunas
Meshejian, Mardi	Santa Fe
Rogers, Richard	Magdalena
Schaller, Anthony Brett	Albuquerque
Stalcup, Eddie	Gallup
Terzuola, Robert	Santa Fe
Trujillo, Albert M.B.	Bosque Farms
Walker, Michael L.	Pueblo Sur Taos
Ware, Tommy	Datil
Wescott, Cody	Las Cruces

NV

Barnett, Van	Reno
Beasley, Geneo	Wadsworth
Cameron, Ron G.	Logandale
Defeo, Robert A.	Henderson
Dellana,	Reno
Duff, Bill	Reno
George, Tom	Henderson
Hrisoulas, Jim	Henderson
Kreibich, Donald L.	Reno
Mount, Don	Las Vegas
Nishiuchi, Melvin S.	Las Vegas
Thomas, Devin	Panaca
Tracy, Bud	Reno
Washburn, Arthur D.	Pioche

NY

Baker, Wild Bill	Boiceville
Cute, Thomas	Cortland
Davis, Barry L.	Castleton
Farr, Dan	Rochester
Faust, Dick	Rochester
Hobart, Gene	Windsor
Isgro, Jeffery	West Babylon
Johnson, Mike	Orient
Johnston, Dr. Robt.	Rochester
Levin, Jack	Brooklyn
Loos, Henry C.	New Hyde Park
Ludwig, Richard O.	Maspeth
Lupole, Jamie G.	Kirkwood
Maragni, Dan	Georgetown
Mccornock, Craig	Willow
Meerdink, Kurt	Barryville
Page, Reginald	Groveland
Pattay, Rudy	Long Beach
Peterson, Karen	Brooklyn
Phillips, Scott C.	Gouverneur
Rachlin, Leslie S.	Elmira
Rappazzo, Richard	Cohoes
Rotella, Richard A.	Niagara Falls
Scheid, Maggie	Rochester
Schippnick, Jim	Sanborn
Schlueter, David	Syracuse
Serafen, Steven E.	New Berlin
Skiff, Steven	Broadalbin
Smith, Lenard C.	Valley Cottage
Smith, Raymond L.	Erin
Summers, Dan	Whitney Pt.
Szilaski, Joseph	Wappingers Falls
Turner, Kevin	Montrose

OH

Babcock, Raymond G.	Vincent
Bailey, Ryan	Galena
Bendik, John	Olmsted Falls
Busse, Jerry	Wauseon
Collins, Lynn M.	Elyria
Coppins, Daniel	Cambridge
Cottrill, James I.	Columbus
Downing, Tom	Cuyahoga Falls
Downs, James F.	Londonderry
Etzler, John	Grafton
Foster, R.L. (Bob)	Mansfield
Francis, John D.	Ft. Loramie
Franklin, Mike	Aberdeen
Geisler, Gary R.	Clarksville
Gittinger, Raymond	Tiffin
Glover, Ron	Mason
Greiner, Richard	Green Springs
Guess, Raymond L.	Mechanicstown
Hinderer, Rick	Wooster
Hudson, Anthony B.	Amanda
Imboden Ii, Howard L.	Dayton
Jones, Roger Mudbone	Waverly
Kiefer, Tony	Pataskala
Longworth, Dave	Hamersville
Loro, Gene	Crooksville
Maienknecht, Stanley	Sardis
Mcdonald, Rich	Columbiana
Mcgroder, Patrick J.	Madison
Mercer, Mike	Lebanon
Messer, David T.	Dayton
Morgan, Tom	Beloit
Panak, Paul S.	Kinsman
Potter, Billy	Nashport
Ralph, Darrel	Galena
Rose, Derek W.	Gallipolis
Rowe, Fred	Amesville
Salley, John D.	Tipp City

Schuchmann, Rick	Cincinnati
Shinosky, Andy	Canfield
Shoemaker, Carroll	Northup
Shoemaker, Scott	Miamisburg
Spinale, Richard	Lorain
Stoddart, W.B. Bill	Fairfield
Strong, Scott	Beavercreek
Summers, Dennis K.	Springfield
Thomas, Kim	Seville
Thourot, Michael W.	Napoleon
Tindera, George	Brunswick
Votaw, David P.	Pioneer
Ward, J.J.	Waverly
Ward, Ron	Loveland
Warther, Dale	Dover
Witsaman, Earl	Stow
Wood, Larry B.	Huber Heights
Wright, L.T.	Steubenville
Yurco, Mike	Canfield

OK

Baker, Ray	Sapulpa
Burke, Dan	Edmond
Carillo, Dwaine	Moore
Crenshaw, Al	Eufaula
Darby, David T.	Cookson
Dill, Dave	Bethany
Englebretson, George	Oklahoma City
Gepner, Don	Norman
Johns, Rob	Enid
Kennedy Jr., Bill	Yukon
Kirk, Ray	Tahlequah
Lairson Sr., Jerry	Ringold
Martin, John Alexander	Okmulgee
Menefee, Ricky Bob	Blawchard
Miller, Michael E.	El Reno
Sanders, A.A.	Norman
Spivey, Jefferson	Yukon
Tomberlin, Brion R.	Norman
Wingo, Gary	Ramona

OR

Bell, Michael	Coquille
Bochman, Bruce	Grants Pass
Brandt, Martin W.	Springfield
Buchanan, Thad	Prineville
Buchman, Bill	Bend
Buchner, Bill	Idleyld Park
Busch, Steve	Oakland
Cameron House,	Salem
Carter, Murray M.	Vernonia
Clark, Nate	Yoncalla
Coon, Raymond C.	Gresham
Davis, Terry	Sumpter
Dowell, T.M.	Bend
Ferdinand, Don	Shady Cove
Gamble, Frank	Salem
Goddard, Wayne	Eugene
Harsey, William H.	Creswell
Hilker, Thomas N.	Williams
Horn, Jess	Eugene
Kelley, Gary	Aloha
Lake, Ron	Eugene
Little, Gary M.	Broadbent
Lockett, Lowell C.	North Bend
Lum, Robert W.	Eugene
Martin, Gene	Williams
Martin, Walter E.	Williams
Miller, Michael K.	Sweet Home
Olson, Darrold E.	Springfield
Rider, David M.	Eugene
Scarrow, Wil	Gold Hill
Schoeningh, Mike	North Powder

Hartman, Arlan (Lanny)	N. Muskegon
Hughes, Daryle	Nunica
Krause, Roy W.	St. Clair Shores
Lankton, Scott	Ann Arbor
Leach, Mike J.	Swartz Creek
Lucie, James R.	Fruitport
Mankel, Kenneth	Cannonsburg
Mills, Louis G.	Ann Arbor
Nix, Robert T.	Wayne
Noren, Douglas E.	Springlake
Parker, Robert Nelson	Rapid City
Repke, Mike	Bay City
Sakmar, Mike	Rochester
Sandberg, Ronald B.	Browntown
Serven, Jim	Fostoria
Sigman, James P.	North Adams
Tally, Grant	Flat Rock
Van Eizenga, Jerry W.	Nunica
Vasquez, Johnny David	Wyandotte
Viste, James	Detroit
Webster, Bill	Three Rivers
Welling, Ronald L	Grand Haven
White, Richard T.	Grosse Pointe Farms
Whittaker, Wayne	Metamore
Whitworth, Ken J.	Sterling Heights
Wood, Webster	Atlanta
Zowada, Tim	Boyne Falls

MN

Davis, Joel	Albert Lea
Goltz, Warren L.	Ada
Griffin, Thomas J.	Windom
Hagen, Philip L.	Pelican Rapids
Hansen, Robert W.	Cambridge
Johnson, R.B.	Clearwater
Knipschield, Terry	Rochester
Maines, Jay	Wyoming
Mickley, Tracy	North Mankato
Rydbom, Jeff	Annandale
Shadley, Eugene W.	Bovey
Steffen, Chuck	St. Michael
Voorhies, Les	Faribault

MO

Bolton, Charles B.	Jonesburg
Buxton, Bill	Kaiser
Conner, Allen L.	Fulton
Cover, Raymond A.	Mineral Point
Cox, Colin J.	Raymore
Davis, W.C.	Raymore
Dippold, Al	Perryville
Driskill, Beryl	Braggadocio
Eaton, Frank L Jr	Farmington
Ehrenberger, Daniel Robert	Mexico
Engle, William	Boonville
Hanson Iii, Don L.	Success
Harris, Jeffery A.	St. Louis
Harrison, Jim (Seamus)	St. Louis
Jones, John A.	Holden
Kinnikin, Todd	House Springs
Knickmeyer, Hank	Cedar Hill
Knickmeyer, Kurt	Cedar Hill
Martin, Tony	Arcadia
Mason, Bill	Excelsior Springs
Mccrackin, Kevin	House Spings
Mccrackin And Son, V.J.	House Spings
Miller, Bob	Oakville
Mulkey, Gary	Branson
Muller, Jody	Pittsburg
Newcomb, Corbin	Moberly
Pryor, Stephen L.	Boss
Ramsey, Richard A.	Neosho
Rardon, A.D.	Polo

Rardon, Archie F.	Polo
Riepe, Richard A.	Harrisonville
Scroggs, James A.	Warrensburg
Sonntag, Douglas W.	Nixa
Steketee, Craig A.	Billings
Stewart, Edward L.	Mexico
Stormer, Bob	St. Peters
Warden, Roy A.	Union
Weddle Jr., Del	St. Joseph
Willis, Bill	Ava

MS

Black, Scott	Picayune
Boleware, David	Carson
Davis, Jesse W.	Sarah
Dickerson, Gordon S.	New Augusta
Evans, Bruce A.	Booneville
Lamey, Robert M.	Biloxi
Lebatard, Paul M.	Vancleave
Pickett, Terrell	Lumberton
Roberts, Michael	Clinton
Roberts, Mike	Clinton
Robinson, Chuck	Picayune
Shiffer, Steve	Leakesville
Skow, H. A. "Tex"	Senatobia
Taylor, Billy	Petal
Vandeventer, Terry L.	Terry
Vardaman, Robert	Hattiesburg
Wehner, Rudy	Collins
Wingo, Perry	Gulfport
Winston, David	Starkville

MT

Barnes, Jack	Whitefish
Barnes, Wendell	Clinton
Barth, J.D.	Alberton
Beam, John R.	Kalispell
Beaty, Robert B.	Missoula
Bell, Don	Lincoln
Bizzell, Robert	Butte
Boxer, Bo	Whitefish
Brooks, Steve R.	Walkerville
Caffrey, Edward J.	Great Falls
Carlisle, Jeff	Simms
Christensen, Jon P.	Shepherd
Colter, Wade	Colstrip
Conklin, George L.	Ft. Benton
Crowder, Robert	Thompson Falls
Dunkerley, Rick	Seeley Lake
Eaton, Rick	Shepherd
Ellefson, Joel	Manhattan
Fassio, Melvin G.	Lolo
Forthofer, Pete	Whitefish
Gallagher, Barry	Lewistown
Harkins, J.A.	Conner
Hill, Howard E.	Polson
Hintz, Gerald M.	Helena
Hulett, Steve	West Yellowstone
Kajin, Al	Forsyth
Kauffman, Dave	Montana City
Luman, James R.	Anaconda
Mcguane Iv, Thomas F.	Bozeman
Mortenson, Ed	Darby
Moyer, Russ	Havre
Munroe, Deryk C.	Bozeman
Nedved, Dan	Kalispell
Patrick, Willard C.	Helena,
Peele, Bryan	Thompson Falls
Peterson, Eldon G.	Whitefish
Piorek, James S.	Rexford
Pursley, Aaron	Big Sandy
Robinson, Robert W.	Polson
Rodewald, Gary	Hamilton

Ruana Knife Works,	Bonne
Smallwood, Wayne	Kalispe
Smith, Josh	Frenchtow
Sweeney, Coltin D.	Missoul
Taylor, Shane	Miles Cit
Thill, Jim	Missoul
Weinand, Gerome M.	Missoul
Woodiwiss, Dorren	Thompson Fall
Yashinski, John L.	Red Lodg

NC

Baker, Herb	Ede
Bauchop, Peter	Car
Britton, Tim	Winston-Saler
Busfield, John	Roanoke Rapid
Chastain, Wade	Horse Sho
Coltrain, Larry D.	Buxto
Daniel, Travis E.	Chocowinit
Drew, Gerald	Asheville
Edwards, Fain E.	Topto
Fox, Paul	Claremor
Gaddy, Gary Lee	Washingto
Goguen, Scott	Newpo
Goode, Brian	Shelb
Greene, Chris	Shelb
Gross, W.W.	Archdal
Gurganus, Carol	Colerai
Gurganus, Melvin H.	Colerai
Guthrie, George B.	Bassemer Cit
Hazen, Mark	Charlott
Kommer, Russ	Farg
Livingston, Robert C.	Murph
Maynard, William N.	Fayetteville
Mcdonald, Robin J.	Fayetteville
Mclurkin, Andrew	Raleigl
Mcnabb, Tommy	Winston-Saler
Mcrae, J. Michael	Mint Hi
Parrish, Robert	Weaverville
Patrick, Chuck	Brasstow
Patrick, Peggy	Brasstow
Scholl, Tim	Angie
Simmons, H.R.	Auror
Sprouse, Terry	Asheville
Sterling, Murray	Mount Air
Summers, Arthur L.	Concor
Sutton, S. Russell	New Ber
Vail, Dave	Hampstead
Wagaman, John K.	Selm
Walker, Don	Burnsville
Warren, Daniel	Cantor
Whitley, L. Wayne	Chocowinit
Williamson, Tony	Siler City
Wilson, Mike	Hayesville
Winkler, Daniel	Blowing Roc
Young, Paul A.	Boon

ND

Pitman, David	Willistor

NE

Jokerst, Charles	Omah
Marlowe, Charles	Omah
Moore, Jon P	Auror
Mosier, Joshua J.	Deshle
Robbins, Howard P.	Elkhorr
Schepers, George B.	Sheltor
Suedmeier, Harlan	Nebraska City
Syslo, Chuck	Omah
Tiensvold, Alan L.	Rushville
Tiensvold, Jason	Rushville
Till, Calvin E. And Ruth	Chadror

NH

Carlson, Kelly	Antrim
Gunn, Nelson L.	Epping
Hill, Steve E.	Goshen
Hitchmough, Howard	Peterborough
Macdonald, John	Raymond
Philippe, D. A.	Cornish
Saindon, R. Bill	Goshen

NJ

Eden, Thomas	Cranbury
Grussenmeyer, Paul G.	Cherry Hill
Kearney, Jarod	Bordentown
Licata, Steven	Noonton
Little, Guy A.	Oakhurst
Mccallen Jr., Howard H.	So Seaside Park
Nelson, Bob	Sparta
Phillips, Jim	Williamstown
Polkowski, Al	Chester
Pressburger, Ramon	Howell
Schilling, Ellen	Hamilton Square
Sheets, Steven William	Mendham
Slee, Fred	Morganville
Viele, H.J.	Westwood
Yeskoo, Richard C.	Summit

NM

Black, Tom	Albuquerque
Cherry, Frank J.	Albuquerque
Coleman, Keith E.	Albuquerque
Cordova, Joseph G.	Peralta
Cumming, Bob	Cedar Crest
Digangi, Joseph M.	Santa Cruz
Duran, Jerry T.	Albuquerque
Dyess, Eddie	Roswell
Fisher, Jay	Clovis
Goode, Bear	Navajo Dam
Gunter, Brad	Tijeras
Hethcoat, Don	Clovis
Hume, Don	Albuquerque
Jones, Bob	Albuquerque
Kimberley, Richard L.	Santa Fe
Lewis, Tom R.	Carlsbad
Macdonald, David	Los Lunas
Meshejian, Mardi	Santa Fe
Rogers, Richard	Magdalena
Schaller, Anthony Brett	Albuquerque
Stalcup, Eddie	Gallup
Terzuola, Robert	Santa Fe
Trujillo, Albert M.B.	Bosque Farms
Walker, Michael L.	Pueblo Sur Taos
Ware, Tommy	Datil
Wescott, Cody	Las Cruces

NV

Barnett, Van	Reno
Beasley, Geneo	Wadsworth
Cameron, Ron G.	Logandale
Defeo, Robert A.	Henderson
Dellana,	Reno
Duff, Bill	Reno
George, Tom	Henderson
Hrisoulas, Jim	Henderson
Kreibich, Donald L.	Reno
Mount, Don	Las Vegas
Nishiuchi, Melvin S.	Las Vegas
Thomas, Devin	Panaca
Tracy, Bud	Reno
Washburn, Arthur D.	Pioche

NY

Baker, Wild Bill	Boiceville
Cute, Thomas	Cortland
Davis, Barry L.	Castleton
Farr, Dan	Rochester
Faust, Dick	Rochester
Hobart, Gene	Windsor
Isgro, Jeffery	West Babylon
Johnson, Mike	Orient
Johnston, Dr. Robt.	Rochester
Levin, Jack	Brooklyn
Loos, Henry C.	New Hyde Park
Ludwig, Richard O.	Maspeth
Lupole, Jamie G.	Kirkwood
Maragni, Dan	Georgetown
Mccornock, Craig	Willow
Meerdink, Kurt	Barryville
Page, Reginald	Groveland
Pattay, Rudy	Long Beach
Peterson, Karen	Brooklyn
Phillips, Scott C.	Gouverneur
Rachlin, Leslie S.	Elmira
Rappazzo, Richard	Cohoes
Rotella, Richard A.	Niagara Falls
Scheid, Maggie	Rochester
Schippnick, Jim	Sanborn
Schlueter, David	Syracuse
Serafen, Steven E.	New Berlin
Skiff, Steven	Broadalbin
Smith, Lenard C.	Valley Cottage
Smith, Raymond L.	Erin
Summers, Dan	Whitney Pt.
Szilaski, Joseph	Wappingers Falls
Turner, Kevin	Montrose

OH

Babcock, Raymond G.	Vincent
Bailey, Ryan	Galena
Bendik, John	Olmsted Falls
Busse, Jerry	Wauseon
Collins, Lynn M.	Elyria
Coppins, Daniel	Cambridge
Cottrill, James I.	Columbus
Downing, Tom	Cuyahoga Falls
Downs, James F.	Londonderry
Etzler, John	Grafton
Foster, R.L. (Bob)	Mansfield
Francis, John D.	Ft. Loramie
Franklin, Mike	Aberdeen
Geisler, Gary R.	Clarksville
Gittinger, Raymond	Tiffin
Glover, Ron	Mason
Greiner, Richard	Green Springs
Guess, Raymond L.	Mechanicstown
Hinderer, Rick	Wooster
Hudson, Anthony B.	Amanda
Imboden Ii, Howard L.	Dayton
Jones, Roger Mudbone	Waverly
Kiefer, Tony	Pataskala
Longworth, Dave	Hamersville
Loro, Gene	Crooksville
Maienknecht, Stanley	Sardis
Mcdonald, Rich	Columbiana
Mcgroder, Patrick J.	Madison
Mercer, Mike	Lebanon
Messer, David T.	Dayton
Morgan, Tom	Beloit
Panak, Paul S.	Kinsman
Potter, Billy	Nashport
Ralph, Darrel	Galena
Rose, Derek W.	Gallipolis
Rowe, Fred	Amesville
Salley, John D.	Tipp City

Schuchmann, Rick	Cincinnati
Shinosky, Andy	Canfield
Shoemaker, Carroll	Northup
Shoemaker, Scott	Miamisburg
Spinale, Richard	Lorain
Stoddart, W.B. Bill	Fairfield
Strong, Scott	Beavercreek
Summers, Dennis K.	Springfield
Thomas, Kim	Seville
Thourot, Michael W.	Napoleon
Tindera, George	Brunswick
Votaw, David P.	Pioneer
Ward, J.J.	Waverly
Ward, Ron	Loveland
Warther, Dale	Dover
Witsaman, Earl	Stow
Wood, Larry B.	Huber Heights
Wright, L.T.	Steubenville
Yurco, Mike	Canfield

OK

Baker, Ray	Sapulpa
Burke, Dan	Edmond
Carillo, Dwaine	Moore
Crenshaw, Al	Eufaula
Darby, David T.	Cookson
Dill, Dave	Bethany
Englebretson, George	Oklahoma City
Gepner, Don	Norman
Johns, Rob	Enid
Kennedy Jr., Bill	Yukon
Kirk, Ray	Tahlequah
Lairson Sr., Jerry	Ringold
Martin, John Alexander	Okmulgee
Menefee, Ricky Bob	Blawchard
Miller, Michael E.	El Reno
Sanders, A.A.	Norman
Spivey, Jefferson	Yukon
Tomberlin, Brion R.	Norman
Wingo, Gary	Ramona

OR

Bell, Michael	Coquille
Bochman, Bruce	Grants Pass
Brandt, Martin W.	Springfield
Buchanan, Thad	Prineville
Buchman, Bill	Bend
Buchner, Bill	Idleyld Park
Busch, Steve	Oakland
Cameron House,	Salem
Carter, Murray M.	Vernonia
Clark, Nate	Yoncalla
Coon, Raymond C.	Gresham
Davis, Terry	Sumpter
Dowell, T.M.	Bend
Ferdinand, Don	Shady Cove
Gamble, Frank	Salem
Goddard, Wayne	Eugene
Harsey, William H.	Creswell
Hilker, Thomas N.	Williams
Horn, Jess	Eugene
Kelley, Gary	Aloha
Lake, Ron	Eugene
Little, Gary M.	Broadbent
Lockett, Lowell C.	North Bend
Lum, Robert W.	Eugene
Martin, Gene	Williams
Martin, Walter E.	Williams
Miller, Michael K.	Sweet Home
Olson, Darrold E.	Springfield
Rider, David M.	Eugene
Scarrow, Wil	Gold Hill
Schoeningh, Mike	North Powder

Schrader, Robert — Bend
Sevey Custom Knife, — Gold Beach
Sheehy, Thomas J. — Portland
Shoger, Mark O. — Beaverton
Smith, Rick — Rogue River
Thompson, Leon — Gaston
Thompson, Tommy — Portland
Vallotton, Butch And Arey — Oakland
Vallotton, Rainy D. — Umpqua
Vallotton, Shawn — Oakland
Vallotton, Thomas — Oakland

PA

Anderson, Gary D. — Spring Grove
Anderson, Tom — Manchester
Appleby, Robert — Shickshinny
Besedick, Frank E. — Ruffsdale
Candrella, Joe — Warminster
Chavar, Edward V. — Bethlehem
Clark, D.E. (Lucky) — Mineral Point
Corkum, Steve — Littlestown
Darby, Rick — Levittown
Evans, Ronald B. — Middleton
Frey Jr., W. Frederick — Milton
Goldberg, David — Ft Washington
Goodling, Rodney W. — York Springs
Gottschalk, Gregory J. — Carnegie
Heinz, John — Upper Black Eddy
Hudson, Rob — Northumberland
Janiga, Matthew A. — Hummelstown
Johnson, John R — New Buffalo
Malloy, Joe — Freeland
Marlowe, Donald — Dover
Mensch, Larry C. — Milton
Miller, Rick — Rockwood
Moore, Ted — Elizabethtown
Morett, Donald — Lancaster
Navagato, Angelo — Camp Hill
Nealy, Bud — Stroudsburg
Neilson, J. — Wyalusing
Nott, Ron P. — Summerdale
Ogden, Bill — Avis
AVIS
Ortega, Ben M. — Wyoming
Parker, J.E. — Clarion
Root, Gary — Erie
Rupert, Bob — Clinton
Sass, Gary N. — Sharpsville
Scimio, Bill — Spruce Creek
Sinclair, J.E. — Pittsburgh
Steigerwalt, Ken — Orangeville
Stroyan, Eric — Dalton
Valois, A. Daniel — Lehighton
Vaughan, Ian — Manheim
Whittaker, Robert E. — Mill Creek
Wilson, Jon J. — Johnstown

RI

Bardsley, Norman P. — Pawtucket
Burak, Chet — E Providence
Dickison, Scott S. — Portsmouth
Mchenry, William James — Wyoming
Olszewski, Stephen — Coventry
Williams, Jason L. — Wyoming
Wright, Richard S. — Carolina

SC

Barefoot, Joe W. — Liberty
Beatty, Gordon H. — Seneca
Branton, Robert — Awendaw
Campbell, Courtnay M. — Columbia
Cannady, Daniel L. — Allendale

Cox, Sam — Gaffney
Denning, Geno — Gaston
Easler Jr., Russell O. — Woodruff
Fecas, Stephen J. — Anderson
Gainey, Hal — Greenwood
George, Harry — Aiken
Gregory, Michael — Belton
Hendrix, Jerry — Clinton
Hendrix, Wayne — Allendale
Herron, George — Springfield
Hucks, Jerry — Moncks Corner
Kay, J. Wallace — Liberty
Knight, Jason — Harleyville
Langley, Gene H. — Florence
Lutz, Greg — Greenwood
Majer, Mike — Hilton Head
Manley, David W. — Central
Mcmanus, Danny — Taylors
Miles Jr., C. R. "Iron Doctor" — Lugoff
Montjoy, Claude — Clinton
Odom Jr, Victor L. — North
Page, Larry — Aiken
Parler, Thomas O. — Charleston
Peagler, Russ — Moncks Corner
Perry, Johnny — Spartanburg
Sears, Mick — Sumter
Thomas, Rocky — Moncks Corner
Tyser, Ross — Spartanburg

SD

Boley, Jamie — Parker
Boysen, Raymond A. — Rapid Ciy
Ferrier, Gregory K. — Rapid City
Sarvis, Randall J. — Fort Pierre
Thomsen, Loyd W. — Oelrichs

TN

Bailey, Joseph D. — Nashville
Baker, Vance — Riceville
Blanchard, G.R. (Gary) — Pigeon Forge
Breed, Kim — Clarksville
Byrd, Wesley L. — Evensville
Canter, Ronald E. — Jackson
Casteel, Dianna — Monteagle
Casteel, Douglas — Monteagle
Centofante, Frank — Madisonville
Claiborne, Ron — Knox
Clay, Wayne — Pelham
Conley, Bob — Jonesboro
Coogan, Robert — Smithville
Copeland, George Steve — Alpine
Corby, Harold — Johnson City
Davey, Kevin — Joelton
Elder Jr., Perry B. — Clarksville
Ewing, John H. — Clinton
Harley, Larry W. — Bristol
Harley, Richard — Bristol
Heflin, Christopher M. — Nashville
Hurst, Jeff — Rutledge
Hutcheson, John — Chattanooga
Johnson, David A. — Pleasant Shade
Johnson, Ryan M. — Hixson
Kemp, Lawrence — Ooletwah
King, Herman — Millington
Levine, Bob — Tullahoma
Marshall, Stephen R. — Mt. Juliet
Mccarty, Harry — Blaine
Mcdonald, W.J. "Jerry" — Germantown
Moulton, Dusty — Loudon
Raley, R. Wayne — Collierville
Ramey, Larry — Chapmansboro
Sampson, Lynn — Jonesborough
Smith, Newman L. — Gatlinburg

Taylor, C. Gray — Fall Branch
Vanderford, Carl G. — Columbia
Walker, John W. — Bon Aqua
Ward, W.C. — Clinton
Wheeler, Gary — Clarksville
Williams Jr., Richard — Morristown
Winter, George — Union City

TX

Adams, William D. — Burton
Alexander, Eugene — Ganado
Allen, Mike "Whiskers" — Malakoff
Appleton, Ron — Bluff Dale
Ashby, Douglas — Dallas
Bailey, Kirby C. — Lytle
Barnes, Marlen R. — Atlanta
Barr, Judson C. — Irving
Batts, Keith — Hooks
Blasingame, Robert — Kilgore
Blum, Kenneth — Brenham
Bradshaw, Bailey — Diana
Bratcher, Brett — Plantersville
Broadwell, David — Wichita Falls
Brooks, Michael — Lubbock
Bullard, Randall — Canyon
Burden, James — Burkburnett
Cairnes Jr., Carroll B. — Palacios
Callahan, F. Terry — Boerne
Cannon, Dan — Dallas
Carpenter, Ronald W. — Jasper
Carter, Fred — Wichita Falls
Champion, Robert — Amarillo
Chase, John E. — Aledo
Chew, Larry — Granbury
Churchman, T.W. (Tim) — Bandera
Cole, James M. — Bartonville
Connor, John W. — Odessa
Connor, Michael — Winters
Cosgrove, Charles G. — Arlington
Costa, Scott — Spicewood
Crain, Jack W. — Granbury
Darcey, Chester L. — College Station
Davidson, Larry — Cedar Hill
Davis, Vernon M. — Waco
Dean, Harvey J. — Rockdale
Dietz, Howard — New Braunfels
Dominy, Chuck — Colleyville
Dyer, David — Granbury
Eldridge, Allan — Ft Worth
Elishewitz, Allen — Canyon Lake
Epting, Richard — College Station
Eriksen, James Thorlief — Garland
Evans, Carlton — Fort Davis
Fant Jr., George — Atlanta
Ferguson, Jim — San Angelo
Fortune Products, Inc., — Marble Falls
Foster, Al — Magnolia
Foster, Norvell C. — San Antonio
Fowler, Jerry — Hutto
Frank, Heinrich H. — Dallas
Fritz, Jesse — Slaton
Fuller, Bruce A. — Baytown
Garner, Larry W. — Tyler
Gault, Clay — Lexington
Goytia, Enrique — El Paso
Graham, Gordon — New Boston
Green, Bill — Sachse
Griffin, Rendon And Mark — Houston
Halfrich, Jerry — San Marcos
Hamlet Jr., Johnny — Clute
Hand, Bill — Spearman
Hawkins, Buddy — Texarkana
Hayes, Scotty — Tesarkana
Haynes, Jerry — San Antonio

Hays, Mark	Austin
Hearn, Terry L.	Lufkin
Hemperley, Glen	Willis
Hicks, Gary	Tuscola
Howell, Jason G.	Lake Jackson
Hudson, Robert	Humble
Hughes, Bill	Texarkana
Hughes, Lawrence	Plainview
Jackson, Charlton R.	San Antonio
Jaksik Jr., Michael	Fredericksburg
Johnson, Gorden W.	Houston
Johnson, Ruffin	Houston
Keller, Bill	San Antonio
Kern, R. W.	San Antonio
Kious, Joe	Kerrville
Knipstein, R.C. (Joe)	Arlington
Ladd, Jim S.	Deer Park
Ladd, Jimmie Lee	Deer Park
Lambert, Jarrell D.	Granado
Laplante, Brett	McKinney
Lay, L.J.	Burkburnett
Lemcke, Jim L.	Houston
Lister Jr., Weldon E.	Boerne
Lively, Tim And Marian	Marble Falls
Locke, Keith	Watauga
Love, Ed	San Antonio
Lovett, Michael	Killeen
Luchak, Bob	Channelview
Luckett, Bill	Weatherford
Marshall, Glenn	Mason
Martin, Michael W.	Beckville
Mcconnell Jr., Loyd A.	Odessa
Mellard, J. R.	Houston
Merz Iii, Robert L.	Katy
Miller, R.D.	Dallas
Mitchell, Wm. Dean	Warren
Moore, James B.	Ft. Stockton
Neely, Greg	Bellaire
Nelson, Dr. Carl	Texarkana
Nolen, R.D. And Steve	Pottsboro
Odgen, Randy W.	Houston
Ogletree Jr., Ben R.	Livingston
Osborne, Warren	Waxahachie
Overeynder, T.R.	Arlington
Ownby, John C.	Plano
Pardue, Joe	Spurger
Patterson, Pat	Barksdale
Pierce, Randall	Arlington
Pollock, Wallace J.	Cedar Park
Polzien, Don	Lubbock
Powell, James	Texarkana
Pugh, Jim	Azle
Ray, Alan W.	Lovelady
Roberts, Jack	Houston
Robinson, Charles (Dickie)	Vega
Rogers, Charles W.	Douglas
Ruple, William H.	Charlotte
Ruth, Michael G	Texarkana
Scott, Al	Harper
Self, Ernie	Dripping Springs
Shipley, Steven A.	Richardson
Sims, Bob	Meridian
Sloan, Shane	Newcastle
Smart, Steve	McKinney
Snody, Mike	Fredericksburg
Stokes, Ed	Hockley
Stone, Jerry	Lytle
Stout, Johnny	New Braunfels
Tham, Phil	Bryan
Theis, Terry	Harper
Thuesen, Ed	Damon
Treiber, Leon	Ingram
Turcotte, Larry	Pampa
Vecera, J R	Thrall
Watson, Daniel	Driftwood

Watts, Johnathan	Gatesville
Watts, Wally	Gatesville
West, Pat	Charlotte
White, Dale	Sweetwater
Whitley, Weldon G.	Odessa
Wilcher, Wendell L.	Palestine
Wilkins, Mitchell	Montgomery
Wilson, Curtis M	Burleson
Wolf Jr., William Lynn	Lagrange
Woodward, Wiley	Colleyville
Yeates, Joe A.	Spring
Zboril, Terry	Caldwell

UT

Allred, Bruce F.	Layton
Black, Earl	Salt Lake City
Ence, Jim	Richfield
Ennis, Ray	Ogden
Erickson, L.M.	Ogden
Hunter, Hyrum	Aurora
Johnson, Steven R.	Manti
Maxfield, Lynn	Layton
Nielson, Jeff V.	Monroe
Nunn, Gregory	Castle Valley
Palmer, Taylor	Blanding
Peterson, Chris	Salina
Rapp, Steven J.	Midvale
Strickland, Dale	Monroe
Velarde, Ricardo	Park City
Winn, Travis A.	Salt Lake City

VA

Apelt, Stacy E.	Norfolk
Arbuckle, James M.	Yorktown
Ballew, Dale	Bowling Green
Batley, Mark S.	Wake
Batson, Richard G.	Rixeyville
Beverly Ii, Larry H.	Spotsylvania
Callahan, Errett	Lynchburg
Catoe, David R.	Norfolk
Chamberlain, Charles R.	Barren Springs
Compton, William E.	Sterling
Davidson, Edmund	Goshen
Douglas, John J.	Lynch Station
Foster, Burt	Bristol
Frazier, Ron	Powhatan
Harris, Cass	Bluemont
Hedrick, Don	Newport News
Hendricks, Samuel J.	Maurertown
Holloway, Paul	Norfolk
Jones, Barry M. And Phillip G.	Danville
Jones, Enoch	Warrenton
Mccoun, Mark	DeWitt
Metheny, H.A. "Whitey"	Spotsylvania
Mills, Michael	Colonial Beach
Murski, Ray	Reston
Norfleet, Ross W.	Richmond
Parks, Blane C.	Woodbridge
Pawlowski, John R.	Newport News
Richter, John C.	Chesapeake
Tomes, P.J.	Shipman
Vanhoy, Ed And Tanya	Abingdon

VT

Haggerty, George S.	Jacksonville
Kelso, Jim	Worcester

WA

Amoureux, A.W.	Northport
Baldwin, Phillip	Snohomish

Begg, Todd M.	Spanaway
Ber, Dave	San Juan Island
Berglin, Bruce D.	Mount Vernon
Bloomquist, R. Gordon	Olympia
Boguszewski, Phil	Lakewood
Boyer, Mark	Bothell
Bromley, Peter	Spokane
Brothers, Robert L.	Colville
Brown, Dennis G.	Shoreline
Brunckhorst, Lyle	Bothell
Bump, Bruce D.	Walla Walla
Butler, John R.	Shoreline
Campbell, Dick	Colville
Chamberlain, John B.	Wenatchee
Chamberlain, Jon A.	E. Wenatchee
Conti, Jeffrey D.	Bonney Lake
Crain, Frank	Spokane
Crossman, Daniel C.	Blakely Island
Crowthers, Mark F.	Rolling Bay
D'Angelo, Laurence	Vancouver
Davis, John	Selah
Diskin, Matt	Freeland
Dole, Roger	Buckley
Evans, Vincent K. And Grace	Cathlamet
Ferry, Tom	Auburn
Frey, Steve	Snohomish
Goertz, Paul S.	Renton
Gray, Bob	Spokane
Greenfield, G.O.	Everett
Hansen, Lonnie	Spanaway
House, Gary	Ephrata
Hurst, Cole	E. Wenatchee
Norton, Don	Port Townsend
O'Malley, Daniel	Seattle
Rader, Michael	Sumner
Rogers, Ray	Wauconda
Schempp, Ed	Ephrata
Schempp, Martin	Ephrata
Schirmer, Mike	Rosalia
Stegner, Wilbur G.	Rochester
Sterling, Thomas J.	Coupeville
Swyhart, Art	Klickitat
Wright, Kevin	Quilcene

WI

Bostwick, Chris T.	Burlington
Brandsey, Edward P.	Milton
Bruner Jr., Fred, Bruner Blades	Fall Creek
Delarosa, Jim	Whitewater
Fiorini, Bill	DeSoto
Genske, Jay	Fond du Lac
Haines, Jeff, Haines Custom Knives	Wauzeka
Hembrook, Ron	Neosho
Johnson, Richard	Germantown
Kanter, Michael	New Berlin
Kohls, Jerry	Princeton
Kolitz, Robert	Beaver Dam
Lary, Ed	Mosinee
Lerch, Matthew	Sussex
Maestri, Peter A.	Spring Green
Martin, Peter	Waterford
Millard, Fred G.	Richland Center
Nelson, Ken	Pittsville
Niemuth, Troy	Sheboygan
Ponzio, Doug	Beloit
R. Boyes Knives,	Menomonee Falls
Revishvili, Zaza	Madison
Ricke, Dave	West Bend
Rochford, Michael R.	Dresser
Schrap, Robert G.	Wauwatosa
Wattelet, Michael A.	Minocqua

WV

Bowen, Tilton	Baker
Carnahan, Charles A.	Green Spring
Derr, Herbert	St. Albans
Drost, Jason D.	French Creek
Drost, Michael B.	French Creek
Elliott, Jerry	Charleston
Jeffries, Robert W.	Red House
Liegey, Kenneth R.	Millwood
Maynard, Larry Joe	Crab Orchard
Mcconnell, Charles R.	Wellsburg
Morris, Eric	Beckley
Pickens, Selbert	Liberty
Reynolds, Dave	Harrisville
Shaver Ii, James R.	Parkersburg
Sigman, Corbet R.	Liberty
Small, Ed	Keyser
Straight, Don	Points
Tokar, Daniel	Shepherdstown
Wilson, R.W.	Weirton
Wyatt, William R.	Rainelle

WY

Alexander, Darrel	Ten Sleep
Ankrom, W.E.	Cody
Archer, Ray And Terri	Medicine Bow
Banks, David L.	Riverton
Barry, Scott	Laramie
Bartlow, John	Sheridan
Bennett, Brett C.	Cheyenne
Draper, Audra	Riverton
Draper, Mike	Riverton
Fowler, Ed A.	Riverton
Friedly, Dennis E.	Cody
Justice, Shane	Sheridan
Kilby, Keith	Cody
Kinkade, Jacob	Cheyenne
Rexroat, Kirk	Wright
Reynolds, John C.	Gillette
Ross, Stephen	Evanston
Spragg, Wayne E.	Lovell

ARGENTINA

Ayarragaray, Cristian L.	(3100) Parana-Entre Rios
Bertolami, Juan Carlos	Neuquen
Gibert, Pedro	San Rafael Mendoza
Kehiayan, Alfredo	CP B1623GXU Buenos Aires
Rho, Nestor Lorenzo	Buenos Aires

AUSTRALIA

Bennett, Peter	Engadine N.S.W. 2233
Brodziak, David	Albany Western Australia
Crawley, Bruce R.	Croydon 3136 Victoria
Cross, Robert	Tamworth 2340 N.S.W.
Del Raso, Peter	Mt. Waverly, Victoria, 3149
Gerner, Thomas	Oxford Western Australia
Gerus, Gerry	Qld. 4870
Giljevic, Branko	N.S.W.
Green, William (Bill)	View Bank Vic.
Harvey, Max	Perth 6155 Western Australia
Husiak, Myron	Victoria
Jones, John	Manly West, QLD 4179
K B S, Knives	Vic 3450
Maisey, Alan	Vincentia 2540 N.S.W.
Mcintyre, Shawn	Hawthorn East Victoria
Spencer, Keith	Chidlow Western Australia
Tasman, Kerley	Western Australia
Zemitis, Joe	2285 Newcastle

AUSTRIA

Poskocil, Helmut	A-3340 Waidhofen/Ybbs

BELGIUM

Dox, Jan	B 2900 Schoten
Monteiro, Victor	1360 Maleves Ste Marie

BRAZIL

Bodolay, Antal	Belo Horizonte MG-31730-700
Bossaerts, Carl	14051-110, Ribeirao Preto
Campos, Ivan	Tatui, Sao Paulo
Dorneles, Luciano Oliverira	Nova Petropolis, RS
Gaeta, Angelo	SP-17201-310
Gaeta, Roberto	Sao Paulo
Garcia, Mario Eiras	Sao Paulo SP-05516-070
Lala, Paulo Ricardo P. and Lala, Roberto P.	SP-19031-260
Neto Jr., Nelson and De Carvalho, Henrique M.	SP-12900-000
Paulo, Fernandes R.	Sao Paulo
Petean, Francisco and Mauricio	SP-16200-000
Ricardo Romano, Bernardes	Itajuba MG
Sfreddo, Rodrigo Menezes	cep g5 150-000
Tkoma, Flavio	Prudonte SP19031-220
Villa, Luiz	Sao Paulo, SP-04537-081
Villar, Ricardo	S.P. 07600-000
Vilar, Ricardo Augusto Ferreira	Mairipora Sao Paulo
Zakharov, Gladiston	Jacaret Sao Paulo

CANADA

Arnold, Joe	London, Ont.
Beauchamp, Gaetan	Stoneham, PQ
Beets, Marty	Williams Lake, BC
Bell, Donald	Bedford, Nova Scotia
Berg, Lothar	Kitchener Ont.
Beshara, Brent (Besh)	Stayner, Ont.
Bold, Stu	Sarnia, Ont.
Boos, Ralph	Edmonton, Alberta
Bourbeau, Jean Yves	Ile Perrot, Quebec
Bradford, Garrick	Kitchener Ont.
Dallyn, Kelly	Calgary AB
Debraga, Jose C.	Aux Lievres Quebec
Debraga, Jovan	Quebec
Deringer, Christoph	Cookshire Quebec
Diotte, Jeff	LaSalle Ontario
Doiron, Donald	Messines PQ
Doucette, R	Brantford Ontario
Doussot, Laurent	Montreal, Quebec
Downie, James T.	Port Franks, Ont.
Dublin, Dennis	Enderby, BC
Freeman, John	Cambridge, Ont.
Frigault, Rick	Niagara Falls Ont.
Garvock, Mark W.	Balderson, Ontario
Gilbert, Chantal	Quebec City Quebec
Haslinger, Thomas	Calgary AB
Hayes, Wally	Orleans, Ont.
Hindmarch, G	Carlyle Sask S0C 0R0
Hofer, Louis	Rose Prairie BC
Jobin, Jacques	Levis Quebec
Kaczor, Tom	Upper London, Ont.
Lambert, Kirby	Regina Saskatchewan S4N X3
Langley, Mick	Qualicum Beach BC
Lay, R.J. (Bob)	Logan Lake, BC
Leber, Heinz	Hudson's Hope, BC
Lightfoot, Greg	Kitscoty AB
Linklater, Steve	Aurora, Ont.
Loerchner, Wolfgang	Bayfield, Or
Lyttle, Brian	High River, A
Maneker, Kenneth	Galiano Island, B.C
Martin, Robb	Elmira, Ontar
Marzitelli, Peter	Langley, B
Massey, Al	Mount Uniacke, Nova Scot
Mckenzie, David Brian	Campbell River
Miville-Deschenes, Alain	Quebe
O'Hare, Sean	Fort Simpson, N
Olson, Rod	High River, A
Painter, Tony	Whitehorse Yuko
Patrick, Bob	S. Surrey, B.C
Pepiot, Stephan	Winnipeg, Ma
Piesner, Dean	Conestogo Or
Roberts, George A.	Whitehorse, Y
Ross, Tim	Thunder Bay, Or
Schoenfeld, Matthew A.	Galiano Island, B.C
St. Amour, Murray	Pembroke On
Stancer, Chuck	Calgary A
Storch, Ed	Alberta T0B 2W
Stuart, Steve	Gores Landing, On
Tichbourne, George	Mississauga, On
Tighe, Brian	St. Catharines On
Toner, Roger	Pickering, On
Treml, Glenn	Thunder Bay, On
Trudel, Paul	Ottawa, On
Vanderkolff, Stephen	Mildmay Ontari
Whitenect, Jody	Nova Scoti
Wile, Peter	Bridgewater, Nova Scoti
Young, Bud	Port Hardy, B

DENMARK

Andersen, Henrik Lefolii	3480, Fredensbor
Anso, Jens	116, 8472 Sporu
Bentzen, Leif	
Dyrnoe, Per	DK 3400 Hilleroe
Henriksen, Hans J.	DK 3200 Helsing
Strande, Poul	Dastrup 4130 Viby S
Vensild, Henrik	DK-8963 Aunin

ENGLAND

Boden, Harry	Derbyshire DE4 2A
Farid R, Mehr	Ker
Hague, Geoff	Wilton Marlborough, Wiltshir
Harrington, Roger	East Susse
Jackson, Jim	Chapel Row Bucklebur RG7 6P
Jones, Charles Anthony	No. Devon E31 4A
Morris, Darrell Price	Devo
Penfold, Mick	Tremar, Cornwall PL14 5S
Wardell, Mick	N Devon EX39 3B
Wise, Donald	East Sussex, TN3 8A
Wood, Alan	Brampton CA8 7H

FRANCE

Bennica, Charles	34190 Moules et Baucel
Chauzy, Alain	21140 Seur-en-Auxio
Doursin, Gerard	Pernes les Fontaine
Ganster, Jean-Pierre	F-67000 Strasbour
Graveline, Pascal and Isabelle	29350 Moelan-sur-Me
Headrick, Gary	Juane Les Pin
Madrulli, Mme Joelle	Salon De Provenc
Reverdy, Nicole and Pierre	
Thevenot, Jean-Paul	Dijo
Viallon, Henri	

GERMANY

Balbach, Markus	35789 Weilmunster Laubuseschbach/Ts

Becker, Franz — 84533, Marktl/Inn
Boehlke, Guenter — 56412 Grossholbach
Borger, Wolf — 76676 Graben-Neudorf
Dell, Wolfgang — D-73277 Owen-Teck
Faust, Joachim — 95497 Goldkronach
Fruhmann, Ludwig — 84489 Burghausen
Greiss, Jockl — D 77773 Schenkenzell
Hehn, Richard Karl — 55444 Dorrebach
Hennicke, — 55578 Wallertheim
   Metallgestaltung
Herbst, Peter — 91207 Lauf a.d. Pegn.
Joehnk, Bernd — 24148 Kiel
Kressler, D.F. — Achim 28832 DE
Neuhaeusler, Erwin — 86179 Augsburg
Rankl, Christian — 81476 Munchen
Rinkes, Siegfried — Markterlbach
Selzam, Frank — Bad Koenigshofen
Steinau, Jurgen — Berlin 0-1162
Tritz, Jean Jose — 20255 Hamburg
Wimpff, Christian — 70574 Stuttgart 70
Wirtz, Achim — D -52146
Zirbes, Richard — D-54526 Niederkail

GREECE

Filippou, Ioannis-Minas — Athens 17122

HOLLAND

Van De Manakker, Thijs — 5759 px
Helenaveen

ISRAEL

Shadmot, Boaz — Arava

ITALY

Albericci, Emilio — 24100, Bergamo
Ameri, Mauro — 16010 Genova
Ballestra, Santino — 18039 Ventimiglia (IM)
Bertuzzi, Ettore — 24068 Seriate (Bergamo)
Bonassi, Franco — Pordenone 33170
Fogarizzu, Boiteddu — 07016 Pattada
Giagu, Salvatore and — 07016 Pattada (SS)
   Deroma Maria Rosaria
Pachi, Francesco — 17046 Sassello (SV)
Puddu, Salvatore — Quartu s Elena (CA)
Riboni, Claudio — Truccazzano (MI)
Scordia, Paolo — Roma
Simonella, Gianluigi — 33085 Maniago
Toich, Nevio — Vincenza
Tschager, Reinhard — I-39100 Bolzano

JAPAN

Aida, Yoshihito — Itabashi-ku, Tokyo 175-0094
Ebisu, Hidesaku — Hiroshima City
Fujikawa, Shun — Osaka 597 0062
Fukuta, Tak — Seki-City, Gifu-Pref
Hara, Kouji — Gifu-Pref. 501-3922
Hirayama, Harumi — Saitama Pref. 335-0001
Hiroto, Fujihara — Hiroshima
Isao, Ohbuchi — Fukuoka
Ishihara, Hank — Chiba Pref.
Kagawa, Koichi — Kanagawa
Kanda, Michio — Yamaguchi 7460033
Kanki, Iwao — Hydugo
Kansei, Matsuno — Gitu-city
Kato, Shinichi — Moriyama-ku Nagoya
Katsumaro, Shishido — Hiroshima
Kawasaki, Akihisa — Kobe

Keisuke, Gotoh — Ohita
Koyama, Captain — Nagoya City 453-0817
   Bunshichi
Mae, Takao — Toyonaka, Osaka
Makoto, Kunitomo — Hiroshima
Matsuno, Kansei — Gifu-City 501-1168
Matsusaki, Takeshi — Nagasaki
Michinaka, Toshiaki — Tottori 680-0947
Micho, Kanda — Yamaguchi
Ryuichi, Kuki — Saitama
Sakakibara, Masaki — Tokyo 156-0054
Shikayama, Toshiaki — Saitama 342-0057
Sugihara, Keidoh — Osaka, F596-0042
Sugiyama, Eddy K. — Ohita
Takahashi, Kaoru — Kamoto Kumamoto
Takahashi, Masao — Gunma 371 0047
Terauchi, Toshiyuki — Fujita-Cho Gobo-Shi
Toshifumi, Kuramoto — Fukuoka
Uchida, Chimata — Kumamoto
Uekama, Nobuyuki — Tokyo
Wada, Yasutaka — Nara prefect 631-0044
Waters, Glenn — Hirosaki City 036-8183
Yoshihara, Yoshindo — Tokyo
Yoshikazu, Kamada — Tokushima
Yoshio, Maeda — Okayama

MEXICO

Scheurer, Alfredo E. Faes — C.P. 16010
Sunderland, Richard — Puerto
Escondido Oaxaca
Young, Cliff — San Miguel De Allende, GTO.

NETHERLANDS

Sprokholt, Rob — Netherlands
Van Den Elsen, Gert — 5012 AJ Tilburg
Van Eldik, Frans — 3632BT Loenen
Van Rijswijk, Aad — 3132 AA Vlaardingen

NEW ZEALAND

Pennington, C.A. — Kainga Christchurch 8009
Reddiex, Bill — Palmerston North
Ross, D.L. — Dunedin
Sandow, Norman E — Howick, Auckland
Sands, Scott — Christchurch 9
Van Dijk, Richard — Harwood Dunedin

NORWAY

Bache-Wiig, Tom — Eivindvik
Sellevold, Harald — N5835 Bergen
Vistnes, Tor

RUSSIA

Kharlamov, Yuri — 300007

SAUDI ARABIA

Kadasah, Ahmed Bin — Jeddah 21441

SLOVAKIA

Albert, Stefan — Filakovo 98604
Bojtos, Arpa D. — 98403 Lucenec
Kovacik, Robert — lucenec
Laoislav, Santa-Lasky — Bystrica
Mojzis, Julius
Pulis, Vladimir — 964 01 Kremnica

SOUTH AFRICA

Arm-Ko Knives, — Marble Ray 4035 KZN
Baartman, George — Limpopo
Bauchop, Robert — Kwazulu-Natal 4278
Beukes, Tinus — Vereeniging 1939
Bezuidenhout, Buzz — Malvern, Queensburgh,
   Natal 4093
Boardman, Guy — New Germany 3619
Brown, Rob E. — Port Elizabeth
Burger, Fred — Kwa-Zulu Natal
De Villiers, Andre — Cascades 3202
   and Kirsten
Dickerson, Gavin — Petit 1512
Fellows, Mike — Mossel Bay 6500
Grey, Piet — Naboomspruit 0560
Harvey, Heather — Belfast 1100
Harvey, Kevin — Belfast 1100
Horn, Des — 7700 Cape Town
Klaasee, Tinus — George 6530
Kojetin, W. — Germiston 1401
Lagrange, Fanie — Table View 7441
Lancaster, C.G. — Free State
Liebenberg, Andre — Bordeauxrandburg 2196
Mackrill, Stephen — Johannesburg
Mahomedy, A. R. — Marble Ray KZN, 4035
Nelson, Tom — Gauteng
Pienaar, Conrad — Bloemfontein 9300
Prinsloo, Theuns — Bethlehem, 9700
Rietveld, Bertie — Magaliesburg 1791
Russell, Mick — Port Elizabeth 6070
Schoeman, Corrie — Danhof 9310
Van Der Westhuizen, Peter — Mossel Bay 6500
Watson, Peter — La Hoff 2570

SWEDEN

Bergh, Roger — 91598 Bygdea
Billgren, Per
Eklund, Maihkel — S-820 41 Farila
Embretsen, Kaj — S-82821 Edsbyn
Hogstrom, Anders T.
Johansson, Anders — S-772 40 Grangesberg
Lundstrom, Jan-Ake — 66010 Dals-Langed
Nilsson, Johnny Walker — Arvidsjaur
Nordell, Ingemar — 82041 Färila
Persson, Conny — 820 50 Loos
Ryberg, Gote — S-562 00 Norrahammar
Styrefors, Mattias
Vogt, Patrik — S-30270 Halmstad

SWITZERLAND

Roulin, Charles — 1233 Geneva
Soppera, Arthur — CH-9631 Ulisbach

UNITED KINGDOM

Heasman, H.G. — Llandudno
Horne, Grace — Sheffield Britian
Maxen, Mick — "Hatfield, Herts"

URUGUAY

Gonzalez, Leonardo Williams — CP 20000
Symonds, Alberto E. — Montevideo 11300

ZIMBABWE

Burger, Pon — Bulawayo

Not all knifemakers are organization-types, but those listed here are in good standing with these organizations.

the knifemakers' guild

2006 voting membership

a Les Adams, Yoshihito Aida, Mike "Whiskers" Allen, Tom Anderson, W. E. Ankrom, Boyd Ashworth, Dick Atkinson

b Santino Ballestra, Norman Bardsley, Van Barnett, A.T. Barr, James J. III Barry, John Bartlow, Gene Baskett, Gaetan Beauchamp, Norman L. Beckett, Raymond Beers, Donald Bell, Tom Black, Andrew Blackton, Gary Blanchard, Arpad Bojtos, Philip Booth, Tony Bose, Dennis Bradley, Edward Brandsey, W. Lowell Jr. Bray, Clint Breshears, Tim Britton, David Brown, Harold Brown, Rick Browne, Fred Jr. Bruner, Jimmie Buckner, R.D. "Dan" Burke, Patrick Burris, John Busfield

c Bill Caldwell, Errett Callahan, Ron Cameron, Daniel Cannady, Ron Canter, Robert Capdepon, Harold J. "Kit" Carson, Fred Carter, Dianna Casteel, Douglas Casteel, Frank Centofante, Jeffrey Chaffee, Joel Chamblin, William Chapo, Alex Chase, Edward Chavar, William Cheatham, Howard F. Clark, Wayne Clay, Vernon Coleman, Blackie Collins, Bob Conley, Gerald Corbit, Harold Corby, George Cousino, Colin Cox, Pat & Wes Crawford, Dan Cruze, Roy D. Cutchin

d George E. Dailey, Charles M. Dake, Alex Daniels, Jack Davenport, Edmund Davidson, Barry Davis, Terry A. Davis, Vernon M. Davis, W. C. Davis, Ralph Jr. D'Elia, Harvey Dean, Dellana, Dan Dennehy, Herbert Derr, Howard Dietz, William Dietzel, Robert Dill, Frank Dilluvio, Al Dippold, David Dodds, Bob Doggett, Tracy Dotson, T. M. Dowell, Larry Downing, Tom Downing, James Downs, Bill Duff, Steve Dunn, Jerry Duran, Fred Durio

e Russell & Paula Easler, Rick Eaton, Allen Elishewitz, Jim Elliott, David Ellis, William B. Ellis, Kaj Embretsen, Jim Ence, Virgil England, William Engle, James T. Eriksen

f Howard Faucheaux, Stephen Fecas, Lee Ferguson, Bill Fiorini, Jay Fisher, Jerry Fisk, Joe Flournoy, Derek Fraley, Michael H. Franklin, John R. Fraps, Ron Frazier, Aaron Frederick, Ralph Freer, Dennis Friedly, Larry Fuegen, Shun Fujikawa, Stanley Fujisaka, Tak Fukuta, Bruce Fuller, Shiro Furukawa

g Frank Gamble, Roger Gamble, William O. Jr. Garner, Ron Gaston, Clay Gault, James "Hoot" Sr. Gibson, Warren Glover, Stefan Gobec, Bruce Goers, David Goldberg, Warren Goltz, Greg Gottschalk, Roger M. Green, Jockl Greiss, Carol Gurganus, Melvin Gurganus, Kenneth Guth

h Philip L. Hagen, Geoffrey Hague, Jeff Hall, Ed Halligan & Son, Tomonori Hamada, Jim Hammond, Koji Hara, J.A. Harkins, Larry Harley, Ralph D. Harris, Rade Hawkins, Richard Hehn, Henry Heitler, Glenn Hemperley, Earl Jay Hendrickson, Wayne Hendrix, Wayne G. Hensley, Peter Herbst, Tim Herman, George Herron, Don Hethcoat, Gil Hibben, Steve E. Hill, R. Hinson & Son, Harumi Hirayama, Howard Hitchmough, Steve Hoel, Kevin Hoffman, D'Alton Holder, J. L. Hollett, Jerry Hossom, Durvyn Howard, Daryle Hughes, Roy Humenick, Joel Humphreys, Joseph Hytovick

i Billy Mace Imel, Michael Irie

j Jim Jacks, Paul Jarvis, John Jensen, Steve Jernigan, Brad Johnson, Ronald Johnson, Ruffin Johnson, Steven R. Johnson, Wm.C. "Bill" Johnson, Enoch D. Jones, Robert Jones

k Edward N. Kalfayan, William Keeton, Bill Keller, Bill Jr. Kennedy, Jot Singh Khalsa, Bill King, Joe Kious, Terry Knipschield, Roy W. Krause, D. F. Kressler, John Kubasek

l Kermit Laurent, Bob Lay, Mike Leach, Matthew J. Lerch, William Letcher, Bill Levengood, Yakov Levin, Bob Levine, Tom Lewis, Steve Linklater, Wolfgang Loerchner, Juan A. Lonewolf, R.W. Loveless, Schuyler Lovestrand, Don Lozier, Robert W. Lum, Larry Lunn, Ernest Lyle

m Stephen Mackrill, Joe Malloy, Dan Maragni, Peter Martin, Randall J. Martin, Kansei Matsuno, Jerry McClure, Charles McConnell, Loyd McConnell, Richard McDonald, Robert J. McDonald, W.J. McDonald, Ken McFall, Frank McGowan, Thomas McGuane, McHenry & Williams, Tommy McNabb, Kurt Meerdink, Mike Mercer, Ted Merchant, Robert L. III Merz, Toshiaki Michinaka, James P. Miller, Steve Miller, Louis Mills, Dan Mink, Jim Minnick, Gunnar Momcilovic, Sidney "Pete" Moon, James B. Moore, Jeff Morgan, C.H. Morris, Dusty Moulton

n Bud Nealy, Corbin Newcomb, Larry Newton, Ron Newton, R.D. & Steve Nolen, Ingemar Nordell, Ross Norfleet, Rick Nowland

o Charles F. Ochs, Ben R. Jr. Ogletree, Warren Osborne, T.R. Overeynder, John Owens

p Francesco Pachi, Larry Page, Robert Papp, Joseph Pardue, Melvin Pardue, Cliff Parker, W. D. Pease, Alfred Pendray, John L. Perry, Eldon Peterson, Kenneth Pfeiffer, Daniel Piergallini, David Pitt, Leon & Tracy Pittman, Al Polkowski, Joe Prince, Jim Pugh, Morris Pulliam

r Jerry Rados, James D. Ragsdale, Steven Rapp, Chris Reeve, John Reynolds, Ron Richard, Dave Ricke, Bertie Rietveld, Willie Rigney, Rex III Robinson, Fred Roe, Richard Rogers, Charles Roulin, Ron Russ, A. G. Russell

s Masaki Sakakibara, Mike Sakmar, Hiroyuki Sakurai, John Salley, Scott Sawby, Maurice & Alan Schrock, Steve Schwarzer, Mark C. Sentz, Yoshinori Seto, Eugene W. Shadley, John I. Shore, Bill Simons, R.J. Sims, James E. Sinclair, Cleston Sinyard, Jim Siska, Fred Slee, Scott Slobodian, J.D. Smith, John W. Smith, Michael J. Smith, Ralph Smith, Jerry Snell, Marvin Solomon, Arthur Soppera, Jim Sornberger, Bill Sowell, Ken Steigerwalt, Jurgen Steinau, Daniel Stephan, Murray Sterling, Barry B. Stevens, Johnny Stout, Keidoh Sugihara, Russ Sutton, Charles Syslo, Joseph Szilaski

t Grant Tally, Robert Terzuola, Leon Thompson, Brian Tighe, Dan Tompkins, John E. Toner, Bobby L. Toole, Dwight Towell, Leon Treiber, Barry Trindle, Reinhard Tschager, Jim Turecek, Ralph Turnbull, Arthur Tycer

v Frans Van Eldik, Edward T. VanHoy, Aad Van Rijswijk, Michael Veit, Ricardo Velarde, Howard Viele, Donald Vogt

w George Walker, James Walker, John W. Walker, Charles B. Ward, Tommy Ware, Daniel Warren, Dale Warther, Charles Weeber, John S. Weever, J. Reese Weiland, Robert Weinstock, Charles L. Weiss, Weldon Whitley, Wayne Whittaker, Donnie R. Wicker, R. W. Wilson, Daniel Winkler, Earl Witsaman, William Wolf, Frank Wojtinowski, Owen Wood, Tim Wright

y Joe Yeates, Yoshindo Yoshihara, George Young, Mike Yurco

z Brad Zinker, Michael Zscherny

american bladesmith society

a Robin E. Ackerson, Lonnie Adams, Kyle A. Addison, Charles L. Adkins, Anthony "Tony" Aiken, Yoichiro Akahori, Douglas A. Alcorn, David Alexander, Mike Alexander, Eugene Alexander, Daniel Allison, Chris Amos, David Anders, Jerome Anders, Gary D. Anderson, Ronnie A. Andress Sr, E. R. (Russ) Andrews II, James M. Arbuckle, Doug Asay, Boyd Ashworth, Ron Austin

b David R. Bacon, Robert Keith Bagley, Marion Bagwell, Brent Bailey, Larry Bailey, Bruce Baker, David Baker, Stephen A. Baker, Randall Baltimore, Dwayne Bandy, Mark D. Banfield, David L. Banks, Robert G. Barker, Reggie Barker, Aubrey G. Barnes Sr., Cecil C. Barnes Jr., Gary Barnes, Marlen R. Barnes, Van Barnett Barnett International, Judson C. Barr, Nyla Barrett, Rick L. Barrett, Michael Barton, Hugh E. Bartrug, Paul C. Basch, Nat Bassett, James L. Batson, R. Keith Batts, Michael R. Bauer, Rick Baum, Dale Baxter, Geneo Beasley, Jim Beaty, Robert B. Beaty, Steve Becker, Bill Behnke, Don Bell, John Bendik, Robert O. Benfield Jr., George Benjamin Jr., Brett Bennett, Rae Bennett, Bruce D. Berglin, Brent Beshara, Chris Bethke, Lora Sue Bethke, Gary Biggers, Ira Lee Birdwell, Hal Bish, William M. Bisher, Jason Bivens, Robert Bizzell, Scott Black, Randy Blair, Dennis Blankenheim, Robert Blasingame, R. Gordon Bloomquist, Josh Blount, Otto Bluntzer, David Bolton, David Boone, Roger E. Bost, Raymond A. Boysen, Bailey Bradshaw, Sanford (Sandy) Bragman, Martin W. Brandt, Robert Branton, Brett Bratcher, W. Lowell Bray Jr., Steven Brazeale, Charles D. Breme, Arthur Britton, Peter Bromley, Charles E. Brooks, Christopher Brown, Dennis G. Brown, Mark D. Brown, Rusty Brown, Troy L. Brown, Steven W. Browning, C. Lyle Brunckhorst, Aldo Bruno, Jimmie H. Buckner, Nick Bugliarello-Wondrich, Bruce D. Bump, Larry Bundrick, Bill Burke, Paul A. Burke, Stephen R. Burrows, John Butler, John R. Butler, Wesley L. Byrd

c Jerry (Buddy) Cabe, Sergio B. Cabrera, Ed Caffrey, Larry Cain, F. Terry Callahan, Robt W. Calvert Jr., Craig Camerer, Ron Cameron, Courtnay M. Campbell, Dan Cannon, Andrew B. Canoy, Jeff Carlisle, Chris Carlson, Eric R. Carlson, William Carnahan, Ronald W. Carpenter, James V. Carriger, Chad Carroll, George Carter, Murray M. Carter, Shayne Carter, Terry Cash, Kevin R. Cashen, P. Richard Chastain, Milton Choate, Jon Christensen, Howard F. Clark, Jim Clary, Joe Click, Russell Coats, Charles Cole, Frank Coleman, Wade Colter, Larry D. Coltrain, Roger N. Comar, Roger Combs, Wm. E. (Bill) Compton, Larry Connelley, John W. Connor, Michael Connor, Charles W. Cook, III, James R. Cook, Robert Cook, James Roscoe Cooper, Jr., Ted Cooper, Joseph G. Cordova, David P. Corrigan, Dr. Timothy L. Costello, William Courtney, Collin Cousino, Gregory G. Covington, Monty L. Crain, Dawnavan M. Crawford, George Crews, Jim Crowell, Peter J. Crowl, Steve Culver, George Cummings, Kelly C. Cupples, John A. Czekala

d George E. Dailey, Mary H. Dake, B. MacGregor Daland, Kelly Dallyn, Sava Damlovac, Alex Daniels, David T. Darby, Chester L. Darcey, David Darpinian, Jim Davidson, Richard T. Davies, Barry Davis, John Davis, Patricia D. Davis, Dudley L. Dawkins, Michael de Gruchy, Angelo De Maria Jr., Harvey J. Dean, Anthony Del Giorno, Josse Delage, Clark B. DeLong, William Derby, Christoph Deringer, Dennis E. Des Jardins, Chuck Diebel, Bill Dietzel, Eric Dincauze, Jason Dingledine, Al Dippold, Matt Diskin, Michael Distin, Luciano Dorneles, Patrick J. Downey, Audra L. Draper, Mike Draper, Joseph D. Drouin, Paul Dubro, Ron Duncan, Calvin Duniphan, Rick Dunkerley, Steve Dunn, Eric Durbin, Kenneth Durham, Fred Durio, David Dyer

e Rick Eaton, Roger Echols, Mike Edelman, Thomas Eden, Gregory K. Edmonson, Randel Edmonson, Mitch Edwards, Lynn Edwards, Joe E. Eggleston, Daniel Robert Ehrenberger, Fred Eisen, Perry B. Elder Jr., Allen Elishewitz, R. Van Elkins, Rickie Ellington, Gordon Elliott, Carroll Ellis, Darren Ellis, Dave Ellis, Roger R. Elrod, Kaj Embretsen, Edward Engarto, Al Engelsman, Richard Epting, David Etchieson, Bruce E. Evans, Greg Evans, Ronald B. Evans, Vincent K. Evans, Wyman Ewing

f John E. Faltay, George Fant Jr., Daniel Farr, Alexander Felix, Gregory K. Ferrier, Robert Thomas Ferry III, Michael J. Filarski, Steve Filicietti, Ioannis-Minas Filippou, Jack Fincher, John Fincher, Ray Fincher, Perry Fink, Sean W. Finlayson, William Fiorini, Jerry Fisk, James O. Fister, John S. Fitch, Dawn Fitch, Mike Fletcher, Joe Flournoy, Charles Fogarty, Don Fogg, Stanley Fortenberry, Burt Foster, Edward K. Foster, Norvell C. Foster, Ronnie E. Foster, Timothy L. Foster, C. Ronnie Fowler, Ed Fowler, Jerry Fowler, Kevin Fox, Walter P. Framski, John M. Frankl, John R. Fraps, Aaron Frederick, Steve Freund, Steve Frey, Rolf Friberg, Rob Fritchen, Daniel Fronefield, Dewayne Frost, Larry D. Fuegen, Bruce A. Fuller, Jack A. Fuller, Richard Furrer

g Barry Gallagher, Jacques Gallant, Jesse Gambee, Tommy Gann, Tommy Gann, Rodney Gappelberg, Jim L. Gardner, Robert J. Gardner, Larry W. Garner, Mike Garner, Timothy P. Garrity, Mark W. Garvock, Bert Gaston, Brett Gatlin, Darrell Geisler, Thomas Gerner, James Gibson, Fabio Giordani, Joel Gist, Kevin Gitlin, Gary Gloden, Wayne Goddard, Jim Gofourth, Scott K. Goguen, David Goldberg, Rodney W. Goodling, Tim Gordon, Thomas L. Gore, Gabe Gorenflo, James T. Gorenflo, Greg Gottschalk, Rayne Gough, Edward Graham, Paul J. Granger, Daniel Gray, Don Greenaway, Jerry Louis Grice, Michael S. Griffin, Larry Groth, Anthony R. Guarnera, Bruce Guidry, Christian Guier, Tom & Gwen Guinn, Garry Gunderson, Johan Gustafsson

h Cyrus Haghjoo, Ed Halligan, N. Pete Hamilton, Timothy J. Hancock, Bill Hand, Don L. Hanson III, Douglas E. Hardy, Larry Harley, Sewell C. Harlin, Paul W. Harm, Brent Harper-Murray, Cass Harris, Jeffrey A. Harris, Tedd Harris, Bill Hart, Sammy Harthman, Heather Harvey, Kevin Harvey, Robert Hatcher, Buddy Hawkins, Rade Hawkins, Rodney Hawkins, Wally Hayes, Charlie E. Haynes, Gary Headrick, Kelly Healy, Chad Heddin, Dion Hedges, Win Heger, Daniel Heiner, John Heinz, E. Jay Hendrickson, Bill Herndon, Harold Herron, Don Hethcoat, Jim B. Hill, John M. Hill, Amy Hinchman, Vance W. Hinds, Donald R. Hinton, Dan Hockensmith, Dr. Georg Hoellwarth, William G. Hoffman, Thomas R. Hogan, Troy Holland, Michael Honey, Un Pyo Hong, John F. Hood, John Horrigan, Robert M. Horrigan, Lawrence House, Gary House, Michael Houston, Jason G. Howell, F. Charles Hubbard, Dale Huckabee, Gov. Mike Huckabee, C. Robbin Hudson, Anthony B. Hudson, Bill Hughes, Daryle Hughes, Tony Hughes, Brad Humelsine, Maurice Hunt, Raymon E. Hunt, Richard D. Hunter, K. Scott Hurst, William R. Hurt, David H. Hwang, Joe Hytovick

i Gary Iames, Hisayuki Ishida

j David Jackson, Jim L. Jackson, Chuck Jahnke, Jr., Karl H. Jakubik, Melvin Jennings Jr., John Lewis Jensen, Mel "Buz" Johns, David A. Johnson, John R. Johnson, Ray Johnson, Thomas Johnson, Clayton W. Johnston, Dr. Robt. Johnston, William Johnston, Chris E. Jones, Enoch Jones, Franklin W. Jones, John Jones, Roger W. Jones, William Burton Jones, Terry J. Jordan, Shane Justice

k Charles Kain, Al J. Kajin, Gus Kalanzis, Barry Kane, David Kazsuk, Jarod Kearney, Robert Keeler, Joseph F. Keeslar, Steven C. Keeslar, Jerry Keesling, Dale Kempf, Larry Kemp, R. W. Kern, Joe Kertzman, Lawrence Keyes, Charles M. Kilbourn, Jr., Keith Kilby, Nicholas Kimball, Richard L. Kimberley, Herman King, David R. King, Fred J. King, Harvey G. King Jr., Kenneth King, Frederick D. Kingery, Donald E. Kinkade, Ray Kirk, Todd Kirk, John Kish, Brad Kliensmid, Russell K. Klingbeil, Hank Knickmeyer, Kurt Knickmeyer, Jason Knight, Steven C. Koster, Bob Kramer, Lefty Kreh, Phil Kretsinger

l Simon Labonti, Jerry Lairson Sr., Curtis J. Lamb, J. D. Lambert, Robert M. Lamey, Leonard D. Landrum, Warren H. Lange, Paul Lansingh, Rodney Lappe, Kermit J. Laurent, Alton Lawrence, Randell Ledbetter, Denis H. LeFranc, Jim L. Lemcke, Jack H. Leverett Jr., Wayne Levin, Bernard Levine, Steve Lewis, Tom Lewis, John J. Lima, Lindy Lippert, Guy A. Little, Tim Lively, Keith Locke, Lowell C. Lockett, Anthony P. Lombardo, Phillip Long, Jonathan A. Loose, Eugene Loro, Jim Lott, Sherry Lott, Jim Lovelace, Ryan Lovell, Steven Lubecki, Bob Luchini, James R. Lucie, James R. Luman, William R. Lyons

m John Mackie, Madame Joelle Madrulli, Takao Mae, Mike Majer, Raymond J. Malaby, John Mallett, Bob Mancuso, Kenneth Mankel, Matt Manley, James Maples, Dan Maragni, Ken Markley, J. Chris Marks, Stephen R. Marshall, Tony Martin, John Alexander Martin, Hal W. Martin, Alan R. Massey, Roger D. Massey, Mick Maxen, Lynn McBee, Daniel McBrearty, Howard H. McCallen Jr., Michael McClure, Sandy McClure, Frederick L. McCoy, Kevin McCrackin, Victor J. McCrackin, Richard McDonald, Robert J. McDonald, Robin J. McDonald, Frank McGowan, Donald McGrath, Patrick T. McGrath, Eric McHugh, Don McIntosh, Neil H. McKee, Tim McKeen, David Brian McKenzie, Hubert W. McLendon, Tommy McNabb, J. Michael McRae, David L. Meacham, Maxie Mehaffey, J. R. Mellard, Walter Merrin, Mardi Meshejian, Ged Messinger, D. Gregg Metheny, Dan Michaelis, Tracy Mickley, Gary Middleton, Bob Miller, Hanford J. Miller, Michael Mills, David Mirabile, Wm. Dean Mitchell, Jim Molinare, Michael Steven Moncus, Charlie Monroe, Keith Montgomery, Lynn Paul Moore, Marve Moore, Michael Robert Moore, Shawn Robert Moore, William F. Moran Jr., Jim Moyer, Russell A. Moyer, James W. Mueller, Jody Muller, Deryk C. Munroe, Jim Mutchler, Ron Myers

n Ryuji Nagoaka, Evan Nappen, Maj. Kendall Nash, Angelo Navagato, Bob Neal, Darby Neaves, Gregory T. Neely, Thomas Conor Neely, James Neilson, Bill Nelson, Lars Nelson, Mark Nevling, Corbin Newcomb, Ron Newton, Tania Nezrick, John Nicoll, Marshall Noble, Douglas E. Noren, H.B. Norris, Paul T. Norris, William North, Vic Nowlan

o Charles F. Ochs III, Julia O'Day, Clyde O'Dell, Vic Odom, Michael O'Herron, Hiroaki Ohta, Michael E. Olive, Todd D. Oliver, Joe Olson, Kent Olson, Richard O'Neill, Robert J. O'Neill, Rich Orton, Philip D. Osattin, Donald H. Osborne, Warren Osborne, Fred Ott, Mac Overton, Donald Owens

p Anthony P. Palermo, Rik Palm, Paul Papich, Ralph Pardington, Cliff Parker, Earl Parker, John Parks, Jimmy D. Passmore, Rob Patton, Jerome Paul, Gary Payton, Michael Peck, Alfred Pendray, Christopher A. Pennington, Johnny Perry, John L. Perry, Conny Persson, Dan L. Petersen, Lloyd Pete C. Peterson, Dan Pfanenstiel, Jim Phillips, Benjamin P. Piccola, Ray Pieper III, Diane Pierce, Dean Piesner, Dietrich Podmajersky, Dietmar Pohl, Clifton Polk, Rusty Polk, Jon R. "Pop" Poplawski, Timothy Potier, Dwight Povistak, James Powell, Robert Clark Powell, Jake Powning, Houston Price, Terry Primos, Jeff Prough, Gerald Puckett, Martin Pullen

q Thomas C. Quakenbush

r Michael Rader, John R. Radford Jr., R. Wayne Raley, Darrel Ralph, Richard A. Ramsey, Gary Randall, James W. Randall Jr., David L. Randolph, Ralph Randow, Mike Reagan, George R. Rebello, Lee Reeves, Roland R. "Rollie" Remmel, Zaza Revishvili, Kirk Rexroat, Scott Reyburn, John Reynolds, Linden W. Rhea, Jim Rice, Stephen E. Rice, Alvin C. Richards Jr., James Richardson, David M. Rider, Richard A. Riepe, Dennis Riley, E. Ray Roberts, Jim Roberts, Don Robertson, Leo D. Robertson, Charles R. Robinson, Michael Rochford, James L. Rodebaugh, James R. Rodebaugh, Gary Rodewald, Charles W. Rogers, Richard Rogers, Willis "Joe" Romero, Frederick Rommel, Troy Ronning, N. Jack Ronzio, Steven Roos, Doun T. Rose, Robert Rosenfeld, Robert N. Rossdeutscher, George R. Roth, Charles Roulin, Kenny Rowe, Clark D. Rozas, Ronald S. Russ, Michael G. Ruth, Michael G. Ruth Jr., Brad Rutherford, Tim Ryan, Wm. Mike Ryan, Raymond B. Rybar Jr., Gerald Rzewnicki

s David Sacks, William Sahli, Ken Sands, Paul Sarganis, Charles R. Sauer, James P. Saviano, Ed Schempp, Ellen Schilling, Tim Scholl, Robert Schrader, Stephen C. Schwarzer, James A. Scroggs, Bert Seale, Turner C. Seale, Jr., David D. Seaton, Steve Seib, Mark C. Sentz, Jimmy Seymour, Rodrigo Menezes Sfreddo, Steve Shackleford, Gary Shaw, James F. Shull, Robert Shyan-Norwalt, Ken Simmons, Brad Singley, Cleston S. Sinyard, Charles Russel Sisemore, Charles J. Smale, Charles Moran Smale, Carel Smith, Clifford Lee Smith, Corey Smith, J.D. Smith, Joshua J. Smith, Lenard C. Smith, Raymond L. Smith, Timothy E. Smock, Michael Tom Snyder, Max Soaper, John E. Soares, Arthur Soppera, Bill Sowell, Randy Spanjer Sr., David R. Sparling, H. Red St. Cyr, Chuck Stancer, Craig Steketee, Daniel Stephan, Tim Stevens, Edward L. Stewart, Rhett & Janie Stidham, Jason M. Stimps, Walter Stockwell, J.B. Stoner, Bob Stormer, Mike Stott, Charles Stout, John K. Stout Jr., Johnny L. Stout, Howard Stover, John Strohecker, Robert E. Stumphy Jr., Harlan Suedmeier, Wayne Suhrbier, Alan L. Sullivan, Fred Suran, Tony Swatton, John Switzer, John D. Switzer, Arthur Swyhart, Mark G. Szarek, Joseph Szilaski

t Scott Taylor, Shane Taylor, Danny O. Thayer, Jean-Paul Thevenot, Brian Thie, David E. Thomas, Devin Thomas, Guy Thomas, Scott Thomas, Hubert Thomason, Robert Thomason, Kinzea L. Thompson, Alan L. Tiensvold, Jason Tiensvold, John Tilton, George Tindera, Dennis Tingle, Dennis P. Tingle, Brion Tomberlin, P. J. Tomes, Kathleen C. Tomey, Mark Torvinen, Lincoln Tracy, Joe E. Travieso III, James J. Treacy, Craig Triplett, Kenneth W. Trisler, James Turpin, Ross Tyser

v Michael V. Vagnino, Jr,, Butch Vallotton, Steve Van Cleve, Jerry W. Van Eizenga, Terry L. Vandeventer, Robert Vardaman, Chris Vidito, Michael Viehman, Gustavo Colodetti Vilal, Ricardo Vilar, Mace Vitale, Patrik Vogt, Bruce Voyles

w Steve "Doc" Wacholz, Lawrence M. Wadler, Adam Waldon, Bill Walker, Don Walker, James L. Walker, Carl D. Ward, Jr., Ken Warner, Robert Lee Washburn Jr., Herman Harold Waters, Lu Waters, Robert Weber, Charles G. Weeber, Fred Weisenborn, Ronald Welling, Eddie Wells, Gary Wendell, Elsie Westlake, Jim Weyer, Nick Wheeler, Wesley Whipple, John Paul White, Lou White, Richard T. White, L. Wayne Whitley, Randy Whittaker, Timothy L. Wiggins, William Burton Wiggins, Jr., Scott Wiley, Dave Wilkes, Craig Wilkins, A. L. Williams, Charles E. Williams, Linda Williams, Michael L. Williams, Edward Wilson, George H. Wilson III, Jeff Wilson, Daniel Winkler, Randy Winsor, George Winter, Ronald E. Woodruff, Steve Woods, Bill Worthen, Terry Wright, Derrick Wulf

z Mark D. Zalesky, Kenneth Zarifes, Matthew Zboray, Terry Zboril, Karl Zimmerman

miniature knifemaker's society

Paul Abernathy, Joel Axenroth, Blade Magazine, Dennis Blaine, Gerald Bodner, Gary Bradburn, Brock Custom Knives, Ivan Campos, Mitzi Cater, Don Cowles, Creations Yvon Vachon, Dennis Cutburth, David Davis, Robert Davis, Gary Denms, Dennis Des Jardins, Eisenberg Jay Publishers, Allen Eldridge, Peter Flores, David Fusco, Eric Gillard, Wayne Goddard, Larah Gray, Gary Greyraven, Tom & Gwen Guinn, Karl Hallberg, Ralph Harris, Richard Heise, Laura Hessler, Wayne Hensley, Tom Hetmanski, Howard Hosick, Albert Izuka, Garry Kelley, Knife World Publishers, R. F. Koebbeman, Terry Kranning, Gary Lack, John LeBlanc, Mike Lee, Les Levinson, Jack Lewis, Mike Ley, Ken Liegey, Henry Loos, Jim Martin, Howard Maxwell, McMullen & Yee Publishing, Ken McFall, Mal Mele, Paul Meyers, Toshiaki Michinaka, Allen G. Miller, Wayne & June Morrison, Mullinnix & Co, National Knife Collectors Assoc., Allen Olsen, Charles Ostendorf, Mike Pazos, Jim Pear, Gordon Pivonka, Jim Pivonka, Prof. Knifemakers Assoc, Jim Pugh, Roy Quincy, John Rakusan, A. D. Rardon, Dawin Richards, Stephen Ricketts, Mark Rogers, Alex Rose, Hank Rummell, Helen Rummell, Sheffield Knifemakers Supply, Sporting Blades, Harry Stalter, Udo Stegemann, Mike Tamboli, Hank Rummell, Paul Wardian, Ken Warner, Michael Wattelet, Ken Wichard Jr. Charles Weiss, Jim Whitehead, Steve Witham, Shirley Whitt, G. T. Williams, Ron Wilson, Dennis Windmiller, Carol Winold, Earl Witsaman, James Woods

professional knifemaker's association

Mike Allen, James Agnew, Usef Arie, Ray B. Archer, Eddie J. Baca, John Bartlow, Donald Bell, Brett C. Bennett, James E. Bliss, Philip Booth, Douglas Brack, Kenneth L. Brock, Ron Burke, Lucas Burnley, Craig Camerer, Tim Cameron, Rod S. Carter, Roger L. Craig, Joel Davis, John Dennehy, Dan Dennehy, Audra Draper, Mike Draper, Ray Ennis, James T. Eriksen, Kirby Evers, John R. Fraps, Scott Gere, Bob Glassman, Sal Glesser, Marge Hartman, Mike Henry, Don Hethcoat, Gary Hicks, Guy Hielscher, Alan Hodges, Don Howard, Tony Howard, Mike Irie, David Johansen, Donald Jones, Jot Singh Khalsa, Harvey King, Steve Kraft, Jim Largent, Neil Lindsay, Mike Lundemann, Jim Magee, Daniel G. May, Jerry & Sandy McClure, Clayton Miller, Skip Miller, Mark Molnar, Ty Montell, Mike Mooney, Gary Moore, Steve Nolen, Rick Nowland, Fred Ott, Rob Patton, Dick Patton, James Poplin, Bill Redd, Terry Roberts, Dennis Riley, Steve Rollert, Charles Sauer, Jerry Schroeder, Eddie F. Stalcup, Craig Steketee, J. C. Stetter, Troy Taylor, Robert Terzuola, Roy Thompson, Loyd W. Thomsen, Jim Thrash, Ed Thuesen, Mark Waites, Dick Waites, Bill Waldrup, Tommy Ware, David Wattenberg, Dan Westlind, Harold J. Wheeler, RW Wilson, Denise Wolford, Monte Zavatta, Michael F Zima, Daniel Zvonek

state/regional associations

alaska knifemakers association

A.W. Amoureux, John Arnold, Bud Aufdermauer, Robert Ball, J.D. Biggs, Lonnie Breuer, Tom Broome, Mark Bucholz, Irvin Campbell, Virgil Campbell, Raymond Cannon, Christopher Cawthorne, John Chamberlin, Bill Chatwood, George Cubic, Bob Cunningham, Gordon S. Dempsey, J.L. Devoll, James Dick, Art Dufour, Alan Eaker, Norm Grant, Gordon Grebe, Dave Highers, Alex Hunt, Dwight Jenkins, Hank Kubaiko, Bill Lance, Bob Levine, Michael Miller, John Palowski, Gordon Parrish, Mark W. Phillips, Frank Pratt, Guy Recknagle, Ron Robertson, Steve Robertson, Red Rowell, Dave Smith, Roger E. Smith, Gary R. Stafford, Keith Stegall, Wilbur Stegner, Norm Story, Robert D. Shaw, Thomas Trujillo, Ulys Whalen, Jim Whitman, Bob Willis

arizona knifemakers association

D. "Butch" Beaver, Bill Cheatham, Dan Dagget, Tom Edwards, Anthony Goddard, Steve Hoel, Ken McFall, Milford Oliver, Jerry Poletis, Merle Poteet, Mike Quinn, Elmer Sams, Jim Sornberger, Glen Stockton, Bruce Thompson, Sandy Tudor, Charles Weiss

arkansas knifemakers association

David Anders, Auston Baggs, Don Bailey, Reggie Barker, Marlen R. Barnes, Paul Charles Basch, Lora Sue Bethke, James Black, R.P. Black, Joel Bradford, Gary Braswell, Paul Brown, Shawn Brown, Troy L. Brown, Jim Butler, Buddy Cabe, Allen Conner, James Cook, Thom Copeland, Gary L. Crowder, Jim Crowell, David T. Darby, Fred Duvall, Rodger Echols, David Etchieson, Lee Ferguson, Jerry Fisk, John Fitch, Joe & Gwen Flournoy, Dewayne Forrester, John Fortenbury, Ronnie Foster, Tim Foster, Emmet Gadberry, Larry Garner, Ed Gentis, Paul Giller, James T. Gilmore, Terry Glassco, D.R. (Rick) Gregg, Lynn Griffith, Arthur J. Gunn, Jr., David Gunnell, Morris Herring, Don "Possum" Hicks, Jim Howington, B. R. Hughes, Ray Kirk, Douglas Knight, Lile Handmade Knives, Jerry Lairson Sr., Claude Lambert, Alton Lawrence, Jim Lemcke, Michael H. Lewis, Willard Long, Dr. Jim Lucie, Hal W. Martin, Tony Martin, Roger D. Massey, Douglas Mays, Howard McCallen Jr., Jerry McClure, John McKeehan, Joe McVay, Bart Messina, Thomas V. Militano, Jim Moore, Jody Muller, Greg Neely, Ron Newton, Douglas Noren, Keith Page, Jimmy Passmore, John Perry, Lloyd "Pete" Peterson, Cliff Polk, Terry Primos, Paul E. Pyle Jr., Ted Quandt, Vernon Red, Tim Richardson, Dennis Riley, Terry Roberts, Charles R. Robinson, Kenny Rowe, Ken Sharp, Terry Shurtleff, Roy Slaughter, Joe D. Smith, Marvin Solomon, Hoy Spear, Charles Stout, Arthur Tycer, Ross Tyser, James Walker, Chuck Ward, Herman Waters, Bryce White, Tillmon T. Whitley III, Mike Williams, Rick Wilson, Terry Wright, Ray Young

australian knifemakers guild inc.

Peter Bald, Wayne Barrett, Peter Bennett, Wayne Bennett, Wally Bidgood, David Brodziak, Neil Charity, Terry Cox, Bruce Crawley, Mark Crowley, Steve Dawson, Malcolm Day, Peter Del Raso, John Dennis, Michael Fechner, Steve Filicietti, Barry Gardner, Thomas Gerner, Branko Giljevic, Eric Gillard, Peter Gordon, Stephen Gregory-Jones, Ben Hall, Mal Hannan, Lloyd Harding, Rod Harris, Glen Henke, Michael Hunt, Robert Hunt,

Myron Husiak, John Jones, Simeon Jurkijevic, Wolf Kahrau, Peter Kandavnieks, Peter Kenny, Tasman Kerley, John Kilby, Murray Lanthois, Anthony Leroy, Greg Lyell, Paul Maffi, Maurice McCarthy, Shawn McIntyre, Ray Mende, Dave Myhill, Adam Parker, John Pattison, Mike Petersen, Murray Shanaughan, Kurt Simmonds, Jim Steele, Rod Stines, David Strickland, Kelvin Thomas, Doug Timbs, Hardy Wangemann, Brendon Ware, Glen Waters, Bob Wilhelm, Joe Zemitis

california knifemakers association

Arnie Abegg, George J. Antinarelli, Elmer Art, Gregory Barnes, Mary Michael Barnes, Hunter Baskins, Gary Biggers, Roger Bost, Clint Breshears, Buzz Brooks, Steven E. Bunyea, Peter Carey, Joe Caswell, Frank Clay, Richard Clow, T.C. Collins, Richard Corbaley, Stephanie Engnath, Alex Felix, Jim Ferguson, Dave Flowers, Logwood Gion, Peter Gion, Joseph Girtner, Tony Gonzales, Russ Green, Tony Guarnera, Bruce Guidry, Dolores Hayes, Bill Herndon, Neal A. Hodges, Richard Hull, Jim Jacks, Lawrence Johnson, David Kazsuk, James P. Kelley, Richard D. Keyes, Michael P. Klein, Steven Koster, John Kray, Bud Lang, Tomas N. Lewis, R.W. Loveless, John Mackie, Thomas Markey, James K. Mattis, Toni S. Mattis, Patrick T. McGrath, Larry McLean, Jim Merritt, Greg Miller, Walt Modest, Russ Moody, Emil Morgan, Gerald Morgan, Mike Murphy, Thomas Orth, Tom Paar, Daniel Pearlman, Mel Peters, Barry Evan Posner, John Radovich, James L. Rodebaugh, Clark D. Rozas, Ron Ruppe, Brian Saffran, Red St. Cyr, James Stankovich, Bill Stroman, Tony Swatton, Gary Tamms, James P. Tarozon, Scott Taylor, Tru-Grit Inc., Tommy Voss, Jessie C. Ward, Wayne Watanabe, Charles Weiss, Steven A. Williams, Harlan M. Willson, Steve Wolf, Barry B. Wood

canadian knifemakers guild

Gaetan Beauchamp, Shawn Belanger, Don Bell, Brent Beshara, Dave Bolton, Conrad Bondu, Darren Chard, Garry Churchill, Guillaume J. Cote, Christoph Deringer, Jeff Diotte, Randy Doucette, Jim Downie, John Dorrell, Eric Elson, Lloyd Fairbairn, Paul-Aime Fortier, Rick Frigault, John Freeman, Mark Garvock, Brian Gilbert, Murray Haday, Tom Hart, Thomas Haslinger, Ian Hubel, Paul Johnston (London, Ont.), Paul Johnston (Smith Falls, Ont.), Jason Kilcup, Kirby Lambert, Greg Lightfoot, Jodi Link, Wolfgang Loerchner, Mel Long, Brian Lyttle, David Macdonald, Michael Mason, Alan Massey, Leigh Maulson, James McGowan, Edward McRae, Mike Mossington, Sean O'Hare, Rod Olson, Neil Ostroff, Ron Post, George Roberts, Brian Russell, Murray St. Armour, Michael Sheppard, Corey Smith, David Smith, Jerry Smith, Walt Stockdale, Matt Stocker, Ed Storch, Steve Stuart, George Tichbourne, Brian Tighe, Robert Tremblay, Glenn Treml, Steve Vanderkloff, James Wade, Bud Weston, Peter Wile

florida knifemaker's association

Dick Atkinson, Barney Barnett, James J. Barry III, Howard Bishop, Andy Blackton, Dennis Blaine, Dennis Blankenhem, Dr. Stephen A. Bloom, Dean Bosworth, John Boyce, Bill Brantley, Lowell Bray, Patrick R. Burris, Norman J. Caesar, Ted Carpenter, Steve Christian, Mark Clark, Lowell Cobb, William Cody, David Cole, Steve Corn, David Cross, Jack Davenport, Kevin Davey, Jim Davis, Kenny Davis, Ralp D'Elia, Bob Doggett, Jim Elliot, William Ellis, Tom M. Enos, Jonathan Feazell, Mike Fisher, Roger Gamble, James "Hoot" Gibson, Pedro Gonzalez, Ernie Grospitch, Fred Harrington, Ralp "Dewey" Harris, Henry Heitler, Kevin Hoffman, Edward O. Holloway, Joe Hytovick, Tom Johanning, Raymond C. Johnson, Richard Johnson, Roy Kelleher, Paul Kent, Bill King, Fred Kingery, John Klingensmith, William S. Letcher, Bill

Levengood, Glenn Long, Gail Lunn, Larry Lunn, Ernie Lyle, Bob Mancuso, Joseph Mandt, Kevin Manley, Michael Matthews, James McNeil, Faustina Mead, Steve Miller, Dan Mink, Steven Morefield, Martin L. Murphy, Gary Nelson, Larry Newton, Clyde Nipper, Praddep Singh Parihar, Cliff Parker, Larry Patterson, Dan Piergallini, Martin Prudente, Bud Pruitt, Terry Lee Renner, Roberto Sanchez, Rusty Sauls, Dennis J. Savage, David Semones, Ann Sheffield, Brad Shepherd, Bill Simons, Stephen J. Smith, Kent Swicegood, Tim Tabor, Michael Tison, Ralph Turnbull, Louis Vallet, Donald Vogt, Doc Wacholz, Reese Weiland, Travis Williamson, Stan Wilson, Denny Young, Brad Zinker

knifemakers' guild of southern africa

Andre DeBeer, Piet Grey, Owen Wood, Jeff Angelo, George Baartman, Francois Basson, Rob Bauchop, George Beechey, Amo Bernard, Buzz Bezuidenhout, Herucus Blomerus, Chris Booysen, Peet Bronkhorst, Rob Brown, Fred Burger, Trevor Burger, William Burger, Andre De Villiers, Gavin Dickerson, Mike Fellows, Leigh Fogary, Andrew Frankland, Brian Geyer, Ettore Gianferrari, Dale Goldschmidt, Frank Goldschmidt, John Grey, Heather Harvey, Kevin Harvey, Dries Hattingh, Gawie Herbst, Thinus Herbst, Greg Hesslewood, Des Horn, Billy Kojetin, Fanie La Grange, Gary Lombard, Steve ombard, A. R, Mahomedy, Peter Mason, George Muller, Gunthr Muller, Tom Nelson, Andries Olivier, Jan Olivier, Christo Oosthuizen, Cedric Pannell, Willie Paulson, Nico Pelzer, Conrad Pienaar, David Pienaar, Jan Potgieter, Lourens Prinsloo, Theuns Prinsloo, Derek Rauch, Chris Reeve, Bertie Rietveld, Dean Riley, John Robertson, Corrie Schoeman, Eddie Scott, Mike Skellern, Carel Smith, Ken Smythe, Graham Spark, Andre Thorburn, Hennie Van Brakel, Fanie Van Der Linde, Johan Van Der Merwe, Van Van Der Merwe, Marius Van Der Vyver, Louis Van Der Walt, Cor Van Ellinckhuijzen, Andre Van Heerden, Gert Vermaak, Erich Vosloo, Desmond Waldeck, John Wilmot, Wollie Wolfaard, Brian Coetzee, Edward Mitchell, Elke Henley, Sharon Burger, Melodie De Witt, Toi Skellern, Roy Dunseith, Nick Grabe, Justin Mason, Rene Vermeulen, Ted Whitfield, Ian Bottomley, Larry Connelly, Stan Gordon, Mark Kretschmer, Steven Lewis, Ken Madden, Hilton Purvis, Melinda Rietveld, Harvey Silk, Willie Ventner.

midwest knifemakers association

E.R. Andrews III, Frank Berlin, Charles Bolton, Tony Cates, Mike Chesterman, Ron Duncan, Larry Duvall, Bobby Eades, Jackie Emanuel, James Haynes, John Jones, Mickey Koval, Ron Lichlyter, George Martoncik, Gene Millard, William Miller, Corbin Newcomb, Chris Owen, A.D. Rardon, Archie Rardon, Max Smith, Ed Stewart, Charles Syslo, Melvin Williams

montana knifemaker's association

Bill Amoureux, Wendell Barnes, James Barth, Bob Beaty, Brett C. Bennett, Arno & Zine Bernard, Robert Bizzell, Peter Bromley, Bruce Bump, Ed Caffrey, C. Camper, John Christensen, Roger Clark, Jack Cory, Bob Crowder, Roger Dole, Rick Dunkerley, Mel Fassio, Tom Ferry, Gary Flohr, Vern Ford, Barry Gallagher, Doc Hagen, Ted Harris, Thomas Haslinger, Sam & Joy Henson, Gerald Hintz, Tori Howe, Al Inman, Dan Kendrick, Doug Klaudt, Mel Long, James Luman, Mike Mann, Jody Martin, Neil McKee, Larry McLaughlin, Mac & Nancy McLaughlin, Gerald Morgan, Ed Mortenson, Deryk Munroe, Dan Nedved, Joe Olson, Daniel O'Malley, Patton Knives, Eldon Peterson, Jim Raymond, Lori Ristinen, James Rodebaugh, Gary Rodewald, Gordon St. Clair, Andy Sarcinella, Charles Sauer, Dean Schroeder, Art Swyhart, Shane Taylor, Jim Thill, Frank Towsley, Bill Waldrup, Michael

Wattelet, Darlene & Gerome Weinand, Daniel Westlind, Nick Wheeler, Michael Young, Fred Zaloudek

new england bladesmiths guild

Phillip Baldwin, Gary Barnes, Paul Champagne, Jimmy Fikes, Don Fogg, Larry Fuegen, Rob Hudson, Midk Langley, Louis Mills, Dan Maragni, Jim Schmidt, Wayne Valachovic and Tim Zowada

north carolina custom knifemakers' guild

Dana C. Acker, Robert E. Barber, Dr. James Batson, Wayne Bernauer, William M. Bisher, Dave Breme, Tim Britton, John (Jack) H. Busfield, E. Gene Calloway, R.C. Chopra, Joe Corbin, Robert (Bob) J.Cumming, Travis Daniel, Rob Davis, Geno Denning, Dexter Ewing, Brent Fisher, Charles F. Fogarty, Don Fogg, Alan Folts, Phillip L. Gaddy, Jim L. Gardner, Norman A. Gervais, Marge Gervais, Nelson Gimbert, Scott Goguen, Mark Gottesman, Ed Halligan, Robert R. Ham, Koji Hara, George Herron, Terrill Hoffman, Stacey Holt, Jesse Houser, Jr., B. R. Hughes, Jack Hyer, Dan Johnson, Tommy Johnson, Barry & Phillip Jones, Barry Jones, Jacob Kelly, Tony Kelly, Robert Knight, Dr. Jim Lucie, Laura Marshall, Dave McKeithan, Andrew McLurkin, Tommy McNabb, Charlie Monroe, Bill Moran, Ron Newton, Victor L. Odom, Jr., Charles Ostendorf, Bill Pate, Howard Peacock, James Poplin, Harry Powell, John W. Poythress, Joan Poythress, Darrel Ralph, Bob Rosenfeld, Bruce M. Ryan, Tim Scholl, Danks Seel, Rodney N. Shelton, J. Wayne Short, Harland & Karen Simmons, Ken & Nancy Simmons, Johnnie Sorrell, Chuck Staples, Murray Sterling, Russ Sutton, Kathleen Tomey, Bruce Turner, Kaiji & Miki Uchida, Dave Vail, Wayne Whitley, James A. Williams, Daniel Winkler, Rob Wotzak

ohio knifemakers association

Raymond Babcock, Van Barnett, Harold A. Collins, Larry Detty, Tom Downing, Jim Downs, Patty Ferrier, Jeff Flannery, James Fray, Bob Foster, Raymond Guess, Scott Hamrie, Rick Hinderer, Curtis Hurley, Ed Kalfayan, Michael Koval, Judy Koval, Larry Lunn, Stanley Maienknecht, Dave Marlott, Mike Mercer, David Morton, Patrick McGroder, Charles Pratt, Darrel Ralph, Roy Roddy, Carroll Shoemaker, John Smith, Clifton Smith, Art Summers, Jan Summers, Donald Tess, Dale

Warther, John Wallingford, Earl Witsaman, Joanne Yurco, Mike Yurco

saskatchewan knifemakers guild

Marty Beets, Art Benson, Doug Binns, Darren Breitkrenz, Clarence Broeksma, Irv Brunas, Emil Bucharsky, Ernie Cardinal, Raymond Caron, Faron Comaniuk, Murray Cook, Sanford Crickett, Jim Dahlin, Herb Davison, Kevin Donald, Brian Drayton, Dallas Dreger, Roger Eagles, Brian Easton, Marvin Engel, Ray Fehler, Rob Fehler, Ken Friedrick, Calvin Granshorn, Vernon Ganshorn, Dale Garling, Alan Goode, Dave Goertz, Darren Greenfield, Gary Greer, Jay Hale, Wayne Hamilton, Phil Haughian, Robert Hazell, Bryan Hebb, Doug Heuer, Garth Hindmarch, John R. Hopkins, Lavern Ilg, Clifford Kaufmann, Meryl Klassen, Bob Kowalke, Todd Kreics, Donald Krueger, Paul Laronge, Patricia Leahy, Ron Lockhart, Pat Macnamara, Bengamin Manton, Ed Mcrac, Len Meeres, Randy Merkley, Arnold Miller, Robert Minnes, Ron Nelson, Brian Obrigewitsch, Bryan Olafson, Blaine Parrry, Doug Peltier, Darryl Perlett, Dean Pickrell, Barry Popick, Jim Quickfall, Bob Robson, Gerry Rush, Geoff Rutledge, Carl Sali, Kim Senft, Eugene Schreiner, Curtis Silzer, Christopher Silzer, David Silzer, Kent Silzer, Don Spasoff, Bob Stewart, Dan Stinnen, Lorne Stadyk, Eugene R. Thompson, Ron Wall, Ken Watt, Trevor, Whitfield, David Wilkes, Merle Williams, Gerry Wozencroft, Ed Zelter, Al Zerr, Brian Zerr, Ronald Zinkhan

south carolina association of knifemakers

Bobby Branton, Gordo Brooks, Daniel L. Cannady, Thomas H. Clegg, John Conn, Geno Denning, Charlie Douan, Jerry G. Hendrix, Wayne Hendrix, George H. Herron, T.J. Hucks, Johnny Johnson, Lonnie Jones, Jason Knight, Col. Thomas D. Kreger, Gene Langley, Eddie Lee, David Manley, William (Bill) Massey, David McFalls, Claude Montjoy, Larry Page, Ricky Rankin, John (Mickey) Reed, Gene Scaffe, Mick Sears, Ralph Smith, S. David Stroud, Robert Stuckey, Rocky Thomas, Woodrow W. Walker, Charlie Webb, Thomas H. Westwood

tennessee knifemakers association

John Bartlow, Doug Casteel, Harold Crisp, Larry Harley, John W. Walker, Harold Woodward, Harold Wright

Hendrickson, E. Jay, 54, 155, 156
Hethcoat, Don, 77
Hilden, Henry, 63, 140, 170
Hill, Steve, 59, 70, 94, 138
Hinderer, Rick, 182
Hindmarch, Garth, 113, 151
Hirayama, Harumi, 62
Hitchmough, Howard, 110, 164
Hoel, Steve, 105, 161
Hoffman, Kevin, 135
Hogstrom, Anders, 72, 112, 141
Holder, D' Alton, 154
Holmes, J.P., 122
House, Gary, 137, 169
Howell, Jason, 109
Hudson, Rob, 91, 111, 116
Ikoma, Flavio Yuji R., 85
Isgro, Jeff, 103
Jarvis, Paul, 98
Jensen, John Lewis, 136
Johnson, S.R. (Steve), 82, 125
Kain, Charles, 108
Kanter, Michael, 63, 67, 90, 142
Keeslar, Joe, 55, 156
Khalsa, Jot Singh, 134, 163
King, Randall, 82
Kious, Joe, 158, 159
Kirk, Ray, 60
Klaasee, Tinus, 92, 140
Knapp, Mark, 61
Knight, Jason, 83
Knipschield, Terry, 105
Koyama, Captain, 96
Krammes, Jeremy, 132
Krein, Tom, 90, 173
Kressler, Dietmar, 82, 123
Lairson Sr., Jerry, 80
Lake, Ron, 106
Lambert, Kirby, 84
Lang, David, 152
Laramie, Mark, 77
Lay, Bob, 63
Lerch, Matthew, 87, 120, 162
Levengood, Bill, 59, 100
Likarich, Steve, 81
Lile, Jimmy, 153
Loerchner, Wolfgang, 133
Loveless, Bob, 125, 179
Lovestrand, Schuyler, Front Cover, 65, 123
Lovett, Michael, 81, 123
Lucie, James, 65
Lundemo, John, 98
Lunn, Larry, 73
Mackrill, Stephen, 155
Mahomedy, A.R., 72
Manaro, Sal, 133
Marlowe, Charles, 23, 154
Martin, Peter, 110
Massey, Roger, 114, 118, 147
Mathews, Charlie, 65, 99
Mathews, Harry, 65, 99

Matsuoka, Scot, 12, 81, 103, 164
Matsusaki, Takeshi, 75
Maxfield, Lynn, 89
Maxwell, Don, 143
Mayo, Tom, 14, 83, 104
McBurnette, Harvey, 56
McClure, Michael, 149
McIntosh, Don, 93, 115
McKee, Neil, 119, 141
Menefee, Rick, 79
Meyer, Christopher, 90
Mickley, Tracy, 71, 90
Mirabile, David, 71, 132
Miville-Deschenes, Alain, 61, 73, 142
Mitsuyuki, Ross, 15
Moon, Sidney "Pete", 66
Mooney, Mike, 58, 67, 87, 153
Moran, William, 80
Morrow, Don, 76
Moulton, Dusty, 56
Mulkey, Gary, 60
Muller, Jody, 56, 95
Murski, Ray, 81, 132
Nappen, Evan F., 43-45
Nealy, Bud, 141
Neilson, J., 64, 68, 78, 88, 93
Nevling, Mark, 112, 169
Newton, Larry, 101
Newton, Ron, 69, 77, 135, 142
Nilsson, Jonny Walker, 99
Norris, Don, 83
O'Brien, Jack, 16-21
O'Hare, Sean, 92, 150
Oliver, A., 167
Olszewski, Stephen, Front Cover
Onion, Ken, 13, 180, 183
Osborne, Don, 109
Osborne, Warren, 162, 164
Ott, Fred, 95, 126
Ouye, Keith, 86, 154
Overeynder, T.R., 76, 138
Panak, Paul, 163
Pardue, Joe
Parker, Cliff, 169, 170
Patrick, Bob, 62
Patterson, Pat, 89
Pease, W.D., 157, 164
Perreault, Dan, 82, 107
Pfanenstiel, Dan, 58, 85
Polk, Cliff, 104
Polk, Rusty, 89, 120
Prinsloo, Lourens, 171
Prinsloo, Theuns, 167
Puddu, Salvatore, 104
Rader, Michael, 69, 95, 96
Ralph, Darrel, 66, 82, 106, 183
Randall, J.W., 112, 170, 171
Rapp, Steven, 115, 158
Reverdy, Pierre, 73
Rexroat, Kirk, 115, 138, 171
Rhea, Lin, 59, 83, 111
Richard, Raymond, 69, 96

Richards, Chuck, 141
Roberts, T.C., 108
Rowe, Fred, 71
Ruth, Mike, 58, 113, 118
Rutherford, Brad, 88, 139
Rybar Jr., Raymond, 69, 138
Saindon, Bill, 141
Sakmar, Mike, 15
Sandow, Norman, 79
Sass, Gary, 62
Sauer, Charles, 74, 137
Schlueter, David, 98
Schneider, Herman J., 166
Schwarzer, Steve, 95, 100, 171
Scroggs, James, 86
Skiff, Steve, 150
Slobodian, Scott, 78, 94, 95, Back Cover
Smith, John W., 148
Smith, Josh, 104, 110, 135, 138
Smith, Raymond, 80
Smith, Rick, 58, 93
Snody, Mike, 184
Solomon, Marvin, 60, 88, 143
St. Amour, Murray, 88
St. Cyr, Red, 114
Stalcup, Eddie, 65, 92, 123
Steinau, Jurgen, 65
Sterling, Murray, 101, 159
Stout, Charles, 70, 89
Stout, Johnny, 103, 157, 159
Stuart, Steve, 72, 112
Szilaksi, Joe, 52, 80
Tabor, Tim, 61, 84, 148
Taylor, C. Gray, 147, Back Cover
Taylor, Shane, 58, 135
Terzuola, Bob, 99
Thomas, Warren, 24
Thomsen, Loyd, 64
Tighe, Brian, 124, 132, 133
Tippetts, Colten, 88, 119, 149
Tomes, P.J., 65, 73, 114
Toner, John, 150, 153
Torres, Henry, 119
Treiber, Leon, 67, 107, 166, 168
Trout, George, 167
Trujillo, Albert, 71
Tschager, Reinhard, 136, 158, 159
Turnbull, Doug, 156
Turnbull, Ralph, 109
Tycer, Art, 60, 121
Tyree, Mike, 151
Vagnino, Michael, 96
Vallotton, Butch, 183
Van Den Elsen, Gert, 94, 97
Van Der Westhuizen, Peter, 93, 108
Vanderkolff, Stephen, Front Cover
Vandeventer, Terry, 112

Velarde, Ricardo, 122
Viele, Howard, 83
Vining, Bill, 106
Vitale, Mace, 86, 117
Wada, Yasutaka, 86
Walker, Jim, 91
Walker, Michael, 107
Wardell, Mick, 93
Ware, Tommy, 119
Warren, Al, 76
Watson, Daniel, 97
Webster, William "Bill", 89
Weinmueller, Hans, 67
Wheeler, Nick, 59
Whitman, Jim, 63
Whitson, Zach, 85, 87
Whittaker, Wayne, 143
Wilson, Stan, 67, 137
Winch, David, 22
Winkler, Daniel, 96, 141
Wirtz, Achim, 94
Wood, Owen, 158
Wright, Richard, 98
Yeang, Kwong, 23
Young, John, 85, 162
Zakabi, Carl, 106
Zemitis, Joe, 142
Zscherny, Mike, 139, 148

leatherworkers/sheathmakers

Bell, Michael, 146
Brandsey, Ed, 146
Cole, Dave, 146
Keeslar, Joe, 145
Kelley, Joann, 144
Marzitelli, Peter, 144
Neilson, Tess, 145
Nevling, Mark, 145
Pulis, Vladimir, 144
Schrap, Robert, 145
Shook, Karen, 146
Smith, Pat, 93
Wattelet, Michael, 144

scrimshanders

Brady, Sandra, 167
Burger, Sharon, 165, 166
Fellows, Mike, 167
Lonewolf, Wei, 166
Lovestrand-Trout, Lauria, Front Cover
Mead, Faustina, 168
Morris, Darrel, 166
Pulis, Vladimir, 167, 168
Roberts, Jack, 166
Stone, Linda Karst, 15, 165, 166, 168
Stothart, Matt, 168
Williams, Gary, 167

The firms listed here are special in the sense that they make or market special kinds of knives made in facilities they own or control either in the U.S. or overseas. Or they are special because they make knives of unique design or function. The second phone number listed is the fax number.

sporting cutlers

A.G. RUSSELL KNIVES INC
1920 North 26th St
Lowell, AR 72745-8489
479-631-0130 800-255-9034; 749-631-8493
ag@agrussell.com; www.agrussell.com
The oldest knife mail-order company, highest quality. Free catalog available. In these catalogs you will find the newest and the best. If you like knives, this catalog is a must.

AL MAR KNIVES
PO Box 2295
Tualatin, OR 97062-2295
503-670-9080; 503-639-4789
www.almarknives.com
Featuring our ultralight ™ series of knives. Sere 2000 ™ Shrike, Sere ™, Operator ™, Nomad ™ and Ultraligh series ™.

ALCAS CORPORATION
1116 E State St
Olean, NY 14760
716-372-3111; 716-373-6155
www.cutco.com
Household cutlery / sport knives

ANZA KNIVES
C Davis
Dept BL 12 PO Box 710806
Santee, CA 92072
619-561-9445; 619-390-6283
sales@anzaknives.com; www.anzaknives.com

B&D TRADING CO.
3935 Fair Hill Rd
Fair Oaks, CA 95628

BARTEAUX MACHETES, INC.
1916 SE 50th St
Portland, OR 97215
503-233-5880
barteaux@machete.com; www.machete.com
Manufacture of machetes, saws, garden tools

BEAR MGC CUTLERY
1111 Bear Blvd. SW
Jacksonville, AL 36265
256-435-2227; 256-435-9348
Lockback, commemorative, multi tools, high tech & hunting knives

BECK'S CUTLERY & SPECIALTIES
Mcgregor Village Center
107 Edinburgh South Dr
Cary, NC 27511
919-460-0203; 919-460-7772
beckscutlery@mindspring.com;
www.beckscutlery.com

BENCHMADE KNIFE CO. INC.
300 Beaver Creek Rd
Oregon City, OR 97045
503-655-6004; 503-655-6223
info@benchmade.com; www.benchmade.com
Sports, utility, law enforcement, military, gift and semi custom

BERETTA U.S.A. CORP.
17601 Beretta Dr
Accokeek, MD 20607
800-528-7453
www.berettausa.com
Full range of hunting & specialty knives

BLACKJACK KNIVES
PO Box 3
Greenville, WV 24945
304-832-6878
www.knifeware.com

BLUE GRASS CUTLERY CORP
20 E Seventh St PO Box 156
Manchester, OH 45144
937-549-2602; 937-549-2709 or 2603
sales @bluegrasscutlery.com
www.bluegrasscutlery.com

Manufacturer of Winchester Knives, John Primble Knives and many contract lines

BOB'S TRADING POST
308 N Main St
Hutchinson, KS 67501
620-669-9441 or 620-474-6466
Tad custom knives with Reichert custom sheaths one at a time one of a kind

BOKER USA INC
1550 Balsam St
Lakewood, CO 80214-5917
303-462-0662;303-462-0668
sales@bokerusa.com;www.bokerusa.com
Wide range of fixed blade and folding knives for hunting, military, tactical and general use

BROWNING
One Browning Pl
Morgan, UT 84050
801-876-2711; 801-876-3331
www.browning.com
Outdoor hunting & shooting products

BUCK KNIVES INC
660 S Lochsa St
Post Falls, ID 83854
800-735-2825
www.buckknives.com
Sports cutlery

BULLDOG BRAND KNIVES
PO Box 23852
Chattanooga, TN 37422
423-894-5102; 423-892-9165
Fixed blade and folding knives for hunting and general use

BUSSE COMBAT KNIFE CO.
11651 CO Rd 12
Wauseon, OH 43567
419-923-6471; 419-923-2337
Simple & very strong straight knife designs for tactical & expedition use
www.bussecombat.com

CAMILLUS CUTLERY CO.
54 Main St.
Camillus, NY 13031
315-672-8111; 315-672-8832
customerservice@camillusknives.com
www.camillusknives.com

CAS IBERIA INC
650 Industrial Blvd.
Sale Creek, TN 37373
423-332-4700; 423-332-7248
www.casiberia.com
Extensive variety of fixed-blade and folding knives for hunting, diving, camping, military and general use.

CASE CUTLERY
W R & Sons
Owens Way
Bradford, PA 16701
800-523-6350; 814-368-1736
consumer-relations @wrcase.com
www.wrcase.com
Folding pocket knives

CHICAGO CUTLERY CO.
5500 Pearl St Ste 400
Rosemont, IL 60018
847-678-8600
www.chicagocutlery.com
Sport & utility knives.

CHRIS REEVE KNIVES
11624 W President Dr. No. B
Boise, ID 83713
208-375-0367; 208-375-0368
crknifo@chrisreeve.com; www.chrisreeve.com
Makers of the award winning Yarborough/ Green Beret Knife; the One Piece Range; and the Sebenza and Mnandi folding knives

COAST CUTLERY CO
2045 SE Ankeny St
Portland, OR 97214
800-426-5858 or 503-234-4545; 503-234-4422
www.coastcutlery.com
Variety of fixed-blade and folding knives and multi-tools for hunting, camping and general use

COLD STEEL INC
3036 Seaborg Ave. Suite A
Ventura, CA 93003
800-255-4716 or 805-650-8481; 805-642-9727
ric@coldsteel.com; www.coldsteel.com
Wide variety of folding lockbacks and fixed-blade hunting, fishing and neck knives, as well as bowies, kukris, tantos, throwing knives, kitchen knives and swords

COLONIAL KNIFE COMPANY DIVISION OF COLONIAL CUTLERY INTERNATIONAL
K.M. Paolantonio
PO Box 960
North Scituate, RI 02857
866-421-6500; 401-421-6555
colonialcutlery @aol.com;
www.colonialcutlery@aol.com or
www.colonialknifecompany.com
Collectors edition specialty knives. Special promotions. Old cutler, barion, trappers, military knives. Industrial knives-electrician etc.

COLUMBIA RIVER KNIFE & TOOL
9720 SW Hillman Ct. Ste 805
Wilsonville, OR 97070
800-891-3100; 503-682-9680
info@crkt.com; www.crkt.com
Complete line of sport, work and tactical knives

CRAWFORD KNIVES
205 N Center
West Memphis, AR 72301
870-732-2452
Folding knives for tactical and general use

DAVID BOYE KNIVES
PO Box 1238
Dolan Springs, AZ 86441
800-853-1617 or 928-767-4273; 928-767-3030
boye@ctaz.com; www.boyeknives.com
Boye Dendritic Cobalt boat knives

DUNN KNIVES
Steve Greene
PO Box 204
Rosville KS 66533
785-584-6856; 785-584-6856
sigreene@earthlink.net; www.dunnknives.com
Custom knives

EMERSON KNIVES, INC.
PO Box 4180
Torrance, CA 90510-4180
310-212-7455; 310-212-7289
www.emersonknives.com
Hard use tactical knives; folding & fixed blades

EXTREMA RATIO SAS
Mauro Chiostri/Maurizio Castrati
Via Tourcoing 40/P
59100 Prato ITALY
0039 0574 58 4639; 0039 0574 58 1312
info@extremaratio.com
Tactical/military knives and sheaths, blades and sheaths to customers specs

FALLKNIVEN AB
Havrevagen 10
S-96142 Boden
SWEDEN
46-92154422; 46-92154433
info@fallkniven.se; www.fallkniven.com
High quality stainless knives

FROG TOOL CO
PO Box 600
Getzville, NY 14068-0600
716-877-2200; 716-877-2591
gatco@buffnet.net; www.frogtool.net
Precision multi tools

FROST CUTLERY CO
PO Box 22636
Chattanooga, Tn 37422
800-251-7768 or423-894-6079; 423-894-9576
www.frostcutleryco.com
*Wide range of fixed-blade and folding knives
with a multitude of handle materials*

GATCO SHARPENERS
PO Box 600
Getzville, Ny 14068
716-877-2200; 716-877-2591
gatco@buffnet.net; www.gatcosharpeners.com
*Precision sharpening systems, diamond
sharpening systems, ceramic sharpening
systems, carbide sharpening systems, natural
Arkansas stones*

GENUINE ISSUE INC.
949 Middle Country Rd
Selden, NY 11784
631-696-3802; 631-696-3803
gicutlery@aol.com
Antique knives, swords

GERBER LEGENDARY BLADES
14200 SW 72nd Ave
Portland, OR 97223
503-639-6161
www.gerberblades.com
*Knives, multi-tools, axes, saws, outdoor
products*

GROHMANN KNIVES LTD.
PO Box 40
Pictou Nova Scotia B0K 1H0
CANADA
888-756-4837 or 902-485-4224; 902-485-5872
*Fixed-blade belt knives for hunting and
fishing, folding pocketknives for hunting and
general use*

GT KNIVES
7734 Arjons Dr
San Diego, CA 92126
858-530-8766; 858-530-8798
gtknives@gtknives.com; www.gtknives.com
Law enforcement & military automatic knives

H&B FORGE CO.
235 Geisinger Rd
Shiloh, OH 44878
419-895-1856
hbforge@direcway.com; www.hbforge.com
*Special order hawks, camp stoves, fireplace
accessories, muzzleloading accroutements*

HISTORIC EDGED WEAPONRY
1021 Saddlebrook Dr
Hendersonville, NC 28739
828-692-0323; 828-692-0600
histwpn@bellsouth.net
*Antique knives from around the world;
importer of puukko and other knives from
Norway, Sweden, Finland and Lapland; also
edged weaponry book "Travels for Daggers"
by Eiler R. Cook*

HONEYCUTT MARKETING, INC., DAN
3165 C-4 S Campbell
Springfield MO 65807
417-887-2635
danhoneycutt@sbcglobal.net
*All kinds of cutlery, military, Randalls. 28 years
young in the cutlery business*

IMPERIAL SCHRADE CORP.
7 Schrade Ct
Ellenville, NY 12428
800-2-Schrade
www.schradeknives.com

JOY ENTERPRISES-FURY CUTLERY
1862 M.L. King Blvd
Riviera Beach, FL 33404
800-500-3879 or 561-863-3205; 561-863-3277
mail@joyenterprises.com;
www.joyenterprises.com; www.furycutlery.com

*Fury ™ Mustang™ extensive variety of fixed-
blade and folding knives for hunting, fishing,
diving, camping, military and general use;
novelty key-ring knives. Muela Sporting
Knives*

KA-BAR KNIVES INC
200 Homer St
Olean, NY 14760
800-282-0130
info@ka-bar.com; www.ka-bar.com

KATZ KNIVES, INC.
PO Box 730
Chandler, AZ 85224-0730
480-786-9334; 480-786-9338
katzkn@aol.com; www.katzknives.com

KELLAM KNIVES CO.
902 S Dixie Hwy
Lantana, FL 33462
800-390-6918; 561-588-3185; 561-588-3186
info@kellamknives.com; www.kellamknives.com
*Largest selection of Finnish knives;
handmade & production*

KERSHAW/KAI CUTLERY CO.
25300 SW Parkway
Wilsonville, OR 97070

MESSEV KLOTZLI
Hohengasse E Ch 3400
Burgdorf
SWITZERLAND
(34) 422-2378; (34) 422-7693
info@klotzli.com; www.klotzli.com
*High-tech folding knives for tactical and
general use*

KNIFEWARE INC
PO Box 3
Greenville, WV 24945
304-832-6878
www.knifeware.com
*Blackjack and Big Country Cross reference
Big Country Knives see Knifeware Inc.*

KNIGHTS EDGE LTD.
5696 N Northwest Highway
Chicago, IL 60646-6136
773-775-3888; 773-775-3339
sales@knightsedge.com;
www.knightsedge.com
*Medieval weaponry, swords, suits of armor,
katanas, daggers*

KNIVES OF ALASKA, INC.
Charles or Jody Allen
3100 Airport Dr
Denison, TX 75020 8623
903-786-7366, 800-572-0980; 903-786-7371
info@knivesofalaska.com;
www.knivesofalaska.com
High quality hunting & outdoorsmen's knives

KUTMASTER KNIVES
Div of Utica Cutlery Co
820 Noyes St
Utica, NY 13502
315-733-4663; 315-733-6602
www.kutmaster.com
*Manufacturer and importer of pocket,
lockback, tool knives and multi-purpose tools*

LAKOTA
620 E Monroe
Riverton, WY 24945
307-856-6559; 307-856-1840
AUS 8-A high-carbon stainless steel blades

LEATHERMAN TOOL GROUP, INC.
PO Box 20595
Portland, OR 97294
503-253-7826; 503-253-7830
mktg@leatherman.com; www.leatherman.com
Multi-tools

LONE WOLF KNIVES
Doug Hutchens
17400 SW Upper Boones Ferry Rd Suite 240
Portland OR 97224
503-431-6777

MARBLE'S OUTDOORS
420 Industrial Park
Gladstone, Mi 49837
906-428-3710; 906-428-3711
marble@up.net; www.marblesoutdoors.com

MASTER CUTLERY INC
701 Penhorn Ave
Secaucus, NJ 07094
201-271-7600; 201-271-7666
www.mastercutlery.com
Largest variety in the knife industry

MASTERS OF DEFENSE KNIFE CO
4850 Brookside Court
Norfolk, VA 23502
800-694-5263; 888-830-2013
cs@blackhawk.com; www.modknives.com
*Fixed-blade and folding knives for tactical and
general use*

MEYERCO MANUFACTURING
4481 Exchange Service Dr
Dallas, TX 75236
214-467-8949; 214-467-9241
www.meyercousa.com
*Folding tactical,rescue and speed-assisted
pocketknives; fixed-blade hunting and fishing
designs; multi-function camping tools and
machetes*

MCCANN INDUSTRIES
132 S 162nd PO Box 641
Spanaway, WA 98387
253-537-6919; 253-537-6993
McCann.machine@worldnet.att.net;
www.mccannindustries.com

MICRO TECHNOLOGY
932 36th Ct. Sw
Vero Beach, FL 32968
772-569-3058; 772-569-7632
sales@microtechknives.com;
www.microtechknives.com
*Manufacturers of the highest quality
production knives*

MORTY THE KNIFE MAN, INC.
4 Manorhaven Blvd
Pt Washington, NY 11050
516-767-2357; 516-767-7058

MUSEUM REPLICAS LTD.
2147 Gees Mill Rd
Conyers, GA 30012
800-883-8838
www.museumreplicas.com
*Historically accurate & battle-ready swords &
daggers*

MYERCHIN MARINE CLASSICS
14765 Nova Scotia Dr
Fontana, CA 92336
909-463-6741; 909-463-6751
myerchin@myerchin.com; www.myerchin.com
Rigging/ Police knives

NATIONAL KNIFE DISTRIBUTORS
125 Depot St
Forest City, NC 28043
800-447-4342 or 828-245-4321; 828-245-5121
nkdi@nkdi.com
*Benchmark pocketknives from Solingen
Germany*

NORMARK CORP
10395 Yellow Circle Dr
Minnetonka, MN 55343
800-874-4451; 612-933-0046
Hunting knives, game shears and skinning ax

ONTARIO KNIFE CO.
26 Empire St
Franklinville, NY 14737
800-222-5233; 800-299-2618
sales@ontarioknife.com; www.ontarioknife.com
*Fixed blades, tactical folders, military &
hunting knives, machetes*

OUTDOOR EDGE CUTLERY CORP.
4699 Nautilus Ct. S #503
Boulder, CO 80301
800-447-EDGE; 303-530-7020
info@outdooredge.com; www.outdooredge.com

PILTDOWN PRODUCTIONS
Errett Callahan
2 Fredonia Ave
Lynchburg, VA 24503
434-528-3444

QUEEN CUTLERY COMPANY
PO Box 500
Franklinville, NY 14737
800-222-5233; 800-299-2618
sales@ontarioknife.com;
www.queencutlery.com
Pocket knives, collectibles, Schatt & Morgan, Robeson, club knives

QUIKUT
PO Box 29
Airport Industrial Park
Walnut Ridge, AR 72476
870-886-6774; 870-886-9162

RANDALL MADE KNIVES
PO Box 1988
Orlando, FL 32802-1988
407-855-8075; 407-855-9054
grandall@randallknives.com;
www.randallknives.com
Handmade fixed-blade knives for hunting, fishing, diving, military and general use

REMINGTON ARMS CO., INC.
870 Remington Drive
PO Box 700
Madison, NC 27025-0700
800-243-9700
www.remigton.com

SANTA FE STONEWORKS
3790 Cerrillos Rd.
Santa Fe, NM 87507
800-257-7625; 505-471-5953; 505-471-0036
knives@rt66.com; www.santafestoneworks.com
Gem stone handles

SARCO CUTLERY LLC
449 Lane Dr
Florence AL 35630
256-766-8099; 256-766-7246
sarcoknives@earthlink.net;
www.sarcoknives.com
Etching and engraving services, club knives. etc. New knives, antique-collectible knives

SOG SPECIALTY KNIVES & TOOLS, INC.
6521 212th St. S.W.
Lynwood, WA 98036
425-771-6230; 425-771-7689
info@sogknives.com; www.sogknives.com
SOG assisted technology, Arc-Lock, folding knives, specialized fixed blades, multi-tools

SPYDERCO, INC.
820 Spyderco Way
Golden, CO 80403

800-525-7770; 303-278-2229
sales@spyderco.com
www.spyderco.com
Knives and sharpeners

SWISS ARMY BRANDS INC.
PO Box 874
One Research Dr
Shelton, CT 06484-0874
800-243-4045; 800-243-4006
www.swissarmy.com
Folding multi-blade designs and multi-tools for hunting, fishing, camping, hiking, golfing and general use. One of the original brands (Victorinox) of Swiss Army Knives

TAYLOR CUTLERY
1736 N Eastman Rd
PO Box 1638
Kingsport, TN 37662-1638
800-251-0254 or 423-247-2406; 423-247-5371
taylor@preferred.com; www.taylorcutlery.com
Fixed-blade and folding knives for tactical, rescue, hunting and general use

TIGERSHARP TECHNOLOGIES
1002 N Central Expwy Suite 499
Richardson TX 75080
469-916-2861; 972-907-0716
chead@tigersharp.com; www.tigersharp.com

TIMBERLINE KNIVES
PO Box 600
Getzville, NY 14068-0600
716-877-2200; 716-877-2591
gatco@buffnet.net; timberlineknives.com;
www.timberlineknives.com
High Technology production knives for professionals, sporting, tradesmen & kitchen use

TINIVES
1725 Smith Rd
Fortson, GA 31808
888-537-9991; 706-322-9892
info@tinives.com; www.tinives.com
High-tech folding knives for tactical, law enforcement and general use

TRU-BALANCE KNIFE CO.
PO Box 140555
Grand Rapids, MI 49514

TURNER, P.J., KNIFE MFG., INC.
PO Box 1549
Afton, WY 83110
307-885-0611
pjtkm@silverstar.com; www.eknife.net

UTICA CUTLERY CO
820 Noyes St
Utica, NY 13503-1537
800-888-4223; 315-733-6602
sales@kutmaster.com

Wide range of folding and fixed-blade designs, multi-tools and steak knives

WARNER, KEN
PO Box 3
Greenville, WV 24945
304-832-6878; 304-832-6550
www.knifeware.com

WENGER NORTH AMERICA
15 Corporate Dr
Orangeburg, NY 10962
800-431-2996 or 845-365-3500; 845-365-3558
www.wengerna.com
One of the official makers of folding multi-blade Swiss Army knives

WILD BOAR BLADES
1701 Broadway PMB 282
Vancouver, WA 98663
888-476-4400 or 360-735-0570; 360-735-0390
wildboarblades@aol.com;
www.wildboarblade.com
Wild Boar Blades is pleased to carry a full line of Kopromed knives and kitchenware imported from Poland

WILLIAM HENRY FINE KNIVES
3200 NE Rivergate
McMinnville, OR 97128
888-563-4500 or 503-434-9700; 503-434-9704
www.williamhenryknives.com
Semi-custom folding knives for hunting and general use; some limited editions

WORLD SURVIVAL INSTITUTE
C Janowsky
Dept BL 12 Box 394
Tok, AK 99780
907-883-4243

WUU JAU CO INC
2600 S Kelly Ave
Edmond, OK 73013
800-722-5760 or 405-359-5031l 877-256-4337 or 405-340-5965
mail@wuujau.com; www.wuujau.com
Wide variety of imported fixed-blade and folding knives for hunting, fishing, camping, and general use. Wholesale to knife dealers only

WYOMING KNIFE CORP.
101 Commerce Dr.
Ft. Collins, CO 80524

XIKAR INC
PO Box 025757
Kansas City MO 64102
888-266-1193; 816-421-3530
info@xikar.com; www.xikar.com
Gentlemen's cutlery and accessories

importers

A. G. RUSSELL KNIVES INC
1920 North 26th St
Lowell, AR 72745-8489
479-631-0130; 800-255-9034; 479-631-8493
ag@agrussell.com; www.agrussell.com
The oldest knife mail-order company, highest quality. Free catalog available. In these catalogs you will find the newest and the best. If you like knives, this catalog is a must. Celebrating 40 years in the industry

ADAMS INTERNATIONAL KNIFEWORKS
8710 Rosewood Hills
Edwardsville, IL 62025
Importers & foreign cutlers

AITOR-BERRIZARGO S.L.
P.I. Eitua PO Box 26
48240 Berriz Vizcaya
SPAIN
946826599; 94602250226
info@aitor.com; www.aitor.com
Sporting knives

ATLANTA CUTLERY CORP.
2147 Gees Mill Rd
Box 839FD
Conyers, GA 30207
770-922-3700; 770-388-0246
www.atlantacutlery.com
Exotic knives from around the world

BAILEY'S
PO Box 550
Laytonville, CA 95454
800-322-4539; 707-984-8115
www.baileys-online.com

BELTRAME, FRANCESCO
Via Molini 27
33085 Maniago PN
ITALY
39 0427 701859
www.italianstiletto.com

BOKER USA, INC.
1550 Balsam St
Lakewood, CO 80214-5917
303-462-0662; 303-462-0668

sales@bokerusa.com; www.bokerusa.com
Ceramic blades

CAMPOS, IVAN DE ALMEIDA
R. Stelio M. Loureiro, 205
Centro, Tatui
BRAZIL
00-55-15-33056867
www.ivancampos.com

C.A.S. IBERIA, INC.
650 Industrial Blvd
Sale Creek, TN 37373
423-332-4700; 423-332-7248
info@casiberia.com; www.casiberia.com

CAS/HANWEI, MUELA
Catoctin Cutlery
PO Box 188
Smithsburg, MD 21783

CLASSIC INDUSTRIES
1325 Howard Ave, Suite 408
Burlingame, CA 94010

COAST CUTLERY CO.
2045 Se Ankeny St
Portland, OR 97214

COLUMBIA PRODUCTS CO.
PO Box 1333
Sialkot 51310
PAKISTAN

COLUMBIA PRODUCTS INT'L
PO Box 8243
New York, NY 10116-8243
201-854-3054 or 201-854-8504; 201-854-7058
nycolumbia@aol.com; http://
columbiaproducts.homestead.com/cat.html
Pocket, hunting knives and swords of all kinds

COMPASS INDUSTRIES, INC.
104 E. 25th St
New York, NY 10010
800-221-9904; 212-353-0826
jeff@compassindustries.com;
www.compassindustries.com
Imported pocket knives

CONAZ COLTELLERIE
Dei F.Lli Consigli-Scarperia
Via G. Giordani, 20
50038 Scarperia (Firenze)
ITALY
36 55 846187; 39 55 846603
conaz@dada.it; www.consigliscarpeia.com
*Handicraft workmanship of knives of the
ancient Italian tradition. Historical and
collection knives*

CONSOLIDATED CUTLERY CO., INC.
696 NW Sharpe St
Port St. Lucie, FL 34983

CRAZY CROW TRADING POST
Po Box 847 Dept 96
Pottsboro, TX 75020
903-786-2287; 903-786-9059
info@crazycrow.com; www.crazycrow.com
*Solingen blades, knife making parts &
supplies*

DER FLEISSIGEN BEAVER
(The Busy Beaver)
Harvey Silk
PO Box 1166
64343 Griesheim
GERMANY
49 61552231; 49 6155 2433
Der.Biber@t-online.de
*Retail custom knives. Knife shows in Germany
& UK*

EMPIRE CUTLERY CORP.
12 Kruger Ct
Clifton, NJ 07013

EXTREMA RATIO SAS
Mauro Chiostri
Mavrizio Castrati
Via Tourcoing 40/p
59100 Prato (PO)
ITALY
0039 0574 58 4639; 0039 0574 581312
info@extremarazio.com; www.extremaratio.com
Tactical & military knives manufacturing

FALLKNIVEN AB
Havrevagen 10
S-96142 Boden
SWEDEN
46 92154422; 46 92154433
info@fallkniven.se
www.fallkniven.com
High quality knives

FREDIANI COLTELLI FINLANDESI
Via Lago Maggiore 41
I-21038 Leggiuno
ITALY

GIESSER MESSERFABRIK GMBH, JOHANNES
Raiffeisenstr 15
D-71349 Winnenden
GERMANY
49-7195-18080; 49-7195-64466
info@giesser.de; www.giesser.de
Professional butchers and chef's knives

HIMALAYAN IMPORTS
3495 Lake Side Dr
Reno, NV 89509
775-825-2279
himimp@aol.com; httpillmembers.aol.com/
himinp/index.html

IVAN DE ALMEIDA CAMPOS-KNIFE DEALER
R. Xi De Agosto
107, Centro, Tatui, Sp 18270
BRAZIL
55-15-251-8092; 55-15-251-4896
campos@bitweb.com.br
Custom knives from all Brazilian knifemakers

JOY ENTERPRISES
1862 M.L. King Blvd
Riviera Beach, FL 33404
561-863-3205/800-500-3879; 561-863-3277
mail@joyenterprises.com;
www.joyenterprises.com
Fury™, Mustang™, Hawg Knives, Muela

KELLAM KNIVES CO.
902 S Dixie Hwy
Lantana, FL 33462
561-588-3185; 800-390-6918; 561-588-3186
info@kellamknives.com; www.kellamknives.com
Knives from Finland; own line of knives

KNIFE IMPORTERS, INC.
PO Box 1000
Manchaca, TX 78652
800-531-5301; 800-266-2373
Wholesale only

KNIGHTS EDGE
5696 N Northwest Hwy
Chicago, IL 60646
773-775-3888; 773-775-3339
www.knightsedge.com
*Exclusive designers of our Rittersteel,
Stagesteel and Valiant Arms and knightedge
lines of weapon*

LEISURE PRODUCTS CORP.
PO Box 1171
Sialkot-51310
PAKISTAN

L. C. RISTINEN
Suomi Shop
17533 Co Hwy 38
Frazee MN 56544
218-538-6633; 218-538-6633
icrist@wcta.net
*Scandinavian cutlery custom antique, books
and reindeer antler*

LINDER, CARL NACHF.
Erholungstr. 10
42699 Solingen
GERMANY
212 330856; 212 337104
info@linder.de; www.linder.de

MARTTIINI KNIVES
PO Box 44 (Marttiinintie 3)
96101 Rovaniemi
FINLAND

MATTHEWS CUTLERY
4401 Sentry Dr., Suite K
Tucker, GA 30084

MESSER KLÖTZLI
PO Box 104
Hohengasse 3, Ch-3402 Burgdorf
SWITZERLAND
034 422 2378; 034 422 7693
info@klotzli.com; www.klotzli.com

MURAKAMI, ICHIRO
Knife Collectors Assn. Japan
Tokuda Nishi 4 Chome, 76 Banchi, Ginancho
Hashimagun, Gifu
JAPAN
81 58 274 1960; 81 58 273 7369
www.gix.orjp/~n-resin/

MUSEUM REPLICAS LIMITED
2147 Gees Mill Rd
Conyers, GA 30012
800-883-8838
www.museumreplicas.com

NICHOLS CO.
PO Box 473, #5 The Green
Woodstock, VT 05091
802-457-3970; 802-457-2051
janjesse@sover.net
*Import & distribute knives from EKA
(Sweden), Helle (Norway), Brusletto
(Norway), Roselli (Finland). Also market Zippo
products, Snow, Nealley axes and hatchets
and snow & Neally axes*

NORMARK CORP.
Craig Weber
10395 Yellow Circle Dr
Minnetonka, MN 55343

PRO CUT
9718 Washburn Rd
Downey, CA 90241
562-803-8778; 562-803-4261
sales@procutdist.com
*Wholesale only. Full service distributor of
domestic & imported brand name cutlery.
Exclusive U.S. importer for both Marto Swords
and Battle Ready Valiant Armory edged
weapons*

PRODUCTORS AITOR, S.A.
Izelaieta 17
48260 Ermua
SPAIN
943-170850; 943-170001
info@aitor.com
Sporting knives

SCANDIA INTERNATIONAL INC.
5475 W Inscription Canyon Dr
Prescott, AZ 86305
928-442-0140; 928-442-0342
frosts@cableone.net; www.frosts-scandia.com
Frosts Knives of Sweden

STAR SALES CO., INC.
1803 N. Central St., PO Box 1503
Knoxville, TN 37901

SVORD KNIVES
Smith Rd., Rd 2
Waiuku, South Auckland
NEW ZEALAND

SWISS ARMY BRANDS LTD.
The Forschner Group, Inc.
One Research Drive
Shelton, CT 06484
203-929-6391; 203-929-3786
www.swissarmy.com

TAYLOR CUTLERY
PO Box 1638
1736 N. Eastman Rd
Kingsport, TN 37662
*Colman Knives along with Smith & Wesson,
Cuttin Horse, John Deere, Zoland knives*

UNITED CUTLERY CORP.
1425 United Blvd
Sevierville, TN 37876
865-428-2532; 865-428-2267
order@unitedcutlery.com;
www.unitedcutlery.com
*Harley-Davidson ® Colt ® , Stanley®, U21 ®,
Rigid Knives ®, Outdoor Life ®, Ford ®,
hunting, camping, fishing, collectible & fantasy
knives*

UNIVERSAL AGENCIES INC
4690 S Old Peachtree Rd, Ste C
Norcross, GA 30071-1517
678-969-9147; 678-969-9148; 678-969-9169
info@uai.org; www.knifesupplies.com;
www.thunderforged.com; www.uai.org
*Serving the cutlery industry with the finest
selection of India Stag, Buffalo Horn,
Thurnderforged ™ Damascus. Mother of
Pearl, Knife Kits and more*

VALOR CORP.
1001 Sawgrass Corp Pkwy
Sunrise, FL 33323-2811
954-377-4925; 954-377-4941
www.valorcorp.com
Wide variety of imported & domestic knives

WENGER N. A.
15 Corporate Dr
Orangeburg, NY 10962
800-431-2996
www.wengerna.com
Swiss Army ™ Knives

WILD BOAR BLADES
1701 Broadway, Suite 282
Vancouver, WA 98663
888-476-4400; 360-735-0570; 360-735-0390
usakopro@aol.com; www.wildboarblades.com
*Wild Boar Blades is pleased to carry a full line
of Kopromed knives and kitchenware
imported from Poland*

ZWILLING J.A.
Henckels Inc
171 Saw Mill River Rd
Hawthorne, NY 10532
914-749-0300; 914-747-9850
info@jahenckels.com; www.jahenckels.com
*Kitchen cutlery, scissors, gadgets, flatware
and cookware*

knife making supplies

AFRICAN IMPORT CO.
Alan Zanotti
22 Goodwin Rd
Plymouth, MA 02360
508-746-8552; 508-746-0404
africanimport@aol.com
Ivory

AMERICAN SIEPMANN CORP.
65 Pixley Industrial Parkway
Rochester, NY 14624
585-247-1640; 585-247-1883
www.siepmann.com
*CNC blade grinding equipment, grinding
wheels, production blade grinding services.
Sharpening stones and sharpening
equipment*

ANCHORAGE CUTLER
Greg Gritten
801 Airport Hts #351
Anchorage, AK 99508
907-277-5843
cutlery@artic.net; www.anchoragecutlery.com
*Custom knife making supplies; ivory,
gemstones, antler, horn, bone*

ART JEWEL ENTERPRISES, LTD.
460 Randy Rd
Carol Stream, IL 60188

ATLANTA CUTLERY CORP.
2147 Gees Mill Rd, Box 839XE
Conyers, GA 30012
800-883-0300

BATAVIA ENGINEERING
PO Box 53
Magaliesburg, 1791
SOUTH AFRICA
27-14-5771294
bertie@batavia.co.za; www.batavia.co.za
*Contact wheels for belt grinders and surface
grinders; damascus and mokume*

BLADEMAKER, THE
Gary Kelley
17485 SW Phesant Ln
Beaverton, OR 97006
503-649-7867
garykelly@theblademaker.com;
www.theblademaker.com
*Period knife and hawk blades for hobbyists &
re-enactors and in dendritic D2 steel.
"Ferroulithic" steel-stone spear point, blades
and arrowheads*

BOONE TRADING CO., INC.
PO Box 669
Brinnon, WA 98320
800-423-1945
www.boonetrading.com
Ivory of all types, bone, horns

BORGER, WOLF
Benzstrasse 8
76676 Graben-Neudorf
GERMANY
wolf@messerschmied.de;
www.messerschmied.de

BOYE KNIVES
PO Box 1238
Dolan Springs, AZ 86441
800-853-1617; 928-767-3030
boye@ctaz.com; www.boyeknives.com
Dendritic steel and Dendritic cobalt

BRONK'S KNIFEWORKS
C. Lyle Brunckhorst
23706 7th Ave SE, Country Village, Suite B

Bothell, WA 98021; 425-402-3484
bronks@net-tech.com;
www.bronksknifeworks.com
Damascus steel

CRAZY CROW TRADING POST
PO Box 847, Dept 96
Pottsboro, TX 75076
903-786-2287; 903-786-9059
info@crazycrow.com; www.crazycrow.com
Solingen blades, knifemaking parts & supples

CUSTOM FURNACES
PO Box 353
Randvaal, 1873
SOUTH AFRICA
27 16 365-5723; 27 16 365-5738
johnlee@custom.co.za
Furnaces for hardening & tempering of knives

CUSTOM KRAFT
PO Box 2337
Riverview, FL 33568
813-671-0661; 727-595-0378
RWPHIL413@earthlink.net;
www.rwcustomknives.com
*Specializes in precision screws and hardware
for folders. Also carrys gemstones and
cabochons for inlay work. Catalog available*

DAMASCUS-USA CHARLTON LTD.
149 Deans Farm Rd
Tyner, NC 27980-9718
252-221-2010
damascususa@intelifort.com;
www.damascususa.com

DAN'S WHETSTONE CO., INC.
418 Hilltop Rd
Pearcy, AR 71964
501-767-1616; 501-767-9598
questions@danswhetstone.com;
www.danswhetstone.com
Natural abrasive Arkansas stone products

DIAMOND MACHINING TECHNOLOGY, INC. DMT
85 Hayes Memorial Dr
Marlborough, MA 01752
800-481-5944; 508-485-3924
dmtsharp@dmtsharp.com; www.dmtsharp.com
*Knife and tool sharpeners - diamond, ceramic
and easy edge guided sharpening kits*

DIXIE GUN WORKS, INC.
PO Box 130
Union City, TN 38281
731-885-0700; 731-885-0440 or 800-238-6785
info@dixiegunworks.com;
www.dixiegunworks.com
Knife and knifemaking supplies

E CHRISTOPHER MFG.
PO Box 685
Union City, TN 38281
731-885-0374; 731-885-0440
*Solingen blades from Germany (ground and
polished)*

EZE-LAP DIAMOND PRODUCTS
3572 Arrowhead Dr
Carson City, NV 89706
775-888-9500; 775-888-9555
sales@eze-lap.com; www.eze-lap.com
Diamond coated sharpening tools

FLITZ INTERNATIONAL, LTD.
821 Mohr Ave
Waterford, WI 53185
800-558-8611; 262-534-2991
info@flitz.com; www.flitz.com
Metal polish, buffing pads, wax

FORTUNE PRODUCTS, INC.
205 Hickory Creek Rd
Marble Falls, TX 78654
830-693-6111; 830-693-6394
www.accusharp.com
AccuSharp knife sharpeners

GILMER WOOD CO.
2211 NW St Helens Rd
Portland, OR 97210
503-274-1271
www.gilmerwood.com

GOLDEN AGE ARMS CO.
PO Box 366, 115 E High St
Ashley, OH 43003

GRS CORP.
D.J. Glaser
PO Box 1153, 900 Overlander St
Emporia, KS 66801
620-343-1084 or 800-835-3519; 620-343-9640
glendo@glendo.com; www.glendo.com
*Engraving, equipment, tool sharpener, books/
videos*

HALPERN TITANIUM INC.
Les and Marianne Halpern
PO Box 214
Three Rivers, MA 01080
413-283-8627; 413-289-2372
info@halperntitanium.com
*Titanium, carbon fiber, G-10, fasteners; CNC
milling*

HARMON, JOE T.
8014 Fisher Dr
Jonesboro, GA 30236

HAWKINS CUSTOM KNIVES & SUPPLIES
110 Buckeye Rd
Fayetteville, GA 30214
770-964-1177; 770-306-2877
radeh@bellsouth.net
www.radehawkinscustomknives.com
All styles

HILTARY DIAMOND INDUSTRIES
7303 E Earll Dr
Scottsdale, AZ 85251
480-945-0700 or 480-994-5752; 480-945-3333
usgrc@qwest.net; www.bigbrainsdont.com

HOUSE OF TOOLS LTD.
#136, 8228 Maclead Tr SE
Calgary, AB
CANADA T2H 2B8

HOV KNIVES & SUPPLIES
Box 8005
S-700 08 Arebro
SWEDEN

INDIAN JEWELERS SUPPLY CO.
Mail Order PO Box 1774, 601 E Coal Ave
Gallup NM 87301
2105 San Mateo Blvd
Albuquerque, NM 87110
505-722-4451; 505-722-4172
orders@ijsinc.com; www.ijsinc.com
Handle materials, tools, metals

INTERAMCO INC.
5210 Exchange Dr
Flint, MI 48507
810-732-8181; 810-732-6116
solutions@interamco.com
Knife grinding and polishing

JANTZ SUPPLY
PO Box 584-K4
Davis, OK 73030-0584
800-351-8900; 580-369-3082
jantz@brightok.net; www.knifemaking.com
Pre shaped blades, kit knives, complete knifemaking supply line

JOHNSON, R.B.
I.B.S. Int'l. Folder Supplies
Box 11
Clearwater, MN 55320
320-558-6128; 320-558-6128
www.customknives.com/r.b.johnson
Threaded pivot pins, screws, taps, etc.

JOHNSON WOOD PRODUCTS
34968 Crystal Rd
Strawberry Point, IA 52076

K&G FINISHING SUPPLIES
PO Box 458
Lakeside, AZ 85929
928-537-8877; 928-537-8066
cs@knifeandgun.com; www.knifeandgun.com
Full service supplies

KOVAL KNIVES, INC.
5819 Zarley St
New Albany, OH 43054
614-855-0777; 614-855-0945
koval@kovalknives.com; www.kovalknives.com
Knifemaking supplies & equipment

KOWAK IVORY
Roland and Kathy Quimby
PO Box 350
Ester, AK 99725
520-723-5827
rlqiv@yahoo.com
Fossil ivories

LITTLE GIANT POWER HAMMER
420 4th Corso
Nebraska City, NE 68410

LIVESAY NEWT
3306 S Dogwood St
Siloam Springs, AR 72761
479-549-3356; 479-549-3357
newt@newtlivesay.com; www.newtlivesay.com
Combat utility knives, titanium knives, sportsmen knives, custom made orders taken on knives and after market Kydex© sheaths for commercial or custom cutlery

LOHMAN CO., FRED
3405 NE Broadway
Portland, OR 97232

M MILLER ORIGINALS
Michael Miller
2960 E Carver Ave
Kingman AZ 86401
928-757-1359
mike@milleroriginals.com
Supplies stabilized juniper burl blocks and scales

MARKING METHODS, INC.
Sales
301 S. Raymond Ave
Alhambra, CA 91803-1531
626-282-8823; 626-576-7564
sales@markingmethods.com;
www.markingmethods.com
Knife etching equipment & service

MASECRAFT SUPPLY CO.
254 Amity St
Meriden, CT 06450
203-238-3049; 203-238-2373
masecraft@masecraftsupply.necoxmail.com;
www.masecraftsupply.com
Natural & specialty synthetic handle materials & more

MEIER STEEL
Daryl Meier
75 Forge Rd
Carbondale, IL 62903
www.meiersteel.com

MOTHER OF PEARL CO.
Joe Culpepper
PO Box 445, 293 Belden Cir
Franklin, NC 28734
828-524-6842; 828-369-7809
mopco@earthlink.net; www.knifehandles.com;
www.stingrayproducts.com
Mother of pearl, bone, abalone, stingray, dyed stag, black clip, ram's horn, mammoth ivory, coral, scrimshaw

NICHOLAS EQUIPMENT CO.
730 E Washington St
Sandusky, OH 44870

NICO BERNARD
PO Box 5151
Nelspruit 1200
SOUTH AFRICA
011-2713-7440099; 011-2713-7440099
bernardn@iafrica.com

NORRIS MIKE
Rt 2 Box 242A
Vanceburg, KY 41179
606-798-1217
Damascus steel

OREGON ABRASIVE & MFG. CO.
12345 NE Sliderberg Rd
Brush Prairie, WA 98606
360-892-1142; 360-892-3025
Tripel grit 3 stone sharpening system

OSO FAMOSO
Box 654
Ben Lomond, CA 95005
831-336-2343
oso@osofamoso.com; www.osofamoso.com
Mammoth ivory bark

OZARK KNIFE & GUN
3165 C-4 S Campbell
Springfield, MO 65807
417-886-CUTT; 417-887-2635
danhoneycutt@sbcglobal.net
28 years in the cutlery business, Missouri's oldest cutlery firm

PAPAI, ABE
5013 N 800 E
New Carlisle, IN 46552

PARAGON INDUSTRIES, INC. L. P.
2011 South Town East Blvd
Mesquite, TX 75149-1122
972-288-7557; 800-876-4328
paragonind@att.net; www.paragonweb.com
Heat treating furnaces for knife makers

POPLIN, JAMES/POP KNIVES & SUPPLIES
103 Oak St
Washington, GA 30673

PUGH, JIM
PO Box 711
Azle, TX 76098
817-444-2679; 817-444-5455
Rosewood and ebony Micarta blocks, rivets for Kydex sheaths, 0-80 screws for folders

RADOS, JERRY
PO Box 531, 7523E 5000 N. Rd
Grant Park, IL 60940
815-405-5061
jerryr@favoravi.com
Damascus steel

REACTIVE METALS STUDIO, INC.
PO Box 890
Clarksdale, AZ 86324
928-634-3434; 928-634-6734
info@reactivemetals.com;
www.reactivemetals.com

R. FIELDS ANCIENT IVORY
Donald Fields
790 Tamerlane St
Deltona, FL 32725
386-532-9070
donaldfields@aol.com
Selling ancient ivories; Mammoth, fossil & walrus

RICK FRIGAULT CUSTOM KNIVES
3584 Rapidsview Dr
Niagara Falls, Ontario
CANADA L2G 6C4
905-295-6695
zipcases@zipcases.com; www.zipcases.com
Selling padded zippered knife pouches with an option to personalize the outside with the marker, purveyor, stores - address, phone number, email web-site or any other information needed. Available in black cordura, mossy oak camo in sizes 4"x2" to 20"x4.5"

RIVERSIDE MACHINE
201M W Stillwell
Dequeen, AR 71832
870-642-7643; 870-642-4023
uncleal@ipa.net; www.riversidemachine.net

ROCKY MOUNTAIN KNIVES
George L. Conklin
PO Box 902, 615 Franklin
Ft. Benton, MT 59442
406-622-3410
bbgrus@ttc-cmc.net
Working knives

RUMMELL, HANK
10 Paradise Lane
Warwick, NY 10990

SAKMAR, MIKE
1451 Clovelly Ave
Rochester, MI 48307
248-852-6775; 248-852-8544
mikesakmar@yahoo.com
Mokume bar stock. Retail & wholesale

SANDPAPER, INC. OF ILLINOIS
270 Eisenhower Ln N, Unit 5B
Lombard, IL 60148
630-629-3320; 630-629-3324
sandinc@aol.com; www.sandpaperinc.com
Abrasive belts, rolls, sheets & discs

SCHEP'S FORGE
PO Box 395
Shelton, NE 68876-0395

SENTRY SOLUTIONS LTD.
33 S Commercial St #401
Manchester, NH 03101-2626
603-626-8888/800-546-8049; 603-626-8889
knives2002@sentrysolutions.com;
www.sentrysolutions.com
Knife care products

SHEFFIELD KNIFEMAKERS SUPPLY, INC.
PO Box 741107
Orange City, FL 32774-1107
386-775-6453; 386-774-5754
www.sheffieldsupply.com

SHINING WAVE METALS
PO Box 563
Snohomish, WA 98291-0563
425-334-5569; 425-334-5569
phb@shiningwave.com; www.shiningwave.com
A full line of Mokune-Gane in precious and non-precious metals for knifemakers, jewelers and other artists

SMITH ABRASIVES, INC.
1700 Sleepy Valley Rd
Hot Springs, AR 71901

SMITH WHETSTONE, INC.
1700 Sleepy Valley Rd
Hot Springs, AR 71901

SMOLEN FORGE, INC.
Nick Smolen
S1735 Vang Rd
Westby, WA 54667
608-634-3569; 608-634-3869
www.smolenforge.com
Damascus billets & blanks, Mokume gane billets

SOSTER SVENSTRUP BYVEJ 16
Dastrup 4130 VIBY SJ
DENMARK
45 46 19 4305; 45 46 19 5319
www.poulstrande.com

STAMASCUS KNIFEWORKS INC.
Ed Van Hoy
24255 N. Fork River
Abingdon, VA 24210
276-944-4885
Blade steels

STOVER, JEFF
PO Box 43
Torrance, CA 90507
310-532-2166
edgedealer@aol.com
Fine custom knives, top makers

TEXAS KNIFEMAKERS SUPPLY
Kevin Thuesen
10649 Haddington Suite 180
Houston TX 77043
713-461-8632
Working straight knives. Hunters including upswept skinners and custom walking sticks

TRU-GRIT, INC.
760 E Francis St #N
Ontario, CA 91761
909-923-4116 or 800-532-3336; 909-923-9932
trugrit1@aol.com; www.trugrit.com

The latest in Norton and 3/M ceramic grinding belts. Also Super Flex, Trizact, Norax and Micron belts to 3000 grit. All of the popular belt grinders. Buffers and variable speed motors. ATS-34, 440C, BG-42, CPM S-30V, 416 and Damascus steel

UNIVERSAL AGENCIES, INC.
4690 S Old Peachtree Rd Ste C
Norcross, GA 30071-1517
678-969-9147 or 678-969-9148; 678-969-9169
info@uai.org; www.knifesupplies.com,
www.thunderforged.com; www.uai.org
Serving the cutlery industry with the finest selection of India Stag, Buffalo Horn, Thunderforged ™ Damascus. Mother of Pearl, Knife Kits and more

WASHITA MOUNTAIN WHETSTONE CO.
PO Box 20378
Hot Springs, AR 71903
501-525-3914; 501-525-0816
wmw@hsnp

WEILAND, J. REESE
PO Box 2337
Riverview, FL 33568
813-671-0661; 727-595-0378

rwphil413@earthlink.net;
www.rwcustomknives.com
Folders, straight knives etc.

WILD WOODS
Jim Fray
PO Box 104
Monclova, OH 43542
419-866-0435

WILSON, R.W.
113 Kent Way
Weirton, WV 26062

WOOD CARVERS SUPPLY, INC.
PO Box 7500-K
Englewood, FL 34295-7500
800-284-6229; 941-698-0329
www.woocarverssupply.com
Over 2,000 unique wood carving tools

WOOD STABILIZING SPECIALISTS INT'L.
Mike & Cara Ludemann
2940 Fayette Ave
Ionia, IA 50645
641-435-4746; 641-435-4759
Mike@Stabilizedwood.com;
www.stabilizedwood.com

mail order sales

A. G. RUSSELL KNIVES INC
1920 North 26th St
Lowell, AR 72745-8489
479-631-0130; 479-631-8493
ag@agrussell.com; www.agrussell.com
The oldest knife mail-order company, highest quality. Free catalog available. In these catalogs you will find the newest and the best. If you like knives, this catalog is a must

ARIZONA CUSTOM KNIVES
Julie Hyman
5099 Medoras Ave
Saint Augustine, FL 32080
904-460-9579
sharptalk@bellsouth.net;
www.arizonacustomknives.com
Color catalog $5 U.S. / $7 Foreign

ARTISAN KNIVES
Ty Young
575 Targhee Twn Rd
Alta, WY 83414
304-353-8111
tyfoto@yahoo.com; www.artisanknives.com
Feature master artisan knives and makers in a unique "coffee table book" style format

ATLANTA CUTLERY CORP.
2147 Gees Mill Rd
Conyers, GA 30012
800-883-0300
www.atlantacutlery.com
Special knives & cutting tools

ATLANTIC BLADESMITHS/PETER STEBBINS
50 Mill Rd
Littleton, MA 01460
978-952-6448
j.galt1100@verizon.ent;
www.atlanticbladesmiths.com
Sell, trade, buy; carefully selected handcrafted, benchmade and factory knives

BALLARD CUTLERY
1495 Brummel Ave.
Elk Grove Village, IL 60007

BECK'S CUTLERY SPECIALTIES
Macgregor Village #109
107 Edinburgh S
Cary, NC 27511
919-460-0203
www.beckscutlery.com
Knives

BLADEGALLERY.COM
107 Central Way
Kirkland WA 98033
877-56-blade
www.bladegallery.com

Bladegallery.com specializes in hand-made one-of-a-kind knives from around the world. We have an emphasis on forged knives and high-end gentlemen's folders

BLUE RIDGE KNIVES
166 Adwolfe Rd
Marion, VA 24354-6664
276-783-6143; 276-783-9298
www.blueridgeknives.com
Wholesale distributor of knives

BOB NEAL CUSTOM KNIVES
PO Box 20923
Atlanta, GA 30320
770-914-7794; 770-914-7796
bob@bobnealcustomknives.com;
www.bobnealcustomknives.com
Exclusive limited edition custom knives-sets & single

BOB'S TRADING POST
308 N Main St
Hutchinson, KS 67501
620-669-9441
bobstradingpost@cox.net
Tad custom knives with reichert custom sheaths one at a time, one of a kind

BOONE TRADING CO., INC.
PO Box 669
Brinnon, WA 98320
800-423-1945
www.boonetrading.com
Ivory scrimshaw horns

CARMEL CUTLERY
Dolores & 6th; PO Box 1346
Carmel, CA 93921
831-624-6699; 831-624-6780
ccutlery@ix.netcom.com;
www.carmelcutlery.com
Quality custom and a variety of production pocket knives, swords; kitchen cutlery; personal grooming items

CLASSIC CUTLERY
5 Logan Rd
Nashua, NH 03063
603-881-3776
yesdragonfly@earthlink.net
Custom knives, gemstones, high quality factory knives

CREATIVE SALES & MFG.
Box 111
Whitefish, MT 59937
406-849-5174; 406-849-5130
www.creativesales.com

CUTLERY SHOPPE
3956 E Vantage Pointe Ln
Meridian, ID 83642
800-231-1272; 208-884-4433
order@cutleryshoppe.com;
www.cutleryshoppe.com
Discount pricing on top quality brands

CUTTING EDGE, THE
1920 North 26th St
Lowell, AR 72745-8489
479-631-0055; 479-636-4618
ce_cuttingedge.com; www.cuttingedge.com
After-market knives since 1968. We offer about 1,000 individual knives for sale each month. Subscription by first class mail, in U.S. $20 per year, Canada or Mexico by air mail, $25 per year. All overseas by air mail, $40 per year. The oldest and the most experienced in the business of buying and selling knives. We buy collections of any size, take knives on consignment. Every month there are 4-8 pages in color featuring the work of top makers

DENTON, J.W.
102 N. Main St, Box 429
Hiawassee, GA 30546
706-896-2292; 706-896-1212
jwdenton@alltel.net
Loveless knives

DUNN KNIVES INC.
PO Box 204
Rossville, KS 66533
785-584-6856; 785-584-6856

EPICUREAN EDGE, THE
107 Central Way
Kirkland, WA 98033
425-889-5980
www.epicureanedge.com
The Epicurean Edge specializes in high-end chef's knives from around the world. We have an empasis on handmade and hard to find knives

FAZALARE, ROY
PO Box 1335
Agoura Hills, CA 91376
818-879-6161 after 7pm
ourfaz@aol.com
Handmade multiblades; older case; Fight'n Rooster; Bulldog brand & Cripple Creek

FROST CUTLERY CO.
PO Box 22636
Chattanooga, TN 37422

GENUINE ISSUE, INC.
949 Middle Country Rd.
Selden, NY 11784
516-696-3802; 516-696-3803
g.l._cutlery.com
All knives

GEORGE TICHBOURNE CUSTOM KNIVES
7035 Maxwell Rd #5
Mississauga Ontario L5S 1R5
CANADA
905-670-0200
sales@tichbourneknives.com;
www.tichbourneknives.com
*Canadian custom knifemaker has full retail
knife store*

GODWIN, INC. G. GEDNEY
2139 Welsh Valley Rd
Valley Forge, PA 19481
610-783-0670; 610-783-6083
www.gggodwin.com
18th century reproductions

GUILD KNIVES
320 Paani Place 1A
Paia, HI 96779
808-877-3109; 808-877-3524
donguild1@aol.com; www.guildkives.com
Purveyor of custom art knives

HAWTHORN GALLERIES, INC.
214 E Walnut St
Springfield, MO 65806
417-866-6688; 417-866-6693
hginc@sbcglobal.net
Heritage Antique Knives

BRUCE VOYLES
PO Box 22171
Chattanooga, TN 37422
423-238-6753; 423-238-6711
bruce@jbrucevoyles.com;
www.jbrucevoyles.com
Knives, knife auctions

HOUSE OF TOOLS LTD.
#136, 8228 Macleod Tr. SE
Calgary, Alberta, Canada
T2H 2B8

HUNTER SERVICES
Fred Hunter
PO Box 14241
Parkville, MD 64152

JENCO SALES, INC.
PO Box 1000
Manchaca, TX 78652
800-531-5301; 800-266-2373
jencosales@sbcglobal.net
Wholesale only

KELLAM KNIVES CO.
902 S Dixie Hwy
Lantana, FL 33462
561-588-3185; 800-390-6918; 561-588-3186
info@kellamknives.com; www.kellamknives.com
*Largest selection of Finnish knives; own line
of folders and fixed blades*

KNIFEART.COM
13301 Pompano Dr
Little Rock AR 72211
501-221-1010; 501-221-2695
www.knifeart.com
*Large internet seller of custom knives &
upscale production knives*

KNIFE IMPORTERS, INC.
PO Box 1000
Manchaca, TX 78652

KNIFEMASTERS CUSTOM KNIVES/J&S FEDER
PO Box 208
Westport, CT 06881
(203) 226-5211; (203) 226-5312
Investment grade custom knives

KNIVES PLUS
2467 I 40 West
Amarillo, TX 79109
800-687-6202
*Retail cutlery and cutlery accessories since
1987*

KRIS CUTLERY
PO Box 133 KN
Pinole, CA 94564
510-223-8968
kriscutlery@attbl.com; www.kriscutlery.com
Japanese, medieval, Chinese & Philippine

CUSTOM KNIFE CONSIGNMENT
PO Box 20923
Atlanta, GA 30320
770-914-7794; 770-914-7796
bob@customknifeconsignment.com;
www.customknifeconsignment.com
We sell your knives

LES COUTEAUX CHOISSIS DE ROBERTS
Ron Roberts
PO Box 273
Mifflin, PA 17058

LONE STAR WHOLESALE
PO Box 587
Amarillo, TX 79105
806-356-9540; 806-359-1603
*Wholesale only; major brands and
accessories*

MATTHEWS CUTLERY
4401 Sentry Dr., Suite K
Tucker, GA 30084

MOORE CUTLERY
PO Box 633
Lockport, IL 60441-0633
708-301-4201; 708-301-4222
gary@knives.cx; www.knives.cx
*Owned & operated by Gary Moore since
1991. (A full-time dealer) Purveyor of high
quality custom & production knives*

MORTY THE KNIFE MAN, INC.
4 Manorhaven Blvd
Port Washington, NY 11050

MUSEUM REPLICAS LTD.
2143 Gees Mill Rd
Conyers, GA 30207
800-883-8838
www.museumreplicas.com
*Historically accurate and battle ready swords
& daggers*

NORDIC KNIVES
1634 CZ Copenhagen Dr.
Solvang, CA 93463
805-688-3612
info@nordicknives.com; www.nordicknives.com
Custom and Randall knives

OAKES WINSTON
431 Deauville Dr
Dayton, OH 45429
937-434-3112
*Dealer in Bose JessHorn, Michael Walker &
other quality knives. Some tactical folders.
$100-$7,000*

PARKER'S KNIFE COLLECTOR SERVICE
6715 Heritage Business Court
Chattanooga, TN 37422
423-892-0448; 423-892-0448
bbknife@bellsouth.net

PEN AND THE SWORD LTD., THE
Po Box 290741
Brooklyn, NY 11229 0741
(718) 382-4847; (718) 376-5745
info@pensword.com
*Custom folding knives, engraving, scrimshaw,
Case knives, English fruit knives, antique
pocket knives*

PLAZA CUTLERY, INC.
3333 S. Bristol St., Suite 2060
South Coast Plaza
Costa Mesa, CA 92626
714-549-3932
dan@plazacutlery.com; www.plazacutlery.com
*Largest selection of knives on the west coast.
Custom makers from beginners to the best.
All customs, William Henry, Strider, Reeves,
Randalls & others available online by phone*

ROBERTSON'S CUSTOM CUTLERY
PO Box 1367
Evans, GA 30809-1367
706-650-0252; 706-860-1623
customknives@comcast.net;
www.robertsoncustomcutlery.com
*World class custom knives, Vanguard knives -
Limited exclusive design*

ROBINSON, ROBERT W.
1569 N. Finley Pt
Polson, MT 59860

SHADOW JAY & KAREN
9719 N Hayden Rd
Scottsdale, AZ 85258
480-947-2136; 480-481-2977
jaykar@cox.net; www.jaykar.com
Diamonds imported direct from Belgium

SMOKY MOUNTAIN KNIFE WORKS
2320 Winfield Dunn Pkwy
Sevierville, TN 37876
865-453-5871; 800-251-9306
info@smkw.com; www.eknifeworks.com
*The world's largest knife showplace, catalog
and website*

**STIDHAM'S KNIVES/DBA MEADOWS' EDGE
KNIFE SHOP**
PO Box 160
Meadows of Dan, VA 24120
276-952-2500; 276-952-6245
rstidham@gate.net;
www.randallknifesociety.com
*Randall, Loveless, Scagel, moran, antique
pocket knives*

STODDARD'S, INC.
Copley Place 25
100 Huntington Ave
Boston, MA 02116
617-536-8688; 617-536-8689
*Cutlery (kitchen, pocket knives, Randall-made
knives, custom knives, scissors & manicure
tools) binoculars, Iwo vision aids, personal
care items (hair brushes, manicure sets
mirrors)*

knife services

appraisers

Levine, Bernard, P.O. Box 2404, Eugene, OR, 97402, 541-484-0294, brlevine@ix.netcom.com

Russell, A.G., Knives Inc, 1920 North 26th St, Lowell, AR, 72745-8489, 479-631-0055, 479-636-4618, ag@agrussell.com, www.agrussell.com

Vallini, Massimo, Via G. Bruno 7, 20154 Milano, ITALY, 02-33614751, massimo_vallini@yahoo.it, Knife expert

custom grinders

Beauchamp, Gaetan, 125 de la Riviere, Stoneham, PQ, G0A 4P0, CANADA, 418-848-1914, (418) 848-6859, knives@gbeauchamp.ca, www.beauchamp.cjb.net

McGowan Manufacturing Company, 4854 N Shamrock Pl #100, Tucson, AZ, 85705, 800-342-4810, 520-219-0884, info@mcgowanmfg.com, www.mcgowanmfg.com, Knife sharpeners, hunting axes

McLuin, Tom, 36 Fourth St., Dracut, MA, 01826, 978-957-4899, tmcluin@attbi.com, www.people.ne.mediaone.net/tmcluin

Peele, Bryan, The Elk Rack, 215 Ferry St. P.O. Box 1363, Thompson Falls, MT, 59873

Schlott, Harald, Zingster Str. 26, 13051 Berlin, GERMANY, 049 030 9293346, harald.schlott@T-online.de, Custom grinder, custom handle artisan, display case/box maker, etcher, scrimshander

Wilson, R.W., P.O. Box 2012, Weirton, WV, 26062

custom handles

Cooper, Jim, 1221 Cook St, Ramona, CA, 92065-3214, 760-789-1097, (760) 788-7992, jamcooper@aol.com

Burrows, Chuck, dba Wild Rose Trading Co, 289 Laposta Canyon Rd, Durango, CO, 81303, 970-259-8396, chuck@wrtcleather.com, www.wrtcleather.com

Fields, Donald, 790 Tamerlane St, Deltona, FL, 32725, 386-532-9070, donaldfields@aol.com, Selling ancient ivories; mammoth & fossil walrus

Grussenmeyer, Paul G., 310 Kresson Rd, Cherry Hill, NJ, 08034, 856-428-1088, 856-428-8997, pgrussentne@comcast.net, www.pgcarvings.com

Holland, Dennis K., 4908-17th Pl., Lubbock, TX, 79416

Imboden II, Howard L., hi II Originals, 620 Deauville Dr., Dayton, OH, 45429

Kelso, Jim, 577 Collar Hill Rd, Worcester, VT, 05682, 802-229-4254, (802) 223-0595

Knack, Gary, 309 Wightman, Ashland, OR, 97520

Marlatt, David, 67622 Oldham Rd., Cambridge, OH, 43725, 740-432-7549

Mead, Dennis, 2250 E. Mercury St., Inverness, FL, 34453-0514

Myers, Ron, 6202 Marglenn Ave., Baltimore, MD, 21206, 410-866-6914

Saggio, Joe, 1450 Broadview Ave. #12, Columbus, OH, 43212, jvsag@webtv.net, www.j.v.saggio@worldnet.att.net, Handle Carver

Schlott, Harald, Zingster Str. 26, 13051 Berlin, GERMANY, 049 030 9293346, harald.schlott@T-online.de, Custom grinder, custom handle artisan, display case/box maker, etcher, scrimshander

Snell, Barry A., 4801 96th St. N., St. Petersburg, FL, 33708-3740

Vallotton, A., 621 Fawn Ridge Dr., Oakland, OR, 97462

Watson, Silvia, 350 Jennifer Lane, Driftwood, TX, 78619

Wilderness Forge, 315 North 100 East, Kanab, UT, 84741, 435-644-3674, bhatting@xpressweb.com

Williams, Gary, (GARBO), PO Box 210, Glendale, KY, 42740-2010

display cases and boxes

Bill's Custom Cases, P O Box 603, Montague, CA, 96064, 530-459-5968, billscustomcases@earthlink.net

Brooker, Dennis, Rt. 1, Box 12A, Derby, IA, 50068

Chas Clements' Custom Leathercraft, Chas, 1741 Dallas St., Aurora, CO, 80010-2018, 303-364-0403, GRYPHONS@HOME.NET, Display case/box maker, Leatherworker, Knife appraiser

Freund, Steve, Tomway LLC, 1646 Tichenor Court, Atlanta, GA, 30338, 770-393-8349, steve@tomway.com, www.tomway.com

Gimbert, Nelson, P.O. Box 787, Clemmons, NC, 27012

McLean, Lawrence, 12344 Meritage Ct, Rancho Cucamonga, CA, 91739, 714-848-5779, lmclean@charter.net

Miller, Michael K., M&M Kustom Krafts, 28510 Santiam Highway, Sweet Home, OR, 97386

Miller, Robert, P.O. Box 2722, Ormond Beach, FL, 32176

Retichek, Joseph L., W9377 Co. TK. D, Beaver Dam, WI, 53916

Robbins, Wayne, 11520 Inverway, Belvidere, IL, 61008

S&D Enterprises, 20 East Seventh St, Manchester, OH, 45144, 937-549-2602, 937-549-2602, sales@s-denterprises.com, www.s-denterprises.com, Display case/box maker. Manufacturer of aluminum display, chipboard type displays, wood displays. Silk screening or acid etching for logos on product.

Schlott, Harald, Zingster Str. 26, 13051 Berlin, GERMANY, 049 030 9293346, harald.schlott@T-online.de, Custom grinder, custom handle artisan, display case/box maker, etcher, scrimshander

engravers

Adlam, Tim, 1705 Witzel Ave., Oshkosh, WI, 54902, 920-235-4589, www.adlamngraving.com

Alfano, Sam, 36180 Henry Gaines Rd., Pearl River, LA, 70452

Allard, Gary, 2395 Battlefield Rd., Fishers Hill, VA, 22626

Alpen, Ralph, 7 Bentley Rd., West Grove, PA, 19390, 610-869-7141

Baron, David, Baron Technology Inc., 62 Spring Hill Rd., Trumbull, CT, 06611, 203-452-0515, bti@baronengraving.com, www.baronengraving.com, Polishing, plating, inlays, artwork

Bates, Billy, 2302 Winthrop Dr. SW, Decatur, AL, 35603, bbrn@aol.com, www.angelfire.com/al/billybates

Bettenhausen, Merle L., 17358 Ottawa, Tinley Park, IL, 60477

Blair, Jim, PO Box 64, 59 Mesa Verde, Glenrock, WY, 82637, 307-436-8115, jblairengrav@msn.com

Bonshire, Benita, 1121 Burlington, Muncie, IN, 47302

Boster, A.D., 3000 Clarks Bridge Rd Lot 42, Gainesville, GA, 30501, 770-532-0958

Brooker, Dennis B., Rt. 1 Box 12A, Derby, IA, 50068

Churchill, Winston G., RFD Box 29B, Proctorsville, VT, 05153

Collins, Michael, Rt. 3075, Batesville Rd., Woodstock, GA, 30188

Cupp, Alana, PO Box 207, Annabella, UT, 84711

Dashwood, Jim, 255 Barkham Rd., Wokingham, Berkshire RG11 4BY, ENGLAND

Dean, Bruce, 13 Tressider Ave., Haberfield, N.S.W. 2045, Sydney, AUSTRALIA, 02 97977608

DeLorge, Ed, 6734 W Main St, Houma, LA, 70360, 504-223-0206

Dickson, John W., PO Box 49914, Sarasota, FL, 34230

Dolbare, Elizabeth, PO Box 502, Dubois, WY, 82513-0502

Downing, Jim, PO Box 4224, Springfield, MO, 65808, 417-865-5953, www.thegunengraver.com, Scrimshander

Duarte, Carlos, 108 Church St., Rossville, CA, 95678

Dubben, Michael, 414 S. Fares Ave., Evansville, IN, 47714

Dubber, Michael W., 8205 Heather Pl, Evansville, IN, 47710-4919

Eklund, Maihkel, Föne 1111, S-82041 Färila, SWEDEN, www.art-knives.com

Eldridge, Allan, 1424 Kansas Lane, Gallatin, TN, 37066

Ellis, Willy B, Willy B's Customs by William B Ellis, 4941 Cardinal Trail, Palm Harbor, FL, 34683, 727-942-6420, www.willyb.com

Engel, Terry (Flowers), PO Box 96, Midland, OR, 97634

Flannery Engraving Co., Jeff, 11034 Riddles Run Rd., Union, KY, 41091, engraving@fuse.net, http://home.fuse.net/engraving/

Foster, Norvell, Foster Enterprises, PO Box 200343, San Antonio, TX, 78220

Fountain Products, 492 Prospect Ave., West Springfield, MA, 01089

Gipe, Sandi, Rt. 2, Box 1090A, Kendrick, ID, 83537

Glimm, Jerome C., 19 S. Maryland, Conrad, MT, 59425

Gournet, Geoffroy, 820 Paxinosa Ave., Easton, PA, 18042, 610-559-0710, www.geoffroygournet.com

Harrington, Fred A., Winter: 3725 Citrus, Summer: 2107 W Frances Rd Mt Morris MI 48458-8215, St. James City, FL, 33956, Winter: 239-283-0721 Summer: 810-686-3008

Henderson, Fred D., 569 Santa Barbara Dr., Forest Park, GA, 30297, 770-968-4866

Hendricks, Frank, 396 Bluff Trail, Dripping Springs, TX, 78620, 512-858-7828

Holder, Pat, 7148 W. Country Gables Dr., Peoria, AZ, 85381

Hudson, Tommy, 1181 E 22nd St. Suite #18, Marysville, CA, 95901, 530-681-6531, twhunson@attbi.com, www.picturetrail.com/tommyhudson

Ingle, Ralph W., 151 Callan Dr., Rossville, GA, 30741, 706-858-0641, riengraver@aol.com, Photographer

Johns, Bill, 1716 8th St, Cody, WY, 82414, 307-587-5090

Kelly, Lance, 1723 Willow Oak Dr., Edgewater, FL, 32132

Kelso, Jim, 577 Coller Hill Rd, Worcester, VT, 05682

Koevenig, Eugene and Eve, Koevenig's Engraving Service, Rabbit Gulch, Box 55, Hill City, SD, 57745-0055

Kostelnik, Joe and Patty, RD #4, Box 323, Greensburg, PA, 15601

Kudlas, John M., 55280 Silverwolf Dr, Barnes, WI, 54873, 715-795-2031, jkudlas@cheqnet.net, Engraver, scrimshander

Limings Jr., Harry, 959 County Rd. 170, Marengo, OH, 43334-9625

Lindsay, Steve, 3714 West Cedar Hills Drive, Kearney, NE, 68847

Lyttle, Brian, Box 5697, High River AB CANADA, T1V 1M7

Lytton, Simon M., 19 Pinewood Gardens, Hemel Hempstead, Herts. HP1 1TN, ENGLAND

Mason, Joe, 146 Value Rd, Brandon, MS, 39042, 601-824-9867, www.joemasonengraving.com

McCombs, Leo, 1862 White Cemetery Rd., Patriot, OH, 45658

McDonald, Dennis, 8359 Brady St., Peosta, IA, 52068

McKenzie, Lynton, 6940 N Alvernon Way, Tucson, AZ, 85718

McLean, Lawrence, 12344 Meritage Ct, Rancho Cucamonga, CA, 91739, 714-848-5779, lmclean@charter.net

Meyer, Chris, 39 Bergen Ave., Wantage, NJ, 07461, 973-875-6299

Minnick, Joyce, 144 N. 7th St., Middletown, IN, 47356

Morgan, Tandie, P.O. Box 693, 30700 Hwy. 97, Nucla, CO, 81424

Morton, David A., 1110 W. 21st St., Lorain, OH, 44052

Moulton, Dusty, 135 Hillview Ln, Loudon, TN, 37774, 865-408-9779

Muller, Jody & Pat, PO Box 35, Pittsburg, MO, 65724, 417-852-4306/417-752-3260, mullerforge@hotmail.com, www.mullerforge.com

Nelida, Toniutti, via G. Pasconi 29/c, Maniago 33085 (PN), ITALY

Nott, Ron, Box 281, Summerdale, PA, 17093

Parsons, Michael R., McKee Knives, 7042 McFarland Rd, Indianapolis, IN, 46227, 317-784-7943

Patterson, W.H., P.O. Drawer DK, College Station, TX, 77841

Peri, Valerio, Via Meucci 12, Gardone V.T. 25063, ITALY

Pilkington Jr., Scott, P.O. Box 97, Monteagle, TN, 37356, 931-924-3400, scott@pilkguns.com, www.pilkguns.com

Poag, James, RR1, Box 212A, Grayville, IL, 62844

Potts, Wayne, 1580 Meade St Apt A, Denver, CO, 80204

Rabeno, Martin, Spook Hollow Trading Co, 530 Eagle Pass, Durango, CO, 81301

Raftis, Andrew, 2743 N. Sheffield, Chicago, IL, 60614

Roberts, J.J., 7808 Lake Dr., Manassas, VA, 20111, 703-330-0448, jjrengraver@aol.com, www.angelfire.com/va2/engraver

Robidoux, Roland J., DMR Fine Engraving, 25 N. Federal Hwy. Studio 5, Dania, FL, 33004

Rosser, Bob, Hand Engraving, 2809 Crescent Ave Ste 20, Homewood, AL, 35209-2526, www.hand-engravers.com

Rudolph, Gil, 20922 Oak Pass Ave, Tehachapi, CA, 93561, 661-822-4949, www.gtraks@csurfers.net

Rundell, Joe, 6198 W. Frances Rd., Clio, MI, 48420

Schickl, L., Ottingweg 497, A-5580 Tamsweg, AUSTRIA, 0043 6474 8583, Scrimshander

Schlott, Harald, Zingster Str. 26, 13051 Berlin, GERMANY, 049 030 9293346, 049 030 9293346, harald.schlott@T-online.de, www.gravur-kunst-atelier.de.vu, Custom grinder, custom handle artisan, display case/box maker, etcher, scrimshander

Schönert, Elke, 18 Lansdowne Pl., Central, Port Elizabeth, SOUTH AFRICA

Shaw, Bruce, P.O. Box 545, Pacific Grove, CA, 93950, 831-646-1937, 831-644-0941

Shostle, Ben, 1121 Burlington, Muncie, IN, 47302

Sinclair, W.P., The Roost Mill Lade, Blyth Bridge, Peeblesshire EH46 7HY, SCOTLAND, 44 0 1721 752787, songdog@clara.net

Smith, Ron, 5869 Straley, Ft. Worth, TX, 76114

Smitty's Engraving, 21320 Pioneer Circle, Hurrah, OK, 73045, 405-454-6968, smittys.engraving@prodigy.net, www.smittys-engraving.us

Spode, Peter, Tresaith Newland, Malvern, Worcestershire WR13 5AY, ENGLAND

Swartley, Robert D., 2800 Pine St., Napa, CA, 94558

Takeuchi, Shigetoshi, 21-14-1-Chome kamimuneoka Shiki shi, 353 Saitama, JAPAN

Theis, Terry, 21452 FM 2093, Harper, TX, 78631, 830-864-4438

Valade, Robert B., 931 3rd Ave., Seaside, OR, 97138, 503-738-7672, (503) 738-7672

Waldrop, Mark, 14562 SE 1st Ave. Rd., Summerfield, FL, 34491

Warenski, Julie, 590 East 500 N., Richfield, UT, 84701, 435-896-5319, julie@warenskiknives.com, www.warenskiknives.com

Warren, Kenneth W., P.O. Box 2842, Wenatchee, WA, 98807-2842, 509-663-6123, (509) 663-6123

Whitehead, James D., 204 Cappucino Way, Sacramento, CA, 95838

Whitmore, Jerry, 1740 Churchill Dr., Oakland, OR, 97462

Winn, Travis A., 558 E. 3065 S., Salt Lake City, UT, 84106

Wood, Mel, P.O. Box 1255, Sierra Vista, AZ, 85636

Zietz, Dennis, 5906 40th Ave., Kenosha, WI, 53144

etchers

Baron Technology Inc., David Baron, 62 Spring Hill Rd., Trumbull, CT, 06611

Fountain Products, 492 Prospect Ave., West Springfield, MA, 01089

Hayes, Dolores, P.O. Box 41405, Los Angeles, CA, 90041

Holland, Dennis, 4908 17th Pl., Lubbock, TX, 79416

Kelso, Jim, 577 Collar Hill Rd, Worcester, VT, 05682

Larstein, Francine, FRANCINE ETCHINGS & ETCHED KNIVES, 368 White Rd, Watsonville, CA, 95076, 800-557-1525/831-426-6046, 831-684-1949, francine@francineetchings.com, www.francineetchings.com

Lefaucheux, Jean-Victor, Saint-Denis-Le-Ferment, 27140 Gisors, FRANCE

Mead, Faustina L., 2550 E. Mercury St., Inverness, FL, 34453-0514, 352-344-4751, scrimsha@infionline.net, www.scrimshaw-by-faustina.com

Myers, Ron, 6202 Marglenn Ave., Baltimore, MD, 21206, (acid) etcher

Schlott, Harald, Zingster Str. 26, 13051 Berlin, GERMANY, 049 030 9293346, harald.schlott@T-online.de, Custom grinder, custom handle artisan, display case/box maker, etcher, scrimshander

Vallotton, A., Northwest Knife Supply, 621 Fawn Ridge Dr., Oakland, OR, 97462

Watson, Silvia, 350 Jennifer Lane, Driftwood, TX, 78619

heat treaters

Bay State Metal Treating Co., 6 Jefferson Ave., Woburn, MA, 01801

Bos Heat Treating, Paul, Shop: 1900 Weld Blvd., El Cajon, CA, 92020, 619-562-2370 / 619-445-4740 Home, PaulBos@BuckKnives.com

Holt, B.R., 1238 Birchwood Drive, Sunnyvale, CA, 94089

Kazou, Okaysu, 12-2 1 Chome Higashi, Ueno, Taito-Ku, Tokyo, JAPAN, 81-33834-2323, 81-33831-3012

Metal Treating Bodycote Inc., 710 Burns St., Cincinnati, OH, 45204

O&W Heat Treat Inc., One Bidwell Rd., South Windsor, CT, 06074, 860-528-9239, (860) 291-9939, owht1@aol.com

Progressive Heat Treating Co., 2802 Charles City Rd, Richmond, VA, 23231, 804-545-0010, 804-545-0012

Texas Heat Treating Inc., 303 Texas Ave., Round Rock, TX, 78664

Texas Knifemakers Supply, 10649 Haddington, Suite 180, Houston, TX, 77043

Tinker Shop, The, 1120 Helen, Deer Park, TX, 77536

Valley Metal Treating Inc., 355 S. East End Ave., Pomona, CA, 91766

Wilderness Forge, 315 North 100 East, Kanab, UT, 84741, 435-644-3674, bhatting@xpressweb.com

Wilson, R.W., P.O. Box 2012, Weirton, WV, 26062

leather workers

Abramson, David, 116 Baker Ave, Wharton, NJ, 07885, lifter4him1@aol.com, www.liftersleather.com

Bruner, Rick, 7756 Aster Lane, Jenison, MI, 49428, 616-457-0403

Burrows, Chuck, dba Wild Rose Trading Co, 289 Laposta Canyon Rd, Durango, CO, 81303, 970-259-8396, chuck@wrtcleather.com

Clements' Custom Leathercraft, Chas, 1741 Dallas St., Aurora, CO, 80010-2018

Cooper, Harold, 136 Winding Way, Frankfort, KY, 40601

Cooper, Jim, 1221 Cook St, Ramona, CA, 92065-3214, 760-789-1097, 760-788-7992, jamcooper@aol.com

Cow Catcher Leatherworks, 3006 Industrial Dr, Raleigh, NC, 27609

Cubic, George, GC Custom Leather Co., 10561 E. Deerfield Pl., Tucson, AZ, 85749, 520-760-0695, gcubic@aol.com

Dawkins, Dudley, 221 N. Broadmoor Ave, Topeka, KS, 66606-1254, 785-235-3871, dawkind@sbcglobal.net, ABS member/knifemaker forges straight knives

Evans, Scott V, Edge Works Mfg, 1171 Halltown Rd, Jacksonville, NC, 28546, 910-455-9834, (910) 346-5660, edgeworks@coastalnet.com, www.tacticalholsters.com

Genske, Jay, 283 Doty St, Fond du Lac, WI, 54935, 920-921-8019/Cell Phone 920-579-0144, jaygenske@hotmail.com, Custom Grinder, Custom Handle Artisan

Hawk, Ken, Rt. 1, Box 770, Ceres, VA, 24318-9630

Homyk, David N., 8047 Carriage Ln., Wichita Falls, TX, 76306

John's Custom Leather, John R. Stumpf, 523 S. Liberty St, Blairsville, PA, 15717, 724-459-6802, 724-459-5996

Kravitt, Chris, HC 31 Box 6484, Rt 200, Ellsworth, ME, 04605-9805, 207-584-3000, 207-584-3000, sheathmkr@aol.com, www.treestumpleather.com, Reference: Tree Stump Leather

Larson, Richard, 549 E. Hawkeye, Turlock, CA, 95380

Layton, Jim, 2710 Gilbert Avenue, Portsmouth, OH, 45662

Lee, Randy, P.O. Box 1873, 270 N 9th West, St. Johns, AZ, 85936, 928-337-2594, 928-337-5002, randylee@randyleeknives.com, info@randyleeknives.com, Custom knifemaker

Long, Paul, 108 Briarwood Ln W, Kerrville, TX, 78028, 830-367-5536, kgebauer@classicnet.net

Mason, Arne, 258 Wimer St., Ashland, OR, 97520, 541-482-2260, (541) 482-7785, www.arnemason.com

McGowan, Liz, 12629 Howard Lodge Dr., Winter Add-2023 Robin Ct Sebring FL 33870, Sykesville, MD, 21784, 410-489-4323

Metheny, H.A. "Whitey", 7750 Waterford Dr., Spotsylvania, VA, 22553, 540-582-3228 Cell 540-542-1440, 540-582-3095, nametheny@aol.com, www.methenyknives.com

Miller, Michael K., 28510 Santiam Highway, Sweet Home, OR, 97386

Mobley, Martha, 240 Alapaha River Road, Chula, GA, 31733

Morrissey, Martin, 4578 Stephens Rd., Blairsville, GA, 30512

Niedenthal, John Andre, Beadwork & Buckskin, Studio 3955 NW 103 Dr., Coral Springs, FL, 33065-1551, 954-345-0447, a_niedenthal@hotmail.com

Neilson, Tess, RR2 Box 16, Wyalusing, PA, 18853, 570-746-4944, www.mountainhollow.net, Doing business as Neilson's Mountain Hollow

Parsons, Michael R., McKee Knives, 7042 McFarland Rd, Indianapolis, IN, 46227, 317-784-7943

Poag, James H., RR #1 Box 212A, Grayville, IL, 62844

Red's Custom Leather, Ed Todd, 9 Woodlawn Rd., Putnam Valley, NY, 10579, 845-528-3783

Rowe, Kenny, 3219 Hwy 29 South, Hope, AR, 71801, 870-777-8216, 870-777-0935, rowesleather@yahoo.com, www.knifeart.com or www.theedgeequipment.com

Schrap, Robert G., 7024 W. Wells St., Wauwatosa, WI, 53213-3717, 414-771-6472, (414) 479-9765, knifesheaths@aol.com, www.customsheaths.com

Strahin, Robert, 401 Center St., Elkins, WV, 26241, *Custom Knife Sheaths

Tierney, Mike, 447 Rivercrest Dr., Woodstock ON CANADA, N4S 5W5

Turner, Kevin, 17 Hunt Ave., Montrose, NY, 10548

Velasquez, Gil, 7120 Madera Dr., Goleta, CA, 93117

Walker, John, 17 Laber Circle, Little Rock, AR, 72210, 501-455-0239, john.walker@afbic.com

Watson, Bill, #1 Presidio, Wimberly, TX, 78676

Whinnery, Walt, 1947 Meadow Creek Dr., Louisville, KY, 40218

Williams, Sherman A., 1709 Wallace St., Simi Valley, CA, 93065

miscellaneous

Hendryx Design, Scott, 5997 Smokey Way, Boise, ID, 83714, 208-377-8044, www.shdsheaths@msn.com
Kydex Sheath Maker

Robertson, Kathy, Impress by Design, PO Box 1367, Evans, GA, 30809-1367, 706-650-0982, (706) 860-1623, impressbydesign@comcast.net, Advertising/graphic designer

Strahin, Robert, 401 Center St., Elkins, WV, 26241, 304-636-0128, rstrahin@copper.net, *Custom Knife Sheaths

photographers

Alfano, Sam, 36180 Henery Gaines Rd., Pearl River, LA, 70452

Allen, John, Studio One, 3823 Pleasant Valley Blvd., Rockford, IL, 61114

Bilal, Mustafa, Turk's Head Productions, 908 NW 50th St., Seattle, WA, 98107-3634, 206-782-4164, (206) 783-5677, mustafa@turkshead.com, www.turkshead.com, Graphic design, marketing & advertising

Bogaerts, Jan, Regenweg 14, 5757 Pl., Liessel, HOLLAND

Box Photography, Doug, 1804 W Main St, Brenham, TX, 77833-3420

Brown, Tom, 6048 Grants Ferry Rd., Brandon, MS, 39042-8136

Butman, Steve, P.O. Box 5106, Abilene, TX, 79608

Calidonna, Greg, 205 Helmwood Dr., Elizabethtown, KY, 42701

Campbell, Jim, 7935 Ranch Rd., Port Richey, FL, 34668

Cooper, Jim, Sharpbycoop.com photography, 9 Mathew Court, Norwalk, CT, 06851, jcooper@sharpbycoop.com, www.sharpbycoop.com

Courtice, Bill, P.O. Box 1776, Duarte, CA, 91010-4776

Crosby, Doug, RFD 1, Box 1111, Stockton Springs, ME, 04981

Danko, Michael, 3030 Jane Street, Pittsburgh, PA, 15203

Davis, Marshall B., P.O. Box 3048, Austin, TX, 78764

Earley, Don, 1241 Ft. Bragg Rd., Fayetteville, NC, 28305

Ehrlich, Linn M., 1850 N Clark St #1008, Chicago, IL, 60614, 312-209-2107

Etzler, John, 11200 N. Island Rd., Grafton, OH, 44044

Fahrner, Dave, 1623 Arnold St., Pittsburgh, PA, 15205

Faul, Jan W., 903 Girard St. NE, Rr. Washington, DC, 20017

Fedorak, Allan, 28 W. Nicola St., Amloops BC CANADA, V2C 1J6

Forster, Jenny, 534 Nantucket Way, Island Lake, IL, 60042, www.thesilkca.msn.com

Fox, Daniel, Lumina Studios, 6773 Industrial Parkway, Cleveland, OH, 44070, 440-734-2118, (440) 734-3542, lumina@en.com

Freiberg, Charley, PO Box 42, Elkins, NH, 03233, 603-526-2767, charleyfreiberg@tos.net

Gardner, Chuck, 116 Quincy Ave., Oak Ridge, TN, 37830

Gawryla, Don, 1105 Greenlawn Dr., Pittsburgh, PA, 15220

Goffe Photographic Associates, 3108 Monte Vista Blvd., NE, Albuquerque, NM, 87106

Graham, James, 7434 E Northwest Hwy, Dallas, TX, 75231, 214-341-5138, jamie@jamiephoto.com, www.jamiephoto.com, Product photographer

Graley, Gary W., RR2 Box 556, Gillett, PA, 16925

Griggs, Dennis, 118 Pleasant Pt Rd, Topsham, ME, 04086, 207-725-5689

Hanusin, John, Reames-Hanusin Studio, PO Box 931, Northbrook, IL, 60065 0931

Hardy, Scott, 639 Myrtle Ave., Placerville, CA, 95667

Hodge, Tom, 7175 S US Hwy 1 Lot 36, Titusville, FL, 32780-8172, 321-267-7989, egdoht@hotmail.com

Holter, Wayne V., 125 Lakin Ave., Boonsboro, MD, 21713, 301-416-2855, mackwayne@hotmail.com

Hopkins, David W, Hopkins Photography inc, 201 S Jefferson, Iola, KS, 66749, 620-365-7443, nhoppy@netks.net

Kerns, Bob, 18723 Birdseye Dr., Germantown, MD, 20874

LaFleur, Gordon, 111 Hirst, Box 1209, Parksville BC CANADA, V0R 270

Lear, Dale, 6544 Cora Mill Rd, Gallipolis, OH, 45631, 740-245-5482, dalelear@yahoo.com, Ebay Sales

LeBlanc, Paul, No. 3 Meadowbrook Cir., Melissa, TX, 75454

Lester, Dean, 2801 Junipero Ave Suite 212, Long Beach, CA, 90806-2140

Leviton, David A., A Studio on the Move, P.O. Box 2871, Silverdale, WA, 98383, 360-697-3452

Long, Gary W., 3556 Miller's Crossroad Rd., Hillsboro, TN, 37342

Long, Jerry, 402 E. Gladden Dr., Farmington, NM, 87401

Lum, Billy, 16307 Evening Star Ct., Crosby, TX, 77532

McCollum, Tom, P.O. Box 933, Lilburn, GA, 30226

Mitch Lum Website and Photography, 4616 25th Ave NE #563, Seattle, WA, 98105, mitch@mitchlum.com, www.mitchlum.com

Moake, Jim, 18 Council Ave., Aurora, IL, 60504

Moya Inc., 4212 S. Dixie Hwy., West Palm Beach, FL, 33405

Norman's Studio, 322 S. 2nd St., Vivian, LA, 71082

Owens, William T., Box 99, Williamsburg, WV, 24991

Palmer Studio, 2008 Airport Blvd., Mobile, AL, 36606

Payne, Robert G., P.O. Box 141471, Austin, TX, 78714

Peterson Photography, Kent, 230 Polk St., Eugene, OR, 97402, kdp@pond.net, www.pond.net/kdp

Pigott, John, 9095 Woodprint LN, Mason, OH, 45040

Point Seven, 810 Seneca St., Toledo, OH, 43608, 519-243-8880, www.pointsevenstudios.com

Rasmussen, Eric L., 1121 Eliason, Brigham City, UT, 84302

Rhoades, Cynthia J., Box 195, Clearmont, WY, 82835

Rice, Tim, PO Box 663, Whitefish, MT, 59937

Richardson, Kerry, 2520 Mimosa St., Santa Rosa, CA, 95405, 707-575-1875, kerry@sonic.net, www.sonic.net/~kerry

Ross, Bill, 28364 S. Western Ave. Suite 464, Rancho Palos Verdes, CA, 90275

Rubicam, Stephen, 14 Atlantic Ave., Boothbay Harbor, ME, 04538-1202

Rush, John D., 2313 Maysel, Bloomington, IL, 61701

Schreiber, Roger, 429 Boren Ave. N., Seattle, WA, 98109

Semmer, Charles, 7885 Cyd Dr., Denver, CO, 80221

Silver Images Photography, 2412 N Keystone, Flagstaff, AZ, 86004

Slobodian, Scott, 4101 River Ridge Dr., P.O. Box 1498, San Andreas, CA, 95249, 209-286-1980, (209) 286-1982, www.slobodianswords.com

Smith, Earl W., 5121 Southminster Rd., Columbus, OH, 43221

Smith, Randall, 1720 Oneco Ave., Winter Park, FL, 32789

Storm Photo, 334 Wall St., Kingston, NY, 12401

Surles, Mark, P.O. Box 147, Falcon, NC, 28342

Third Eye Photos, 140 E. Sixth Ave., Helena, MT, 59601

Thurber, David, P.O. Box 1006, Visalia, CA, 93279

Tighe, Brian, RR 1, Ridgeville ON CANADA, L0S 1M0, 905-892-2734, www.tigheknives.com

Towell, Steven L., 3720 N.W. 32nd Ave., Camas, WA, 98607, 360-834-9049, sltowell@netscape.net

Valley Photo, 2100 Arizona Ave., Yuma, AZ, 85364

Verno Studio, Jay, 3030 Jane Street, Pittsburgh, PA, 15203

Ward, Chuck, 1010 E North St, PO Box 2272, Benton, AR, 72018, 501-778-4329, chuckbop@aol.com

Weyer International, 2740 Nebraska Ave., Toledo, OH, 43607, 800-448-8424, (419) 534-2697, law-weyerinternational@msn.com, Books

Wise, Harriet, 242 Dill Ave., Frederick, MD, 21701

Worley, Holly, Worley Photography, 6360 W David Dr, Littleton, CO, 80128-5708, 303-257-8091, 720-981-2800, hsworley@aol.com, Products, Digital & Film

scrimshanders

Adlam, Tim, 1705 Witzel Ave., Oshkosh, WI, 54902, 920-235-4589, www.adlamngraving.com

Alpen, Ralph, 7 Bentley Rd., West Grove, PA, 19390, 610-869-7141

Anderson, Terry Jack, 10076 Birnamwoods Way, Riverton, UT, 84065-9073

Bailey, Mary W., 3213 Jonesboro Dr., Nashville, TN, 37214, mbscrim@aol.com, www.members.aol.com/mbscrim/scrim.html

Baker, Duane, 2145 Alum Creek Dr., Cambridge Park Apt. #10, Columbus, OH, 43207

Barrows, Miles, 524 Parsons Ave., Chillicothe, OH, 45601

Brady, Sandra, P.O. Box 104, Monclova, OH, 43542, 419-866-0435, (419) 867-0656, sandyscrim@hotmail.com, www.knifeshows.com

Beauchamp, Gaetan, 125 de la Riviere, Stoneham, PQ, G0A 4P0, CANADA, 418-848-1914, (418) 848-6859, knives@gbeauchamp.ca, www.beauchamp.cjb.net

Bellet, Connie, PO Box 151, Palermo, ME, 04354 0151, 207-993-2327, phwhitehawk@gwl.net

Benade, Lynn, 2610 Buckhurst Dr, Beachwood, OH, 44122, 216-464-0777, llbnc17@aol.com

Bonshire, Benita, 1121 Burlington Dr., Muncie, IN, 47302

Boone Trading Co. Inc., P.O. Box 669, Brinnon, WA, 98320, 800-423-1945, ww.boonetrading.com

Bryan, Bob, 1120 Oak Hill Rd., Carthage, MO, 64836

Byrne, Mary Gregg, 1018 15th St., Bellingham, WA, 98225-6604

Cable, Jerry, 332 Main St., Mt. Pleasant, PA, 15666

Caudill, Lyle, 7626 Lyons Rd., Georgetown, OH, 45121

Cole, Gary, PO Box 668, Naalehu, HI, 96772, 808-929-9775, 808-929-7371, www.community.webshots.com/album/11836830uqyeejirsz

Collins, Michael, Rt. 3075, Batesville Rd., Woodstock, GA, 30188

Conover, Juanita Rae, P.O. Box 70442, Eugene, OR, 97401, 541-747-1726 or 543-4851, juanitaraeconover@yahoo.com

Courtnage, Elaine, Box 473, Big Sandy, MT, 59520

Cover Jr., Raymond A., Rt. 1, Box 194, Mineral Point, MO, 63660

Cox, J. Andy, 116 Robin Hood Lane, Gaffney, SC, 29340

Dietrich, Roni, Wild Horse Studio, 1257 Cottage Dr, Harrisburg, PA, 17112, 717-469-0587, ronimd@aol

DiMarzo, Richard, 2357 Center Place, Birmingham, AL, 35205

Dolbare, Elizabeth, PO Box 502, Dubois, WY, 82513-0502

Eklund, Maihkel, Föne 1111, S-82041 Färila, SWEDEN, +46 6512 4192, maihkel.eklund@swipnet.se, www.art-knives.com

Eldridge, Allan, 1424 Kansas Lane, Gallatin, TN, 37066

Ellis, Willy b, Willy B's Customs by William B Ellis, 4941 Cardinal Trail, Palm Harbor, FL, 34683, 727-942-6420, www.willyb.com

Fisk, Dale, Box 252, Council, ID, 83612, dafisk@ctcweb.net

Foster Enterprises, Norvell Foster, P.O. Box 200343, San Antonio, TX, 78220

Fountain Products, 492 Prospect Ave., West Springfield, MA, 01089

Gill, Scott, 925 N. Armstrong St., Kokomo, IN, 46901

Halligan, Ed, 14 Meadow Way, Sharpsburg, GA, 30277, ehkiss@bellsouth.net

Hands, Barry Lee, 26192 East Shore Route, Bigfork, MT, 59911

Hargraves Sr., Charles, RR 3 Bancroft, Ontario CANADA, K0L 1C0

Harless, Star, c/o Arrow Forge, P.O. Box 845, Stoneville, NC, 27048-0845

Harrington, Fred A., Summer: 2107 W Frances Rd,   Mt Morris MI 48458 8215, Winter: 3725 Citrus, St. James City, FL, 33956, Winter 239-283-0721, Summer 810-686-3008

Hergert, Bob, 12 Geer Circle, Port Orford, OR, 97465, 541-332-3010, hergert@harborside.com, www.scrimshander.com

Hielscher, Vickie, 6550 Otoe Rd, P.O. Box 992, Alliance, NE, 69301, 308-762-4318, hielscher@premaonline.com

High, Tom, 5474 S. 112.8 Rd., Alamosa, CO, 81101, 719-589-2108, scrimshaw@vanion.com, www.rockymountainscrimshaw.com, Wildlife Artist

Himmelheber, David R., 11289 40th St. N., Royal Palm Beach, FL, 33411

Holland, Dennis K., 4908-17th Place, Lubbock, TX, 79416

Hutchings, Rick "Hutch", 3007 Coffe Tree Ct, Crestwood, KY, 40014, 502-241-2871, baron1@bellsouth.net

Imboden II, Howard L., 620 Deauville Dr., Dayton, OH, 45429, 937-439-1536, Guards by the "Last Wax Technic"

Johnson, Corinne, W3565 Lockington, Mindora, WI, 54644

Johnston, Kathy, W. 1134 Providence, Spokane, WA, 99205

Karst Stone, Linda, 903 Tanglewood Ln, Kerrville, TX, 78028-2945, 830-896-4678, 830-257-6117, karstone@ktc.com

Kelso, Jim, 577 Coller Hill Rd, Worcester, VT, 05682

Kirk, Susan B., 1340 Freeland Rd., Merrill, MI, 48637

Koevenig, Eugene and Eve, Koevenig's Engraving Service, Rabbit Gulch, Box 55, Hill City, SD, 57745-0055

Kostelnik, Joe and Patty, RD #4, Box 323, Greensburg, PA, 15601

Lemen, Pam, 3434 N. Iroquois Ave., Tucson, AZ, 85705

Martin, Diane, 28220 N. Lake Dr., Waterford, WI, 53185

McDonald, René Cosimini-, 14730 61 Court N., Loxahatchee, FL, 33470

McFadden, Berni, 2547 E Dalton Ave, Dalton Gardens, ID, 83815-9631

McGowan, Frank, 12629 Howard Lodge Dr., Winter Add-2023 Robin Ct Sebring FL 33870, Sykesville, MD, 21784, 863-385-1296

McGrath, Gayle, PMB 232 15201 N Cleveland Ave, N Ft Myers, FL, 33903

McLaran, Lou, 603 Powers St., Waco, TX, 76705

McWilliams, Carole, P.O. Box 693, Bayfield, CO, 81122

Mead, Faustina L., 2550 E. Mercury St., Inverness, FL, 34453-0514, 352-344-4751, scrimsha@infionline.net, www.scrimshaw-by-faustina.com

Mitchell, James, 1026 7th Ave., Columbus, GA, 31901

Moore, James B., 1707 N. Gillis, Stockton, TX, 79735

Ochonicky, Michelle "Mike", Stone Hollow Studio, 31 High Trail, Eureka, MO, 63025, 636-938-9570, www.bestofmissourihands.com

Ochs, Belle, 124 Emerald Lane, Largo, FL, 33771, 727-530-3826, chuckandbelle@juno.com, www.oxforge.com

Pachi, Mirella, Via Pometta 1, 17046 Sassello (SV), ITALY, 019 720086, WWW.PACHI-KNIVES.COM

Parish, Vaughn, 103 Cross St., Monaca, PA, 15061

Peterson, Lou, 514 S. Jackson St., Gardner, IL, 60424

Poag, James H., RR #1 Box 212A, Grayville, IL, 62844

Polk, Trena, 4625 Webber Creek Rd., Van Buren, AR, 72956

Purvis, Hilton, P.O. Box 371, Noordhoek, 7979, SOUTH AFFRIC, 27 21 789 1114, hiltonp@telkomsa.net, www.kgsa.co.za/member/hiltonpurvis

Ramsey, Richard, 8525 Trout Farm Rd, Neosho, MO, 64850

Ristinen, Lori, 14256 County Hwy 45, Menahga, MN, 56464, 218-538-6608, lori@loriristinen.com, www.loriristinen.com

Roberts, J.J., 7808 Lake Dr., Manassas, VA, 22111, 703-330-0448, jjrengraver@aol.com, www.angelfire.com/va2/engraver

Rudolph, Gil, 20922 Oak Pass Ave, Tehachapi, CA, 93561, 661-822-4949, www.gtraks@csurfers.net

Rundell, Joe, 6198 W. Frances Rd., Clio, MI, 48420

Saggio, Joe, 1450 Broadview Ave. #12, Columbus, OH, 43212, 614-481-1967, jvsaggio@earthlink.net, www.j.v.saggio@worldnet.att.net

Sahlin, Viveca, Konstvaktarevagem 9, S-772 40 Grangesberg, SWEDEN, 46 240 23204, www.scrimart.use

Satre, Robert, 518 3rd Ave. NW, Weyburn SK CANADA, S4H 1R1

Schlott, Harald, Zingster Str. 26, 13051 Berlin, 929 33 46, GERMANY, 049 030 9293346, 049 030 9293346, harald.schlott@t-online.de, www.gravur-kunst-atelier.de.vu

Schulenburg, E.W., 25 North Hill St., Carrollton, GA, 30117

Schwallie, Patricia, 4614 Old Spartanburg Rd. Apt. 47, Taylors, SC, 29687

Selent, Chuck, P.O. Box 1207, Bonners Ferry, ID, 83805

Semich, Alice, 10037 Roanoke Dr., Murfreesboro, TN, 37129

Shostle, Ben, 1121 Burlington, Muncie, IN, 47302

Sinclair, W.P., 3, The Pippins, Warminster, Wiltshire BA12 8TH, ENGLAND

Smith, Peggy, 676 Glades Rd., #3, Gatlinburg, TN, 37738

Smith, Ron, 5869 Straley, Ft. Worth, TX, 76114

Stahl, John, Images In Ivory, 2049 Windsor Rd., Baldwin, NY, 11510, 516-223-5007, imivory@msn.com, www.imagesinivory.org

Steigerwalt, Jim, RD#3, Sunbury, PA, 17801

Stuart, Stephen, 15815 Acorn Circle, Tavares, FL, 32778, 352-343-8423, (352) 343-8916, inkscratch@aol.com

Talley, Mary Austin, 2499 Countrywood Parkway, Memphis, TN, 38016, matalley@midsouth.rr.com

Thompson, Larry D., 23040 Ave. 197, Strathmore, CA, 93267

Toniutti, Nelida, Via G. Pascoli, 33085 Maniago-PN, ITALY

Tucker, Steve, 3518 W. Linwood, Turlock, CA, 95380

Tyser, Ross, 1015 Hardee Court, Spartanburg, SC, 29303

Velasquez, Gil, Art of Scrimshaw, 7120 Madera Dr., Goleta, CA, 93117

Wilderness Forge, 475 NE Smith Rock Way, Terrebonne, OR, 97760, bhatting@xpressweb.com

Williams, Gary, PO Box 210, Glendale, KY, 42740, 270-369-6752, garywilliam@alltel.net

Winn, Travis A., 558 E. 3065 S., Salt Lake City, UT, 84106

Young, Mary, 4826 Storeyland Dr., Alton, IL, 62002

organizations

AMERICAN BLADESMITH SOCIETY
c/o Jan DuBois; PO Box 1481; Cypress, TX 77410-1481; 281-225-9159;
Web: www.americanbladesmith.com

AMERICAN KNIFE & TOOL INSTITUTE*
David Kowalski, Comm. Coordinator, AKTI; DEPT BL2, PO Box 432, Iola,
WI 54945-0432;715-445-3781; communications@akti.org; www.
akti.org

AMERICAN KNIFE THROWERS ALLIANCE
c/o Bobby Branton; 4976 Seewee Rd; Awendaw, SC 29429

ARIZONA KNIFE COLLECTOR'S ASSOCIATION
c/o D'Alton Holder, President, 7148 W. Country Gables Dr., Peoria, AZ
. 85381 www.akca.net

ART KNIFE COLLECTOR'S ASSOCIATION
c/o Mitch Weiss, Pres.; 2211 Lee Road, Suite 104; Winter Park, FL 32789

BAY AREA KNIFE COLLECTOR'S ASSOCIATION
Doug Isaacson, B.A.K.C.A. Membership, 36774 Magnolia, Newark, CA
94560 www.bakca.org

ARKANSAS KNIFEMAKERS ASSOCIATION
David Etchieson, 60 Wendy Cove, Conway, AR 72032
www.arkansasknifemakers.com

AUSTRALASIAN KNIFE COLLECTORS
PO BOX 149 CHIDLOW 6556 WESTERN AUSTRALIA TEL: (08) 9572
7255   FAX: (08) 9572 7266   International Inquiries: TEL: + 61 8
9572 7255   FAX: + 61 8 9572 7266   akc@knivesaustralia.com.au

CALIFORNIA KNIFEMAKERS ASSOCIATION
c/o Clint Breshears, Membership Chairman; 1261 Keats St; Manhattan
Beach CA 90266; 310-372-0739; breshears@mindspring.com
Dedicated to teaching and improving knifemaking

CANADIAN KNIFEMAKERS GUILD
c/o Peter Wile; RR # 3; Bridgewater N.S. CANADA B4V 2W2; 902-543-
1373; www.ckg.org

CUTTING EDGE, THE
1920 N 26th St; Lowell AR 72745; 479-631-0055; 479-636-4618; ce-
info@cuttingedge.com
*After-market knives since 1968. We offer about 1,000 individual
knives each month. The oldest and the most experienced in the
business of buying and selling knives. We buy collections of any size,
take knives on consignment or we will trade. Web:
www.cuttingedge.com*

FLORIDA KNIFEMAKERS ASSOCIATION
c/o President, Dan Mink, PO Box 861, Crystal beach, Florida, 34681
(727) 786 5408 www.floridaknifemakers.org

JAPANESE SWORD SOCIETY OF THE U.S.
PO Box 712; Breckenridge, TX 76424

KNIFE COLLECTORS CLUB INC, THE
1920 N 26th St; Lowell AR 72745; 479-631-0130; 479-631-8493;
ag@agrussell.com Web:www.club@k-c-c.com
*The oldest and largest association of knife collectors. Issues limited
edition knives, both handmade and highest quality production, in very
limited numbers. The very earliest was the CM-1, Kentucky Rifle*

KNIFE WORLD
PO Box 3395; Knoxville, TN 37927; 800-828-7751; 865-397-1955; 865-
397-1969; knifepub@knifeworld.com
*Publisher of monthly magazine for knife enthusiasts and world's
largest knife/cutlery bookseller. Web: www.knifeworld.com*

KNIFEMAKERS GUILD
c/o Beverly Imel, Knifemakers Guild, Box 922, New Castle, IN 47362;
(765) 529-1651 www.knifemakersguild.com

KNIFEMAKERS GUILD OF SOUTHERN AFRICA, THE
c/o Carel Smith; PO Box 1744; Delmars 2210; SOUTH AFRICA;
carelsmith@therugby.co.za Web:www.kgsa.co.za

KNIVES ILLUSTRATED
265 S. Anita Dr., Ste. 120; Orange, CA 92868; 714-939-9991; 714-939-
9909; knivesillustrated@yahoo.com; Web:www.knivesillustrated.com
*All encompassing publication focusing on factory knives, new
handmades, shows and industry news, plus knifemaker features, new*

MONTANA KNIFEMAKERS' ASSOCIATION, THE
14440 Harpers Bridge Rd; Missoula, MT 59808; 406-543-0845
*Annual book of custom knife makers' works and directory of knife
making supplies; $19.99*

NATIONAL KNIFE COLLECTORS ASSOCIATION
PO Box 21070; Chattanooga, TN 37424; 423-892-5007; 423-899-9456;
info@nationalknife.org; Web: www.nationalknife.org

NEO-TRIBAL METALSMITHS
PO Box 44095; Tucson, AZ 85773-4095

NEW ENGLAND CUSTOM KNIFE ASSOCIATION
George R. Rebello, President; 686 Main Rd; Brownville, ME 04414; Web:
www.knivesby.com/necka.html

NORTH CAROLINA CUSTOM KNIFEMAKERS GUILD
c/o 2112 Windy Woods Drive, Raleigh, NC 27607 (919) 834-4693
www.ncknifeguild.org

NORTH STAR BLADE COLLECTORS
PO Box 20523, Bloomington, MN 55420

OHIO KNIFEMAKERS ASSOCIATION
c/o Jerry Smith, Anvils and Ink Studios, P.O. Box 7887, Columbus, Ohio
43229-7887 www.geocities.com/ohioknives/

OREGON KNIFE COLLECTORS ASSOCIATION
www.oregonknifeclub.org

RANDALL KNIFE SOCIETY
PO Box 158, Meadows of Dan, VA 24120 email: payrks@gate.net

ROCKY MOUNTAIN BLADE COLLECTORS ASSOCIATION
Mike Moss. Pres., P.O. Box 324, Westminster, CO 80036

**RESOURCE GUIDE AND NEWSLETTER / AUTOMATIC
KNIVES**
*2269 Chestnut St., Suite 212; San Francisco, CA 94123; 415-731-
0210; Web: www.thenewsletter.com*

SOUTH CAROLINA ASSOCIATION OF KNIFEMAKERS
c/o Victor Odom, Jr., Post Office Box 572, North, SC 29112 (803) 247-
5614 www.scak.org

SOUTHERN CALIFORNIA BLADES
SC Blades, PO Box 1140, Lomita, CA 90717 www.scblades.com

TEXAS KNIFEMAKERS & COLLECTORS ASSOCIATION
2254 Fritz Allen Street, Fort Worth, Texas 76114 www.tkca.org

TACTICAL KNIVES
Harris Publications; 1115 Broadway; New York, NY 10010

TRIBAL NOW!
Neo-Tribal Metalsmiths; PO Box 44095; Tucson, AZ 85733-4095

WEYER INTERNATIONAL BOOK DIVISION
2740 Nebraska Ave; Toledo, OH 43607-3245

publications

BLADE
700 E. State St., Iola, WI 54990-0001; 715-445-2214;
www.blademag.com
The world's No. 1 knife magazine.

KNIFE WORLD
PO Box 3395, Knoxville, TN 37927

KNIVES ILLUSTRATED
265 S. Anita Dr., Ste. 120, Orange, CA 92868; 714-939-9991;
knivesillustrated@yahoo.com Web:www.knivesillustrated.com
*All encompassing publication focusing on factory knives, new
handmades, shows and industry news*

**RESOURCE GUIDE AND NEWSLETTER / AUTOMATIC
KNIVES**
2269 Chestnut St., Suite 212, San Francisco, CA 94123;
415-731-0210; Web:www.thenewsletter.com

TACTICAL KNIVES
Harris Publications, 1115 Broadway, New York, NY 10010

WEYER INTERNATIONAL BOOK DIVISION
2740 Nebraska Ave Toledo OH 43607-3245